CONTINUUM & THE PUBLISHERS ASSOCIATION

DIRECTORY OF PUBLISHING

2012

UNITED KINGDOM AND THE REPUBLIC OF IRELAND

continuum

Continuum International Publishing Group
The Tower Building
11 York Road
London SE1 7NX

80 Maiden Lane
Suite 704
New York, NY 10038

Thirty-seventh edition 2012

British Library Cataloguing-in-Publication Data
A catalogue entry for this book is available from the British Library.

ISBN: 978 1 4411 9792 4

Research and editing by Peter Gill
Text processing and typesetting by John Ainslie Consultancy
Printed and bound in Great Britain by MPG Books Group

DIRECTORY OF PUBLISHING

2012

7000000140945

Contents

1 Introduction

FOREWORD

The 37th edition of the *Directory of Publishing*, published by Continuum in association with The Publishers Association, provides an indispensable guide to book publishing in the United Kingdom and Republic of Ireland and contains details of nearly 900 publishers. In addition to the detailed entries on publishers, the *Directory* offers in depth coverage of the wider UK book trade, and lists over 500 organizations associated with the industry, including packagers, distributors, library suppliers, authors' agents and translation services. An appendix analyses publishers by field of speciality. Indexes include ISBN prefix numbers; names of key personnel and publishers' imprints; and a listing of UK publishers by postcode.

The directory is updated annually. Previous entrants are sent last year's entry and new entrants a questionnaire. We are grateful to all those who have provided information for this edition. We have done all we can to ensure accuracy and completeness, but cannot accept responsibility for errors or omissions that escaped us. New entrants either approached the publisher or were discovered by monitoring various sources – the trade press, publishers' catalogues, exhibitions, book fairs, and the files of the Publishers Association itself.

As in the previous edition we have not excluded all organizations which have failed to reply to our mailings. Instead we have re-run their 2011 entries and marked them with an asterisk. However, such organizations will be deleted from the next edition if they fail to update their entries for the second year running.

Underlined entries are members of the Publishers Association.

We welcome all comments and suggestions from readers for improvements. We are also happy to receive details of possible new entries, but please note these must meet our criteria for inclusion. Publishers should either be a Publishers Association or Foilsiú Éireann member or be of a certain size, publishing at least 5 new titles a year or employing at least 4 people.

All organizations are entered free of charge.

Continuum

HOW TO OBTAIN BRITISH BOOKS

This introduction is particularly intended for booksellers ordering from a British publisher for the first time.

HOW TO ORDER

1 If you have not previously ordered from a publisher, you should write for details on:

trade discounts;
credit facilities;
catalogue mailing.

Please enclose in your letter information including:

name and address of your bank;
names and addresses of one or two publishers, preferably British, with whom you already do business. In certain circumstances you may be directed to a local stockist, agent or representative.

2 When the publisher agrees to supply you, your order should include:

your full name and address;
order date and order number;
dispatch instructions: where you want the books to be sent and where you want the invoice sent;
carriage instructions:
   surface post
   special carrier (e.g. shipper)
   air freight
invoicing instructions:
   if you want a separate invoice by airmail
   minimum number of copies you require
full details of the book:
   number of copies you need
   title
   author/editor
   cased/limp/paperback
   international standard book number (ISBN)

3 Orders Clearing, Mardev Ltd, Quadrant House, The Quadrant, Sutton, Surrey SM2 5AS (tel: +44 (0)20 8652 3899, fax: +44 (0)20 8652 4597, email: enquiries@mardev.com, web site: http://www.mardevlists.com) have an Orders Clearing system: by sending all your orders for different publishers to the one address, you can save yourself money. Similarly, Orders Clearing operates a service for the payment of publishers' accounts, the Overseas Booksellers' Clearing House (OBCH). Booksellers may send one cheque for various accounts and OBCH will then distribute the payments to the different publishers.

4 An Orders Clearing Service is also offered by the Booksellers Order Distribution Ltd (BOD). Their address is 49 Victoria Road, Aldershot, Hampshire GU11 1SJ (tel: +44 (0)1252 20697, fax: +44 (0)1252 20697).

5 Nielsen BookNet provides a range of e-commerce services that allow electronic trading between booksellers, distributors, publishers, libraries and other suppliers, regardless of their size and location. Services include BookNet for booksellers and publishers/ distributors, TeleOrdering and EDI messaging. Contact Nielsen BookData, 3rd Floor, Midas House, 62 Goldsworth Road, Woking, GU21 6LQ (tel: +44 (0)870 777 8710, fax: +44 (0)870 777 8711, email: sales@nielsenbookdata.co.uk, website: http://www.bookdata.co.uk).

FOR REFERENCE

1 **Nielsen BookData:**
Provides monthly and quarterly content-rich book information for English-language titles published internationally. Available on CD-ROM and online by subscription from Nielsen BookData, 3rd Floor, Midas House, 62 Goldsworth Road, Woking, GU21 6LQ (tel: +44 (0)870 777 8710, fax: +44 (0)870 777 8711, email: sales@nielsenbookdata.co.uk, website: http://www.bookdata.co.uk).

2 **The Bookseller:**
The British book trade journal, published weekly by Bookseller Publications, containing correspondence, articles, trade news, together with a list of books published each week (web site: http://www.theBookseller.com). See also section 6.12 for details of other periodicals and reference books of the trade.

3 **British National Bibliography:**
A subject list of new British books arranged by Dewey classification. Published weekly with interim cumulations and an annual cumulation by the British Library, National Bibliographic Service, Boston Spa, Wetherby, West Yorkshire LS23 7BQ (tel: +44 (0)1937 546585, fax: +44 (0)1937 546586, email: nbs-info@bl.uk, web site: http://www.bl.uk).

4 Individual publishers will normally provide catalogues of their own publications on request.

HOW TO PAY

You can pay by:

cheque, bank draft or letter of credit
bill of exchange drawn by the publisher on your giro or postal account
international money order/postal order

IMPORTANT

Please make sure that:

the publisher receives the *full amount* of the invoice value, free of all bank charges and transfer fees;
you pay *promptly*;
if you have any problems, raise them *promptly*;
if you have any difficulty in paying, consult your local bank manager, or the British Embassy, Consulate or High Commission.

WHEN YOU HAVE DIFFICULTY IN OBTAINING BRITISH BOOKS

1   If you have a problem of a *general* nature, please write to the Publishers Association, 29b Montague Street, London WC1B 5BH (email: mail@publishers.org.uk, tel: +44 (0)20 7691 9191, fax: +44 (0)20 7691 9199). The Association cannot intervene in problems which may arise between individual booksellers and publishers.

2   British Council

Your nearest office may be able to help you with enquiries about UK publishing. Details of its network of offices are available from: British Council Information Centre, tel: +44 (0)161 957 7755, fax: +44 (0)161 957 7762, email: general.enquiries@britishcouncil.org, minicom: +44 (0)161 957 7188, web site: http://www.britishcouncil.org.

PUBLISHERS' ABBREVIATED ANSWERS

Most publishers use one of the answers below when books are not available, and give an explanation of their answer codes at the bottom of the invoice.

NK	Not known, not ours, or so far in the future or so long out of print that it is unknown to the trade department
OO/TF	On order, to follow shortly
B8 *or* **BDG8**	Binding, will be available in August
B/ND	Binding (no date)
RP/June *or* **RP/6**	Reprint available in June
RP/2M	Reprint available in 2 months
NYP	Not yet published
NEP	New edition in preparation
RPUC	Reprint under consideration
OP	Out of print
OO/USA	On order, to be supplied by USA
TOP	Temporarily out of print
OS	Out of stock
RP/ND	Reprinting, no date

TECHNICAL TERMS

Firm

Books are normally supplied 'firm'. This means you will accept the books, pay for them, and will not be able to return them.

See-safe or On approval

Some publishers are prepared to supply books on the basis that they are paid for at normal credit terms, but if the books remain unsold they may be returned with the publisher's authorization for crediting against future orders. You will be expected to return the books at your own expense. You should always obtain in writing details from publishers of any such agreements they are prepared to offer to their customers.

Standing Orders

Some publishers operate a scheme which allows a bookseller automatically to receive books in given subjects as they are published. These are normally supplied 'on approval'. You should write to individual publishers for details of their schemes.

Continuation Orders

Continuation Orders can be placed for books published in series and multi-volume works. This means that each new volume that appears will be sent to you automatically.

Pro-forma Invoice

Some publishers may prefer to supply initial orders by means of a pro-forma invoice which has to be paid before the books are sent.

THE PUBLISHERS ASSOCIATION

29b Montague Street, London WC1B 5BW
Telephone: +44 (0)20 7691 9191 **Fax:** +44 (0)20 7691 9199
Email: mail@publishers.org.uk
Web site: http://www.publishers.org.uk

Chief Executive: Richard Mollet
Director of Educational, Academic & Professional Publishing: Graham Taylor
Director of International and Trade Services: Emma House

Making the case for UK publishers
– **The Publishers Association** is the leading organisation working on the behalf of book, journal and electronic publishers based in the UK. We bring publishers together to discuss the critical issues facing the industry and to define the practical policies, which will drive our lobbying and campaigns in the UK and internationally. The aim of The Publishers Association is to ensure a secure future for the UK publishing industry.
– **Acting for the Industry:** The PA's mission is to strengthen the trading environment for UK publishers by ensuring that the needs and concerns of the industry are heard at all levels of Government in the UK, in Europe and internationally. We are actively involved in issues such as: copyright legislation; the adaptation of legislation to digital technology; copyright licensing arrangements for education, business, and public bodies; legislation on VAT, e-commerce and other issues affecting publishers; funding for learning and information resources in schools, colleges and universities; the promotion of books and reading; export promotion of books and journals; anti-piracy campaigns (terrestrial and internet); efficiency in supply and marketing; the protection of freedom to publish.
– **Front Line Information:** PA posts front line information to our website and communicates with members through our regular e-mail bulletins. The Members Only section of the PA website contains detailed information prepared exclusively for members including: the latest market statistics, copyright law updates, comments on current government policy, PA briefs and reports on market concerns, anti-piracy action updates, digital rights information, and updates on EU legislation.

Home and Export Markets
Market development is at the heart of the PA's activities, which include:
– **International trade fairs**, operating with UK Trade & Investment a subsidy scheme for companies wishing to exhibit. Additionally, our TurnKey Exhibition Services offer publishers a complete exhibition service for major fairs.

– **Market intelligence**, including online access to the Global Publishing Information website (http://www.publishers.org.uk/gpi.nsf), and exclusive access to the Aid Digest.
– **Trade delegations and seminars** organised with UK Trade & Investment support, to gain knowledge of and exposure in growth markets such as China, Africa, Asia and Eastern Europe.
– **Home trade initiatives**, such as World Book Day, which result in a significant increase in sales, particularly of children's books, during the period of promotion.

Join the PA now – add your voice, have your say
As a PA member you can add your voice and have your say on the vital issues affecting our industry today. Membership is open to any company registered in the UK engaged in book, journal or electronic publishing as a bona fide and continuing operation. Subscription rates are based on turnover, with special introductory rates for new members and discounted rates for journal publishers.

The International Division
The International Division actively supports the international sales activities of PA members. We act against piracy, and on copyright and trade barrier issues, organise trade missions and UK representation at international trade fairs.

Trade Publishers Council
The Trade Publishers Council determines PA policy on consumer market matters, and acts on specific issues with the objectives of expanding the market and increasing efficiency. Other trade groups include our Children's Book Group, Christian Books Group and Digital Directors' Group.

Academic and Professional Division
The Academic and Professional Division provides a forum for higher education, monograph, journal and reference publishers. We represent publishers' concerns to key stakeholders, conduct market research and run a number of events.

The Educational Publishers Council
The Educational Publishers Council provides a voice for school and college publishers. We campaign for better funding for learning resources and represent the industry in the development of the electronic market, as well as running seminars and compiling market statistics.

2   Publishers

2001

AA PUBLISHING
[trading as AA Media Ltd]
Fanum House, Basingstoke, Hants
RG21 4EA
Telephone: 01256 491578
Fax: 01256 322575
Email: AAPublish@TheAA.com
Web Site: www.theAA.com

Distribution (UK):
Littlehampton Book Services Ltd,
Faraday Close, Durrington, Worthing,
West Sussex BN13 3RB

Personnel:
R. C. A. Miles (Chief Executive)
D. Watchus (Publisher)
T. A. Lee (Sales & Marketing Director)
R. Firth (Production Director)
M. Poulter (Finance Director)
S. Gold (Human Resources Director)

Atlases & Maps; Guide Books; Natural
History; Photography; Transport; Travel &
Topography

Imprints, Series & ISBNs:
Automobile Association: 978 0 7495, 978 0
  86145
Travel Series: Citypacks: 978 0 7495
Travel Series: Essentials: 978 0 7495
Travel Series: Key Guides: 978 0 7495
Travel Series: Spiral Guides: 978 0 7495

Distributor for:
AAA Road Maps of USA, Canada, Mexico;
  Thomas Cook; Scottish Tourist Board

2002

*ACAIR LTD
Unit 7, 7 James Street, Stornoway,
Isle of Lewis HS1 2QN
Telephone: 01851 703020
Fax: 01851 703294
Email: info@acairbooks.com
Web Site: www.acairbooks.com

Distribution:
BookSource, 50 Cambuslang Road,
Glasgow G32 8NB
Telephone: 0845 370 0067
Fax: 0845 370 0068

Personnel:
Norma Macleod (Editor)
Margaret Anne Macleod (Designer)
Margaret Martin (Administrator)
Donalda Riddell (Stock)

Children's Books; Educational & Textbooks;
Fiction; History & Antiquarian; Poetry

Imprints, Series & ISBNs:
978 0 86152

Book Trade Association Membership:
Publishing Scotland; Booksellers
Association

2003

*ACCENT PRESS LTD
The Old School, Upper High Street,
Bedlinog CF46 6RY
Telephone: 01443 710930
Fax: 01443 710940
Email: info@accentpress.co.uk
Web Site: www.accentpress.co.uk

Distribution:
Macmillan Distribution (MDL), Brunel Road,
Houndmills, Basingstoke, Hants RG21 6XS
Telephone: 01256 802692
Email: trade@macmillan.co.uk

Personnel:
Hazel Cushion (Managing Director)
Robert Cushion (Finance Director)
Karen Smart (Administration)
Alison Stokes (Production)

Biography & Autobiography; Children's
Books; Cookery, Wines & Spirits; Crafts &
Hobbies; Crime; Educational & Textbooks;
Fiction; Guide Books; Humour; Industry,
Business & Management; Medical (incl. Self
Help & Alternative Medicine); Poetry

Associated Companies:
Curriculum Concepts UK; Green Fuse;
  Wedding Bible Co; Xcite Books

Overseas Representation:
All Arab countries: Peter Ward
Australia & New Zealand: Exisle Publishing
Central & Eastern Europe: Tony Moggach
Indian Subcontinent: Maya Publishers
Singapore, Malaysia, Thailand & Indonesia:
  PMS Publishers Marketing Services,
  Singapore
Spain, Portugal & Gibraltar: Iberian Book
  Services

Book Trade Association Membership:
Booksellers Association; Independent
Publishers Guild

2004

ACUMEN PUBLISHING LTD
4 Saddler Street, Durham DH1 3NP
Telephone: 0191 383 1889
Fax: 0191 386 2542
Email:
  steven.gerrard@acumenpublishing.co.uk
Web Site: www.acumenpublishing.co.uk

**Warehouse, Trade Enquiries, Orders &
Distribution:**
Marston Book Services, 160 Milton Park,
Abingdon, Oxon OX14 4YN
Telephone: 01235 465521
Fax: 01235 465555
Email: trade.orders@marston.co.uk
Web Site: www.marston.co.uk

Personnel:
Steven Gerrard (Publisher)
Kate Williams (Prepress Manager)
Tristan Palmer (Senior Editor)

Academic & Scholarly; Biography &
Autobiography; Educational & Textbooks;
History & Antiquarian; Philosophy; Politics &
World Affairs; Reference Books, Directories
& Dictionaries; Religion & Theology;
Sociology & Anthropology

New Titles: 25 (2010) , 30 (2011)

Imprints, Series & ISBNs:
978 1 84465, 978 1 902683

Overseas Representation:
Australia & New Zealand: Palgrave
  Macmillan, South Yarra, Vic, Australia
Austria, Germany & Switzerland: Bernd
  Feldmann, Oranienburg, Germany
Belgium, Luxembourg & Netherlands: Fred
  Hermans, AG Bovenkarspel, Netherlands
Botswana, Lesotho, Namibia, South Africa,
  Swaziland & Zimbabwe: The African
  Moon Press, Kelvin, South Africa
Brunei, Cambodia, Indonesia, Laos,
  Philippines, Singapore, Thailand &
  Vietnam: APD Singapore Pte Ltd,
  Singapore
China, Hong Kong, Korea & Taiwan: Asia
  Publishers Services Ltd, Hong Kong
Eastern Europe: Laszlo Horvath, Budapest,
  Hungary
France, Italy, Portugal & Spain: Flavio
  Marcello Publishers' Agents &
  Consultants, Padua, Italy
Greece, Cyprus & Malta: Charles Gibbes
  Associates, Louslitges, France
India: Maya Publishers Pvt Ltd, New Delhi,
  India
Japan: Tim Burland, Tokyo, Japan
Middle East: Avicenna Ltd, Oxford, UK
Scandinavia: Colin Flint Ltd, Harlow, UK
USA & Canada: McGill-Queen's University
  Press, Montreal, PQ, Canada

Book Trade Association Membership:
Independent Publishers Guild

2005

ADAM MATTHEW DIGITAL LTD
Pelham House, London Road,
Marlborough, Wiltshire SN8 2AG
Telephone: 01672 511921

Fax: 01672 511663
Email: david@amdigital.co.uk
Web Site: www.amdigital.co.uk

Personnel:
William Pidduck (Chairman)
David Tyler (Managing Director)
Khal Rudin (Sales & Marketing Director)

Academic & Scholarly; Electronic
(Educational); Electronic (Professional &
Academic); Gender Studies; History &
Antiquarian; Literature & Criticism; Military
& War

New Titles: 18 (2010) , 14 (2011)
No of Employees: 29
Annual Turnover: £5.4M

Associated Companies:
USA: Adam Matthew Education Inc.

Overseas Representation:
Italy: Licosa SPA, Florence, Italy
Japan: Maruzen Co Ltd, Tokyo, Japan
Korea: GDI, Seoul, Republic of Korea
Taiwan: Transmission Books & Microforms
  Co Ltd, Taipei, Taiwan

2006

*ADAMSON PUBLISHING LTD
8 The Moorings, Norwich NR3 3AX
Telephone: 01603 623336
Fax: 01603 624767
Email: stephen@adamsonbooks.com
Web Site: www.adamsonbooks.com

Personnel:
Stephen Adamson (Chairman)

Educational & Textbooks; Electronic
(Educational); Reference Books, Directories
& Dictionaries

Imprints, Series & ISBNs:
978 0 948543

2007

ADLARD COLES NAUTICAL
[an imprint of Bloomsbury Publishing PLC]
50 Bedford Square, London WC1B 3DP
Telephone: 020 7758 0200
Fax: 020 7758 0333
Web Site: www.adlardcoles.com

Personnel:
Richard Charkin (Managing Director)
Janet Murphy (Editorial Director)
David Ward (Sales Director (Home))
David Wightman (Sales Director
  (International))

Nautical

New Titles: 38 (2010) , 37 (2011)
No of Employees: 4

Imprints, Series & ISBNs:
978 0 7136, 978 1 4081

Parent Company:
Bloomsbury Publishing PLC

Associated Companies:
Thomas Reed Publications; Reeds Almanac

Overseas Representation:
See: Bloomsbury Publishing PLC, London, UK

2008

*ADVANCE MATERIALS
41 East Hatley, Sandy, Bedfordshire
SG19 3JA
Telephone: 01767 652140
Fax: 01767 652937
Email: office@advancematerials.co.uk
Web Site: www.advancematerials.co.uk

Orders:
NBN International, Estover Road, Plymouth, Devon PL6 7PY
Telephone: 01752 202300
Fax: 01752 202330
Email: orders@nbninternational.com
Web Site: www.nbninternational.com

Personnel:
Mrs Jennifer Ollerenshaw (*Director*)
Dr Timothy Ollerenshaw (*IT Manager*)
Mrs Helen Edwards (*Administrator*)

Educational & Textbooks; Languages & Linguistics

Imprints, Series & ISBNs:
978 0 9532440, 978 0 9547695, 978 0 9559265, 978 0 9565431

Overseas Representation:
Australia & New Zealand: Foreign Language Bookshop Pty Ltd, Melbourne, Vic, Australia
North America: IB Source, Chicago, IL, USA

Book Trade Association Membership:
Independent Publishers Guild

2009

AEON BOOKS
118 Finchley Road, London W5 4YX
Telephone: 020 7431 1075
Fax: 020 7435 9076
Email: shop@karnacbooks.com
Web Site: www.karnacbooks.com

Warehouse, Distribution:
Marston Book Services Ltd,
160 Milton Park, Abingdon, Oxfordshire
OX14 4SD
Telephone: 01235 465500
Fax: 01235 465555
Email: enquiries@marston.co.uk
Web Site: www.marston.co.uk

Personnel:
Oliver Rathbone (*Managing Director*)

Magic & the Occult

Imprints, Series & ISBNs:
978 1 904658

Overseas Representation:
USA: Stylus Publishing Inc, Sterling, VA, USA

Book Trade Association Membership:
Booksellers Association

2010

AIR-BRITAIN (HISTORIANS) LTD
41 Penshurst Road, Leigh, Tonbridge, Kent
TN11 8HL

Telephone: 01732 835637
Fax: 01732 835637
Email: mike@absales.demon.co.uk
Web Site: www.air-britain.com

Personnel:
Michael Graham Rice (*Sales Director*)
Howard Nash (*Director*)
Dr Chris Chatfield (*Director*)
Don Schofield (*Treasurer*)
Geoff Negus (*Chairman*)

Aviation; Military & War

Imprints, Series & ISBNs:
978 0 85130

Overseas Representation:
Australia & New Zealand: Aviation Worldwide, Oamaru, New Zealand

2011

ALBAN BOOKS LTD
14 Belford Road, Edinburgh EH4 3BL
Telephone: 0131 226 2217
Fax: 0131 225 5999
Email: sales@albanbooks.com
Web Site: www.albanbooks.com

Warehouse, Invoicing, Customer Services:
c/o Marston Book Services Ltd,
160 Milton Park, Abingdon, Oxon
OX14 4SD
Telephone: 01235 465500
Fax: 01235 465555

Personnel:
Jonny Gallant (*Managing Director*)
Nigel Parkinson (*Sales Manager*)
Elaine Reid (*Marketing Manager*)
Margaret Reid (*Accounts & Special Orders*)
Katie Gordon (*Sales & Marketing Assistant*)
Alison Wilson (*Sales & Marketing Assistant*)

Academic & Scholarly; Children's Books; Educational & Textbooks; Fiction; Philosophy; Reference Books, Directories & Dictionaries; Religion & Theology

No of Employees: 6

Distributor for:
USA: Abingdon Press; Augsburg Fortress Publishers; Ave Maria Press; Wm B. Eerdmans Publishing Co; Hendrickson Publishers; Orbis Books

Book Trade Association Membership:
Publishing Scotland

2012

*ALBYN PRESS
2 Caversham Street, Chelsea, London
SW3 4AH
Telephone: 020 7351 4995
Fax: 020 7351 4995
Email:
leonard.holdsworth@btopenworld.com

Personnel:
James Hughes (*Editorial Director*)
Leonard Holdsworth (*Production*)
Margaret Fletcher (*Sales*)

Fiction; Fine Art & Art History; Geography & Geology; Guide Books; History & Antiquarian; Illustrated & Fine Editions; Literature & Criticism; Poetry; Reference Books, Directories & Dictionaries; Transport

Imprints, Series & ISBNs:
978 0 284

Parent Company:
Christchurch Publishers Ltd

Associated Companies:
Charles Skilton Publishing Group; Tallis Press

Book Trade Association Membership:
Independent Publishers Guild

2013

IAN ALLAN PUBLISHING LTD
Riverdene Business Park, Molesey Road, Hersham, Surrey KT12 4RG
Telephone: 01932 266600
Fax: 01932 266601
Email: info@ianallanpublishing.co.uk
Web Site: www.ianallanpublishing.com

Distribution:
Littlehampton Book Services,
Faraday Close, Durrington, Worthing,
West Sussex BN13 3RB
Telephone: 01903 828800 (trade orders)
Fax: 01903 828802
Email: orders@lbsltd.co.uk

Representation (UK, Wales & Ireland):
DJ Segrue, 1st Floor, 9 Church Road,
Stanmore, Middlesex HA7 4AR
Telephone: 020 8420 6548
Fax: 020 8420 6458
Email: danh@djsegrueltd.co.uk

Representation (Scotland):
Alan Scollan, Earnockmuir Cottage,
Meikle Earnock Road, Hamilton ML3 8RL
Telephone: 01698 459371

Personnel:
David Allan (*Chairman*)
Iain Aitken (*Managing Director*)
Nick Grant (*Publisher*)
Nigel Passmore (*Sales Manager*)
Jacqueline Vanhinsbergh (*Marketing Manager*)
Alan Butcher (*Production Manager*)
Emily McMillan (*Marketing Manager*)

Atlases & Maps; Aviation; History & Antiquarian; Military & War; Nautical; Reference Books, Directories & Dictionaries; Sports & Games; Transport

New Titles: 125 (2010) , 55 (2011)

Imprints, Series & ISBNs:
Ian Allan: 978 0 7110
Classic Publications: 978 1 903223
Lewis Masonic (only available from Midland Counties Publications): 978 0 85318
Midland Publishing: 978 1 85780
OPC: 978 0 86093

Parent Company:
Ian Allan Group Ltd

Distributor for:
KRB (formerly Kestrel Railway Books); Millstream; Noodle Books; Pendragon; Polygon Press; Red Kite; Runpast; John Sullivan

Overseas Representation:
Australia, New Zealand & Papua New Guinea: DLS Australia (Pty) Ltd, Braeside, Vic, Australia
Austria, Belgium, France, Germany, Netherlands & Switzerland: European Marketing Services, London, UK
Canada & USA: Bookmasters Distribution Services, Ashland, Ohio, USA
Central & Eastern Europe: Tony Moggach, InterMedia Americana (IMA) Ltd, London, UK
Middle & Far East: Julian Ashton, Ashton International Marketing Services, Sevenoaks, Kent, UK
Scandinavia: Gill Angell & Stewart Siddall, Angell Eurosales, Berwick-on-Tweed, UK
South Africa: Zytek Publishing (pty), Johannesburg, South Africa
Spain, Portugal, Gibraltar, Italy, Malta, Greece, Slovenia, Croatia, Bosnia & Montenegro: Bookport Associates, Corsico (MI), Italy
USA (Aviation titles only): Specialty Press, North Branch, MN, USA

USA (Masonic titles only): Atlas Books (a division of BookMasters Inc), Ashland, OH, USA
USA (Military titles only): Casemate Publishers & Book Distributors LLC, Havertown, PA, USA

Book Trade Association Membership:
Booksellers Association; Independent Publishers Guild

2014

*PHILIP ALLAN PUBLISHERS LTD
Market Place, Deddington, Oxon OX15 0SE
Telephone: 01869 338652
Fax: 01869 338803
Email: sales@philipallan.co.uk
Web Site: www.philipallan.co.uk

Personnel:
Paul Cherry (*Editorial Director*)
Ceri Jenkins (*Marketing Manager*)

Educational & Textbooks

Imprints, Series & ISBNs:
Philip Allan Updates: 978 0 86003, 978 1 84489

Parent Company:
Hodder Education

Book Trade Association Membership:
Educational Publishers Council

2015

J. A. ALLEN
[an imprint of Robert Hale Ltd]
45–47 Clerkenwell Green, London
EC1R 0HT
Telephone: 020 7251 2661
Fax: 020 7490 4958
Email: allen@halebooks.com
Web Site: www.allenbooks.co.uk

Warehouse & Shipping:
Combined Book Services Ltd, Units I/K, Paddock Wood Distribution Centre, Paddock Wood, Tonbridge, Kent TN12 6UU
Telephone: 01892 837171
Fax: 01892 837272
Email: orders@combook.co.uk

Personnel:
Lesley Gowers (*Publisher*)

Animal Care & Breeding; Sports & Games; Veterinary Science

Imprints, Series & ISBNs:
978 0 85131

Parent Company:
Robert Hale Ltd

Overseas Representation:
See: Robert Hale Ltd, London, UK

2016

ALLISON & BUSBY
13 Charlotte Mews, London W1T 4EJ
Telephone: 020 7580 1080
Fax: 020 7580 1180
Email: susie@allisonandbusby.com
Web Site: www.allisonandbusby.com

Warehouse & Distribution:
Turnaround Publisher Services Ltd, Unit 3, Olympia Trading Estate, Coburg Road, London N22 6TZ
Telephone: 020 8829 3000
Fax: 020 8881 5088
Email: orders@turnaround-uk.com

Personnel:
Susie Dunlop (*Publishing Director & UK Sales*)
Chiara Priorelli (*Publicity & Online Marketing Manager*)

Lara Crisp (*Managing Editor*)
Lesley Crooks (*Sales & Digital Manager*)
Sara Magness (*Editorial Administrator*)
Christina Griffiths (*Art Editor*)

Biography & Autobiography; Children's Books; Crime; Fiction; Humour; Science Fiction

New Titles: 90 (2010) , 90 (2011)
No of Employees: 6

Imprints, Series & ISBNs:
978 0 7490, 978 0 85031

Parent Company:
Spain: Editorial Prensa Iberica SA

Overseas Representation:
Africa, Middle East & Gulf: InterMedia Americana (IMA) Ltd, London, UK
Australia: DLS Australia
Canada: Georgetown Publications Inc, Toronto, Ont, Canada
France, Belgium & Netherlands: Michael Geoghegan, London, UK
Germany: Gabriele Kern Publishers Services, Frankfurt-am-Main, Germany
India: Maya Publishers Pvt Ltd, New Delhi, India
Italy: Ted Dougherty, London, UK
Scandinavia: Angell Eurosales, Berwick-on-Tweed, UK
South & South East Europe, Eastern Europe & Egypt: IMA
Spain, Portugal & Malta: Peter Prout Iberian Book Services, Madrid, Spain
USA: International Publishers Marketing Inc, Sterling, VA, USA

Book Trade Association Membership:
Independent Publishers Guild

2017 ▬▬▬▬▬▬▬

ALMA BOOKS LTD
London House,
243–253 Lower Mortlake Road, Richmond,
Surrey TW9 2LL
Telephone: 020 8948 9550
Fax: 020 8948 5599
Email: info@almabooks.com
Web Site: www.almabooks.com

Personnel:
Alessandro Gallenzi (*Managing Director*)
Elisabetta Minervini (*Sales & Marketing Director*)

Biography & Autobiography; Crime; Fiction; Humour; Poetry

New Titles: 15 (2010) , 20 (2011)
Annual Turnover: £650,000

Imprints, Series & ISBNs:
978 1 84688

Associated Companies:
UK: Herla Publishing

Overseas Representation:
Australia: Bloomsbury, Australia
South Africa: Jonathan Ball, South Africa
USA & Canada: Trafalgar Square Publishing / IPG, Chicago, IL, USA

Book Trade Association Membership:
Independent Publishers Guild

2018 ▬▬▬▬▬▬▬

AMBER BOOKS LTD
Bradley's Close, 74–77 White Lion Street,
London N1 9PF
Telephone: 020 7520 7600
Fax: 020 7520 7606 & 7607
Email: enquiries@amberbooks.co.uk
Web Site: www.amberbooks.co.uk

Personnel:
Stasz Gnych (*Managing Director*)

Sara Ballard (*Rights Director*)
Peter Thompson (*Head of Production*)
Charles Catton (*Publishing Manager*)
Mark Batley (*Design Manager*)
Terry Forshaw (*Picture Manager*)

Animal Care & Breeding; Atlases & Maps; Aviation; Children's Books; Crafts & Hobbies; Crime; Electronic (Entertainment); Fashion & Costume; History & Antiquarian; Illustrated & Fine Editions; Military & War; Nautical; Reference Books, Directories & Dictionaries; Sports & Games; Transport

Imprints, Series & ISBNs:
978 1 906626, 978 1 907446, 978 1 908273

Book Trade Association Membership:
Book Packagers Association

2019 ▬▬▬▬▬▬▬

*AMBERWOOD PUBLISHING LTD
Unit 4, Stirling House, Sunderland Quay,
Culpeper Close, Medway City Estate,
Rochester, Kent ME2 4HN
Telephone: 01634 290115
Fax: 01634 290761
Email: books@amberwoodpublishing.com
Web Site:
www.amberwoodpublishing.com

Warehouse:
Mulberry Court, Stour Road, Bournemouth,
Dorset
Telephone: 01202 488333
Fax: 01202 476872
Email: pauline@bio-health.co.uk

Personnel:
June Crisp (*Managing Director*)
Henry Crisp (*Company Secretary*)
Victor Perfitt (*Chairman*)
Pauline Parrot (*Administration & Accounts, Dispatch*)

Health & Beauty; Medical (incl. Self Help & Alternative Medicine)

Imprints, Series & ISBNs:
978 0 9517723, 978 1 899308

2020 ▬▬▬▬▬▬▬

AMERICAN PSYCHIATRIC PUBLISHING INC
5 Victoria House, 138 Watling Street East,
Towcester NN12 6BT
Telephone: 01327 357770
Fax: 01327 359572
Email: appi@oppuk.co.uk
Web Site: www.appi.org

Warehouse & Distribution:
NBN International, 10 Thornbury Road,
Plymouth PL6 7PP
Telephone: 01752 202301
Fax: 01752 202331
Email: orders@nbninternational.com
Web Site: www.nbninternational.com

Personnel:
Gary Hall (*Manager*)

Academic & Scholarly; Educational & Textbooks; Medical (incl. Self Help & Alternative Medicine); Psychology & Psychiatry; Reference Books, Directories & Dictionaries

New Titles: 29 (2011)

Imprints, Series & ISBNs:
978 0 89042, 978 1 58562

Parent Company:
USA: American Psychiatric Publishing Inc

2021 ▬▬▬▬▬▬▬

*A. M. S. EDUCATIONAL LTD
38 Parkside Road, Leeds LS6 4NB
Telephone: 0113 275 9900
Fax: 0113 275 7799
Email: admin@amseducational.co.uk
Web Site: www.amseducational.com

Orders (for Senter & Propagator):
38 Parkside Road, Leeds LS6 4NB
Telephone: 0113 275 9900
Fax: 0113 275 7799
Email: www.amseducational.co.uk
Web Site: www.senter.co.uk

Personnel:
Stan Sharp (*Managing Director*)
Margaret Sharp (*Finance Director*)
Victoria Keys (*Publishing Manager*)

Aviation; Biography & Autobiography; Children's Books; Educational & Textbooks; History & Antiquarian; Military & War; Poetry

Imprints, Series & ISBNs:
A.M.S. Educational: 978 1 86029
Educational Fun Factory: 978 1 86029
Falconwood Series: 978 1 900899
Leopard Learning: 978 1 899929
New Education Press (N.E.P.): 978 0 946947
Propagator Press: 978 1 86029
Senter Series: 978 1 902751

Distributor for:
Prim-Ed Publishing
New Zealand: Sunshinebooks UK
UK: Claire Publications; Desktop Publications

Book Trade Association Membership:
Independent Publishers Guild

2022 ▬▬▬▬▬▬▬

ANDERSEN PRESS LTD
20 Vauxhall Bridge Road, London
SW1V 2SA
Telephone: 020 7840 8701
Fax: 020 7233 6263
Email:
andersenpublicity@randomhouse.co.uk
Web Site: www.andersenpress.co.uk

Warehouse, Orders & Payments:
TBS Ltd, Colchester Road, Frating Green,
Colchester, Essex CO7 7DW
Telephone: 01206 255678
Fax: 01206 255930

Address for Returns Requests:
Sales Department,
Random House Children's Books,
61–63 Uxbridge Road, London W5 5SA
Telephone: 020 8231 6800
Fax: 020 8231 6767
Web Site: www.andersenpress.co.uk

Personnel:
Klaus Flugge (*Managing & Publisher*)
P. W. Durrance (*Director*)
Rona Selby (*Editorial Director*)
Mark Hendle (*Company Secretary*)
Sarah Pakenham (*Rights & Permission*)
Clare Simms (*Marketing & Publicity*)
Charlie Sheppard (*Editorial Director, Fiction*)

Children's Books

New Titles: 80 (2010) , 92 (2011)
No of Employees: 10
Annual Turnover: £3.7M

Imprints, Series & ISBNs:
Andersen Press: 978 0 86264, 978 0 905478, 978 1 84270, 978 1 84939
Andersen Young Readers' Library: 978 0 86264, 978 0 905478, 978 1 84270, 978 1 84939
Children's Picture Books: 978 0 86264, 978 0 905478, 978 1 84270, 978 1 84939

Associated Companies:
Random House

Overseas Representation:
Other overseas markets – see: Random House Group Ltd, London, UK
USA: Lerner Publishing Group, USA; Trafalgar House, USA

2023 ▬▬▬▬▬▬▬

CHRIS ANDREWS PUBLICATIONS LTD
15 Curtis Yard, North Hinksey Lane, Oxford
OX2 0LX
Telephone: 01865 723404
Fax: 01865 725294
Email: chris.andrews1@btclick.com
Web Site: www.cap-ox.co.uk

Personnel:
Chris Andrews (*Director*)
Virginia Andrews (*Director*)
Annabel Matthews (*Personal Assistant*)

Travel & Topography

Imprints, Series & ISBNs:
978 0 9509643, 978 0 9540331, 978 1 905385, 978 1 906725

Book Trade Association Membership:
Independent Publishers Guild

2024 ▬▬▬▬▬▬▬

ANGLO-SAXON BOOKS
Hereward, 11 Black Bank Road,
Little Downham, Ely, Cambs CB6 2UA
Telephone: 07576 452901
Email: tony@asbooks.co.uk
Web Site: www.asbooks.co.uk

Personnel:
Tony Linsell (*Contact*)

Academic & Scholarly; Educational & Textbooks; History & Antiquarian; Languages & Linguistics; Magic & the Occult; Military & War; Poetry; Reference Books, Directories & Dictionaries; Religion & Theology

New Titles: 4 (2010) , 4 (2011)

Imprints, Series & ISBNs:
Anglo-Saxon Books: 978 1 898281
Athelney: 978 1 903313

Overseas Representation:
USA & Canada: The David Brown Book Co, Oakville, CT, USA

2025 ▬▬▬▬▬▬▬

*ANN ARBOR PUBLISHERS LTD
PO Box 1, Belford, Northumberland
NE70 7JX
Telephone: 01668 214460
Fax: 01668 214484
Email: enquiries@annarbor.co.uk
Web Site: www.annarbor.co.uk

Personnel:
Peter D. Laverack (*Managing Director*)

Academic & Scholarly; Educational & Textbooks; Psychology & Psychiatry

Imprints, Series & ISBNs:
978 0 87879, 978 0 931421, 978 1 900506

Distributor for:
Academic Therapy Publications; Ann Arbor Publishers; High Noon Books; PAR; Pro-Ed; SlossEn; Western Psychological Services

Book Trade Association Membership:
BEEA

2026

*ANOVA BOOKS
The Old Magistrates Court,
10 Southcombe Street, London W14 0RA
Telephone: 020 7605 1400
Fax: 020 7605 1401
Email: customerservices@anovabooks.com
Web Site: www.anovabooks.com

Warehouse, Trade orders & enquiries:
HarperCollins, Westerhill Road,
Bishopbriggs, Glasgow G64 2QT
Telephone: 0141 306 3100
Email: uk.orders@harpercollins.co.uk

Personnel:
Mr Jonathan White *(Sales & Marketing Director)*
Ms Komal Patel *(Senior Publicity & Marketing Manager)*
Miss Joanna Hutchinson *(Digital Marketing Executive)*
Ms Sinead Hurley *(Head of Foreign Rights)*

Animal Care & Breeding; Architecture & Design; Children's Books; Cinema, Video, TV & Radio; Cookery, Wines & Spirits; Crafts & Hobbies; Do-It-Yourself; Fashion & Costume; Fine Art & Art History; Gardening; History & Antiquarian; Humour; Military & War; Music; Photography; Sports & Games

Imprints, Series & ISBNs:
Batsford
Collins & Brown: 978 1 84340
Conway: 978 1 84486
National Trust
Pavilion: 978 1 86205
Portico: 978 1 86105
Robson: 978 1 86105
Salamander (packager)

Overseas Representation:
Australia: HarperCollins Publishers, Pymble, NSW, Australia
Belgium, France, Netherlands & Luxembourg: Ted Dougherty, London, UK
Carribbean, Mexico & Central America: Humphrys Roberts Associates, London, UK
Central & Eastern Europe: CLB Marketing Services, Budapest, Hungary
Far East: Ashton International Marketing, Kent, UK
Germany, Switzerland & Austria: Gabriele Kern Publishers Services, Frankfurt, Germany
Italy, Greece, Spain, Portugal & Cyprus: Padovani Books, Italy
New Zealand: HarperCollins Publishers (NZ), Glenfield, Auckland, New Zealand
Scandinavia: McNeish Publishing Services, East Sussex, UK
Singapore & Malaysia: Pansing Distribution, Times Centre, Singapore
South Africa (Batsford, Conway, Robson): Trinity Books, Randburg, South Africa
South Africa (Collins & Brown, National Trust, Pavilion, Portico, Simplicity Books): Wild Dog Press, Johannesburg, South Africa
USA & Canada (Batsford, Collins & Brown, Conway): Sterling Distribution, New York, NY, USA
USA & Canada (National Trust, Pavilion, Portico, Robson, Simplicity Books): Trafalgar Square, IPG, Chicago, IL, USA

Book Trade Association Membership:
Independent Publishers Guild

2027

ANSHAN LTD
6 Newlands Road, Tunbridge Wells, Kent TN4 9AT
Telephone: 01892 557767
Fax: 01892 530358
Email: info@anshan.co.uk

Web Site: www.anshan.co.uk

Warehouse:
CBS, Unit D,
Paddock Wood Distribution Centre,
Paddock Wood, Tonbridge, Kent TN12 6UU
Telephone: 01892 837171
Fax: 01892 837272
Email: orders@combook.co.uk
Web Site: www.combook.co.uk

Representation (UK):
Quantum Publishing Solutions Ltd,
2 Cheviot Road, Paisley PA2 8AN

Personnel:
Shân White *(Managing Director)*
Andrew White *(Sales Director)*

Academic & Scholarly; Biography & Autobiography; Chemistry; Computer Science; Educational & Textbooks; Engineering; Environment & Development Studies; Mathematics & Statistics; Medical (incl. Self Help & Alternative Medicine); Physics; Psychology & Psychiatry; Reference Books, Directories & Dictionaries; Scientific & Technical

Imprints, Series & ISBNs:
978 1 848290, 978 1 904798, 978 1 905740

Overseas Representation:
Australia & New Zealand: Contact Anshan Direct
Central Europe & Ireland: Contact Anshan Direct
China: China Publishers Services Ltd, Hong Kong
Greece & Eastern Europe: Philip Tyers
Japan (Medical titles): Nankodo Co Ltd, Tokyo, Japan
Japan (Science titles): United Publishers Services Ltd, Tokyo, Japan
Scandinavia: Colin Flint Ltd, Harlow, UK
Taiwan: Unifacmanu Trading Co Ltd, Taipei, Taiwan
USA: Princeton Selling Group Inc, Wayne, PA, USA

2028

ANTHEM PRESS
[an imprint of Wimbledon Publishing Company]
75–76 Blackfriars Road, London SE1 8HA
Telephone: 020 7401 4200
Fax: 020 7401 4225
Email: info@wpcpress.com
Web Site: www.anthempress.com

Personnel:
Mr Tej Sood *(Managing Director)*

Academic & Scholarly; Atlases & Maps; Chemistry; Economics; Educational & Textbooks; Electronic (Educational); Electronic (Professional & Academic); Engineering; Environment & Development Studies; Gender Studies; Geography & Geology; Industry, Business & Management; Law; Literature & Criticism; Mathematics & Statistics; Medical (incl. Self Help & Alternative Medicine); Physics; Poetry; Politics & World Affairs; Reference Books, Directories & Dictionaries; Scientific & Technical; Sociology & Anthropology

New Titles: 100 (2011)
No of Employees: 10+

Imprints, Series & ISBNs:
Anthem Press: 978 1 84331, 978 1 898855
Anthem Press India: 978 81 905835, 978 81 907570
Wimbledon Publishing Co: 978 1 84331
WPC Classics: 978 1 898855

Book Trade Association Membership:
Publishers Association; Independent Publishers Guild

2029

ANTIQUE COLLECTORS' CLUB LTD
Sandy Lane, Old Martlesham, Woodbridge, Suffolk IP12 4SD
Telephone: 01394 389950
Fax: 01394 389999
Email: sales@antique-acc.com
Web Site: www.accdistribution.com

Personnel:
Diana Steel *(Managing Director)*
Sarah Smye *(Marketing Director)*
Vanessa Shorten *(Financial Director)*
James Smith *(Sales Director)*
Marco Jellinek *(Business Development Director)*
John Brancati *(General Manager, USA)*

Antiques & Collecting; Architecture & Design; Children's Books; Cookery, Wines & Spirits; Fashion & Costume; Fine Art & Art History; Gardening; Humour; Natural History; Photography; Reference Books, Directories & Dictionaries

Imprints, Series & ISBNs:
978 0 902028, 978 0 907462, 978 1 85149, 978 1 870673

Distributor for:
24 Ore Cultura (Motta); Acanthus Press; ACR Edition; Umberto Allemandi; Arnoldsche Verlagsanstalt; Arsenale Editrice; Artmedia Press; Ashmolean Museum Publications; The Azur Corporation Ltd; Beta Plus; George Braziller; Centro Di; Images; Lannoo Publishers; PI Global; River Books; Scala; Stichting Kunstboek; Vivays Publishing; Waanders

Overseas Representation:
All other territories: Antique Collectors' Club, Woodbridge, Suffolk, UK
Australia: Peribo Pty Ltd, Mount Kuring-Gai, NSW, Australia
Central Europe (excluding Russia): Csaba & Jackie Lengyel de Bagota, Budapest, Hungary
Far East (including Hong Kong, Taiwan, Philippines & China): Asia Publishers Services Ltd, Hong Kong
France: Interart SARL, Paris, UK
Germany, Austria & Switzerland: Michael Klein, Vilsbiburg, Germany
India: The Variety Book Depot, New Delhi, India
Iran: Jahan Adib Publishing, Tehran, Iran
Italy, Spain, Portugal & Greece: Penny Padovani, London, UK
Japan & South Korea: Ralph & Sheila Summers, Woodford Green, Essex, UK
Malaysia: APD Kuala Lumpur Pte Ltd, Selangor, Malaysia
Near & Middle East & Turkey: Avicenna Partnership, Dumfries, UK
Netherlands: Libridis Group / Nilsson & Lamm BV, Weesp, Netherlands
New Zealand: Book Reps NZ Ltd, Auckland, New Zealand
Republic of Ireland & Northern Ireland: Robert Towers, Monkstown, Co Dublin, Republic of Ireland
Scandinavia & Iceland: Elisabeth Harder-Kreimann, Hamburg, Germany
South & Central America, Caribbean & Mexico: InterMedia Americana (IMA) Ltd, London, UK
South East Asia (including Singapore, Thailand, Vietnam, Cambodia, Indonesia & Brunei): APD Singapore Pte Ltd, Singapore
USA: Antique Collectors Club, New York, NY, USA
West, Central & East Africa (excluding Sudan): InterMedia Africa Ltd (IMA), London, UK

Book Trade Association Membership:
Independent Publishers Guild

2030

ANVIL PRESS POETRY LTD
Neptune House, 70 Royal Hill, London SE10 8RF
Telephone: 020 8469 3033
Email: anvil@anvilpresspoetry.com
Web Site: www.anvilpresspoetry.com

Distribution:
NBN International, Thornbury Road, Plymouth, Devon PL6 7PP
Telephone: 01752 20230
Fax: 01752 202333
Email: orders@nbninternational.com
Web Site: www.nbninternational.com

Personnel:
Peter Jay *(Managing Director: Editorial, Administration & Production)*
Kit Yee Wong *(Administrative Manager)*

Poetry

New Titles: 11 (2010) , 7 (2011)
No of Employees: 2

Imprints, Series & ISBNs:
Anvil Editions: 978 0 85646, 978 0 900977
Poetica: 978 0 85646, 978 0 900977

Overseas Representation:
Australia: Eleanor Brasch Enterprises, Artarmon, NSW, Australia
Eastern Europe, Greece & Israel: Tony Moggach, InterMedia Americana (IMA) Ltd, London, UK
France, Benelux, Germany, Austria & Switzerland: Ted Dougherty, London, UK
Republic of Ireland: Robert Towers, Monkstown, Co Dublin, Republic of Ireland
Spain: Peter Prout Iberian Book Services, Madrid, Spain
USA: Consortium Book Sales & Distribution Inc, Minneapolis, MN, USA

Book Trade Association Membership:
Independent Publishers Guild

2031

APPLETREE PRESS LTD
The Old Potato Station,
14 Howard Street South, Belfast BT7 1AP
Telephone: 028 9024 3074
Fax: 028 9024 6756
Email: reception@appletree.ie
Web Site: www.appletree.ie

Distribution:
Gill and Macmillan, Republic of Ireland
Telephone: +353 (0)1 500 9500
Fax: +353 (0)1 500 9599
Email: sales@gillmacmillan.ie
Web Site: www.gillmacmillan.ie

Personnel:
John Murphy *(Managing Director)*
Jean Brown *(Editor)*
Paul McAvoy *(Production Manager)*
Mark Elliott *(Sales Manager)*

Cookery, Wines & Spirits; Guide Books; History & Antiquarian; Humour; Reference Books, Directories & Dictionaries; Sports & Games; Travel & Topography

New Titles: 12 (2010) , 12 (2011)
No of Employees: 10

Imprints, Series & ISBNs:
978 0 86281, 978 0 904651

Overseas Representation:
Australia & New Zealand: Peribo Pty Ltd, Mount Kuring-Gai, NSW, Australia
France, Belgium, Scandinavia, Germany, Austria, Switzerland & Spain: Appletree Press, Belfast, UK
Greece, Cyprus, Israel, Russia, Eastern Europe & the Baltic States: IMA, Greece

Italy: Penguin Italia srl, Milan, Italy
Netherlands: Novelty Books, Weesp,
Netherlands
Republic of Ireland: Compass Independent
Book Sales Ltd, Naas, Co Kildare,
Republic of Ireland
USA & Canada: Independent Publishers
Group (IPG), Chicago, IL, USA

Book Trade Association Membership:
Publishing Ireland (Foilsiú Éireann)

2032 ▬▬▬▬▬▬▬

ARCADIA BOOKS LTD
15–16 Nassau Street, London W1W 7AB
Telephone: 020 7436 9898
Email: info@arcadiabooks.co.uk
Web Site: www.arcadiabooks.co.uk

Distribution:
Turnaround, Unit 3, Olympia Trading Estate,
Coburg Road, London N22 6TZ
Telephone: 020 8829 3000
Fax: 020 8881 5088
Email: orders@turnaround-uk.com
Web Site: www.turnaround-uk.com

Personnel:
Gary Pulsifer *(Publisher)*
Daniela de Groote *(Associate Publisher)*
Angeline Rothermundt *(Editor Director)*
Andrew Hayward *(Financial Director)*

*Biography & Autobiography; Crime;
Fiction; Gay & Lesbian Studies; Gender
Studies; Photography; Politics & World
Affairs; Travel & Topography*

New Titles: 35 (2010) , 35 (2011)
No of Employees: 4

Imprints, Series & ISBNs:
978 1 900850, 978 1 905147
Arcadia Books
BlackAmber
Bliss Books
EuroCrime
Maia Press

Overseas Representation:
Australia/New Zealand: Tower Too, NSW,
Australia
Israel (selected titles only): Steimatzky Ltd,
Bnei Brak, Israel
North America: Dufour Editions, Chester
Springs, PA, USA
South Africa: Quartet Sales & Marketing,
Johannesburg, South Africa

Book Trade Association Membership:
Independent Publishers Guild; English PEN –
Writers in Prison & Books to Prisoners
Committee; BTBS (The Book Trade Charity)

2033 ▬▬▬▬▬▬▬

ARCHAEOPRESS LTD
Gordon House, 276 Banbury Road, Oxford
OX2 7ED
Telephone: 01865 311914
Fax: 01865 311914
Email: bar@archaeopress.com
Web Site: www.archaeopress.com

Personnel:
Dr David Davison *(Director)*

Archaeology

Imprints, Series & ISBNs:
Archaeopress: 978 1 905739
British Archaeological Reports: 978 1 4073

Overseas Representation:
Worldwide: Hadrian Books Ltd, Oxford, UK

2034 ▬▬▬▬▬▬▬

*ARCHETYPE PUBLICATIONS LTD
6 Fitzroy Square, London W1T 5HJ
Telephone: 020 7380 0800

Fax: 020 7380 0500
Email: info@archetype.co.uk
Web Site: www.archetype.co.uk

Personnel:
James Black *(Managing Director)*

*Academic & Scholarly; Archaeology; Fine
Art & Art History; Scientific & Technical*

Imprints, Series & ISBNs:
978 1 873132, 978 1 904982

Overseas Representation:
USA (All titles): Antique Collectors Club Ltd,
Easthampton, MA, USA; JG Publishing
Services, Los Angeles, CA, USA

2035 ▬▬▬▬▬▬▬

**ARCHITECTURAL ASSOCIATION
PUBLICATIONS**
36 Bedford Square, London WC1B 3ES
Telephone: 020 7887 4021
Fax: 020 7414 0782
Email: publications@aaschool.ac.uk
Web Site: www.aaschool.ac.uk

Personnel:
Marilyn Sparrow *(Sales & Marketing
Manager)*
Kirsten Morphet *(Publications Co-ordinator)*
Pamela Johnston *(Editor)*
Thomas Weaver *(Editor)*

Architecture & Design

New Titles: 20 (2010) , 12 (2011)
No of Employees: 4

Imprints, Series & ISBNs:
Architectural Association: 978 1 870890,
978 1 902902, 978 1 907896
Bedford Press: 978 1 907414

Parent Company:
Architectural Association Inc

Overseas Representation:
Australia: Robyn Ralton, Collingwood, Vic,
Australia
France: Muriel Fischer, Paris, France
Germany & Austria: Kurt Salchli, Berlin,
Germany
Netherlands & Belgium: Berend Bosch,
Noordwijk, Netherlands
Southern Europe: Bookport Associates,
Milan, Italy

Book Trade Association Membership:
Publishers Association

2036 ▬▬▬▬▬▬▬

ARCHIVE PUBLISHING
Unit 3, Stone Lane Industrial Estate,
Wimborne, Dorset BH21 1HB
Telephone: 01202 848352
Email: orders@archivepublishing.co.uk
Web Site: www.transpersonalbooks.com

*Children's Books; Fiction; Medical (incl. Self
Help & Alternative Medicine); Music;
Psychology & Psychiatry*

New Titles: 2 (2010) , 4 (2011)
No of Employees: 0

Imprints, Series & ISBNs:
978 0 9542712, 978 1 906289

Book Trade Association Membership:
Booksellers Association; Independent
Publishers Guild

2037 ▬▬▬▬▬▬▬

ARENA BOOKS (PUBLISHERS)
6 Southgate Green, Bury St Edmunds,
Suffolk IP33 2BL
Telephone: 01284 754123
Fax: 01284 754123

Email: arenabooks@tiscali.co.uk
Web Site: www.arenabooks.co.uk

Personnel:
James Farrell *(Managing Director)*
Robert Corfe *(Director)*
Russell Corfe *(Editor)*
June Hardy *(Sales Manager)*

*Academic & Scholarly; Economics; Fiction;
History & Antiquarian; Industry, Business &
Management; Literature & Criticism;
Military & War; Philosophy; Politics & World
Affairs; Religion & Theology; Science
Fiction; Sociology & Anthropology; Travel &
Topography*

Imprints, Series & ISBNs:
978 0 9538460, 978 0 9543161, 978 0
9556055, 978 1 906791

Overseas Representation:
Egypt: Abdul Radder Al-Bakkar, Cairo,
Egypt
Poland: Graal Sp, Warsaw, Poland
USA: Ingram Publisher Services, La Vergne,
TN, USA

Book Trade Association Membership:
Independent Publishers Guild

2038 ▬▬▬▬▬▬▬

ASHGATE PUBLISHING LTD
Wey Court East, Union Road, Farnham,
Surrey GU9 7PT
Telephone: 01252 736600
Fax: 01252 736736
Email: info@ashgatepublishing.com
Web Site: www.ashgate.com

Warehouse & Mailing Shop, Orders:
Ashgate Publishing Direct Sales,
Bookpoint Ltd, 39 Milton Park, Abingdon,
Oxon OX14 4TD
Telephone: 01235 400400
Fax: 01235 400454

Personnel:
Nigel Farrow *(Chairman)*
Rachel Lynch *(Managing Director)*
Jonathan Norman *(Publisher: Business
(Gower))*
Lucy Myers *(Managing Director – Lund
Humphries)*
Adrian Shanks *(Editorial, Production &
Digital Director)*
Darren Wise *(Finance/Accounting Director)*
Anne Nolan *(Ashgate Marketing Director)*
Richard Dowling *(Sales Director)*
Jo Burges *(Systems Director)*

*Academic & Scholarly; Architecture &
Design; Aviation; Bibliography & Library
Science; Economics; Educational &
Textbooks; Electronic (Professional &
Academic); Environment & Development
Studies; Fine Art & Art History; Gender
Studies; Geography & Geology; History &
Antiquarian; Illustrated & Fine Editions;
Industry, Business & Management; Law;
Literature & Criticism; Military & War;
Music; Philosophy; Politics & World Affairs;
Reference Books, Directories &
Dictionaries; Religion & Theology; Sociology
& Anthropology; Theatre, Drama & Dance;
Transport*

New Titles: 800 (2011)
No of Employees: 120

Imprints, Series & ISBNs:
Arena: 978 1 85742
Ashgate Publishing: 978 0 7546, 978 1
84014
Avebury: 978 0 291, 978 1 85628, 978 1
85972
Dartmouth: 978 1 85521
Gower Publishing: 978 0 566, 978 1 85904
Gregg International: 978 0 576
Gregg Revivals: 978 0 7512
Lund Humphries: 978 0 85331

Scolar Press: 978 0 85967, 978 1 85928
Variorum: 978 0 86078
Wildwood House: 978 0 7045

Parent Company:
Ashgate Publishing Group

Associated Companies:
Gower Publishing Co Ltd; Lund Humphries;
Scolar Fine Art Ltd
USA: Ashgate Publishing Co

Overseas Representation:
*Australia, South East Asia, Malaysia,
Philippines, China, Hong Kong, Taiwan,
Myanmar (Burma) & South Korea:*
Ashgate Publishing Asia-Pacific,
Newport, NSW, Australia
India: Maya Publishers Pvt Ltd, New Delhi,
India
Japan: United Publishers Services Ltd,
Tokyo, Japan
USA: Ashgate Publishing Co, Burlington,
VT, USA

Book Trade Association Membership:
Independent Publishers Guild

2039 ▬▬▬▬▬▬▬

ASHGROVE PUBLISHING
27 John Street, London WC1N 2BX
Telephone: 020 7242 4820
Email: ashgrovepublishing@gmail.com

Warehouse & Distribution:
Orca Book Services, Unit 3A,
Fleets Corner Industrial Estate, Fleetsbridge,
Poole, Dorset BH17 0HL
Telephone: 01202 785714
Fax: 01202 672076
Email:
tradeorders@orcabookservices.co.uk
Web Site: www.orcabookservices.co.uk

Personnel:
Brad Thompson *(Managing Director)*

*Audio Books; Biography & Autobiography;
Cookery, Wines & Spirits; Fiction; Health &
Beauty; Medical (incl. Self Help &
Alternative Medicine); Military & War;
Psychology & Psychiatry; Religion &
Theology*

New Titles: 6 (2010) , 8 (2011)
No of Employees: 2
Annual Turnover: £30,000

Imprints, Series & ISBNs:
978 0 906798, 978 1 85398

Parent Company:
Hollydata Publishers Ltd

Associated Companies:
Childrens Corner Ltd

Overseas Representation:
Worldwide: Star Book Sales, Whimple,
Exeter, UK

2040 ▬▬▬▬▬▬▬

***ASHMOLEAN MUSEUM
PUBLICATIONS**
Ashmolean Museum, Beaumont Street,
Oxford OX1 2PH
Telephone: 01865 278010
Fax: 01865 278106
Email: publications@ashmus.ox.ac.uk
Web Site: www.ashmolean.org

Warehouse, Trade Enquiries & Orders:
Antique Collectors Club, Sandy Lane,
Old Martlesham, Woodbridge, Suffolk
IP12 4SD
Telephone: 01394 389950
Fax: 01394 389999
Email: sales@antique-acc.com
Web Site: www.accdistribution.com

Personnel:
D. McCarthy (Commercial Manager)
E. Jolliffe (Deputy, Editorial, Production, Web Editor Publishing Manager)
K. Wodehouse (Picture Library Manager)

Academic & Scholarly; Archaeology; Fine Art & Art History; History & Antiquarian

Imprints, Series & ISBNs:
978 0 900090, 978 0 907849, 978 1 85444

Parent Company:
Ashmolean Museum, University of Oxford

Overseas Representation:
Australia: Inbooks, c/o James Bennett Pty Ltd, Belrose, NSW, Australia
Europe: Antique Collectors Club, Suffolk, UK
USA: Antique Collectors Club Ltd, Easthampton, MA, USA

Book Trade Association Membership:
Booksellers Association; Independent Publishers Guild; Museums & Galleries Publishing Group

2041 ▬▬▬▬

ASIAN-E LTD
2nd floor, 3 Brindley Place, Birmingham B1 2JB
Telephone: 0121 698 8524
Fax: 0121 698 8593
Web Site: www.asian-e.co.uk

Book Trade Association Membership:
Publishers Association

2042 ▬▬▬▬

ASSOCIATION FOR LEARNING TECHNOLOGY
Gipsy Lane, Headington, Oxford OX3 0BP
Telephone: 01865 484125
Fax: 01865 484165
Email: admin@alt.ac.uk
Web Site: www.alt.ac.uk

Personnel:
Seb Schmoller (Chief Executive)

Academic & Scholarly

Imprints, Series & ISBNs:
Beyond Control (Research Proceeding): 978 0 9545870

2043 ▬▬▬▬

ASSOCIATION FOR SCOTTISH LITERARY STUDIES
c/o Dept of Scottish Literature, University of Glasgow,
7 University Gardens, Glasgow G12 8QH
Telephone: 0141 330 5309
Fax: 0141 330 5309
Email: office@asls.org.uk
Web Site: www.asls.org.uk

Trade Enquiries:
BookSource, 50 Cambuslang Road, Glasgow G32 8NB
Telephone: 0845 370 0063
Fax: 0845 370 0064
Email: orders@booksource.net
Web Site: www.booksource.net

Personnel:
Mr Duncan Jones (Director)

Academic & Scholarly; Educational & Textbooks; Fiction; Languages & Linguistics; Literature & Criticism; Poetry; Theatre, Drama & Dance

New Titles: 5 (2010) , 8 (2011)
No of Employees: 2
Annual Turnover: £147,265

Imprints, Series & ISBNs:
978 0 948877, 978 1 906841
ASLS Annual Volumes (series)
New Writing Scotland (series)
Occasional Papers (series)
Scotnotes (series)

Book Trade Association Membership:
Publishing Scotland

2044 ▬▬▬▬

ATLANTIC BOOKS
Ormond House, 26–27 Boswell Street, London WC1N 3JZ
Telephone: 020 7269 1610
Fax: 020 7430 0916
Email: enquiries@groveatlantic.co.uk
Web Site: www.atlantic-books.co.uk

Distribution:
TBS Ltd, Colchester Road, Frating Green, Colchester, Essex CO7 7DW
Telephone: 01206 255678
Fax: 01206 255930
Email: sales@tbs-ltd.co.uk
Web Site: www.thebookservice.co.uk

Personnel:
Toby Mundy (Chief Executive Officer & Publisher)
Vanessa Kerr (Rights Director)
Nicolas Cheetham (Publishing Director, Corvus)
Margaret Stead (Publishing Director, Atlantic)
Alan Craig (Production)
Karen Duffy (Publicity)
Ravi Mirchandani (Editor-in-Chief)

Biography & Autobiography; Crime; Economics; Fiction; History & Antiquarian; Humour; Industry, Business & Management; Law; Literature & Criticism; Mathematics & Statistics; Military & War; Music; Natural History; Philosophy; Poetry; Politics & World Affairs; Psychology & Psychiatry; Reference Books, Directories & Dictionaries; Religion & Theology; Science Fiction; Sports & Games; Transport

Imprints, Series & ISBNs:
978 1 84354

Overseas Representation:
Australia: Allen & Unwin
Europe: Faber & Faber, London, UK
Far East: Julian Ashton, Ashton International Marketing Services, Sevenoaks, Kent, UK
New Zealand: Allen & Unwin
Republic of Ireland: Repforce Ireland, Irishtown, Dublin, Republic of Ireland
South Africa: Penguin Group SA, Rosebank, South Africa

Book Trade Association Membership:
Publishers Association; Independent Publishers Guild

2045 ▬▬▬▬

ATLANTIC EUROPE PUBLISHING CO LTD
Greys Court Farm, Greys Court, Henley on Thames, Oxon RG9 4PG
Telephone: 01491 628188
Fax: 01491 628189
Email: info@atlanticeurope.com
Web Site: www.AtlanticEurope.com & www.CurriculumVisions.com

Personnel:
Dr B. J. Knapp (Director)

Chemistry; Children's Books; Educational & Textbooks; Electronic (Educational); Environment & Development Studies; Geography & Geology; History & Antiquarian; Mathematics & Statistics; Physics; Reference Books, Directories &

Dictionaries; Religion & Theology; Scientific & Technical

Imprints, Series & ISBNs:
978 1 86214, 978 1 869860

2046 ▬▬▬▬

*ATTIC PRESS
[an imprint of Cork University Press]
c/o Cork University Press,
Youngline Industrial Estate, Pailaduff Road, Togher, Cork, Republic of Ireland
Telephone: +353 (0)21 490 2980
Fax: +353 (0)21 431 5329
Web Site: www.corkuniversitypress.com

Representation (Republic of Ireland & Northern Ireland):
Mullet Fitzpatrick, 58 New Vale Cottages, Shankhill, Dublin, Republic of Ireland

Orders & Distribution:
Gill & Macmillan, Hume Avenue, Park West, Dublin 12, Republic of Ireland

Personnel:
Mike Collins (Publications Director)

Biography & Autobiography; Cookery, Wines & Spirits; Gender Studies; Music; Politics & World Affairs

Imprints, Series & ISBNs:
978 0 946211, 978 0 9535353, 978 1 85594

Parent Company:
Republic of Ireland: Cork University Press

Overseas Representation:
Netherlands & Germany: Brigitte Axster, Frankfurt, Germany
UK: Quantum Publishing Solutions Ltd, Paisley, UK
UK (excluding Northern Ireland): Marston Book Services Ltd, Abingdon, UK
USA: Dufour Editions Inc, Chester Springs, PA, USA

Book Trade Association Membership:
Publishing Ireland (Foilsiú Éireann)

2047 ▬▬▬▬

AUDIBLE.CO.UK
Colet Court, 100 Hammersmith Road, London W6 7JP
Telephone: 020 8956 2828
Fax: 020 8956 2829
Web Site: www.audible.co.uk

Book Trade Association Membership:
Publishers Association

2048 ▬▬▬▬

*AUDIO-FORUM – THE LANGUAGE SOURCE
World Microfilms, PO Box 35488, St John's Wood, London NW8 6WD
Telephone: 020 7586 4499
Email: microworld@ndirect.co.uk
Web Site: www.microworld.uk.com

Personnel:
S. C. Albert (Director)

Academic & Scholarly; Languages & Linguistics

Imprints, Series & ISBNs:
with Sussex Publications: 978 1 86013

Associated Companies:
Sussex Publications Ltd; World Microfilms Publications Ltd

2049 ▬▬▬▬

AUDIOGO LTD
[The Home of BBC Audiobooks]

St James House, The Square, Lower Bristol Road, Bath BA2 3BH
Telephone: 01225 878000
Fax: 01225 878003
Email: info@audiogo.co.uk
Web Site: www.audiogo.co.uk

Personnel:
Mike Bowen (Managing Director)
Jan Paterson (Publishing Director)
Nick Forster (Sales & Marketing Director)
Tracy Leeming (Operations Director)
Bradley Whittock (Finance Director)

Audio Books

Imprints, Series & ISBNs:
Cover to Cover Cassettes (Audio Cassettes & CDs): 978 1 85549
Radio Collection (Audio Cassettes, CDs & MP3 CDs): 978 0 563
Word for Word (Audio Cassettes & CDs)

Overseas Representation:
USA: AudioGO Ltd, USA

Book Trade Association Membership:
Publishers Association

2050 ▬▬▬▬

AURELIAN INFORMATION LTD
4(A) Alexandra Mansions, West End Lane, London NW6 1LU
Telephone: 020 7794 8609
Fax: 020 7794 8609
Email: paul@aurelian.org.uk
Web Site: www.dircon.co.uk/aurelian/

Distribution:
Wyvern DM Ltd, Harrier House, Sedgeway Business Park, Witchford, Ely, Cambs CB6 2HY
Telephone: Database enquiries: 01353 667733
Fax: 01353 669030 (Database enquiries)
Web Site: www.dircon.co.uk/aurelian/

Personnel:
Paul Petzold (Director)
Julia Kaufmann OBE (Company Secretary)

Industry, Business & Management; Reference Books, Directories & Dictionaries

Imprints, Series & ISBNs:
Aurelian: 978 1 899247
National Charities Database: 978 1 899247

2051 ▬▬▬▬

*AUREUS PUBLISHING LTD
Castle Court, Castle-upon-Alun, St Bride's Major, Vale of Glamorgan CF32 0TN
Telephone: 01656 880033
Fax: 01656 880033
Email: info@aureus.co.uk
Web Site: www.aureus.co.uk

Personnel:
Meuryn Hughes (Director)

Biography & Autobiography; Fine Art & Art History; Music; Sports & Games

Imprints, Series & ISBNs:
978 1 899750

2052 ▬▬▬▬

AURORA METRO PUBLICATIONS LTD
67 Grove Avenue, Twickenham, London TW1 4HX
Telephone: 020 3261 0000
Fax: 020 8898 0735
Email: info@aurorametro.com
Web Site: www.aurorametro.com

Distribution:
Central Books, 99 Wallis Road, Hackney,
London E9 5LN
Telephone: 020 8986 4854
Fax: 020 8533 5821
Email: info@centralbooks.com &
orders@centralbooks.com
Web Site: www.centralbooks.com

Personnel:
Cheryl Robson *(Publisher)*
Steve Robson *(Sales & Marketing)*
Rebecca Gillieron *(Managing Editor)*
Sumedha Mane *(Administrator)*

*Academic & Scholarly; Children's Books;
Cinema, Video, TV & Radio; Cookery, Wines
& Spirits; Educational & Textbooks; Fiction;
Gay & Lesbian Studies; Gender Studies;
Humour; Reference Books, Directories &
Dictionaries; Theatre, Drama & Dance;
Travel & Topography*

Imprints, Series & ISBNs:
Aurora Metro Press: 978 0 9515877, 978 0
9536757, 978 0 9542330, 978 0
9546912, 978 0 9551566, 978 1 906582
Supernova Books: 978 0 9566329

Overseas Representation:
Australia: Int Books, 3 Charles St, Coburg
North, Victoria, Australia
Canada: Playwrights Press Canada, Toronto,
Ont, Canada
USA: TCG/Consortium, St Paul, MN, USA

Book Trade Association Membership:
Independent Publishers Guild

2053

*AURUM PRESS
7 Greenland Street, London NW1 0ND
Telephone: 020 7284 7160
Fax: 020 7485 4902
Email:
firstname.secondname@aurumpress.co.
uk
Web Site: www.aurumpress.co.uk

Distribution & Warehouse:
Littlehampton Book Services,
Columbia Building, Faraday Close,
Durrington, Worthing, West Sussex
BN13 3RB
Telephone: 01903 828800
Fax: 01903 828801

Personnel:
W. J. McCreadie *(Managing Director)*
Graham Eames *(Sales Director)*
Graham Coster *(Editorial Director)*

*Architecture & Design; Biography &
Autobiography; Cinema, Video, TV &
Radio; Cookery, Wines & Spirits; Crafts &
Hobbies; Fashion & Costume; Gardening;
Health & Beauty; Humour; Military & War;
Music; Natural History; Photography;
Sports & Games; Transport; Travel &
Topography*

Imprints, Series & ISBNs:
978 1 84513, 978 1 85410, 978 1 902538,
978 1 903221, 978 1 906417

Parent Company:
Quarto Group Plc

Overseas Representation:
*Africa (excluding South Africa) & Eastern
Europe:* InterMedia Americana (IMA) Ltd,
London, UK
Australia: Bookwise International, Adelaide,
SA, Australia
Canada: Manda Group, Toronto, Ont,
Canada
Europe: Bill Bailey Publishers
Representatives, Newton Abbot, UK
Far East: Ashton International Marketing
Services, Sevenoaks, Kent, UK

Latin America & Caribbean: Humphrys
Roberts Associates, London, UK
New Zealand: Hachette Livre New Zealand,
Auckland, New Zealand
Scandinavia: McNeish Publishing
International, East Sussex, UK
South Africa: Trinity Books CC, Randburg,
South Africa
USA: IPG Trafalgar Square, Chicago, IL, USA

Book Trade Association Membership:
Independent Publishers Guild

2054

***AUSTIN & MACAULEY PUBLISHERS
LTD**
CGC-33–01, 25 Canada Square,
Canary Wharf, London E14 5LB
Telephone: 020 7038 8212
Fax: 020 7038 8100
Email: editors@austinmacauley.com
Web Site: www.austinmacauley.com

Personnel:
Annette Longman *(Chief Editor)*
Serena Brotherton *(Executive Editor)*
Ross Malik *(Marketing Executive)*

*Academic & Scholarly; Accountancy &
Taxation; Agriculture; Animal Care &
Breeding; Antiques & Collecting; Audio
Books; Bibliography & Library Science;
Biography & Autobiography; Biology &
Zoology; Children's Books; Cinema, Video,
TV & Radio; Computer Science; Cookery,
Wines & Spirits; Crime; Do-It-Yourself;
Economics; Educational & Textbooks;
English as a Foreign Language;
Environment & Development Studies;
Fashion & Costume; Fiction; Fine Art & Art
History; Gardening; Gay & Lesbian Studies;
Health & Beauty; Humour; Industry;
Business & Management; Literature &
Criticism; Magic & the Occult; Mathematics
& Statistics; Medical (incl. Self Help &
Alternative Medicine); Military & War;
Natural History; Nautical; Philosophy;
Poetry; Politics & World Affairs; Psychology
& Psychiatry; Reference Books, Directories &
Dictionaries; Religion & Theology; Science
Fiction; Scientific & Technical; Sociology &
Anthropology; Sports & Games; Theatre,
Drama & Dance; Travel & Topography;
Vocational Training & Careers*

2055

AUTHENTIC MEDIA
52 Presley Way, Crownhill, Milton Keynes
MK8 0ES
Email: info@authenticmedia.co.uk
Web Site: www.authenticmedia.co.uk

Orders:
Trust Media Distribution (Formerly STL
Distribution), PO Box 300,
Kingstown Broadway, Carlisle, Cumbria
CA3 0HA
Telephone: 01228 512512
Fax: 01228 514949
Web Site:
www.trustmediadistribution.co.uk

Personnel:
Malcolm Down *(Publisher)*
Sarah Gallagher *(Marketing Co-ordinator,
Authentic (General) – Administration)*
Mike Parsons *(Paternoster (Academic)
Editorial)*
Liz Williams *(Authentic (General) – Editorial)*
Peter Little *(Production Controller)*
Richard Durham *(Data Administrator)*
Becky Fawcett *(Editorial Administrator)*

*Academic & Scholarly; Biography &
Autobiography; Children's Books; Religion
& Theology*

Imprints, Series & ISBNs:
Authentic Bibles: 978 0 85009

Authentic Lifestyle: 978 1 85078, 978 1
86024
Paternoster: 978 1 84227, 978 1 85364

Overseas Representation:
India: OM Book Services, Delhi, India
USA: STL Inc, Waynesboro, GA, USA

Book Trade Association Membership:
Booksellers Association

2056

*AUTHORHOUSE UK LTD
500 Avebury Boulevard, Milton Keynes,
Bucks MK9 2BE
Telephone: 01908 309250
Fax: 01908 309259
Web Site: www.authorhouse.co.uk

Personnel:
Tim Davies *(Managing Director)*
Daniel Cooke *(Business Development
Director)*

*Biography & Autobiography; Children's
Books; Cookery, Wines & Spirits; Crime;
Fiction; Humour; Poetry; Religion &
Theology; Science Fiction*

Imprints, Series & ISBNs:
978 1 4208, 978 1 4259, 978 1 4343

Parent Company:
USA: Author Solutions Inc

Associated Companies:
USA: Authorhouse (USA); iUniverse;
Trafford; Wordclay; Xlibris

2057

*AVA PUBLISHING (UK) LTD
56A Chapel Road, Worthing, West Sussex
BN11 1BE
Telephone: 01903 204455
Fax: 01903 237346
Email: enquiries@avabooks.com
Web Site: www.avabooks.com

Personnel:
Brian Morris *(Publisher)*
Terry Hancock *(Finance Manager)*
Caroline Walmsley *(Editor in Chief)*

*Architecture & Design; Cinema, Video, TV &
Radio; Educational & Textbooks; Electronic
(Educational); Fashion & Costume; Industry,
Business & Management; Photography;
Reference Books, Directories & Dictionaries*

Imprints, Series & ISBNs:
978 2 88479, 978 2 940373, 978 2
940411, 978 2 940439

Parent Company:
Switzerland: AVA Publishing SA

Overseas Representation:
USA & Canada: Ingram Publisher Services,
La Vergne, TN, USA
World (excluding North America): Thames
& Hudson Ltd, London, UK

2058

AWARD PUBLICATIONS LTD
The Old Riding School, Welbeck Estate,
Worksop, Notts S80 3LR
Telephone: 01909 478170
Fax: 01909 484632
Email: info@awardpublications.co.uk
Web Site: www.awardpublications.co.uk

Personnel:
Anna Wilkinson *(Managing Director)*
Richard Carman *(International Sales
Director)*
David Meggs *(UK Sales Director)*
Adam Wilde *(Production Manager)*

*Children's Books; Reference Books,
Directories & Dictionaries*

New Titles: 50 (2010) , 50 (2011)
No of Employees: 14

Imprints, Series & ISBNs:
Award: 978 0 86163, 978 1 84135
Horus: 978 1 899762

2059

AXIS EDUCATION
5 Knights Park, Hussey Road,
Battlefield Enterprise Park, Shrewsbury
SY1 3TE
Telephone: 01743 460021
Fax: 01743 454890
Web Site: www.axiseducation.co.uk

Book Trade Association Membership:
Publishers Association

2060

B SMALL PUBLISHING LTD
The Book Shed, 36 Leyborne Park, Kew,
Richmond, Surrey TW9 3HA
Telephone: 020 8948 2884
Fax: 020 8948 6458
Web Site: www.bsmall.co.uk

**Sales Representation, UK Trade
Enquiries & Orders:**
Bounce! Sales & Marketing Ltd,
14 Greville Street, London EC1N 8SB
Telephone: 020 7138 3650
Fax: 020 7138 3658
Email: sales@bouncemarketing.co.uk
Web Site: www.bouncemarketing.co.uk

Personnel:
Catherine Bruzzone *(Publisher & Managing
Director)*
Sam Hutchinson *(General Manager)*

*Children's Books; Crafts & Hobbies; English
as a Foreign Language; Languages &
Linguistics*

New Titles: 9 (2010) , 7 (2011)
No of Employees: 2

Imprints, Series & ISBNs:
978 1 874735, 978 1 902915, 978 1
905710

Overseas Representation:
Australia (languages only): Intext Book Co
Pty Ltd, Hawthorn, Vic, Australia
South Africa: Phambili Agencies CC,
Johannesburg, South Africa

Book Trade Association Membership:
Independent Publishers Guild

2061

**BERNARD BABANI (PUBLISHING)
LTD**
The Grampians, Shepherds Bush Road,
London W6 7NF
Telephone: 020 7603 2581/7296
Fax: 020 7603 8203
Email: enquiries@babanibooks.com
Web Site: www.babanibooks.com

Personnel:
Michael H. Babani *(Sales, Production,
Managing Director)*

*Computer Science; Crafts & Hobbies;
Educational & Textbooks; Electronic
(Educational); Electronic (Entertainment);
Electronic (Professional & Academic);
Engineering; Mathematics & Statistics;
Scientific & Technical*

Imprints, Series & ISBNs:
Babani Press: 978 0 85934, 978 0 900162

Associated Companies:
Bernards (Publishers) Ltd

Book Trade Association Membership:
Independent Publishers Guild

2062

BADGER PUBLISHING LTD
[a division of Haven Books Ltd]
Suite G08, Business & Technology Centre,
Bessemer Drive, Stevenage SG1 2DX
Telephone: 01438 791037
Fax: 01438 791036
Email: enquiries@badger-publishing.co.uk
Web Site: www.badger-publishing.co.uk

Personnel:
Susan Ross (*Director & Publisher*)
Jean Constantine (*Sales & Marketing Manager*)
Danny Pearson (*Senior Editor*)

Children's Books; Educational & Textbooks

Imprints, Series & ISBNs:
978 1 84424, 978 1 84691, 978 1 85880,
978 1 84926, 978 1 86509

Parent Company:
UK: Haven Books Ltd

Book Trade Association Membership:
Publishers Association; Educational
Publishers Council

2063

CHARLES BAKER BOOKS
c/o 47 Bury New Road, Prestwich,
Manchester M25 9JY

Book Trade Association Membership:
Publishers Association

2064

BALBERRY PUBLISHING
322 Old Brompton Road, London SW5 9JH
Telephone: 020 7373 7781
Fax: 020 7373 4930

Book Trade Association Membership:
Publishers Association

2065

THE BANNER OF TRUTH TRUST
3 Murrayfield Road, Edinburgh EH12 6EL
Telephone: 0131 337 7310
Fax: 0131 346 7484
Email: info@banneroftruth.co.uk
Web Site: www.banneroftruth.co.uk

Warehouse:
17 Bankhead Drive,
Sighthill Industrial Estate, Edinburgh
EH11 4DW
Telephone: 0131 442 2945
Fax: 0131 442 2945
Email: info@banneroftruth.co.uk
Web Site: www.banneroftruth.co.uk

Personnel:
John Rawlinson (*General Manager*)
Jonathan Watson (*Editor*)

Religion & Theology

New Titles: 25 (2010) , 25 (2011)
No of Employees: 10

Imprints, Series & ISBNs:
978 0 85151, 978 1 84871

Associated Companies:
USA: The Banner of Truth

Overseas Representation:
New Zealand: Sovereign Grace Books,
Auckland, New Zealand
Nigeria: Amazing Grace Ltd, Kano, Nigeria

Philippines: Evangelical Outreach Inc,
Quezon City, Philippines
South Africa: Barnabas Book Room, Durban
North, South Africa; Farel Distributors
(Pty) Ltd, North Riding, South Africa
USA: The Banner of Truth, Carlisle, PA, USA

2066

*BARDDAS
Pen-Rhiw, 71 Pentrepoeth Road, Morriston,
Swansea SA6 6AE
Telephone: 01792 792829
Fax: 01792 792829
Email: alan.llwyd@googlemail.com

Assistant Officer:
Bod Aeron, Heol Pen-Sarn, Y Bala,
Gwynedd LL23 7SR
Telephone: 01678 521051
Fax: 01678 521051
Email: elwyn@barddas.fsnet.co.uk
Web Site: www.barddas.com

Personnel:
Alan Llwyd (*Administrative Officer*)
Elwyn Edwards (*Assistant Officer*)

Poetry

Imprints, Series & ISBNs:
978 1 900437

2067

BAREFOOT BOOKS
294 Banbury Road, Oxford OX2 7ED
Telephone: 01865 311100
Fax: 01865 514965
Email: info@barefootbooks.com
Web Site: www.barefootbooks.com

Trade Sales (Orders):
Littlehampton Book Services Ltd,
Faraday Close, Durrington, Worthing,
West Sussex BN13 3RB
Telephone: 01903 828800
Fax: 01903 828801

Personnel:
Tessa Strickland (*Editor-in-Chief*)
Nancy Traversy (*Managing Director*)
Gautam Bhasin (*European General Manager*)

Audio Books; Children's Books; Educational & Textbooks

Imprints, Series & ISBNs:
978 1 84148, 978 1 84686, 978 1 898000,
978 1 901223, 978 1 902283, 978 1
905236

Overseas Representation:
Australia: Willow Connection Pty Ltd,
Brookvale, NSW, Australia
East Africa: A–Z Africa Book Services,
Rotterdam, Netherlands
Europe (Trade), Indian Subcontinent & Middle East: Gabriele Kern Publishers
Services, Frankfurt-am-Main, Germany;
Jenny Padovani, Barcelona, Spain; Penny
Padovani, Montanare di Cortona, Italy
Latin America & Caribbean: David Williams,
InterMedia Americana (IMA) Ltd,
London, UK
New Zealand: Addenda Ltd, Grey Lynn,
New Zealand
Republic of Ireland & Northern Ireland:
Conor Hackett, Dublin, Republic of
Ireland
South Africa: Phambili Agencies CC,
Germiston, South Africa; Salmonberry
Press, South Africa
*South East Asia, Far East, North Asia, Hong
Kong, Singapore, Brunei & Malaysia
(Libraries), Singapore, Brunei & Malaysia
(Trade & Special Sales):* Chris Ashdown,
Publishers Marketing Services Pte Ltd,
Singapore

South East, Far East & North Asia:
Publishers International Marketing,
London, UK
USA: Barefoot Books Inc, Cambridge, MA,
USA

2068

BARNY BOOKS
Hough on the Hill, Grantham NG32 2BB
Telephone: 01400 250246
Fax: 01400 251737
Email: barnybooks@barnybooks.co.uk
Web Site: www.barnybooks.co.uk

Orders & Invoices:
76 Cotgrave Lane, Tollerton, Nottingham
NG12 4FY
Telephone: 0115 937 5147
Email: info@barnybooks.co.uk
Web Site: www.barnybooks.co.uk

Personnel:
Molly Burkett (*Editor*)
Jayne Thompson (*Business Manager*)

*Biography & Autobiography; Children's
Books; Cookery, Wines & Spirits; Fiction;
Gardening; History & Antiquarian;
Humour; Industry, Business &
Management; Medical (incl. Self Help &
Alternative Medicine); Military & War;
Transport*

New Titles: 13 (2010) , 15 (2011)
No of Employees: 2
Annual Turnover: £15,000

Imprints, Series & ISBNs:
978 0 948204, 978 1 906542
Events, People to be Remembered (Joseph
Banks – Sir John Hawrins)
Once upon a Wartime (Series): 978 1
903172

2069

BATSFORD
[an imprint of Anova Books Group]
10 Southcombe Street, London W14 0RA
Telephone: 020 7605 1400
Fax: 020 7605 1401
Email: reception@anovabooks.com
Web Site: www.anovabooks.com

Distribution, Warehouse & Enquiries:
HarperCollins Distribution, Campsie View,
Westerhill Road, Bishopbriggs, Glasgow
G64 2QT
Telephone: 0141 306 3100
Fax: 0141 306 3767

Personnel:
Tina Persaud (*Publisher*)
Komal Patel (*Senior Marketing Manager*)
Sinead Hurley (*Head of International Rights*)

*Archaeology; Architecture & Design; Crafts
& Hobbies; Fashion & Costume;
Gardening; History & Antiquarian*

Imprints, Series & ISBNs:
978 0 7134

Parent Company:
Anova Books Co Ltd

Overseas Representation:
Australia: Capricorn Link (Australia) Pty Ltd,
Windsor, NSW, Australia
Canada: Sterling Publishing Co Inc, New
York, NY, USA
Eastern Europe: Tony Moggach, InterMedia
Americana (IMA) Ltd, London, UK
Far East: Ashton International Marketing
Services, Sevenoaks, Kent, UK
France, Netherlands & Luxembourg: Ted
Dougherty, London, UK
Germany, Switzerland & Austria: Gabriele
Kern Publishers Services, Frankfurt-am-
Main, Germany

Mexico & Central America: Christopher
Humphrys, Humphrys Roberts
Associates, London, UK
New Zealand: HarperCollins (NZ) Ltd,
Glenfield, Auckland, New Zealand
Scandinavia & Italy: McNeish Publishing
International, East Sussex, UK
Singapore: Pansing Distribution Sdn Bhd,
Singapore
South Africa: Trinity Books CC, Randburg,
South Africa
South America: Terry Roberts, Cotia SP,
Brazil
Spain, Portugal, Malta & Greece: Penny
Padovani, London, UK

Book Trade Association Membership:
Independent Publishers Guild

2070

*BBH PUBLISHING LTD
[trading as The Francis Frith Collection]
Frith's Barn, Teffont, Salisbury, Wilts
SP3 5QP
Telephone: 01722 716376
Fax: 01722 716881
Email: sales@francisfrith.co.uk
Web Site: www.francisfrith.co.uk

Personnel:
John Buck (*Managing Director*)
Jason Buck (*Development Director*)
John Brewer (*Financial Controller*)
Julia Skinner (*Managing Editor*)
Isobel Buck (*IP Rights Manager*)
Sandra Sanger (*Office Sales Manager*)

*History & Antiquarian; Photography; Travel
& Topography*

Imprints, Series & ISBNs:
978 1 84589, 978 1 85937

2071

*BEAM EDUCATION
Delta Place, 27 Bath Road, Cheltenham
GL53 7TH
Telephone: 01242 278100
Fax: 01242 278650
Email: info@beam.co.uk
Web Site: www.beam.co.uk

Personnel:
Adrian Maddison (*Manager*)
Liz Free (*Professional Development Lead*)
Holly Haynes (*Professional Development
Admin.*)
Ellie Hanwell (*BEAM Administrator*)

*Educational & Textbooks; Mathematics &
Statistics*

Imprints, Series & ISBNs:
978 1 906224
Peter Clarke: 978 1 906224

Parent Company:
UK: Nelson Thornes Ltd

2072

RUTH BEAN PUBLISHERS
Victoria Farmhouse, Carlton, Bedford
MK43 7LP
Telephone: 01234 720356
Fax: 01234 720590
Email: ruthbean@onetel.com

Personnel:
Ruth Bean (*Publisher*)
Nigel Bean (*Sales Manager*)

*Academic & Scholarly; Antiques &
Collecting; Crafts & Hobbies; Fashion &
Costume; Theatre, Drama & Dance*

New Titles: 1 (2011)

Imprints, Series & ISBNs:
978 0 903585

Book Trade Association Membership:
Independent Publishers Guild

2073

BEAUTIFUL BOOKS LTD
36–38 Glasshouse Street, London W1B 5DL
Telephone: 020 7734 4448
Fax: 020 3070 0764
Email: simon@beautiful-books.co.uk
Web Site: www.beautiful-books.co.uk

Distribution:
Turnaround Publisher Services, Unit 3,
Olympia Trading Estate, Coburg Road,
London N22 6TZ
Telephone: 020 8829 3000
Fax: 020 8881 5088
Email: claire@turnaround-uk.com
Web Site: www.turnaround-uk.com

Personnel:
Simon Petherick *(Publisher)*
Tamsin Griffiths *(Production Manager)*
Ryan Davies *(Publicity Manager)*
Sara Di Girolamo *(Rights and Digital Officer)*
Ian Roberts *(Sales Manager)*

*Audio Books; Biography & Autobiography;
Cinema, Video, TV & Radio; Fashion &
Costume; Fiction; Humour; Literature &
Criticism; Music; Psychology & Psychiatry;
Reference Books, Directories &
Dictionaries; Sociology & Anthropology;
Travel & Topography*

New Titles: 21 (2010) , 30 (2011)
No of Employees: 5
Annual Turnover: £400,000

Imprints, Series & ISBNs:
Beautiful Books: 978 1 905636, 978 1
  907616
Bloody Books: 978 1 905636, 978 1
  907616
Burning House: 978 1 905636, 978 1
  907616

Overseas Representation:
Australia & New Zealand: Peribo Pty Ltd,
  Mount Kuring-Gai, NSW, Australia
Europe (including Ireland): Turnaround
  Publisher Services Ltd, London, UK
North America: IPG/Trafalgar Square
  Publishing, Chicago, USA

2074

*BEDFORD FREEMAN WORTH (BFW)
at Palgrave Macmillan, Houndmills,
Basingstoke, Hants RG21 6XS
Telephone: 01256 302983

Trade Orders & Warehouse:
Macmillan Direct, Customer Services,
Brunel Road, Houndmills, Basingstoke,
Hants RG21 6XS
Telephone: 01256 302699
Fax: 01256 364733
Email: mdl@macmillan.co.uk
Web Site: www.macmillan-mdl.co.uk

Personnel:
Margaret Hewinson *(Publishing Director
  (College))*

*Academic & Scholarly; Biology & Zoology;
Chemistry; Geography & Geology;
Mathematics & Statistics; Physics;
Psychology & Psychiatry*

Imprints, Series & ISBNs:
978 0 7167

Parent Company:
USA: W. H. Freeman & Co

Distributor for:
Palgrave Macmillan; University Science
  Books; Worth Publishers
USA: Sinauer Associates

Overseas Representation:
Australia & New Zealand: Macmillan
  Education Australia, South Yarra, Vic,
  Australia
USA: W. H. Freeman & Co, New York, USA

Book Trade Association Membership:
International Group of Scientific, Medical &
Technical Publishers

2075

THE BELMONT PRESS
29 Tenby Avenue, Harrow HA3 8RU
Telephone: 020 8907 4700
Fax: 020 8907 7354
Web Site: www.waterways.co.uk &
  www.belmont1948.co.uk

Personnel:
John Lawes *(Managing Director)*
Mark Lawes *(Technical Director)*

*Atlases & Maps; Children's Books; History &
Antiquarian; Nautical; Transport; Travel &
Topography*

New Titles: 6 (2010) , 6 (2011)

Imprints, Series & ISBNs:
Belmont series of books: 978 0 905366
Navigator series of maps: 978 0 905366
Working Waterways series: 978 0 905366

Parent Company:
Belmont (1948) Ltd

Associated Companies:
Belmont Books; Chris Deucher; John
  Reeve; Waterway Books; Waterways
  Book Service

Distributor for:
Enigma Publishing; Remus Publishing; W.H.
  Walker & Bros; Robert Wilson Designs;
  Working Waterways Series

2076

BENE FACTUM PUBLISHING LTD
PO Box 58122, London SW8 5WZ
Telephone: 020 7720 6767
Email: inquiries@bene-factum.co.uk
Web Site: www.bene-factum.co.uk

Representation:
Compass DSA, 13 Progress Business Park,
Whittle Parkway, Slough SL1 6DQ
Telephone: 01628 559500
Fax: 01628 663876
Email: sales@compass-dsa.co.uk

Distribution:
Marston Book Services, PO Box 269,
Abingdon, Oxon OX14 4YN
Telephone: 01235 465500
Fax: 01235 465555
Email: direct.orders@marston.co.uk

Personnel:
Anthony Weldon *(Managing Director)*

*Antiques & Collecting; Aviation; Biography
& Autobiography; Children's Books;
Cookery, Wines & Spirits; Fashion &
Costume; Fine Art & Art History;
Gardening; History & Antiquarian;
Humour; Illustrated & Fine Editions;
Industry, Business & Management; Law;
Medical (incl. Self Help & Alternative
Medicine); Military & War; Poetry;
Reference Books, Directories &
Dictionaries; Travel & Topography;
Vocational Training & Careers*

New Titles: 6 (2010) , 12 (2011)

Imprints, Series & ISBNs:
978 0 9522754, 978 1 903071

Book Trade Association Membership:
Independent Publishers Guild

2077

BERG PUBLISHERS
[A member of the Bloomsbury Group]
Berg Publishers, Bloomsbury Plc,
50 Bedford Square, London WC1B 3DP
Telephone: 020 7631 5600
Fax: 020 7631 5800
Email: kathryn.earle@bloomsbury.com
Web Site: www.bergpublishers.com

Distribution & Returns:
Macmillan Distribution Ltd (MDL),
Brunel Road, Houndmills, Basingstoke,
Hants RG21 6XS
Telephone: 01256 302692
Fax: 01256 812521/812558 (Home),
01256 842084 (Export)
Email: trade@macmillan.co.uk
Web Site:
www.macmillandistribution.co.uk

Personnel:
Kathryn Earle *(Managing Director, Berg and
  Visual Arts, and New Business Director,
  Academic & Professional Division)*
Geraldine Billingham *(Editorial Director)*
Jennifer Howell *(Head of Marketing)*
Ken Bruce *(Head of Production)*
Emily Medcalf *(International Sales Manager)*
Helen Toone *(E-Content and Systems
  Manager, Project Manager, Berg Fashion
  Library)*

*Academic & Scholarly; Architecture &
Design; Cinema, Video, TV & Radio;
Educational & Textbooks; Electronic
(Professional & Academic); Fashion &
Costume; Fine Art & Art History;
Photography; Sociology & Anthropology*

Imprints, Series & ISBNs:
978 0 485, 978 0 85496, 978 1 84520, 978
  1 84788, 978 1 85973

Parent Company:
Bloomsbury Publishing Plc

Distributor for:
USA: Fairchild Books

Overseas Representation:
Australia & New Zealand: Bloomsbury
  Australia
China: China Publishers' Services, Beijing, P.
  R. of China
Europe: Durnell Marketing Ltd, Tunbridge
  Wells, UK
Hong Kong, Philippines & Thailand: The
  White Partnership, Tunbridge Wells, UK
India: Maya Publishers Pvt Ltd, New Delhi,
  India
Japan: Eureka Press, Kyoto, Japan
Korea: Information & Culture Korea (ICK),
  Seoul, Republic of Korea
Middle East & North Africa: International
  Publishing Services (IPS) Middle East Ltd,
  Dubai, UAE
Pakistan: World Press, Lahore, Pakistan
Rest of Africa: Tula Publishing Ltd, Oxford,
  UK
Singapore & Malaysia: Penguin Books,
  Singapore
South Africa: Book Promotions, Cape Town,
  South Africa
Taiwan: Unifacmanu Trading Co Ltd, Taipei,
  Taiwan
USA: Bloomsbury

Book Trade Association Membership:
Independent Publishers Guild; ALPSP

2078

*BERGHAHN BOOKS
3 Newtec Place, Magdalen Road, Oxford
OX4 1RE
Telephone: 01865 250011
Fax: 01865 250056
Email: publisher@berghahnbooks.com
Web Site: www.berghahnbooks.com

Warehouse & Orders:
Marston Book Services, PO Box 269,
Abingdon, Oxon OX14 4YN
Telephone: 01235 465500
Fax: 01235 465555
Email: enquiries@marston.co.uk

Also at:
150 Broadway, Suite 812, New York,
NY 10038, USA
Telephone: +1 (212) 233 6004
Fax: +1 (212) 233 6007
Web Site: berghahnbooks.com

Personnel:
Marion Berghahn *(Managing Director)*
Mark Stanton *(Managing Editor)*
Kayleigh Chalcroft *(Publicity/Marketing
  Associate)*
Lore Cortis *(Rights Manager)*
Rupert Jones-Parry *(International Sales
  Director)*
Vivian Berghahn *(Editorial Director)*
Melissa Spinelli *(Production Manager)*
Ann Przyzycki *(Editorial Associate)*
Martha Hoffman *(Journal Manager)*
Katherine Elgart *(Publicity/Marketing
  Assistant)*
Gabriel Stuart *(Journal Marketing Assistant)*

*Academic & Scholarly; Biography &
Autobiography; Cinema, Video, TV &
Radio; Economics; Electronic (Professional &
Academic); Environment & Development
Studies; Gender Studies; History &
Antiquarian; Languages & Linguistics;
Literature & Criticism; Military & War;
Politics & World Affairs; Religion &
Theology; Sociology & Anthropology;
Theatre, Drama & Dance; Travel &
Topography*

Imprints, Series & ISBNs:
978 1 57181, 978 1 84545

Distributor for:
India: Social Science Press
Israel: Yad Vashem
UK: Durkheim Press

Overseas Representation:
Australia & New Zealand: Woodslane Pty
  Ltd, Warriewood, NSW, Australia
Benelux: Jos de Jong, Belgium
Canada: Renouf Books, Ottawa, Ont,
  Canada
China & Hong Kong: Inspirees Bowen,
  Beijing, P. R. of China
Eastern Europe: László Horváth Publishers
  Representative, Budapest, Hungary
Europe: Berghahn Books, Oxford, UK
Germany (stockholding): Missing Link
  International Booksellers, Bremen,
  Germany
Greece & Cyprus: Charles Gibbes
  Associates, London, UK
India: Sara Books Pvt Ltd, New Delhi, India
Italy & France: Flavio Marcello Publishers'
  Agents & Consultants, Padua, Italy
Japan (stockholding): United Publishers
  Services Ltd, Tokyo; Kinokuniya Ltd,
  Tokyo, Japan
Latin/Central America: Cranbury
  International LLC, Montpelier, VT, USA
Middle East & Turkey: Avicenna Partnership,
  Oxford, UK
Scandinavia: David Towle International,
  Stockholm, Sweden
South Africa: The African Moon Press,
  South Africa
Spain & Portugal: Iberian Book Services,
  Madrid, Spain
Taiwan: Unifacmanu Trading Co Ltd, Taipei,
  Taiwan

2079

BIBLE READING FELLOWSHIP
15 The Chambers, Vineyard, Abingdon,
Oxon OX14 3FE
Telephone: 01865 319700
Fax: 01865 319701

Email: enquiries@brf.org.uk
Web Site: www.brf.org.uk

Distribution:
Trust Media Distribution, Kingstown,
Broadway, Carlisle CA3 0HA
Telephone: 01228 512512
Fax: 01228 514949
Email: info@tmdistribution.co.uk
Web Site: www.tmdistribution.co.uk

Personnel:
R. Fisher (Chief Executive Officer)
Karen Laister (Deputy Chief Executive)
Sue Doggett (Commissioning Editor)
Naomi Starkey (Commissioning Editor)
Olivia Warburton (Commissioning Editor &
    Editorial Services Team Leader)

Children's Books; Educational & Textbooks;
Religion & Theology

New Titles: 58 (2010) , 71 (2011)
No of Employees: 21
Annual Turnover: £1M

Imprints, Series & ISBNs:
978 0 7459, 978 0 85746, 978 1 84101
Barnabas
Barnabas for Children: , 978 0 85746
Barnabas in Schools: , 978 0 85746
Day by Day with God
Foundations21: , 978 0 85746
Guidelines
Messy Church: , 978 0 85746
New Daylight
People's Bible Commentary Series
Quiet Spaces
The Upper Room

Overseas Representation:
Australia: Willow Connection Pty Ltd,
    Brookvale, NSW, Australia
New Zealand: Scripture Union Wholesale,
    Wellington, New Zealand
USA: The Bible Reading Fellowship, Winter
    Park, FL, USA

2080

JOSEPH BIDDULPH PUBLISHER
32 Stryd Ebeneser, Pontypridd CF37 5PB
Telephone: 01443 662559

Personnel:
Joseph Biddulph (Sole Proprietor)

Academic & Scholarly; Architecture &
Design; Languages & Linguistics; Poetry;
Reference Books, Directories &
Dictionaries; Religion & Theology

Imprints, Series & ISBNs:
Joseph Biddulph Publisher: 978 1 897999
Languages Information Centre: 978 0
948565

2081

**BIOHEALTHCARE PUBLISHING
(OXFORD) LTD**
Hexagon House, Avenue 4, Station Lane,
Witney, Oxon OX28 4BN
Telephone: 01993 848726
Fax: 01865 884448
Email: info@biohealthcarepublishing.com
Web Site:
    www.biohealthcarepublishing.com

Personnel:
Dr Glyn Jones (Managing Director)
Dr Melinda Taylor (Finance Director)

Academic & Scholarly; Chemistry; Industry,
Business & Management; Medical (incl. Self
Help & Alternative Medicine); Scientific &
Technical

Imprints, Series & ISBNs:
978 1 907568

Overseas Representation:
China: Benjamin Pan, CPM, Beijing, P. R. of
    China
India: Ravindra Saxena, Sara Books, Delhi,
    India
Japan: Ben Kato, Tokyo, Japan
Middle East: Avicenna, Oxford, UK
North America: Martin Hill, New York, NY,
    USA
Republic of Korea: Se-Yung Jun, ICK, Seoul,
    Republic of Korea
South East Asia: Steven Goh, APAC,
    Singapore
Southern Europe: Mare Nostrum,
    Harrogate, UK
Taiwan: UNIFCCMANU, Taipei, Taiwan

2082

BIRLINN LTD
West Newington House,
10 Newington Road, Edinburgh EH9 1QS
Telephone: 0131 668 4371
Fax: 0131 668 4466
Email: info@birlinn.co.uk
Web Site: www.birlinn.co.uk

Distribution:
BookSource, 50 Cambuslang Road,
Glasgow G32 8NB
Telephone: 0845 370 0067
Fax: 0845 370 0068
Email: info@booksource.net
Web Site: www.booksource.net

Personnel:
Hugh Andrew (Managing Director)
Rona Stewart (Finance)
Liz Short (Production)
Neville Moir (Publisher)
Andrew Simmons (Editorial)
Vikki Reily (Sales)
Maria White (Rights)
Jan Rutherford (Publicity)
Laura Poynton (Sales Director)

Fiction; Guide Books; History &
Antiquarian; Humour; Illustrated & Fine
Editions; Military & War; Poetry

Imprints, Series & ISBNs:
Birlinn: 978 1 84158, 978 1 874744
Birlinn General (Military & Adventure titles):
    978 1 84341
John Donald: 978 0 85976
John Donald (Print on demand titles): 978 1
    904607
Mercat: 978 1 84183
Polygon: 978 0 7486, 978 0 9544075, 978
    1 84697, 978 1 904598

Associated Companies:
John Donald Publishers Ltd; Polygon

Distributor for:
Maclean Press

Overseas Representation:
Australia: UNIREPS University and Reference
    Publishers' Services, Sydney, NSW,
    Australia
Austria, Belgium, France, Germany, Greece,
    Italy, Luxembourg, Netherlands &
    Switzerland: Ted Dougherty, London, UK
Canada: Vanwell Publishing Ltd, St
    Catharines, Ont, Canada
Denmark, Finland, Iceland, Norway,
    Portugal, Spain, Sweden & Eastern
    Europe: Bill Bailey Publishers
    Representatives, Newton Abbot, UK
USA (academic): Interlink Publishing Group
    Inc, Northampton, MA, USA
USA (for military & adventure titles only):
    Casemate Publishers & Book Distributors
    LLC, Havertown, PA, USA

Book Trade Association Membership:
Independent Publishers Guild

2083

BITTER LEMON PRESS
37 Arundel Gardens, London W11 2LW
Telephone: 020 7727 7927
Fax: 020 7460 2164
Email: books@bitterlemonpress.com
Web Site: www.bitterlemonpress.com

Crime; Fiction

New Titles: 7 (2010) , 6 (2011)

Book Trade Association Membership:
Independent Publishers Guild

2084

*BLACK ACE BOOKS
PO Box 7547, Perth PH2 1AU
Telephone: 01821 642822
Fax: 01821 642101
Web Site: www.blackacebooks.com

Personnel:
Hunter Steele (Publisher & Rights)
Boo Wood (Publicity & Sales)

Academic & Scholarly; Biography &
Autobiography; Fiction; History &
Antiquarian; Philosophy

Imprints, Series & ISBNs:
978 1 872988

Overseas Representation:
Italy: Piergiorgio Nicolazzini Literary Agency,
    Milan, Italy
Japan: The English Agency (Japan) Ltd,
    Tokyo, Japan

2085

BLACK DOG PUBLISHING LTD
10A Acton Street, London WC1X 9NG
Telephone: 020 7713 5097
Fax: 020 7713 8682
Web Site: www.blackdogonline.com

Warehouse & Distribution:
Marston Book Services, PO Box 269,
Abingdon, Oxon OX14 4YN
Telephone: 01235 465500
Fax: 01235 465555
Email: direct.orders@marston.co.uk

Architecture & Design; Cinema, Video, TV &
Radio; Crafts & Hobbies; Environment &
Development Studies; Fashion & Costume;
Fine Art & Art History; Gardening;
Illustrated & Fine Editions; Music;
Photography; Travel & Topography

New Titles: 48 (2010) , 50 (2011)
No of Employees: 15

Imprints, Series & ISBNs:
978 1 904772, 978 1 906155, 978 1
    907317
Architecture & Urbanism (Serial books): 978
    1 901033
Artworld
-De, -Dis, -Ex: 978 1 901033
Labels Unlimited
Revisions: 978 1 901033
Serial Books Design: 978 1 901033

Overseas Representation:
Asia: Asia Publishers Services and APD
    Singapore Ltd
Australia & New Zealand: Peribo Pty Ltd,
    Mount Kuring-Gai, NSW, Australia
Canada & USA: Perseus Group, Jackson,
    TN, USA
Europe & New Zealand: Marston Book
    Services Ltd, Abingdon, UK
France: Critiques Livres Distribution,
    Bagnolet, France
UK: Yale Representation Ltd

2086

BLACK SPRING PRESS LTD
Curtain House, 134–146 Curtain Road,
London EC2A 3AR
Telephone: 020 7613 3066
Fax: 020 7613 0028
Email: general@blackspringpress.co.uk
Web Site: www.blackspringpress.co.uk

Distribution:
Turnaround Publisher Services Ltd, Unit 3,
Olympia Trading Estate, Coburg Road,
London N22 6TZ
Telephone: 020 8829 3000
Fax: 020 8881 5088
Email: orders@turnaround-uk.com
Web Site: www.turnaround-psl.com

Personnel:
Robert Hastings (Publisher)

Biography & Autobiography; Cinema,
Video, TV & Radio; Fiction; Music

Imprints, Series & ISBNs:
978 0 948238

Overseas Representation:
Europe, Middle East & Far East: Turnaround
    Publisher Services Ltd, London, UK

2087

*A. & C. BLACK (PUBLISHERS) LTD
36 Soho Square, London W1D 3QY
Telephone: 020 7758 0200
Fax: 020 7758 0222
Web Site: www.acblack.com

Distribution:
Macmillan Distribution (MDL), Brunel Road,
Houndmills, Basingstoke, Hants RG21 6XT
Telephone: 01256 302699
Fax: 01256 812521
Email: direct@acblack.com

Personnel:
Nigel Newton (Chairman)
Jill Coleman (Managing Director)
Jonathan Glasspool (Deputy Managing
    Director)
Janet Murphy (Adlard Coles Nautical
    Director)
Oscar Heini (Production Director)
David Wightman (Rights, Sales & Marketing
    Director)
Colin Adams (Group Finance Director)
Chris Facey (Finance Director)
Jayne Parsons (Children's Books Director)
Rosanna Bortoli (Head of Publicity &
    Marketing)

Architecture & Design; Children's Books;
Crafts & Hobbies; Educational & Textbooks;
English as a Foreign Language; Fashion &
Costume; Fine Art & Art History; Health &
Beauty; Humour; Music; Natural History;
Nautical; Reference Books, Directories &
Dictionaries; Sports & Games; Theatre,
Drama & Dance

Imprints, Series & ISBNs:
Adlard Coles Nautical
The Arden Shakespeare
Andrew Brodie Publications
Featherstone Education
Know the Game
Methuen Drama
New Mermaids
Thomas Reeds
Whitaker's Almanacks
Who's Who
Wisden Cricketer's Almanack

Parent Company:
Bloomsbury Plc

Distributor for:
Little Tiger Press; V & A Publications;
    Wisden

Overseas Representation:
Australia & New Zealand: Allen & Unwin Pty Ltd, Crows Nest, NSW, Australia
Canada (excluding V&A titles): Penguin Group Canada, Toronto, Ont, Canada
Central & Eastern Europe: Grazyna Soszynska, Penguin Poland, Poznan-Baranowo, Poland
France (excluding V&A titles): Jean-Luc Morel, Penguin France, Paris, France
Germany: Edith Strommen, Penguin Books Deutschland GmbH, Frankfurt am Main, Germany
Germany & Austria: Klaus Melz, Penguin Books Deutschland GmbH, Mannheim, Germany
India (excluding V&A titles): Penguin Books India, New Delhi, India
Italy: Umberto Vigoni, Penguin Italia srl, Milan, Italy
Laos, Cambodia, Vietnam & Thailand: Keith Hardy, International Sales Dept, Penguin UK, London, UK
Malaysia (excluding V&A titles): Penguin Books Malaysia, c/o Pearson Malaysia Sdn Bhd, Selangor Darul Ehsan, Malaysia
Middle East, Hong Kong, Thailand & Indonesia: Sarah Davison-Aitkins, International Sales Dept, Penguin UK, London, UK
Netherlands, Belgium & Luxembourg: Feico Deutekom, Penguin Books BV, Amsterdam, Netherlands
Portugal: Adelino Abrantos, Penguin Books SA, Madrid, Spain
Republic of Ireland: Brian Blennerhassett, Butler Sims Ltd, Dublin, Republic of Ireland
Scandinavia & Latin America: Tamsin Pagella, International Sales Dept, Penguin UK, London, UK
Singapore (excluding V&A titles): Penguin Books Singapore, c/o Pearson Education South Asia Pte Ltd, Singapore
South America, Latin America & Caribbean: David Williams, InterMedia Americana (IMA) Ltd, London, UK
South East Europe & Africa: Amy Elkington, International Sales Dept, Penguin UK, London, UK
South Korea, Taiwan, Japan, China & Philippines: Yvonne Francis, International Sales Dept, Penguin UK, London, UK
Southern Africa: Book Promotions (Pty) Ltd/ Horizon Books (Pty) Ltd, Cape Town, South Africa
Spain: Javier Rivera, Penguin Books SA, Madrid, Spain
Switzerland & Malta: Kathy John, International Sales Dept, Penguin UK, London, UK
USA (excluding V&A titles): Consortium Book Sales & Distribution, Minneapolis, MN, USA

Book Trade Association Membership:
Publishers Association; Educational Publishers Council; Music Publishers Association

2088

*BLACKSTAFF PRESS
4C Heron Wharf, Sydenham Business Park, Belfast BT3 9LE
Telephone: 028 9045 5006
Fax: 028 9046 6237
Email: info@blackstaffpress.com
Web Site: www.blackstaffpress.com

Distribution (UK & Northern Ireland):
Gill & Macmillan, Hume Avenue, Park West, Dublin 12, Republic of Ireland
Telephone: +353 (0)1 500 9500
Fax: +353 (0)1 500 9599
Email: sales@gillmacmillan.ie
Web Site: www.gillmacmillan.ie

Personnel:
Patricia Horton *(Managing Editor)*
Helen Wright *(Editor)*

Michelle Griffin *(Production Editor)*
Sarah Bowers *(Publicist)*

Academic & Scholarly; Agriculture; Archaeology; Biography & Autobiography; Cinema, Video, TV & Radio; Cookery, Wines & Spirits; Crime; Fiction; Geography & Geology; Guide Books; Health & Beauty; History & Antiquarian; Humour; Illustrated & Fine Editions; Literature & Criticism; Mathematics & Statistics; Medical (incl. Self Help & Alternative Medicine); Military & War; Music; Natural History; Photography; Poetry; Politics & World Affairs; Reference Books, Directories & Dictionaries; Religion & Theology; Sports & Games; Theatre, Drama & Dance; Travel & Topography

Imprints, Series & ISBNs:
978 0 85640

Parent Company:
CDS

Overseas Representation:
All other areas: Blackstaff Press, Belfast, UK
USA: Dufour Editions Inc, Chester Springs, PA, USA

Book Trade Association Membership:
Publishing Ireland (Foilsiú Éireann); Booksellers Association; Independent Publishers Guild

2089

BLACKTHORN PRESS
Blackthorn House, Middleton Road, Pickering, North Yorks YO18 8AL
Telephone: 01751 474043
Email: blackthornpress@yahoo.com
Web Site: www.blackthornpress.com

Personnel:
Alan Avery *(Proprietor)*

Fine Art & Art History; History & Antiquarian; Literature & Criticism

New Titles: 6 (2010) , 6 (2011)
No of Employees: 3

Imprints, Series & ISBNs:
978 0 9540535

2090

JOHN BLAKE PUBLISHING LTD
[incorporating Smith Gryphon Publishers Ltd & Metro Publishing Ltd]
3 Bramber Court, 2 Bramber Road, London W14 9PB
Telephone: 020 7381 0666
Fax: 020 7381 6868
Email: rosie@blake.co.uk
Web Site: www.johnblakepublishing.co.uk

Distribution:
Littlehampton Book Services, Faraday Close, Durrington, Worthing, West Sussex BN13 3RB
Telephone: 01903 828800
Fax: 01903 828802
Email: orders@lbsltd.co.uk
Web Site: www.lbsltd.co.uk

Personnel:
John Blake *(Managing Director)*
Rosie Virgo *(Deputy Managing Director)*
Ray Mudie *(Sales Director)*
Michelle Signore *(Editor-in-Chief)*
Joanna Kennedy *(Accounts Executive)*
Clare Tillyer *(Head of Marketing)*
Stuart Finglass *(Sales & Logistics Manager)*
John Wordsworth *(Editor)*
Moira Ashcroft *(Production)*
Liz Mallett *(Head of Publicity)*

Audio Books; Biography & Autobiography; Cookery, Wines & Spirits; Crime; Humour; Music; Sports & Games

New Titles: 100 (2010) , 100 (2011)
No of Employees: 12

Imprints, Series & ISBNs:
978 1 84358, 978 1 84454, 978 1 85782

Associated Companies:
Metro Books; Smith Gryphon Publishers Ltd

Overseas Representation:
Australia: Alpa Books, St Agnes, Australia
Germany: Michael Mellor, Munich, Germany
New Zealand: Bookreps, Auckland, New Zealand
South Africa: Peter Hyde Associates (Pty) Ltd, Cape Town, South Africa
USA: Trafalgar Publishing, Chicago, IL, USA

Book Trade Association Membership:
Booksellers Association; Independent Publishers Guild

2091

*BLOODAXE BOOKS LTD
Highgreen, Tarset, Northumberland NE48 1RP
Telephone: 01434 240500 (editorial) 01678 521550 (sales)
Fax: 01434 240505 (editorial) 01678 521544 (sales)
Email: editor@bloodaxebooks.com (editorial), sales@bloodaxebooks.com
Web Site: www.bloodaxebooks.com

Warehouse, Trade Enquiries & Orders:
Littlehampton Book Services, Faraday Close, Durrington, Worthing, West Sussex BN13 3RB
Telephone: 01903 828800
Fax: 01903 828802
Email: orders@lbsltd.co.uk

Personnel:
Simon Thirsk *(Chairman)*
Neil Astley *(Managing Director)*
Alison Davis *(Company Secretary)*
Bethan Jones *(Finance Manager)*
Christine Macgregor *(Publicity Manager)*
Suzanne Fairless-Aitken *(Permissions & Foreign Rights)*
Jean Smith *(Finance & Sales Assistant)*
Rebecca Hodkinson *(Prizes & Administration)*
Annette Charpentier *(Marketing)*

Literature & Criticism; Poetry

Imprints, Series & ISBNs:
Bloodaxe Books: 978 0 906427, 978 1 85224
Pandon Press: 978 1 85557

Associated Companies:
Pandon Press Ltd

Overseas Representation:
Australia: John Reed Book Distribution, Tea Gardens, NSW, Australia
Caribbean: Hugh Dunphy, Kingston, Jamaica
Europe: Michael Geoghegan, London, UK
India: Surit Mitra, New Delhi, India
Italy, Spain & Portugal: Penny Padovani, London, UK
North America: Dufour Editions Inc, Chester Springs, PA, USA
Republic of Ireland: Repforce Ireland, Irishtown, Dublin, Republic of Ireland
South & Central America, Africa (excluding South Africa), Eastern Europe, Middle East, Turkey, Israel, Greece & Cyprus: InterMedia Americana (IMA) Ltd, London, UK

2092

*BLOOMSBURY PUBLISHING PLC
36 Soho Square, London W1D 3QY
Telephone: 020 7494 2111

Fax: 020 7434 0151
Web Site: www.bloomsbury.com

Distributor:
Macmillan Distribution (MDL), Houndmills, Basingstoke, Hants RG21 6XS
Telephone: 01256 329242
Fax: 01256 364733

Personnel:
Nigel Newton *(Chief Executive Director)*
Richard Charkin *(Executive Director)*
Alexandra Pringle *(Editor-in-Chief)*
Kathleen Furran *(Marketing Director)*
Colin Adams *(Finance Director)*
Ruth Logan *(Rights Director)*
Colin Midson *(Publicity Director)*
Penny Edwards *(Production Director)*
David Ward *(Sales Director)*
Sarah Odedina *(Children's Director)*

Audio Books; Biography & Autobiography; Children's Books; Cinema, Video, TV & Radio; Cookery, Wines & Spirits; Fiction; Health & Beauty; History & Antiquarian; Humour; Literature & Criticism; Military & War; Music; Politics & World Affairs; Reference Books, Directories & Dictionaries; Theatre, Drama & Dance

Imprints, Series & ISBNs:
978 0 7475

Parent Company:
USA: Bloomsbury

Associated Companies:
A & C Black
Germany: Berlin Verlag

Overseas Representation:
Africa & Middle East: Penguin International Sales, London, UK
Australia & New Zealand: Allen & Unwin Pty Ltd, Sydney, NSW, Australia
Canada: Penguin Group Canada, Toronto, Ont, Canada
Central & Eastern Europe: Grazyna Soszynska, Penguin Poland, Poznan-Baranowo, Poland
France, Morocco, Tunisia & Algeria: Jean-Luc Morel, Penguin Group, Roissy, France
Germany & Austria: Uli Hoernemann, Berlin Verlag, Berlin, Germany
Hong Kong, Macau, China, Philippines, Thailand, Indonesia, Vietnam, Cambodia, Taiwan & Korea: Yvonne Francis, Penguin International Sales, London, UK
India: Penguin Books India, New Delhi, India
Italy: Penguin Italia srl, Milan, Italy
Japan: Lisa Finch, Bloomsbury International Sales, Bloomsbury Publishing, London, UK
Netherlands, Belgium & Luxembourg: Penguin Books BV, Amsterdam, Netherlands
Pakistan: Julian Russ, Tula Publishing Ltd, Oxford, UK
Republic of Ireland & Northern Ireland: Louise Dobbin, Repforce Ireland, Irishtown, Dublin, Republic of Ireland
Scandinavia: Sarah Davison-Aitkens, Penguin International Sales, London, UK
Singapore & Malaysia: Penguin Books Malaysia, c/o Pearson Malaysia Sdn Bhd, Selangor Darul Ehsan, Malaysia; Penguin Books Singapore, c/o Pearson Education South Asia Pte Ltd, Singapore
South Africa: Jonathan Ball Publishers (Pty) Ltd, Johannesburg, South Africa
South East Europe, Cyprus, Greece, Gibraltar, Turkey, Israel, Caribbean & Latin America: Tamsin Pagella, Penguin International Sales, London, UK
Spain & Portugal: Geraldine Kilpatrick, Penguin Books SA, Madrid, Spain
Sri Lanka: Shan Rajaguru, Colombo, Sri Lanka
Switzerland & Malta: Kathy John, Penguin International Sales, London, UK

Book Trade Association Membership:
Publishers Association; Independent
Publishers Guild

BLUE OCEAN PUBLISHING
St John's Innovation Centre, Cowley Road,
Cambridge CB4 0WS
Telephone: 01763 208887
Email:
blueoceanpublishing@btconnect.com
Web Site: www.blueoceanpublishing.biz

Personnel:
Miss Angela Wilde (Publisher)

Academic & Scholarly; Children's Books;
Cookery, Wines & Spirits; Crafts & Hobbies;
Educational & Textbooks; History &
Antiquarian; Industry, Business &
Management; Literature & Criticism;
Poetry; Religion & Theology; Theatre,
Drama & Dance

New Titles: 2 (2010) , 4 (2011)

Imprints, Series & ISBNs:
978 0 9556430, 978 1 907527

BLUE SKY PRESS
57 Longfield Avenue, Fareham, Hants
PO14 1BU
Telephone: 07816 411341
Email: blueskypress@BurgessMcCain.com
Web Site: www.blueskypress.co.uk &
www.thealicefactor.com

Personnel:
Victoria Stone (Executive Assistant)
Cfyn Markwick-Day (Managing Editor)

Fiction; Music; Poetry

Parent Company:
UK: Burgess McCain Ltd

BLUEBERRY PRESS LTD
17 Cheltenham Avenue, Catshill,
Bromsgrove, Worcs B61 0RU
Telephone: 07795 360294
Email:
andrew.corcoran@blueberrypress.co.uk
Web Site: www.blueberrypress.co.uk

Personnel:
Andrew Corcoran (Director)

Academic & Scholarly; Educational &
Textbooks; Fiction

New Titles: 4 (2010)
Annual Turnover: £20,000

Imprints, Series & ISBNs:
978 0 9564572

BML
[a division of Bowker]
St Andrew's House,
18–20 St Andrew Street, London
EC4A 3AG
Telephone: 020 7832 1782
Email: jo@bookmarketing.co.uk
Web Site: www.bookmarketing.co.uk

Personnel:
Jo Henry (Managing Director)
Steve Bohme (Research Director)

Academic & Scholarly; Electronic
(Professional & Academic); Reference
Books, Directories & Dictionaries

New Titles: 3 (2010) , 3 (2011)
No of Employees: 4

Annual Turnover: £450,000

Imprints, Series & ISBNs:
978 1 873517

Parent Company:
UK: Bowker

Book Trade Association Membership:
Booksellers Association; Independent
Publishers Guild

BODLEIAN LIBRARY PUBLISHING
Osney One, Osney Mead, Oxford OX2 0EW
Telephone: 01865 283850
Fax: 01865 277620
Email: publishing@bodleian.ox.ac.uk
Web Site: www.bodleianbookshop.co.uk

Trade Enquiries & Orders:
Turpin Distribution Ltd, Pegasus Drive,
Stratton Business Park, Biggleswade, Beds
SG18 8TQ
Telephone: 01767 604968
Fax: 01767 601640
Email: custserv@turpin-distribution.com
Web Site: www.turpin-distribution.com

Representation (UK Book Trade):
Yale University Press

Personnel:
Samuel Fanous (Publisher)
Deborah Susman (Managing Editor)
Su Wheeler (Marketing & Sales Co-
ordinator)

Academic & Scholarly; Antiques &
Collecting; Architecture & Design;
Biography & Autobiography; Children's
Books; Fine Art & Art History; History &
Antiquarian; Humour; Literature &
Criticism; Military & War; Natural History;
Politics & World Affairs; Reference Books,
Directories & Dictionaries; Sports & Games

New Titles: 10 (2010) , 21 (2011)
No of Employees: 5

Imprints, Series & ISBNs:
978 1 85124
Original Rules
Postcards from...
Treasures of the Bodleian Library

Parent Company:
University of Oxford

Overseas Representation:
Australia & New Zealand: Inbooks, Australia
USA & Canada: Chicago University Press,
Chicago, IL, USA

Book Trade Association Membership:
Independent Publishers Guild; Association
of Cultural Enterprises

BONACIA LTD
Remus House, Coltsfoot Drive, Woodston,
Peterborough PE2 9BF
Telephone: 01733 890099
Fax: 01733 313524
Email: info@bonacia.co.uk
Web Site: www.Bonacia.co.uk

Personnel:
Morgan Walton (Director)
Rosie Walton (Director)
Kirsty Ogden (Accounts Manager)

Poetry

Imprints, Series & ISBNs:
Bookprinting UK
Forward Poetry
Leavers Books
Need2Know
New Fiction

Poetry Rivals
Proprint
School Artists
School Products
Young Writers

Book Trade Association Membership:
Booksellers Association

BOOK CASTLE PUBLISHING LTD
2a Sycamore Business Park, Copt Hewick,
North Yorkshire HG4 5DF
Telephone: 01582 344321
Fax: 01582 344318
Email: info@bookcastlepublishing.co.uk
Web Site:
www.bookcastlepublishing.co.uk

Personnel:
Paul Bowes (Publisher, Manager)
Sally Siddons (External Sales & Marketing
Production Manager)

Biography & Autobiography; History &
Antiquarian; Travel & Topography

New Titles: 3 (2010) , 2 (2011)
No of Employees: 1

Imprints, Series & ISBNs:
978 0 9509773, 978 1 871199, 978 1
903747, 978 1 906632

BORTHWICK PUBLICATIONS
Borthwick Institute, University of York,
Heslington, York YO10 5DD
Telephone: 01904 321166
Web Site: www.york.ac.uk/borthwick

Personnel:
Christopher Webb (General Editor)

Academic & Scholarly; Archaeology;
Educational & Textbooks; History &
Antiquarian; Law; Religion & Theology

New Titles: 4 (2010) , 4 (2011)

Imprints, Series & ISBNs:
Borthwick List & Indexes: 978 0 903857
Borthwick Papers: 978 0 903857
Borthwick Publications: 978 1 09
Borthwick Studies in History: 978 0 903857
Borthwick Texts & Calendars: 978 0 903857
Borthwick Wallets: 978 0 903857
Monastic Research Bulletin: 978 0 903857

Parent Company:
University of York

*BOSSINEY BOOKS LTD
Hillside, Langore, Launceston, Cornwall
PL15 8LD
Telephone: 01566 774176
Email: bossineybooks@btinternet.com
Web Site: www.bossineybooks.com

Distribution:
Tor Mark Press, PO Box 4, Redruth,
Cornwall TR16 5YX
Telephone: 01209 822101
Fax: 01209 822035
Email: office@tormark.co.uk
Web Site: www.tormark.co.uk

Personnel:
Jane White (Director)
Paul White (Director)

Cookery, Wines & Spirits; Guide Books;
History & Antiquarian; Magic & the Occult

Imprints, Series & ISBNs:
978 1 899383, 978 1 906474
Tamar Books

Book Trade Association Membership:
Independent Publishers Guild

BOWKER (UK) LTD
St Andrew's House,
18–20 St Andrew Street, London
EC4A 3AG
Telephone: 020 7832 1770
Fax: 020 7832 1710
Email: sales@bowker.co.uk
Web Site: www.bowker.com

Personnel:
Doug McMillan (Managing Director)
Pam Roud (Sales Director)
Jo Grange (Marketing Manager)

Academic & Scholarly; Bibliography &
Library Science; Electronic (Educational);
Electronic (Professional & Academic)

Imprints, Series & ISBNs:
978 0 8352

Associated Companies:
USA: R. R. Bowker LLC; Cambridge
Information Group

Overseas Representation:
see: www.bowker.co.uk, UK

Book Trade Association Membership:
Booksellers Association; CILIP

*MARION BOYARS PUBLISHERS LTD
24 Lacy Road, London SW15 1NL
Telephone: 020 8788 9522
Fax: 020 8789 8122
Email: catheryn@marionboyars.com
Web Site: www.marionboyars.co.uk

Distribution:
Central Books, 99 Wallis Road, London
E9 5LN
Telephone: 020 8986 4854
Fax: 020 8533 5821
Email: orders@centralbooks.com

Personnel:
Catheryn Kilgarriff (Managing Director)
Rebecca Gillieron (Editorial Manager)
Katharine Bright-Holmes (Editorial
Manager)
Kit Maude (Sales Co-ordinator Manager)

Biography & Autobiography; Children's
Books; Cinema, Video, TV & Radio; Fiction;
Literature & Criticism; Music; Philosophy;
Theatre, Drama & Dance

Imprints, Series & ISBNs:
978 0 7145

Associated Companies:
USA: Marion Boyars Publishers Inc

Overseas Representation:
Australia & New Zealand: Tower Books Pty
Ltd, Frenchs Forest, NSW, Australia
France, Germany & Switzerland: Michael
Geoghegan, London, UK
Italy, Spain, Portugal & Greece: Penny
Padovani, London, UK
South Africa: Stephan Phillips (Pty) Ltd,
Cape Town, South Africa
USA: Consortium Book Sales & Distribution
Inc, MN, USA

Book Trade Association Membership:
Independent Publishers Guild

BOYDELL & BREWER LTD
PO Box 9, Woodbridge, Suffolk IP12 3DF
Telephone: 01394 610600
Fax: 01394 610316
Email: trading@boydell.co.uk

Web Site: www.boydellandbrewer.com

Personnel:
P. Clifford *(Managing Director)*
M. J. Richards *(Sales Director)*
C. L. Palmer *(Editorial Director)*
W. Ellis *(Accounts Director)*
J. M. Jordan *(Customer Orders Manager)*
M. L. Webb *(Production Manager)*
Dr M. Middeke *(Senior Commissioning Editor)*

Academic & Scholarly; Archaeology; Architecture & Design; History & Antiquarian; Literature & Criticism; Military & War; Music; Philosophy; Reference Books, Directories & Dictionaries; Travel & Topography

New Titles: 225 (2011)
No of Employees: 19

Imprints, Series & ISBNs:
Boydell Press: 978 0 85115
D. S. Brewer: 978 0 85991
Camden House: 978 1 57113
Companion Guides: 978 1 900639
James Currey: 978 1 84701
Tamesis: 978 1 85566
York Medieval Press: 978 1 903153

Associated Companies:
USA: Boydell & Brewer Inc; University of Rochester Press

Distributor for:
Bedfordshire Historical Record Society; Henry Bradshaw Society; Burke's Peerage; Canterbury & York Society; Church of England Record Society; Early English Text Society; Ecclesiastical History Society; Lincoln Records Society; Plumbago Books; Royal Historical Society; Scholarly Digital Editions; Scottish Text Society; Suffolk Records Society; Surtees Society; Toccata Press; Victoria County History; Yorkshire Archaeological Society
USA: University of Rochester Press

Overseas Representation:
Australia: Inbooks, Brookvale, NSW, Australia
Belgium, Luxembourg & Netherlands: Kemper Conseil Publishing, Leidschendam, Netherlands
Eastern Europe: Marek Lewinson, Warsaw, Poland
France: Mare Nostrum, Paris, France
Germany, Austria & Switzerland: Bernd Feldmann, Oranienburg, Germany
Greece & Cyprus: Charles Gibbes Associates, Louslitges, France
India & Sri Lanka: Viva Group, New Delhi, India
Italy: David Pickering, Mare Nostrum Publishing Consultants, Rome, Italy
Middle East & North Africa: Publishers International Marketing, Storrington, UK
Pakistan: T.M.L. Publishers' Consultants & Representatives, Lahore, Pakistan
Philippines: Edwin Makabenta, Quezon City, Philippines
Republic of Ireland: Global Book Marketing, London, UK
Scandinavia: Colin Flint Ltd, Publishers Scandinavian Consultancy, Cambridge, UK
South East Asia & Korea: Publishers International Marketing, London, UK
Spain & Portugal: Iberian Book Services, Madrid, Spain

Book Trade Association Membership:
Independent Publishers Guild

2105 ▬▬▬▬▬▬

BRADT TRAVEL GUIDES LTD
1st Floor, IDC House, The Vale, Chalfont St Peter, Bucks SL9 9RZ
Telephone: 01753 893444

Fax: 01753 892333
Email: info@bradtguides.com
Web Site: www.bradtguides.com

Orders to:
NBN International, 10 Thornbury Road, Plymouth PL6 7PP
Telephone: 01752 202301
Fax: 01752 202331
Email: orders@nbninternational.com

Personnel:
Donald Greig *(Executive Director)*
Peter Jay *(Finance Director)*
Adrian Phillips *(Publishing Director)*

Guide Books; Travel & Topography

Imprints, Series & ISBNs:
Bradt Travel Guides: 978 1 84162

Overseas Representation:
Africa (excluding South Africa, Namibia, & Zimbabwe): A–Z Africa Book Services, Rotterdam, Netherlands
Australia: Woodslane Pty Ltd, Warriewood, NSW, Australia
Austria: Freytag & Berndt, Vienna, Austria
Belgium: Craenen bvba, Herent (Winksele), Belgium
Eastern Europe: CLB Marketing Services, Budapest, Hungary
France: Cartothèque EGG, Notre Dame D'Oé, France
Germany & Luxembourg: Durnell Marketing Ltd, Tunbridge Wells, UK
Israel: Steinhard Katzir, Netanya, Israel
Netherlands: Nilsson & Lamm BV, Weesp, Netherlands
Portugal: Iberian Book Services, Madrid, Spain
Scandinavian Europe: Angell Eurosales, Berwick-on-Tweed, UK
Singapore: Pansing Distribution Pte Ltd, Singapore
South & Central America: David Williams, InterMedia Americana (IMA) Ltd, London, UK
South Africa: Jacana Media, Johannesburg, South Africa
Spain: Altair, Barcelona, Spain
Switzerland: Distribution OLF SA, Fribourg, Switzerland
USA & Canada: Globe Pequot Press, Guilford, CT, USA

Book Trade Association Membership:
Independent Publishers Guild

2106 ▬▬▬▬▬▬

NICHOLAS BREALEY PUBLISHING
3–5 Spafield Street, London EC1R 4QB
Telephone: 020 7239 0360
Fax: 020 7239 0370
Email: rights@nicholasbrealey.com
Web Site: www.nicholasbrealey.com

Orders & Warehouse:
TBS Ltd, Colchester Road, Frating Green, Colchester, Essex CO7 7DW
Telephone: 01206 256000
Fax: 01206 819587

Personnel:
Nicholas Brealey *(Managing Director)*
Andrew Menniss *(Sales Manager)*
Sally Lansdell *(Publishing Manager)*

Biography & Autobiography; Economics; Industry, Business & Management; Psychology & Psychiatry; Travel & Topography; Vocational Training & Careers

Imprints, Series & ISBNs:
Nicholas Brealey: 978 1 85788
Nicholas Brealey International
Davies-Black: 978 0 89106
Industrial Society (acquired titles): 978 0 85290
Intercultural Press

Parent Company:
UK: NB Ltd

Associated Companies:
USA: NB Publishing Inc

Overseas Representation:
Asia (excluding Singapore & Malaysia): Sales East, Bangkok, Thailand
Australia: Allen & Unwin Pty Ltd, Sydney, NSW, Australia
Europe (excluding Scandinavia) & Switzerland: Michael Geoghegan, London, UK
India: Research Press, New Delhi, India
Republic of Ireland: Gill Simpson, Dublin, Republic of Ireland
Scandinavia: Angell Eurosales, Berwick-on-Tweed, UK
Singapore & Malaysia: Horizon Books Pte Ltd, Singapore
South Africa: Wild Dog Press, Highlands North, South Africa
USA: National Book Network, Lanham, MD, USA; Nicholas Brealey Publishing North America, Boston, MA, USA

Book Trade Association Membership:
Independent Publishers Guild

2107 ▬▬▬▬▬▬

*BREWIN BOOKS LTD
Doric House, 56 Alcester Road, Studley, Warwickshire B80 7LG
Telephone: 01527 854228
Fax: 01527 852746
Email: admin@brewinbooks.com
Web Site: www.brewinbooks.com

Warehouse:
Supaprint Works, Unit 19, Enfield Industrial Estate, Redditch, Worcs B97 6BZ
Telephone: 01527 62212
Fax: 01527 60451
Email: admin@supaprint.com
Web Site: www.supaprint.com

Personnel:
Alan Brewin *(Managing Director)*
Alistair Brewin *(Art, Book Design & Production Director)*
Julie Brewin *(Company Secretary)*

Biography & Autobiography; Fiction; History & Antiquarian; Military & War; Transport

Imprints, Series & ISBNs:
Alton Douglas Books: 978 1 85858
Brewin Books: 978 0 947731, 978 0 9505570, 978 1 85858
History-into-Print: 978 1 85858

Distributor for:
City of Birmingham Libraries; Hunt End Books

2108 ▬▬▬▬▬▬

BRIDGE BOOKS
61 Park Avenue, Wrexham LL12 7AW
Telephone: 01978 358661 & 0845 166 2851
Email: enquiries@bridgebooks.co.uk

Distribution:
Welsh Books Council, Glanrafon Industrial Estate, Llanbadarn, Aberystwyth, Ceredigion SY23 3AQ
Telephone: 01970 624455

Personnel:
W. Alister Williams *(Partner)*
Susan A. Williams *(Partner)*

Aviation; History & Antiquarian; Military & War; Travel & Topography

New Titles: 10 (2011)

Imprints, Series & ISBNs:
978 0 9508285, 978 1 84494, 978 1 872424

2109 ▬▬▬▬▬▬

BRILLIANT PUBLICATIONS
Unit 10, Sparrow Hall Farm, Edlesborough, Dunstable LU6 2ES
Telephone: 01525 222292
Fax: 01525 222720
Email: info@brilliantpublications.co.uk
Web Site: www.brilliantpublications.co.uk

Sales & Distribution:
Brilliant Publications, Mendlesham Industrial Estate, Norwich Road, Mendlesham. Suffolk IP14 5ND
Telephone: 01449 766629
Fax: 01449 767122
Email: orders@tradecounter.co.uk

Personnel:
Priscilla Hannaford *(Publisher)*
Richard Dorrance *(Finance Director)*
Alison Marshall *(Marketing)*

Educational & Textbooks; Languages & Linguistics

Imprints, Series & ISBNs:
978 0 85747, 978 1 897675, 978 1 903853, 978 1 905780

Book Trade Association Membership:
Publishers Association; Educational Publishers Council; Independent Publishers Guild

2110 ▬▬▬▬▬▬

BRITISH ASSOCIATION FOR ADOPTION & FOSTERING
[BAAF]
Saffron House, 6–10 Kirby Street, London EC1N 8TS
Telephone: 020 7421 2602
Fax: 020 7421 2601
Email: shaila.shah@baaf.org.uk
Web Site: www.baaf.org.uk

Trade Enquiries:
Turnaround Distribution, Unit 3, Olympia Trading Estate, Coburg Road, London N22 6TZ
Telephone: 020 8829 3000
Fax: 020 8881 5088
Email: orders@turnaround-uk.com

Personnel:
David Holmes *(Chief Executive)*
Shaila Shah *(Director of Publications)*

Academic & Scholarly; Children's Books; Psychology & Psychiatry; Reference Books, Directories & Dictionaries; Sociology & Anthropology

New Titles: 30 (2010) , 30 (2011)
No of Employees: 120

Imprints, Series & ISBNs:
978 0 903534, 978 1 873868, 978 1 903699, 978 1 905664, 978 1 907585

Overseas Representation:
Australia (selected titles): Innovative Resources, Bendigo, Vic, Australia

Book Trade Association Membership:
The Publishers Forum for the Voluntary Sector

2111 ▬▬▬▬▬▬

BRITISH GEOLOGICAL SURVEY
Keyworth, Nottingham NG12 5GG
Telephone: 0115 936 3241 (sales) & 0115 936 3147 (returns)
Fax: 0115 936 3488

Email: sales@bgs.ac.uk & ikp@bgs.ac.uk (returns)
Web Site: www.bgs.ac.uk & www.geologyshop.com (online shop)

Distribution & Representation:
Cordee Ltd, 11 Jacknell Road, Dodswell Bridge Industrial Estate, Hinckley, Leics LE10 3BS
Telephone: 01455 611185
Fax: 01455 635687
Email: info@cordee.co.uk
Web Site: www.cordee.co.uk

Personnel:
Prof John Ludden (Director)
Jim Rayner (Head of Graphic Communication)
Chris Luton (Copyright & IPR)
Ivan Page (Sales Manager)

Atlases & Maps; Geography & Geology; Guide Books; Scientific & Technical

New Titles: 25 (2010) , 25 (2011)

Imprints, Series & ISBNs:
British Geological Survey (Books & Reports): 978 0 85272
British Geological Survey (Maps): 978 0 7518

Parent Company:
Natural Environment Research Council

Distributor for:
Durham County Council

2112 ▬▬▬▬▬▬

BRITISH LIBRARY
96 Euston Road, London NW1 2DB
Telephone: 020 7412 7535
Fax: 020 7412 7768
Email: blpublications@bl.uk
Web Site: www.bl.uk

Orders:
The British Library, Turpin Distribution Ltd, Stratton Business Park, Pegasus Drive, Biggleswade, Beds SG18 8QB
Telephone: 01767 604955
Fax: 01767 601640
Email: custserv@turpin-distribution.com
Web Site: www.turpin-distribution.com

Personnel:
David Way (Head of Publishing)
Catherine Britton (Editorial & Rights)
Martin Oestreicher (Sales)
Lara Speicher (Editorial)

Academic & Scholarly; Bibliography & Library Science; Biography & Autobiography; Fine Art & Art History; History & Antiquarian; Illustrated & Fine Editions

Imprints, Series & ISBNs:
Bibliography of British Newspapers: 978 0 7123
The British Library: 978 0 7123
British Library Guides: 978 0 7123
British Library Occasional Papers: 978 0 7123
The British Library Studies in Medieval Culture: 978 0 7123
The British Library Studies in the History of the Book: 978 0 7123
Corpus of British Medieval Library Catalogues: 978 0 7123
The Panizzi Lectures: 978 0 7123

Overseas Representation:
Australia: InBooks, Belrose, NSW, Australia
USA & Canada: University of Chicago Press, Chicago, IL, USA

Book Trade Association Membership:
Booksellers Association; Independent Publishers Guild

2113 ▬▬▬▬▬▬

BRITISH MUSEUM PRESS
38 Russell Square, London WC1B 3QQ
Telephone: 020 7323 1234
Fax: 020 7436 7315
Email: publicity@britishmuseum.co.uk
Web Site: www.britishmuseum.org/ publishing

Trade Distributor:
Littlehampton Book Services, Faraday Close, Durrington, Worthing, West Sussex BN13 3RB
Telephone: 01903 828501
Fax: 01903 828801/2
Email: enquiries@lbsltd.co.uk

Personnel:
Brian Oldman (Managing Director)
Helen Watts (Finance & Administration Director)
Rosemary Bradley (Publishing Director)
Coralie Hepburn (Editorial)
Susan Walby (Head of Production)
Sheila McKenna (Head of Sales, Marketing & Rights)
Sarah Morgan (Marketing/Publicity)

Academic & Scholarly; Antiques & Collecting; Archaeology; Children's Books; Fine Art & Art History; History & Antiquarian; Natural History; Reference Books, Directories & Dictionaries; Sociology & Anthropology

Imprints, Series & ISBNs:
978 0 7141

Parent Company:
The British Museum Co Ltd

Overseas Representation:
USA (Trade orders): British Museum Press, London, UK
Worldwide (excluding USA): Thames & Hudson (Distributors) Ltd, Farnborough, Hants, UK

Book Trade Association Membership:
Publishers Association

2114 ▬▬▬▬▬▬

***BROOKLANDS BOOKS LTD**
PO Box 146, Cobham, Surrey KT11 1LG
Telephone: 01932 865051
Fax: 01932 868803
Email: sales@brooklands-books.com
Web Site: www.brooklands-books.com

Personnel:
I. Dowdeswell (Director)
J. Powell (Director)
B. Cleveland (Sales Manager)

Aviation; Military & War; Transport

Imprints, Series & ISBNs:
978 1 85520

Parent Company:
USA: Robert Bentley Publishers; Cartech; SA Design

Distributor for:
USA: Robert Bentley Inc; SA Design

Overseas Representation:
Southern Europe: Bookport Associates, Corsico (MI), Italy

2115 ▬▬▬▬▬▬

BROWN DOG BOOKS
6 The Old Dairy, Melcombe Road, Bath BA2 3LR
Telephone: 01225 478444
Fax: 01225 478440
Email: sales@manning-partnership.co.uk
Web Site: www.manning-partnership.co.uk

Personnel:
Garry Manning (Managing Director)
Roger Hibbert (Sales & Marketing Director)
Heather Morris (Editorial Director)
Karen Twissell (Office Manager)
James Wheeler (Sales Manager)

Children's Books; Cookery, Wines & Spirits; Humour; Sports & Games

Imprints, Series & ISBNs:
Brown Dog Books: 978 1 903056
Nightingale: 978 1 903222

Parent Company:
Manning Partnership Ltd

Distributor for:
Portugal: Impala
UK: Anness; Carroll & Brown; G2; Hometown World; Interpet Publishing; Ivy Press; Nightingale Press; Search Press
USA: Mathew Price; Source Books

2116 ▬▬▬▬▬▬

BROWN, SON & FERGUSON, LTD
4–10 Darnley Street, Glasgow G41 2SD
Telephone: 0141 429 1234
Fax: 0141 420 1694
Email: info@skipper.co.uk
Web Site: www.skipper.co.uk

Personnel:
T. Nigel Brown (Chairman & Production Director)
Richard P. B. Brown (Director)

Nautical; Theatre, Drama & Dance

New Titles: 4 (2010) , 1 (2011)
No of Employees: 11
Annual Turnover: £1.24M

Imprints, Series & ISBNs:
978 0 85174, 978 1 84927

Associated Companies:
James Munro & Co

Book Trade Association Membership:
Publishing Scotland

2117 ▬▬▬▬▬▬

***BROWN & WHITTAKER PUBLISHING**
Stronsaule, Tobermory, Isle of Mull PA75 6PR
Telephone: 01688 302381
Email: olivebrown@msn.com
Web Site: www.brown-whittaker.co.uk

Personnel:
Olive Brown (Partner)
Jean Whittaker (Partner)

Archaeology; Biography & Autobiography; Biology & Zoology; Cookery, Wines & Spirits; Guide Books; History & Antiquarian; Natural History; Poetry

Imprints, Series & ISBNs:
978 0 9528428, 978 0 9532775, 978 1 904353

Book Trade Association Membership:
Publishing Scotland

2118 ▬▬▬▬▬▬

BRYNTIRION PRESS
Bryntirion, Bridgend, Mid Glamorgan CF31 4DX
Telephone: 01656 655886
Fax: 01656 665919

Representation:
Evangelical Press, Faverdale North, Darlington DL3 0PH
Telephone: 01325 380232

Fax: 01325 466153
Email: sales@evangelical-press.org

Personnel:
Sharon Barnes (Press Officer)

Religion & Theology

New Titles: 3 (2010) , 3 (2011)
No of Employees: 1
Annual Turnover: £15,000

Parent Company:
Evangelical Movement of Wales

Distributor for:
Association of Christian Teachers of Wales

Book Trade Association Membership:
Booksellers Association; Undeb Cyhoeddwyr a Llyfrwerthwyr Cymru (The Union of Welsh Publishers and Booksellers)

2119 ▬▬▬▬▬▬

BURNS & OATES
see: Continuum International Publishing Group

2120 ▬▬▬▬▬▬

BUTTERFINGERS BOOKS
30 Tor View Avenue, Glastonbury, Somerset BA6 8AF
Telephone: 01458 830900
Email: laurie@butterfingersbooks.co.uk
Web Site: www.butterfingers.co.uk

Personnel:
L. H. R. Collard (Rights Director)

Educational & Textbooks; Sports & Games

New Titles: 1 (2010) , 1 (2011)

Imprints, Series & ISBNs:
978 0 9513240, 978 1 898591

Distributor for:
Switzerland: Jonglerie Diffusion
UK: Circusstuff
USA: Brian Dubé Inc; Renegade Juggling

Overseas Representation:
North America: Brian Dube Inc, New York, NY, USA

2121 ▬▬▬▬▬▬

CABI
Nosworthy Way, Wallingford, Oxon OX10 8DE
Telephone: 01491 832111
Fax: 01491 833508 & 829292 (order fulfilment)
Email: publishing@cabi.org
Web Site: www.cabi.org/

Personnel:
Ms Caroline McNamara (Executive & Commercial Director)
Ms Andrea Powell (Executive & Publishing Director)
Shaun Hobbs (Director, Plantwise Knowledge Bank)
Elizabeth Dodsworth (Knowledge for Development Director)
Nigel Farrar (Editorial Director)

Academic & Scholarly; Agriculture; Animal Care & Breeding; Biology & Zoology; Environment & Development Studies; Medical (incl. Self Help & Alternative Medicine); Scientific & Technical; Veterinary Science

Imprints, Series & ISBNs:
978 0 85198, 978 0 85199, 978 1 84593

Parent Company:
CAB International

Distributor for:
International Food Information Service;
Royal Society of Edinburgh

Overseas Representation:
Africa: CABI Africa, Nairobi, Kenya
All other areas: Commercial Department,
Wallingford, UK
Asia: CABI South East & East Asia, Serdang,
Malaysia
*Australia, New Zealand & Papua New
Guinea:* DA Information Services Pty Ltd,
Mitcham, Vic, Australia
Canada: CABI North America, Cambridge,
MA, USA
Caribbean: CABI Caribbean & Latin
America, Curepe, Trinidad
*Denmark, Finland, Iceland, Norway &
Sweden:* Colin Flint Ltd, Harlow, UK
Germany, Austria & Switzerland: Missing
Link International Booksellers, Bremen,
Germany
India: Book Marketing Services, Chennai,
India
Middle East (excluding Iran): James & Lorin
Watt Ltd, Publishing Consultants,
Oxford, UK
South Africa: Academic Marketing Services
(Pty) Ltd, Craighall, South Africa
*USA, Central America, Caribbean, Mexico,
Puerto Rico & Guam:* Oxford University
Press, Cary, NC, USA

Book Trade Association Membership:
Booksellers Association

2122 ━━━━━━━

*CALYPSO PUBLICATIONS
2 Gatcombe Road, London N19 4PT
Telephone: 020 7281 4948
Fax: 020 7281 4948
Email: Gerald@calypso.org.uk &
enquiries@calypso.org.uk
Web Site: www.calypso.org.uk/ourbooks &
www.calypso.org.uk/bookshop

Personnel:
G. H. Jennings *(Proprietor)*

*Academic & Scholarly; Animal Care &
Breeding; Biology & Zoology; Crafts &
Hobbies; Educational & Textbooks; Natural
History; Reference Books, Directories &
Dictionaries; Scientific & Technical; Travel &
Topography; Veterinary Science*

Imprints, Series & ISBNs:
978 0 906301, 978 1 902788

Parent Company:
The Calypso Organization

Overseas Representation:
Australia: Andrew Isles Bookshop,
Melbourne, Vic, Australia
Cyprus: Soloneion Book Centre, Nicosia,
Cyprus
USA: The Aquatic Bookshop, Placerville,
CA, USA

2123 ━━━━━━━

***CAMBRIDGE ARCHIVE EDITIONS
LTD**
7 Ashley House, The Broadway,
Farnham Common, Slough SL2 3PQ
Telephone: 01753 646633
Fax: 01753 646746
Email: info@archiveeditions.co.uk
Web Site: www.archiveeditions.co.uk

Personnel:
Jeanette Wood *(Head of Customer
Relations & Finance)*
Ann Greenwood *(Production Manager)*
Jessica Lagan *(Publisher)*

*Academic & Scholarly; History &
Antiquarian; Politics & World Affairs*

Imprints, Series & ISBNs:
978 1 84097, 978 1 85207

Parent Company:
UK: Cambridge University Press

2124 ━━━━━━━

CAMBRIDGE UNIVERSITY PRESS
The Edinburgh Building, Shaftesbury Road,
Cambridge CB2 8RU
Telephone: 01223 312393
Fax: 01223 315052
Email: information@cambridge.org
Web Site: www.cambridge.org

Orders:
Telephone: 01223 325577
Fax: 01223 325151
Email: intcustserve@cambridge.org
Web Site: www.cambridge.org

Personnel:
Stephen R. R. Bourne *(Chief Executive of the
Press)*
Christopher Boughton *(Managing Director,
Asia-Pacific)*
Andrew Brown *(Managing Director,
Academic)*
Hanri Pieterse *(Managing Director,
Cambridge Learning)*
Andrew Gilfillan *(Managing Director,
Europe, Middle East & Africa)*
Steven Miller *(Chief Financial Officer)*
Richard Ziemacki *(President, Americas)*
Kevin Taylor *(Director of Legal Services &
Governance)*
Peter Davison *(Corporate Affairs Director)*
Richard Fisher *(Academic & Professional
Director)*
Michael Peluse *(ELT Director)*
Tony Lund *(Director, Asia)*
Mark Maddocks *(Chief Information Officer)*
Simon Ross *(Journals Director)*
Rohan Seery *(Academic Sales & Marketing
Director)*
Simon Read *(Education Director)*
Howard Buckley *(Chief Financial Officer,
EMEA)*
Cathy Armor *(Human Resources Director)*
Sandra Ward *(Operations Director)*
Peter Phillips *(Chief Operating Officer)*

*Academic & Scholarly; Archaeology;
Architecture & Design; Biology & Zoology;
Chemistry; Computer Science; Economics;
Educational & Textbooks; Electronic
(Educational); Electronic (Professional &
Academic); Engineering; English as a
Foreign Language; Environment &
Development Studies; Fine Art & Art
History; Gender Studies; Geography &
Geology; History & Antiquarian; Industry,
Business & Management; Languages &
Linguistics; Law; Literature & Criticism;
Mathematics & Statistics; Medical (incl. Self
Help & Alternative Medicine); Music;
Natural History; Philosophy; Physics; Politics
& World Affairs; Psychology & Psychiatry;
Reference Books, Directories &
Dictionaries; Religion & Theology; Scientific
& Technical; Sociology & Anthropology;
Theatre, Drama & Dance*

New Titles: 4000 (2010) , 4000 (2011)
No of Employees: 1950
Annual Turnover: £250M

Imprints, Series & ISBNs:
978 0 521, 978 1 107
Cambridge Library Collection: 978 1 108

Associated Companies:
Hong Kong: Cambridge Knowledge (China)
Ltd; United Publishers Services Ltd
India: Cambridge University Press India (Pvt)
Ltd
Japan: Cambridge University Press Japan KK
Mexico: ELT Trading SA de CV
South Africa: Cambridge University Press
South Africa (Pty) Ltd
UK: Cambridge Hitachisoft Educational

Solutions PLC; Cambridge Printing
Services Ltd; Cambridge University Press
(Holdings) Ltd; Oncoweb Ltd

Book Trade Association Membership:
Publishers Association; Booksellers
Association; Educational Publishers
Council; International Group of Scientific,
Medical & Technical Publishers;
Independent Publishers Guild; Association
of Learned & Professional Society
Publishers; BML; IBD

2125 ━━━━━━━

*CAMERON BOOKS
PO Box 1, Moffat, Dumfriesshire DG10 9SU
Telephone: 01683 220808
Fax: 01683 220012
Email: jh@cameronbooks.co.uk
Web Site: www.cameronbooks.co.uk

Personnel:
Jill Hollis *(Director)*

*Antiques & Collecting; Architecture &
Design; Fine Art & Art History; Natural
History*

Imprints, Series & ISBNs:
Cameron & Hollis: 978 0 906506

2126 ━━━━━━━

CAMRA BOOKS
230 Hatfield Road, St Albans, Herts
AL1 4LW
Telephone: 01727 867201
Fax: 01727 867670
Email: camra@camra.org.uk
Web Site: www.camra.org.uk

UK Distribution:
Macmillan Distribution (MDL), Houndmills,
Basingstoke, Hampshire RG21 6XS
Telephone: 01256 329242
Fax: 01256 328339

Personnel:
Tony Jerome *(Head of Marketing)*
Simon Hall *(Head of Publishing)*
Chris Lewis *(Marketing Officer)*

*Biography & Autobiography; Cookery,
Wines & Spirits; Guide Books; Reference
Books, Directories & Dictionaries; Travel &
Topography*

New Titles: 6 (2010) , 8 (2011)
No of Employees: 25

Imprints, Series & ISBNs:
978 1 85249

Parent Company:
Campaign for Real Ale Ltd

Overseas Representation:
USA: Trafalgar (Independent Publishers
Group) Chicago, IL, USA

Book Trade Association Membership:
Independent Publishers Guild

2127 ━━━━━━━

CANONGATE BOOKS
14 High Street, Edinburgh EH1 1TE
Telephone: 0131 557 5111
Fax: 0131 557 5211
Email: info@canongate.co.uk
Web Site: www.meetatthegate.com

Warehouse & Orders:
The Book Service Ltd, Distribution Centre,
Colchester Road, Frating Green, Colchester,
Essex CO7 7DW
Telephone: 01206 256000
Fax: 01206 255715
Email: helpdesk@tbs-ltd.co.uk
Web Site: www.thebookservice.co.uk

Personnel:
Jamie Byng *(Publisher)*
Susie Tastard *(Acting Finance Director)*
Caroline Gorham *(Production Director)*
Polly Collingridge *(Rights Director)*
Jenny Todd *(Sales & Marketing Director)*
Anya Serota *(Publishing Director (Fiction))*
Nick Davies *(Editorial Director (Non-Fiction))*
Alex Young *(Head of Marketing)*
Angela Robertson *(Head of Publicity)*
Norah Perkins *(Managing Editor)*

*Audio Books; Biography & Autobiography;
Cinema, Video, TV & Radio; Crime; Fiction;
Fine Art & Art History; History &
Antiquarian; Humour; Illustrated & Fine
Editions; Literature & Criticism; Music;
Philosophy; Poetry; Politics & World Affairs;
Psychology & Psychiatry; Religion &
Theology; Travel & Topography*

New Titles: 50 (2010) , 50 (2011)
No of Employees: 39

Imprints, Series & ISBNs:
Canongate: 978 0 86241, 978 1 84195
Canongate Classics: 978 0 86241, 978 1
84195
Canons: 978 0 86241, 978 0 85786
Myths: 978 0 86241, 978 1 84195

Associated Companies:
Australia: Text Publishing
USA: Canongate US

Overseas Representation:
Australia: Penguin Books Australia Ltd,
Camberwell, Vic, Australia
Canada: Penguin Group Canada, Toronto,
Ont, Canada
Eastern Europe: Csaba & Jackie Lengyel de
Bagota, Budapest, Hungary
Far East: Julian Ashton, Ashton
International Marketing Services,
Sevenoaks, Kent, UK
India: Rave Media, Nandan Jha, India
Latin America & Caribbean: InterMedia
Americana (IMA) Ltd, London, UK
Netherlands, Africa & Pakistan: Export Sales
Department, Canongate Books,
Edinburgh, UK
New Zealand: Penguin Books (New
Zealand) Ltd, Auckland, New Zealand
Northern Europe: Bridget Lane, Faber &
Faber, London, UK
South Africa: Penguin Books South Africa,
Gardenview, South Africa
Southern Europe: Melissa Elders, Faber &
Faber, London, UK
USA: Publishers Group West, Berkeley, CA,
USA

Book Trade Association Membership:
Publishers Association; Publishing
Scotland; Independent Publishers Guild

2128 ━━━━━━━

*CAPALL BANN PUBLISHING
Auton Farm, Milverton, Somerset TA4 1NE
Telephone: 01823 401528
Fax: 01823 401529
Email: enquiries@capallbann.co.uk
Web Site: www.capallbann.co.uk

Personnel:
Jon Day *(Sales & Rights Publisher)*
Julia Day *(Administration & Editorial
Publisher)*

*Animal Care & Breeding; Archaeology;
Cookery, Wines & Spirits; Crafts & Hobbies;
Educational & Textbooks; Environment &
Development Studies; Gardening; Gender
Studies; Guide Books; Health & Beauty;
History & Antiquarian; Magic & the Occult;
Medical (incl. Self Help & Alternative
Medicine); Music; Natural History;
Philosophy; Psychology & Psychiatry;
Religion & Theology; Theatre, Drama &
Dance*

Imprints, Series & ISBNs:
978 1 86163, 978 1 898307

Overseas Representation:
Australia (New Age): Brumby Books
Holdings Pty Ltd, Kilsyth South, Vic,
Australia
South Africa: Bacchus Books, Cresta, South
Africa
USA: Holmes Publishing Group, Edmunds,
WA, USA; New Leaf Distributing Co,
Lithia Springs, GA, USA

2129

*CAPSTONE GLOBAL LIBRARY LTD
Halley Court, Jordan Hill, Oxford OX2 8EJ
Telephone: 01865 311366
Fax: 01865 314272
Email: information@cambridge.org
Web Site: www.heinemannlibrary.co.uk

*Academic & Scholarly; Educational &
Textbooks*

Book Trade Association Membership:
Publishers Association

2130

CAPUCHIN CLASSICS
128 Kensington Church Street, London
W8 4BH
Telephone: 020 7221 7166
Fax: 020 7792 9288
Email: info@stacey-international.co.uk
Web Site: www.stacey-international.co.uk

Personnel:
Patrick Kelly *(Managing Director)*
Christina Forde *(Designer)*
Hannah Young *(Editor)*
David Birkett *(Sales & Marketing)*
Liz Holmes *(Production Manager)*
Emma Howard *(Editor)*
Zak Kadrou *(Editorial Assistant)*

*Academic & Scholarly; Archaeology;
Biography & Autobiography; Children's
Books; Cookery, Wines & Spirits; Fiction;
Gardening; Guide Books; History &
Antiquarian; Natural History; Politics &
World Affairs; Reference Books, Directories
& Dictionaries; Religion & Theology; Travel
& Topography*

New Titles: 30 (2010) , 20 (2011)
No of Employees: 8
Annual Turnover: £500,000

Parent Company:
UK: Stacey Publishing Ltd

Overseas Representation:
Australia: Peribo, NSW, Australia
Europe: Durnell Marketing, Tunbridge
Wells, UK
South Africa: Stephan Philips, Cape Town,
South Africa
South America & Caribbean: Intermedia
Americana, London, UK
USA: Midpoint, New York, NY, USA

Book Trade Association Membership:
Independent Publishers Guild

2131

CAREL PRESS LTD
4 Hewson Street, Carlisle, Cumbria
CA2 5AU
Telephone: 01228 538928
Fax: 01228 591816
Email: office@carelpress.co.uk
Web Site: www.carelpress.com &
www.shortershakespeare.com

Personnel:
Chas White *(Publisher)*
Mrs Ann Batey *(Office Manager)*

*Atlases & Maps; Educational & Textbooks;
Electronic (Educational); Languages &
Linguistics; Literature & Criticism;
Mathematics & Statistics; Reference Books,
Directories & Dictionaries; Sports & Games;
Theatre, Drama & Dance*

Imprints, Series & ISBNs:
978 1 872365, 978 1 905600

Distributor for:
Arc Theatre Co; ODT Inc (Maps); One Page
Book Co

Book Trade Association Membership:
Independent Publishers Guild

2132

*CARLTON PUBLISHING GROUP
20 Mortimer Street, London W1T 3JW
Telephone: 020 7612 0400
Fax: 020 7612 0408
Email: sales@carltonbooks.co.uk
Web Site: www.carltonbooks.co.uk

Distribution:
HarperCollins Publishers, PO Box Glasgow
G4 0NB
Telephone: 0141 306 3100
Fax: 0141 306 3767
Email: uk.orders@harpercollins.co.uk

Personnel:
J. Goodman *(Chairman/Publisher)*
B. Rasmussen *(Managing Director)*
P. Murray Hill *(Publishing Director)*
R. Porter *(Design Director)*
A. Whitton *(Financial Director)*
J. Greenhough *(Sales Director)*

*Antiques & Collecting; Architecture &
Design; Biography & Autobiography;
Children's Books; Cinema, Video, TV &
Radio; Cookery, Wines & Spirits; Crafts &
Hobbies; Crime; Electronic (Entertainment);
Fashion & Costume; Fine Art & Art History;
Health & Beauty; History & Antiquarian;
Humour; Illustrated & Fine Editions; Military
& War; Music; Natural History;
Photography; Sports & Games; Transport*

Imprints, Series & ISBNs:
978 1 85868
Carlton Books: 978 1 84222
Andre Deutsch: 978 0 233
Goodman Books: 978 1 84796
Prion: 978 1 85375

Parent Company:
Jonathan Goodman Publishing

Overseas Representation:
All Other Markets: Gunnar Lie & Associates
Ltd, London, UK
Australia & New Zealand: c/o Jonathan
Goodman, Carlton Publishing Group,
London, UK
North America & Foreign Language: c/o
Belinda Rasmussen, Carlton Publishing
Group, London, UK

2133

CARNEGIE PUBLISHING LTD
Carnegie House, Chatsworth Road,
Lancaster LA1 4SL
Telephone: 01524 840111
Email: anna@carnegiepublishing.com
Web Site: www.carnegiepublishing.com

Personnel:
Alistair Hodge *(Managing Director)*
Anna Goddard *(Marketing Director)*
Lucy Frontani *(Book Design Manager)*

*Academic & Scholarly; Archaeology;
Cookery, Wines & Spirits; History &
Antiquarian; Industry, Business &
Management; Military & War; Natural
History*

New Titles: 12 (2010) , 12 (2011)
No of Employees: 8
Annual Turnover: £500,000

Imprints, Series & ISBNs:
Carnegie Publishing Ltd: 978 1 85936
Crucible Books: 978 1 905472
Palatine Books: 978 1 874181
Scotforth Books: 978 1 904244

Book Trade Association Membership:
Publishers Association

2134

JON CARPENTER PUBLISHING
Alder House, Market Street, Charlbury
OX7 3PH
Telephone: 01608 819117
Fax: 01608 811969
Email: jon@joncarpenter.co.uk

Trade Orders:
Central Books, 99 Wallis Road, London
E9 5LN
Telephone: 020 8986 4854
Fax: 020 8533 5821
Email: orders@centralbooks.com

Personnel:
Jon Carpenter *(Publisher)*

*Academic & Scholarly; Cookery, Wines &
Spirits; Economics; Environment &
Development Studies; History &
Antiquarian; Medical (incl. Self Help &
Alternative Medicine); Philosophy; Politics &
World Affairs; Sociology & Anthropology*

New Titles: 8 (2010) , 8 (2011)
No of Employees: 1

Imprints, Series & ISBNs:
Jon Carpenter: 978 0 9549727, 978 1
897766, 978 1 906067
Wychwood Press: 978 1 902279

Distributor for:
Australia: Envirobook Pty

Overseas Representation:
Australia: Envirobook, Annandale, NSW,
Australia
USA: Independent Publishers Group (IPG),
Chicago, IL, USA

Book Trade Association Membership:
Booksellers Association

2135

CARROLL & BROWN LTD
20 Lonsdale Road, London NW6 6RD
Telephone: 020 7372 0900
Fax: 020 7372 0460
Email: mail@carrollandbrown.co.uk
Web Site: www.carrollandbrown.co.uk

Personnel:
Amy Carroll *(Managing Director)*
Chrissie Lloyd *(Art Director)*
Simonne Waud *(Sales, Rights Director)*
Derek Thornhill *(UK Sales Director)*

*Animal Care & Breeding; Cookery, Wines &
Spirits; Health & Beauty; Medical (incl. Self
Help & Alternative Medicine)*

Imprints, Series & ISBNs:
978 1 903258, 978 1 904760

Associated Companies:
Carroll & Brown Publishers Ltd

Overseas Representation:
Worldwide: Derek Thornhill, Carroll &
Brown Ltd, London, UK

Book Trade Association Membership:
Independent Publishers Guild; Book
Packagers Association

2136

THE CATHOLIC TRUTH SOCIETY
[Publishers to the Holy See]
40–46 Harleyford Road, London SE11 5AY
Telephone: 020 7640 0042
Fax: 020 7640 0046
Email: info@cts-online.org.uk
Web Site: www.cts-online.org.uk

Retail Bookshop,
25 Ashley Place, London SW1P 1LT
Telephone: 020 7834 1363
Fax: 020 7821 7398
Email: bookshop@cts-online.org.uk
Web Site: www.cts-online.org.uk

Personnel:
Rt Rev Paul Hendricks *(Chairman)*
Fergal Martin *(General Secretary)*
John Dilger *(Hon Treasurer & Director)*
Stephen Campbell *(Production Manager)*
Richard Brown *(Sales and Marketing
Manager)*
Pierpaolo Finaldi *(Commissioning Editor)*
Rebecca Binney *(Editorial Assistant)*

*Biography & Autobiography; Children's
Books; Guide Books; History &
Antiquarian; Reference Books, Directories &
Dictionaries; Religion & Theology*

Imprints, Series & ISBNs:
978 0 85183
Catholic Truth Society: 978 1 86082

Distributor for:
Vatican City: L' Osservatore Romano

Overseas Representation:
Australia & New Zealand: St Pauls
Publications, Strathfield, NSW, Australia
North America: Ignatius Press, CA, USA

Book Trade Association Membership:
Booksellers Association

2137

CATNIP PUBLISHING
14 Greville Street, London EC1N 8SB
Telephone: 020 7138 3650
Fax: 020 7138 3658

Book Trade Association Membership:
Publishers Association

2138

*CAXTON PUBLISHING GROUP LTD
20 Bloomsbury Street, London WC1B 3JH
Telephone: 020 7636 7171
Fax: 020 7636 1922
Email: office@caxtonpublishing.com
Web Site: www.caxtonpublishing.com

Personnel:
Finbarr McCabe *(Managing Director)*
James Birney *(Sales Director)*

*Antiques & Collecting; Architecture &
Design; Atlases & Maps; Aviation;
Children's Books; Cookery, Wines & Spirits;
Crafts & Hobbies; Crime; Do-It-Yourself;
Fiction; Fine Art & Art History; Gardening;
Magic & the Occult; Medical (incl. Self Help
& Alternative Medicine); Military & War;
Natural History; Reference Books,
Directories & Dictionaries; Transport*

Imprints, Series & ISBNs:
Brockhampton Press: 978 1 84186
Caxton Editions: 978 1 84067
Chaucer Press: 978 1 904449
Knight Paperbacks: 978 1 84067
Mercury Books: 978 1 904668
TimeLife: 978 1 84447

2139

CBD RESEARCH LTD
Chancery House, 15 Wickham Road,
Beckenham, Kent BR3 5JS
Telephone: 020 8650 7745
Fax: 020 8650 0768
Email: cbd@cbdresearch.com
Web Site: www.cbdresearch.com

*Crime; Reference Books, Directories &
Dictionaries*

Imprints, Series & ISBNs:
978 0 9554514
CBD Research: 978 0 900246
Chancery House Press: 978 0 900246

Book Trade Association Membership:
Independent Publishers Guild; Data
Publishers Association

2140

CENGAGE LEARNING EMEA LTD
Cheriton House, North Way, Andover,
Hants SP10 5BE
Telephone: 01264 332424
Fax: 01264 342745
Web Site: www.cengage.co.uk

Personnel:
Jill Jones *(Chief Executive Officer &
President)*
Chad Bonney *(Chief Financial Officer)*
Andrew Robinson *(Sales Director)*
Carrie Willicome *(Customer Service
Director)*
Rossella Proscia *(Marketing Director)*
Linden Harris *(Publishing Director)*
Pedja Paulicic *(Digital Solutions Director)*

*Academic & Scholarly; Accountancy &
Taxation; Biology & Zoology; Chemistry;
Economics; Educational & Textbooks;
Engineering; English as a Foreign
Language; Health & Beauty; Industry,
Business & Management; Mathematics &
Statistics; Physics; Psychology & Psychiatry;
Reference Books, Directories &
Dictionaries; Vocational Training & Careers*

Distributor for:
Brooks/Cole; Cengage Learning; Course
Technology; Delmar Learning; Gale;
Heinle; South Western; Wadsworth

Book Trade Association Membership:
Publishers Association

2141

***CENTRE FOR ALTERNATIVE
TECHNOLOGY PUBLICATIONS**
Machynlleth, Powys SY20 9AZ
Telephone: 01654 705980
Fax: 01654 702782
Email: allan.shepherd@cat.org.uk
Web Site: www.cat.org.uk/catpubs

Distribution:
Central Books, 99 Wallis Road, London
E9 5LN
Telephone: 0845 458 9911
Fax: 0845 458 9912
Email: contactus@centralbooks.com
Web Site: www.centralbooks.com

Personnel:
Graham Preston *(Production Manager)*
Allan Shepherd *(Publisher)*
Annika Lundqvist *(Publishing Assistant)*

*Architecture & Design; Do-It-Yourself;
Educational & Textbooks; Environment &
Development Studies; Gardening; Travel &
Topography*

Imprints, Series & ISBNs:
New Futures: 978 1 898049, 978 1 902175

Overseas Representation:
USA & Canada: New Society Publishers,
Gabriola Island, BC, Canada

Book Trade Association Membership:
Independent Publishers Guild

2142

**CENTRE FOR ECONOMIC POLICY
RESEARCH**
3rd Floor, 77 Bastwick Street, London
EC1V 3PZ
Telephone: 020 7183 8801
Fax: 020 7183 8820
Email: cepr@cepr.org
Web Site: www.cepr.org

Personnel:
Stephen Yeo *(Chief Executive Officer)*
Anil Shamdasani *(Publications Manager)*

*Academic & Scholarly; Economics; Industry,
Business & Management; Politics & World
Affairs*

New Titles: 20 (2010) , 20 (2011)
No of Employees: 15

Imprints, Series & ISBNs:
978 0 9557009, 978 1 898128, 978 1
907142

Overseas Representation:
USA & Canada: The Brookings Institution,
Washington, DC, USA
Worldwide: Central Books, London, UK

2143

CENTRE FOR POLICY ON AGEING
25–31 Ironmonger Row, London EC1V 3QP
Telephone: 020 7553 6500
Fax: 020 7553 6501
Email: cpa@cpa.org.uk
Web Site: www.cpa.org.uk/

Warehouse, Trade Enquiries & Orders:
Central Books, 99 Wallis Road, London
E9 5LN
Telephone: 0845 458 9911
Fax: 0845 458 9912
Email: orders@centralbooks.com
Web Site: www.centralbooks.co.uk

Personnel:
Gillian Crosby *(Director)*
Nat Lievesley *(Manager)*

*Academic & Scholarly; Electronic
(Professional & Academic); Sociology &
Anthropology*

Imprints, Series & ISBNs:
978 0 904139, 978 1 901097

Book Trade Association Membership:
Independent Publishers Guild

2144

*CHALKSOFT LTD
PO Box 49, Spalding, Lincs PE11 1NZ
Telephone: 01775 769518
Fax: 01775 762618
Email: chalksoft@clara.co.uk
Web Site: www.chalksoft.clara.co.uk

Personnel:
David Baldwin *(Managing Director)*
Mrs Gillian Baldwin *(Sales & Rights, Office
Manager)*

*Academic & Scholarly; Animal Care &
Breeding; Children's Books; Educational &
Textbooks; Electronic (Educational);
Gardening; Geography & Geology;
Mathematics & Statistics; Music; Natural
History; Scientific & Technical*

Imprints, Series & ISBNs:
Chalksoft: 978 1 85116

Nene Valley Publishing: 978 1 85116
School Garden Co: 978 1 85116
SGC Books: 978 1 85116

Associated Companies:
Nene Valley Publishing; School Garden Co

Book Trade Association Membership:
Independent Publishers Guild

2145

CHANNEL VIEW PUBLICATIONS LTD
St Nicholas House, 31–34 High Street,
Bristol BS1 2AW
Telephone: 0117 315 8562
Fax: 0117 315 8563
Email: info@channelviewpublications.com
Web Site:
www.channelviewpublications.com

Distribution:
Marston Book Services, PO Box 269,
Unit 160, Milton Park, Abingdon
OX14 4YN
Telephone: 01235 465500
Fax: 01235 465555
Email: trade.order@marston.co.uk
Web Site: www.marston.co.uk

Personnel:
Tommi Grover *(Managing Director)*
Anna Roderick *(Editorial Director)*
Elinor Robertson *(Marketing Manager)*
Sarah Williams *(Production Manager)*
Laura Longworth *(Publishing Assistant)*

*Academic & Scholarly; Educational &
Textbooks; Environment & Development
Studies; Languages & Linguistics;
Psychology & Psychiatry; Sociology &
Anthropology; Travel & Topography*

New Titles: 48 (2010) , 44 (2011)
No of Employees: 5
Annual Turnover: £600,000

Imprints, Series & ISBNs:
Channel View Publications: 978 1 84541
Multilingual Matters: 978 0 905028, 978 1
84769, 978 1 85359

Overseas Representation:
Australia: DA Information Services Pty Ltd,
Mitcham, Vic, Australia
Canada: University of Toronto Press, North
York, Ont, Canada
China: Sarah Zhao, Meme Media, P. R. of
China
Hong Kong: Aromix Books, Hong Kong
Iran: Kowkab Publishers, Tehran, Iran
Japan: Koro Komori, Japan
Korea: Se-Yung Jun, Seoul, Republic of
Korea
Malaysia: Publishers Marketing Services,
Selangor, Malaysia
Singapore: Publishers Marketing Services
Pte Ltd, Singapore
USA: UTP, Tonawanda, NY, USA

Book Trade Association Membership:
Independent Publishers Guild; Association
of Learned & Professional Society Publishers

2146

**CHARTERED INSTITUTE OF
PERSONNEL & DEVELOPMENT**
151 The Broadway, London SW19 1JQ
Telephone: 020 8612 6564
Fax: 020 8543 4371
Email: publishing@cipd.co.uk
Web Site: www.cipd.co.uk/bookstore

Distribution:
McGraw-Hill Education,
McGraw-Hill House,
Shoppenhangers Road, Maidenhead, Berks
SL6 2QL
Telephone: 01628 502700
Fax: 01628 770224
Web Site: www.cipd.co.uk/bookstore

Personnel:
Stephen Dunn *(Head of Publishing)*
Elizabeth Wright *(Commissioning Manager)*
Jeff Wood *(Operations Manager)*
Sinead Burke *(Sales & Marketing Manager)*
Georgie Smith *(Senior Operations Executive)*
Sumayya Patel *(Operations Executive)*
Thomas Pether *(Operations Co-ordinator)*
Nicole Pellicena *(Senior Sales & Marketing
Executive)*
Justin Stahley *(Sales & Marketing Executive)*
Bernadette Bauskis *(Sales & Marketing
Administrator)*
Holly Spice *(Senior Commissioning Editor)*
Kirsty Smy *(Commissioning Editor)*
Abi Sugden *(Assistant Commissioning
Editor)*
Rebecca Wood *(Online Content Editor)*
Heidi Partridge *(Commissioning Assistant)*
Phill Thompson *(Journals Executive)*
Margaret Marriott *(Commissioning
Manager)*

*Academic & Scholarly; Educational &
Textbooks; Industry, Business &
Management*

No of Employees: 18

Imprints, Series & ISBNs:
978 1 84398

Overseas Representation:
Worldwide: McGraw-Hill Education,
Maidenhead, UK

2147

**THE CHARTERED INSTITUTE OF
PUBLIC FINANCE & ACCOUNTANCY**
3 Robert Street, London WC2N 6RL
Telephone: 020 7543 5600
Fax: 020 7543 5607
Email: sara.hackwood@cipfa.org.uk
Web Site: www.cipfa.org.uk/shop

Personnel:
Ms Sara Hackwood *(Publications Manager)*

Accountancy & Taxation; Economics

Imprints, Series & ISBNs:
978 0 85299, 978 1 84508

2148

CHATHAM PUBLISHING
3 Barham Avenue, Elstree, Herts WD6 3PW
Telephone: 020 8455 5559
Email: michael@frontline-books.com
Web Site: www.chathampublishing.com

Trade Enquiries & Orders:
Pen and Sword Books, 57 Church Street,
Barnsley, South Yorkshire S70 2AS
Telephone: 01226 734222
Email: trade@pen-and-sword.co.uk

Personnel:
Lionel Leventhal *(Publisher)*

Military & War; Nautical; Transport

Imprints, Series & ISBNs:
978 1 86176

Parent Company:
Lionel Leventhal Ltd

Overseas Representation:
Australia & New Zealand: Peribo Pty Ltd,
Mount Kuring-Gai, NSW, Australia
*Austria, Switzerland, Czech & Slovak
Republics, Hungary, Poland, Croatia,
Slovenia, Spain (including Gibraltar) &
Portugal:* Sandro Salucci, Florence, Italy
Canada: Vanwell Publishing Ltd, St
Catharines, Ont, Canada
New Zealand: South Pacific Books (Imports)
Ltd, Auckland, New Zealand
South Africa: Peter Renew, Titles SA,
Johannesburg, South Africa

USA: MBI Publishing Co, St Paul, MN, USA

2149 ▬▬▬▬

*CHEMCORD LTD
16 Inch Keith, St Leonards, East Kilbride,
Glasgow G74 2JZ
Telephone: 01355 235447
Fax: 01355 235447
Email: office@chemcord.co.uk
Web Site: www.chemcord.co.uk

Personnel:
Jim Melrose *(Director)*
Douglas Buchanan *(Director)*
Pat Buchanan *(Sales Manager & Company
Secretary)*

Educational & Textbooks

2150 ▬▬▬▬

CHICKEN HOUSE PUBLISHING LTD
2 Palmer Street, Frome, Somerset
BA11 1DS
Telephone: 01373 454488
Fax: 01373 454499
Email: chickenhouse@doublecluck.com
Web Site: www.doublecluck.com

Warehouse, Trade Enquiries & Orders:
HarperCollins Publishers,
Customer Services, 103 Westerhill Road,
Bishopbriggs, Glasgow G64 2QT
Telephone: 0844 576 8121
Fax: 0844 576 8131
Email: uk.orders@harpercollins.co.uk

Personnel:
Barry Cunningham *(Managing Director)*
Rachel Hickman *(Deputy Managing
Director)*
Imogen Cooper *(Head of Fiction)*
Elinor Bagenal *(Head of Rights)*
Esther Waller *(Publishing Manager)*
Laura Myers *(Sales & Marketing Manager)*
Tina Waller *(Digital Marketing Coordinator)*

Children's Books

New Titles: 22 (2010) , 17 (2011)
No of Employees: 8

Imprints, Series & ISBNs:
978 1 903434, 978 1 904442, 978 1
905294, 978 1 906427, 978 1 908435

Parent Company:
USA: Scholastic

Overseas Representation:
Bermuda: Mary Winchell, Flatts, Bermuda
Central & Eastern Europe & Israel: Vincent
Walsh, Yellow Brick Media, Scarborough,
UK
Hong Kong & China: Jolie Li, Scholastic
Asia, Causeway Bay, Hong Kong
Jamaica & other Caribbean Islands: Sharon
Neita, The Book Merchant Ltd, Kingston,
Jamaica
Japan: Keiko Niwano, Scholastic, Saitama,
Japan
Korea: Helen Yang, Scholastic Asia, Seoul,
Republic of Korea
Latin America: Janine Kelly, Scholastic,
Buenos Aires, Argentina
Middle East & Northern Africa: Michelle
Alwan & Bassem Badran, Bab Idriss,
Beirut, Lebanon
Philippines: Henry Chua, Scholastic, Makati
City, Philippines
Puerto Rico: Darlene Vazquez, Caribe
Grolier/Scholastic Inc, Santurce, Puerto
Rico
Singapore, Malaysia & Indonesia: Selina
Lee, Scholastic, Kuala Lumpur, Malaysia
Southern & East Africa: Brian Mey,
Scholastic, Cape Town, South Africa
Taiwan: Sonia Dung, Scholastic, Taipei,
Taiwan
Thailand: Maneerat Kurdmanee, Scholastic
Asia, Bangkok, Thailand

West Africa: Joyce Agyare, Scholastic,
Tema, Ghana

2151 ▬▬▬▬

**CHILD'S PLAY (INTERNATIONAL)
LTD**
Ashworth Road, Bridgemead, Swindon,
Wilts SN5 7YD
Telephone: 01793 616286
Fax: 01793 512795
Email: office@childs-play.com
Web Site: www.childs-play.com

Personnel:
Neil Burden *(Publisher, Chief Executive)*
Paul Gerrish *(Sales Director)*
Claire Matthews *(Production Manager)*
Beth Cox *(Education Manager)*
Adriana Twinn *(Chair)*
Sue Baker *(Editor)*
Annie Kubler *(Artistic Director)*
Nicola Gardner *(Data Processing Manager)*

Children's Books

New Titles: 45 (2010) , 40 (2011)
No of Employees: 22
Annual Turnover: £2.2M

Imprints, Series & ISBNs:
Child's Play: 978 0 85953, 978 1 84643,
978 1 904550

Overseas Representation:
Australia: Child's Play Australia, Terrey Hills,
NSW, Australia
Canada: Monarch Books of Canada Ltd,
Downsview, Ont, Canada
New Zealand: Nationwide Book
Distributors, Oxford, New Zealand
South Africa: Phambili Agencies CC,
Germiston, South Africa
United Arab Emirates: Child's Play Dubai,
Dubai, UAE
USA: Child's Play Inc, Auburn, ME, USA

Book Trade Association Membership:
Booksellers Association; Educational
Publishers Council; Independent Publishers
Guild

2152 ▬▬▬▬

CHRISTIAN EDUCATION
1020 Bristol Road, Selly Oak, Birmingham
B29 6LB
Telephone: 0121 472 4242
Fax: 0121 472 7575
Email: enquiries@christianeducation.org.uk
Web Site: www.christianeducation.org.uk

Personnel:
Peter Fishpool *(Chief Executive Officer)*
Azhar Lodhi *(Design & Production)*
Anstice Hughes *(Managing Editor)*
Gill Neuenhaus *(Finance Officer)*
Diane Horton *(Office, Sales &
Administration Manager)*
Stephen Pett *(RE Adviser)*
Pete Johnson *(Sales Administrator)*
Rosemary Rivett *(Director of Professional
Services)*
Lat Blaylock *(RE Adviser)*
Fiona Moss *(RE Adviser)*

*Academic & Scholarly; Children's Books;
Educational & Textbooks; Electronic
(Professional & Academic); Religion &
Theology*

New Titles: 9 (2010) , 13 (2011)
No of Employees: 14
Annual Turnover: £1M

Imprints, Series & ISBNs:
Christian Education Publications: 978 1
904024, 978 1 905893
International Bible Reading Association:
978 1 904024
RE Today Services: 978 1 904024

Associated Companies:
UK: Christian Education Publications; RE
Today Services

Book Trade Association Membership:
Publishers Association; Educational
Publishers Council; Christian Booksellers
Convention

2153 ▬▬▬▬

CHRISTIAN FOCUS PUBLICATIONS
Geanies House, Fearn, Tain, Ross-shire
IV20 1TW
Telephone: 01862 871011
Fax: 01862 871699
Email: info@christianfocus.com
Web Site: www.christianfocus.com

Distribution:
Trust Media Distribution, PO Box 300,
Kingstown Broadway, Carlisle, Cumbria
CA3 0QS
Telephone: 0800 282728
Fax: 0800 282530
Email: salesline@tmdistribution.co.uk
Web Site: www.TMDistribution.co.uk

Personnel:
William MacKenzie *(Managing Director)*
Anthony Gosling *(Sales & Marketing
Manager)*
Willie Mackenzie *(Director of Publishing
(Adult Editorial))*
Jonathan Dunbar *(Production Manager)*
Catherine Mackenzie *(Children's Editor)*
Daniel van Straaten *(Design Manager)*
Philip Magee *(Marketing Manager)*

*Biography & Autobiography; Children's
Books; Educational & Textbooks; History &
Antiquarian; Religion & Theology; Sports &
Games*

Imprints, Series & ISBNs:
978 0 906731, 978 1 84550, 978 1 85792,
978 1 871676
Christian Focus
Christian Focus 4 Kids
Christian Heritage
Mentor

Parent Company:
UK: Balintore Holdings

Overseas Representation:
Australia: CLC Australia, Kippa-Ring, Qld,
Australia; Koorong, Blackburn South,
Vic, Australia; Reformers Bookshop,
Stanmore, Australia; Word,
Nunawading, Vic, Australia
Far East: Chris Ashdown, Publishers'
International Marketing, Ferndown,
Dorset, UK
New Zealand: Soul Distributors, Auckland,
New Zealand
South Africa: Struik Christian Books, Cape
Town, South Africa
USA & Canada: LG & G Group, LLC,
Waxhaw, North Carolina, USA; STL
Distribution, Elizabethton, TN, USA

Book Trade Association Membership:
Evangelical Christian Publishers Association
(USA); Christian Booksellers Association
(USA)

2154 ▬▬▬▬

CHURCH HOUSE PUBLISHING
The Archbishops' Council, Church House,
Great Smith Street, London SW1P 3AZ
Telephone: 020 7898 1451
Fax: 020 7898 1449
Email: publishing@churchofengland.org
Web Site: www.chpublishing.co.uk

Sales, Customer Service & Warehouse:
Norwich Books & Music,
13a Hellesdon Park Road, Norwich
NR6 5DR
Telephone: 01603 785923

Fax: 01603 785915
Email:
orders@norwichbooksandmusic.co.uk
Web Site: www.chpublishing.co.uk

See also:
SCM-Canterbury Press

Personnel:
Thomas Allain-Chapman *(Publishing
Manager)*

*Reference Books, Directories &
Dictionaries; Religion & Theology*

Imprints, Series & ISBNs:
978 0 7151
In association with Saint Andrew Press: 978
0 9562821

Parent Company:
UK: The Archbishops' Council

Associated Companies:
UK: Hymns Ancient & Modern Ltd

Overseas Representation:
Australia & New Zealand: Rainbow Book
Agencies, Preston, Vic, Australia
Canada: Bayard/Novalis Distribution,
Toronto, Ont, Canada
USA: Westminster John Knox Press,
Louisville, KY, USA

Book Trade Association Membership:
Independent Publishers Guild; Christian
Suppliers' Group

2155 ▬▬▬▬

CHURCH OF IRELAND PUBLISHING
Church of Ireland House, Church Avenue,
Rathmines, Dublin 6, Republic of Ireland
Telephone: +353 (0)1 492 3979
Fax: +353 (0)1 492 4770
Email: susan.hood@rcbdub.org
Web Site: www.cip.ireland.anglican.org

Personnel:
Susan Hood *(Publications Officer)*

*Academic & Scholarly; Children's Books;
History & Antiquarian; Religion & Theology*

New Titles: 6 (2010) , 4 (2011)
No of Employees: 1

Imprints, Series & ISBNs:
978 1 904884

Book Trade Association Membership:
Publishing Ireland (Foilsiú Éireann)

2156 ▬▬▬▬

CICERONE PRESS LTD
2 Police Square, Milnthorpe, Cumbria
LA7 7PY
Telephone: 01539 562069
Fax: 01539 563417
Email: info@cicerone.co.uk
Web Site: www.cicerone.co.uk

Personnel:
Jonathan Williams *(Managing Director)*
Lesley Williams *(Sales & Marketing Director)*

*Guide Books; Sports & Games; Travel &
Topography*

Imprints, Series & ISBNs:
978 0 902363, 978 1 84965, 978 1 85284

Overseas Representation:
Europe: Bill Bailey Publishers
Representatives, Newton Abbot, UK
France: Editeur, Vaison la Romaine, France
Netherlands: Nilsson & Lamm BV, Houten,
Netherlands
Spain: Map Iberia FeB SL, Avila, Spain
USA: Midpoint Trade Books Inc, New York,
USA

Book Trade Association Membership:
Independent Publishers Guild

2157

*CILT, THE NATIONAL CENTRE FOR LANGUAGES
111 Westminster Bridge Road, London
SE1 7HR
Telephone: 0845 612 5885
Fax: 0845 612 5995
Email: books@cilt.org.uk
Web Site: www.cilt.org.uk

Distribution & Orders:
Central Books Ltd, 99 Wallis Road, London
E9 5LN
Telephone: 0845 458 9911
Fax: 0845 458 9912
Email: mo@centralbooks.com
Web Site: www.centralbooks.com

Personnel:
Teresa Tinsley (Director, Communications)
Tamzin Caffrey (Head of Marketing, Press & Publishing)
Rick Sutton (Publishing Manager)
Julie Manandhar (Marketing Co-ordinator)

Academic & Scholarly; Educational & Textbooks; Languages & Linguistics; Vocational Training & Careers

Imprints, Series & ISBNs:
Advanced Pathfinder
Classic Pathfinder
Curriculum Guides
Info Tech
New Pathfinder
Pathfinder
Reflections on Practice
Resource File
Young Pathfinder

Book Trade Association Membership:
Educational Publishers Council

2158

CITY & GUILDS
1 Giltspur Street, London EC1A 9DD
Telephone: 020 7294 2540
Web Site: www.cityandguilds.com

Book Trade Association Membership:
Publishers Association

2159

CLAIRE PUBLICATIONS
Unit 8, Tey Brook Centre, Great Tey,
Colchester, Essex CO6 1JE
Telephone: 01206 211020
Fax: 01206 212755
Email: mail@clairepublications.com
Web Site: www.clairepublications.com

Personnel:
Noel Graham (Production Managing Director)
Luba Medcalf (Finance)
Dorcas Smith (Rights)

Educational & Textbooks; Electronic (Educational); Languages & Linguistics; Mathematics & Statistics

Book Trade Association Membership:
British Educational Supplies Association

2160

CLAIRVIEW BOOKS LTD
Hillside House, The Square, Forest Row,
East Sussex RH18 5ES
Telephone: 0870 486 3526
Email: office@clairviewbooks.com
Web Site: www.clairviewbooks.com

Personnel:
Sevak Gulbekian (Chief Editor)

Agriculture; Cookery, Wines & Spirits; Environment & Development Studies; Health & Beauty; Medical (incl. Self Help & Alternative Medicine); Military & War; Politics & World Affairs; Religion & Theology

New Titles: 8 (2010) , 7 (2011)
No of Employees: 1
Annual Turnover: £60,000

Imprints, Series & ISBNs:
978 1 905570

Overseas Representation:
Australia: Footprint Books, Melbourne, Vic, Australia
Canada: Tri-Fold Books, Ont, Canada
New Zealand: Ceres Books, Auckland, New Zealand
South Africa: Stephan Phillips Ltd, Cape Town, South Africa
USA: Steinerbooks, New York, NY, USA

Book Trade Association Membership:
Independent Publishers Guild

2161

T. & T. CLARK
see: Continuum International Publishing
Group

2162

JAMES CLARKE & CO
PO Box 60, Cambridge CB1 2NT
Telephone: 01223 350865
Fax: 01223 366951
Email: publishing@jamesclarke.co.uk &
orders@jamesclarke.co.uk
Web Site: www.james.clarke.co.uk

Personnel:
Adrian Brink (Managing Director)

Academic & Scholarly; Bibliography & Library Science; Biography & Autobiography; History & Antiquarian; Literature & Criticism; Philosophy; Reference Books, Directories & Dictionaries; Religion & Theology

New Titles: 35 (2010) , 28 (2011)
No of Employees: 6

Imprints, Series & ISBNs:
978 0 227

Associated Companies:
The Lutterworth Press

Overseas Representation:
USA: The David Brown Book Co (DBBC), Oakville, CT, USA

Book Trade Association Membership:
Publishers Association; Independent
Publishers Guild

2163

*CLASS PUBLISHING
The Exchange, Express Park, Bristol Road,
Bridgwater, Somerset TA6 4RR
Telephone: 01278 427800
Fax: 01278 421077
Email: post@class.co.uk
Web Site: www.class.co.uk

Trade Enquiries & Orders & Distribution:
Macmillan Distribution (MDL), Brunel Road,
Houndmills, Basingstoke, Hants RG21 6XS
Telephone: 01256 329242
Fax: 01256 331413
Email: mdl@macmillan.co.uk
Web Site: www.macmillan-mdl.co.uk

Personnel:
Richard Warner (Managing Director)
Rebecca Hirst (Healthcare Marketing Manager)

Sylvia Hotchin (Legal Customer Services Manager)
Lorna Downing (European Manager, Jones & Bartlett International)

Health & Beauty; Law; Medical (incl. Self Help & Alternative Medicine)

Imprints, Series & ISBNs:
978 1 85959, 978 1 872362

Associated Companies:
Class Health; Class Legal; Jones & Bartlett
International; Jones & Bartlett Learning

Book Trade Association Membership:
Independent Publishers Guild

2164

CLEAR ANSWER MEDICAL PUBLISHING LTD
128a Queens Court, Queensway, London
W2 4QS
Telephone: 020 7229 0893
Email: info@camp-books.com

Personnel:
Dr Frank Seibert-Alves (Managing Director)
Mrs Catarina A. Seibert-Alves (Company Secretary)

Academic & Scholarly; Biology & Zoology; Educational & Textbooks; Medical (incl. Self Help & Alternative Medicine)

New Titles: 2 (2011)

Imprints, Series & ISBNs:
978 1 903573

Book Trade Association Membership:
Independent Publishers Guild

2165

*CLÓ IAR-CHONNACHTA
Indreabhán, Conamara, Co Galway,
Republic of Ireland
Telephone: +353 (0)91 593307
Fax: +353 (0)91 593362
Email: cic@iol.ie
Web Site: www.cic.ie

Representation:
AIS, 31 Fenian Street, Dublin 2,
Republic of Ireland
Telephone: +353 (0)1 661 6522
Fax: +353 (0)1 661 2378

Personnel:
Micheal Ó Conghaile (Managing Director, Rights)
Bridget Bhreathnach (Sales & Marketing)
Deirdre Ní Thuathail (General Manager)

Audio Books; Biography & Autobiography; Children's Books; Educational & Textbooks; Fiction; Gay & Lesbian Studies; History & Antiquarian; Languages & Linguistics; Literature & Criticism; Music; Photography; Poetry; Theatre, Drama & Dance; Travel & Topography

Imprints, Series & ISBNs:
978 1 874700, 978 1 900693, 978 1
902420, 978 1 905560

Overseas Representation:
USA: Dufour Editions Inc, Chester Springs,
PA, USA

Book Trade Association Membership:
Publishing Ireland (Foilsiú Éireann)

2166

*COACHWISE LTD
Chelsea Close, off Amberley Road, Armley,
Leeds LS12 4HP
Telephone: 0113 231 1310
Fax: 0113 203 8826

Email: enquiries@coachwise.ltd.uk
Web Site: www.coachwise.ltd.uk

Personnel:
Tony Byrne (Managing Director)
Kath Leonard (Commercial Director)
Melanie Mallinson (Marketing & Mail Order Director)
Martin Betts (Head of Publications & Design)
Terry Hartley (Print Manager)

Academic & Scholarly; Children's Books; Educational & Textbooks; Electronic (Educational); Sports & Games

Imprints, Series & ISBNs:
978 1 905540, 978 1 902523

Parent Company:
UK: The National Coaching Foundation

Distributor for:
UK: The Association for Physical Education;
The National Coaching Foundation

Overseas Representation:
USA: Soccer Learning Systems, Pleasanton,
CA, USA

Book Trade Association Membership:
Publishers Association

2167

COASTAL PUBLISHING
[Sillson Communications Ltd]
The Studio, Puddletown Road, Wareham,
Dorset BH20 6AE
Telephone: 01929 554195
Fax: 01929 554502
Email: orders@coastalpublishing.co.uk
Web Site: www.coastalpublishing.co.uk

Geography & Geology; Photography; Travel & Topography

New Titles: 2 (2011)
No of Employees: 6

2168

*COIS LIFE
62 Páirc na Rós, Ascaill na Cille,
Dún Laoghaire, Co Dublin,
Republic of Ireland
Telephone: +353 (0)1 280 7951
Fax: +353 (0)1 280 7951
Email: eolas@coislife.ie
Web Site: www.coislife.ie

Trade - Wholesaler:
Áis, 31 Fenian Street, Dublin 2,
Republic of Ireland
Telephone: +353 (0)1 661 6522

Personnel:
C. Nic Pháidín (Company Secretary)
S. Ó Cearnaigh (Chairman)

Academic & Scholarly; Audio Books; Children's Books; Educational & Textbooks; Fiction; Languages & Linguistics; Literature & Criticism; Poetry; Theatre, Drama & Dance

Imprints, Series & ISBNs:
978 1 901176, 978 1 907494

Book Trade Association Membership:
Publishing Ireland (Foilsiú Éireann)

2169

*COLLINS & BROWN
Anova Books, 10 Southcombe Street,
London W14 0RA
Telephone: 020 7605 1400
Fax: 020 7605 1401
Email: customerservices@anovabooks.com
Web Site: www.anovabooks.com

Warehouse & Trade Orders:
HarperCollins, Glasgow
Telephone: 0141 306 3100
Fax: 0141 306 1401

Personnel:
Katie Cowan (*Associate Publisher*)
Jonathan White (*Head of Sales & Marketing*)

Animal Care & Breeding; Cookery, Wines & Spirits; Crafts & Hobbies; Do-It-Yourself; Fashion & Costume; Fiction; Health & Beauty; Magic & the Occult; Medical (incl. Self Help & Alternative Medicine); Music; Photography; Reference Books, Directories & Dictionaries; Sports & Games; Theatre, Drama & Dance

Imprints, Series & ISBNs:
978 1 84340

Parent Company:
Anova Books

Overseas Representation:
Australia: HarperCollins Publishers, Pymble, NSW, Australia
Belgium, France, Netherlands & Luxembourg: Anova Books, London, UK
Caribbean, Mexico & Central America: Christopher Humphrys, Humphrys Roberts Associates, London, UK
Eastern Europe: Csaba Lengyel de Bagota, CLB Marketing Services, Budapest, Hungary
Far East: Julian Ashton, Ashton International Marketing Services, Sevenoaks, Kent, UK
Germany, Switzerland & Austria: Gabriele Kern Publishers Services, Frankfurt-am-Main, Germany
India: Mr Seshadri, Overleaf, New Delhi, India
Italy, Spain, Portugal & Greece: Padovani Books Ltd, London, UK
New Zealand: HarperCollins (NZ) Ltd, Glenfield, Auckland, New Zealand
Pakistan: Tahir M. Lodhi, Lahore, Pakistan
Russia & Baltic States: Tony Moggach, InterMedia Americana (IMA) Ltd, London, UK
Scandinavia: Katie McNeish, McNeish Publishing International, East Sussex, UK
Singapore & Malaysia: Pansing Distribution Sdn Bhd, Singapore
South Africa: Trinity Books CC, Randburg, South Africa
South America: Terry Roberts, Humphrys Roberts Associates, Cotia SP, Brazil
USA & Canada: Sterling Publishing Co Inc, New York, NY, USA

Book Trade Association Membership:
Independent Publishers Guild

2170 ▬▬▬▬▬

COLLINS GEO
[a division of HarperCollins Publishers]
Westerhill Road, Bishopbriggs, Glasgow G64 2QT
Telephone: 0141 306 3576
Fax: 020 8237 4209
Email:
elizabeth.mclachlan@harpercollins.co.uk
Web Site: www.collinsbartholomew.com

Personnel:
Sheena Barclay (*Managing Director*)
James Graves (*Production Director*)
Judith House (*Marketing Manager*)
Tom Fussell (*Commercial Director*)

Atlases & Maps; Educational & Textbooks; Electronic (Educational); Environment & Development Studies; Geography & Geology; Guide Books; Travel & Topography

Imprints, Series & ISBNs:
Bartholomew: 978 0 7028
Collins Cartographic: 978 0 00

Collins Longman: 978 0 00
Nicholson: 978 0 7028
Times Books: 978 0 7230

Parent Company:
HarperCollins

Overseas Representation:
Australia: HarperCollins Publishers, Pymble, NSW, Australia
Canada: HarperCollins Publishers, Toronto & Scarborough, Ont, Canada
Denmark: Scanvik Books ApS, Copenhagen, Denmark
France: Editions Geographiques Generales, Paris, France
Germany & Austria: Internationales Landkartenhaus Geocenter, Stuttgart, Germany
India: Maya Publishers Pvt Ltd, New Delhi, India; Rupa, New Delhi, India
Italy: InterOrbis Media Distribution srl Ed, Corsico (Milan), Italy
Japan: Maruzen Co Ltd, Tokyo, Japan
Netherlands: Nilsson & Lamm BV, Weesp, Netherlands
New Zealand: HarperCollins (NZ) Ltd, Glenfield, Auckland, New Zealand
Singapore & Malaysia: MPH Distributors, Singapore
South Africa: Jonathan Ball, HarperCollins Publishers, Johannesburg & Jeppestown, South Africa
Sweden: Lantmateriet Kartbutiken, Stockholm & Vällingby, Sweden
Thailand: Asia Book Co Ltd, Bangkok, Thailand
USA: Hammond Inc, Maplewood, NJ, USA

Book Trade Association Membership:
Publishers Association; Publishing Scotland

2171 ▬▬▬▬▬

COLOUR HEROES LTD
Unit 6, Longbridge House Farm, Stillington Road, Easingwold, York YO61 3ET
Telephone: 01347 824459
Fax: 01347 822543
Email: info@colourheroes.com
Web Site: www.colourheroes.com

Personnel:
Lorraine Ives (*Sales & Marketing Director*)
Les Ives (*Creative Director*)
Nichola Theakstone (*Business Development Manager*)

Archaeology; Educational & Textbooks; Fiction; Guide Books; History & Antiquarian; Military & War; Natural History

New Titles: 4 (2010) , 4 (2011)
No of Employees: 5

2172 ▬▬▬▬▬

COLOURPOINT BOOKS
Colourpoint House, Jubilee Business Park, 21 Jubilee Road, Newtownards, Co Down BT23 4YH
Telephone: 028 9182 6339
Fax: 028 9182 1900
Email: info@colourpoint.co.uk
Web Site: www.colourpoint.co.uk

Representation:
Bookworld, Unit 10, Hodfar Road, Sandy Lane Industrial Estate, Stourport on Severn, Worcs DY13 9QB
Telephone: 01299 823330

Distribution:
MIMO Distribution (as principal address)
Telephone: 028 9182 0505
Email: sales@mimodistribution.co.uk

Personnel:
Norman Johnston (*Partner*)
Sheila Johnston (*Partner*)
Wesley Johnston (*Editorial Partner*)

Malcolm Johnston (*Finance Partner*)
Denise Martin (*Company Administrator*)

Biography & Autobiography; Educational & Textbooks; Fiction; History & Antiquarian; Transport

Imprints, Series & ISBNs:
978 1 898392, 978 1 904242, 978 1 906578

Distributor for:
MIMO Distribution

Book Trade Association Membership:
Irish Educational PA

2173 ▬▬▬▬▬

COLUMBA
55A Spruce Avenue, Stillorgan Industrial Park, Blackrock, Co Dublin, Republic of Ireland
Telephone: +353 (0)1 294 2556
Fax: +353 (0)1 294 2564
Email: info@columba.ie
Web Site: www.columba.ie

Personnel:
Séan O Boyle (*Managing Director & Publisher*)
Patricia Lowth (*Accounts Payable*)
Michael Brennan (*Sales Manager*)

Academic & Scholarly; History & Antiquarian; Religion & Theology

Imprints, Series & ISBNs:
The Columba Press: 978 0 948183, 978 1 85607
Currach Press: 978 1 85607

Overseas Representation:
Australia: Rainbow Books, Melbourne, Vic, Australia
New Zealand: Pleroma, Central Hawkes Bay, New Zealand
USA & Canada: Dufour Editions Inc, Chester Springs, PA, USA

Book Trade Association Membership:
Publishing Ireland (Foilsiú Éireann); Booksellers Association

2174 ▬▬▬▬▬

COMMONWEALTH SECRETARIAT
Marlborough House, Pall Mall, London SW1Y 5HX
Telephone: 020 7747 6342
Fax: 020 7839 9081
Email: publications@commonwealth.int
Web Site: www.thecommonwealth.org/publications

Orders:
BEBC Distribution, Albion Close, Parkstone, Poole, Dorset BH12 3LL
Telephone: 01202 724292
Email: commonwealth@bebc.co.uk
Web Site: www.bebcdistribution.co.uk

Personnel:
Nicola Perou (*Acting Publications Manager*)

Academic & Scholarly; Agriculture; Economics; Electronic (Educational); Environment & Development Studies; Gender Studies; Industry, Business & Management; Law; Politics & World Affairs; Reference Books, Directories & Dictionaries; Scientific & Technical

Imprints, Series & ISBNs:
978 0 85092, 978 1 84859, 978 1 84929

Distributor for:
UK: Commonwealth Association of Tax Administrators; Commonwealth Foundation

Overseas Representation:
Botswana: Malburg Book Agency, Gaborone, Botswana
Canada: Renouf Publishing Co Ltd, Ottawa, Ont, Canada
Egypt: The Middle East Readers Information Center, MERIC, Cairo, Egypt
Germany: Missing Link Versandbuchhandlung, Bremen, Germany
Ghana: F. Reimmer Book Services, Accra, Ghana
Hong Kong: Transglobal Publishers Services Ltd, Hong Kong
Iberia: Iberian Book Services, Madrid, Spain
India: Parrot Reads Publishers, New Delhi, India
Japan: Far Eastern Booksellers, Tokyo, Japan
Kenya: Legacy Books, Nairobi, Kenya
Malaysia: KL Book Distributors, Kuala Lumpur, Malaysia
Nepal: Everest Media International Services P. Ltd, Kathmandu, Nepal
Nigeria: Mosuro The Booksellers Ltd, Ibadan, Nigeria
Pakistan: Book Bird Publishers Representatives, Lahore, Pakistan
Singapore: Horizon Books Pte Ltd, Singapore; Select Books Pte Ltd, Singapore
South Africa: Hargraves Library Service, Claremont & Cape Town, South Africa
Switzerland: Munstergass-Buchhandlung, Bern, Switzerland
Taiwan: Tycoon Information Inc, Taipei, Taiwan
Tanzania: E & D Vision Publishing Ltd, Dar es Salaam, Tanzania
Trinidad & Tobago: Systematics Studies Ltd, St Augustine, Trinidad
Uganda: Gustro Ltd, Kampala, Uganda
USA: Stylus Publishing Inc, Sterling, VA, USA

Book Trade Association Membership:
Publishers Association; Independent Publishers Guild

2175 ▬▬▬▬▬

*COMPENDIUM PUBLISHING LTD
43 Frith Street, London W1D 4SA
Telephone: 020 7287 4570
Fax: 0845 130 3173
Email: info@compendiumpublishing.com
Web Site:
www.compendiumpublishing.com

Personnel:
Alan Greene (*Managing Director*)
Simon Forty (*Editor*)
Bill Lucas (*Sales Director*)

Architecture & Design; History & Antiquarian; Military & War; Music; Philosophy; Photography; Travel & Topography

Imprints, Series & ISBNs:
Compendium Publishing

Overseas Representation:
Australia: Herron, Queensland, Australia
Central & South America, Caribbean: David Williams, London, UK
Europe excluding Germany: Book Port Associates, Corsico, Italy
Germany, Austria & Switzerland: Publishers Services, Frankfurt, Germany
Hong Kong & China: United Century Book Services, Chaiwan, Hong Kong
India, Bangladesh & Sri Lanka: Research Press, New Delhi, India
Middle East, North Africa & Israel: Peter Ward Book Exports, London, UK
Philippines, Korea & Taiwan: Marketing Services for Publishers, Pasig City, Philippines
Singapore, Malaysia, Indonesia & Brunei: Marketing Services for Publishers Pte Ltd, Singapore
South Africa: Wild Dog Press, Lyndhurst, South Africa

2176

CONRAN OCTOPUS
[a division of Octopus Publishing Group]
Endeavour House,
189 Shaftesbury Avenue, London
WC2H 8JY
Telephone: 020 7632 5400
Email: info@octopus-publishing.co.uk
Web Site: www.octopusbooks.co.uk

Distribution:
Littlehampton Book Services Ltd,
Faraday Close, Durrington, Worthing,
West Sussex BN13 3TG
Telephone: 01903 828500
Fax: 01903 828802

Personnel:
Denise Bates (Group Publishing Director)
Jonathan Christie (Art Director)

Architecture & Design; Cookery, Wines &
Spirits; Crafts & Hobbies; Gardening

Imprints, Series & ISBNs:
Conran: 978 1 84091

Parent Company:
UK: Hachette UK

Overseas Representation:
See: Octopus Publishing Group, London, UK

2177

CONSTABLE & ROBINSON LTD
55–56 Russell Square, London, WC1B 4HP
Telephone: 020 7268 9700
Email: general@constablerobinson.com &
  sales@constablerobinson.com
Web Site: www.constablerobinson.com

Warehouse & Distribution:
TBS Ltd, Colchester Road, Frating Green,
Colchester, Essex CO7 7DW
Telephone: 01206 256000
Fax: 01206 819587

Personnel:
Nick Robinson (Publisher)
Pete Duncan (Managing Director)
Nova Jayne Robinson (Online-Publishing
  Director)
Adrian Andrews (Finance Director)
Martin Palmer (Group Sales Director)
Leo Hollis (History Editor)
Eryl Humphrey Jones (Rights Director)
Sam Evans (Publicity Director)
Haydn Jones (Sales Director)
Rob Nichols (Marketing Director)
Krystyna Green (Senior Commissioning
  Editor: Robinson – Crime – Fiction & Non-
  Fiction)
Duncan Proudfoot (Non-Fiction Editor)
James Gurbutt (Publisher, Corsair imprint)
Andreas Campomar (Editorial Director, Non-
  Fiction)
Fritha Saunders (Editor, Psychology)
Hugh Barker (Special Sales Manager)

Biography & Autobiography; Fiction;
Gardening; Humour; Illustrated & Fine
Editions; Medical (incl. Self Help &
Alternative Medicine); Military & War;
Psychology & Psychiatry; Science Fiction

Imprints, Series & ISBNs:
Constable: 978 1 84901, 978 1 84119, 978
  1 84529, 978 1 85487
Corsair: 978 1 84901
Magpie Books: 978 1 84901, 978 1 84119,
  978 1 85487
Right Way: 978 0 7160
Robinson: 978 1 84901, 978 1 84119, 978
  1 84529, 978 1 85487

Overseas Representation:
Australia (Constable & Robinson – Library
  Supplies): Murdoch Books

Australia (Constable & Robinson – Retail):
  Walker Books
Central & Eastern Europe, Russia, CIS,
  Middle East, North & Central America,
  France, Italy & Greece: Walker Books
India: Penguin India
Japan & China: Timberham, Ferndown, UK
Japan, China & South East Asia: Publishers
  International Marketing, London, UK
New Zealand, Scandinavia, Iceland, Spain &
  Portugal: Murdoch Books
Republic of Ireland: Vivienne Lavery,
  Blackrock, Co Dublin, Republic of Ireland
South Africa: Penguin Books South Africa,
  Parklands, South Africa
West Indies & West Africa: Kelvin van
  Hasselt Publishing Services, Briningham,
  Norfolk, UK
Western Europe: Michael Geoghegan,
  London, UK

Book Trade Association Membership:
Publishers Association; Independent
Publishers Guild

2178

**THE CONTINUUM INTERNATIONAL
PUBLISHING GROUP LTD**
[a Bloomsbury Company]
The Tower Building, 11 York Road, London
SE1 7NX
Telephone: 020 7922 0880
Fax: 020 7922 0881
Email: info@continuumbooks.com
Web Site: www.continuumbooks.com

Distribution:
Orca Book Services, Stanley House,
3 Fleets Lane, Poole, Dorset BH15 3AJ
Telephone: 01202 665432
Fax: 01202 666219
Web Site: www.orcabookservices.co.uk

Personnel:
Bob Marsh (Finance Director)
Robin Baird-Smith (Publishing Director)
Ken Rhodes (Sales & Marketing Director)
Anna Fleming (Publisher)
Sarah Campbell (Publisher)
Elizabeth White (Special Sales & Rights
  Manager)
Louise Cameron (Production Director)

Academic & Scholarly; Bibliography &
Library Science; Biography &
Autobiography; Cinema, Video, TV &
Radio; Economics; Educational &
Textbooks; Electronic (Educational);
Electronic (Professional & Academic);
History & Antiquarian; Languages &
Linguistics; Literature & Criticism; Music;
Philosophy; Politics & World Affairs;
Reference Books, Directories &
Dictionaries; Religion & Theology; Theatre,
Drama & Dance

Imprints, Series & ISBNs:
Athlone: 978 0 485
A. & C. Black (New Testament
  Commentaries): 978 0 7136
Burns & Oates: 978 0 86012
Cassell Academic: 978 0 304
Cassell Reference: 978 0 304
Geoffrey Chapman: 978 0 225
Claridge Press: 978 0 582
T. & T. Clark International: 978 0 567
Continuum: 978 0 8264, 978 1 4411
Continuum Collection: 978 1 84714
Hambledon Continuum: 978 1 84725
Leicester University Press: 978 0 7185
Mansell: 978 0 7201
Mowbray: 978 0 264
Network Continuum Education: 978 1
  85539
Pinter
Sheed & Ward: 978 0 7220
Sheffield Academic Press: 978 1 84127, 978
  1 85075
Thoemmes Continuum: 978 1 84371, 978
  1 85506
Trinity Press International: 978 1 56338

Parent Company:
UK: Bloomsbury Publishing PLC

Associated Companies:
USA: The Continuum International
Publishing Group Inc

Overseas Representation:
Australia: Palgrave Macmillan, Melbourne,
  Vic, Australia
Australia (Religion titles only): Rainbow
  Books, Melbourne, Vic, Australia
Austria, Greece & Cyprus: Tyers Book Sales,
  UK
Eastern Europe: Jacek Lewinson, Warsaw,
  Poland
India & Sri Lanka: Palgrave Macmillan, New
  Delhi, India
Japan: United Publishers Services Ltd,
  Tokyo, Japan
Korea: Information & Culture Korea (ICK),
  Seoul, Republic of Korea
Mexico, Central & South America:
  Cranbury International LLC, Montpelier,
  VT, USA
Middle East, North Africa & Malta:
  International Publishing Services (IPS)
  Middle East Ltd, Dubai, UAE
Netherlands, Belgium, Germany, France,
  Switzerland, Italy, Israel & Caribbean:
  The Continuum International Publishing
  Group Ltd, London, UK
Nigeria: Bounty Press Ltd, Ibadan, Nigeria
Pakistan: T.M.L. Publishers' Consultants &
  Representatives, Lahore, Pakistan
Scandinavia: Colin Flint Ltd, Publishers
  Scandinavian Consultancy, Cambridge,
  UK
Southeast & East Asia: Taylor & Francis Asia
  Pacific, Singapore
Southern Africa: Book Promotions (Pty) Ltd/
  Horizon Books (Pty) Ltd, Cape Town,
  South Africa
Spain, Portugal & Gibraltar: Iberian Book
  Services, Madrid, Spain

Book Trade Association Membership:
Independent Publishers Guild

2179

DAVID C. COOK (UK)
Lottbridge Drove, Eastbourne, East Sussex
BN23 6NT
Telephone: 01323 437700
Fax: 01323 411970
Email: books@kingsway.co.uk
Web Site: www.kingsway.co.uk

Trade Orders:
Kingsway, 26–28 Lottbridge Drove,
Eastbourne, East Sussex BN23 6NT
Telephone: 01323 437700
Fax: 01323 411970
Email: tradeorders@kingsway.co.uk
Web Site: www.kingsway.co.uk

Personnel:
John Paculabo (Chief Executive Officer)
Jonathan Brown (Business Development
  Director)
Bill Owen (Finance & Administration
  Manager)
Miriam Doherty (Books, Card & Gift
  Manager)

Biography & Autobiography; Religion &
Theology

New Titles: 5 (2010) , 5 (2011)
No of Employees: 55
Annual Turnover: £8M

Imprints, Series & ISBNs:
David C. Cook: 978 0 78140, 978 0 78143,
  978 0 78144, 978 0 78145, 978 1
  43470, 978 1 55513, 978 1 56292, 978
  1 58919
Kingsway: 978 0 85476, 978 0 85491, 978
  0 86065, 978 0 86239, 978 0 902088,
  978 1 84291

Distributor for:
22 Media; Barbour Publishing Inc.; Beacon
  Hill Press; Charisma House; Dernier
  Publishers; Faithwords; Freeman Smith;
  Gospel Light & Regal Books; Guideposts/
  Ideals; Influence; Kregal; Lifeway,
  Broadman & Holmon; Moody; NavPress;
  New Leaf Publishing Group; Standard
  Publishing; Worthy Publishing

Overseas Representation:
Australia: Kennedy International, NSW,
  Australia
Canada: David C. Cook Distribution
  Canada, Paris, Ont, Canada
South Africa: Struik Christian Books Pty Ltd,
  Maitland, Cape Town, South Africa

2180

**COORDINATION GROUP
PUBLICATIONS LTD (CGP LTD)**
Kirkby-in-Furness, Cumbria LA17 7WZ
Telephone: 01229 715700
Fax: 01229 716958
Email: customerservices@cgpbooks.co.uk
Web Site: www.cgpbooks.co.uk

Personnel:
Graham Servante (Managing Director)
Jane Barnes (Publishing Director)

Educational & Textbooks

No of Employees: 150
Annual Turnover: £13M

Imprints, Series & ISBNs:
978 1 84146, 978 1 84762

Associated Companies:
USA: CGP Study; Coordination Group
  Publications Inc (trading as CGP
  Education)

2181

COPPER BEECH PUBLISHING LTD
PO Box 159, East Grinstead, Sussex
RH19 4FS
Telephone: 01342 314734
Fax: 01342 312196
Email: sales@copperbeechpublishing.co.uk
Web Site:
  www.copperbeechpublishing.co.uk

Personnel:
Jan Barnes (Rights)
Julie Hird (Editorial)
Elizabeth Moreira (Finance)

Cookery, Wines & Spirits; Fashion &
Costume; Gardening; History &
Antiquarian; Sports & Games; Transport

Imprints, Series & ISBNs:
978 0 9516295, 978 1 898617
English Eccentricities
The Etiquette Collection

Book Trade Association Membership:
Independent Publishers Guild

2182

CORK UNIVERSITY PRESS
Youngline Industrial Estate, Pailaduff Road,
Togher, Cork, Republic of Ireland
Telephone: +353 (0)21 490 2980
Fax: +353 (0)21 431 5329
Email: corkuniversitypress@ucc.ie
Web Site: www.corkuniversitypress.com

**Orders & Distribution (Republic of
Ireland, Northern Ireland & Europe):**
Gill & Macmillan Distribution,
Hume Avenue, Park West, Dublin 12,
Republic of Ireland
Telephone: +353 (0)1 500 9500
Fax: +353 (0)1 500 9596

Representation (Republic of Ireland & Northern Ireland):
Robert Towers, 2 The Crescent, Monkstown, Co Dublin, Republic of Ireland
Telephone: +353 (0)1 280 6532
Fax: +353 (0)1 280 6020

Personnel:
Mike Collins (Publications Director)
Maria O'Donovan (Production Editor)

Academic & Scholarly; Archaeology; Architecture & Design; Atlases & Maps; Biography & Autobiography; Cinema, Video, TV & Radio; Cookery, Wines & Spirits; Economics; Environment & Development Studies; Fine Art & Art History; Gardening; Gay & Lesbian Studies; Gender Studies; Geography & Geology; History & Antiquarian; Literature & Criticism; Military & War; Music; Natural History; Philosophy; Photography; Psychology & Psychiatry; Sports & Games; Theatre, Drama & Dance

Imprints, Series & ISBNs:
Atrium
Attic Press
Field Day Essays: 978 0 902561, 978 1 85918
Irish Narratives: 978 0 902561, 978 1 85918
Undercurrents: 978 0 902561, 978 1 85918

Overseas Representation:
Japan: United Publishers Services Ltd, Tokyo, Japan
North America: Stylus Publishing LLC, Herndon, VA, USA
UK & Europe: Quantum Publishing Solutions Ltd, Paisley, UK
UK (excluding Northern Ireland) (Distribution): Marston Book Services Ltd, Abingdon, UK

Book Trade Association Membership:
Publishing Ireland (Foilsiú Éireann)

2183

CORNWALL EDITIONS LTD
8 Langurtho Road, Fowey, Cornwall PL23 1EQ
Telephone: 01726 832483
Fax: 01726 832483
Email: info@cornwalleditions.co.uk
Web Site: www.cornwalleditions.co.uk

Personnel:
Ian Grant (Publisher)
Judy Martin (Customer Services Manager)

Archaeology; Children's Books; Fiction; History & Antiquarian; Natural History

Imprints, Series & ISBNs:
Cornwall Editions: 978 1 904880
Ian Grant Publishers: 978 1 904880

Book Trade Association Membership:
Independent Publishers Guild

2184

COUNCIL FOR BRITISH ARCHAEOLOGY
St Mary's House, 66 Bootham, York YO30 7BZ
Telephone: 01904 671417
Fax: 01904 671384
Email: books@britarch.ac.uk
Web Site: www.britarch.ac.uk

Distribution:
Central Books Ltd, 99 Wallis Road, London E9 5LN
Telephone: 0845 458 9910
Fax: 0845 458 9912
Email: mo@centralbooks.com
Web Site: www.centralbooks.com

Personnel:
Michael Heyworth (Director)
Peter Olver (Finance Director)
Gill Chitty (Head of Conservation)
Cherida Plumb (Head of Development)
Catrina Appleby (Publications Officer)
Sophie Cringle (Marketing and Events Officer)
Marcus Smith (Information Officer)
Mike Pitts (British Archaeology Magazine Editor)
Nicky Milsted (Young Archaeologists' Club Magazine Editor)
Suzie Thomas (Community Archaeology Support Officer)

Archaeology

Imprints, Series & ISBNs:
Archaeology of York
British and Irish Archaeological Bibliography
British Archaeology
CBA Research Reports: 978 1 902771
Practical Handbooks in Archaeology: 978 1 902771

Book Trade Association Membership:
Association of Learned & Professional Society Publishers

2185

COUNTRYSIDE BOOKS
2 Highfield Avenue, Newbury, Berks RG14 5DS
Telephone: 01635 43816
Fax: 01635 551004
Email: info@countrysidebooks.co.uk
Web Site: www.countrysidebooks.co.uk

Personnel:
Nicholas Battle (Publisher)
Suzanne Battle (Partner)
Jackie Arrowsmith (Sales Manager)
Paula Leigh (Managing Editor)
Deb Marshman (Publicity Manager)

Architecture & Design; Aviation; Guide Books; History & Antiquarian; Humour; Military & War; Reference Books, Directories & Dictionaries; Sociology & Anthropology; Transport; Travel & Topography

Imprints, Series & ISBNs:
978 0 86368, 978 0 905392, 978 1 84674, 978 1 85306, 978 1 85455

Parent Company:
Countryside Books UK

Distributor for:
Boomerang Family Ltd; Cube Publications Ltd; The Dovecote Press; Historical Publications Ltd; Kent County Council; Meridian Books; Power Publications

Overseas Representation:
USA & Canada: The David Brown Book Co, Oakville, CT, USA

Book Trade Association Membership:
Independent Publishers Guild

2186

*COUNTYVISE LTD
14 Appin Road, Birkenhead CH41 9HH
Telephone: 0151 647 3333
Fax: 0151 647 8286
Email: info@birkenheadpress.co.uk
Web Site: www.countyvise.co.uk

Personnel:
John Emmerson (Managing Director)
Jean Emmerson (Director)

Academic & Scholarly; Biography & Autobiography; Children's Books; Crime; Fiction; History & Antiquarian; Humour; Natural History; Nautical; Poetry; Religion & Theology; Sports & Games; Transport

Imprints, Series & ISBNs:
978 0 907768, 978 1 901231, 978 1 906823
Appin Press: 978 1 906205
Liver Press: 978 1 871201
Merseyside Port Folios: 978 0 9516129
Picton Press (Liverpool): 978 1 873245

2187

COURSEWARE4TRAINERS LTD
The Orchard Glasshouse, South Willingham, Market Rasen, Lincs LN8 6NG
Telephone: 01507 313501
Fax: 01507 313332
Email: paul.ferguson@courseware4trainers.co.uk
Web Site: www.courseware4trainers.co.uk

No of Employees: 4

Book Trade Association Membership:
Publishers Association

2188

CREATIVE CONTENT LTD
8 The Cornfields, Hatch Warren, Basingstoke, Hants RG22 4QB
Telephone: 01256 466641

Electronic (Professional & Academic)

New Titles: 15 (2010)

Book Trade Association Membership:
Publishers Association

2189

CRÉCY PUBLISHING LTD
Unit 1A, Ringway Trading Estate, Shadowmoss Road, Manchester M22 5LH
Telephone: 0161 499 0024
Fax: 0161 499 0298
Email: books@crecy.co.uk
Web Site: www.crecy.co.uk

Personnel:
Jeremy M. Pratt (Managing Director)
Gill Richardson (Customer Services and Editorial Manager)
Chris Tordoff (Marketing Manager)

Aviation; History & Antiquarian; Military & War; Nautical; Transport

Imprints, Series & ISBNs:
Airdata Publications: 978 0 85979
Airplan Flight Equipment Ltd: 978 1 874783
Crécy: 978 0 947554
Flight Recorder Publications
Goodall Publications: 978 0 907579
Hikoki Publications: 978 1 902109
Nostalgia Road: 978 1 903016, 978 1 908347

Distributor for:
Aerospace Masterbooks; Air Research Publications; Airplan Flight Equipment Ltd; Airtime Publishing; Aviation Publications Inc; Camber Publications Ltd; Independent Books; Leandoer + Ekholm; Pacific Century; Specialty Press

Overseas Representation:
Australia: J. B. Wholesalers, Bibra Lake, WA, Australia
Canada: Vanwell Publishing Ltd, St Catharines, Ont, Canada
Eastern Europe: Tony Moggach, UK
Europe: Bookport Associates, Corsico (MI), Italy
New Zealand: South Pacific Books (Imports) Ltd, Auckland, New Zealand
USA: Specialty Press, North Branch, MN, USA
Western Europe: Anselm Robinson, UK

2190

CRESSRELLES PUBLISHING CO LTD
10 Station Road Industrial Estate, Colwall, Malvern WR13 6RN
Telephone: 01684 540154
Email: simon@cressrelles.co.uk
Web Site: www.cressrelles.co.uk

Personnel:
Simon Smith (Sales Director)
Leslie Smith (Director)

Theatre, Drama & Dance

New Titles: 12 (2010) , 12 (2011)
No of Employees: 2

Imprints, Series & ISBNs:
Actinic Press
Cressrelles: 978 0 85956
J. Garnet Miller: 978 0 85343
Kenyon-Deane: 978 0 7155
New Playwrights' Network: 978 0 86319, 978 0 903653, 978 0 906660

Distributor for:
USA: Anchorage Press Inc

Overseas Representation:
Australia: Origin Theatrical, Sydney, NSW, Australia
New Zealand: Play Bureau of New Zealand Ltd, New Plymouth, New Zealand
Republic of Ireland: Drama League of Ireland, Dublin, Republic of Ireland
South Africa: Dalro (Pty) Ltd, Braamfontein, South Africa
USA: Bakers Plays, Quincy, MA, USA

2191

*CRIMSON PUBLISHING
2nd Floor, Westminster House, Kew Road, Richmond, Surrey TW9 2ND
Telephone: 020 8334 1600
Fax: 020 8334 1601
Email: info@crimsonpublishing.co.uk
Web Site: www.crimsonpublishing.co.uk

Bookshop Orders:
Portfolio Books, 2nd Floor, Westminster House, Kew Road, Richmond, Surrey TW9 2ND
Telephone: 020 8334 1730
Fax: 020 8334 1609
Email: info@portfoliobooks.com
Web Site: www.portfoliobooks.com

Personnel:
David Lester (Managing Director)
Allison Harper (Financial Director)
Jo Jacomb (Production Manager – Trotman)
Sally Rawlings (Production Manager – Crimson)
Lucy Smith (Marketing Director)
Alison Yates (Senior Commissioning Editor)
Hugh Brune (Sales Director)

Biography & Autobiography; Crafts & Hobbies; Educational & Textbooks; Electronic (Educational); Guide Books; Health & Beauty; Industry, Business & Management; Reference Books, Directories & Dictionaries; Travel & Topography; Vocational Training & Careers

Imprints, Series & ISBNs:
Crimson / Vacation Work / Pathfinder Guides / Crimson Short Walks: 978 1 85458
Pocket Bibles
Trotman: 978 1 84455
Trotman Education: 978 1 906041
White Ladder

Overseas Representation:
Australia: Woodslane Pty Ltd, Warriewood, NSW, Australia
Benelux: Nilsson & Lamm BV, Weesp, Netherlands

South Africa: Trinity Books CC, Randburg, South Africa
USA: Letter Soup Rights Agency, Woodbury, MN, USA

2192

*CROSSBOW EDUCATION LTD
41 Sawpit Lane, Brocton, Staffs ST17 0TE
Telephone: 01785 660902
Fax: 01785 661431
Email: sales@crossboweducation.co.uk
Web Site: www.crossboweducation.co.uk

Also at:
Crossbow Education Ltd,
Tollgate Business Centre, Tollgate Drive,
Stafford ST16 3HS
Telephone: 0845 269 7272
Email: orders@crossboweducation.co.uk
Web Site: crossboweducation.com

Personnel:
Robert Hext *(Co-Director: UK & USA)*
Anne Hext *(Co-Director: UK & USA)*
Pelle Johansson *(UK General Manager)*
Ruth Johansson *(UK Finance & Wages)*
Mark Poyser *(UK General Sales)*
Robin York *(US Manager)*

Academic & Scholarly; Educational & Textbooks

Imprints, Series & ISBNs:
978 1 900891

Overseas Representation:
USA: Crossbow Education Corp, Cornelius, NC, USA

Book Trade Association Membership:
Educational Publishers Council

2193

CROWN HOUSE PUBLISHING LTD
Crown Buildings, Bancyfelin,
Carmarthenshire SA33 5ND
Telephone: 01267 211345
Fax: 01267 211882
Email: books@crownhouse.co.uk
Web Site: www.crownhouse.co.uk

Distribution:
Grantham Book Services, Trent Road,
Grantham, Lincolnshire NG31 7XQ
Telephone: 01476 541 080
Fax: 01476 541 061
Email: orders@gbs.tbs-ltd.co.uk

Personnel:
David Bowman *(Managing Director)*
Caroline Lenton *(Sales & Marketing Director)*

Academic & Scholarly; Medical (incl. Self Help & Alternative Medicine); Psychology & Psychiatry

New Titles: 34 (2010) , 25 (2011)
No of Employees: 12

Distributor for:
UK: The Developing Co; The Quest Institute
USA: Free Spirit; Kagan Professional Development; Kendall Hunt Publishing; Meta Publications; Science & Behaviour Books; Westwood Publishing

Overseas Representation:
Australasia: Footprint Books Pty Ltd, NSW, Australia
Central & Eastern Europe: IMA Publishers' Sales Representation, London, UK
Hong Kong & Macau: Transglobal Publishers Services Ltd, Hong Kong
India: Research Press, New Delhi, India
Israel: Probook Ltd
Malaysia: Publishers Marketing Services Pte Ltd, Malaysia
Philippines, Korea & Taiwan: I. J. Sagun Enterprises Inc, Philippines

Singapore: Publishers Marketing Services Pte Ltd, Singapore
South Africa: Juta & Co, Claremont, South Africa
Spain, Portugal & Gibraltar: Iberian Book Services, Spain

Book Trade Association Membership:
Booksellers Association; Independent Publishers Guild

2194

THE CROWOOD PRESS LTD
The Stable Block, Crowood Lane,
Ramsbury, Marlborough, Wiltshire SN8 2HR
Telephone: 01672 520320
Fax: 01672 520280
Email: enquiries@crowood.com
Web Site: www.crowood.com

Distribution:
Grantham Book Services, Trent Road,
Grantham, Lincs NG31 7XQ
Telephone: 01476 541000
Fax: 01476 541060
Email: orders@gbs.tbs-ltd.co.uk
Web Site: www.crowood.com

Personnel:
John Dennis *(Chairman)*
Ken Hathaway *(Managing Director)*
Julie Sankey *(Sales & Marketing)*

Agriculture; Animal Care & Breeding; Antiques & Collecting; Aviation; Crafts & Hobbies; Do-It-Yourself; Gardening; Military & War; Natural History; Nautical; Sports & Games; Theatre, Drama & Dance; Transport

Imprints, Series & ISBNs:
978 0 946284, 978 1 84797, 978 1 85223, 978 1 86126

Overseas Representation:
Australia: Peribo Pty Ltd, Mount Kuring-Gai, NSW, Australia
Canada: Vanwell Publishing Ltd, St Catharines, Ont, Canada
Scandinavia: Angell Eurosales, Berwick-on-Tweed, UK
Singapore, Malaysia & Brunei: Publishers Marketing Services Pte Ltd, Singapore
South Africa: Peter Hyde Associates (Pty) Ltd, Cape Town, South Africa
Southern Europe: Bookport Associates, Corsico (MI), Italy
USA: Trafalgar Square Publishing, North Pomfret, VT, USA
Western Europe: Anselm Robinson, London, UK

2195

*G. L. CROWTHER
224 South Meadow Lane, Preston PR1 8JP
Telephone: 01772 257126

Personnel:
G. L. Crowther *(Sole Proprietor/Executive)*

Atlases & Maps; Geography & Geology; Transport

Imprints, Series & ISBNs:
National Series of Waterway Tramway and Railway Atlases: 978 1 85615

2196

CRW PUBLISHING LTD
6 Turville Barns, Eastleach, Cirencester, Glos GL7 3QB
Telephone: 01367 850448
Email: clive.reynard@btinternet.com
Web Site: www.collectors-library.com

Trade Orders:
Macmillan Distribution (MDL), Brunel Road, Basingstoke, Hants RG21 6XS

Telephone: 01256 302692 & 0845 070 5656 (automated line – orders & availability)
Fax: 01256 812558
Email: orders@macmillan.co.uk

Personnel:
Ken Webb *(Production Director)*
Marus Clapham *(Editorial Director)*
Clive Reynard *(Sales Director)*
Cameron Brown *(Chairman, Director)*

Children's Books; Fiction; Humour

Imprints, Series & ISBNs:
Collector's Library: 978 1 904633, 978 1 904919, 978 1 905716, 978 1 907360
Collector's Library Editions/Cases/Omnibus Editions: 978 1 904633, 978 1 904919, 978 1 905716

Overseas Representation:
Australia: Alpa Books, Australia
Far East: Pan Macmillan Asia, Hong Kong
Germany, Eastern Europe, Russia, Benelux, Austria & Switzerland: Pan Macmillan, London, UK
Greece: Bookport Associates
New Zealand: David Bateman Ltd, Auckland, New Zealand
Scandinavia: Anglo-Nordic Books Ltd
Spain, Portugal & Italy: Penguin Books SA, Madrid, Spain

2197

*CSA WORD
[the trading name for CSA Telltapes Ltd]
6a Archway Mews, London SW15 2PE
Telephone: 020 8871 0220
Fax: 020 8877 0712
Email: info@csaword.co.uk
Web Site: www.csaword.co.uk

Distribution:
Orca Book Services, Unit A3, Fleets Corner, Poole, Dorset BH17 0HL
Telephone: 01202 665432
Fax: 01202 666219
Email: orders@orca-book-services.co.uk

Personnel:
Clive Stanhope *(Managing Director)*
Victoria Williams *(Sales Manager)*
Vanessa Brown *(Production Manager)*

Audio Books

Imprints, Series & ISBNs:
978 1 873859, 978 1 901768, 978 1 904605, 978 1 906147, 978 1 934997

Overseas Representation:
USA & Canada: Publishers Group West, Berkeley, CA, USA

2198

*CUALANN PRESS
6 Corpach Drive, Dunfermline, Fife KY12 7XG
Telephone: 01383 733724
Fax: 01383 733724
Email: info@cualann.com & cualann@btinternet.com
Web Site: www.cualann.com

Personnel:
Brid Hetherington *(Director)*

Biography & Autobiography; History & Antiquarian; Military & War; Sports & Games; Travel & Topography

Imprints, Series & ISBNs:
978 0 9535036, 978 0 9544416, 978 0 9554273

2199

CYHOEDDIADAU'R GAIR
Ael y Bryn, Chwilog, Pwilheli, Gwynedd LL53 6SH

Telephone: 01766 819120
Fax: 01766 819120
Email: aled@ysgolsul.com
Web Site: www.ysgolsul.com

Personnel:
Aled Davies *(Director)*

Children's Books; Religion & Theology

Imprints, Series & ISBNs:
978 1 85994

Parent Company:
Welsh Sunday School Council

Overseas Representation:
Worldwide: Welsh Books Council, Aberystwyth, UK

Book Trade Association Membership:
Independent Publishers Guild

2200

DANCE BOOKS LTD
Charwell House, Wilsom Road, Alton, Hampshire GU34 2PP
Telephone: 01420 525 299
Fax: 01420 540 272
Email: dwl@dancebooks.co.uk
Web Site: www.dancebooks.co.uk

Warehouse, Trade Enquiries & Orders:
Vine House Distribution, Waldenbury, North Common, Chailey, East Sussex BN8 4DR
Telephone: 01825 723398
Fax: 01825 724188
Email: sales@vinehouseuk.co.uk
Web Site: www.vinehouseuk.co.uk

Personnel:
John O'Brien *(Chairman)*
David Leonard *(Managing, Editorial & Production Director)*
Richard Holland *(Sales Director)*

Academic & Scholarly; Music; Theatre, Drama & Dance

New Titles: 10 (2010) , 10 (2011)
No of Employees: 4

Imprints, Series & ISBNs:
978 0 903102, 978 1 85273

Distributor for:
USA: Dance Horizons; Princeton Book Co

Overseas Representation:
Australia: Footprint Books Pty Ltd, Warriewood, NSW, Australia
USA: Princeton Book Co, Hightstown, NJ, USA

2201

*DARTON, LONGMAN & TODD LTD
1 Spencer Court,
140–142 Wandsworth High Street, London SW18 4JJ
Telephone: 020 8875 0155
Fax: 020 8875 0133
Email: audep@darton-longman-todd.co.uk
Web Site: www.dltbooks.com

Distribution:
Norwich Books and Music,
St Mary's Works, St Mary's Plain, Norwich NR3 3BH
Telephone: 01603 612914

Personnel:
Margot Crowther *(Accounts Director)*
Brendan Walsh *(Editorial Director)*
Helen Porter *(Managing Editor Director)*
Ken Ruskin *(Production Director)*
Aude Pasquier *(Sales & Marketing Director)*

*Academic & Scholarly; Biography &
Autobiography; Educational & Textbooks;
Philosophy; Psychology & Psychiatry;
Religion & Theology*

Imprints, Series & ISBNs:
978 0 232

Overseas Representation:
*Africa, Caribbean Commonwealth, Far East
& South Africa:* Kelvin van Hasselt
Publishing Services, Briningham, Norfolk,
UK
Australia: Rainbow Books, Fairfield, Vic,
Australia
Canada: Novalis Inc, Toronto, Ont, Canada
Malta: Preca Library, Societas Doctrinae
Christianae, M.U.S.E.U.M., Bajda, Malta
New Zealand: Pleroma Christian Supplies,
Otane, Central Hawkes Bay, New Zealand

2202 ■■■■■

THE DAVENANT PRESS
PO Box 323, Burford OX18 4XN
Telephone: 01865 292148
Fax: 01993 824129
Email: judith@history.u-net.com
Web Site: www.davenantpress.co.uk

Personnel:
Judith Ann Loades *(Proprietor)*

*Academic & Scholarly; Animal Care &
Breeding; Archaeology; Biography &
Autobiography; Educational & Textbooks;
History & Antiquarian; Literature &
Criticism; Politics & World Affairs; Religion
& Theology*

New Titles: 8 (2010) , 26 (2011)

Imprints, Series & ISBNs:
Davenant Press (General Academic Titles):
978 1 85944
Notes on English Literature: 978 1 85944
Notes on History: 978 1 85944
Notes on Politics: 978 1 85944

Book Trade Association Membership:
Booksellers Association

2203 ■■■■■

*DAY ONE PUBLICATIONS
Ryelands Road, Leominster HR6 8NZ
Telephone: 01568 613740
Fax: 01568 611473
Email: info@dayone.co.uk
Web Site: www.dayone.co.uk

Personnel:
John Roberts *(Director)*
Mark Roberts *(Managing Director)*
Jim Holmes *(Marketing & Sales Manager)*

*Audio Books; Biography & Autobiography;
Children's Books; Guide Books; Religion &
Theology; Travel & Topography*

Imprints, Series & ISBNs:
978 0 902548, 978 1 84625, 978 1 903087

Parent Company:
Day One Christian Ministries

Overseas Representation:
Canada: Sola Scriptura Ministries, Guelph,
Ont, Canada
USA: Day One Christian Ministries (Inc),
Greenville, SC, USA

Book Trade Association Membership:
Booksellers Association; Christian
Booksellers Convention (UK); CBA (USA)

2204 ■■■■■

*DEDALUS LTD
Langford Lodge, St Judith's Lane, Sawtry,
Cambs PE28 5XE
Telephone: 01487 832382

Email: info@dedalusbooks.com
Web Site: www.dedalusbooks.com

Distribution, Warehouse & Invoicing:
Central Books Ltd, 99 Wallis Road, London
E9 5LN
Telephone: 0845 458 9911
Fax: 0845 458 9912
Email: orders@centralbooks.com

UK Sales:
Turnaround Publisher Services Ltd, Unit 3,
Olympia Trading Estate, Coburg Road,
London N22 6TZ
Telephone: 020 8829 3000
Fax: 020 8881 5088

Personnel:
Robert Irwin *(Editorial Director)*
Juri Gabriel *(Chairman & Rights Director)*
Eric Lane *(Managing Director)*
Mike Mitchell *(Translations Director)*

*Biography & Autobiography; Cookery,
Wines & Spirits; Fiction; Gardening;
Literature & Criticism; Travel & Topography*

Imprints, Series & ISBNs:
Dedalus Concept Books: 978 1 903517,
978 1 907650
Dedalus Euro Shorts
Dedalus European Classics: 978 0 946626,
978 1 873982
Empire of the Senses: 978 0 946626, 978 1
873982
Europe 1992–2012: 978 0 946626, 978 1
873982
Modern English Fiction: 978 0 946626, 978
1 873982

Overseas Representation:
Australia & New Zealand: Peribo Pty Ltd,
Mount Kuring-Gai, NSW, Australia
Canada: Disticor Book Division, Toronto,
Ont, Canada
*France, Belgium, Germany, Switzerland,
Austria, Netherlands & Eastern Europe:*
Michael Geoghegan, London, UK
Scandinavia: Angel Eurosales, Berwick-on-
Tweed, UK
Spain, Portugal, Greece & Italy: Penny
Padovani, London, UK
USA: SCB Distributors, Gardena, CA, USA

Book Trade Association Membership:
Independent Publishers Guild

2205 ■■■■■

DELANCEY PRESS LTD
23 Berkeley Square, London W1J 6HE
Telephone: 020 7665 6605
Email: delanceypress@aol.com
Web Site: www.delanceypress.co.uk &
www.peoplesbookprize.com

Personnel:
Tatiana Wilson *(Managing Director:
Marketing)*
Jackie Crouch *(Finance)*
Rupert Jones-Parry *(Rights Manager)*
Alexandra Shelly *(Editor)*

*Children's Books; Fiction; Humour;
Psychology & Psychiatry*

Imprints, Series & ISBNs:
978 0 9539119, 978 1 907205

Book Trade Association Membership:
Publishers Association; Booksellers
Association

2206 ■■■■■

DELTA ALPHA PUBLISHING LTD
19H John Spencer Square, London N1 2LZ
Telephone: 020 7359 1822
Fax: 020 7359 1822
Email: dap@deltaalpha.com
Web Site: www.deltaalpha.com

Personnel:
Damien Abbott *(Director)*
Deborah Lloyd *(Marketing Manager)*
John Knox *(Marketing Manager)*

*Economics; Law; Photography; Reference
Books, Directories & Dictionaries*

Imprints, Series & ISBNs:
978 0 9668946

Associated Companies:
USA: Delta Alpha Publishing

Overseas Representation:
Australia: Delta Alpha, Scarborough, Qld,
Australia
USA: Port City Fulfilment, Kimball, MI, USA

Book Trade Association Membership:
Independent Publishers Guild; Publisher
Marketing Association, USA; Australian PA

2207 ■■■■■

DELTA ELT PUBLISHING LTD
Hoe Lane, Peaslake, Surrey GU5 9SW
Telephone: 01306 731770
Web Site: www.deltapublishing.co.uk

*Educational & Textbooks; English as a
Foreign Language; Languages & Linguistics*

Imprints, Series & ISBNs:
978 1 900783, 978 1 905085

2208 ■■■■■

RICHARD DENNIS PUBLICATIONS
The New Chapel, Shepton Beauchamp,
Ilminster, Somerset TA19 0JT
Telephone: 01460 240044
Email:
books@richarddennispublications.com
Web Site:
www.richarddennispublications.com

Personnel:
Richard Dennis *(Production)*
Sharon Pearce *(Administration)*
Tracie Welch *(Accounts)*
Magnus Dennis *(Photographer)*
Buchan Dennis *(Marketing)*

*Academic & Scholarly; Antiques &
Collecting; Architecture & Design;
Biography & Autobiography; Fine Art & Art
History; History & Antiquarian; Illustrated &
Fine Editions*

New Titles: 2 (2010) , 2 (2011)
No of Employees: 5

Imprints, Series & ISBNs:
978 0 903685, 978 0 9553741

Overseas Representation:
USA: Antique Collectors Club Ltd,
Easthampton, MA, USA

2209 ■■■■■

DENOR PRESS LTD
3 Hillcourt Avenue London N12 8EY
Telephone: 07768 855995
Fax: 020 8446 4504
Email: denor@dial.pipex.com
Web Site: www.denorpress.com

Personnel:
Lucille Leader *(Production & Editorial
Director)*
Dr Geoffrey Leader *(Director)*
Philip Woolfson *(Consultant/Accountant)*

*Academic & Scholarly; Biography &
Autobiography; Educational & Textbooks;
Fiction; Medical (incl. Self Help & Alternative
Medicine); Music*

New Titles: 2 (2010) , 2 (2011)
No of Employees: 2

Imprints, Series & ISBNs:
978 0 9526056

Distributor for:
UK: Leading Note Productions

Overseas Representation:
USA: Lightning Source Inc (US), Lavergne,
TN, USA

2210 ■■■■■

*J M DENT
[imprint of The Orion Publishing Group Ltd]
Orion House, 5 Upper St Martins Lane,
London WC2H 9EA
Telephone: 020 7240 3444
Fax: 020 7240 4822

Trade Counter & Warehouse:
Littlehampton Book Services Ltd,
Faraday Close, Durrington, Worthing,
West Sussex BN13 3RB
Telephone: 01903 828500
Fax: 01903 828625

*Academic & Scholarly; Biography &
Autobiography; Children's Books;
Economics; Fiction; Gardening; History &
Antiquarian; Law; Literature & Criticism;
Music; Reference Books, Directories &
Dictionaries; Scientific & Technical*

Imprints, Series & ISBNs:
J M Dent: 978 0 460
Everyman Paperbacks: 978 0 460

Parent Company:
The Orion Publishing Group Ltd

Overseas Representation:
see: The Orion Publishing Group Ltd,
London, UK

2211 ■■■■■

**THE DERBY BOOKS PUBLISHING CO
LTD**
3 The Parker Centre, Mansfield Road,
Derby DE21 4SZ
Telephone: 01332 384235
Fax: 01332 292755
Email: sales@dbpublishing.co.uk
Web Site: www.dbpublishing.co.uk

Personnel:
Stephen Caron *(Chairman & Managing
Director)*
Jane Caron *(Finance Director)*
Jo Rush *(Sales & Marketing)*
Carole Vernon *(Administration)*

*Biography & Autobiography; Guide Books;
Sports & Games; Transport*

Imprints, Series & ISBNs:
978 0 907969, 978 1 85983, 978 1 873626

2212 ■■■■■

*DIONYSIA PRESS LTD
7 Duddingston House Courtyard,
127 Milton Road West, Edinburgh
EH15 1JG

Personnel:
Eve Smith *(Director)*
Denise Smith *(Director: Marketing, Editorial,
Secretary)*

Literature & Criticism

Imprints, Series & ISBNs:
978 1 903171

Distributor for:
Greece: Dionysia Press

Overseas Representation:
Greece: Dionysia Zervanou, Athens, Greece

Book Trade Association Membership:
Publishing Scotland

2213

DISCOVERY WALKING GUIDES LTD
10 Tennyson Close, Dallington,
Northampton NN5 7HJ
Web Site: www.walking.demon.co.uk

Also at:
DWG Ltd, c/o Mailshot Services,
21 Upper Priory Street, Northampton
NN1 2PT

Personnel:
David Brawn (Company Secretary)
Ros Brawn (Director)

Atlases & Maps; Guide Books; Travel &
Topography

New Titles: 16 (2010) , 18 (2011)

Imprints, Series & ISBNs:
Bus & Touring Maps: 978 1 904946
Tour & Trail Maps: 978 1 904946
Walk! Guide Books: 978 1 904946

Overseas Representation:
Spain: Map Iberia FeB SL, Avila, Spain

2214

DITTO INTERNATIONAL LTD
7 Regents Hall, St Mary's Avenue,
Stony Stratford, Bucks MK11 1EB
Telephone: 01908 563766
Email: info@dittointernational.co.uk
Web Site: www.dittointernational.co.uk

Personnel:
Mrs Pauline Carpenter (Director)
Mrs Anita Epple (Director)

Academic & Scholarly; Educational &
Textbooks

New Titles: 2 (2010)
No of Employees: 2

2215

DJØF
5 Victoria House, 138 Watling Street East,
Towcester NN12 6BT
Telephone: 01327 357770
Fax: 01327 359572

Warehouse & Distribution:
Marston Book Services, 160 Milton Park,
PO Box 269, Abingdon OX14 4YN
Telephone: 01235 465577
Fax: 01235 465555
Web Site: www.djoef-forlag.dk

Personnel:
Gary Hall (Manager)

Economics; Industry, Business &
Management; Law

Parent Company:
Denmark: DJØF Publishing

2216

*ERIC DOBBY PUBLISHING LTD
Random Acres, Slip Mill Lane, Hawkhurst,
Kent TN18 5AD
Telephone: 01580 753387
Fax: 01580 753387
Email: eric@ericdobbypublishing.com

Distribution:
Publishers Group UK, 8 The Arena,
Mollison Avenue, Enfield, Middx EN3 7NL
Telephone: 020 8804 0400
Fax: 020 8804 0044
Web Site: www.pguk.co.uk

Personnel:
Eric Dobby (Managing Director, Sales &
Rights)
Tracey Dobby (Director Administration)

Architecture & Design; Crime; Fashion &
Costume; Military & War; Reference Books,
Directories & Dictionaries

Imprints, Series & ISBNs:
978 1 85882

Associated Companies:
Medway Publishing Ltd

Overseas Representation:
Australia: Woodslane, Mona Vale, NSW,
Australia
Benelux: Jos de Jong, Just in Time
Promotions, Heenstal, Netherlands
Eastern Europe: Dr László Horváth
Publishers Representative, Budapest,
Hungary
Italy, Greece & Cyprus: Charles Gibbes
Associates, London, UK
Middle East & Malta: Avicenna Partnership,
Oxford, UK
Scandinavia: David Towle International
South Africa: Palgrave Macmillan,
Johannesburg, South Africa
South East Asia: Asia Publishers Services
Ltd, Hong Kong
South West Asia: APD Singapore Pte Ltd,
Singapore
Spain, Portugal & Gibraltar: Iberian Book
Services, Madrid, Spain

2217

DONHEAD PUBLISHING LTD
Lower Coombe, Donhead St Mary,
Shaftesbury, Dorset SP7 9LY
Telephone: 01747 828422
Fax: 01747 828522
Web Site: www.donhead.com

Personnel:
Jill Pearce (Managing Director & Publisher)
Chris Hall (Finance Director)
Vicky Morland (Publishing Manager)

Architecture & Design; Scientific & Technical

New Titles: 5 (2010) , 5 (2011)
No of Employees: 3

Imprints, Series & ISBNs:
978 1 873394

Overseas Representation:
Germany, Switzerland, Austria: Fraunhofer
IRB, Stuttgart, Germany
USA: Port City Fulfilment, Kimball, MI, USA

Book Trade Association Membership:
Independent Publishers Guild

2218

THE DOVECOTE PRESS
Stanbridge, Wimborne Minster, Dorset
BH21 4JD
Telephone: 01258 840549
Fax: 01258 840958
Email: online@dovecotepress.com
Web Site: www.dovecotepress.com

Personnel:
David Burnett (Managing Director)
Elizabeth Dean (Secretary)

Archaeology; Biography & Autobiography;
Geography & Geology; Guide Books;
History & Antiquarian; Military & War;
Natural History; Transport; Travel &
Topography

Imprints, Series & ISBNs:
978 0 946159, 978 1 874336, 978 1
904349

2219

*ASHLEY DRAKE PUBLISHING LTD
PO Box 733, Cardiff CF14 7ZY
Telephone: 029 2021 8187
Email: post@ashleydrake.com
Web Site: www.ashleydrake.com

Distribution:
NBN International, Estover Road, Plymouth
PL6 7PY
Web Site: www.nbninternational.com

Personnel:
Ashley Drake (Managing Director)
Siwan Wyn (Company Secretary)

Academic & Scholarly; Biography &
Autobiography; Children's Books; Cookery,
Wines & Spirits; Educational & Textbooks;
History & Antiquarian; Industry, Business &
Management; Languages & Linguistics;
Literature & Criticism; Military & War;
Politics & World Affairs; Psychology &
Psychiatry; Sports & Games; Theatre,
Drama & Dance

Imprints, Series & ISBNs:
Y Ddraig Fach: 978 1 899877
Gwasg Addysgol Cymru: 978 1 899869
Hisarlik Press: 978 1 874312
Morgan Publishing: 978 1 903532
Scandinavian Academic Press: 978 1
904609
St David's Press (formerly Ashley Drake
Publishing): 978 1 902719
Welsh Academic Press: 978 1 86057

Overseas Representation:
North America: ISBS, Portland OR, USA

2220

DRAMATIC LINES
PO Box 201, Twickenham TW2 5RQ
Telephone: 020 8296 9502
Fax: 020 8296 9503
Email: mail@dramaticlinespublishers.co.uk
Web Site: www.dramaticlines.co.uk

Personnel:
John Nicholas (Managing Editor)
Heather Stephens (Sales, Marketing &
Production)
Irene Palko (Development)

Children's Books; Educational & Textbooks;
History & Antiquarian; Theatre, Drama &
Dance

2221

*DREF WEN CYF/LTD
28 Church Road, Whitchurch, Cardiff
CF14 2EA
Telephone: 029 2061 7860
Fax: 029 2061 0507
Email: gwilym@drefwen.com
Web Site: www.drefwen.com

Personnel:
Roger Boore (Director)
Anne Boore (Director)
Gwilym Boore (Director)
Alun Boore (Director)
Rhys Boore (Director)

Audio Books; Children's Books; Educational
& Textbooks; Fiction

Imprints, Series & ISBNs:
978 0 85596, 978 0 946962

Book Trade Association Membership:
Cwlwm Cyhoeddwyr Cymru (Union of
Welsh Publishers)

2222

GERALD DUCKWORTH & CO LTD
90–93 Cowcross Street, London EC1M 6BF
Telephone: 020 7490 7300

Fax: 020 7490 0080
Email: info@duckworth-publishers.co.uk
Web Site: www.ducknet.co.uk

Distribution:
Grantham Book Services, Trent Road,
Grantham, Lincs NG31 7XQ

Personnel:
Peter Mayer (Owner & Managing Director)
Ray Davies (Production Director)
Jon Jackson (Editorial Director)
Ben Slight (Sales & Marketing Executive)
Suzannah Rich (Publicity Manager)
Jessica Thompson (Acting Publicity
Manager)

Architecture & Design; Biography &
Autobiography; Children's Books; Cinema,
Video, TV & Radio; Crime; Economics;
Fashion & Costume; Fiction; Fine Art & Art
History; History & Antiquarian; Humour;
Illustrated & Fine Editions; Literature &
Criticism; Magic & the Occult; Military &
War; Music; Natural History; Philosophy;
Physics; Politics & World Affairs; Reference
Books, Directories & Dictionaries; Religion &
Theology; Science Fiction; Sports & Games;
Theatre, Drama & Dance; Travel &
Topography

No of Employees: 7

Imprints, Series & ISBNs:
Duckworth: 978 0 7156

Overseas Representation:
Australia & New Zealand: Bloomsbury,
Sydney, Australia
Central & Eastern Europe: Penguin Poland,
Poznan-Baranowo, Poland
France, Morocco, Algeria & Tunisia:
Penguin Group, Amsterdam, Netherlands
Germany & Austria: Uli Hoernemann, Belin
Verlag, Berlin, Germany
Holland, Belgium & Luxembourg: Penguin
Benelux, Amsterdam, Netherlands
India: Penguin Books India, New Delhi, India
Italy: Penguin Italia, Milano, Italy
Middle East: Penguin Group (Arabia),
Dubai, UAE
Scandinavia & Switzerland: Penguin
International Sales, London, UK
Singapore & Malaysia: Penguin Books
Singapore, Singapore
South Africa: Book Promotions Pty Ltd, Diep
River, South Africa
Spain & Portugal: Penguin Books S.A.,
Madrid, Spain

Book Trade Association Membership:
Independent Publishers Guild

2223

DUNEDIN ACADEMIC PRESS
Hudson House, 8 Albany Street, Edinburgh
EH1 3QB
Telephone: 0131 473 2397
Fax: 01250 870920
Email: mail@dunedinacademicpress.co.uk
Web Site:
www.dunedinacademicpress.co.uk

Representation (UK):
Compass Academic Ltd,
The Barley Mow Centre,
10 Barley Mow Passage, Chiswick, London
W4 4PH
Telephone: 020 8994 6477
Fax: 020 8400 6132
Email: AS@compass-academic.co.uk

**Distribution (excluding North America
& Australasia):**
Dunedin Academic Press, c/
o Turpin Distribution, Pegasus Drive,
Stratton Business Park, Biggleswade, Beds
SG18 8TQ
Telephone: 01767 604951
Fax: 01767 601640
Email: books@turpin-distribution.com

Personnel:
Anthony Kinahan (*Director*)
Norman Steven (*Director*)

Academic & Scholarly; Geography & Geology; Languages & Linguistics; Medical (incl. Self Help & Alternative Medicine); Sociology & Anthropology

New Titles: 9 (2010) , 20 (2011)
No of Employees: 0

Imprints, Series & ISBNs:
Dunedin Academic Press: 978 1 903765, 978 1 906716, 978 1 78046
Terra Publishing: 978 1 903544

Overseas Representation:
Arab World & Iran: Dar Kreidieh, Beirut, Lebanon
Australasia: Inbooks, c/o James Bennett Pty Ltd, Belrose, NSW, Australia
Benelux: Netwerk Academic Book Agency, Rotterdam, Netherlands
China & Taiwan: China Publishing Services, Hong Kong
Hong Kong & Macau: Transglobal Publishers Services Ltd, Hong Kong
India, Bangladesh, Indonesia, Sri Lanka, Singapore, Pakistan, Thailand: The White Partnership, Tunbridge Wells, Kent, UK
Korea, Taiwan & Philippines: Edwin Makabenta, Quezon City, Philippines
North America: International Specialized Book Services Inc, Portland, OR, USA
Republic of Ireland & Northern Ireland: Brookside Publishing Services, Dublin, Republic of Ireland
Scandinavia: Jan Norbye, Ølstykke, Denmark
Spain & Portugal: Chris Humphrys, Gaucin, Spain

Book Trade Association Membership:
Publishing Scotland; International Group of Scientific, Medical & Technical Publishers

2224 ━━━━━

*EAGLE PUBLISHING LTD
3–4 The Drove, West Wilts Trading Estate, Westbury, Wilts BA13 4JE
Telephone: 01225 899141
Fax: 01225 768811
Email: eaglepublishing@btconnect.com

Distributors:
IVP Books, Norton Street, Nottingham NG7 3HR
Telephone: 0115 978 1054
Fax: 0115 942 2694
Web Site: www.ivpbooks.com

Personnel:
David Wavre (*Managing Director*)

Religion & Theology

Imprints, Series & ISBNs:
978 0 86347

Overseas Representation:
Australia & South Africa: IVP Books, Nottingham, UK
New Zealand: Scripture Union Wholesale, Wellington, New Zealand
Republic of Ireland: Columba Book Service, Blackrock, Co Dublin, Republic of Ireland

2225 ━━━━━

*EARTHSCAN
Dunstan House, 14A St Cross Street, London EC1N 8XA
Telephone: 020 7841 1930
Fax: 020 7242 1474
Email: earthinfo@earthscan.co.uk
Web Site: www.earthscan.co.uk

Distribution:
Macmillan Distribution (MDL), Brunel Road, Houndmills, Basingstoke, Hants RG21 6XS

Telephone: 01256 329242
Fax: 01256 842084
Email: orders@macmillan.co.uk

Personnel:
Edward Milford (*Executive Chairman*)
Jonathan Sinclair Wilson (*Managing Director*)
Gina Mance (*Head of Production*)
Veruschka Selbach (*Head of Sales & Marketing*)

Academic & Scholarly; Agriculture; Architecture & Design; Atlases & Maps; Biology & Zoology; Economics; Educational & Textbooks; Electronic (Professional & Academic); Engineering; Environment & Development Studies; Geography & Geology; Industry, Business & Management; Law; Natural History; Politics & World Affairs; Reference Books, Directories & Dictionaries; Scientific & Technical; Sociology & Anthropology; Transport

Imprints, Series & ISBNs:
Earthscan: 978 1 84407, 978 1 85383
James & James: 978 0 907383, 978 1 873936, 978 1 902916

Overseas Representation:
Africa (excluding North & South Africa): Tony Moggach, InterMedia Africa Ltd (IMA), London, UK
Australia, New Zealand & Papua New Guinea: New South Books, Moorebank, NSW, Australia
Canada: UBC Press, Georgetown, Ont, Canada
China & Hong Kong: China Publishers Services Ltd, Hong Kong
India: Vinod Vasishtha, Viva Books, New Delhi, India
Japan: Tim Burland, Tokyo, Japan; United Publishers Services Ltd, Tokyo, Japan
Korea: Se-Yung Jun, Information & Culture Korea (ICK), Seoul, Republic of Korea
Latin America & Caribbean: Ethan Atkin, Cranbury International LLC, Montpelier, VT, USA
Malaysia & Brunei: UBSD, Selangor, Malaysia
Middle East & North Africa: Zoe Kaviani, International Publishing Services (IPS) Middle East Ltd, Dubai, UAE
Pakistan, Afghanistan & Tajikistan: Book Bird Publishers Representatives, Lahore, Pakistan
Philippines: Megatexts Phil Inc, Cebu City, Philippines
South Africa: Jacana Media, Johannesburg, South Africa
Taiwan: Unifacmanu Trading Co Ltd, Taipei, Taiwan
USA: Stylus Publishing LLC, Herndon, VA, USA

Book Trade Association Membership:
Independent Publishers Guild

2226 ━━━━━

ECO-LOGIC BOOKS
Mulberry House, 19 Maple Grove, Bath BA2 3AF
Telephone: 01225 484472
Fax: 0871 522 7054
Web Site: www.eco-logicbooks.com

Personnel:
Peter Andrews (*Publisher*)

Agriculture; Architecture & Design; Crafts & Hobbies; Environment & Development Studies; Gardening

New Titles: 3 (2011)

Imprints, Series & ISBNs:
978 1 899233

Distributor for:
Australia: Holmgren Design Services
UK: Common Ground
USA: Alan C. Hood & Co Inc; Mole Publishing Co; Oasis Design; Trucking Turtle Publishing

2227 ━━━━━

ECO PUBLISHING INTERNATIONAL LTD
PO Box 56891, London N13 9AJ
Email:
mail@ecopublishinginternational.com
Web Site:
www.ecopublishinginternational.com

Personnel:
Malcolm Watson (*Chairman*)

Educational & Textbooks; Environment & Development Studies

Imprints, Series & ISBNs:
978 1 947049

Book Trade Association Membership:
Publishers Association

2228 ━━━━━

EDINBURGH UNIVERSITY PRESS
22 George Square, Edinburgh EH8 9LF
Telephone: 0131 650 4218
Fax: 0131 650 3286
Email: marketing@eup.ed.ac.uk
Web Site: www.euppublishing.com

New Titles: 120 (2010) , 130 (2011)

2229 ━━━━━

*EDUCATIONAL PLANNING BOOKS LTD
PO Box 63, Hathersage, Hope Valley, Derbyshire S32 1DJ
Telephone: 01433 651010
Fax: 01433 650000
Email: sales@epb-ltd.co.uk

Warehouse:
Bamford Works, Bamford, Hope Valley, Derbyshire S33 0EB
Telephone: 01433 651010
Fax: 01433 650000
Email: sales@epb-ltd.co.uk
Web Site: www.edplanbooks.com

Personnel:
G. N. S. Garner (*Managing Director*)

Educational & Textbooks

Book Trade Association Membership:
Publishers Association

2230 ━━━━━

EGMONT UK LTD
239 Kensington High Street, London W8 6SA
Telephone: 020 7761 3500
Fax: 020 7761 3510
Email: info@euk.egmont.com
Web Site: www.egmont.co.uk

Egmont Press & Sales Departments:
3rd Floor, Beaumont House, Kensington Village, Avonmore Road, London W14 8TS
Telephone: 020 7605 6600
Fax: 020 7605 6601

Personnel:
Rob McMenemy (*Senior Vice-President, Egmont English Language & Central Europe*)
Jimmy Weir (*Chief Financial Officer*)
Gillian Laskier (*Group Sales Director*)
Cally Poplak (*Managing Director, Egmont Press*)

David Riley (*Managing Director, Egmont Publishing Group*)
Debbie Cook (*Director of Magazines*)

Children's Books

Imprints, Series & ISBNs:
Dean: 978 0 603
Egmont: 978 1 4052
Mammoth: 978 0 7497
Methuen: 978 0 416

Parent Company:
Denmark: Egmont Fonden

Book Trade Association Membership:
Publishers Association; Booksellers Association

2231 ━━━━━

EGON PUBLISHERS LTD
618 Leeds Road, Outwood, Wakefield WF1 2LT
Telephone: 01924 871697
Fax: 01924 871697
Email: information@egon.co.uk
Web Site: www.egon.co.uk

Personnel:
Mr Colin Redman (*Managing Director*)
Mrs Rachel Redman (*Company Secretary*)

Educational & Textbooks

New Titles: 5 (2010)
No of Employees: 2
Annual Turnover: £40,000

Imprints, Series & ISBNs:
978 0 905858, 978 1 899998, 978 1 904160, 978 1 907656

Associated Companies:
UK: SEN Marketing

Distributor for:
UK: Brand Books

Overseas Representation:
Australia: Silvereye Publications, Avalon, NSW, Australia
New Zealand: Acquila Enterprises, Auckland, New Zealand
Singapore: September 21, Braddell Tech, Singapore

2232 ━━━━━

ELAND PUBLISHING LTD
3rd Floor, 61 Exmouth Market, London EC1R 4QL
Telephone: 020 7833 0762
Fax: 020 7833 4434
Email: info@travelbooks.co.uk
Web Site: www.travelbooks.co.uk

Trade Distribution:
Grantham Book Services, Trent Road, Grantham, Lincs NG31 7XG
Telephone: 01476 541080
Fax: 01476 541061
Email: orders@gbs.tbs-ltd.co.uk

Personnel:
Rose Baring (*Production Director*)
Barnaby Rogerson (*Co-Publisher*)
Stephanie Allen (*Publicity Director*)
Lucy Underhill (*Financial Director*)

Travel & Topography

Imprints, Series & ISBNs:
978 0 907871

Associated Companies:
UK: Baring & Rogerson; Sickle Moon Books

Overseas Representation:
Australia & New Zealand: New South Books, NSW, Australia
Eastern Europe, Russia & Sub-Saharan

Africa: Tony Moggach, London, UK
France, Benelux, Germany, Austria & Switzerland: Ted Dougherty, London, UK
Italy, Spain, Portugal, Greece & Gibraltar: Jenny & Penny Padovani, London, UK
Mexico, Central & Southern America: David Williams, InterMedia Americana (IMA) Ltd, London, UK
Middle East, North Africa, Turkey & Iran: Peter Ward Book Exports, London, UK
Thailand, Burma, Laos & Vietnam: Orchid Press, Bangkok, Thailand
USA & Canada: Dufour Editions Inc, Chester Springs, PA, USA

Book Trade Association Membership:
Independent Publishers Guild

2233 ▬

*ELECTRIC WORD PLC
33–41 Dallington Street, London EC1V 0BB
Telephone: 020 7954 3420
Fax: 0845 450 6140
Web Site: www.electricwordplc.com

Academic & Scholarly

2234 ▬

EDWARD ELGAR PUBLISHING LTD
The Lypiatts, 15 Lansdown Road, Cheltenham, Glos GL50 2JA
Telephone: 01242 226934
Fax: 01242 262111
Email: info@e-elgar.co.uk
Web Site: www.e-elgar.co.uk

Distribution:
Marston Book Services Ltd, PO Box 269, Abingdon, Oxon OX14 4YN
Telephone: 01235 465500
Fax: 01235 465555
Email: client@marston.co.uk
Web Site: www.marston.co.uk

Personnel:
Edward Elgar *(Chairman)*
Tim Williams *(Managing Director)*
Sandy Elgar *(Personnel Director & Secretary)*
Alex Pettifer *(Editorial Director)*
Julie Leppard *(Head of Editorial & Production Service)*
Francine O'Sullivan *(Senior Commissioning Editor)*
Ruth Kirk *(Rights & Permissions)*
Hilary Quinn *(Marketing, Publicity & Sales)*

Academic & Scholarly; Agriculture; Economics; Educational & Textbooks; Electronic (Professional & Academic); Environment & Development Studies; Industry, Business & Management; Law; Reference Books, Directories & Dictionaries; Transport

New Titles: 310 (2010) , 378 (2011)
No of Employees: 58

Imprints, Series & ISBNs:
978 0 85793, 978 1 78100, 978 1 84064, 978 1 84376, 978 1 84542, 978 1 84720, 978 1 84844, 978 1 84980, 978 1 85278, 978 1 85898

Associated Companies:
USA: Edward Elgar Publishing Inc

Overseas Representation:
Japan: United Publishers Services Ltd, Tokyo, Japan
North & South America: Edward Elgar Publishing Inc, Northampton, MA, USA
Singapore, Malaysia, Thailand, Indonesia, Philippines, Brunei, Vietnam, Myanmar, Laos & Cambodia: Taylor & Francis Asia Pacific, Singapore

2235 ▬

ELLIOTT & THOMPSON
27 John Street, London WC1N 2BX

Telephone: 020 7831 5013
Email: info@eandtbooks.com
Web Site: www.eandtbooks.com

Personnel:
Lorne Forsyth *(Chairman)*
Olivia Bays *(Publisher)*
Nick Sidwell *(Publishing Executive)*

Biography & Autobiography; Cookery, Wines & Spirits; Economics; History & Antiquarian; Industry, Business & Management; Military & War; Music; Natural History; Politics & World Affairs; Sports & Games

New Titles: 14 (2010) , 20 (2011)
No of Employees: 3

Imprints, Series & ISBNs:
978 1 904027, 978 1 907642

Overseas Representation:
German-language European territories: Gabriele Kern
Middle East & Far East (ex. Singapore & Malaysia): Faber & Faber
Singapore and Malaysia: Penguin Group
South Africa: Penguin Group
South America, Central America & Caribbean: David Williams
UK & Ireland: Frances Lincoln
USA: Trafalgar Square

Book Trade Association Membership:
Independent Publishers Guild

2236 ▬

*ELM PUBLICATIONS
Seaton House, Kings Ripton, Huntingdon PE28 2NJ
Telephone: 01487 773359
Fax: 01487 773359
Email: elm@elm-training.co.uk
Web Site: www.elm-training.co.uk

Personnel:
Sheila Ritchie *(Home & Export Sales Managing Director)*
Duncan Ritchie *(IT Director/Secretary)*
Jacqueline Wieczovek *(Sales Manager)*

Educational & Textbooks; Electronic (Educational); Industry, Business & Management; Transport; Travel & Topography

Imprints, Series & ISBNs:
978 0 946139, 978 0 9505828, 978 1 85450

Parent Company:
Elm Consulting Ltd

Book Trade Association Membership:
Booksellers Association

2237 ▬

ELSEVIER LTD
The Boulevard, Langford Lane, Kidlington, Oxford OX5 1GB
Telephone: 01865 843000
Fax: 01865 853010
Email: initial.surname@elsevier.com
Web Site: www.elsevier.com

Also at:
32 Jamestown Road, London NW1 7BY
Telephone: 020 7424 4200
Fax: 020 7424 4431

Also at:
20–22 East Street, Edinburgh EH7 4BQ
Telephone: 0131 524 1700
Fax: 0131 524 1800

Academic & Scholarly; Chemistry; Educational & Textbooks; Medical (incl. Self Help & Alternative Medicine); Scientific & Technical

Imprints, Series & ISBNs:
Academic Press: 978 0 12
Churchill-Livingstone: 978 0 443
Elsevier Advanced Technology: 978 0 08
Elsevier Applied Science: 978 0 08
Elsevier Trends Journals: 978 0 08
Harcourt Health Sciences
Harcourt Ltd
Harcourt Publishers Ltd
Mosby: 978 0 7243
Pergamon: 978 0 08
W. B. Saunders: 978 0 7020
Scutari Press

Parent Company:
Netherlands: Elsevier BV

Associated Companies:
USA: Elsevier Inc

Overseas Representation:
Australia: Elsevier Australia, Marrickville, NSW, Australia
Brazil: Editora Campus Ltda, Rio de Janeiro, Brazil
India: Elsevier India, New Delhi, India
Japan: Elsevier Japan, Tokyo, Japan
Korea: Elsevier, Seoul, Republic of Korea
Pakistan: Rae & Sons Publishers Representatives, Lahore, Pakistan

Book Trade Association Membership:
Publishers Association; International Group of Scientific, Medical & Technical Publishers; STM

2238 ▬

*EMERALD GROUP PUBLISHING LTD
Howard House, Wagon Lane, Bingley, West Yorkshire BD16 1WA
Telephone: 01274 777700
Web Site: www.emeraldinsight.com

Personnel:
Martin Fojt *(Chairman)*
John Peters *(Chief Executive Officer)*
Niki Haunch *(Head of Editorial)*
Moyna Keenan *(Head of Corporate Communications)*

Academic & Scholarly; Accountancy & Taxation; Archaeology; Computer Science; Economics; Educational & Textbooks; Electronic (Educational); Electronic (Professional & Academic); Engineering; Environment & Development Studies; Industry, Business & Management; Languages & Linguistics; Philosophy; Psychology & Psychiatry; Sociology & Anthropology; Transport; Vocational Training & Careers

2239 ▬

*ENCYCLOPAEDIA BRITANNICA (UK) LTD
2nd Floor, Unity Wharf, 13 Mill Street, London SE1 2BH
Telephone: 020 7500 7800
Fax: 020 7500 7578
Email: enquiries@britannica.co.uk
Web Site: www.britannica.co.uk

Distributors:
Encyclopaedia Britannica (UK) Ltd, Unit Y, Paddock Wood Distribution Centre, Paddock Wood, Tonbridge, Kent TN12 6UU
Telephone: 01892 839814
Fax: 01892 837272
Email: britannica@combook.co.uk

Personnel:
Ian Grant *(Managing Director)*
Jane Helps *(Operations Vice-President)*
Patrick McGuire *(Sales & Distribution Manager)*
Diane Franklyn *(Consumer Sales Director)*
Chrysandra Halstead *(Marketing Executive Manager)*

Atlases & Maps; Children's Books; Electronic (Educational); Reference Books, Directories & Dictionaries

Imprints, Series & ISBNs:
978 0 85229, 978 1 59339, 978 1 84326, 978 2 85229

Parent Company:
USA: Encyclopaedia Britannica Inc

Distributor for:
France: Encyclopaedia Universalis

Overseas Representation:
Germany, Austria, Switzerland & Netherlands: Ted Dougherty, London, UK
Italy: Mare Nostrum Publishing Consultants, Rome, Italy
Scandinavia: Colin Flint Ltd, Harlow, UK
South-East Europe, North Africa & Middle East (excluding GCC): Avicenna Partnership, Oxford, UK
Spain & Portgual: Iberian Book Services, Madrid, Spain
Sub-Saharan Africa (excluding South Africa), Eastern Europe (excluding Russia): InterMedia Americana (IMA) Ltd, London, UK

Book Trade Association Membership:
Independent Publishers Guild

2240 ▬

ENERGY INSTITUTE
61 New Cavendish Street, London W1G 7AR
Telephone: 020 7467 7100
Fax: 020 7255 1472
Web Site: www.energypublishing.org

Personnel:
Erica Sciolti *(Publishing Manager)*

Academic & Scholarly; Aviation; Chemistry; Electronic (Professional & Academic); Engineering; Environment & Development Studies; Industry, Business & Management; Reference Books, Directories & Dictionaries; Scientific & Technical

Imprints, Series & ISBNs:
978 0 85293

Book Trade Association Membership:
Association of Learned & Professional Society Publishers

2241 ▬

ENGLISH HERITAGE
The Engine House, Fire Fly Avenue, Swindon SN2 2EH
Telephone: 01793 414619
Email: robin.taylor@english-heritage.org.uk
Web Site: www.english-heritage.org.uk

Distribution:
Central Books, 99 Wallis Road, London E9 5LN
Telephone: 0845 458 9910
Fax: 020 8533 5821
Email: eh@centralbooks.com

Personnel:
Robin Taylor *(Managing Editor)*
John Hudson *(Head of Publishing)*
Clare Blick *(Sales & Publicity Manager)*

Academic & Scholarly; Archaeology; Architecture & Design; Educational & Textbooks; Guide Books; History & Antiquarian; Military & War; Travel & Topography

No of Employees: 11

Imprints, Series & ISBNs:
978 1 84802, 978 1 85074, 978 1 873592, 978 1 905624

Overseas Representation:
Australia: James Bennett Pty Ltd, Belrose, NSW, Australia
Benelux: Roy de Boo, Hooge Mierde, Netherlands
Scandinavia: Jan Norbye, Olstykke, Denmark
Spain and Portugal: Peter Prout, Iberian Book Services, Madrid, Spain
USA: The David Brown Book Co, Oakville, CT, USA

Book Trade Association Membership:
Association of Learned & Professional Society Publishers

2242

ENITHARMON PRESS
26b Caversham Road, London NW5 2DU
Telephone: 020 7482 5967
Fax: 020 7284 1787
Email: info@enitharmon.co.uk
Web Site: www.enitharmon.co.uk

Warehouse:
Central Books, 99 Wallis Road, London E9 5LN
Telephone: 020 8986 4854
Fax: 020 8533 5821

Personnel:
Stephen Stuart-Smith (*Director*)
Isabel Brittain (*Director*)
Larissa Attisso (*Sales and Administration*)
Peter Target (*Publicity*)
Anne Stewart (*Finance*)

Fiction; Illustrated & Fine Editions; Literature & Criticism; Poetry

New Titles: 10 (2010) , 15 (2011)
No of Employees: 5

Imprints, Series & ISBNs:
978 1 870612, 978 1 900564, 978 1 904634, 978 1 907587

Associated Companies:
Enitharmon Editions Ltd; London Magazine Editions

Overseas Representation:
USA & Canada: Dufour Editions Inc, Chester Springs, PA, USA

2243

EQUINOX PUBLISHING LTD
Unit S3, Kelham House, 3 Lancaster Street, Sheffield, South Yorkshire S3 8AF S3 8AF
Telephone: 0114 272 5957
Fax: 0560 345 9046
Email: jjoyce@equinoxpub.com
Web Site: www.equinoxpub.com

Distribution:
Marston Book Services Ltd, PO Box 269, Abingdon, Oxon OX14 4YN
Telephone: 01235 465521
Fax: 01235 465555
Email: trade.orders@marston.co.uk

Personnel:
Janet Joyce (*Publisher*)
Valerie Hall (*Editorial & Rights*)
Yvonne Nazareth (*Journals*)
Sarah Hussell (*Journal Customer Services*)

Academic & Scholarly; Archaeology; Biography & Autobiography; Cookery, Wines & Spirits; Educational & Textbooks; Electronic (Professional & Academic); Gender Studies; History & Antiquarian; Languages & Linguistics; Music; Philosophy; Reference Books, Directories & Dictionaries; Religion & Theology; Sociology & Anthropology

New Titles: 40 (2010) , 45 (2011)
No of Employees: 4

Imprints, Series & ISBNs:
Equinox: 978 1 84553, 978 1 904768, 978 1 908049
Southover Press

Distributor for:
J R Collis Publications; Contact Pastoral Trust; Vanias Editions

Overseas Representation:
Australia & New Zealand: Eleanor Brasch Enterprises, Artarmon, NSW, Australia
China, Hong Kong & Taiwan: Ian Taylor & Associates, Beijing, P. R. of China
Europe: Andrew Durnell Marketing Ltd, Tunbridge Wells, UK
India: Maya Publishers Pvt Ltd, New Delhi, India
Japan: United Publishers Services Ltd and Tim Burland, Tokyo, Japan
Middle East: Avicenna Partnership Ltd, Oxford, UK
North America: The David Brown Book Co, Oakville, CT, USA
Singapore, Malaysia & Brunei: Publishers Marketing Services Pte Ltd, Singapore
South Africa, Botswana, Lesotho, Namibia, Swaziland & Zimbabwe: Chris Reinders, The African Moon Press, Kelvin, South Africa

Book Trade Association Membership:
Independent Publishers Guild; Association of Learned & Professional Society Publishers (UK Serials Interest Group)

2244

THE ERSKINE PRESS
The White House, Sandfield Lane, Eccles, Norwich, Norfolk NR16 2PB
Telephone: 01953 887277
Fax: 01953 888361
Email: erskpres@aol.com
Web Site: www.erskine-press.com

Personnel:
Crispin de Boos (*Director*)
Lesley de Boos (*Commissioning Editor*)

Academic & Scholarly; Biography & Autobiography; Crime; History & Antiquarian; Illustrated & Fine Editions; Medical (incl. Self Help & Alternative Medicine); Military & War; Natural History; Travel & Topography

New Titles: 4 (2010) , 6 (2011)
No of Employees: 2
Annual Turnover: £40,000

Imprints, Series & ISBNs:
Archival Facsimiles: 978 0 948285, 978 1 85297
Erskine Press: 978 0 948285, 978 1 85297

Parent Company:
jack afrika Publishing Ltd

2245

ESPRESSO EDUCATION
200 Shepherds Bush Road, Hammersmith, London W6 7NL
Telephone: 020 7870 4515

No of Employees: 105

Book Trade Association Membership:
Publishers Association

2246

ETHICS INTERNATIONAL PRESS LTD
[publishes for Centre for Business & Public Sector Ethics]
St Andrews Castle,
St Andrews Street South, Bury St Edmunds, Suffolk IP33 3PH
Telephone: 01954 710086
Fax: 01954 710103

Email: info@ethicspress.com
Web Site: www.ethicspress.com

Personnel:
Dr Rosamund Thomas (*Director*)
Robert Willis (*Marketing Manager*)
Christopher Thomas (*General Manager*)

Academic & Scholarly; Educational & Textbooks; Electronic (Educational); Electronic (Professional & Academic); Environment & Development Studies; Industry, Business & Management; Law; Politics & World Affairs; Vocational Training & Careers

Imprints, Series & ISBNs:
978 1 871891
Teaching Ethics (Book series)

Associated Companies:
Ethics International MultiMedia Ltd

Book Trade Association Membership:
Publishers Association

2247

*EUROMONITOR INTERNATIONAL
60–61 Britton Street, London EC1M 5UX
Telephone: 020 7251 8024
Fax: 020 7608 3149
Email: info@euromonitor.com
Web Site: www.euromonitor.com

Personnel:
Trevor Fenwick (*Managing Director*)
Robert Senior (*Chairman*)
David Gudgin (*Director*)

Economics; Industry, Business & Management; Reference Books, Directories & Dictionaries

Imprints, Series & ISBNs:
978 0 86338, 978 1 84264

Associated Companies:
Dubai: Euromonitor International
Lithuania: Euromonitor International
P. R. of China: Euromonitor International (Shanghai) Co Ltd
Singapore: Euromonitor International (Asia) Pte Ltd
USA: Euromonitor International Inc

Book Trade Association Membership:
Data Publishers Association; European Association of Directory Publishers

2248

EVANS PUBLISHING GROUP
2A Portman Mansions, Chiltern Street, London W1U 6NR
Telephone: 020 7487 0920
Fax: 020 7487 0921
Email: sales@evansbrothers.co.uk
Web Site: www.evansbooks.co.uk

Personnel:
Danny Daly (*Chief Operating Officer*)
Brian Jones (*International Director*)
Andrew Macmillan (*UK Sales Director*)
Sarah Ramiah (*Accountant*)
Ms Su Swallow (*UK Publisher*)
Jason McGovern (*Export Sales Manager*)
Ms Jenny Mulvanny (*Production Manager*)
Ms Britta Martins-Simon (*Foreign Rights Manager*)

Children's Books; Educational & Textbooks; Electronic (Educational)

New Titles: 100 (2010) , 200 (2011)
No of Employees: 14
Annual Turnover: £3M

Imprints, Series & ISBNs:
Cherrytree: 978 1 84234
Evans: 978 0 237

Zero to Ten: 978 1 84089

Associated Companies:
Kenya: Evans Brothers (Kenya) Ltd
Nigeria: Evans Brothers (Nigeria Publishers) Ltd
Sierra Leone: Evans Brothers (Sierra Leone) Ltd

Book Trade Association Membership:
Publishers Association; Educational Publishers Council

2249

EVERYMAN'S LIBRARY
Northburgh House, 10 Northburgh Street, London EC1V 0AT
Telephone: 020 7566 6350
Fax: 020 7490 3708
Email: books@everyman.uk.com

Trade Orders & Enquiries:
Grantham Book Services, Trent Road, Grantham, Lincs NG31 7XQ
Telephone: 01476 541000
Fax: 01476 541061
Web Site: www.granthambookservices.co.uk

Personnel:
David Campbell (*Managing Director*)
Clémence Jacquinet (*Editorial (Travel Guides)*)
Jane Holloway (*Editorial (Classics)*)

Academic & Scholarly; Children's Books; Fiction; Guide Books; Illustrated & Fine Editions; Literature & Criticism; Philosophy; Poetry; Science Fiction; Travel & Topography

Imprints, Series & ISBNs:
Everyman Children's Classics
Everyman Classics
Everyman Guides
Everyman Pocket Classics
Everyman Pocket Poets
Everyman Wodehouse

Parent Company:
USA: Alfred A. Knopf

Overseas Representation:
Worldwide (excluding North America): Random House International (Everyman's Library), UK

2250

EX LIBRIS PRESS
11 Regents Place, Bradford on Avon, Wiltshire BA15 1ED
Telephone: 01225 865191
Email: roger.jones@ex-librisbooks.co.uk
Web Site: www.ex-librisbooks.co.uk

Stockists:
Gardners Books, 1 Whittle Drive, Willingdon Drove, Eastbourne, East Sussex BN23 6QH
Telephone: 01323 521777
Fax: 01323 521666

Personnel:
Roger Jones (*Proprietor*)

Archaeology; Biography & Autobiography; Cookery, Wines & Spirits; Gardening; Geography & Geology; Guide Books; History & Antiquarian; Natural History; Nautical; Poetry; Transport; Travel & Topography

New Titles: 2 (2010) , 4 (2011)

Imprints, Series & ISBNs:
978 1 906641
ELSP (Ex Libris Self Publishing)
Seaflower Books: 978 0 948578, 978 0 9506563, 978 1 903341

2251

EXECUTIVE GRAPEVINE INTERNATIONAL LTD
Rosanne House, Parkway,
Welwyn Garden City AL8 6HG
Telephone: 01707 351451
Fax: 01707 390143
Web Site: www.askgrapevine.com

Personnel:
Helen Barrett *(Chief Executive Officer)*
Anna Weston *(Managing Director)*
Sabrina Ponte *(Director, Sales & Marketing)*
Sally Griffin *(Chief Operating Officer)*

*Industry, Business & Management;
Reference Books, Directories & Dictionaries*

New Titles: 3 (2010) , 2 (2011)
No of Employees: 28

Imprints, Series & ISBNs:
978 1 903530, 978 1 903550

Book Trade Association Membership:
Data Publishers Association

2252

*EXLEY PUBLICATIONS LTD
16 Chalk Hill, Watford, Herts WD19 4BG
Telephone: 01923 474480
Fax: 01923 818733
Web Site: www.helenexleygiftbooks.com

Warehouse:
Trade Counter, The Airfield, Norwich Road,
Mendlesham, Suffolk IP14 5NA
Telephone: 01449 766629
Fax: 01449 767122

Personnel:
Helen M. Exley *(Managing Director & Editorial)*
Richard A. Exley *(Finance & Production Director)*
Lincoln Exley *(Associate/Export Sales Director)*
Charlotte Smith *(Head of UK Sales Manager)*
Keith Allen-Jones *(Foreign Rights Director)*

Humour

Imprints, Series & ISBNs:
978 1 84634, 978 1 85015, 978 1 86187

Associated Companies:
France: Exley SA
USA: Exley Giftbooks

Overseas Representation:
Australia: Card & Paper House, Australia;
New Holland Publishers Pty Ltd, French's
Forest, NSW, Australia
Canada: Pierre Belvedere, Montreal,
Canada
Hong Kong: Pacific Century Distribution
Ltd, Hong Kong
India: Maya Publishers Pvt Ltd, New Delhi,
India
Israel: Astra Agency, Jerusalem, Israel
Korea: Union Enterprise Co Ltd, Seoul,
Republic of Korea
Lebanon: Librarie Samir Editeur, Beirut,
Lebanon
Malta: Audio Visual Centre Ltd, Sliema,
Malta
New Zealand: David Bateman Ltd,
Auckland, New Zealand
Pakistan: Mackwin & Co, Karachi, Pakistan
Philippines: Balatbat & Sons International,
Filinvest, Philippines
Republic of Ireland: Island Publications Ltd,
Dublin, Republic of Ireland
Singapore: Cards n Such Pte Ltd, Singapore
Southern Africa: Struik Book Distributors,
Johannesburg, South Africa
Spain: Editorial Edaf SA, Madrid, Spain
Vietnam: Fahasa Companie, Ho Chi Minh
City, Vietnam

Book Trade Association Membership:
Independent Publishers Guild

2253

EXPRESS PUBLISHING
Liberty House, New Greenham Park,
Newbury, Berks RG19 6HW
Telephone: 01635 817363
Fax: 01635 817463
Web Site: www.expresspublishing.co.uk

Book Trade Association Membership:
Publishers Association

2254

F+W MEDIA INTERNATIONAL, LTD (FORMERLY DAVID & CHARLES)
[A subsidiary of F+W Media, Inc.]
Brunel House, Forde Close, Newton Abbot,
Devon TQ12 4PU
Telephone: 01626 323200
Fax: 01626 323317
Web Site: www.fwmedia.co.uk

Trade Orders & Enquiries:
Customer Services, Trade Department, GBS,
Trent Road, Grantham, Lincolnshire
NG31 7QX
Telephone: 01476 541080
Fax: 0117 654 1061
Email: orders@gbs.tbs-ltd.co.uk

Personnel:
James Woollam *(Managing Director)*
Richard Dodman *(Sales & New Business
Director and Trade Community Leader)*
Ali Myer *(Editorial & Design Director)*

*Cookery, Wines & Spirits; Crafts & Hobbies;
History & Antiquarian; Humour;
Photography; Transport*

Imprints, Series & ISBNs:
David & Charles: 978 0 7153

Parent Company:
USA: F+W Media, Inc.

Distributor for:
Italy: White Star Edizione
UK: Reader's Digest Books
USA: Adams Media; Dover Publications;
F+W Media (North Light Books, Writer's
Digest Books, Betterway Books); Krause
Publications; Sellers

Overseas Representation:
Asia, Middle East: Michelle Morrow Curreri,
Beverly, MA, USA
Australia: Capricorn Link (Australia) Pty Ltd,
Windsor, NSW, Australia
Belgium, France & Netherlands: Ted
Dougherty, London, UK
Cyprus, Gibraltar, Spain and Portugal: Jenny
Padovani Frias, Barcelona, Spain
*Denmark, Finland, Norway, Sweden &
Netherlands (Foreign Rights Agent):*
Candida Buckley, Leeds, Kent, UK
Denmark, Sweden, Norway & Finland:
Angell Eurosales, Berwick-on-Tweed, UK
Eastern Europe: Bill Bailey Publishers
Representatives, Newton Abbot, UK
Germany, Austria & Switzerland: Gabriele
Kern Publishers Services, Frankfurt-am-
Main, Germany
India, Bangladesh, Nepal & Sri Lanka: Maya
Publishers Pvt Ltd, New Delhi, India
Italy & Greece: Penny Padovani, London, UK
Latin America & Caribbean: David Williams,
London, UK
*Mauritius, Kenya, Gambia, Botswana &
Zimbabwe:* Export Sales Manager, David
& Charles Ltd, Newton Abbot, UK
New Zealand: David Bateman Ltd,
Auckland, New Zealand
South Africa: Trinity Books CC, Randburg,
South Africa
USA & Canada: F + W Media Inc, Cincinnati,
USA

Book Trade Association Membership:
Independent Publishers Guild

2255

*FABER & FABER LTD
Bloomsbury House,
74–77 Great Russell Street, London
WC1B 3DA
Telephone: 020 7927 3800
Fax: 020 7927 3801
Email: mailbox@faber.co.uk
Web Site: www.faber.co.uk

Accounts:
16 Burnt Mill, Elizabeth Way, Harlow, Essex
CM20 2HX
Fax: 01279 417366
Web Site: www.faber.co.uk

Distribution & Orders:
TBS Ltd, Colchester Road, Frating Green,
Colchester, Essex CO7 7DW
Telephone: 01206 256004
Fax: 01206 255912

Personnel:
Stephen Page *(Chief Executive)*
Walter Donohue *(Publisher & Film Director)*
Valerie Eliot *(Director)*
Julian Loose *(Editorial, Fiction & Non-Fiction
Director)*
Lee Brackstone *(Director)*
David Tebbutt *(Finance Director)*
Nigel Marsh *(Publishing Services Director)*
Jason Cooper *(Rights Director)*
Will Atkinson *(Sales & Marketing Director)*
Rachel Alexander *(Publicity Director)*
Belinda Matthews *(Music Director)*
Paul Keegan *(Editorial: Poetry)*
Julia Haydon-Wells *(Editorial: Children's)*
Dinah Wood *(Editorial: Plays)*

*Biography & Autobiography; Children's
Books; Cinema, Video, TV & Radio;
Cookery, Wines & Spirits; Fiction; Literature
& Criticism; Music; Poetry; Politics & World
Affairs; Theatre, Drama & Dance*

Imprints, Series & ISBNs:
978 0 571

Associated Companies:
USA: Faber & Faber Inc

Distributor for:
De la Mare Publishing Ltd; Sanctuary
Publishing; Screenpress Publishing
USA: Faber & Faber Inc

Overseas Representation:
*Argentina, Bermuda, Bolivia, Brazil, Central
America, Chile, Columbia, Ecuador,
French West Indies, Jamaica, Mexico,
Paraguay, Peru, Uruguay & Venezuela:*
InterMedia Americana (IMA) Ltd,
London, UK
*Asia (including Japan, Korea, Taiwan &
Hong Kong):* Julian Ashton, Sevenoaks,
Kent, UK
Australia: Allen & Unwin Pty Ltd, Crows
Nest, NSW, Australia
Canada: Penguin Group Canada, Toronto,
Ont, Canada
*Central Europe, Netherlands, Belgium,
Luxembourg, Switzerland & Scandinavia:*
Bunmi Oke, Faber & Faber, London, UK
*Eastern Europe (excluding Russia & Baltic
States):* Csaba Lengyel de Bagota,
Budapest, Hungary
France, Germany & Austria: Patrick Keogh,
Faber & Faber, London, UK
India: Penguin Books India, New Delhi, India
Italy: Penguin Italia srl, Milan, Italy
*Middle East (including Israel & Iran), North
Africa, Malta & Turkey:* Peter Ward Book
Exports, London, UK
New Zealand: Allen & Unwin Pty Ltd,
Auckland, New Zealand
Pakistan: Faber & Faber, London, UK
Republic of Ireland: Gill Hess Ltd, Skerries,
Co Dublin, Republic of Ireland

Singapore & Malaysia: Penguin Singapore,
Singapore
Southern Africa: Book Promotions Pty Ltd,
Cape Town, South Africa
Spain & Portugal: Penguin Spain, Madrid,
Spain
*Thailand, Cambodia, Laos, Vietnam &
Myanmar:* Keith Hardy, Hardy Bigfoss
International Co Ltd, Bangkok, Thailand
USA: Faber & Faber Inc, A Division of Farrer,
Strauss & Giroux, New York, USA

Book Trade Association Membership:
Publishers Association

2256

FABIAN SOCIETY
11 Dartmouth Street, London SW1H 9BN
Telephone: 020 7227 4900
Fax: 020 7976 7153
Email: info@fabian-society.org.uk
Web Site: www.fabians.org.uk

Personnel:
Andrew Harrop *(General Secretary)*
Phil Mutero *(Sales)*
Tom Hampson *(Editorial Director)*

*Academic & Scholarly; Economics;
Environment & Development Studies;
Philosophy; Politics & World Affairs*

New Titles: 8 (2010) , 8 (2011)
No of Employees: 12
Annual Turnover: £800,000

Imprints, Series & ISBNs:
Fabian Pamphlet: 978 0 7163

Associated Companies:
NCLC Publishers Ltd

Distributor for:
NCLC Publishers Ltd

Book Trade Association Membership:
Booksellers Association

2257

*FACET PUBLISHING
7 Ridgmount Street, London WC1E 7AE
Telephone: 020 7255 0590
Fax: 020 7255 0591
Email: info@facetpublishing.co.uk
Web Site: www.facetpublishing.co.uk

Warehouse:
Bookpoint Ltd, 130 Milton Park, Abingdon,
Oxon OX14 4SB
Telephone: 01235 827702
Fax: 01235 827703
Email: facet@bookpoint.co.uk

Personnel:
John Woolley *(Managing Director (CILIP
Enterprises))*
Helen Carley *(Publisher)*
Sarah Busby *(Commissioning Editor)*
James Williams *(Marketing Manager)*
Kathryn Beecroft *(Production Manager)*
Rohini Ramachandran *(Sales Manager)*
Lin Franklin *(Desk Editor)*
June York *(Typesetter)*

*Academic & Scholarly; Bibliography &
Library Science; Educational & Textbooks;
Electronic (Professional & Academic);
Reference Books, Directories & Dictionaries*

Imprints, Series & ISBNs:
978 1 85604

Parent Company:
CILIP (Chartered Institute of Library and
Information Professionals)

Overseas Representation:
Australia & New Zealand: Inbooks, c/o
James Bennett Pty Ltd, Belrose, NSW,
Australia

Canada & USA: Neal-Schuman Publishers Inc, New York, NY, USA
Eastern Europe: Marek Lewinson, Warsaw, Poland
India: Book Marketing Services, Chennai, India
Japan: United Publishers Services Ltd, Tokyo, Japan
Middle East: International Publishing Services (IPS) Middle East Ltd, Dubai, UAE
South East Asia: Taylor & Francis Asia Pacific, Singapore
Spain & Portugal: Iberian Book Services, Madrid, Spain

Book Trade Association Membership:
Publishers Association; Independent Publishers Guild

2258 ━━━━━

*FAMILY PUBLICATIONS
Denis Riches House, 66 Sandford Lane, Kennington, Oxford OX1 5RP
Telephone: 0845 0500 879
Fax: 01865 321325
Web Site: www.familypublications.co.uk

Personnel:
Colin Mason *(Managing Director)*

Biography & Autobiography; History & Antiquarian; Religion & Theology

Imprints, Series & ISBNs:
978 1 871217, 978 1 907380

Overseas Representation:
Australia: Freedom Publishing, North Melbourne, Vic, Australia

2259 ━━━━━

A. & A. FARMAR
78 Ranelagh Village, Dublin 6, Republic of Ireland
Telephone: +353 (0)1 496 3625
Fax: +353 (0)1 497 0107
Email: afarmar@iol.ie
Web Site: www.aafarmar.ie

Trade Orders (Republic of Ireland):
Gill and Macmillan, Hume Avenue, Park West, Dublin 12, Republic of Ireland
Telephone: +353 (0)1 500 9500
Fax: +353 (0)1 500 9599
Email: sales@gillmacmillan.ie

Personnel:
Anna Farmar *(Editorial)*
Tony Farmar *(Production)*

Academic & Scholarly; History & Antiquarian

No of Employees: 2

Imprints, Series & ISBNs:
978 1 899047, 978 1 906353

Overseas Representation:
UK (Trade Orders): Central Books Ltd, London, UK

Book Trade Association Membership:
Publishing Ireland (Foilsiú Éireann)

2260 ━━━━━

*FASTPRINT
9 Culley Court, Bakewell Road, Orton Southgate, Peterborough PE2 6XD
Telephone: 01733 237867
Fax: 01733 234309
Email: info@upfrontpublishing.com
Web Site: www.upfrontpublishing.com

Personnel:
Andy Cork *(Managing Director)*
Simon Potter *(Publishing Manager)*
Pauline Tebbott *(Publishing Assistant)*

Biography & Autobiography; Fiction; Poetry; Religion & Theology

Imprints, Series & ISBNs:
Fastprint: 978 1 84426
Upfront: 978 1 84426

Parent Company:
Print on Demand – Worldwide

Book Trade Association Membership:
Independent Publishers Guild

2261 ━━━━━

FHG GUIDES LTD
Abbey Mill Business Centre, Seedhill, Paisley PA1 1TJ
Telephone: 0141 887 0428
Fax: 0141 889 7204
Email: admin@fhguides.co.uk
Web Site: www.holidayguides.com

Book Trade Representative:
Martin Kaye, Kuperard Publishers, 59 Hutton Grove, London N12 8DS
Telephone: 020 8446 2440
Fax: 020 8446 2441
Email: martin@kuperard.co.uk

Personnel:
G. Pratt *(Publishing Director)*

Guide Books; Sports & Games; Travel & Topography

New Titles: 8 (2010) , 8 (2011)
No of Employees: 12

Imprints, Series & ISBNs:
978 1 85055

Parent Company:
Kuperard Publishers

Book Trade Association Membership:
Periodical Publishers Association

2262 ━━━━━

*FIELL PUBLISHING LTD
51 Sulgrave Road, London W6 7QH
Telephone: 020 7603 4247
Fax: 020 7602 4268
Web Site: www.fiell.com

Architecture & Design; Fashion & Costume; Photography; Travel & Topography

2263 ━━━━━

FIFTH DIMENSION LTD
[t/a Dimensional Entertainment]
Marston House, 28 Marston Road, Blakenhall, Wolverhampton, West Midlands WV2 4NL
Telephone: 0788 874 2758

Book Trade Association Membership:
Publishers Association

2264 ━━━━━

FILAMENT PUBLISHING LTD
16 Croydon Road, Waddon, Croydon, Surrey CR0 4PA
Telephone: 020 8688 2598
Fax: 020 7183 7186
Email: info@filamentpublishing.com
Web Site: www.filamentpublishing.com

Representation (UK):
Gardners Books, 1 Whittle Drive, Eastbourne, East Sussex BN23 6QH

Personnel:
Christopher Day *(Director)*
Bernard Marchant *(Finance)*
Zara Thatcher *(Editor)*
Andrew White *(Production)*
Catriona Cotton *(Book keeper)*

Academic & Scholarly; Accountancy & Taxation; Audio Books; Biography & Autobiography; Crafts & Hobbies; Educational & Textbooks; Electronic (Professional & Academic); Industry, Business & Management; Medical (incl. Self Help & Alternative Medicine); Military & War; Philosophy; Religion & Theology; Sports & Games; Theatre, Drama & Dance; Vocational Training & Careers

New Titles: 12 (2010) , 20 (2011)
No of Employees: 5
Annual Turnover: £150,000

Imprints, Series & ISBNs:
978 1 905493

Book Trade Association Membership:
Independent Publishers Guild

2265 ━━━━━

*FINDHORN PRESS LTD
Delft Cottage, Dyke, Forres, Moray IV36 2TF
Telephone: 01309 690582
Fax: 0131 777 2711
Email: info@findhornpress.com
Web Site: www.findhornpress/

Personnel:
Thierry Bogliolo *(Publisher)*
Carol Shaw *(Marketing & Publicity Manager)*
Sabine Weeke *(Rights, Editorial Manager)*

Animal Care & Breeding; Cookery, Wines & Spirits; Gardening; Gay & Lesbian Studies; Guide Books; Health & Beauty; Medical (incl. Self Help & Alternative Medicine); Religion & Theology

Imprints, Series & ISBNs:
978 0 905249, 978 1 84409, 978 1 899171

Overseas Representation:
Australia: Brumby Books Holdings Pty Ltd, Kilsyth South, Vic, Australia
New Zealand: Ceres Books, Ellerslie, New Zealand
North America: Independent Publishers Group (IPG), Chicago, IL, USA
Republic of Ireland & Europe: Deep Books Ltd, London, UK
Singapore: Pen International Ltd, Singapore, Singapore
South Africa: Faradawn CC, Saxonwold, South Africa
USA: New Leaf Distributing Co, Lithia Springs, GA, USA

Book Trade Association Membership:
Independent Publishers Guild

2266 ━━━━━

FIRST & BEST IN EDUCATION
Earlstrees Court, Earlstrees Road, Corby, Northants NN17 4HH
Telephone: 01536 399011 (Orders & Accounts), 399004 (Editorial)
Fax: 01536 399012
Email: sales@firstandbest.co.uk
Web Site: www.shop.firstandbest.co.uk

Personnel:
Jane Edmonds *(Finance Manager)*
Tony Attwood *(Managing Director)*
Anne Cockburn *(Senior Editor)*

Educational & Textbooks; Electronic (Educational)

Imprints, Series & ISBNs:
978 1 86083

Parent Company:
UK: Hamilton House Mailings Ltd

Book Trade Association Membership:
Educational Publishers Council

2267 ━━━━━

FIVE LEAVES PUBLICATIONS
PO Box 8786, Nottingham NG1 9AW
Telephone: 0115 969 3597
Email: info@fiveleaves.co.uk
Web Site: www.fiveleaves.co.uk

Personnel:
Ross Bradshaw *(Publisher)*
Pippa Hennessy *(Marketing)*

Academic & Scholarly; Children's Books; Crime; Fiction; History & Antiquarian; Poetry; Politics & World Affairs

New Titles: 20 (2010) , 28 (2011)

Imprints, Series & ISBNs:
Bromley House Editions: 978 1 905512
Crime Express: 978 1 905512
Five Leaves Publications: 978 0 907123, 978 1 905512
Richard Hollis: 978 1 905512
New London Editions: 978 1 905512

Overseas Representation:
Iberia: Iberian Book Representation

2268 ━━━━━

*FLAMBARD PRESS
Holy Jesus, City Road, Newcastle upon Tyne NE1 2AJ
Telephone: 0191 233 3865
Email: editor@flambardpress.co.uk
Web Site: www.flambardpress.co.uk

Personnel:
Peter Lewis *(Company Secretary)*
Margaret Lewis *(Editor)*
Will Mackie *(Managing Editor)*

Biography & Autobiography; Crime; Fiction; Fine Art & Art History; Photography; Poetry

Imprints, Series & ISBNs:
978 1 873226, 978 1 906601

Book Trade Association Membership:
Independent Publishers Guild

2269 ━━━━━

FLORIS BOOKS TRUST LTD
15 Harrison Gardens, Edinburgh EH11 1SH
Telephone: 0131 337 2372
Fax: 0131 347 9919
Email: floris@florisbooks.co.uk
Web Site: www.florisbooks.co.uk

Warehouse & Orders:
BookSource, 50 Cambuslang Road, Glasgow G32 8NB
Telephone: 0845 370 0067
Fax: 0845 370 0068
Email: orders@booksource.net

Personnel:
Katy Lockwood-Holmes *(Publisher)*
Sally Polson *(Editorial)*

Academic & Scholarly; Children's Books; Crafts & Hobbies; Gardening; Health & Beauty; Medical (incl. Self Help & Alternative Medicine); Philosophy; Religion & Theology

Imprints, Series & ISBNs:
978 0 86315, 978 0 903540, 978 0 906155

Distributor for:
USA: Biodynamic Farming & Gardening Association; Lindisfarne Press

Overseas Representation:
Australia: Footprint Books Pty Ltd, Warriewood, NSW, Australia
New Zealand: Ceres Books, Ellerslie, New Zealand

USA (all titles): Steiner Books Inc, Herndon, VA, USA

Book Trade Association Membership:
Publishing Scotland

2270 ▬▬▬

FOOD TRADE PRESS LTD
Station House, Hortons Way, Westerham, Kent TN16 1BZ
Telephone: 01959 563944
Fax: 01959 561285
Web Site: www.foodtradepress.com

Personnel:
Adrian Binsted *(Publishing Director)*

Agriculture; Chemistry; Reference Books, Directories & Dictionaries; Scientific & Technical

New Titles: 10 (2010) , 10 (2011)
No of Employees: 6

Imprints, Series & ISBNs:
978 0 900379, 978 0 903962

Associated Companies:
Attwood & Binsted Ltd

Distributor for:
Campden BRI; Leatherhead Food International
Denmark: Mercantila Publishing AS
Italy: Chiriotti Editori Srl
Spain: Montagud Editores SA
Switzerland: Binsted Frères SA
USA: American Association of Cereal Chemists; American Institute of Baking; Chemical Publishing Co Inc; CTI Publications Inc; Food & Nutrition Press Inc; Food Processors Institute; Edward E. Judge & Sons

2271 ▬▬▬

*FOOTPRINT TRAVEL GUIDES
6 Riverside Court, Lower Bristol Road, Bath BA2 3DZ
Telephone: 01225 469141
Fax: 01225 469461
Email: contactus@footprintbooks.com
Web Site: www.footprinttravelguides.com

UK Trade Sales Agent:
GeoCenter International Ltd,
Meridian House, Churchill Way West, Basingstoke, Hants RG21 6YR
Telephone: 01256 817987
Fax: 01256 817988
Email: sales@geocenter.co.uk
Web Site: www.geocenter.co.uk

Personnel:
Andy Riddle *(Managing Director)*
Patrick Dawson *(Commercial Director)*
Alan Murphy *(Publisher)*
Liz Harper *(Marketing Manager)*

Guide Books; Sports & Games; Travel & Topography

Imprints, Series & ISBNs:
978 0 900751
Footprint Handbooks: 978 1 900949, 978 1 903471, 978 1 904777, 978 1 906098

Parent Company:
USA: Morris Communications LLC

Associated Companies:
UK: Compass Maps Ltd
USA: Globe Pequot Press

Distributor for:
UK: Wexas International
USA: Globe Pequot Press; Insiders' Guides

Overseas Representation:
Australia & New Zealand: Woodslane Pty Ltd, Warriewood, NSW, Australia

Belgium: Craenen bvba, Herent (Winksele), Belgium
Canada: Manda Group, Toronto, Ont, Canada
Europe: Bill Bailey Publishers Representatives, Newton Abbot, UK
Israel: SKP, Tel Aviv, Israel
Latin America: InterMedia Americana (IMA) Ltd, London, UK
Middle East: Peter Ward Book Exports
Netherlands: Nilsson & Lamm BV, Weesp, Netherlands
Singapore & Malaysia: Pansing Distribution Pte Ltd, Singapore
South Africa: Faradawn CC, Saxonwold, South Africa
South East Asia: DDP, Paris, France
USA: Globe Pequot Press, Guilford, CT, USA

2272 ▬▬▬

FORENSIC SCIENCE SOCIETY
Clarke House, 18A Mount Parade, Harrogate HG1 1BX
Telephone: 01423 506068
Fax: 01423 566391
Email: journal@forensic-science-society.org.uk
Web Site: www.forensic-science-society.org.uk

Personnel:
Dr Niamh Nic Daéid *(Hon Editor)*

Scientific & Technical

New Titles: 4 (2010) , 4 (2011)
No of Employees: 6

2273 ▬▬▬

THE FOSTERING NETWORK
87 Blackfriars Road, London SE1 8HA
Telephone: 020 7620 6400
Fax: 020 7620 6401

Personnel:
Lucy Peake *(Head of External Affairs)*
Gill Cronin *(Marketing & Membership)*

Educational & Textbooks; Psychology & Psychiatry; Vocational Training & Careers

Imprints, Series & ISBNs:
978 0 946015

2274 ▬▬▬

W. FOULSHAM & CO LTD
The Oriel, Capital Point, 33 Bath Road, Slough, Berks SL1 3UF
Telephone: 01753 526769
Fax: 01753 535003
Email: marketing@foulsham.com
Web Site: www.foulsham.com

Distribution:
Macmillan Distribution (MDL), Houndmills, Basingstoke RG21 2XS
Telephone: 01256 329242
Fax: 01256 812558
Email: mdl@macmillan.co.uk
Web Site: www.mdl.macmillan.co.uk

Personnel:
Barry Belasco *(Managing Director)*
Graham Darlow *(Production Manager)*
Sue Wilkins *(Office Systems Manager)*

Accountancy & Taxation; Antiques & Collecting; Cookery, Wines & Spirits; Crafts & Hobbies; Do-It-Yourself; Gardening; Guide Books; Health & Beauty; Humour; Industry, Business & Management; Magic & the Occult; Medical (incl. Self Help & Alternative Medicine); Military & War; Poetry; Psychology & Psychiatry; Reference Books, Directories & Dictionaries; Sports & Games; Travel & Topography

Imprints, Series & ISBNs:
Foulsham: 978 0 572

Quantum: 978 0 572

Overseas Representation:
Australia: Capricorn Link (Australia) Pty Ltd, Windsor, NSW, Australia
Belgium, Germany, Luxembourg, Netherlands, Switzerland & Austria: Robbert J. Pleysier, Heerde, Netherlands
Cambodia, Laos, Myanmar, Thailand, Philippines & Vietnam: Ashton International Marketing Services, Sevenoaks, Kent, UK
Canada: Codasat, Vancouver, BC, Canada
Caribbean: Macmillan Caribbean Ltd, Oxford, UK
Central & Eastern Europe: Dr László Horváth Publishers Representative, Budapest, Hungary
Central & South America: InterMedia Americana (IMA) Ltd, London, UK
Far East, Singapore & Malaysia: Ashton International Marketing Services, Sevenoaks, Kent, UK
India: Maya Publishers Pvt Ltd, New Delhi, India
Middle East: Richard Carman Associates, Northwich, UK
New Zealand: Southern Publishers Group, Auckland, New Zealand
South Africa: Trinity Books, PO Box 242, Randburgh 2125, South Africa
Sub-Saharan Africa: InterMedia Africa Ltd (IMA), London, UK
USA: Associated Publishers Group, Nashville, TN, USA

2275 ▬▬▬

FOUR COURTS PRESS
7 Malpas Street, Dublin 8, Republic of Ireland
Telephone: +353 (0)1 453 4668
Fax: +353 (0)1 453 4672
Email: info@fourcourtspress.ie
Web Site: www.fourcourtspress.ie

Distribution:
Gill & Macmillan, Hume Avenue, Park West, Dublin 12, Republic of Ireland
Telephone: +353 (0)1 500 9555
Fax: +353 (0)1 500 9599
Email: info@fourcourtspress.ie
Web Site: www.fourcourtspress.ie

Personnel:
Martin Healy *(Managing Director)*
Anthony Tierney *(Marketing)*
Martin Fanning *(Editorial)*
Michael Potterton *(Editorial)*
Meghan Donaldson *(Marketing)*

Academic & Scholarly; Archaeology; Fine Art & Art History; History & Antiquarian; Law; Literature & Criticism; Military & War; Music; Philosophy; Reference Books, Directories & Dictionaries; Religion & Theology

New Titles: 55 (2010) , 58 (2011)
No of Employees: 5

Imprints, Series & ISBNs:
978 0 906127, 978 1 84682, 978 1 85182
Four Courts Press
Open Air

Overseas Representation:
USA: International Specialized Book Services Inc, Portland, OR, USA

2276 ▬▬▬

SAMUEL FRENCH LTD
52 Fitzroy Street, London W1T 5JR
Telephone: 020 7387 9373
Fax: 020 7387 2161
Email: theatre@samuelfrench-london.co.uk
Web Site: www.samuelfrench-london.co.uk

Personnel:
Vivien Goodwin *(Managing Director)*
Amanda Smith *(Editorial Director)*

Theatre, Drama & Dance

New Titles: 35 (2010) , 30 (2011)
No of Employees: 30

Imprints, Series & ISBNs:
Acting Editions: 978 0 573

Parent Company:
Samuel French Inc

Distributor for:
USA: Samuel French Inc

Overseas Representation:
Australia: The Dominie Group, Brookvale, NSW, Australia
East Africa: Phoenix Players Ltd, Nairobi, Kenya
Malta: Dingli Co International, Valletta, Malta
New Zealand: Play Bureau of New Zealand Ltd, New Plymouth, New Zealand
Republic of Ireland: Drama League of Ireland, Dublin, Republic of Ireland
South Africa, Namibia, Swaziland, Botswana & Lesotho: Dalro (Pty) Ltd, Braamfontein, South Africa
Zimbabwe: National Theatre Organization, Harare, Zimbabwe

Book Trade Association Membership:
Publishers Association; Booksellers Association

2277 ▬▬▬

FRIENDS OF THE EARTH
26–28 Underwood Street, London N1 7JQ
Telephone: 020 7490 1555
Fax: 020 7490 0881
Web Site: www.foe.co.uk

Personnel:
Adam Bradbury *(Publications Manager)*

Academic & Scholarly; Educational & Textbooks; Environment & Development Studies; Gardening; Reference Books, Directories & Dictionaries; Transport

Imprints, Series & ISBNs:
978 1 85750

2278 ▬▬▬

*GADFLY ENTERTAINMENT LTD
15–19 Cavendish Square, London W1G 0DD
Email: info@gadfly-ent.com
Web Site: www.gadfly-ent.com

2279 ▬▬▬

GALACTIC CENTRAL PUBLICATIONS
25a Copgrove Road, Leeds, West Yorkshire LS8 2SP
Telephone: 0113 248 8124
Email: philsp@philsp.com
Web Site: www.philsp.com

Personnel:
Phil Stephensen-Payne *(Publisher)*

Bibliography & Library Science

Imprints, Series & ISBNs:
978 1 871133

Overseas Representation:
USA: Chris Drumm, Polk City, IA, USA

2280 ▬▬▬

THE GALLERY PRESS
Loughcrew, Oldcastle, Co Meath, Republic of Ireland
Telephone: +353 (0)49 854 1779

Fax: +353 (0)49 854 1779
Email: gallery@indigo.ie
Web Site: www.gallerypress.com

Personnel:
Peter Fallon *(Editorial, Production Director)*
Jean Barry *(Administration)*
Suella Wynne *(Administration)*
Anne Duggan *(Sales & Accounts)*

Poetry; Theatre, Drama & Dance

New Titles: 12 (2010) , 10 (2011)
No of Employees: 4

Imprints, Series & ISBNs:
978 0 902996, 978 0 904011, 978 1 85235

Book Trade Association Membership:
Publishing Ireland (Foilsiú Éireann)

2281 ■

GALORE PARK PUBLISHING LTD
19–21 Sayers Lane, Tenterden, Kent
TN30 6BW
Telephone: 01580 764242
Fax: 01580 764142
Email: info@galorepark.co.uk
Web Site: www.galorepark.co.uk

Personnel:
Nicholas Oulton *(Managing Director)*
Aidan Gill *(Editorial Director)*
Natalie Friend *(Marketing Manager / Public Relations)*
Helen Standen *(Financial Controller)*
Denise Hart *(Operations Director)*
Ben Barton *(Sales and Marketing Director)*
Nigel Green *(Digital Publishing Director)*

Children's Books; Educational & Textbooks; Electronic (Educational)

New Titles: 20 (2010) , 20 (2011)
No of Employees: 21

Imprints, Series & ISBNs:
Galore Park Publishing: 978 1 902984
Gresham Books
Iseb Publications: 978 1 902984

Parent Company:
Galore Park (Holdings) Ltd

Associated Companies:
Gresham Books Ltd

Distributor for:
UK: The Good Schools Guide; Learning Together; ZimZamZoum

Book Trade Association Membership:
Publishers Association; Booksellers
Association; Educational Publishers
Council; Independent Publishers Guild

2282 ■

GARNET PUBLISHING LTD
8 Southern Court, South Street, Reading
RG1 4QS
Telephone: 0118 959 7847
Fax: 0118 959 7356 (Trade Enquiries & Orders)
Web Site: www.garnetpublishing.co.uk

Personnel:
Nadia Khayat *(Managing Director)*
Arash Hejazi *(Publisher)*

Architecture & Design; Cookery, Wines & Spirits; Fiction; Guide Books; History & Antiquarian; Literature & Criticism; Photography; Politics & World Affairs; Religion & Theology; Sociology & Anthropology; Travel & Topography

New Titles: 12 (2010) , 9 (2011)
No of Employees: 4

Imprints, Series & ISBNs:
Garnet Publishing: 978 1 85964, 978 1
873938, 978 1 902932
Ithaca Press: 978 1 85964, 978 1 873938.
978 1 902932
South Street Press: 978 1 85964, 978 1
873938, 978 1 902932

Associated Companies:
Garnet Education; Ithaca Press; South
Street Press

Overseas Representation:
USA (Trade): IPM, Dulles, VA, USA
Worldwide: Salt Way Publishing Ltd, Glos,
UK

Book Trade Association Membership:
Publishers Association; Independent
Publishers Guild

2283 ■

GATEHOUSE MEDIA LTD
PO Box 965, Warrington, Cheshire
WA4 9DE
Telephone: 01925 267778
Fax: 01925 267778
Email: info@gatehousebooks.com
Web Site: www.gatehousebooks.com

Personnel:
Catherine White *(Managing Director)*

*Audio Books; Educational & Textbooks;
English as a Foreign Language*

Imprints, Series & ISBNs:
Gatehouse Books: 978 1 84231

Overseas Representation:
Canada: Grass Roots Press, Edmonton, Alb,
Canada
USA: Peppercorn Books & Press, Hartford,
MI, USA

Book Trade Association Membership:
Publishers Association

2284 ■

THE GEOGRAPHICAL ASSOCIATION
160 Solly Street, Sheffield S1 4BF
Telephone: 0114 296 0088
Fax: 0114 296 7176
Email: info@geography.org.uk
Web Site: www.geography.org.uk

Personnel:
David Lambert *(Chief Executive)*
John Lyon *(Programme Director)*
Richard Gill *(Business Manager)*
Ruth Totterdell *(Publications Manager)*
Dorcas Turner *(Assistant Editor)*
Anna Grandfield *(Production Editor)*

*Atlases & Maps; Educational & Textbooks;
Electronic (Educational); Geography &
Geology; Guide Books; Travel & Topography*

New Titles: 9 (2010) , 7 (2011)
No of Employees: 15

Imprints, Series & ISBNs:
978 1 84377

2285 ■

GEOGRAPHY PUBLICATIONS
24 Kennington Road, Templeogue,
Dublin 6W, Republic of Ireland
Telephone: +353 (0)1 456 6085
Fax: +353 (0)1 456 6085
Email: books@geographypublications.com
Web Site:
www.geographypublications.com

Personnel:
William Nolan *(Contact)*

Academic & Scholarly; Archaeology; Atlases

*& Maps; Biography & Autobiography;
Educational & Textbooks; Geography &
Geology; History & Antiquarian; Languages
& Linguistics; Reference Books, Directories
& Dictionaries*

Imprints, Series & ISBNs:
History & Society Series: 978 0 906602

2286 ■

THE GEOLOGICAL SOCIETY
Unit 7, Brassmill Enterprise Centre,
Brassmill Lane, Bath BA1 3JN
Telephone: 01225 445046
Fax: 01225 442836
Email: sales@geolsoc.org.uk
Web Site: www.geolsoc.org.uk/bookshop

Personnel:
Neal Marriott *(Director of Publishing)*
Samantha Kaye *(Marketing Co-ordinator)*
Angharad Hills *(Commissioning Editor)*
Sarah Gibbs *(Senior Production Editor)*
Dawn Angel *(Sales & Customer Services
Supervisor)*

*Academic & Scholarly; Engineering;
Environment & Development Studies;
Geography & Geology; Scientific &
Technical*

New Titles: 20 (2010) , 27 (2011)
No of Employees: 14

Imprints, Series & ISBNs:
Geological Society: 978 0 903317, 978 1
86239, 978 1 897799

Distributor for:
USA: American Association of Petroleum
Geologists; Geological Society of
America; SEPM

Overseas Representation:
India: EWP, New Delhi, India
South East Asian Territories: The White
Partnership
Spain & Portugal: Iberian Book Services,
Madrid, Spain
USA: AAPG, Tulsa, USA; Princeton Selling
Group Inc, Wayne, PA, USA

Book Trade Association Membership:
Association of Learned & Professional
Society Publishers

2287 ■

STANLEY GIBBONS
399 Strand, London WC2R 0LX
Telephone: 020 7836 8444
Fax: 020 7836 8444
Email: enquiries@stanleygibbons.co.uk
Web Site: www.stanleygibbons.com

Publishing, Mail Order:
7 Parkside, Christchurch Road, Ringwood,
Hants BH24 3SH
Telephone: 01425 472363
Fax: 01425 470247
Email: rswain@stanleygibbons.co.uk
Web Site: www.stanleygibbons.com

Personnel:
Michael Hall *(Chief Executive)*
Mark Henley *(Finance Director)*
Donal Duff *(Chief Operating Officer)*
Richard Purkis *(Company Secretary)*
Keith Heddle *(Sales & Marketing Director)*
Robert Swain *(Publisher)*

*Crafts & Hobbies; Reference Books,
Directories & Dictionaries*

Imprints, Series & ISBNs:
978 0 85259

Parent Company:
UK: Stanley

Associated Companies:
UK: Benham; Fraser's

Overseas Representation:
Australia: Renniks Publications Pty Ltd,
Banksmeadow, NSW, Australia
Belgium: N. V. deZittere (DZT)/Davo, Tielt
(Brabant), Belgium
Canada: Unitrade Associates, Toronto, Ont,
Canada
Denmark: Samlerforum/Davo, Karup,
Denmark
Finland: Davo C/o Kapylan, Helsinki, Finland
France: ARPHI/Davo, Viroflay, France
Germany: Schaubek Verlag Leipzig,
Markranstaedt, Germany
Italy: Ernesto Marini SRL, Genoa, Italy
Japan: Japan Philatelic, Tokyo, Japan
Netherlands: Uitgeverij Davo BV, Deventer,
Netherlands
New Zealand: House of Stamps,
Paraparaumu, New Zealand; Philatelic
Distributors, New Plymouth, New
Zealand
Norway: Skanfil A/S, Haugesund, Norway
Saudi Arabia: Arabian Stamp Centre,
Riyadh, Saudi Arabia
Singapore: C S Philatelic Agency, Singapore
Sweden: Chr Winther Sorensen AB,
Knaered, Sweden
USA: Filatco, Appleton, WI, USA

2288 ■

GIBSON SQUARE
See website
Telephone: 020 7096 1100
Fax: 020 7993 2214
Email: info@gibsonsquare.com
Web Site: www.gibsonsquare.com

Warehouse:
Littlehampton Book Services,
Faraday Close, Durrington, Worthing,
West Sussex BN13 3RB
Telephone: 01903 828500
Fax: 01903 828802
Email: orders@lbsltd.co.uk
Web Site: www.lbsltd.co.uk

Personnel:
Camille Pandian

*Biography & Autobiography; Cinema,
Video, TV & Radio; Crime; Economics; Fine
Art & Art History; Gay & Lesbian Studies;
Health & Beauty; History & Antiquarian;
Humour; Medical (incl. Self Help &
Alternative Medicine); Philosophy; Politics &
World Affairs; Psychology & Psychiatry;
Sociology & Anthropology; Theatre, Drama
& Dance; Travel & Topography*

Imprints, Series & ISBNs:
978 1 903933, 978 1 906142

Overseas Representation:
Australia: Tower Books Pty Ltd, Frenchs
Forest, NSW, Australia
Canada & USA: NBN, Blue Ridge Summit,
PA, USA
New Zealand: Addenda Ltd, Grey Lynn,
New Zealand

Book Trade Association Membership:
Independent Publishers Guild

2289 ■

GILL & MACMILLAN
Hume Avenue, Park West, Dublin 12,
Republic of Ireland
Telephone: +353 (0)1 500 9500
Fax: +353 (0)1 500 9599
Email: ftobin@gillmacmillan.ie
Web Site: www.gillmacmillan.ie

Personnel:
M. H. Gill *(Chairman)*
M. D. O'Dwyer *(Managing Director)*
A. Murray *(Educational Publishing Director)*
P. A. Thew *(Marketing & Sales Director)*

B. D. Curtin *(Company Secretary/Financial Director)*
M. O'Keeffe *(Production Director)*
F. M. Tobin *(General Publishing Director)*
J. Manning *(Distribution Director)*

Academic & Scholarly; Biography & Autobiography; Cookery, Wines & Spirits; Economics; Educational & Textbooks; Guide Books; History & Antiquarian; Humour; Politics & World Affairs; Psychology & Psychiatry; Reference Books, Directories & Dictionaries

New Titles: 134 (2010) , 131 (2011)
No of Employees: 70
Annual Turnover: €10.5M

Imprints, Series & ISBNs:
Gill & Macmillan: 978 0 7171
Newleaf: 978 0 7171
RíRá: 978 0 7171

Overseas Representation:
Australia: Brumby Books Holdings Pty Ltd, Kilsyth South, Vic, Australia
India, Pakistan & Sri Lanka: Pan Macmillan, New Delhi, India
Middle East, South East & North Asia: Pan Macmillan Asia, Hong Kong
New Zealand: New Holland Publishers (NZ) Ltd, Auckland, New Zealand
South Africa: Pan Macmillan SA Pty Ltd, Johannesburg, South Africa
UK: Bounce! Sales & Marketing Ltd, London, UK

Book Trade Association Membership:
Publishing Ireland (Foilsiú Éireann)

2290 ▬▬▬

*GLMP LTD
GLMP House, PO Box 225, Abergele, Conwy County LL18 9AY
Telephone: 01745 832863
Fax: 01745 826606
Web Site: www.studymates.co.uk

Warehouse, Trade Enquiries & Orders:
NBN International, 10 Estover Road, Plymouth PL6 9PY
Telephone: 01752 202301
Fax: 01752 202331
Email: orders@nbninternational.com

Representation (UK):
Compass Academic Ltd,
West Newington House,
10 Newington Road, Edinburgh EH9 1QS
Telephone: 0131 668 3777

Personnel:
Dr Graham Lawler *(Managing Director)*
Dr Judith Lawler *(Finance Director)*

Academic & Scholarly; Audio Books; Biology & Zoology; Chemistry; Educational & Textbooks; Electronic (Educational); English as a Foreign Language; History & Antiquarian; Industry, Business & Management; Languages & Linguistics; Law; Literature & Criticism; Mathematics & Statistics; Medical (incl. Self Help & Alternative Medicine); Military & War; Physics; Poetry; Politics & World Affairs; Religion & Theology; Scientific & Technical; Sociology & Anthropology; Theatre, Drama & Dance

Imprints, Series & ISBNs:
Aber Education: 978 1 84285
Mr Educator: 978 1 84285
Studymates Professional: 978 1 84285

Overseas Representation:
Australia & New Zealand: Footprint Books Pty Ltd, Sydney, NSW, Australia
Caribbean: David Williams Intermedia Ltd, UK

Book Trade Association Membership:
Independent Publishers Guild

2291 ▬▬▬

GLOWWORM BOOKS & GIFTS LTD
Unit 2, 5 Youngs Road,
East Mains Industrial Estate, Broxburn, West Lothian EH52 5LY
Telephone: 01506 857570
Fax: 01506 858100
Web Site: www.glowwormbooks.co.uk

Personnel:
Katrena Allan *(Managing Director)*
Gordon Allan *(Production Director)*

Children's Books

New Titles: 1 (2011)

Imprints, Series & ISBNs:
978 0 9557559, 978 1 871512

2292 ▬▬▬

ALAN GODFREY MAPS
Prospect Business Park, Leadgate, Consett DH8 7PW
Telephone: 01207 583388
Fax: 01207 583399
Email: godfreyedition@btinternet com
Web Site: www.alangodfreymaps.co.uk

Personnel:
Alan Godfrey *(Contact)*

Atlases & Maps; History & Antiquarian

New Titles: 120 (2010) , 100 (2011)
No of Employees: 4

Imprints, Series & ISBNs:
978 0 85054, 978 0 907554, 978 1 84151, 978 1 84784

Overseas Representation:
Australia: Mapworks, North Essendon, Vic, Australia
Germany: GeoCenter Touristik Medienservice GmbH, Stuttgart, Germany

Book Trade Association Membership:
British Cartographic Society

2293 ▬▬▬

GODSFIELD PRESS LTD
Endeavour House,
189 Shaftesbury Avenue, London WC2H 8JY
Telephone: 020 7632 5400
Email: info@octopus-publishing.co.uk
Web Site: www.octopusbooks.co.uk

Personnel:
Denise Bates *(Group Publishing Director)*
Clare Churly *(Managing Editor)*
John Saunders-Griffiths *(Foreign Rights Director)*

Magic & the Occult; Medical (incl. Self Help & Alternative Medicine); Religion & Theology

Imprints, Series & ISBNs:
978 1 85675

Parent Company:
Hachette UK

Overseas Representation:
see:: Octopus Publishing Group, London, UK

2294 ▬▬▬

VICTOR GOLLANCZ LTD
Orion House, 5 Upper St Martins Lane, London WC2H 9EA
Telephone: 020 7240 3444

Fax: 020 7240 5822
Web Site: www.orionbooks.co.uk

Warehouse, Trade Enquiries & Orders:
see The Orion Publishing Group Ltd

Personnel:
Lisa Milton *(Managing Director)*
Dallas Manderson *(Group Sales Director)*
Mark Streatfeild *(Export Sales Director)*
Dominic Smith *(UK Sales Director)*
Simon Spanton *(Deputy Publishing Director)*
Gillian Redfearn *(Editorial Director)*
Clare Jarvis *(Finance Director)*

Fiction; Science Fiction

Imprints, Series & ISBNs:
Victor Gollancz Ltd: 978 0 575
VGSF: 978 0 575

Parent Company:
The Orion Publishing Group Ltd

Overseas Representation:
see: The Orion Publishing Group Ltd, London, UK

2295 ▬▬▬

GOMER
Llandysul, Ceredigion SA44 4JL
Telephone: 01559 363090
Fax: 01559 363758
Email: gwasg@gomer.co.uk
Web Site: www.gomer.co.uk

Personnel:
J. H. Lewis *(Director)*
Jonathan Lewis *(Managing Director)*
Roderic Lewis *(Director)*
Carol Bignell *(Accounts)*
Meinir James *(Head of Marketing)*
Dylan Williams *(Head of Publishing)*

Biography & Autobiography; Children's Books; History & Antiquarian; Languages & Linguistics; Literature & Criticism; Photography; Poetry; Reference Books, Directories & Dictionaries; Sports & Games; Transport; Travel & Topography

New Titles: 110 (2010) , 125 (2011)
No of Employees: 55

Imprints, Series & ISBNs:
978 1 84851, 978 1 85902, 978 1 84323

Parent Company:
J. D. Lewis & Sons Ltd

Associated Companies:
Lewis Printers

Book Trade Association Membership:
Booksellers Association; Independent Publishers Guild; Cwlwm Cyhoeddwyr Cymru (Welsh Publishers)

2296 ▬▬▬

THE GOOD FOOD GUIDE
[a division of Peto Place Publishing Ltd]
2 Marylebone Road, London NW1 4DF
Telephone: 020 7770 7000
Fax: 020 7770 7600
Email: editors@thegoodfoodguide.co.uk
Web Site: www.thegoodfoodguide.co.uk

Send orders to:
Littlehampton Book Services Ltd,
Faraday Close, Durrington, Worthing, West Sussex BN13 3RB
Telephone: 01903 828500
Web Site: www.lbsltd.co.uk

Cookery, Wines & Spirits; Guide Books

New Titles: 2 (2010) , 3 (2011)

Imprints, Series & ISBNs:
978 1 84490

Parent Company:
UK: Peto Place Investments

Associated Companies:
UK: Which? Ltd

2297 ▬▬▬

GOTHIC IMAGE PUBLICATIONS
PO Box 2568, Glastonbury, Somerset BA6 8XR
Telephone: 01458 831281
Fax: 01458 833385
Email: publications@gothicimage.co.uk
Web Site: www.gothicimage.co.uk

Trade Orders:
Deep Books Ltd, Unit 3,
Goose Green Trading Estate,
47 East Dulwich Road, London SE22 9BN
Telephone: 020 8693 0234
Fax: 020 8693 1400
Email: sales@deep-books.co.uk

Personnel:
Frances Howard-Gordon *(Editorial & Commissioning Director)*
Jamie George *(Export Sales Director)*
Diana Macleash *(Financial Controller)*

Biography & Autobiography; Fine Art & Art History; Guide Books; Magic & the Occult; Philosophy; Politics & World Affairs; Psychology & Psychiatry; Religion & Theology; Travel & Topography

Imprints, Series & ISBNs:
Traveller's Guide Series: 978 0 906362

Associated Companies:
UK: Gothic Image Ltd (Retail Shop); Gothic Image Tours (Tour Operator)

Overseas Representation:
Europe: Deep Books Ltd, London, UK
USA: SCB Distributors, Gardena, CA, USA

Book Trade Association Membership:
Booksellers Association

2298 ▬▬▬

GOWER PUBLISHING CO LTD
Wey Court East, Union Road, Farnham, Surrey GU9 7PT
Telephone: 01252 736600
Fax: 01252 736736
Email: info@gowerpublishing.com
Web Site: www.gowerpublishing.com

Customer Service Department/World Distribution:
Bookpoint Ltd, 39 Milton Park, Abingdon, Oxon OX14 4TD
Telephone: 01235 400400
Fax: 01235 400454
Email: gower@bookpoint.co.uk
Web Site: www.gowerpublishing.com

Personnel:
N. A. E. Farrow *(Chairman)*
Rachel Lynch *(Managing Director)*
Darren Wise *(Finance Director)*
Richard Dowling *(Sales Director)*
Josephine Burgess *(Director – Publishing Systems)*
Jonathan Norman *(Publishing Director)*
Susan White *(Marketing Manager)*
Keith Towndrow *(Foreign Rights)*

Accountancy & Taxation; Architecture & Design; Economics; Educational & Textbooks; Electronic (Professional & Academic); Engineering; Industry, Business & Management; Vocational Training & Careers

Imprints, Series & ISBNs:
Ashgate: 978 0 7546
Gower: 978 0 566, 978 0 7546
Lund Humphries: 978 0 85331

Parent Company:
Ashgate Publishing Co Ltd

Associated Companies:
USA: Ashgate Publishing Co

Overseas Representation:
Africa (excluding South Africa & North Africa): InterMedia Africa Ltd (IMA), London, UK
Central & Eastern Europe: Dr László Horváth Publishers Representative, Budapest, Hungary
India: Maya Publishers Pvt Ltd, New Delhi, India
Iran: Kowkab Publishers, Tehran, Iran
Japan: United Publishers Services Ltd, Tokyo, Japan
Korea: Information & Culture Korea (ICK), Seoul, Republic of Korea
Middle East: Publishers International Marketing, Burmarsh, UK
North & South America: Ashgate Publishing Co, Burlington, VT, USA
Pakistan: Book Bird Publishers Representatives, Lahore, Pakistan
South East Asia, Myanmar (Burma), China, Hong Kong, South Korea, Australia & New Zealand: Ashgate Publishing Asia-Pacific, Newport, NSW, Australia

Book Trade Association Membership:
Independent Publishers Guild

2299 ▬▬▬

GRACEWING PUBLISHING
Gracewing House, 2 Southern Avenue, Leominster, Herefordshire HR6 0QF
Telephone: 01568 616835
Fax: 01568 613289
Email: gracewingx@aol.com
Web Site: www.gracewing.co.uk

Personnel:
Tom Longford *(Managing Director)*
Jo Ashworth *(Publishing Manager)*
Adrian Hodnett *(Customer Service Manager)*
Mary Clewer *(Accounts Manager)*
Monica Manwaring *(Publicity Manager)*

Academic & Scholarly; Architecture & Design; Biography & Autobiography; Guide Books; History & Antiquarian; Philosophy; Religion & Theology

Imprints, Series & ISBNs:
978 0 85244

Distributor for:
Ignatius Press; Mercer University Press; Newman House; OSV; Smyth & Helwys; St Bedes; Templegate

Overseas Representation:
Australia: Freedom Publishing, North Melbourne, Vic, Australia
USA: Liturgy Training Publications, Chicago, IL, USA

2300 ▬▬▬

GRAFFEG
[Imprint of Peter Gill and Associates]
2 Radnor Court, 256 Cowbridge Road East, Cardiff CF5 1GZ
Telephone: 029 2078 5156
Fax: 029 2039 8101
Email: info@graffeg.com
Web Site: www.graffeg.com

Personnel:
Peter Gill *(Managing Director)*
Vanessa Bufton *(Marketing Executive)*
Sarah Evans *(Production and Editorial Executive)*
Matthew Howard *(Sales and Marketing Manager)*

Architecture & Design; Cookery, Wines &

Spirits; Gardening; Geography & Geology; Guide Books; Natural History; Photography; Sports & Games; Travel & Topography

New Titles: 3 (2010) , 5 (2011)
No of Employees: 4
Annual Turnover: £100,000

Imprints, Series & ISBNs:
978 0 9544334, 978 1 905582

Parent Company:
UK: Peter Gill and Associates

Overseas Representation:
USA & Canada: Antique Collectors' Club, Woodbridge, Suffolk, UK

Book Trade Association Membership:
Booksellers Association; Independent Publishers Guild

2301 ▬▬▬

W. F. GRAHAM (NORTHAMPTON) LTD
2 Pondwood Close, Moulton Park, Northampton NN3 6RT
Telephone: 01604 645537
Fax: 01604 648414
Email: books@wfgraham.co.uk
Web Site: www.wfgraham.co.uk

Personnel:
Tim Graham *(Managing Director)*
Ian Wilson *(General Manager)*
Jonathan Newman *(General Manager)*

Children's Books

New Titles: 10 (2010) , 10 (2011)
No of Employees: 5

Imprints, Series & ISBNs:
978 1 85128

Overseas Representation:
West Indies: Humphrys Roberts Associates, London, UK

2302 ▬▬▬

*GRANADA LEARNING
The Chiswick Centre,
414 Chiswick High Road, London W4 5TF
Telephone: 020 8996 3333
Fax: 020 8742 8546
Web Site: www.gl-assessment.co.uk

Educational & Textbooks

Book Trade Association Membership:
Publishers Association

2303 ▬▬▬

GRANTA BOOKS
12 Addison Avenue, London W11 4QR
Telephone: 020 7605 1360
Fax: 020 7605 1361
Email: rights@granta.com
Web Site: www.granta.com

Trade Orders:
TBS Ltd, Distribution Centre, Colchester Road, Frating Green, Colchester, Essex CO7 7DW
Telephone: 01206 255678
Fax: 01206 255930
Email: mdl@macmillan.co.uk

Personnel:
Brigid Macleod *(Sales)*
Pru Rowlandson *(Publicity)*
Sarah Wasley *(Production)*
Angela Rose *(Rights)*
Sara Holloway *(Editorial)*

Biography & Autobiography; Fiction; Politics & World Affairs; Travel & Topography

Imprints, Series & ISBNs:
Granta Books: 978 1 86207
Granta Magazine
Portobello Books: 978 1 84627

Parent Company:
Granta Publications; Portobello Books

Associated Companies:
Granta Magazine

Overseas Representation:
Australia & New Zealand: Allen & Unwin Pty Ltd, Sydney, NSW, Australia
Canada: House of Anansi, Toronto, Ont, Canada
Europe: International Sales Director, Miles Poynton, Faber & Faber, London, UK
Indian Subcontinent: Penguin Books India, New Delhi, India
Northern Europe: Bridget Lane, Faber & Faber, London, UK
Republic of Ireland: Repforce Ireland, Irishtown, Dublin, Republic of Ireland
South Africa: Penguin Books South Africa (Pty) Ltd, Johannesburg, South Africa
Southern Europe: Melissa Elders, Faber & Faber, London, UK
USA, Middle East, Eastern Europe, Africa (excluding South Africa), Latin America & Caribbean: sales@granta.com, UK

2304 ▬▬▬

GRANTA EDITIONS
25–27 High Street, Chesterton, Cambridge CB4 1ND
Telephone: 01223 352790
Fax: 01223 460718
Email: granta@bpccam.co.uk
Web Site: www.grantaeditions.co.uk

Personnel:
Colin Walsh *(Managing Director)*
Jo Littlechild *(Marketing Manager)*
Susan Buck *(Accounts Manager)*

Academic & Scholarly; Accountancy & Taxation; Agriculture; Antiques & Collecting; Archaeology; Architecture & Design; Atlases & Maps; Aviation; Biography & Autobiography; Cookery, Wines & Spirits; Do-It-Yourself; Economics; Educational & Textbooks; Engineering; Environment & Development Studies; Fashion & Costume; Fine Art & Art History; Guide Books; Health & Beauty; History & Antiquarian; Illustrated & Fine Editions; Industry, Business & Management; Law; Medical (incl. Self Help & Alternative Medicine); Music; Natural History; Nautical; Photography; Physics; Psychology & Psychiatry; Reference Books, Directories & Dictionaries; Scientific & Technical; Sociology & Anthropology; Sports & Games; Theatre, Drama & Dance; Transport; Travel & Topography; Veterinary Science

New Titles: 6 (2010) , 10 (2011)

Imprints, Series & ISBNs:
978 0 906782, 978 1 85757

Parent Company:
Book Production Consultants Ltd

Associated Companies:
Book Connections Ltd

2305 ▬▬▬

GREEN BOOKS
Foxhole, Dartington, Totnes, Devon TQ9 6EB
Telephone: 01803 863260
Fax: 01803 863843
Email: sales@greenbooks.co.uk
Web Site: www.greenbooks.co.uk

UK Trade Distribution:
Central Books, 99 Wallis Road, London E9 5LN
Telephone: 0845 458 9911
Fax: 0845 458 9912
Email: info@centralbooks.com
Web Site: www.centralbooks.com

Personnel:
John Elford *(Publisher)*
Bee West *(Sales Manager)*
Amanda Cuthbert *(Commissioning Editor)*
Stacey Hedge *(Marketing & Publicity Manager)*

Architecture & Design; Biography & Autobiography; Cookery, Wines & Spirits; Do-It-Yourself; Economics; Environment & Development Studies; Fine Art & Art History; Gardening; Guide Books; Health & Beauty; Literature & Criticism; Natural History; Philosophy; Poetry; Politics & World Affairs; Reference Books, Directories & Dictionaries; Travel & Topography

New Titles: 16 (2010) , 16 (2011)
No of Employees: 4
Annual Turnover: £650,000

Imprints, Series & ISBNs:
Green Books: 978 1 903998, 978 1 907448, 978 0 85784
Green Books & Resurgence Books: 978 1 870098
Green Earth Books: 978 1 900322
Themis Books: 978 0 9527302

Distributor for:
USA: Chelsea Green Publishing Co

Overseas Representation:
Australia: Brumby Books Holdings Pty Ltd, Kilsyth South, Vic, Australia
New Zealand: Ceres Books, Ellerslie, New Zealand
USA: Chelsea Green Publishing Co, White River Junction, VT, USA

Book Trade Association Membership:
Independent Publishers Guild

2306 ▬▬▬

W. GREEN THE SCOTTISH LAW PUBLISHER
[a Thomson Reuters Company]
21 Alva Street, Edinburgh EH2 4PS
Telephone: 0131 225 4879
Fax: 0131 225 2104
Email: alan.bett@thomsonreuters.com
Web Site: www.wgreen.co.uk

Personnel:
Mrs Gilly Grant *(Director)*
Alan Bett *(Marketing Manager)*
Janet Campbell *(Publisher)*

Law

Imprints, Series & ISBNs:
978 0 414

Parent Company:
International Thomson Corporation

Overseas Representation:
Australia: The Law Book Co Ltd, North Ryde, Australia
Bangladesh: Karim International, Dhaka, Bangladesh
Botswana: Kerrison Book Services, Gabarone, Botswana
Canada: Carswell Publishing Ltd, Scarborough, Ont, Canada
Ghana: J. A. Amoah, Accra, Ghana
India: N. M. Tripathi Pte Ltd, Bombay, India
Israel: Steimatzky Ltd, Bnei Brak, Israel
Japan: Macmillan Shuppan KK, Tokyo, Japan
Kenya, Tanzania, Uganda & Mauritius: Kelvin van Hasselt Publishing Services, Briningham, Norfolk, UK

Malawi, Zambia & Zimbabwe: Barbie Keene, Harare, Zimbabwe
Malaysia, Singapore & Brunei: Malayan Law Journal Pte Ltd, Singapore
Pakistan: Pakistan Law House, Karachi, Pakistan

Book Trade Association Membership:
Publishing Scotland

2307

GREENHILL BOOKS / LIONEL LEVENTHAL LTD
5A Accommodation Road, London NW11 8ED
Telephone: 020 8455 5559
Email: michael@frontline-books.com
Web Site: www.greenhillbooks.com

Warehouse:
Pen and Sword Books, 57 Church Street, Barnsley, South Yorkshire S70 2AS
Telephone: 01226 734222
Email: trade@pen-and-sword.co.uk

Personnel:
Michael Leventhal *(Director)*

Aviation; History & Antiquarian; Military & War

Parent Company:
Lionel Leventhal Ltd

Associated Companies:
Chatham Publishing

Overseas Representation:
Australia & New Zealand: Peribo Pty Ltd, Mount Kuring-Gai, NSW, Australia
Austria, Switzerland, Czech & Slovak Republics, Hungary, Poland, Croatia, Slovenia, Spain (including Gibraltar) & Portugal: Sandro Salucci, Florence, Italy
Belgium: De Krijger, Erps, Belgium
Canada: Vanwell Publishing Ltd, St Catharines, Ont, Canada
New Zealand: South Pacific Books (Imports) Ltd, Auckland, New Zealand
South Africa: Peter Renew, Titles SA, Johannesburg, South Africa
USA: MBI Publishing Co, St Paul, MN, USA

2308

GREENLEAF PUBLISHING
Aizlewood's Mill, Nursery Street, Sheffield S3 8GG
Telephone: 0114 282 3475
Fax: 0114 282 3476
Email: sales@greenleaf-publishing.com
Web Site: www.greenleaf-publishing.com

Personnel:
Jayney Bown *(Office Manager)*
Dean Bargh *(Editorial Director)*
John Stuart *(Managing Director)*
Tom Harryman *(Distribution Manager/ Admin Asssitant)*

Academic & Scholarly; Educational & Textbooks; Environment & Development Studies; Industry, Business & Management; Scientific & Technical

Imprints, Series & ISBNs:
978 1 874719, 978 1 906093

Overseas Representation:
Australia: DA Information Services Pty Ltd, Mitcham, Vic, Australia
India: Viva Books, New Delhi, India
Taiwan: Unifacmanu Trading Co Ltd, Taipei, Taiwan
USA & Canada: Renouf Publishing Co Ltd, Ottawa, Ont, Canada

2309

GRESHAM BOOKS LTD
19–21 Sayers Lane, Tenterden, Kent TN30 6BW
Telephone: 01580 767596
Fax: 01580 764142
Email: info@gresham-books.co.uk
Web Site: www.gresham-books.co.uk

Personnel:
Mr Nicholas Oulton *(Managing Director)*

History & Antiquarian; Music; Religion & Theology

New Titles: 44 (2010) , 40 (2011)
No of Employees: 2
Annual Turnover: £250,000

Imprints, Series & ISBNs:
978 0 905418, 978 0 946095, 978 0 9502121

Parent Company:
UK: Galore Park Publishing Ltd

Book Trade Association Membership:
Booksellers Association; Educational Publishers Council; Independent Publishers Guild

2310

*GRUB STREET
4 Rainham Close, London SW11 6SS
Telephone: 020 7924 3966 & 7738 1008
Fax: 020 7738 1009
Email: post@grubstreet.co.uk
Web Site: www.grubstreet.co.uk

Distribution:
Littlehampton Book Services Ltd, Faraday Close, Durrington, Worthing, West Sussex BN13 3RB
Telephone: 01903 828500
Fax: 01903 828802
Email: ...@lbsltd.co.uk
Web Site: www.lbsltd.co.uk

Personnel:
John Davies *(Director)*
Anne Dolamore *(Sales & Marketing)*

Aviation; Cookery, Wines & Spirits; Military & War

Imprints, Series & ISBNs:
978 0 948817, 978 1 898697, 978 1 902304, 978 1 904010, 978 1 904943, 978 1 906502

Overseas Representation:
Asia & Middle East: Grub Street, London, UK
Australia: Capricorn Link (Australia) Pty Ltd, Windsor, NSW, Australia
Canada: Vanwell Publishing Ltd, St Catharines, Ont, Canada
New Zealand: Nationwide Book Distributors, New Zealand
North & West Europe: EMS (Anselm Robinson), London, UK
Republic of Ireland: Vivienne Lavery, Blackrock, Co Dublin, Republic of Ireland
Scandinavia: Angell Eurosales, Berwick-on-Tweed, UK
South Africa: Penguin Books South Africa (Pty) Ltd, Johannesburg, South Africa
Southern Europe: Jenny & Penny Padovani, London, UK
USA: Casemate Publishers & Book Distributors LLC, Havertown, PA, USA

Book Trade Association Membership:
Independent Publishers Guild; BA (Associate Member)

2311

GUILDHALL PRESS
Unit 15, Rath Mor Centre, Bligh's Lane, Derry BT48 0LZ
Telephone: 028 7136 4413
Fax: 028 7137 2949
Email: info@ghpress.com
Web Site: www.ghpress.com

Personnel:
Paul Hippsley *(Project & Managing Editor, Marketing Manager)*

Academic & Scholarly; Biography & Autobiography; Children's Books; Crime; Educational & Textbooks; Fiction; Gay & Lesbian Studies; Guide Books; History & Antiquarian; Humour; Literature & Criticism; Music; Photography; Poetry; Politics & World Affairs; Theatre, Drama & Dance

Imprints, Series & ISBNs:
978 0 946451

Overseas Representation:
Australia: Irish Book Centre, Melbourne, Australia
USA: Irish Books & Media Inc, Minneapolis, MN, USA

Book Trade Association Membership:
Publishing Ireland (Foilsiú Éireann)

2312

GULLANE CHILDREN'S BOOKS
See: Meadowside Children's Books

2313

GWASG GWENFFRWD
PO Box 21, Corwen LL21 9WZ
Telephone: 0845 330 6754

Personnel:
Dr H. G. A. Hughes *(Director of Research)*

Academic & Scholarly; Bibliography & Library Science; Biography & Autobiography; Children's Books; Educational & Textbooks; Electronic (Professional & Academic); English as a Foreign Language; History & Antiquarian; Languages & Linguistics; Literature & Criticism; Poetry; Politics & World Affairs; Reference Books, Directories & Dictionaries; Religion & Theology; Sociology & Anthropology; Travel & Topography

New Titles: 6 (2010) , 6 (2011)
No of Employees: 4

Imprints, Series & ISBNs:
978 0 9501861, 978 1 85651

2314

GWASG GWYNEDD
Hafryn, Llwyn Hudol, Pwllheli, Gwynedd LL53 5YE
Telephone: 01758 612483

Personnel:
Alwyn Elis *(Managing Director)*
Nan Elis *(Editor)*

Biography & Autobiography; Children's Books

New Titles: 10 (2010) , 10 (2011)
No of Employees: 5

Imprints, Series & ISBNs:
978 0 86074

2315

*HACHETTE CHILDREN'S BOOKS
338 Euston Road, London NW1 3BH
Telephone: 020 7873 6000

Fax: 020 7873 6024
Email: gm@hachettechildrens.co.uk

Distribution Centre:
Bookpoint Ltd, 130 Milton Park, Abingdon, Oxon OX14 4SB
Telephone: 01235 400400
Fax: 01235 400445

Personnel:
Marlene Johnson *(Managing Director)*
Les Phipps *(Group Sales Director)*
Andrew Sharp *(Group Rights Director)*
Charmian Allwright *(Group Production Director)*
Anne McNeil *(Publishing (Picture Books & Fiction) Director)*
Susan Barry *(Marketing Director)*
Rachel Cooke *(Franklin Watts Director)*
Anne Marimuthu *(Finance Director)*
Paul Litherland *(Trade Sales Director)*
Penny Morris *(Orchard Books Director)*

Audio Books; Children's Books; Educational & Textbooks; Fiction; Fine Art & Art History; Poetry; Reference Books, Directories & Dictionaries

Imprints, Series & ISBNs:
Aladdin/Watts
Animal Ark Series
Felicity Wishes range
Franklin Watts
Hodder Children's Books: 978 0 340
Hodder Home Learning Series
Hodder Wayland
Kipper range: 978 0 340
Orchard Books
Rainbow Magic

Parent Company:
Hachette UK

Distributor for:
Aladdin

Overseas Representation:
Africa, West Indies, South & Central America: Tony Moggach, InterMedia Americana (IMA) Ltd, London, UK
Australia: Hachette Livre Australia, Sydney, NSW, Australia
Australia & New Zealand: Watts ANZ, Sydney, NSW, Australia
Brazil (paperbacks): Agencia Siciliano de Livros, São Paulo, Brazil
Canada (trade & paperbacks): McArthur & Co Publishers Ltd, Toronto, Ont, Canada
Eastern Europe: David Williams, InterMedia Americana (IMA) Ltd, London, UK
Germany, Switzerland & Austria: Gabriele Kern Publishers Services, Frankfurt-am-Main, Germany
Hong Kong: Publishers' Associates Ltd, Hong Kong
India: Ajay Parmar, New Delhi, India
Israel: Steimatzky Ltd, Bnei Brak, Israel
Italy, Spain, Portugal & Gibraltar: Penny Padovani, London, UK
Japan & Korea: Yasy Murayama, Ageo, Japan
Netherlands (trade): Nilsson & Lamm BV, Weesp, Netherlands
New Zealand: Hachette Livre New Zealand, Auckland, New Zealand
Norway, Sweden, Finland, Denmark, Iceland, Netherlands & France: Angell Eurosales, Berwick-on-Tweed, UK
Pakistan (paperbacks): Liberty Books (Pvt) Ltd, Karachi, Pakistan
Republic of Ireland & Northern Ireland: Repforce Ireland Ltd, Monkstown, Republic of Ireland
Singapore & Malaysia: APD Singapore Pte Ltd, Singapore
South Africa: Jonathan Ball Publishers (Pty) Ltd, Jeppestown, South Africa; Pan Macmillan SA Pty Ltd, Hyde Park, South Africa
South Africa & Southern Africa (Wayland): Pan Macmillan SA Pty Ltd, Hyde Park, South Africa

Southern Africa (trade): Jonathan Ball Publishers (Pty) Ltd, Johannesburg, South Africa

Book Trade Association Membership:
Publishers Association; Educational Publishers Council

2316

HACHETTE SCOTLAND
2A Christie Street, Paisley PA1 1NB
Telephone: 0141 552 8082
Email:
bob.mcdevitt@hachettescotland.co.uk
Web Site: www.hachettescotland.co.uk

Personnel:
Bob McDevitt *(Publisher)*
Gillian McKay *(Regional Sales Manager)*

Biography & Autobiography; Cookery, Wines & Spirits; Crime; Fiction; History & Antiquarian; Humour; Military & War; Music; Sports & Games

Imprints, Series & ISBNs:
978 0 7553

Parent Company:
UK: Hachette UK

Overseas Representation:
British Commonwealth of Nations (including Canada): Darragh Deering, Headline Export Sales, London, UK

Book Trade Association Membership:
Publishers Association; Publishing Scotland

2317

PETER HADDOCK PUBLISHING
Pinfold Lane, Bridlington, East Yorkshire YO16 6BT
Telephone: 01262 678121
Fax: 01262 400043
Web Site: www.phpublishing.co.uk

Personnel:
Rodney Noon *(Managing Director)*
Peter Thornton *(Shipping Manager)*
Jason Hickey *(Customer Services Manager)*
Carolyn Meah *(Commercial Director)*

Children's Books; Reference Books, Directories & Dictionaries

Imprints, Series & ISBNs:
978 0 7105
Big Time

Parent Company:
D. C. Thomson & Co Ltd

Book Trade Association Membership:
Booksellers Association

2318

HALBAN PUBLISHERS
22 Golden Square, Piccadilly, London W1F 9JW
Telephone: 020 7437 9300
Fax: 020 7437 9512
Email: books@halbanpublishers.com
Web Site: www.halbanpublishers.com

Distribution:
Littlehampton Book Services,
Faraday Close, Durrington, Worthing,
West Sussex BN13 3RB
Telephone: 01903 828842
Fax: 01903 828621
Email: sales@lbsltd.co.uk

Personnel:
Peter Halban *(Director)*
Martine Halban *(Director)*

Biography & Autobiography; Fiction; History & Antiquarian; Literature &

Criticism; Philosophy; Politics & World Affairs; Religion & Theology

New Titles: 8 (2010) , 9 (2011)

Imprints, Series & ISBNs:
978 1 870015, 978 1 905559

Overseas Representation:
Australia: Allen & Unwin Pty Ltd, Crows Nest, NSW, Australia
Canada: McArthur & Co Publishers Ltd, Toronto, Ont, Canada
Caribbean: Humphrys Roberts Associates, London, UK
East & West Africa: Richard Carman Associates, Northwich, UK
Eastern Europe: Csaba & Jackie Lengyel de Bagota, Budapest, Hungary
Europe (excluding Scandinavia & Netherlands): c/o Florence Chatelain, The Orion Publishing Group Ltd, London, UK
India, Sri Lanka & Bangladesh: Maya Publishers Pvt Ltd, New Delhi, India
Japan, South East Asia, Far East & Pakistan: Ralph & Sheila Summers, Woodford Green, Essex, UK
Middle East & North Africa: Peter Ward Book Exports, London, UK
Netherlands: Consul Books, Blaricum, Netherlands
New Zealand: Hodder Moa Beckett Publishers (NZ) Ltd, Auckland, New Zealand
Republic of Ireland: Gill Hess Ltd, Skerries, Co Dublin, Republic of Ireland
Russia, Baltic States & former USSR: Tony Moggach, IMA, London, UK
Scandinavia: Pernille Larsen (Books for Europe), Roskilde, Denmark
South Africa: Jonathan Ball Publishers (Pty) Ltd, Johannesburg, South Africa
South America: Humphrys Roberts Associates, Cotia SP, Brazil
USA & other territories: Export Department, The Orion Publishing Group Ltd, London, UK

Book Trade Association Membership:
Independent Publishers Guild

2319

HALDANE MASON LTD
PO Box 34196, London NW10 3YB
Telephone: 020 8459 2131
Fax: 020 8728 1216
Email: info@haldanemason.com
Web Site: www.haldanemason.com

Warehouse, Trade Enquiries & Orders:
Vine House Distribution Ltd,
The Old Mill House, Mill Lane, Uckfield,
East Sussex TN22 5AA
Telephone: 01825 767396
Fax: 01825 765649
Email: sales@vinehouseuk.co.uk

Personnel:
Ron Samuel *(Director)*
Ms Sydney Francis *(Director)*

Children's Books; Cookery, Wines & Spirits; Crafts & Hobbies; Educational & Textbooks; Health & Beauty; Medical (incl. Self Help & Alternative Medicine); Natural History; Sports & Games

Imprints, Series & ISBNs:
978 1 902463, 978 1 905339
Haldane Mason
Red Kite Books

Book Trade Association Membership:
Independent Publishers Guild

2320

ROBERT HALE LTD
Clerkenwell House,
45–47 Clerkenwell Green, London
EC1R 0HT

Telephone: 020 7251 2661
Fax: 020 7490 4958
Email: enquire@halebooks.com
Web Site: www.halebooks.com

Warehouse & Returns:
Combined Book Services, Units I/K,
Paddock Wood Distribution Centre,
Paddock Wood, Tonbridge, Kent TN12 6UU
Telephone: 01892 837171
Fax: 01892 837272
Email: orders@combook.co.uk

Personnel:
John Hale *(Chairman)*
Gill Jackson *(Managing Director)*
Robert Kynaston *(Finance Director)*
Robert Hale *(Production Director)*
Nick Chaytor *(Rights Manager)*

Animal Care & Breeding; Antiques & Collecting; Biography & Autobiography; Cinema, Video, TV & Radio; Crafts & Hobbies; Crime; Fiction; Fine Art & Art History; Gardening; History & Antiquarian; Humour; Magic & the Occult; Military & War; Music; Natural History; Photography; Politics & World Affairs; Reference Books, Directories & Dictionaries; Sports & Games; Transport; Travel & Topography

New Titles: 270 (2010) , 270 (2011)
No of Employees: 20

Imprints, Series & ISBNs:
J. A. Allen: 978 0 85131
Robert Hale: 978 0 7090, 978 0 7091
NAG: 978 0 7198

Distributor for:
Phoenix

Overseas Representation:
Australia: DLS Australia (Pty) Ltd, Braeside, Vic, Australia
France, Germany, Netherlands, Austria & Switzerland: Ted Dougherty, London, UK
Ireland: Andrew Russell, Holywell, Dromore, Bantry, Republic of Ireland
Italy, Spain, Portugal, Greece & Gibraltar: Penny Padovani, London, UK
New Zealand: South Pacific Books (Imports) Ltd, Auckland, New Zealand
South Africa: Trinity Books CC, Randburg, South Africa
USA: Independent Publishers Group, 814 N Franklin St, Chicago, ILL 60610, USA

Book Trade Association Membership:
Independent Publishers Guild; Faber Factory

2321

*HALSGROVE
Halsgrove House, Ryelands Estate,
Bagley Road, Wellington, Somerset
TA21 9PZ
Telephone: 01823 653777
Fax: 01823 665294
Email: sales@halsgrove.com
Web Site: www.halsgrove.com

Personnel:
Julian Davidson *(Managing Director)*
Steven Pugsley *(Chairman)*
Simon Butler *(Publisher)*

Archaeology; Aviation; Biography & Autobiography; Fine Art & Art History; Guide Books; History & Antiquarian; Illustrated & Fine Editions; Military & War; Natural History; Travel & Topography

Imprints, Series & ISBNs:
Halsgrove: 978 1 84114
Halstar: 978 0 906690
Rylands: 978 0 906551

Parent Company:
UK: D. A. A. Halsgrove Ltd

Associated Companies:
UK: Halstar Ltd

Distributor for:
UK: Halsgrove; Halstar; Ryelands

2322

HAMBLEDON CONTINUUM LTD
see: Continuum International Publishing Group

2323

*HANBURY PLAYS
Keeper's Lodge, Broughton Green,
Droitwich, Worcs WR9 7EE
Telephone: 01527 821564
Email: hanburyplays@tiscali.co.uk
Web Site: www.hanburyplays.co.uk

Personnel:
Brian J. Burton *(Proprietor)*

Theatre, Drama & Dance

Imprints, Series & ISBNs:
978 0 85197, 978 0 907926, 978 1 85205

Distributor for:
USA: Contemporary Drama Service; Pioneer Drama Service

Overseas Representation:
Australia: The Dominie Group, Brookvale, NSW, Australia
Malta: Dingli Co International, Valletta, Malta
New Zealand: Play Bureau of New Zealand Ltd, New Plymouth, New Zealand

2324

*HARDEN'S LTD
14 Buckingham Street, London WC2N 6DF
Telephone: 020 7839 4763
Fax: 020 7839 7561
Email: rh@hardens.com
Web Site: www.hardens.com

Personnel:
Richard Harden *(Director)*
Peter Harden *(Director)*

Guide Books; Reference Books, Directories & Dictionaries

Imprints, Series & ISBNs:
978 1 873721

2325

*HARLEQUIN MILLS & BOON LTD
Eton House, 18–24 Paradise Road,
Richmond, Surrey TW9 1SR
Telephone: 020 8288 2800
Fax: 020 8288 2899
Web Site: www.millsandboon.co.uk

Personnel:
Mandy Ferguson *(Managing Director)*
Stuart Barber *(Finance & IS Director, Company Secretary)*
Karin Stoecker *(Editorial Director)*
Jackie McGee *(Human Resources Director)*
Clare Somerville *(Retail Sales & Marketing Director)*
Angela Meredith *(Retail Operations & Production Director)*
Tim Cooper *(Direct Marketing Director)*
Ian Roberts *(Sales Director)*

Fiction

Book Trade Association Membership:
Publishers Association

2326

JOHN HARPER PUBLISHING LTD
27 Palace Gates Road, London N22 7BW
Telephone: 020 8881 4774

Email: orders@johnharperpublishing.co.uk
Web Site:
www.johnharperpublishing.co.uk

Book Orders:
Turpin Distribution Services Ltd,
Stratton Business Park, Pegasus Drive,
Biggleswade SG18 8QB
Telephone: 01767 604951
Email: custserv@turpin-distribution.com

*Academic & Scholarly; Educational &
Textbooks; Politics & World Affairs*

Imprints, Series & ISBNs:
978 0 9543811, 978 0 9551144, 978 0
9556202, 978 0 9564508

Book Trade Association Membership:
Independent Publishers Guild

2327 ▬▬▬▬▬▬

*HARPERCOLLINS PUBLISHERS LTD
77–85 Fulham Palace Road, London
W6 8JB
Telephone: 020 8741 7070
Fax: 020 8307 4440
Email: enquiries@harpercollins.co.uk
Web Site: www.harpercollins.co.uk

**Registered Office (Warehouse, Trade
Orders & Distribution, Finance):**
Westerhill Road, Bishopbriggs, Glasgow
G64 2QR
Telephone: 0141 772 3200
Fax: 0141 772 3200 x3119

Personnel:
Victoria Barnsley (*Chief Executive Officer*)
Keith Mullock (*Chief Operating Officer*)
Charlie Redmayne (*Executive Vice-President
& Chief Digital Officer*)
Robert Scriven (*Managing Director,
Languages*)
Mario Santos (*Managing Director,
Children's*)
Belinda Budge (*Managing Director &
Publisher, Harper Fiction & Harper Non-
Fiction*)
John Bond (*Managing Director, Press Books*)
David Roche (*Managing Director, Group
Sales & Trade Marketing*)
Nigel Ward (*Managing Director, Education*)
Katie Fulford (*Managing Director, Special
Projects*)
James Graves (*Global Sourcing Director*)
Lucy Vanderbilt (*Rights Director*)
Sylvia May (*Group International Sales
Director*)
Helen Ellis (*Publicity Director, Harper Press*)
Julian Thomas (*Information Technology
Director*)
Sean Plunkett (*Group Supply Chain
Director*)
Ed Kielbasiewicz (*Finance Director*)
Siobhan Kenny (*Communications Director*)
Julia Wisdom (*Harper Fiction, Crime
Publishing Director*)
Susan Watt (*Harper Fiction Publishing
Director*)
Jonathan Taylor (*Harper Sport Publishing
Director*)
Jane Johnson (*Harper Fiction, Voyager
Publishing Director*)
Nick Pearson (*Fourth Estate Publishing
Director*)
David Brawn (*Tolkien & Estates Publishing
Director*)
Ann-Janine Murtagh (*Publisher, Children's
Books*)
Clare Smith (*Harper Press Fiction Publishing
Director*)
Arabella Pike (*Harper Press Non-Fiction
Publishing Director*)
Lynne Drew (*Harper Fiction Publishing
Director*)

Academic & Scholarly; Animal Care &

*Breeding; Antiques & Collecting;
Architecture & Design; Atlases & Maps;
Audio Books; Biography & Autobiography;
Biology & Zoology; Chemistry; Children's
Books; Cinema, Video, TV & Radio;
Cookery, Wines & Spirits; Crafts & Hobbies;
Crime; Do-It-Yourself; Economics;
Educational & Textbooks; Electronic
(Educational); Electronic (Entertainment);
Electronic (Professional & Academic);
English as a Foreign Language;
Environment & Development Studies;
Fiction; Fine Art & Art History; Gardening;
Gender Studies; Geography & Geology;
Guide Books; Health & Beauty; History &
Antiquarian; Humour; Illustrated & Fine
Editions; Industry, Business &
Management; Languages & Linguistics;
Literature & Criticism; Magic & the Occult;
Medical (incl. Self Help & Alternative
Medicine); Military & War; Music; Natural
History; Photography; Physics; Poetry;
Politics & World Affairs; Psychology &
Psychiatry; Reference Books, Directories &
Dictionaries; Religion & Theology; Science
Fiction; Scientific & Technical; Sports &
Games; Travel & Topography*

Imprints, Series & ISBNs:
Collins
Collins Classics
Collins Crime
Collins Dictionaries COBUILD
Collins New Naturalist Library
Collins Teacher
Collins/Times Maps & Atlases
CollinsEducation
CollinsGems
Fourth Estate
Harper Perennial
Harper Sport
Harper Thorsons/Harper Element
HarperCollins
HarperCollins Audio
HarperCollins Children's Books
HarperCollins Entertainment
HarperCollins Non-Fiction
Janes
Times Books
Tolkien
Voyager

Parent Company:
News Corporation

Overseas Representation:
Australia: HarperCollins Publishers, Pymble,
NSW, Australia
Canada: HarperCollins Publishers, Toronto
& Scarborough, Ont, Canada
India: HarperCollins Publishers India Pvt Ltd,
New Delhi, India
New Zealand: HarperCollins (NZ) Ltd,
Glenfield, Auckland, New Zealand
USA: HarperCollins Publishers, New York,
USA
Worldwide (except countries listed):
HarperCollins Publishers Ltd, Glasgow &
London, UK

Book Trade Association Membership:
Publishers Association

2328 ▬▬▬▬▬▬

*HARRIMAN HOUSE
3A Penns Road, Petersfield, Hants
GU32 2EW
Telephone: 01730 233870
Fax: 01730 233880
Email: info@harriman-house.com
Web Site: www.harriman-house.com

Personnel:
Myles Hunt (*Managing Director*)
Suzanne Anderson (*Rights*)
Louise Hinchen (*Publicity & Marketing*)
Nick Read (*Head of Production*)
Craig Pearce (*Editor*)
Chris Parker (*Sales & New Media*)

*Accountancy & Taxation; Economics;
Industry, Business & Management*

Imprints, Series & ISBNs:
978 0 85719, 978 1 897597, 978 1
905641, 978 1 906659

Overseas Representation:
Central & Eastern Europe: Tony Moggach,
Publishers Sales Representation, London,
UK
Spain, Portugal & Gibraltar: Peter Prout,
Iberian Book Services, Madrid, Spain
West Africa: Joseph Makope, InterMedia
Americana (IMA) Ltd, London, UK
*Western Europe (including Austria,
Belgium, France, Germany, Greece, Italy,
Luxembourg, Malta, Netherlands &
Switzerland):* Ted Dougherty, London, UK

2329 ▬▬▬▬▬▬

HART PUBLISHING
16C Worcester Place, Oxford OX1 2JW
Telephone: 01865 517530
Fax: 01865 510710
Email: mail@hartpub.co.uk
Web Site: www.hartpub.co.uk

Personnel:
Richard Hart (*Joint Owner & Managing
Director*)
Jane Parker (*Joint Owner, Sales & Marketing
Director*)

Academic & Scholarly; Law

New Titles: 92 (2010) , 112 (2011)

Imprints, Series & ISBNs:
978 1 84113, 978 1 84946, 978 1 901362

Distributor for:
Belgium: Intersentia

Overseas Representation:
Africa: Tula Publishing Ltd
Benelux: Intersentia, Antwerp, Belgium
Canada: Codasat, c/o University Toronto
Press Distribution, Downsview, Ont,
Canada
Central & Eastern Europe: Jacek Lewinson,
Poland
*Greece, Turkey, Arab Middle East & North
Africa:* Avicenna Partnership Ltd, UK
Italy & France: Mare Nostrum Publishing
Consultants, Rome, Italy
Scandinavia: Colin Flint Ltd, Harlow, UK
South East Asia: STM Publisher Services Pte
Ltd, Singapore
Spain & Portugal: Peter Prout Iberian Book
Services, Madrid, Spain
USA: International Specialized Book
Services Inc, Portland, OR, USA

Book Trade Association Membership:
Independent Publishers Guild

2330 ▬▬▬▬▬▬

HARVARD UNIVERSITY PRESS
Vernon House, 23 Sicilian Avenue, London
WC1A 2QS
Telephone: 020 7306 0603
Fax: 020 7306 0604
Email: info@harvardup.co.uk
Web Site: www.hup.harvard.edu

Orders & Warehouse:
c/o John Wiley & Sons,
European Distribution Centre,
Bognor Regis, West Sussex PO22 9NQ
Telephone: 01243 779777
Fax: 01243 829121
Email: cs-books@wiley.co.uk

Personnel:
Richard Howells (*Sales Director*)
Rebekah White (*Publicity & Promotion
Manager*)

Academic & Scholarly; Biography &

*Autobiography; Biology & Zoology;
Cinema, Video, TV & Radio; Economics;
Fine Art & Art History; Gender Studies;
Health & Beauty; History & Antiquarian;
Law; Literature & Criticism; Military & War;
Music; Natural History; Philosophy; Politics
& World Affairs; Psychology & Psychiatry;
Reference Books, Directories &
Dictionaries; Religion & Theology; Sociology
& Anthropology*

Imprints, Series & ISBNs:
Belknap: 978 0 674
Harvard University Press: 978 0 674
Loeb Classical Library: 978 0 674

Parent Company:
USA: Harvard University Press

Overseas Representation:
China: Everest International Publishing
Services, Beijing, P. R. of China
*Germany, Austria, Switzerland, Italy, Spain
& Portugal:* Uwe Lüdemann, Berlin,
Germany
Hong Kong: Jane Lam, Aromix Books, Hong
Kong
Israel: Rodney Franklin Agency, Tel Aviv,
Israel
Japan: Rockbook, Tokyo, Japan
Malaysia: Simon Tay, Apex Knowledge,
Selangor, Malaysia
Middle East (excluding Greece & Israel):
Avicenna Partnership, Oxford, UK
North America, Mexico & Central America:
Harvard University Press, Cambridge,
MA, USA
*Poland, Hungary, Croatia, Slovenia,
Slovakia, Czech Republic, Russia,
Lithuania, Latvia, Estonia, Romania,
Serbia, Albania & Bosnia Herzegovina:*
Ewa Ledóchowicz, Konstancin-Jeziorna,
Poland
*Scandinavia, Netherlands, Luxembourg,
Belgium & France:* Fred Hermans,
Bovenkarspel, Netherlands
South Africa: Cory Voigt Associates,
Johannesburg, South Africa
South East Asia: Joseph Goh, IGP Services,
Singapore
South Korea: Se-Yung Jun & Min-Hwa Yoo,
Seoul, Republic of Korea
Taiwan: B. K. Norton, Taipei, Taiwan

Book Trade Association Membership:
Independent Publishers Guild

2331 ▬▬▬▬▬▬

HARVEY MAP SERVICES LTD
12–22 Main Street, Doune, Perthshire
FK16 6BJ
Telephone: 01786 841202
Fax: 01786 841098
Email: sh@harveymaps.co.uk
Web Site: www.harveymaps.co.uk

Personnel:
Susan Harvey (*Managing Director*)
Jacci Cameron (*Office Manager*)

Atlases & Maps; Sports & Games

New Titles: 8 (2010) , 9 (2011)
No of Employees: 8
Annual Turnover: £600,000

Imprints, Series & ISBNs:
978 1 85137

Distributor for:
Canada: Chrismar Inc
Denmark: Compukort

Book Trade Association Membership:
International Map Trade Association

2332 ▬▬▬▬▬▬

HAWKER PUBLICATIONS
Culvert House, Culvert Road. London
SW11 5DH

Telephone: 020 7720 2108
Fax: 020 7498 3023
Email: kate@hawkerpublications.com
Web Site: www.careinfo.org

Distribution:
NBN Plymbridge Ltd, Estover Road,
Plymouth, Devon PL6 7PZ
Telephone: 01752 202300

Personnel:
Dr R. Hawkins (*Managing Director*)
P. Petker (*Sales Director*)

*Health & Beauty; Medical (incl. Self Help &
Alternative Medicine); Vocational Training &
Careers*

New Titles: 3 (2010)
No of Employees: 20

Imprints, Series & ISBNs:
Better Care Guides: 978 1 874790
Hawker Publications: 978 1 874790

Overseas Representation:
Australia: Basing House Books,
Hammondville, NSW, Australia

2333 ▬▬▬

*HAWTHORN PRESS
Hawthorn House, 1 Lansdown Lane,
Stroud, Glos GL5 1BJ
Telephone: 01453 757040
Fax: 01453 751138
Email: info@hawthornpress.com
Web Site: www.hawthornpress.com

Distribution & Sales:
BookSource, 50 Cambuslang Road,
Glasgow G32 8NB
Telephone: 0845 370 0063
Fax: 0845 370 0064
Email: orders@booksource.net

Personnel:
Martin Large (*Director*)
Judy Large (*Director*)
Farimah Englefield (*Finance Manager*)
Claire Percival (*Administrator*)

*Academic & Scholarly; Children's Books;
Crafts & Hobbies; Educational & Textbooks;
Gardening; Gender Studies; Industry,
Business & Management; Medical (incl. Self
Help & Alternative Medicine); Music;
Politics & World Affairs; Psychology &
Psychiatry; Religion & Theology; Sociology
& Anthropology*

Imprints, Series & ISBNs:
978 1 903458, 978 1 907359
Conflict & Peace Building: 978 1 869890
Early Years Education: 978 1 869890
Family Activities & Crafts: 978 1 869890
Parenting & Child Health: 978 1 869890
Psychology & Self Help: 978 1 869890
Rudolf Steiner Education: 978 1 869890

Overseas Representation:
Australia: Footprint Books Pty Ltd,
Warriewood, NSW, Australia
Canada: Tri-fold Books, Guelph, Ont,
Canada
New Zealand: Ceres Books, Ellerslie, New
Zealand
South Africa: Peter Hyde Associates (Pty)
Ltd, Cape Town, South Africa; Rudolf
Steiner Publications, Bryanston, South
Africa
USA (all titles): Steiner Books Inc, Herndon,
VA, USA

Book Trade Association Membership:
Independent Publishers Guild

2334 ▬▬▬

HAYNES PUBLISHING
Sparkford, Nr Yeovil, Somerset BA22 7JJ
Telephone: 01963 440635

Fax: 01963 440825
Email: sales@haynes.co.uk
Web Site: www.haynes.co.uk

Customer Services (Trade):
Telephone: 01963 442080
Fax: 01963 440001
Email: sales@haynes.co.uk
Web Site: www.haynes.co.uk

Personnel:
J Haynes (*Chairman*)
James Bunkum (*Finance Director & Group
Company Secretary*)
Jeremy Yates-Round (*Managing Director –
UK & Europe; Sales & Marketing Director*)
Nigel Clements (*Production Director*)
Matthew Minter (*Motor Trade Division,
Editorial Director*)
Mark Hughes (*Book Trade Division, Editorial
Director*)
Graham Cook (*Overseas Sales & Rights
Director*)
Eric Oakley (*Chief Executive Officer*)

*Animal Care & Breeding; Architecture &
Design; Atlases & Maps; Aviation;
Biography & Autobiography; Children's
Books; Computer Science; Cookery, Wines
& Spirits; Crafts & Hobbies; Crime; Do-It-
Yourself; Electronic (Entertainment);
Electronic (Professional & Academic);
Gardening; Guide Books; Health & Beauty;
History & Antiquarian; Humour; Medical
(incl. Self Help & Alternative Medicine);
Military & War; Music; Nautical;
Photography; Reference Books, Directories
& Dictionaries; Scientific & Technical; Sports
& Games; Transport; Travel & Topography*

New Titles: 126 (2010) , 130 (2011)
No of Employees: 72
Annual Turnover: £33.3M

Imprints, Series & ISBNs:
G. T. Foulis: 978 0 85429
Haynes: 978 1 84425, 978 1 85010, 978 1
85960, 978 0 85733
J. H. Haynes & Co Ltd: 978 0 85696, 978 0
900550
Oxford Illustrated Press: 978 0 902280, 978
0 946609, 978 1 85509
Patrick Stephens Ltd: 978 0 85059, 978 1
85260

Parent Company:
UK: Haynes Publishing Group P.L.C.

Overseas Representation:
Australia: Haynes Manuals Inc, Padstow,
NSW, Australia
Sweden: Haynes Publishing Nordiska AB,
Uppsala, Sweden
USA: Haynes Manuals Inc, Newbury Park,
CA, USA
USA (non-Manual titles only): MBI
Publishing Co, St Paul, MN, USA

Book Trade Association Membership:
Booksellers Association

2335 ▬▬▬

HAYWARD PUBLISHING
Southbank Centre, Belvedere Road, London
SE1 8XX
Telephone: 020 7921 0826
Fax: 020 7921 0700
Email:
deborah.power@southbankcentre.co.uk
Web Site: www.southbankcentre.co.uk

Personnel:
Deborah C. Power (*Sales Manager*)
Faye Robson (*Publications Co-ordinator*)
Mary Richards (*Art Publisher*)
Nadine Monem (*Acting Art Publisher*)

*Architecture & Design; Fine Art & Art
History; Photography*

New Titles: 8 (2010) , 7 (2011)

No of Employees: 3

Imprints, Series & ISBNs:
978 1 85332

Book Trade Association Membership:
Booksellers Association; Association of
Cultural Enterprises

2336 ▬▬▬

HB PUBLICATIONS
PO Box 21660, London SW16 1WJ
Telephone: 020 8769 1585
Fax: 020 8769 2320
Web Site: www.hbpublications.com

Book Trade Association Membership:
Publishers Association

2337 ▬▬▬

HEADLINE BOOK PUBLISHING LTD
338 Euston Road, London NW1 3BH
Telephone: 020 7873 6000
Fax: 020 7873 6124
Email: headline.books@headline.co.uk
Web Site: www.headline.com &
www.madaboutbooks.com

Book Trade Association Membership:
Publishers Association

2338 ▬▬▬

*HEART OF ALBION PRESS
2 Cross Hill Close, Wymeswold,
Loughborough LE12 6UJ
Telephone: 01509 880725
Email: albion@indigogroup.co.uk
Web Site: www.hoap.co.uk

Personnel:
R. N. Trubshaw (*Owner*)

*Archaeology; Electronic (Educational);
Guide Books; History & Antiquarian; Magic
& the Occult; Philosophy; Psychology &
Psychiatry; Religion & Theology; Sociology
& Anthropology*

Imprints, Series & ISBNs:
Alternative Albion: 978 1 872883, 978 1
905646
Explore Books: 978 1 872883, 978 1
905646
Heart of Albion: 978 1 872883, 978 1
905646

2339 ▬▬▬

ROGER HEAVENS
125 Keddington Road, Louth, Lincolnshire
LN11 0BL
Telephone: 01507 606102
Fax: 01507 606102
Web Site: www.booksoncricket.net

Personnel:
Roger Heavens (*Proprietor*)
Sally Heavens (*Editor*)
Roger Packham (*Editor*)

Academic & Scholarly; Sports & Games

New Titles: 3 (2010) , 3 (2011)
No of Employees: 1
Annual Turnover: £25,000

Imprints, Series & ISBNs:
Roger Heavens: 978 1 900592
RH Business Books: 978 1 900592

Overseas Representation:
Australia: Roger Page, Yallambe, Vic,
Australia

2340 ▬▬▬

HELION & CO LTD
26 Willow Road, Solihull, West Midlands
B91 1UE

Telephone: 0121 705 3393
Fax: 0121 711 4075
Email: info@helion.co.uk
Web Site: www.helion.co.uk

Personnel:
Duncan Rogers (*Managing Director*)
Wilfrid Rogers (*General Manager*)

*Academic & Scholarly; History &
Antiquarian; Military & War*

Imprints, Series & ISBNs:
978 1 874622, 978 1 906033, 978 1
907677

Distributor for:
Aegis Consulting/Aberjona Press; Eagle
Editions; Reid Air Publishing; Vanwell
Publishing

Overseas Representation:
Australia & New Zealand: Crusader Trading
Pty Ltd, Weston, ACT, Australia
*Austria, France, Switzerland, Benelux,
Germany, Eastern Europe, Greece, Italy,
Portugal, Spain, Gibraltar, Slovenia &
Croatia:* Casemate Publishing UK,
Newbury, UK
Canada: Vanwell Publishing Ltd, St
Catharines, Ont, Canada
USA: Casemate Publishers & Book
Distributors LLC, Havertown, PA, USA

2341 ▬▬▬

*HELTER SKELTER PUBLISHING LTD
PO Box 50497, London W8 9FA
Telephone: 0794 1206045
Email: sales@helterskelterpublishing.com
Web Site:
www.helterskelterpublishing.com

Personnel:
Graeme Milton (*Director*)
Michael O'Connell (*Company Secretary*)

Music

Imprints, Series & ISBNs:
978 1 900924, 978 1 905139

2342 ▬▬▬

HEMMING INFORMATION SERVICES
32 Vauxhall Bridge Road, London
SW1V 2SS
Telephone: 020 7973 6604
Fax: 020 7233 5053
Email: l.alderson@hgluk.com
Web Site: www.hgluk.com

Also at:
8 The Old Yarn Mills, Sherborne, Dorset
DT9 3RQ
Telephone: 01935 816030
Fax: 01935 817200
Email: info@hisdorset.com

Personnel:
Graham Bond (*Managing Director*)
Linda Alderson (*Production Director*)
Mike Burton (*Editorial Director (Local
Government titles)*)
Emma Sabin (*Sales Director*)
Dean Wanless (*Senior Editor*)

Reference Books, Directories & Dictionaries

No of Employees: 120

Imprints, Series & ISBNs:
978 0 7079

Parent Company:
Hemming Group Ltd

Book Trade Association Membership:
Data Publishers Association; European
Directory Publishers Association

2343

IAN HENRY PUBLICATIONS LTD
20 Park Drive, Romford, Essex RM1 4LH
Telephone: 01708 749119
Fax: 01708 736213
Email: info@ian-henry.com
Web Site: www.ian-henry.com

Personnel:
Ian Wilkes (*Publisher & Managing Director*)

Cookery, Wines & Spirits; Educational &
Textbooks; Fiction; History & Antiquarian;
Humour; Medical (incl. Self Help &
Alternative Medicine); Theatre, Drama &
Dance; Transport

New Titles: 1 (2010) , 1 (2011)

Imprints, Series & ISBNs:
978 0 86025

Distributor for:
UK: Havering Museum

2344

*THE HERBERT PRESS
[an imprint of A. & C. Black]
36 Soho Square, London W1D 3QY
Telephone: 020 7758 0263
Email: sjames@acblack.com

Personnel:
Nigel Newton (*Chairman*)
Jill Coleman (*Managing Director*)
Susan James (*Publisher*)

Architecture & Design; Fashion & Costume;
Fine Art & Art History; Illustrated & Fine
Editions

Imprints, Series & ISBNs:
Design Handbooks: 978 0 7136, 978 0
906969, 978 1 871569
The Herbert History of Art & Architecture:
978 0 7136, 978 0 906969, 978 1
871569

Parent Company:
A. & C. Black Plc

Associated Companies:
Bloomsbury

Overseas Representation:
Australia: Allen & Unwin Pty Ltd, Sydney,
NSW, Australia
Europe: Penguin Group, London, UK
USA: Bloomsbury Academic USA

2345

NICK HERN BOOKS
The Glasshouse, 49a Goldhawk Road,
London W12 8QP
Telephone: 020 8749 4953
Fax: 020 8735 0250
Email: info@nickhernbooks.demon.co.uk
Web Site: www.nickhernbooks.co.uk

Distribution:
Grantham Book Services Ltd, Trent Road,
Grantham, Lincs NG31 7XQ
Telephone: 01476 541000
Fax: 01476 541060
Email: orders@gbs.tbs-ltd.co.uk

Personnel:
Nick Hern (*Managing Director*)
Matt Applewhite (*Commissioning Editor*)
Robin Booth (*Marketing & Publicity
Manager*)
Ian Higham (*Sales Manager*)

Cinema, Video, TV & Radio; Theatre, Drama
& Dance

New Titles: 70 (2010) , 70 (2011)
No of Employees: 8

Imprints, Series & ISBNs:
978 1 84842, 978 1 85459

Distributor for:
Canada: Playwrights Press Canada
USA: Drama Book Publishers; Theatre
Communications Group

Overseas Representation:
Australia: Currency Press, Sydney, Australia
Canada: Playwrights Press Canada, Toronto,
Ont, Canada
USA: Theatre Communications Group, New
York, USA

Book Trade Association Membership:
Independent Publishers Guild

2346

HIGHLAND BOOKS
Two High Pines, Knoll Road, Godalming,
Surrey GU7 2EP
Telephone: 01483 424560
Fax: 01483 424388
Email: info@highlandbks.com
Web Site: www.highlandbks.com

Distribution / Trade Orders:
STL Distribution, PO Box 300,
Kingstown Broadway, Carlisle, Cumbria
CA3 0QS
Telephone: 01228 611511
Fax: 01228 514949
Email: info@highlandbks.com
Web Site: www.stldistribution.co.uk

Personnel:
Philip Ralli (*Director*)

Biography & Autobiography; Children's
Books; Fiction; Religion & Theology

New Titles: 6 (2010) , 6 (2011)
No of Employees: 2

Imprints, Series & ISBNs:
Highland: 978 0 946616, 978 1 897913
Usharp: 978 1 905496

Overseas Representation:
South Africa: Methodist Wholesale, Cape
Town, South Africa

2347

HINTON HOUSE PUBLISHERS LTD
Newman House, 4 High Street,
Buckingham MK18 1NT
Telephone: 01280 822557
Fax: 0560 313 5274
Email: info@hintonpublishers.com
Web Site: www.hintonpublishers.com

Personnel:
Sarah Miles (*Publisher*)

Educational & Textbooks; Languages &
Linguistics; Medical (incl. Self Help &
Alternative Medicine); Psychology &
Psychiatry

Imprints, Series & ISBNs:
978 1 906531

Overseas Representation:
Malaysia: Publishers Marketing Services Pte
Ltd, Kuala Lumpur, Malaysia
Singapore: SpEd LLP, Singapore

Book Trade Association Membership:
Publishers Association

2348

HIPPOPOTAMUS PRESS
22 Whitewell Road, Frome, Somerset
BA11 4EL
Telephone: 01373 466653
Fax: 01373 466653
Email: rjhippopress@aol.com

Personnel:
R. John (*Publisher*)
M. Pargitter (*Editor*)
Anna Martin (*Editorial Assistant*)

Literature & Criticism; Poetry

New Titles: 2 (2010) , 3 (2011)
No of Employees: 3

Imprints, Series & ISBNs:
978 0 904179

Distributor for:
Austria: University of Salzburg Press
USA: Ramparts Inc

2349

HISTORICAL PUBLICATIONS LTD
32 Ellington Street, London N7 8PL
Telephone: 020 7607 1628
Fax: 020 7609 6451
Email:
richardson@historicalpublications.co.uk
Web Site:
www.historicalpublications.co.uk

Distribution:
Countryside Books, 2 Highfield Avenue,
Newbury, Berks RG14 5DS
Telephone: 01635 43816
Fax: 01635 551004
Email: info@countrysidebooks.co.uk
Web Site: www.countrysidebooks.co.uk

Personnel:
John Richardson (*Managing Director*)
Helen English (*Secretary*)

Academic & Scholarly; Architecture &
Design; History & Antiquarian; Travel &
Topography

New Titles: 6 (2010) , 3 (2011)
No of Employees: 2
Annual Turnover: £100,000

Imprints, Series & ISBNs:
978 0 948667, 978 1 905286

2350

HOBNOB PRESS
PO Box 1838, East Knoyle, Salisbury
SP3 6FA
Telephone: 01747 830015
Email: john@hobnobpress.co.uk
Web Site: www.hobnobpress.co.uk

Personnel:
John Chandler (*Sole Trader*)

Academic & Scholarly; Archaeology; Guide
Books; History & Antiquarian; Literature &
Criticism; Travel & Topography

New Titles: 9 (2010) , 12 (2011)
No of Employees: 0

Imprints, Series & ISBNs:
978 0 946418, 978 1 906978

Distributor for:
Wiltshire Buildings Record; Wiltshire Record
Society

2351

*HODDER EDUCATION
338 Euston Road, London NW1 3BH
Telephone: 020 7873 6000
Fax: 020 7873 6299 & 6325
Web Site: www.hoddereducation.co.uk

Distribution Centre:
Bookpoint Ltd, 130 Milton Park, Abingdon,
Oxon OX14 4SB
Telephone: 01235 400400
Fax: 01235 400445

Personnel:
Thomas Webster (*Chief Executive Director*)
Elisabeth Tribe (*Managing Director, Schools*)
C. P. Shaw (*Managing Director, Tertiary*)
Alyssum Ross (*Business Operations Director*)
David Swarbrick (*Managing Director,
Consumer Learning*)
John Mitchell (*Scotland – Hodder Gibson
Director*)
Robert Sulley (*Editorial Director, Science &
International*)
Tim Mahar (*Sales & Marketing Director,
Trade*)
Janice Tolan (*Schools & FE, Sales &
Marketing Director*)
Jim Belben (*Schools Director (Humanities &
Modern Languages)*)
Steve Connolly (*Editorial Digital Publishing
Director*)
Alex Jones (*Finance Director*)
Paul Cherry (*Philip Allan Director*)
Vivian Marr (*Editorial Director, Consumer
Languages*)

Academic & Scholarly; Accountancy &
Taxation; Animal Care & Breeding; Antiques
& Collecting; Archaeology; Atlases & Maps;
Audio Books; Aviation; Biology & Zoology;
Chemistry; Cinema, Video, TV & Radio;
Computer Science; Cookery, Wines &
Spirits; Crafts & Hobbies; Do-It-Yourself;
Economics; Educational & Textbooks;
Electronic (Educational); Electronic
(Professional & Academic); English as a
Foreign Language; Environment &
Development Studies; Gardening; Gender
Studies; Geography & Geology; Health &
Beauty; History & Antiquarian; Industry,
Business & Management; Languages &
Linguistics; Law; Literature & Criticism;
Mathematics & Statistics; Medical (incl. Self
Help & Alternative Medicine); Natural
History; Philosophy; Physics; Politics &
World Affairs; Psychology & Psychiatry;
Reference Books, Directories &
Dictionaries; Religion & Theology; Scientific
& Technical; Sociology & Anthropology;
Sports & Games; Vocational Training &
Careers

Imprints, Series & ISBNs:
Philip Allan: 978 0 86003, 978 1 84489
Arnold: 978 0 7131
Chambers: 978 0 550
Harrap: 978 0 245
Hodder & Stoughton: 978 0 340
Hodder & Stoughton Educational: 978 0
340
Hodder Arnold: 978 0 340
Hodder Gibson: 978 0 7169
Hodder Murray: 978 0 340
John Murray: 978 0 7195
Teach Yourself: 978 0 340

Parent Company:
Hodder Headline Plc/Hachette Livre

Associated Companies:
Headline Book Publishing Ltd; Hodder &
Stoughton

Overseas Representation:
All other international queries: Rebecca
Duprey, International Sales Manager,
Hodder, London, UK
Antigua (School FE Medical Trade): The Best
of Books, St John's, Antigua
Argentina: Kel Ediciones SA (Agents),
Buenos Aires, Argentina
Australia (FE/Medical/Trade): Hachette Livre
Australia, Sydney, NSW, Australia
Australia (Livewires): Cambridge University
Press, Australia
Australia (School – excluding Livewires):
Cengage (Australia), NSW, Australia
Bangladesh (School/FE/Medical/Trade):
Ansania Mission Book Distribution
House, Bangladesh
Barbados (School/FE/Medical/Trade): Julie
White, Barbados
*Benelux, Italy & Scandinavia (FE Medical
Trade):* Ben Doming, Hodder, London, UK

Cameroon (School/FE/Medical/Trade): Macmillan Publishers Cameroon Ltd, Limbe, Cameroon
Canada (FE/Medical/Trade, excluding Teach Yourself): Oxford University Press Canadian Branch, Don Mills, Ont, Canada
Canada (School – excluding Modern Languages): Bacon & Hughes Ltd, Ottawa, Ont, Canada
Canada (School – Modern Languages only): The Resource Centre, Waterloo, Canada
Canada (Teach Yourself): McGraw-Hill, Canada
Caribbean (Trade) & South America (School/FE/Medical/Trade): Humphrys Roberts Associates, London, UK
China (School/FE/Medical/Trade): Ian Taylor Associates Ltd, London, UK
Egypt (School): Macmillan Publishers Egypt Ltd, Cairo, Egypt
Ethiopia (School/FE/Medical/Trade): Etcon Ltd, Ethiopia
Europe (School): Gill Dee, International Schools Sales Manager, Hodder, London, UK
France, Spain & Portugal (FE/Medical/Trade): Anne Kelsall, Hodder, London, UK
Germany, Austria & Switzerland (School/FE/Medical/Trade): Giana Elyea, Hodder, London, UK
Ghana (School/FE/Medical/Trade): EPP Book Services Ltd, Accra, Ghana
Greece & Cyprus (FE/Medical/Trade): Zitsa Seraphimidi, J & L Watt, Paleo Faliro, Greece
Hong Kong (School/FE/Medical/Trade) & Taiwan (School): Asia Publishers Services Ltd, Hong Kong
Hong Kong (School): Pilot Publishers Services Ltd, Kowloon, Hong Kong
India (School/FE/Trade, excluding Teach Yourself): Viva Group, New Delhi, India
India (Medical): Jaypee Brothers Medical Publishers (Pte) Ltd, New Delhi, India
India (Teach Yourself): Hachette India, New Delhi, India
Iran (FE/Medical/Trade): Farhad Maftoon, Tehran, Iran
Israel (FE/Medical/Trade): Rodney Franklin Agency, Tel Aviv, Israel
Jamaica (School/FE/Medical/Trade): Kingston Bookshop, Kingston, Jamaica
Japan (School/FE/Trade): United Publishers Services Ltd, Tokyo, Japan
Japan (Medical): Nankodo Co Ltd, Tokyo, Japan
Korea (School/FE/Medical/Trade): Information & Culture Korea (ICK), Seoul, Republic of Korea
Malawi (School/FE/Medical/Trade): Bookland International, Malawi
Maldives (School/FE/Medical/Trade): Asrafee Bookshop, Maldives
Mauritius (School/FE/Medical/Trade): Editions le Printemps, Vacoas, Mauritius
Middle East (FE/Medical/Trade): James & Lorin Watt Ltd, Publishing Consultants, Oxford, UK
Middle East (School): Gill Dee, Hodder, London, UK
Namibia, Swaziland, Botswana, Lesotho & South Africa (School/FE/Medical): Macmillan South Africa Publishers (Pty) Ltd, Braamfontein, South Africa
Namibia, Swaziland, Botswana, Lesotho, South Africa & Zimbabwe (Trade): Pan Macmillan SA Pty Ltd, Hyde Park, South Africa
New Zealand (School/FE/Medical/Trade): Hachette Livre New Zealand, Auckland, New Zealand
Nigeria (School/FE/Medical/Trade): Bounty Press Ltd, Ibadan, Nigeria
Pakistan (School/FE/Medical/Trade): Andrew White, The White Partnership, Tunbridge Wells, UK
Republic of Ireland (School/FE/Medical/Trade): Vivienne Lavery, Blackrock, Co Dublin, Republic of Ireland
Scandinavia, Benelux & Eastern Europe (FE/

Medical/Trade): Jacek Lewinson, Warsaw, Poland
Singapore, Indonesia, Brunei, Malaysia, Thailand & Philippines (School/FE/Medical): APD Malaysia, Malaysia; APD Singapore Pte Ltd, Singapore
Singapore, Indonesia, Brunei, Malaysia, Thailand & Philippines (Trade): Pansing Distribution Pte Ltd, Singapore
St Lucia (School FE Medical Trade): Nathaniel's Books, St Lucia
Tanzania (School/FE/Medical/Trade): Macmillan Aidan Ltd, Dar es Salaam, Tanzania
Trinidad & Tobago (School/FE/Medical/Trade): RIK Services Ltd, San Fernando, Trinidad
Turkey (Medical): Nobel Tip Kitabevlen, Turkey
Uganda (School/FE/Medical/Trade): Macmillan Uganda Ltd, Kampala, Uganda
USA (FE/Medical): Oxford University Press Inc USA, New York, NY, USA
USA (Teach Yourself): McGraw-Hill, Chicago, IL, USA
USA (Trade – excluding Teach Yourself): Trafalgar Square Publishing / IPG, Chicago, IL, USA
Zambia (School/FE/Medical/Trade): Macmillan Zambia, Lusaka, Zambia

Book Trade Association Membership:
Educational Publishers Council; International Group of Scientific, Medical & Technical Publishers

2352 ▬▬▬▬▬▬▬

HODDER FAITH
338 Euston Road, London NW1 3BH
Telephone: 020 7873 6000
Fax: 020 7873 6059
Email: hodderfaith-sales@hodder.co.uk
Web Site: www.hodderfaith.com

Distribution:
Bookpoint Ltd, 130 Milton Park, Abingdon, Oxon OX14 4SB
Telephone: 01235 400400
Fax: 01235 400445

Personnel:
Jamie Hodder-Williams (CEO)
Ian Metcalfe (Publishing Director)
Lucy Hale (Sales Director)

Biography & Autobiography; Fiction; History & Antiquarian; Philosophy; Religion & Theology

Imprints, Series & ISBNs:
Hodder & Stoughton: 978 0 340
Hodder Windblown: 978 0 340

Parent Company:
Hachette UK Ltd

Associated Companies:
Hachette UK; Headline Book Publishing Ltd

Distributor for:
USA: FaithWords

Overseas Representation:
Australia: Hachette Australia, Sydney, NSW, Australia
Canada: Hachette Canada, New York, USA
India: Hachette India, Mumbai, India
New Zealand: Hachette New Zealand, Auckland, New Zealand
Singapore: Pansing Distribution Sdn Bhd, Singapore
Southern Africa: Jonathan Ball Publishers (Pty) Ltd, Johannesburg, South Africa
USA: Trafalgar Square Publishing, North Pomfret, VT, USA

Book Trade Association Membership:
Publishers Association; Booksellers Association; ECPA

2353 ▬▬▬▬▬▬▬

HODDER GIBSON
[An imprint of Hodder Education]
2A Christie Street, Paisley PA1 1NB
Telephone: 0141 848 1609
Fax: 0141 889 6315
Email: hoddergibson@hodder.co.uk
Web Site: www.hoddereducation.co.uk

Distribution:
Bookpoint, 130 Milton Park, Abingdon, Oxon OX14 4SB
Telephone: 01235 400400
Fax: 01235 400454
Email: education@bookpoint.co.uk

Personnel:
John Mitchell (Managing Director)
Jim Donnelly (Sales Manager)
Ian MacLean (Sales Representative)
Elizabeth Hayes (Project Editor (Scotland))
Ella Austin (Editorial Assistant)

Academic & Scholarly; Educational & Textbooks; Electronic (Educational)

New Titles: 24 (2010) , 23 (2011)
No of Employees: 5

Imprints, Series & ISBNs:
formerly Robert Gibson & Sons: 978 0 7169
Hodder: 978 0 340

Parent Company:
Hachette UK

Book Trade Association Membership:
Publishers Association; Publishing Scotland; Educational Publishers Council

2354 ▬▬▬▬▬▬▬

HODDER & STOUGHTON GENERAL
338 Euston Road, London NW1 3BH
Telephone: 020 7873 6141
Fax: 020 7873 6195

Distribution Centre:
Bookpoint Ltd, 130 Milton Park, Abingdon, Oxon OX14 4SB
Telephone: 01235 400400
Fax: 01235 400445

Personnel:
Jamie Hodder-Williams (Managing Director)
Lisa Highton (Publisher)
Lucy Hale (Sales Director)
Karen Geary (Publicity Director)
Auriol Bishop (Creative Director)
Helen Dance (Chief Operating Officer)
Carolyn Mays (Fiction Director)
Rowena Webb (Non-Fiction Director)
Rupert Lancaster (Audio Director)
Carole Welch (Sceptre Director)
Jason Bartholomew (Subsidiary Rights)
Roland Philipps (John Murray Director)

Audio Books; Biography & Autobiography; Cinema, Video, TV & Radio; Cookery, Wines & Spirits; Crime; Fiction; History & Antiquarian; Humour; Military & War; Politics & World Affairs; Science Fiction; Sports & Games

Imprints, Series & ISBNs:
Coronet
Hodder & Stoughton: 978 0 340
Mullholland
John Murray
Saltyard
Sceptre: 978 0 340
Two Roads

Parent Company:
Hachette UK Ltd

Associated Companies:
Headline Book Publishing Ltd
France: Hachette Livre

Overseas Representation:
Australia: Hachette Australia, Sydney, NSW, Australia
Canada (trade & paperbacks): Hachette Canada, Toronto, Ont, Canada
Caribbean: Humphreys Roberts Associates, London, UK
Eastern Europe: CLB, Budapest, Hungary
India: Hachette India, New Delhi, India
New Zealand: Hachette New Zealand, Auckland, New Zealand
Singapore: Pansing Distribution Sdn Bhd
South America: Intermedia Americana, London, UK
Southern Africa (trade): Jonathan Ball Publishers (Pty) Ltd, Jeppestown, South Africa
USA: Trafalgar Square, Chicago, IL, USA

Book Trade Association Membership:
Publishers Association

2355 ▬▬▬▬▬▬▬

ALISON HODGE PUBLISHERS
2 Clarence Place, Penzance, Cornwall TR20 8XA
Telephone: 01736 368093
Email: info@alison-hodge.co.uk
Web Site: www.alisonhodgepublishers.co.uk

Distribution:
Tormark, Redruth, Cornwall TR16 5HY
Telephone: 01209 822101
Fax: 01209 822035
Email: sales@tormark.co.uk

Personnel:
Alison Hodge (Publisher)

Biography & Autobiography; Cookery, Wines & Spirits; Fine Art & Art History; Gardening; Geography & Geology; Guide Books; History & Antiquarian; Natural History; Photography; Sports & Games; Travel & Topography

New Titles: 5 (2010) , 6 (2011)

Imprints, Series & ISBNs:
978 0 906720
The County Gardens Guides Inspirations Series
Pocket Cornwall

Overseas Representation:
Australia and New Zealand (surfing titles only): Woodslane, Warriewood, NSW, Australia
Europe: Bill Bailey Publishers Representatives, Newton Abbot, UK

2356 ▬▬▬▬▬▬▬

*HOLLAND PUBLISHING PLC
18 Bourne Court, Southend Road, Woodford Green, Essex IG8 8HD
Telephone: 020 8551 7711
Fax: 020 8551 1266
Email: sales@holland-publishing.co.uk
Web Site: www.holland-publishing.co.uk

Personnel:
J. W. Holland (Managing Director)
Mrs S. M. Holland (Company Secretary)

Children's Books; Educational & Textbooks; Electronic (Educational); Electronic (Entertainment)

Imprints, Series & ISBNs:
978 1 85038
Christmas is Fun
Colouring is Fun
Creative Colouring
Doodle Design
Halloween is Fun
Learning is Fun
Little Star Creations
Phonics is Fun
Puzzle Zone

2357

HOLO BOOKS
Clarendon House, 52 Cornmarket, Oxford
OX1 3HJ
Telephone: 01865 513681
Fax: 01865 554199
Email: holobooks@yahoo.co.uk
Web Site: www.holobooks.co.uk

Orders:
Central Books, 99 Wallis Road, London
E9 5LN
Telephone: 020 8986 4854
Fax: 020 8533 5821
Email: orders@centralbooks.com
Web Site: www.centralbooks.co.uk

Personnel:
Susanna Hoe (Partner)
Derek Roebuck (Partner)
Leonie Harries (Manager)

Academic & Scholarly; Archaeology;
Biography & Autobiography; Gender
Studies; Guide Books; History &
Antiquarian; Humour; Law; Travel &
Topography

New Titles: 2 (2010)

Imprints, Series & ISBNs:
The Arbitration Press
Of Islands and Women Series
The Women's History Press

Distributor for:
Hong Kong: Roundhouse Publications
(Asia)
USA: Bear Creek Books

Overseas Representation:
Hong Kong: Far East Media, Hong Kong
USA: Wm. W. Gaunt & Sons Inc, Holmes
Beach, FL, USA

2358

HONNO (WELSH WOMEN'S PRESS)
Unit 14, Creative Units,
Aberystwyth Arts Centre, Penglais Campus,
Aberystwyth, Ceredigion SY23 3GL
Telephone: 01970 623150
Fax: 01970 623150
Email: post@honno.co.uk
Web Site: www.honno.co.uk

Secretary (Honorary):
Ailsa Craig, Heol y Cawl, Dinas Powys,
Vale of Glamorgan CF6 4AH
Telephone: 029 2051 5014
Fax: 029 2051 5014
Email: post@honno.co.uk
Web Site: www.honno.co.uk

Personnel:
Helena Earnshaw (maternity leave)
(Marketing Manager (acting: Stephanie
Tillotson))
Caroline Oakley (Editor)
Lesley Rice (maternity leave) (Production &
Administration (acting: Sarah Morton))
Frances Lewis (Finance)

Biography & Autobiography; Crime; Fiction

New Titles: 11 (2010) , 9 (2011)
No of Employees: 4
Annual Turnover: £45,000

Imprints, Series & ISBNs:
Honno Classic Fiction: 978 1 870206, 978 1
906784
Honno Modern Fiction: 978 1 870206, 978
1 906784
Honno Voices: 978 1 870206, 978 1
906784

Book Trade Association Membership:
Independent Publishers Guild; Union of
Welsh Booksellers & Publishers

2359

HOPSCOTCH
[a division of MA Education]
St Jude's Church, Dulwich Road, Herne Hill,
London SE24 0PB
Telephone: 020 7738 5454
Fax: 020 7778 8317
Email: angela.s@markallengroup.com
Web Site: www.hopscotchbooks.com

Sales & Distribution:
Unit A 1–5 Dinton Business Park,
Catherine Ford Road, Dinton, Nr Salisbury
SP3 5HZ
Telephone: 01722 716935
Fax: 01722 716812
Email: sales@hopscotchbooks.com
Web Site: www.hopscotchbooks.com

Personnel:
Angela Shaw (Associate Publisher)

Educational & Textbooks; Electronic
(Educational)

New Titles: 21 (2011)
No of Employees: over 50

Imprints, Series & ISBNs:
978 1 902239, 978 1 904307, 978 1
905390

Parent Company:
UK: Mark Allen Group

2360

THE HORIZON PRESS
3 Peak Business Centre,
Moor Farm Road West, Ashbourne,
Derbyshire DE6 1HD
Telephone: 01335 347349
Fax: 01335 347303
Email: books@thehorizonpress.co.uk

Trade Enquiries:
Grantham Book Services, Trent Road,
Grantham, Lincs NG31 7XQ
Telephone: 01476 541080
Email: orders@gbs.tbs-ltd.co.uk

Trade Enquiries (alternative):
Tiptree Book Services

Personnel:
Lindsey Porter (Managing Director)
Chris Gilbert (Sales & Marketing Manager)
Stella Porter (Office Manager)

Antiques & Collecting; Aviation; Guide
Books; History & Antiquarian; Nautical;
Transport; Travel & Topography

New Titles: 25 (2011)

Imprints, Series & ISBNs:
Landmark Collectors Library: 978 1 84306
Landmark Countryside Collection: 978 1
84306
Landmark Visitors Guides: 978 1 84306

2361

HOW TO BOOKS LTD
Spring Hill House, Spring Hill Road,
Begbroke, Oxford OX5 1RX
Telephone: 01865 375794
Fax: 01865 379162
Email: info@howtobooks.co.uk
Web Site: www.howtobooks.co.uk

Customer Services:
Grantham Book Services, Trent Road,
Grantham, Lincs NG31 7XG
Telephone: 01476 541080
Fax: 01476 541061
Email: orders@gbs.tbs-ltd.co.uk
Web Site: www.howtobooks.co.uk

Sales Representation (UK & Ireland):
Compass DSA Ltd,
13 Progress Business Centre,
Whittle Parkway, Slough SL1 6DQ
Telephone: 01628 559500
Fax: 01628 663876
Email: sales@compass-dsa.co.uk

Personnel:
Giles Lewis (Managing Director)
Nikki Read (Editorial Director)
Chris Kinsey (eCommerce Manager)

Animal Care & Breeding; Antiques &
Collecting; Cookery, Wines & Spirits; Do-It-
Yourself; Educational & Textbooks;
Gardening; Guide Books; Health & Beauty;
Industry, Business & Management;
Literature & Criticism; Medical (incl. Self
Help & Alternative Medicine); Reference
Books, Directories & Dictionaries; Travel &
Topography; Vocational Training & Careers

New Titles: 35 (2010) , 36 (2011)
No of Employees: 5

Imprints, Series & ISBNs:
How To Books: 978 1 84528, 978 1 85703,
978 1 905862
Spring Hill: 978 1 84528, 978 1 85703, 978
1 905862

Parent Company:
UK: How To Ltd

Overseas Representation:
Africa: Kelvin van Hasselt Publishing
Services, Briningham, Norfolk, UK
Australia & New Zealand: Footprint Books
Pty Ltd, Sydney, NSW, Australia
Austria, Germany & Benelux: Robbert J.
Pleysier, Heerde, Netherlands
China, Hong Kong, Indonesia, Japan, Korea,
Philippines & Thailand: Chris Ashdown,
Ferndown, UK
Eastern Europe & Greece: Tony Moggach,
InterMedia Americana (IMA) Ltd,
London, UK
France, Switzerland, Italy & Malta: Ted
Dougherty, Export Sales Agency, London,
UK
Latin America & West Indies: David
Williams, InterMedia Americana (IMA)
Ltd, London, UK
Malaysia & Singapore: Pansing Distribution
Pte Ltd, Singapore
Middle East & Turkey: Publishers
International Marketing, Polfages, France
South Africa: Phambili CC, Kensington,
South Africa
Spain & Portugal: Peter Prout, Iberian Book
Services, Madrid, Spain
USA: Parkwest Publications Inc, Miami, FL,
USA

Book Trade Association Membership:
Independent Publishers Guild

2362

HUMAN KINETICS EUROPE LTD
107 Bradford Road, Stanningley, Leeds
LS28 6AT
Telephone: 0113 255 5665
Fax: 0113 255 5885
Email: hk@hkeurope.com
Web Site: www.humankinetics.com/

Personnel:
Sara Cooper (Managing Director)
Sian Partridge (Sales Manager)
Graham Wilson (Finance Manager)
Karen Ingram (Customer Services Manager)
Rory Aspell (Marketing Manager)
Peter Murphy (Editorial Manager)

Academic & Scholarly; Educational &
Textbooks; Electronic (Educational);
Electronic (Professional & Academic);
Health & Beauty; Medical (incl. Self Help &
Alternative Medicine); Psychology &
Psychiatry; Scientific & Technical; Sports &
Games; Theatre, Drama & Dance

New Titles: 120 (2010) , 120 (2011)
No of Employees: 16
Annual Turnover: £2.2M

Imprints, Series & ISBNs:
978 0 7360, 978 0 87322, 978 0 88011,
978 0 918438, 978 0 931250

Parent Company:
USA: Human Kinetics Inc

Associated Companies:
Australia: Human Kinetics
Canada: Human Kinetics
New Zealand: Human Kinetics

Overseas Representation:
Australia: Human Kinetics (Australia),
Torrens Park, SA, Australia
Brazil (academic): Tecmedd, São Paulo,
Brazil
Canada: Human Kinetics (Canada),
Windsor, Ont, Canada
China (including Hong Kong): AA Media
Services, Shanghai, P. R. of China
India: Disvan Enterprises, New Delhi, India
Iran: Kowkab Publishers, Tehran, Iran
Japan: Eureka Press, Kyoto, Japan
Korea: Daehan Media Co Ltd, Seoul,
Republic of Korea
New Zealand: Human Kinetics (New
Zealand), Auckland, New Zealand
Singapore & Malaysia: Icon Books
Singapore Pte Ltd, Singapore
South Africa (academic): Academic &
Professional Book Distributor,
Johannesburg, South Africa
South Africa (trade): Real Books CC,
Johannesburg, South Africa
Taiwan: Unifacmanu Trading Co Ltd, Taipei,
Taiwan
Thailand, Indonesia, Bangladesh, Brunei &
Philippines: Alkem Co (S) Pte Ltd,
Singapore
USA: Human Kinetics, Champaign, IL, USA

Book Trade Association Membership:
Independent Publishers Guild

2363

JOHN HUNT PUBLISHING LTD
Laurel House, Jacklyns Lane, Alresford,
Hants SO24 9JH
Fax: 01962 773769
Email: office1@o-books.net
Web Site: www.o-books.net

Personnel:
John Hunt (Publisher)
Kate Rowlandson (Manager)
Catherine Harris (Sales Manager)

Children's Books; Fiction; Magic & the
Occult; Medical (incl. Self Help & Alternative
Medicine); Philosophy; Psychology &
Psychiatry; Religion & Theology; Sociology
& Anthropology

New Titles: 150 (2010) , 200 (2011)
No of Employees: 5
Annual Turnover: £1M

Imprints, Series & ISBNs:
Circle Books
John Hunt: 978 1 84298
O-Books: 978 1 903816
Zero Books

Overseas Representation:
Australia: Brumby Books Holdings Pty Ltd,
Kilsyth South, Vic, Australia
New Zealand: Peaceful Living Publications,
Auckland, New Zealand
Singapore: STP Distributors Pte Ltd,
Singapore
South Africa: Alternative Books CC,
Ferndale, South Africa
USA & Canada: NBN, Blue Ridge Summit,
PA, USA

Book Trade Association Membership:
Independent Publishers Guild

2364 ▬▬▬▬▬▬▬▬▬

C. HURST & CO (PUBLISHERS) LTD
41 Great Russell Street, London WC1B 3PL
Telephone: 020 7255 2201
Email: michael@hurstpub.co.uk
Web Site: www.hurstpub.co.uk

Distribution:
Marston Book Services, PO Box 269,
Abingdon, Oxon OX14 4YN
Telephone: 01235 465500
Fax: 01235 465555

Personnel:
Michael Dwyer (Managing Director & Publisher)
Kathleen May (Marketing Director)
Daisy Leitch (Managing Editor)

Academic & Scholarly; Gender Studies; Military & War; Politics & World Affairs; Religion & Theology; Sociology & Anthropology

Imprints, Series & ISBNs:
978 0 903983, 978 0 905838, 978 1 85065

Distributor for:
Signal Books

Overseas Representation:
Australia: UNIREPS University and Reference Publishers' Services, Sydney, NSW, Australia
Benelux, France & Suisse Romande: Michael Geoghegan, London, UK
China & Hong Kong: Access Asia Media Services, Beijing, P. R. of China
Eastern Europe: Ewa Ledóchowicz, Konstancin-Jeziorna, Poland
Greece, Malta, Italy & Cyprus: Charles Gibbes Associates, Louslitges, France
Japan: United Publishers Services Ltd, Tokyo, Japan
Middle East: Avicenna Partnership, Oxford, UK
Nordic countries: Colin Flint Ltd, Harlow, UK
Republic of Ireland: Geoff Bryan, Dublin, Republic of Ireland
South East Asia: Taylor & Francis Ltd, Singapore
Southern Africa: Bacchus Books, Johannesburg, South Africa
Spain & Portugal: Iberian Book Services, Madrid, Spain

Book Trade Association Membership:
Independent Publishers Guild

2365 ▬▬▬▬▬▬▬▬▬

HYMNS ANCIENT & MODERN LTD
13–17 Long Lane, London EC1A 9PN
Telephone: 020 7776 7551
Fax: 020 7776 7556
Web Site: www.hymnsam.co.uk

Warehouse & Distribution:
Norwich Books & Music,
13a Hellesdon Park Road, Norwich, Norfolk
NR6 5DR
Telephone: 01603 785925
Fax: 01603 785915
Email: info@norwichbooksandmusic.co.uk
Web Site:
www.norwichbooksandmusic.co.uk

Personnel:
Dominic Vaughan (Group Chief Executive Officer)
Michael Addison (Sales & Marketing Director)
Christine Smith (Publishing Director)
Stephen Rogers (Production Manager)
Brenda Medhurst (Financial Director)
Aude Pasquier (UK Sales Manager)

Rebecca Goldsmith (Rights Administrator)
Natalie Watson (SCM Press Commissioning Editor)

Academic & Scholarly; Biography & Autobiography; Educational & Textbooks; Music; Philosophy; Reference Books, Directories & Dictionaries; Religion & Theology

New Titles: 120 (2011)
No of Employees: 60
Annual Turnover: £6.5M

Imprints, Series & ISBNs:
Canterbury Press, Norwich: 978 1 85311
Church House Publishing: 978 0 7151
Hymns Ancient & Modern: 978 0 907547
Religious and Moral Education Press: 978 0 900274, 978 1 85175
SCM Press: 978 0 334
St Andrew Press

Distributor for:
Acora; Cairns; Canterbury Press, Church House Publishing; Church Publishing Inc; Churches Together in Britain & Ireland; Concilium; Darton, Longman & Todd; Epworth Press; HarperCollins Religious; Joint Liturgical Studies; Royal School of Church Music (RSCM); SCM Press; SLG Press; Westminster John Knox Press

Overseas Representation:
Australia (Canterbury Press, Norwich): Rainbow Books, Fairfield, Vic, Australia
Canada (SCM Press & Canterbury Press, Norwich): Novalis Inc, Toronto, Ont, Canada
Continental Europe (Canterbury Press & SCM Press): Durnell Marketing Ltd, Tunbridge Wells, UK
New Zealand (Canterbury Press, Norwich): Church Book Stores, Auckland, New Zealand
Republic of Ireland (Canterbury Press & SCM Press): Columba Book Service, Blackrock, Co Dublin, Republic of Ireland
South Africa (SCM Press): Pearson, South Africa
USA (SCM Press & Canterbury Press, Norwich): Westminster John Knox Press, Louisville, KY, USA

Book Trade Association Membership:
Publishers Association; Publishing Scotland; Independent Publishers Guild

2366 ▬▬▬▬▬▬▬▬▬

HYPATIA PUBLICATIONS
[including Patten Press & Jamieson Library imprints]
Jamieson Library, Old Post Office, Newmill, Penzance, Cornwall TR20 8XN
Telephone: 01736 360549
Fax: 01736 333307
Email: info@hypatia-trust.org.uk
Web Site: www.hypatia-trust.org.uk

Warehouse:
Jamieson Library, Old Post Office, Newmill, Penzance, Cornwall TR20 8XN
Telephone: 01736 360549
Email: booksales@hypatia-trust.org.uk
Web Site: www.hypatia-trust.org.uk

Personnel:
Dr Melissa Hardie (Director)
Donna Anton (IT Director)

Academic & Scholarly; Bibliography & Library Science; Biography & Autobiography; Educational & Textbooks; Fine Art & Art History; History & Antiquarian; Reference Books, Directories & Dictionaries

New Titles: 2 (2010) , 2 (2011)
No of Employees: 2
Annual Turnover: £20,000

Imprints, Series & ISBNs:
978 1 872229

Parent Company:
UK: The Hypatia Trust

Associated Companies:
UK: Jamieson Library; Patten Press

Overseas Representation:
USA: Malcolm Summers, VT, USA

2367 ▬▬▬▬▬▬▬▬▬

*ICHEME
165–189 Railway Terrace, Rugby
CV21 3HQ
Telephone: 01788 578214
Fax: 01788 560833
Email: claudia@icheme.org
Web Site: www.icheme.org

Personnel:
Claudia Flavell-While (Publications Director)
Jacqueline Cressey (Marketing Manager)

Engineering; Scientific & Technical

Imprints, Series & ISBNs:
978 0 85295

Overseas Representation:
Australia & New Zealand: DA Information Services Pty Ltd, Mitcham, Vic, Australia
USA & Canada: Princeton Selling Group Inc, Wayne, PA, USA

2368 ▬▬▬▬▬▬▬▬▬

ICON BOOKS LTD
Omnibus Business Centre,
39–41 North Road, London N7 9DP
Telephone: 020 7697 9695
Fax: 020 7697 9501
Email: info@iconbooks.co.uk
Web Site: www.iconbooks.co.uk

Distribution:
TBS Distribution Centre, Colchester Road, Frating Green, Colchester, Essex CO7 7DW
Telephone: 01206 255678 (UK trade) & 255644 (Export)
Fax: 01206 255930 (UK trade) & 255916 (Export)
Email: sales@tbs-ltd.co.uk & export@tbs-ltd.co.uk

UK Rights (Icon & Wizard titles):
The Marsh Agency, 50 Albemarle Street, London W1S 4BD
Telephone: 020 7493 4361
Fax: 020 7495 8961
Email: steph@patersonmarsh.co.uk

Sales Representation (UK):
Faber & Faber, Bloomsbury House, 74–77 Great Russell Street, London WC1B 3DA
Telephone: 020 7465 0045
Fax: 020 7465 0034
Email: sales@faber.co.uk

Personnel:
Peter Pugh (Chairman)
Simon Flynn (Managing Director)
Duncan Heath (Editorial Director)
Andrew Furlow (Sales & Marketing Director)
Henry Lord (Publicity Manager)

Academic & Scholarly; Aviation; Biography & Autobiography; Chemistry; Children's Books; Crime; Economics; Educational & Textbooks; Fiction; Gender Studies; Geography & Geology; Health & Beauty; History & Antiquarian; Humour; Languages & Linguistics; Literature & Criticism; Mathematics & Statistics; Military & War; Natural History; Philosophy; Physics; Poetry; Politics & World Affairs; Psychology & Psychiatry; Reference Books, Directories & Dictionaries; Religion & Theology; Science Fiction; Scientific & Technical; Sociology &

Anthropology; Sports & Games

Imprints, Series & ISBNs:
978 1 84046, 978 1 84831

Associated Companies:
Wizard Books

Overseas Representation:
Australasia: Allen & Unwin Pty Ltd, Sydney, NSW, Australia
Canada: Penguin Group Canada, Toronto, Ont, Canada
Singapore & Malaysia: Penguin Books Singapore, Jurong, Singapore
South Africa: Book Promotions Ltd, Johannesburg, South Africa
USA (Rights – Icon & Wizard titles): Carol Mann Agency, New York, NY, USA
USA (Totem Books): Consortium, Minneapolis, MN, USA

Book Trade Association Membership:
Independent Publishers Guild

2369 ▬▬▬▬▬▬▬▬▬

ICSA INFORMATION & TRAINING LTD
16 Park Crescent, London W1B 1AH
Telephone: 020 7612 7020
Fax: 020 7323 1132
Email: publishing@icsa.co.uk
Web Site: www.icsabookshop.co.uk

Distribution, Orders, Customer Service & Accounts:
Marston Book Services Ltd, PO Box 269, Abingdon, Oxon OX14 4YN
Telephone: 01235 465500
Fax: 01235 465555
Email: direct.order@marston.co.uk

Personnel:
Clare Grist Taylor (Joint Managing Director)
Susan Richards (Joint Managing Director)
Fiona Tucker (Commissioning Editor)
Kelly Jones (Production Editor)
Ella Pocock (Publishing Assistant)
Joanne Glover (Assistant Marketing Manager)

Educational & Textbooks; Industry, Business & Management

Imprints, Series & ISBNs:
978 0 902197, 978 1 85418, 978 1 86072

Book Trade Association Membership:
Independent Publishers Guild

2370 ▬▬▬▬▬▬▬▬▬

*IHS BRE PRESS
Garston, Watford, Herts WD25 9XX
Telephone: 01923 664761
Fax: 01923 662477
Email: brepress@ihs.com
Web Site: www.brebookshop.com

Sales & Customer Service:
IHS BRE Press, Willoughby Road, Bracknell, Berks RG12 8FB
Telephone: 01344 328038
Fax: 01344 328005
Email: brepress@ihs.com
Web Site: www.brebookshop.com

Personnel:
Nick Clarke (Publisher)

Architecture & Design; Environment & Development Studies; Scientific & Technical

Imprints, Series & ISBNs:
BRE Press: 978 1 86081
IHS BRE Press: 978 1 84806

Parent Company:
UK: IHS Global Ltd

2371

*IHS JANE'S
163 Brighton Road, Coulsdon, Surrey
CR5 2YH
Telephone: 020 8700 3745
Fax: 020 8763 1006
Web Site: www.IHS.com

Personnel:
Michael Dell (Director)
Amanda Castle (Public Relations)
Sean Howe (Publishing Director)

Aviation; Electronic (Professional &
Academic); Industry, Business &
Management; Military & War; Nautical;
Politics & World Affairs; Reference Books,
Directories & Dictionaries; Transport

Imprints, Series & ISBNs:
978 0 7106

Parent Company:
IHS

Overseas Representation:
Australia & New Zealand: IHS Jane's,
Rozelle, NSW, Australia
Egypt: IHS Jane's, Cairo, Egypt
India: IHS Jane's, New Delhi, India
Indonesia, Korea, Malaysia, Singapore &
Taiwan: IHS Jane's, Singapore
Japan: IHS Jane's, Japan
Kuwait & Saudi Arabia: IHS Jane's, Dubai,
UAE
North & South America: IHS Jane's,
Alexandria, VA, USA
Worldwide (excluding countries listed): IHS
Jane's, UK

Book Trade Association Membership:
Data Publishers Association

2372

THE ILEX PRESS LTD
210 High Street, Lewes, East Sussex
BN7 2NS
Telephone: 01273 487440
Fax: 01273 487441
Web Site: www.ilex-press.com

**Sales & Distribution, Trade Enquiries &
Orders:**
Trade Distribution & Accounts,
Thames & Hudson (Distributors),
44 Clockhouse Road, Farnborough, Hants
GU14 7QZ
Telephone: 01252 541602
Fax: 01252 541602
Email:
customerservices@thameshudson.co.uk

Personnel:
Alastair Campbell (Publisher)
Stephen Paul (Director)
Roly Allen (Associate Publisher)

Atlases & Maps; Computer Science; Crafts
& Hobbies; Electronic (Entertainment); Fine
Art & Art History; Photography; Reference
Books, Directories & Dictionaries

Imprints, Series & ISBNs:
978 1 904705

2373

IMPERIAL COLLEGE PRESS
57 Shelton Street, Covent Garden, London
WC2H 9HE
Telephone: 020 7836 3954
Fax: 020 7836 2020
Email: edit@icpress.co.uk
Web Site: www.icpress.co.uk

Trade Enquiries & Orders:
World Scientific Publishing,
57 Shelton Street, Covent Garden, London
WC2H 9HE
Telephone: 020 7836 0888

Fax: 020 7836 2020
Email: sales@wspc.co.uk
Web Site: www.wspc.co.uk

Personnel:
Prof K. K. Phua (Chairman)
Laurent Chaminade (Publisher)
Kellye Curtis (Commissioning Editor)
Jackie Downs (Senior Editor)

Academic & Scholarly; Biology & Zoology;
Chemistry; Computer Science; Economics;
Electronic (Educational); Electronic
(Professional & Academic); Engineering;
Environment & Development Studies;
Industry, Business & Management;
Mathematics & Statistics; Medical (incl. Self
Help & Alternative Medicine); Physics;
Scientific & Technical

No of Employees: 10

Imprints, Series & ISBNs:
978 1 86094

Parent Company:
Singapore: World Scientific

Overseas Representation:
Hong Kong: World Scientific Publishing
(HK) Co Ltd, Hong Kong
India: World Scientific Publishing Co Pte Ltd,
Bangalore, India
Singapore: World Scientific Publishing Co
Pte Ltd, Singapore
Taiwan: World Scientific Publishing Co Pte
Ltd, Taipei, Taiwan
USA: World Scientific Publishing Co Inc,
River Edge, NJ, USA

2374

IMPRINT ACADEMIC
PO Box 200, Exeter, Devon EX5 5HY
Telephone: 01392 851550
Fax: 01392 851178
Email: sandra@imprint.co.uk
Web Site: www.imprint.co.uk

Personnel:
J. K. B. Sutherland (Partner)
K. A. Sutherland (Partner)
A. Freeman (Managing Editor)
S. Good (Administrator)
D. Hall (Print Processor)
A. Roppert (Print Manager)
J. Pomroy (Packaging)
D. Pomroy (Binder)

Academic & Scholarly; Philosophy; Politics &
World Affairs; Psychology & Psychiatry;
Religion & Theology; Scientific & Technical;
Sociology & Anthropology

New Titles: 40 (2010) , 30 (2011)
No of Employees: 6

Imprints, Series & ISBNs:
Idealist Studies: 978 0 907845, 978 1
84540
Imprint Art: 978 0 907845, 978 1 84540
Societas: 978 0 907845, 978 1 84540

Overseas Representation:
USA: Ingram Publisher Services Inc,
Chambersburg, PA, USA; Philosophy
Documentation Center, Charlottesville,
VA, USA

2375

**IMRAY LAURIE NORIE & WILSON
LTD**
Wych House, The Broadway, St Ives,
Huntingdon PE27 5BT
Telephone: 01480 462114
Fax: 01480 496109
Email: enquiries@ imray.com
Web Site: www.imray.com

Personnel:
William Wilson (Managing Director)

Mrs E. N. Wilson (Director)
Ian Rippington (Sales Director)
Mrs Emma Woodfield (Accountant)

Geography & Geology; Nautical; Sports &
Games; Transport; Travel & Topography

New Titles: 10 (2011)
No of Employees: 24

Imprints, Series & ISBNs:
978 0 85288, 978 1 84623

Distributor for:
Ordnance Survey; J. M. Pearson & Sons;
RCC Pilotage Foundation; RYA Royal
Yachting Association; United Kingdom
Hydrographic Office
France: Editions du Briel; Editions Vagnon;
Euromapping; Fluviacarte
Netherlands: ANWB; Hydrographic Office
Norway: Hydrographic Office
Republic of Ireland: Irish Cruising Club
UK: Clyde Cruising Club; Royal Yachting
Association
USA: Cruising Guide Publications;
Seaworthy Publications; University of
Hawaii Press

Overseas Representation:
Australia: Boat Books (Australia) Pty Ltd,
Melbourne, Vic, Australia; Boat Books
(Australia) Pty Ltd, Sydney, NSW,
Australia
Belgium: The Boathouse, Nieuwpoort,
Belgium
France: Accastillage Diffusion, St-Martin de
Crau, France; Groupe Calade Diffusion,
Aix-en-Provence, France
Greece: AP Marine, Thessaloniki, Greece;
Contract Yacht Services, Levkas, Greece;
Lalizas, Piraeus PC, Greece; Tecrep
Marine SA, Piraeus, Greece
Italy: Edizioni Il Frangente, Verona, Italy
Netherlands: Vrolijk Watersport BV,
Scheveningen, Netherlands
New Zealand: Trans-Pacific Marine Ltd,
Auckland, New Zealand
Republic of Ireland: Viking Marine, Dublin,
Republic of Ireland
Spain: Flint Suministros SL, Barcelona, Spain
USA: Bluewater Books and Charts, Fort
Lauderdale, FL, USA; Paradise Cay

Book Trade Association Membership:
International Map Trade Association; British
Cartographic Society

2376

IN EASY STEPS LTD
4 Chapel Court, 42 Holly walk,
Leamington Spa, Warks CV32 4YS
Telephone: 01926 831557
Fax: 01926 817005
Email: info@ineasysteps.com
Web Site: www.ineasysteps.com

Distribution:
Bookpoint Ltd, 130 Milton Park, Abingdon,
Oxon OX14 4SB
Telephone: 01235 400400
Fax: 01235 832068

Personnel:
Sevanti Kotecha (Director)

Accountancy & Taxation; Computer
Science; Crafts & Hobbies; Educational &
Textbooks; Electronic (Professional &
Academic); Industry, Business &
Management; Photography; Reference
Books, Directories & Dictionaries; Scientific
& Technical; Vocational Training & Careers

New Titles: 25 (2010) , 25 (2011)
No of Employees: 4

Imprints, Series & ISBNs:
Complete Guides: 978 1 874029
In Easy Steps: 978 1 84078, 978 1 874029

Overseas Representation:
Australia & New Zealand: Woodslane Pty
Ltd, Warriewood, NSW, Australia
India: Tata McGraw-Hill, Utar Paradesh,
India
South Africa: Intersoft Simon (Pty) Ltd,
Johannesburg, South Africa
South East Asia: McGraw-Hill Education,
Singapore
USA: Publishers Group West, Berkeley, CA,
USA

Book Trade Association Membership:
Independent Publishers Guild

2377

**INCORPORATED COUNCIL OF LAW
REPORTING FOR ENGLAND AND
WALES**
Megarry House, 119 Chancery Lane,
London WC2A 1PP
Telephone: 020 7242 6471
Fax: 020 7831 5247
Email: postmaster@iclr.co.uk
Web Site: www.iclr.co.uk

Personnel:
Kevin Laws (Secretary)
Rebecca Herle (Head of Marketing &
Operations)
Stephen Mitchell (Facilities & Production
Manager)
Clive Scowen (Editor)
Helen Yates (Agency Subscriptions & Sales)
Louise Carlin (Campaign Manager)
Claire Honey (Subscription & Sales
Administrator)

Law

Overseas Representation:
Australia: Thomson Legal & Regulatory,
Rozelle, NSW, Australia
Canada: Carswell (a Thomson Reuters
company), Scarborough, Ont, Canada

2378

INDEPENDENT MUSIC PRESS
PO Box 69, Church Stretton, Shropshire
SY6 6WZ
Telephone: 01694 720049
Email: martin@impbooks.com
Web Site: www.impbooks.com

Biography & Autobiography; Fashion &
Costume; Music

2379

INDEPENPRESS PUBLISHING LTD
25 Eastern Place, Brighton BN2 1GJ
Telephone: 0845 108 0530
Fax: 01273 261434
Email: info@penpress.co.uk
Web Site: www.penpress.co.uk,
www.pulppress.co.uk &
www.indepenpress.co.uk

Personnel:
Lynn Ashman (Director)
Grace Rafael (Director)
Linda Lloyd (Senior Editor)
Danny Bowman (Pulp Press Rights)

Biography & Autobiography; Children's
Books; Cookery, Wines & Spirits; Crafts &
Hobbies; Crime; Do-It-Yourself; Educational
& Textbooks; Fiction; Gay & Lesbian
Studies; Health & Beauty; Humour;
Industry, Business & Management;
Literature & Criticism; Magic & the Occult;
Medical (incl. Self Help & Alternative
Medicine); Military & War; Music;
Philosophy; Poetry; Politics & World Affairs;
Reference Books, Directories &
Dictionaries; Religion & Theology; Science
Fiction; Sports & Games; Theatre, Drama &
Dance; Travel & Topography

New Titles: 150 (2010) , 150 (2011)

No of Employees: 8

Imprints, Series & ISBNs:
978 1 900796, 978 1 904018, 978 1
904754, 978 1 905203, 978 1 906206,
978 1 906710, 978 1 907172, 978 1
907499
Indepenpress
Pen Press
Pink Press
Pulp Press

Book Trade Association Membership:
Booksellers Association; Independent
Publishers Guild

2380

INSTANT-BOOKS UK LTD
10 Tennyson Close, Dallington,
Northampton NN5 7HJ
Email: instant.books@ntlworld.com
Web Site: www.instant-books.org

Personnel:
David Brawn (Company Secretary, Director)
Ros Brawn (Director)
P. Tomlinson (Director)
J. Cawley (Director)
N. Robbins-Cherry (Director)
G. Robbins-Cherry (Director)

Atlases & Maps; Crafts & Hobbies;
Environment & Development Studies;
Guide Books; Travel & Topography

New Titles: 12 (2010), 10 (2011)

Imprints, Series & ISBNs:
Instant-Book Editions: 978 1 84834
Tour & Trail Maps: 978 1 84834
Walk! Guidebooks: 978 1 84834

2381

**INSTITUTE FOR EMPLOYMENT
STUDIES**
Sovereign House, Church Street, Brighton
BN1 1UJ
Telephone: 01273 763400
Fax: 01273 763401
Email: iesbooks@employment-
studies.co.uk
Web Site: www.employment-studies.co.uk

Distributors:
Gardners Books Ltd, 1 Whittle Drive,
Eastbourne BN23 6QH
Telephone: 01323 521555
Fax: 01323 521666
Email: sales@gardners.com
Web Site: www.gardners.com

Personnel:
Lorna Hardy (Information Manager)

Academic & Scholarly; Industry, Business &
Management

Imprints, Series & ISBNs:
IES Report Series: 978 1 85184

2382

INSTITUTE OF ACOUSTICS
77A St Peter's Street, St Albans, Herts
AL1 3BN
Telephone: 01727 848195
Fax: 01727 850553
Email: ioa@ioa.org.uk
Web Site: www.ioa.org.uk

Personnel:
Kevin Macan-Lind (Chief Executive)
Ian Bennett (Editor)
Dennis Baylis (Advertising Manager)

Academic & Scholarly; Scientific & Technical

No of Employees: 10

2383

**INSTITUTE OF EDUCATION
(PUBLICATIONS), UNIVERSITY OF
LONDON**
20 Bedford Way, London WC1H 0AL
Telephone: 020 7911 5383
Email: ioepublications@ioe.ac.uk
Web Site: www.ioe.ac.uk/publications

Trade Enquiries, Orders & Distribution:
Central Books Ltd, 99 Wallis Road, London
E9 5LN
Telephone: 0845 458 9911
Fax: 0845 458 9912
Email: info@centralbooks.com
Web Site: www.centralbooks.com

Personnel:
Jim Collins (Publisher)
Nicole Edmondson (Assistant Publications
Editor)
Sally Sigmund (Marketing Manager)

Academic & Scholarly; Educational &
Textbooks; Sociology & Anthropology;
Vocational Training & Careers

Imprints, Series & ISBNs:
Bedford Way Papers (series): 978 0 85473
Inaugural Professorial Lectures (series): 978
0 85473
Issues in Practice (series): 978 0 85473
Viewpoints (series): 978 0 85473

Overseas Representation:
North America: Stylus Publishing Inc,
Sterling, VA, USA

Book Trade Association Membership:
Independent Publishers Guild

2384

**INSTITUTE OF EMPLOYMENT
RIGHTS**
4th Floor, Jack Jones House, 1 Islington,
Liverpool L3 8EG
Telephone: 0151 207 5265
Fax: 0151 207 5264
Email: office@ier.org.uk
Web Site: www.ier.org.uk

Personnel:
Carolyn Jones (Director)
Treena Johnson (Administration Officer)

Academic & Scholarly; Economics; Law;
Politics & World Affairs

Imprints, Series & ISBNs:
Workers in Cuba: unions and labour
relations: 978 1 906703

2385

**INSTITUTE OF FOOD SCIENCE &
TECHNOLOGY**
5 Cambridge Court,
210 Shepherds Bush Road, London W6 7NJ
Telephone: 020 7603 6316
Fax: 020 7602 9936
Email: info@ifst.org
Web Site: www.ifst.org

Personnel:
Jon Poole (Chief Executive)
Angela Winchester (Communications
Officer)

Scientific & Technical

Imprints, Series & ISBNs:
978 0 905367

Book Trade Association Membership:
Association of Learned Society Publishers

2386

**INSTITUTE OF MATHEMATICS AND
ITS APPLICATIONS**
Catherine Richards House,
16 Nelson Street, Southend-on-Sea, Essex
SS1 1EF
Telephone: 01702 354020
Fax: 01702 354111
Email: post@ima.org.uk
Web Site: www.ima.org.uk

Personnel:
David Youdan (Executive Director)

Mathematics & Statistics

New Titles: 1 (2010), 1 (2011)
No of Employees: 18

Imprints, Series & ISBNs:
978 0 905091

Book Trade Association Membership:
Association of Learned & Professional
Society Publishers

2387

**INSTITUTE OF PHYSICS &
ENGINEERING IN MEDICINE**
Fairmount House, 230 Tadcaster Road, York
YO24 1ES
Telephone: 01904 610821
Fax: 01904 612279
Email: office@ipem.ac.uk
Web Site: www.ipem.ac.uk

Personnel:
R. W. Neilson (General Secretary)
M. Goodall (Publications Co-ordinator)

Engineering; Medical (incl. Self Help &
Alternative Medicine); Physics; Scientific &
Technical

New Titles: 3 (2010), 7 (2011)
No of Employees: 10

Imprints, Series & ISBNs:
IPEM Report Series: 978 1 903613

Book Trade Association Membership:
Association of Learned & Professional
Society Publishers

2388

**INSTITUTION OF ENGINEERING AND
TECHNOLOGY (IET)**
Michael Faraday House, Six Hills Way,
Stevenage, Herts SG1 2AY
Telephone: 01438 767328
Fax: 01438 765515
Email: books@theiet.org
Web Site: www.theiet.org

Trade Enquiries & Orders:
PO Box 96, Stevenage, Herts SG1 2SD
Telephone: 01438 767328
Fax: 01438 767375
Email: sales@theiet.org
Web Site: www.theiet.org

Warehouse:
7 Fulton Close, Argyle Way, Stevenage,
Herts
Telephone: 01438 355029
Fax: 01438 355034

Personnel:
Daniel Smith (Head of Academic Publishing)
Amanda Weaver (Head of Practitioner
Publishing)
Afroditi Forti (Sales Manager)

Academic & Scholarly; Computer Science;
Educational & Textbooks; Electronic
(Professional & Academic); Engineering;
Industry, Business & Management;
Scientific & Technical

Imprints, Series & ISBNs:
978 0 85296, 978 0 86341, 978 0 901223,
978 0 906048, 978 1 84919

Associated Companies:
USA: INSPEC Inc

Overseas Representation:
USA & Canada: Princeton Selling Group Inc,
Wayne, PA, USA

Book Trade Association Membership:
Booksellers Association; International
Group of Scientific, Medical & Technical
Publishers; Association of Learned &
Professional Society Publishers

2389

INTELLECT LTD
The Mill, Parnall Road, Fishponds, Bristol
BS16 3JG
Telephone: 0117 958 9910
Fax: 0117 958 9911
Email: info@intellectbooks.com
Web Site: www.intellectbooks.com/

Distribution:
Gardners Books, 1 Whittle Drive,
Eastbourne BN23 6QH
Telephone: 01323 521777
Fax: 01323 521666
Email: custcare@gardners.com
Web Site: www.gardners.com

Personnel:
Masoud Yazdani (Chairman & Editor-in-
Chief)
May Yao (Operations Director)

Academic & Scholarly; Architecture &
Design; Cinema, Video, TV & Radio;
Computer Science; Educational &
Textbooks; Electronic (Educational);
Electronic (Professional & Academic);
Environment & Development Studies;
Gender Studies; History & Antiquarian;
Languages & Linguistics; Literature &
Criticism; Philosophy; Scientific & Technical;
Sociology & Anthropology; Theatre, Drama
& Dance

Imprints, Series & ISBNs:
978 0 89391, 978 1 56750, 978 1 84150,
978 1 871516
Advances in Art & Urban Futures
Advances in Human Computer Interaction
Bahá'í Books (series)
Changing Media, Changing Europe (series)
Computers and the History of Art (series)
Decode Books (series)
ECREA (series)
Elm Bank Publications
European Studies Series
Intellect Play Series
Progress in Neural Networks
Readings in Art and Design Education
(series)
Studies in Popular Culture (series)
Theatre & Consciousness (series)
Trends in Functional Programming
Venton

Overseas Representation:
Australasia: Inbooks, Sydney, NSW,
Australia
North America: University of Chicago Press,
Chicago, IL, USA

Book Trade Association Membership:
Independent Publishers Guild

2390

INTERNATIONAL MEDICAL PRESS
36 St Mary at Hill, London EC3R 8DU
Telephone: 020 7398 0700
Fax: 020 7398 0701
Email: info@intmedpress.com
Web Site: www.intmedpress.com

Academic & Scholarly; Electronic

(Professional & Academic); Medical (incl. Self Help & Alternative Medicine)

Imprints, Series & ISBNs:
978 1 901769

Book Trade Association Membership:
Publishers Association

2391

*INTERNATIONAL NETWORK FOR THE AVAILABILITY OF SCIENTIFIC PUBLICATIONS (INASP)
58 St Aldates, Oxford OX1 1ST
Telephone: 01865 249909
Fax: 01865 251060
Email: inasp@inasp.info
Web Site: www.inasp.info/

Personnel:
Tag McEntegart (Executive Director)
Julie Walker (Head of Publishing Support Senior Programme)
Sioux Cumming (Publishing Support Programme Officer)

Academic & Scholarly; Bibliography & Library Science; Educational & Textbooks; Electronic (Professional & Academic); Reference Books, Directories & Dictionaries

Imprints, Series & ISBNs:
978 1 902928

Book Trade Association Membership:
Association of Learned & Professional Society Publishers

2392

*IOP PUBLISHING
Dirac House, Temple Back, Bristol BS1 6BE
Telephone: 0117 929 7481
Fax: 0117 929 4318
Email: custserv@iop.org
Web Site: www.iop.org

Personnel:
Jerry Cowhig (Managing Director)
Michael Bray (Financial Director)
Karen O'Flaherty (Group Human Resources Director)
Nicola Gulley (Editorial Director)
James Walker (Group IT Director)

Computer Science; Electronic (Professional & Academic); Mathematics & Statistics; Physics; Scientific & Technical

Parent Company:
The Institute of Physics

Associated Companies:
USA: IOP Publishing Inc

Overseas Representation:
Japan (books): Eastern Book Service Inc, Tokyo, Japan
Japan (journals): Maruzen Co Ltd, Tokyo, Japan
Other Territories (books): Enquiries, Institute of Physics Publishing, Bristol, UK
Pakistan (books): Pak Book Corporation, Lahore, Pakistan
South East Asia, New Zealand & Australia (books): Hemisphere Publication Services, Singapore
USA & Canada (books): IOP Publishing, Williston, VT, USA
USA, Canada & Mexico (journals): American Institute of Physics, Melville, NY, USA

Book Trade Association Membership:
Publishers Association; International Group of Scientific, Medical & Technical Publishers; Association of Learned & Professional Society Publishers

2393

IPS EDUCATIONAL PUBLISHING
Unit 19, Edison Road, Aylesbury, Bucks HP19 8TE
Telephone: 01296 395777

Personnel:
Geoff Walters (Sales Manager)

Educational & Textbooks

New Titles: 9 (2010)

Book Trade Association Membership:
Publishers Association

2394

IRISH ACADEMIC PRESS
2 Brookside, Dundrum Road, Dublin 14, Republic of Ireland
Telephone: +353 (0)1 298 9937
Fax: +353 (0)1 298 2783
Email: info@iap.ie
Web Site: www.iap.ie

Academic & Scholarly; Biography & Autobiography; Gender Studies; History & Antiquarian; Literature & Criticism; Military & War; Politics & World Affairs; Religion & Theology; Sociology & Anthropology; Theatre, Drama & Dance

Imprints, Series & ISBNs:
978 0 7165

Book Trade Association Membership:
Publishing Ireland (Foilsiú Éireann)

2395

IRWELL PRESS LTD
59A High Street, Clophill, Beds MK45 4BE
Telephone: 01525 861888
Fax: 01525 862044
Email: George@irwellpress.co.uk
Web Site: www.irwellpress.co.uk

Personnel:
George Reeve (Director)
Chris Hawkins (Director)

Transport

Imprints, Series & ISBNs:
978 1 871608, 978 1 903266, 978 1 906919

Overseas Representation:
Australia: Train World Property, East Brighton, Vic, Australia

2396

ISIS PUBLISHING LTD
Unit 7, Centremead, Osney Mead, Oxford OX2 0ES
Telephone: 01865 250333
Fax: 01865 790358
Email: pauline.horne@isis-publishing.co.uk
Web Site: www.isis-publishing.co.uk

Distribution:
Ulverscroft Large Print Books Ltd, The Green, Bradgate Road, Anstey, Leicester LE7 7FU
Telephone: 0116 236 4325
Fax: 0116 234 0205
Email: sales@ulverscroft.co.uk
Web Site: www.ulverscroft.co.uk

Personnel:
Robert Thirlby (Chief Executive Director)
Pauline Horne (Distribution, General, Sales & Marketing Manager)
Lorna Dubose (Finance Manager)
Becky Curtis (Editorial – General Books Manager)
Catherine Thompson (Studio/Post Production Manager)

Audio Books; Biography & Autobiography; Crime; Fiction; Humour; Military & War; Poetry; Science Fiction

Imprints, Series & ISBNs:
978 0 7531, 978 1 4450, 978 1 84559, 978 1 85089, 978 1 85695

Parent Company:
Ulverscroft Group Ltd

Overseas Representation:
Australia: Ulverscroft Large Print Books (Australia) Pty Ltd, Crows Nest, NSW, Australia
Canada: Stricker Books, Toronto, Ont, Canada
Denmark: Bierman & Bierman A/S, Grindsted, Denmark
Japan: PIC, Tokyo, Japan
New Zealand: Ulverscroft Large Print Books Ltd, Fielding, New Zealand
Norway: Lydlitteratur, Nesoya, Norway
Republic of Ireland: Ulverscroft Large Print Books Ltd, Dublin, Republic of Ireland
South Africa (Audio): Book Talk Pty Ltd, Parkhurst, South Africa
Sweden: Bibliotekstjanst AB, Lund, Sweden
USA (Audio & Large print): Ulverscroft Large Print Books (USA) Inc, West Seneca, NY, USA

2397

THE ISLAMIC TEXTS SOCIETY
Miller's House, Kings Mill Lane, Great Shelford, Cambridge CB22 5EN
Telephone: 01223 842425
Fax: 01223 842425
Email: mail@its.org.uk
Web Site: www.its.org.uk

Distribution:
Orca Book Services Ltd, Unit A3, Fleets Corner, Poole, Dorset BH17 0HL
Telephone: 01202 665432
Fax: 01202 666219
Email: orders@orcabookservices.co.uk

Personnel:
Fatima Azzam (Trust Secretary)
Mohamed Eldakrouri (General Manager)

Academic & Scholarly; Law; Religion & Theology

No of Employees: 2

Overseas Representation:
USA: Independent Publishers Group (IPG), Chicago, IL, USA

Book Trade Association Membership:
Publishers Association

2398

IT GOVERNANCE PUBLISHING
Unit 3, Clive Court, Bartholomew's Walk, Cambridgeshire Business Park, Ely CB7 4EH
Telephone: 0845 070 1750
Fax: 01353 662667
Email: acalder@itgovernance.co.uk
Web Site: itgovernance.co.uk

Electronic (Professional & Academic)

New Titles: 34 (2010)

Parent Company:
UK: IT Governance Ltd

Book Trade Association Membership:
Publishers Association

2399

ITHACA PRESS
[Books on The Middle East]
8 Southern Court, South Street, Reading RG1 4QS
Telephone: 0118 959 7847

Fax: 0118 959 7356 (Trade Enquiries & Orders)
Web Site: www.ithacapress.co.uk

Representation (UK):
Compass Academic,
The Barley Mow Centre,
10 Barley Mow Passage, Chiswick, London W4 4PH
Telephone: 020 8994 6477

Personnel:
Nadia Khayat (Managing Director)
Arash Hejazi (Publisher)

Academic & Scholarly; Economics; Gender Studies; History & Antiquarian; Languages & Linguistics; Law; Literature & Criticism; Poetry; Politics & World Affairs; Religion & Theology; Sociology & Anthropology

New Titles: 5 (2010) , 16 (2011)
No of Employees: 4

Imprints, Series & ISBNs:
978 0 86372, 978 0 903729

Parent Company:
Garnet Publishing Ltd

Overseas Representation:
USA (academic): International Specialized Book Services Inc, Portland, OR, USA
Worldwide: Salt Way Publishing Ltd, Glos, UK

Book Trade Association Membership:
Independent Publishers Guild

2400

IVP
IVP Book Centre, Norton Street, Nottingham NG7 3HR
Telephone: 0115 978 1054
Fax: 0115 942 2694
Email: ivp@ivpbooks.com
Web Site: www.ivpbooks.com

Personnel:
Brian Wilson (Chief Executive Officer)
George Russell (Finance & Operations)

Academic & Scholarly; Biography & Autobiography; Reference Books, Directories & Dictionaries; Religion & Theology

No of Employees: 33

Imprints, Series & ISBNs:
Apollos: 978 0 85110, 978 0 85111, 978 1 84474
IVP: 978 0 85110, 978 0 85111, 978 1 84474

Distributor for:
Bible Society; Christian Medical Fellowship; Dorling Kindersley Religious; Good Book Company; HarperCollins Religious; Piquant
Australia: Matthias Media; Youthworks
Denmark: Scandinavia Publishing House
UK: Hodder Faith
USA: Crossway Books; IVP; NavPress

Overseas Representation:
East Africa: Keswick Book Society, Nairobi, Kenya
Netherlands: ASAF Import 3, Westervoort, Netherlands
New Zealand: Soul Distributors, Auckland, New Zealand
Philippines: Evangelical Outreach Inc, Quezon City, Philippines; Overseas Missionary Fellowship, Manila, Philippines
Singapore: Bethesda Book Centre, Singapore
South Africa: Protestant Book Centre, Cape Town, South Africa

Sweden: Din Bok –
Formsamlingsbokhandeln, Goteborg,
Sweden
USA: InterVarsity Press, Downers Grove, IL,
USA

Book Trade Association Membership:
Christian Suppliers' Group; Evangelical
Christian Publishers Association

2401

IWA PUBLISHING

[Wholly owned subsidiary of the
International Water Association (IWA)]
Alliance House, 12 Caxton Street, London
SW1H 0QS
Telephone: 020 7654 5500
Fax: 020 7654 5555
Email: publications@iwap.co.uk
Web Site: www.iwapublishing.com

Orders:
Portland Customer Services,
Commerce Way, Whitehall Industrial Estate,
Colchester CO2 8HP
Telephone: 01206 796351
Fax: 01206 799331
Email: sales@portland-services.com

Personnel:
Michael Dunn (*Publisher, Managing
Director & Commissioning Editor*)
Michelle Jones (*Publications Manager*)
Ian Morgan (*Marketing Manager*)
David Burns (*Digital Marketing Manager*)
Victoria Beddow (*Digital Publishing
Assistant*)

*Academic & Scholarly; Electronic
(Professional & Academic); Engineering;
Industry, Business & Management;
Reference Books, Directories &
Dictionaries; Scientific & Technical*

New Titles: 40 (2010), 35 (2011)

Imprints, Series & ISBNs:
978 1 84339, 978 1 900222, 978 1 78040

Parent Company:
International Water Association

Overseas Representation:
Australia & New Zealand: Australian Water
Association, Artarmon, NSW, Australia;
DA Information Services Pty Ltd,
Mitcham, Vic, Australia
*China, Korea, Vietnam, Thailand, Malaysia,
Philippines, Singapore:* Tony Poh, STM
Publisher Services Pte Ltd, Singapore
India: Kailash Balani, Aditya Books Pvt Ltd,
New Delhi, India
Japan: Kay Kato Associates, Kanagawa,
Japan
Latin America: Robert Wing, Systems Link
International, Opa-Locka, Florida, USA
Middle East: Zoe Kaviani, International
Publishing Services Ltd, Dubai, UAE
North America: Martin P. Hill Consulting,
New York, NY, USA
Taiwan: Ta Tong Book Co Ltd, Taipei, Taiwan

Book Trade Association Membership:
Association of Learned & Professional
Society Publishers

2402

JAMES & JAMES (PUBLISHERS) LTD

[an imprint of Third Millennium Information
Group]
2–5 Benjamin Street, London EC1M 5QL
Telephone: 020 7336 0144
Fax: 020 7608 1188
Email: mj@tmiltd.com
Web Site: www.tmiltd.com

Personnel:
Hamish MacGibbon (*Chairman*)

Academic & Scholarly; History &

*Antiquarian; Industry, Business &
Management*

New Titles: 15 (2010), 18 (2011)
No of Employees: 10
Annual Turnover: £1.07M

Imprints, Series & ISBNs:
978 1 906507

Parent Company:
Third Millennium Information Ltd

2403

JANUS PUBLISHING CO LTD

105–107 Gloucester Place, London
W1U 6BY
Telephone: 020 7486 6633
Fax: 020 7486 6090
Email: publisher@januspublishing.co.uk
Web Site: www.januspublishing.co.uk

Distribution/Sales:
25 Winnock Road, Colchester, Essex
CO1 2BG
Telephone: 01206 578856
Fax: 01206 573221
Email: sales@januspublishing.co.uk
Web Site: www.januspublishing.co.uk

Personnel:
Jeannie Leung (*Managing, Rights &
Permissions Director*)
Tina Brand (*Sales Director*)

*Academic & Scholarly; Biography &
Autobiography; Children's Books; Crime;
Do-It-Yourself; Economics; Educational &
Textbooks; Fiction; Fine Art & Art History;
History & Antiquarian; Humour; Literature
& Criticism; Magic & the Occult; Medical
(incl. Self Help & Alternative Medicine);
Military & War; Nautical; Philosophy;
Poetry; Politics & World Affairs; Religion &
Theology; Science Fiction; Sociology &
Anthropology; Sports & Games; Theatre,
Drama & Dance*

Imprints, Series & ISBNs:
Empiricus Books: 978 1 902835
Janus Books: 978 1 85756

Parent Company:
Junction Books Ltd

Overseas Representation:
India: Ane Books Pvt Ltd, New Delhi, India
Malaysia, Singapore & Brunei: Proof Line
(M) Sdn Bhd, Petaling Jaya, Malaysia
Philippines: IJ Sagun Enterprises Inc
South Africa: Vuga Booksellers, Durban,
South Africa

Book Trade Association Membership:
Booksellers Association; Independent
Publishers Guild

2404

JARNDYCE BOOKSELLERS

46 Great Russell Street, London WC1B 3PA
Telephone: 020 7631 4220
Fax: 020 7631 1882
Email: books@jarndyce.co.uk
Web Site: www.jarndyce.co.uk

Personnel:
Brian Lake (*Partner*)
Janet Nassau (*Partner*)

*Academic & Scholarly; Bibliography &
Library Science; Economics; Fiction;
Languages & Linguistics; Literature &
Criticism; Poetry; Reference Books,
Directories & Dictionaries; Sociology &
Anthropology*

Imprints, Series & ISBNs:
978 1 900718

Book Trade Association Membership:
Antiquarian Booksellers' Association;
Provincial Booksellers' Fairs Association

2405

JOLLY LEARNING LTD

Tailours House, High Road, Chigwell, Essex
IG7 6DL
Telephone: 020 8501 0405
Fax: 020 8500 1696
Email: chris@jollylearning.co.uk
Web Site: www.jollylearning.co.uk

Personnel:
Christopher Jolly (*Managing Director*)
Diane Harding (*Accounts Manager*)
Androula Stratton (*Marketing Manager*)
Angela Hockley (*Editorial Manager*)

*Educational & Textbooks; Electronic
(Educational)*

Annual Turnover: £3M

Imprints, Series & ISBNs:
978 1 84414, 978 1 870946, 978 1 903619

Overseas Representation:
USA: Jolly Learning Ltd, c/o American
International Distribution Corporation,
Williston, VT, USA

Book Trade Association Membership:
Independent Publishers Guild

2406

*JONES & BARTLETT INTERNATIONAL

The Exchange, Express Park, Bristol Road,
Bridgwater TA6 4RR W6 7PA
Telephone: 01278 427800
Fax: 01278 421077
Email: ldowning@jblearning.com
Web Site: www.jblearning.com

Warehouse, Trade Enquiries & Orders:
Macmillan Distribution (MDL), Brunel Road,
Houndmills, Basingstoke RG21 6XS
Telephone: 01256 329242
Fax: 01256 331413
Email: mdl@macmillan.co.uk
Web Site: www.macmillan-mdl.co.uk

Personnel:
Richard Warner (*Managing Director*)
Lorna Downing (*European Manager*)
Chris Gribble (*Sales Manager*)
Sarah Burne (*Operations Manager*)

*Biology & Zoology; Chemistry; Computer
Science; Educational & Textbooks;
Geography & Geology; Law; Mathematics
& Statistics; Medical (incl. Self Help &
Alternative Medicine); Physics; Psychology
& Psychiatry; Scientific & Technical; Sports &
Games; Vocational Training & Careers*

Imprints, Series & ISBNs:
978 0 7637, 978 0 86729

Parent Company:
USA: Jones & Bartlett Inc

2407

JORDAN PUBLISHING LTD

21 St Thomas Street, Bristol BS1 6JS
Telephone: 0117 918 1530
Fax: 0117 925 0486
Web Site: www.jordanpublishing.co.uk

Personnel:
Will Ricketts (*Managing Director*)
Stuart Harrison (*Head of Marketing & Sales*)
Achim Bosse (*Editorial Manager*)

*Accountancy & Taxation; Crime; Electronic
(Professional & Academic); Industry,
Business & Management; Law*

Imprints, Series & ISBNs:
Family Law: 978 0 85308, 978 1 84661
Jordans: 978 0 85308, 978 1 84661

Parent Company:
West of England Trust

2408

RICHARD JOSEPH PUBLISHERS LTD

PO Box 15, Torrington, Devon EX38 8ZJ
Telephone: 01805 625750
Fax: 01805 625376
Email: office@sheppardsconfidential.com
Web Site:
www.sheppardsconfidential.com

Personnel:
Richard Joseph (*Managing Director*)
(to be appointed) (*Compiler*)
Claire Hudson (*Production Manager*)

Reference Books, Directories & Dictionaries

Imprints, Series & ISBNs:
Sheppard: 978 1 872699

2409

S. KARGER AG

c/o London Liaison Office, 4 Rickett Street,
London SW6 1RU
Telephone: 020 7386 0500
Fax: 020 7610 3337
Email: uk@karger.ch
Web Site: www.karger.com

Personnel:
Dr Thomas Karger (*President*)
Gabriella Karger (*Chief Executive Officer*)
Ralph Weil (*Chief Executive Officer*)
Moritz Thommen (*Sales & Marketing*)
Hermann Vonlanthen (*Production*)
Thomas Nold (*Editor*)

*Mathematics & Statistics; Medical (incl. Self
Help & Alternative Medicine); Psychology &
Psychiatry*

New Titles: 150 (2010), 150 (2011)
No of Employees: 300

Imprints, Series & ISBNs:
978 3 8055

Parent Company:
Switzerland: S. Karger AG

Overseas Representation:
Australia: DA Information Services Pty Ltd,
Mitcham, Vic, Australia
Baltic States: Bookshop Krisostomus, Tartu,
Estonia
China & Taiwan: Karger China, Beijing, P. R.
of China
France: Librairie Médi-Sciences SARL, Paris,
France
Germany: S. Karger GmbH, Freiburg,
Germany
*Gulf Council countries, Iran, Middle East,
North Africa & Turkey:* Trans Middle East
International Distribution Co Ltd,
Amman, Jordan
India, Bangladesh & Sri Lanka: Medscience
India, New Delhi, India
Japan: Karger Japan Inc, Tokyo, Japan
Pakistan: Tahir M. Lodhi, Lahore, Pakistan
Republic of Ireland: S. Karger AG, London,
UK
Singapore: APAC Publishers Services Pte
Ltd, Singapore
South & Central America: Cranbury
International LLC, Montpelier, VT, USA
*South Africa, Botswana, Namibia,
Zimbabwe:* Medical Book Marketing,
Craighall, South Africa
South East Asia: Karger Regional Office,
Malaysia
Switzerland (Head Office): S. Karger AG,
Basel, Switzerland
Thailand: S. Karger AG / Karger Libri,
Bangkok, Thailand

USA: S. Karger Publishers Inc, Unionville, USA

2410

KARNAC BOOKS LTD
118 Finchley Road, London NW3 5HT
Telephone: 020 7431 1075
Fax: 020 7435 9076
Email: shop@karnacbooks.com
Web Site: www.karnacbooks.com

Personnel:
Oliver Rathbone *(Managing Director)*
Alex Massey *(Sales Director)*

Gender Studies; Psychology & Psychiatry

New Titles: 80 (2010) , 90 (2011)
No of Employees: 11

Imprints, Series & ISBNs:
Clunie Press: 978 0 946439, 978 1 85575
Harris Meltzer Trust: 978 1 85575
Institute of Psycho-Analysis, London: 978 0 946439, 978 1 85575
International Psychoanalytical Association: 978 1 85575
Karnac Books: 978 0 946439, 978 1 85575, 978 1 78049
Library of Analytical Psychology: 978 0 946439, 978 1 85575
Maresfield Library: 978 0 946439, 978 1 85575
Systemic Thinking Theory & Practice Series: 978 0 946439, 978 1 85575
Tavistock Clinic Series: 978 1 85575
Tavistock Institute of Marital Studies (TIMS): 978 0 946439, 978 1 85575
UKCP Series: 978 1 85575
Winnicott Studies (Series): 978 0 946439, 978 1 85575

Distributor for:
Carl Auer International; Tavistock Institute of Marital Studies; Zeig Tucker & Co

Book Trade Association Membership:
Booksellers Association; Independent Publishers Guild

2411

KENYON-DEANE
10 Station Road Industrial Estate, Colwall, Malvern, Worcs WR13 6RN
Telephone: 01684 540154
Email: simon@cressrelles.co.uk
Web Site: www.cressrelles.co.uk

Personnel:
Leslie Smith *(Finance, Production, Editorial & Rights Manager)*
Simon Smith *(Sales & Marketing Manager)*

Theatre, Drama & Dance

New Titles: 3 (2010) , 3 (2011)
No of Employees: 2

Imprints, Series & ISBNs:
978 0 7155

Parent Company:
Cressrelles Publishing Co Ltd

Distributor for:
USA: Anchorage Press

Overseas Representation:
Australia: Origin Theatrical, Sydney, NSW, Australia
New Zealand: Play Bureau of New Zealand Ltd, New Plymouth, New Zealand
Republic of Ireland: Drama League of Ireland, Dublin, Republic of Ireland
South Africa: Dalro (Pty) Ltd, Braamfontein, South Africa
USA: Bakers Plays, Quincy, MA, USA

2412

KEW PUBLISHING
[Royal Botanic Gardens, Kew]
Herbarium, 3rd Floor Wing E,
Royal Botanic Gardens, Kew, Richmond, Surrey TW9 3AE
Telephone: 020 8332 5751 & 5776 (sales enquiries)
Fax: 020 8332 5646
Email: publishing@kew.org
Web Site: www.kew.org & www.kewbooks.com

Personnel:
Gina Fullerlove *(Head of Publishing)*
John Harris *(Sales, Marketing & Business Development)*
Lloyd Kirton *(Production Controller)*
Lydia White *(Publishing Assistant)*

Academic & Scholarly; Biology & Zoology; Children's Books; Fine Art & Art History; Gardening; Natural History; Reference Books, Directories & Dictionaries; Scientific & Technical

New Titles: 20 (2010) , 16 (2011)
No of Employees: 10
Annual Turnover: £500,000

Imprints, Series & ISBNs:
978 1 84246

Parent Company:
UK: Royal Botanic Gardens, Kew

Overseas Representation:
All territories (excluding USA, Canada & Mexico): Marston Book Services Ltd, Abingdon, Oxon, UK
USA, Canada & Mexico: University of Chicago Press, Chicago, IL, USA

Book Trade Association Membership:
Independent Publishers Guild; Association of Cultural Enterprises

2413

*HILDA KING EDUCATIONAL
Ashwells Manor Drive, Penn, Bucks HP10 8EU
Telephone: 01494 813947 & 817947
Fax: 01494 813947
Email: rkinged@aol.com
Web Site: www.hildaking.co.uk

Personnel:
Hilda King *(Director)*
R. E. King *(Executive)*

Educational & Textbooks

Imprints, Series & ISBNs:
978 1 873533

2414

LAURENCE KING PUBLISHING LTD
361–373 City Road, London EC1V 1LR
Telephone: 020 7841 6900
Fax: 020 7841 6939
Email: enquiries@laurenceking.com
Web Site: www.laurenceking.com

Personnel:
Nick Perren *(Chairman)*
Laurence King *(Managing Director)*
John Stoddart *(Financial Director)*
Felicity Awdry *(Production Director)*
Philip Cooper *(Editorial Director)*
Kara Hattersley-Smith *(Editorial – College & Fine Art Director)*
Janet Pilch *(Rights Manager)*
Lewis Gill *(Publicity Manager)*
Simon Gwynn *(Sales Manager)*
Eleanor Muir *(Marketing Manager)*
Amy Capelin *(Rights Manager)*

Architecture & Design; Fashion & Costume; Fine Art & Art History

New Titles: 60 (2010) , 70 (2011)
No of Employees: 44

Imprints, Series & ISBNs:
Portfolio (series)
Portfolio Skills (series)

Book Trade Association Membership:
Publishers Association

2415

THE KING'S ENGLAND PRESS
Cambertown House, Commercial Road, Goldthorpe, Rotherham S63 9BL
Telephone: 01484 663790
Fax: 01484 663790
Email: steve@kingsengland.com
Web Site: www.kingsengland.com & www.pottypoets.com

Personnel:
Steve Rudd *(Managing Director)*
Debbie Nunn *(Company Secretary)*

Archaeology; Children's Books; History & Antiquarian; Poetry; Travel & Topography

Imprints, Series & ISBNs:
978 1 872438

2416

JESSICA KINGSLEY PUBLISHERS
116 Pentonville Road, London N1 9JB
Telephone: 020 7833 2307
Fax: 020 7837 2917
Email: post@jkp.com
Web Site: www.jkp.com

Trade Enquiries & Orders:
Macmillan Distribution (MDL), Brunel Road, Houndmills, Basingstoke, Hants RG21 6XS
Telephone: 01256 302985
Fax: 01256 841426
Email: trade@macmillan.co.uk
Web Site: www.macmillandistribution.co.uk

Personnel:
Jessica Kingsley *(Managing Director)*
Dee Brigham *(Company Secretary)*
Helen Longmate *(Marketing and Sales Director & Rights Manager)*
Jemima Kingsley *(Director)*
Despina Pechlivanidis *(Sales Manager)*
Octavia Kingsley *(Production Director)*

Academic & Scholarly; Children's Books; Educational & Textbooks; Health & Beauty; Law; Medical (incl. Self Help & Alternative Medicine); Psychology & Psychiatry; Religion & Theology; Sociology & Anthropology; Sports & Games; Vocational Training & Careers

Imprints, Series & ISBNs:
Children in Charge: 978 1 85302
Community, Culture and Change: 978 1 84310
Forensic Focus: 978 1 85302
Jessica Kingsley Publishers: 978 1 84310, 978 1 85302
Research Highlights in Social Work: 978 1 85302
Singing Dragon: 978 1 84819

Associated Companies:
USA: Jessica Kingsley Publishers Inc

Overseas Representation:
Australia & New Zealand: Footprint Books Pty, Warriewood, NSW, Australia
Canada: UBC Press, Toronto, Ontario, Canada
Europe: Durnell Marketing Ltd, Tunbridge Wells, UK
Japan: United Publishers Services Ltd

Singapore, Malaysia, Hong Kong, Taiwan, China, Philippines & Korea: Taylor and Francis, Singapore
USA: Jessica Kingsley Publishers Inc, Philadelphia, USA

Book Trade Association Membership:
Publishers Association; Educational Publishers Council

2417

SEAN KINGSTON PUBLISHING
57 Orchard Way, Wantage, Oxon OX12 8ED
Telephone: 01235 770787
Email: mail@seankingston.co.uk
Web Site: www.seankingston.co.uk/publishing.html

Personnel:
Dr Sean Kingston *(Publisher)*
Selina Kingston *(Marketing)*

Academic & Scholarly; Sociology & Anthropology

New Titles: 6 (2010) , 6 (2011)
No of Employees: 2

Imprints, Series & ISBNs:
978 0 9545572, 978 0 9556400, 978 1 907774

2418

KOGAN PAGE LTD
120 Pentonville Road, London N1 9JN
Telephone: 020 7278 0433
Fax: 020 7837 6348
Email: kpinfo@koganpage.com
Web Site: www.koganpage.com

Distribution Centre:
The Book Service Ltd, Colchester Road, Frating Green, Colchester, Essex CO7 7DW
Telephone: +44 (0)1206 256000
Fax: +44 (0)1206 255715
Web Site: www.thebookservice.co.uk

Personnel:
Philip Kogan *(Chairman)*
Helen Kogan *(Managing Director)*
Mark Briars *(Financial Director)*
Martin Klopstock *(Publishing Services Director)*
Matthew Smith *(Publishing Director)*
John Sadler *(Commercial Director)*

Academic & Scholarly; Accountancy & Taxation; Economics; Educational & Textbooks; Electronic (Educational); Electronic (Professional & Academic); Industry, Business & Management; Reference Books, Directories & Dictionaries; Transport; Vocational Training & Careers

New Titles: 145 (2010) , 145 (2011)

Imprints, Series & ISBNs:
978 0 7494

Overseas Representation:
Australia & NZ: Woodslane
China: China Publisher Services
Ghana: EPP
Japan, Taiwan & Philippines: The White Partnership
Nigeria: Rombic
Singapore & Malaysia: Pansing
South Africa: Book Promotions
UK: Compass Academic
USA & Canada: Kogan Page USA, Philadelphia, USA

Book Trade Association Membership:
Publishers Association; Independent Publishers Guild; Data Publishers Association

2419

KUBE PUBLISHING LTD
Markfield Conference Centre, Ratby Lane,
Markfield, Leicestershire LE67 9SY
Telephone: 01530 249230
Fax: 01530 249656
Email: info@kubepublishing.com
Web Site: www.kubepublishing.com

Personnel:
Mr Haris Ahmad (Director)
Mr Anwar Cara (Sales & Production
    Executive)
Mr Khalid Manzoor (Distribution & Sales
    Executive)
Miss Rufeedah Cara (Administration)
Mr Yahya Birt (Commissioning Editor)

Academic & Scholarly; Audio Books;
Children's Books; Economics; Educational &
Textbooks; Fiction; Law; Religion &
Theology

New Titles: 11 (2010) , 13 (2011)
No of Employees: 8

Imprints, Series & ISBNs:
The Islamic Foundation: 978 0 86037
Kube Publishing: 978 1 84774
Revival: 978 0 9536768

Parent Company:
UK: The Islamic Foundation

Distributor for:
Pakistan: Institute of Policy Studies; Islamic
    Book Publishers
USA: Foundation for Islamic Knowledge;
    International Institute of Islamic Thought

Overseas Representation:
Middle East: CIEL S.a.r.l, Beirut, Lebanon
Pakistan: Paradise Books & Distribution,
    Karachi, Pakistan
USA & Canada: Consortium Sales &
    Distribution, Minneapolis, MN, USA

2420

KYLE BOOKS
23 Howland Street, London W1T 4AY
Telephone: 020 7692 7215
Fax: 020 7692 7260
Email: general.enquiries@kylebooks.com
Web Site: www.kylebooks.com

Distribution:
Littlehampton Book Services Ltd,
Faraday Close, Durrington, West Sussex
BN13 3RB
Telephone: 01903 828800
Fax: 01903 828801
Email: orders@lbsltd.co.uk
Web Site: www.lbsltd.co.uk

Personnel:
Kyle Cathie (Managing Director)
Julia Barder (Sales & Marketing Director)
Catherine Heygate (Rights Director)
Judith Hannam (Senior Commissioning
    Editor)

Cookery, Wines & Spirits; Crafts & Hobbies;
Gardening; Health & Beauty; Reference
Books, Directories & Dictionaries; Sports &
Games

Imprints, Series & ISBNs:
978 1 85626
Kyle Books: 978 0 85783

Distributor for:
UK: Duncan Petersen Publishing Ltd

Overseas Representation:
Australia: Simon & Schuster (Australia) Pty
    Ltd, Pymble, NSW, Australia
India: Penguin Books India, New Delhi, India
New Zealand: New Holland Publishers (NZ)
    Ltd, Auckland, New Zealand

Singapore: Pansing Distribution, Singapore
South Africa: Penguin Books South Africa
    (Pty) Ltd, Johannesburg, South Africa
USA & Canada: National Book Network,
    Lanham, MD, USA

2421

*PETER LANG LTD
Evenlode Court, Main Road,
Long Hanborough, Witney, Oxon OX29 8SZ
Telephone: 01993 880088
Fax: 01993 882040
Email: oxford@peterlang.com
Web Site: www.peterlang.net

Personnel:
Graham Speake (Publishing Director)
Hannah Godfrey (Commissioning Editor)
Nick Reynolds (Commissioning Editor)
Mette Bundgaard (Production Manager)
Peggy Struck (Sales & Marketing Manager)

Academic & Scholarly

Imprints, Series & ISBNs:
978 3 03911

Parent Company:
Switzerland: Peter Lang

Associated Companies:
Belgium: P. I. E. – Peter Lang SA
Germany: Peter Lang GmbH
USA: Peter Lang Publishing Inc

Overseas Representation:
Worldwide: Peter Lang, Pieterlen,
    Switzerland

Book Trade Association Membership:
Independent Publishers Guild

2422

LAPWING PUBLICATIONS
1 Ballysillan Drive, Belfast BT14 8HQ
Telephone: 028 9050 0796
Email: lapwing.poetry@ntlworld.com
Web Site: www.lapwingpoetry.com.

Personnel:
Dennis Greig (Editor & Production
    Management)
Rene Greig (Editor)
Adam Rudden (Editor & Internet Services
    Management)

Poetry

New Titles: 40 (2010) , 39 (2011)
No of Employees: 0

Imprints, Series & ISBNs:
978 1 898472, 978 1 905425, 978 1
    907276

2423

LAW REPORTS INTERNATIONAL LTD
Eden House, 2 St Aldate's Courtyard,
Oxford OX1 1BN
Telephone: 01865 794638
Fax: 01865 794628
Email: lawreports@clara.co.uk
Web Site: www.lawreports.com

Personnel:
Mrs Sarah Smith (Production Editor)
Mrs Sarah Snell (Senior Editor)
Julia Savage (Editor)
Jack Robinson (Editor)
Peter Bowden (Editor)
Dr Alan Milner (Editor in Chief & Director)
Mrs Patricia Milner (Company Secretary &
    Director)

Law

New Titles: 10 (2011)
No of Employees: 7

Imprints, Series & ISBNs:
978 1 870584, 978 1 902907, 978 1
    906585

Distributor for:
Zambia: The Zambia Law Journal

2424

LAW SOCIETY PUBLISHING
113 Chancery Lane, London WC2A 1PL
Telephone: 020 7841 5472
Fax: 020 7841 5450
Email: publishing@lawsociety.org.uk
Web Site: www.lawsociety.org.uk/
    bookshop

Distribution:
Prolog, PO Box 99, Sudbury, Suffolk
CO10 2SN
Telephone: 0870 850 1422
Fax: 01787 313995

Personnel:
Stephen Honey (Publishing Manager)
Sarah Foulkes (Production Manager)
Millie Patel (Marketing Manager)
Janet Noble (Senior Commissioning Editor)
Ben Mullane (Commissioning Editor)
Simon Blackett (Commissioning Editor)
Sarah Marling (Marketing Executive)

Law

New Titles: 24 (2010) , 25 (2011)
No of Employees: 500

Imprints, Series & ISBNs:
The Law Society: 978 1 85328

Parent Company:
The Law Society

Book Trade Association Membership:
Data Publishers Association

2425

LEARNING MATTERS LTD
20 Cathedral Yard, Exeter EX1 1HB
Telephone: 01392 215560
Fax: 01392 215561
Email: info@learningmatters.co.uk
Web Site: www.learningmatters.co.uk

Distribution:
BEBC Distribution, 15 Albion Close,
Parkstone, Poole BH12 3LL
Telephone: 0845 230 9000
Fax: 01202 715556
Email: learningmatters@bebc.co.uk
Web Site: www.bebc.co.uk

Personnel:
Jonathan Harris (Managing Director)
Zoe Seaton (Sales & Marketing Manager)

Academic & Scholarly; Educational &
Textbooks; Electronic (Professional &
Academic); Psychology & Psychiatry;
Sociology & Anthropology

Imprints, Series & ISBNs:
978 0 85725, 978 1 84445, 978 1 903300

Overseas Representation:
Australia: Palgrave Macmillan, South Yarra,
    Vic, Australia
Barbados: Days Bookstore, Bridgetown,
    Barbados
Ghana: EPP Books Services Ltd, Accra,
    Ghana
Jamaica: The Book Merchant Ltd, Kingston,
    Jamaica
Malaysia: APD Kuala Lumpur Pte Ltd,
    Selangor, Malaysia
Singapore: APD Singapore Pte Ltd,
    Singapore
USA: ISBS, Portland, OR, USA

Book Trade Association Membership:
Independent Publishers Guild

2426

*LEARNING TOGETHER
18 Shandon Park, Belfast BT5 6NW
Telephone: 028 9040 2086
Fax: 028 9040 2086
Email: info@learningtogether.co.uk
Web Site: www.learningtogether.co.uk

Distribution:
Orca Book Services, Unit A3, Fleets Corner,
Poole, Dorset BH17 0HL
Telephone: 01202 665432
Fax: 01202 666219
Email: mail@orcabookservices.co.uk

Representation:
c/o Alan Goodworth, Roundhouse Group,
Millstone, Limers Lane, Northam,
North Devon EX39 2RG
Telephone: 01237 474474
Fax: 01237 474774
Email: roundhouse.group@ukgateway.net

Personnel:
Janet McConkey (Managing Director)
Stephen McConkey (Author/Publisher)

Educational & Textbooks

Imprints, Series & ISBNs:
Practice Tests In Series: 978 1 873385

Book Trade Association Membership:
Publishers Association; Educational
Publishers Council

2427

*LEATHERHEAD FOOD RESEARCH
Randalls Road, Leatherhead, Surrey
KT22 7RY
Telephone: 01372 822556 & 822241
    (Sales)
Fax: 01372 822272
Email: publications@leatherheadfood.com
Web Site: www.leatherheadfood.com

Personnel:
Dr Paul Berryman (Chief Executive Officer)
Victoria Emerton (Knowledge Services
    Manager)

Law; Scientific & Technical

Imprints, Series & ISBNs:
978 0 905748, 978 1 904007, 978 1
    905224

2428

LEGAL ACTION GROUP
242 Pentonville Road, London N1 9UN
Telephone: 020 7833 2931
Fax: 020 7837 6094
Email: lag@lag.org.uk
Web Site: www.lag.org.uk

Personnel:
Steve Hynes (Director)
Esther Pilger (Publisher)
Nim Moorthy (Marketing Manager)
Adam Wilson (Customer Services Executive)
Andrew Troszok (Customer Services
    Executive)

Law

New Titles: 4 (2010) , 35 (2011)
No of Employees: 9
Annual Turnover: £800,000

Imprints, Series & ISBNs:
978 0 905099, 978 1 903307

Book Trade Association Membership:
Independent Publishers Guild

2429

*LEGEND PRESS
2 London Wall Buildings, London
EC2M 5UU
Telephone: 020 7448 5137
Email: info@legendpress.co.uk
Web Site: www.legendpress.co.uk

Personnel:
Tom Chalmers (Managing Director)

Fiction

Imprints, Series & ISBNs:
978 0 9551032, 978 1 906558

Book Trade Association Membership:
Independent Publishers Guild

2430

*LETTERLAND INTERNATIONAL LTD
Stonebridge House, 28–32 Bridge Street,
Leatherhead, Surrey KT22 8BZ
Telephone: 01223 262675
Fax: 01223 264126
Email: info@letterland.com
Web Site: www.letterland.com

Distribution:
Grantham Book Services, Trent Road,
Grantham, Lincs NG31 7XQ
Telephone: 01476 541080
Fax: 01476 541061
Email: orders@letterland.com
Web Site:
www.granthambookservices.co.uk

Personnel:
Mark Wendon (Director)
Thomas Wendon (Marketing Director)
Jonathan Wendon (Production Manager)
Lisa Chapman (Editor)

Children's Books; Educational & Textbooks;
Electronic (Educational); English as a
Foreign Language

Imprints, Series & ISBNs:
978 0 907345, 978 1 86209

Overseas Representation:
Australia: Ed Source, Bassendean, WA,
   Australia
Canada: Educan, Weston, Ont, Canada
China: Ian Taylor & Associates, Beijing, P. R.
   of China
Hong Kong: ETC Educational Technology
   Connection (HK) Ltd, Tai Koo Shing,
   Hong Kong
Japan: J & N English Club, Shizuoka-ken,
   Japan
Korea: Infobooks, Seoul, Republic of Korea
Middle East & North Africa: International
   Publishers Representatives (IPR) Ltd,
   Nicosia, Cyprus
New Zealand: Wakelin Educational Services,
   Ashburton, New Zealand
Nigeria: Kcxploits, Lagos, Nigeria
Singapore: Tumble Tots (Asia) Pty Ltd,
   Singapore, Singapore
South Africa: Educational Ideas,
   Johannesburg, South Africa
Taiwan: Hello! Book Club, Taipei County,
   Taiwan
USA: Letterland International, Enfield, NH,
   USA

Book Trade Association Membership:
Publishers Association; Educational
Publishers Council; Independent Publishers
Guild; International Reading Association

2431

DEWI LEWIS PUBLISHING
8 Broomfield Road, Heaton Moor,
Stockport SK4 4ND
Telephone: 0161 442 9450
Fax: 0161 442 9450
Email: mail@dewilewispublishing.com

Web Site: www.dewilewispublishing.com

Trade Enquiries & Orders:
Turnaround, Unit 3 Olympia Trading Estate,
Coburg Road, London N22 6TZ
Telephone: 020 8829 3000
Fax: 020 8881 5088
Email: orders@turnaround-uk.com
Web Site: www.turnaround-uk.com

Personnel:
Dewi Lewis (Publisher)
Caroline Warhurst (Sales & Marketing
   Director)

Architecture & Design; Fine Art & Art
History; Illustrated & Fine Editions;
Photography; Reference Books, Directories
& Dictionaries; Sports & Games

Imprints, Series & ISBNs:
978 1 899235, 978 1 904587

Overseas Representation:
Germany: Visual Books Sales Agency, Berlin,
   Germany
New Zealand: Southern Publishers Group,
   Auckland, New Zealand
North America: Consortium Book Sales &
   Distribution Inc, St Paul, MN, USA

2432

LEXUS LTD
60 Brook Street, Glasgow G40 2AB
Telephone: 0141 556 0440
Fax: 0141 556 2202
Email:
peterterrell@lexusforlanguages.co.uk
Web Site: www.lexusforlanguages.co.uk

Personnel:
Peter Terrell (Publisher)
Elfreda Crehan (Production Editor)

Children's Books; Educational & Textbooks;
Languages & Linguistics; Reference Books,
Directories & Dictionaries

New Titles: 2 (2011)
No of Employees: 2

Imprints, Series & ISBNs:
Chinese Classroom: 978 1 904737
Travelmates: 978 1 904737

2433

*LIBERTIES PRESS
Guinness Enterprise Centre, Taylor's Lane,
Dublin 8, Republic of Ireland
Telephone: +353 (0)1 415 1286
Email: sean@libertiespress.com
Web Site: www.libertiespress.com

Personnel:
Sean O'Keeffe (Director)
Peter O'Connell (Director)

Architecture & Design; Cookery, Wines &
Spirits; Health & Beauty; History &
Antiquarian; Literature & Criticism; Politics
& World Affairs; Religion & Theology;
Sports & Games

Imprints, Series & ISBNs:
978 0 9545335, 978 1 905483

Parent Company:
Republic of Ireland: Liberties Media Ltd

Book Trade Association Membership:
Publishing Ireland (Foilsiú Éireann)

2434

LIBRARIO PUBLISHERS LTD
Brough House, Kinloss, Moray IV36 2UA
Telephone: 01343 850178
Email: amlawson@librario.com
Web Site: www.librario.com

Personnel:
Mark Lawson (Managing Director)
Mrs Rosemary Lawson (Sales Director)
Mrs Janet Barcis (Bookkeeper)

Crime; Fiction; History & Antiquarian;
Medical (incl. Self Help & Alternative
Medicine); Military & War; Natural History;
Nautical

Imprints, Series & ISBNs:
978 0 9542960, 978 1 904440, 978 1
   906775

Overseas Representation:
UDSA / Canada: Creative Books
   International

2435

*LIFE OF RILEY PRODUCTIONS LTD
62 Wilson Street, London EC2A 2BU
Telephone: 01787 478337

Electronic (Educational)

2436

THE LILLIPUT PRESS LTD
62–63 Sitric Road, Arbour Hill, Dublin 7,
Republic of Ireland
Telephone: +353 (0)1 671 1647
Fax: +353 (0)1 671 1233
Email: info@lilliputpress.ie
Web Site: www.lilliputpress.ie

Distributors (Trade Orders):
Gill & Macmillan, Hume Avenue,
Park West, Dublin 12, Republic of Ireland
Telephone: +353 (0)1 500 9500
Fax: +353 (0)1 500 9599

Personnel:
Antony Farrell (Managing Director &
   Publisher)
David Dickson (Director)
Vincent Hurley (Director)
Terence Brown (Director)
Vivienne Guinness (Director)
Kathy Gilfillan (Director)
Daniel Caffrey (Director)
Fiona Dunne (Editor)
Kitty Lyddon (Office Manager)

Academic & Scholarly; Architecture &
Design; Biography & Autobiography;
Fiction; Fine Art & Art History; History &
Antiquarian; Illustrated & Fine Editions;
Literature & Criticism; Music; Photography;
Reference Books, Directories & Dictionaries

Imprints, Series & ISBNs:
978 0 946640, 978 1 84351, 978 1
   874675, 978 1 901866

Distributor for:
UK: The Houyhnhnm Press

Overseas Representation:
France: Lora Fountain Literary Agent, Paris,
   France
UK: Central Books Ltd, London, UK

Book Trade Association Membership:
Publishing Ireland (Foilsiú Éireann)

2437

LION HUDSON PLC
Wilkinson House, Jordan Hill Road, Oxford
OX2 7DR
Telephone: 01865 302750
Fax: 01865 302757
Email: info@lionhudson.com
Web Site: www.lionhudson.com

Personnel:
Alice Lawhead (Non-Executive Director)
Paul Clifford (Managing Director)
Nicholas Jones (Deputy Managing Director)
Suzanne Wilson-Higgins (UK Sales &
   Marketing Director)

Roy McCloughry (Chairman)
Jonathan Carr (Production Manager)
Robert Wendover (Export Sales Manager)
Paul Whitton (International & Subsidiary
   Rights)
Caroline Gregory (Financial Controller)

Biography & Autobiography; Children's
Books; Educational & Textbooks; Fiction;
Religion & Theology

New Titles: 160 (2010), 155 (2011)
No of Employees: 53
Annual Turnover: £9M

Imprints, Series & ISBNs:
Aslan: 978 0 7459, 978 0 85648
Candle: 978 1 85985
Lion: 978 0 7459, 978 0 85648
Lion Children's: 978 0 7459, 978 0 85648
Monarch: 978 1 85424

Overseas Representation:
Australia: New Book Distributors, Sydney,
   Australia
New Zealand: New Holland Publishers (NZ)
   Ltd, Auckland, New Zealand
South Africa: Pearson Education, Cape
   Town, South Africa

Book Trade Association Membership:
Independent Publishers Guild

2438

LISU
Loughborough University, Loughborough,
Leics LE11 3TU
Telephone: 01509 635680
Fax: 01509 635699
Email: lisu@lboro.ac.uk
Web Site: www.lboro.ac.uk/departments/
   dis/lisu

Personnel:
Claire Creaser (Director)

Bibliography & Library Science; Reference
Books, Directories & Dictionaries

Imprints, Series & ISBNs:
978 0 948848, 978 1 905499
LISU Reports: 978 1 901786

Parent Company:
Loughborough University

2439

LITTLE, BROWN BOOK GROUP
100 Victoria Embankment, London
EC4Y 0DY
Telephone: 020 7911 8000
Fax: 020 7911 8100
Email: info@littlebrown.co.uk
Web Site: www.littlebrown.co.uk,
   www.orbitbooks.co.uk &
   www.virago.co.uk

Distribution Centre:
Littlehampton Book Services Ltd,
Faraday Close, Durrington, West Sussex
BN13 3RB
Telephone: 01903 828511
Fax: 01903 828801
Email: orders@lbsltd.co.uk

Personnel:
Ursula Mackenzie (Chief Executive Officer)
David Kent (Chief Operating Officer)
Diane Spivey (Rights Director)
Duncan Spilling (Design Director)
Robert Manser (Group Sales, Marketing &
   Publishing Director)
Richard Beswick (Managing Director – Little
   Brown & Abacus)
Tim Holman (Publisher – Orbit)
Lennie Goodings (Publisher – Virago)
Antonia Hodgson (Editor-in-Chief – Sphere
   non-fiction)
Nick Ross (Production Director)
Maddie Mogford (Legal Director)

Emily-Jane Taylor (Finance Director)
Rebecca Saunders (Editorial Director –
Sphere fiction)
Emma Beswetherick (Editorial Director –
Piatkus fiction)
Tim Whiting (Publishing Director – LB/
Abacus & Piatkus non-fiction)

Audio Books; Biography & Autobiography;
Crime; Fiction; History & Antiquarian;
Humour; Literature & Criticism; Military &
War; Music; Politics & World Affairs;
Psychology & Psychiatry; Science Fiction;
Sports & Games; Travel & Topography

New Titles: 500 (2010) , 550 (2011)
No of Employees: 145

Imprints, Series & ISBNs:
Abacus: 978 0 349
Atom: 978 1 904233, 978 1 905654
Audio Books: 978 1 4055
Bulfinch: 978 0 8212
Little, Brown: 978 0 316, 978 1 4087
Orbit: 978 1 84149, 978 1 85723
Piatkus: 978 0 7499
Sphere Hardbacks: 978 1 84744
Sphere Paperbacks: 978 0 7515
Virago: 978 1 84408, 978 1 85381, 978 1
86049

Parent Company:
France: Hachette Livre Group of Companies

Overseas Representation:
Africa: A–Z Africa Book Services,
Rotterdam, Netherlands
Australia: Hachette Livre Australia, Sydney,
NSW, Australia
Canada: Hachette Canada, New York, NY,
USA
Caribbean, Central & South America: Jerry
Carrillo Inc, USA
China: Wei Zhao, New York, NY, USA
France & Scandinavia: Melanie Boesen,
Hachette US, Denmark
Germany, Sweden & Middle East: Simon
McArt, Little, Brown Book Group,
London, UK
India: Hachette India, Gurgaon, India
Italy: Penguin Italia srl, Milan, Italy
Japan, Thailand, Indonesia, Hong Kong,
Korea & Taiwan: Gilles Fauveau, Japan
New Zealand: Hachette Livre New Zealand,
Auckland, New Zealand
Singapore & Malaysia: Penguin Books
Singapore, Jurong, Singapore
South Africa: Penguin Books SA (Pty) Ltd,
Denver Ext 4, South Africa
Spain & Portugal: Penguin Books SA,
Madrid, Spain
Switzerland, Belgium, Netherlands,
Gibraltar, Malta & Cyprus: Rachel Hurn,
Little, Brown Book Group, London, UK

Book Trade Association Membership:
Publishers Association; Booksellers
Association; Book Marketing Ltd

2440

LITTLE TIGER PRESS
[an imprint of Magi Publications]
1 The Coda Centre, 189 Munster Road,
London SW6 6AW
Telephone: 020 7385 6333
Fax: 020 7385 7333
Email: info@littletiger.co.uk
Web Site: www.littletigerpress.com

Distribution:
Macmillan Distribution (MDL), Brunel Road,
Houndmills, Basingstoke, Hants RG21 6XS
Telephone: 01256 302692
Fax: 01256 812558
Email: mdl@macmillan.co.uk

Personnel:
Monty Bhatia (Proprietor)
David Bucknor (Sales Director)
Aude Lavielle (Rights Director)
Yolande Denny (Production Director)

Jude Evans (Publisher)
Jill Coleman (Managing Director)

Children's Books

Imprints, Series & ISBNs:
Caterpillar Books: 978 1 84857
Little Tiger Press: 978 1 84506, 978 1
85430, 978 1 84895
Stripes Publishing: 978 1 84715

Parent Company:
Magi Publications

Overseas Representation:
Australia: Global Language Books, Yennora,
NSW, Australia
Malaysia, Singapore & Brunei: Pansing
Distribution Ptd Ltd, Times Centre,
Singapore
New Zealand: South Pacific Book
Distributors Ltd, Auckland, New Zealand
Southern Africa: Titles SA, Johannesburg,
South Africa

2441

**THE LITTMAN LIBRARY OF JEWISH
CIVILIZATION**
PO Box 645, Oxford OX2 0UJ
Telephone: 01865 514688
Fax: 01865 722964
Email: info@littman.co.uk
Web Site: www.littman.co.uk

Distribution:
NBN International, 10 Thornbury Road,
Plymouth PL6 7PY
Telephone: 01752 202300
Fax: 01752 202333
Email: orders@nbninternational.com
Web Site: www.nbninternational.com

Personnel:
Ludo Craddock (Chief Executive Officer)
Connie Webber (Managing Editor)
Colette Littman (Director)
Robert Littman (Director)

Academic & Scholarly; Biography &
Autobiography; Educational & Textbooks;
Fine Art & Art History; History &
Antiquarian; Literature & Criticism; Music;
Philosophy; Politics & World Affairs;
Religion & Theology; Sociology &
Anthropology; Theatre, Drama & Dance

New Titles: 9 (2010) , 10 (2011)

Imprints, Series & ISBNs:
978 1 874774, 978 1 904113, 978 1
906764

Overseas Representation:
Australia & New Zealand: DA Information
Services, Mitcham, Vic, Australia
Israel: The Hebrew University Magnes Press,
Jerusalem, Israel
USA & Canada: International Specialized
Book Services Inc, Portland, OR, USA

Book Trade Association Membership:
Independent Publishers Guild

2442

LIVERPOOL UNIVERSITY PRESS
4 Cambridge Street, Liverpool L69 7ZU
Telephone: 0151 794 2233
Fax: 0151 794 2235
Email: lup@liv.ac.uk
Web Site: http://www.liverpool-
unipress.co.uk

Sales & Distribution:
Marston Book Services, PO Box 269,
Abingdon, Oxon OX14 4YN
Telephone: 01235 465500
Fax: 01235 465555
Email: trade.order@marston.co.uk
Web Site: www.marston.co.uk

Personnel:
Anthony Cond (Managing Director)
Jennifer Howard (Sales & Marketing
Manager)
Justine Greig (Finance and Administration
Manager)
Helen Tookey (Production Manager)
Patrick Brereton (Production Editor)
Clare Hooper (Journals Publishing Manager)
Janet Smith (Sales & Marketing Co-
ordinator)
Alison Welsby (Commissioning Editor)
Charly Paige (Marketing Executive)
Karen Phair (Finance Assistant)

Academic & Scholarly; Architecture &
Design; Educational & Textbooks; Fine Art &
Art History; History & Antiquarian;
Languages & Linguistics; Literature &
Criticism; Poetry; Politics & World Affairs;
Science Fiction; Sociology & Anthropology

New Titles: 4050 (2010)
No of Employees: 9

Imprints, Series & ISBNs:
978 0 85323, 978 1 84631

Overseas Representation:
Australia and New Zealand: InBooks,
Frenchs Forest, NSW 2086, Australia
Benelux & Germany: Roy de Boo, Hooge
Mierde, Netherlands
Central & Latin America: InterMedia
Americana (IMA) Ltd, London, UK
Eastern and Central Europe and the ex-
Soviet Republics: Laszlo Horvath,
Budapest, Hungary
India: Viva Group, New Delhi, India
Malaysia: Yuha Associates, Selangor Darul
Ehsan, Malaysia
North America and Mexico: University of
Chicago Press, Chicago, USA
South East Asia, Korea, Taiwan, China and
Hong Kong: Tony Poh, STM Publisher
Services Pte Ltd, Yew Mei Green,
Singapore
Spain & Portugal: Iberian Book Services,
Madrid, Spain
Taiwan: Ta Tong Book Company Ltd, Taipei,
Taiwan
The Middle East, North Africa and Turkey:
Avicenna Partnership Ltd, Oxford, UK
UK and Ireland: Quantum Publishing Ltd,
London, UK

Book Trade Association Membership:
Independent Publishers Guild

2443

***LIVING TIME® MEDIA
INTERNATIONAL**
Units 18c–19c, Wem Business Park,
New Street, Wem, Shropshire SY4 5JX
Telephone: 01939 236623
Fax: 01939 234873 & 01743 244921
Email: livingtime@email.com
Web Site: www.livingtime.co.uk

Global Rights (for Europe & USA):
5 Portland Crescent, Shrewsbury,
Shropshire SY2 5NG
Telephone: 07877 851410
Fax: 01743 244921
Email: livingtime@europe.com
Web Site: www.livingtime.co.uk

Personnel:
Alderson Smith (Head of Publishing/Chief
Executive)
Edouard d'Araille (Editor-in-Chief)
John Hargreaves (International Sales
Executive)
James Hartley (Foreign & Subsidiary Rights
Executive)
Jack Goldstein (Film Rights Executive (USA))
Carolyn Eden (Children's Book Rights
Executive)

Academic & Scholarly; Biography &
Autobiography; Children's Books; Cinema,

Video, TV & Radio; Crime; Educational &
Textbooks; Electronic (Educational);
Electronic (Entertainment); English as a
Foreign Language; Fiction; History &
Antiquarian; Literature & Criticism;
Philosophy; Poetry; Psychology &
Psychiatry; Science Fiction

Imprints, Series & ISBNs:
Living Time® Digital: 978 1 906904
Living Time® Media International: 978 1
905820
Living Time® Press: 978 1 903331

Parent Company:
Living Time®

Associated Companies:
The Academy of the 3rd Millennium™;
Fortune Street®; Living Time Vision
(LTV); Living Time® America; Living
Time® Design; Living Time® Docufilms;
Living Time® Films Ltd; Living Time®
Legal; Living Time® Music

Overseas Representation:
Worldwide: Jack Goldstein, Living Time®
America, Hollywood, CA, USA

2444

LOGASTON PRESS
Little Logaston, Woonton, Almeley,
Herefordshire HR3 6QH
Telephone: 01544 327344
Email: logastonpress@btinternet.com
Web Site: www.logastonpress.co.uk

Personnel:
Andy Johnson (Proprietor)
Karen Johnson (Proprietor)

Archaeology; Architecture & Design; Fine
Art & Art History; Guide Books; History &
Antiquarian; Natural History; Reference
Books, Directories & Dictionaries

Imprints, Series & ISBNs:
Monuments in the Landscape Series: 978 0
9510242, 978 1 873827, 978 1 904396,
978 1 906663

2445

LOMOND BOOKS LTD
14 Freskyn Place,
East Mains Industrial Estate, Broxburn
EH52 5NF
Telephone: 01506 855955
Fax: 01506 855965
Email: sales@lomondbooks.co.uk
Web Site: www.lomondbooks.com

Personnel:
Trevor Maher (Director)
Duncan Baxter (Sales Director)
Jackie Brown (Operations Director)
Arthur Robertson (Buyer)

Children's Books; Cookery, Wines & Spirits;
Crafts & Hobbies; Guide Books; History &
Antiquarian; Humour; Illustrated & Fine
Editions; Natural History; Reference Books,
Directories & Dictionaries

Imprints, Series & ISBNs:
978 1 84204

Book Trade Association Membership:
Booksellers Association

2446

LONDUBH BOOKS
18 Casimir Avenue, Harold's Cross,
Dublin 6W, Republic of Ireland
Email: info@londubh.ie
Web Site: www.londubh.ie

Distribution:
Compass IBS, Naas, Co Kildare,
Republic of Ireland

Personnel:
Jo O'Donoghue (*Publisher*)
David Parfrey (*Production*)

Biography & Autobiography; Health & Beauty; History & Antiquarian; Medical (incl. Self Help & Alternative Medicine); Travel & Topography

New Titles: 16 (2010) , 8 (2011)
No of Employees: 2

Imprints, Series & ISBNs:
978 1 907535

Book Trade Association Membership:
Publishing Ireland (Foilsiú Éireann)

2447 ▬

LUATH PRESS LTD
543/2 Castlehill, The Royal Mile, Edinburgh EH1 2ND
Telephone: 0131 225 4326
Fax: 0131 225 4324
Email: gavin.macdougall@luath.co.uk
Web Site: www.luath.co.uk

Distribution:
HarperCollins, Westerhill Road, Bishopbriggs, Glasgow G64 2QR
Telephone: 0870 787 1722
Fax: 0870 787 1723
Email: enquiries@harpercollins.co.uk
Web Site: b2b.harpercollins.co.uk

Personnel:
Gavin MacDougall (*Director, Rights & Overseas Distribution*)
Christine Wilson (*Production & Editorial*)
Hannah Sim (*Sales & Marketing*)
Robin Jones (*Press & Events*)

Biography & Autobiography; Children's Books; Cinema, Video, TV & Radio; Cookery, Wines & Spirits; Crime; Economics; Fiction; Gardening; Geography & Geology; Guide Books; History & Antiquarian; Humour; Languages & Linguistics; Literature & Criticism; Magic & the Occult; Medical (incl. Self Help & Alternative Medicine); Military & War; Music; Natural History; Photography; Poetry; Politics & World Affairs; Sports & Games; Theatre, Drama & Dance; Travel & Topography; Veterinary Science

New Titles: 30 (2010) , 30 (2011)

Imprints, Series & ISBNs:
Let's Explore: 978 0 946487, 978 1 84282
Luath: 978 0 946487, 978 1 84282, 978 1 906307, 978 1 905222, 978 1 906817, 978 1 908373
Luath Guides to Scotland: 978 0 946487
Luath Storyteller: 978 1 84282, 978 1 905222
On the Trail of: 978 0 946487, 978 1 84282
The Quest for: 978 0 946487, 978 1 84282
Scots in
Viewpoints
Walk with Luath: 978 0 946487
Wild Lives: 978 0 946487

Overseas Representation:
Australia & New Zealand: Luath Press Ltd, Edinburgh, UK
Canada: McArthur & Co, Toronto, Canada
USA: Ingram Publisher Services, Nashville, TN, USA

Book Trade Association Membership:
Publishing Scotland; Independent Publishers Guild

2448 ▬

LUND HUMPHRIES
Ashgate Publishing Group, Wey Court East, Union Road, Farnham, Surrey GU9 7PT
Telephone: 01252 331551
Fax: 01252 736736

Email: info@lundhumphries.com
Web Site: www.lundhumphries.com

Trade Distribution:
Bookpoint Ltd, 39 Milton Park, Abingdon, Oxon OX14 4TD
Telephone: 01235 400400
Fax: 01235 400413
Email: orders@bookpoint.co.uk

Personnel:
Nigel Farrow (*Chairman, Ashgate Publishing*)
Lucy Myers (*Managing Director*)

Academic & Scholarly; Antiques & Collecting; Architecture & Design; Fine Art & Art History; Photography

Imprints, Series & ISBNs:
978 1 84822

Parent Company:
Ashgate Publishing

Overseas Representation:
Australia & Far East: Ashgate Publishing Asia-Pacific, Warriewood, NSW, Australia
Central & Eastern Europe: Dr László Horváth Publishers Representative, Budapest, Hungary
Finland, Sweden, Norway, Denmark & Iceland: Andrew Durnell Marketing Ltd, Tunbridge Wells, UK
France & Netherlands: Casemate Books, Newbury, UK
Germany, Austria, Switzerland, Italy, Greece, Luxembourg & Belgium: Ted Dougherty, London, UK
India: Maya Publishers Pvt Ltd, New Delhi, India
Japan (stockholding agents): United Publishers Services Ltd, Tokyo, Japan
Korea: Information & Culture Korea (ICK), Seoul, Republic of Korea
Middle East: Publishers International Marketing, Polfages, France
New Zealand: South Pacific Books (Imports) Ltd, Auckland, New Zealand
South Africa: Peter Hyde Associates (Pty) Ltd, Cape Town, South Africa
South America & Africa (excluding South Africa): InterMedia Americana (IMA) Ltd, London, UK
Spain & Portugal: Jenny Padovani, Barcelona, Spain
USA & Canada: Lund Humphries, Burlington, VT, USA

2449 ▬

THE LUTTERWORTH PRESS
PO Box 60, Cambridge CB1 2NT
Telephone: 01223 350865
Fax: 01223 366951
Email: publishing@lutterworth.com
Web Site: www.lutterworth.com

Trade Enquiries & Orders:
James Clarke & Co, PO Box 60, Cambridge CB1 2NT
Telephone: 01223 350865
Fax: 01223 366951
Email: orders@jamesclarke.co.uk
Web Site: www.lutterworth.com

Personnel:
Adrian Brink (*Managing Director*)

Academic & Scholarly; Antiques & Collecting; Architecture & Design; Biography & Autobiography; Children's Books; Crafts & Hobbies; Educational & Textbooks; Fine Art & Art History; History & Antiquarian; Illustrated & Fine Editions; Literature & Criticism; Military & War; Natural History; Philosophy; Politics & World Affairs; Reference Books, Directories & Dictionaries; Religion & Theology; Sports & Games

Imprints, Series & ISBNs:
Acorn Editions: 978 0 906554
Patrick Hardy: 978 0 7444
The Lutterworth Press: 978 0 7188

Parent Company:
James Clarke & Co Ltd

Overseas Representation:
USA: The David Brown Book Co (DBBC), Oakville, CT, USA

Book Trade Association Membership:
Independent Publishers Guild

2450 ▬

McCRIMMON PUBLISHING CO LTD
10–12 High Street, Great Wakering, Essex SS3 0EQ
Telephone: 01702 218956
Fax: 01702 216082
Email: info@mccrimmons.com
Web Site: www.mccrimmons.com

Bookshop:
All Saints Pastoral Centre, London Colney, St Albans, Herts
Telephone: 01727 827612
Fax: 01727 827612
Email: (as above)
Web Site: (as above)

Personnel:
Joan McCrimmon (*Secretary*)
Don McCrimmon (*Sales Director*)
Nick Snode (*Graphic Designer*)
Sue Anderson (*Accounts*)
Louise Madden (*Bookshop Manager*)
Caroline Lee (*Sales Ledger*)
Robert Mossop (*Warehouse*)

Children's Books; Educational & Textbooks; Electronic (Educational); Music; Religion & Theology

Imprints, Series & ISBNs:
978 0 85597

Distributor for:
USA: LTP Publications; Printery House Inc

Overseas Representation:
Australia: John Garrett Publishing, Mulgrave, Vic, Australia
Hong Kong: Catholic Truth Society, Hong Kong
New Zealand: Pleroma Christian Supplies, Otane, Central Hawkes Bay, New Zealand
South Africa: The Catholic Bookshop, Cape Town, South Africa

2451 ▬

McGRAW-HILL EDUCATION
Shoppenhangers Road, Maidenhead, Berks SL6 2QL
Telephone: 01628 502500
Fax: 01628 770224
Web Site: www.mcgraw-hill.co.uk

Personnel:
John Donovan (*UK/Northern & Central Europe Managing Director*)
Thanos Blintzios (*MEA Managing Director*)
Lefteris Souris (*Sales & Marketing Director, MEA*)
Emma Gibson (*General Manager Professional/Medical & Open University Press*)
Alice Duijser (*HE Sales & Marketing Director*)
Shona Mullen (*General Manager, Content & Digital Development EMEA*)

Academic & Scholarly; Accountancy & Taxation; Architecture & Design; Aviation; Biology & Zoology; Chemistry; Computer Science; Economics; Educational & Textbooks; Electronic (Educational); Electronic (Professional & Academic); Engineering; English as a Foreign Language; Geography & Geology; Industry, *Business & Management; Law; Mathematics & Statistics; Medical (incl. Self Help & Alternative Medicine); Philosophy; Physics; Politics & World Affairs; Psychology & Psychiatry; Reference Books, Directories & Dictionaries; Scientific & Technical; Sociology & Anthropology; Transport; Vocational Training & Careers*

Imprints, Series & ISBNs:
978 0 07

Parent Company:
USA: McGraw-Hill Inc

Associated Companies:
Open University Press
Australia: McGraw-Hill Education
Canada: McGraw-Hill Ryerson Ltd
Colombia: McGraw-Hill/InterAmericana (Colombia) SA
India: McGraw-Hill Education (India) Pvt Ltd
Italy: McGraw-Hill Libri Italia srl
Japan: McGraw-Hill Book Co
Mexico: Libros McGraw-Hill de Mexico SA de CV
Portugal: McGraw-Hill/Interamericana de Portugal Ltda
Singapore: McGraw-Hill International Book Co
Spain: McGraw-Hill Interamericana de España SAU
USA: Wm. C. Brown; Brown & Benchmark; Irwin; Irwin Professional; Osborne/McGraw-Hill
Venezuela: McGraw-Hill/InterAmericana (Venezuela) SA

Distributor for:
USA: Amacom; Berrett-Koehler; R & D Books

Book Trade Association Membership:
Publishers Association; Booksellers Association

2452 ▬

MACMILLAN CHILDREN'S BOOKS LTD
20 New Wharf Road, London N1 9RR
Telephone: 020 7014 6000
Fax: 020 7014 6001
Web Site: www.panmacmillan.com

Trade Enquiries:
Macmillan Distribution (MDL), Houndmills, Basingstoke, Hants RG21 6XS
Telephone: 01256 329242
Fax: 01256 840154
Email: mdl@macmillan.co.uk

Personnel:
Belinda Rasmussen (*Publisher, MCB*)
Ian Mitchell (*Production Director*)
Kate Mackenzie (*Rights Director*)
Anne Glenn (*Art Director*)
Rebecca McNally (*Publishing Director, Fiction*)
Suzanne Carnell (*Editorial, Picture & Gift Books Director*)
Gaby Morgan (*Editorial, Poetry & Non-Fiction Director*)
Martina Challis (*Publishing Director, Kingfisher*)
Ed Ripley (*Sales Director*)

Audio Books; Children's Books; Poetry

New Titles: 227 (2010) , 226 (2011)
No of Employees: 11

Imprints, Series & ISBNs:
Campbell Books: 978 0 330, 978 0 333
Kingfisher: 978 0 7534
Macmillan Children's Books: 978 0 330, 978 0 333
Young Picador: 978 0 330, 978 0 333

Parent Company:
Macmillan Ltd

Associated Companies:
Macmillan Education Ltd; Macmillan Publishers Ltd; Palgrave Macmillan Ltd; Pan Macmillan Ltd

Book Trade Association Membership:
Publishers Association; Children's Book Circle; PA Children's Book Group

2453

MACMILLAN EDUCATION
Macmillan Oxford, Between Towns Road, Oxford OX4 3PP
Telephone: 01865 405700
Fax: 01865 405701
Web Site: www.macmillaneducation.com

Distribution:
Macmillan Distribution (MDL), Houndmills, Basingstoke, Hants RG21 6XS
Telephone: 01256 329242
Fax: 01256 840154
Email: mdl@macmillan.co.uk

Personnel:
Simon Allen (*Chief Executive Macmillan Education*)
Jeremy Dieguez (*Managing Director, Europe*)
Mark Chalmers (*Group Finance Director, Mac Ed*)
Paul Emmett (*Finance Director ELT*)
Kate Melliss (*Publisher, Spain*)
Flavio Centofanti (*Regional Director, Middle East*)
Jo Greig (*International Marketing Director*)
Steven Maginn (*Regional Director, East Asia*)
Karen Hadley (*Business Systems Director*)
Anne Young (*Production Director*)
Sharon Jervis (*Publisher, Latin America*)
Martin Powter (*Company Secretary*)
Nick Evans (*Commercial Director, Africa*)
Dan Wilson (*Regional Director – Latin America*)

Atlases & Maps; Biology & Zoology; Chemistry; Children's Books; Educational & Textbooks; English as a Foreign Language; Environment & Development Studies; Geography & Geology; History & Antiquarian; Languages & Linguistics; Mathematics & Statistics; Physics; Reference Books, Directories & Dictionaries; Vocational Training & Careers

New Titles: 1562 (2010), 1566 (2011)
No of Employees: 200

Imprints, Series & ISBNs:
978 0 333
Macmillan Education
Macmillan Heinemann ELT

Parent Company:
Macmillan Ltd

Associated Companies:
Macmillan Children's Books; Macmillan Publishers Ltd; Palgrave Macmillan; Pan Macmillan

Overseas Representation:
See: Macmillan Publishers Ltd, Basingstoke, UK

Book Trade Association Membership:
Publishers Association

2454

MACMILLAN PUBLISHERS LTD
Brunel Road, Houndmills, Basingstoke, Hants RG21 6XS
Telephone: 01256 329242
Fax: 01256 842754
Web Site: www.macmillan.co.uk

Personnel:
Dr A. Thomas (*Chief Executive Officer*)
D. J. G. Knight (*Managing Director, Palgrave*)
W. H. Farries (*Group Central Finance Director, Macmillan*)
S. C. Inchcombe (*Managing Director, Nature Publishing Group*)
S. J. Allen (*Managing Director, Macmillan Education*)
A. Forbes Watson (*Managing Director, Pan Macmillan*)
C. E. Fleming (*Company Secretary*)
J. M. Wheeldon (*Chief Finance Officer*)
R. Jacobs (*Group Legal Counsel*)

Academic & Scholarly; Architecture & Design; Audio Books; Biography & Autobiography; Biology & Zoology; Chemistry; Children's Books; Cinema, Video, TV & Radio; Computer Science; Cookery, Wines & Spirits; Crafts & Hobbies; Crime; Economics; Educational & Textbooks; Electronic (Professional & Academic); Engineering; English as a Foreign Language; Environment & Development Studies; Fiction; Fine Art & Art History; Gardening; Gender Studies; Guide Books; Health & Beauty; History & Antiquarian; Humour; Languages & Linguistics; Law; Literature & Criticism; Mathematics & Statistics; Medical (incl. Self Help & Alternative Medicine); Military & War; Music; Natural History; Philosophy; Physics; Poetry; Politics & World Affairs; Psychology & Psychiatry; Reference Books, Directories & Dictionaries; Religion & Theology; Science Fiction; Scientific & Technical; Sociology & Anthropology; Sports & Games; Theatre, Drama & Dance; Travel & Topography

Imprints, Series & ISBNs:
Boxtree
Campbell Books
Kingfisher
Macmillan
Macmillan Children's Books
Macmillan Digital Audio
Macmillan Education
Macmillan English Campus
Macmillan New Writing
Nature
Nature Publishing Group
Palgrave Macmillan
Pan Macmillan
Picador
Priddy Books
Rodale
Sidgwick & Jackson
Think Books
Tor

Parent Company:
Germany: Georg von Holtzbrinck GmbH

Associated Companies:
Argentina: Editorial Estrada SA; Editorial Puerto de Palos SA; Macmillan Publishers SA
Australia: Macmillan Distribution Services Pty Ltd; Macmillan Publishers Australia Pty Ltd; Macquarie Library Pty Ltd; Macquarie Online Pty Ltd; Pan Macmillan Australia Pty Ltd
Botswana: Macmillan Botswana Publishing Co (Pty) Ltd
Brazil: Macmillan do Brasil
Colombia: Macmillan Publishers SAS
Egypt: Macmillan Publishers Egypt Ltd
Hong Kong: Macmillan New Asia Publishers Ltd; Macmillan Publishers (China) Ltd
India: Macmillan Publishers India Ltd; MPS Ltd
Japan: Macmillan Language House Ltd; Nature Japan KK
Mexico: Ediciones Castillo SA de CV; Editorial Macmillan Publishers SA de CV
Mozambique: Macmillan Mozambique Lda
Namibia: Macmillan Education Namibia Publishers (Pty) Ltd
New Zealand: Macmillan Publishers New Zealand Ltd
Nigeria: Northern Nigerian Publishing Co Ltd
Peru: Macmillan Publishers SA
Poland: Macmillan Polska Sp.Z.O.O.
Republic of Ireland: Gill & Macmillan Ltd
Republic of Korea: Macmillan Korea Publishers Ltd
South Africa: Macmillan South Africa Publishers (Pty) Ltd; Pan Macmillan South Africa Publishers (Pty) Ltd
Spain: Macmillan Iberia SA
Swaziland: Macmillan Boleswa Publishers Pty Ltd
UK: Macmillan Distribution Ltd
USA: Bedford, Freeman & Worth Publishing Group LLC; Tom Doherty Associates LLC; Farrar, Straus & Giroux LLC; Henry Holt and Co LLC; Holtzbrinck Publishers LLC; ICC Inc; Macmillan Academic Publishing Inc; Macmillan Publishers Inc; Nature America Inc; St Martin's Press LLC; Stockton Press Inc
Zambia: Macmillan Publishers (Zambia) Ltd
Zimbabwe: College Press Publishers (Pvt) Ltd

Distributor for:
see: Macmillan Children's Books; Macmillan Education; Palgrave Macmillan; Pan Macmillan

Overseas Representation:
Australia: Macmillan Education Australia, South Yarra, Vic, Australia; Pan Macmillan (Australia) Pty Ltd, Sydney, NSW, Australia
Austria, Germany & Switzerland: Annika Fesch, Stuttgart, Germany
Botswana: Macmillan Botswana Publishing Co Ltd, Gaborone, Botswana
Brazil: Macmillan do Brasil, São Paulo, Brazil
China: Macmillan Ltd, Beijing Office, Beijing, P. R. of China; Macmillan Publishers (China) Ltd, Hong Kong; Pan Macmillan Asia, Hong Kong
Colombia: Macmillan Publishers SAS, Bogota, Colombia
Cyprus: Char. J. Philippides & Son Ltd, Nicosia, Cyprus
Dubai: Macmillan Education Dubai, Dubai, UAE
Egypt: Macmillan Publishers Egypt Ltd, Cairo, Egypt
France: Laila Belyazid, Paris, France
France & Netherlands: Anne Georges, Brussels, Belgium
Greece: Apollo Distributors, Athens, Greece
Hong Kong: Macmillan Education, East Asia, Hong Kong; Macmillan Production Asia, Hong Kong
Hungary: Edit Szabo, Budapest, Hungary
India: Macmillan Publishers India Ltd, Bangalore, India; Palgrave Macmillan, New Delhi, India
Iran: Sepehr Bookshop, Tehran, Iran
Italy: Macmillan Publishers Ltd, Milan, Italy
Japan: Macmillan Language House, Tokyo, Japan; Nature Japan, Tokyo, Japan
Kenya: Moran (E.A.) Publishers Ltd, Nairobi, Kenya
Korea: Macmillan Korea Publishers Ltd, Seoul, Republic of Korea
Mexico & Central America: Macmillan Publishers SA de CV, Mexico DF, Mexico
Mozambique: Macmillan Mozambique Lda, Mozambique
Namibia: Macmillan Education Namibia Publishers (Pty) Ltd, Windhoek, Namibia
Netherlands, Belgium & Luxembourg: Daan Timmermans, Amsterdam, Netherlands
New Zealand: Macmillan Publishers New Zealand Ltd, Auckland, New Zealand
Pakistan: Book Bird Publishers Representatives, Lahore, Pakistan
Peru: Macmillan Publishers SA, Lima, Peru
Poland: Macmillan Polska, Warsaw, Poland
Republic of Ireland: Gill & Macmillan Ltd, Dublin, Republic of Ireland
Saudi Arabia: Elmia Bookstores, Riyadh, Saudi Arabia
Singapore: Pansing Distribution Sdn Bhd, Singapore
South Africa: Macmillan South Africa Publishers (Pty) Ltd, Braamfontein, South Africa; Pan Macmillan SA Pty Ltd, Hyde Park, South Africa
Swaziland: Macmillan Boleswa Publishers (Pty) Ltd, Manzini, Swaziland
Taiwan: Macmillan Taiwan Ltd, Taipei, Taiwan
Turkey: Macmillan Publishers Ltd, Istanbul, Turkey
Zambia: Macmillan Zambia, Lusaka, Zambia
Zimbabwe: College Press Publishers (Pvt) Ltd, Harare, Zimbabwe

Book Trade Association Membership:
Publishers Association; Independent Publishers Guild

2455

MAGNA LARGE PRINT BOOKS
Magna House, Long Preston, Skipton, North Yorks BD23 4ND
Telephone: 01729 840225 & 840526
Fax: 01729 840683
Email: dallen@magnaprint.co.uk
Web Site: www.ulverscroft.co.uk

Personnel:
Robert Thirlby (*Chairman*)
Diane Allen (*General Manager*)
David Mellin (*Accounts*)

Audio Books; Fiction

New Titles: 288 (2010), 288 (2011)
No of Employees: 14

Imprints, Series & ISBNs:
Audio: 978 1 85903
Large Print: 978 0 7505, 978 1 84262

Parent Company:
Ulverscroft Large Print Books

Distributor for:
Mills & Boon Large Print

Overseas Representation:
Worldwide: Ulverscroft Large Print Books, UK

2456

MAINSTREAM PUBLISHING CO (EDINBURGH) LTD
7 Albany Street, Edinburgh EH1 3UG
Telephone: 0131 557 2959
Fax: 0131 556 8720
Email:
seonaid.macleod@mainstreampublishing.com
Web Site:
www.mainstreampublishing.com

Distribution, Trade Enquiries & Orders:
TBS Ltd, Colchester Road, Frating Green, Colchester, Essex CO7 7DW
Telephone: 01206 255600
Fax: 01206 255930

Personnel:
Bill Campbell (*Joint Managing Director, Editorial*)
Peter MacKenzie (*Joint Managing Director, Sales*)
Fiona Brownlee (*Marketing & Rights, Publicity Director*)
Ailsa Bathgate (*Editorial Director*)
Douglas Nicoll (*Company Accountant*)
Neil Graham (*Production Manager*)
Fiona Atherton (*Publicity Manager*)

Biography & Autobiography; Cinema, Video, TV & Radio; Cookery, Wines & Spirits; Crime; Fine Art & Art History; Guide Books; Health & Beauty; History & Antiquarian; Humour; Illustrated & Fine Editions; Literature & Criticism; Medical (incl. Self Help & Alternative Medicine); Military & War; Music; Photography; Politics & World Affairs; Psychology & Psychiatry; Sports & Games; Travel & Topography

New Titles: 43 (2010)

No of Employees: 15

Imprints, Series & ISBNs:
978 0 906391, 978 1 84018, 978 1 84596, 978 1 85158
Mainstream Digital: 978 1 78057, 978 1 845968, 978 1 845969, 978 1 907195

Associated Companies:
Random House UK

Overseas Representation:
Australia: Random House Australia Pty Ltd, Sydney, NSW, Australia
Canada: Random House of Canada Ltd, Mississauga, Ont, Canada
Caribbean & Latin America: Random House Inc, New York, NY, USA
Germany, Switzerland, Austria, Belgium, Denmark, Finland & Luxembourg: Jörg Riekenbrauk, Cologne, Germany
Hong Kong, Taiwan, South Korea & China: Stanson Yeung, Random House of Canada Ltd, Toronto, Ont, Canada
India, Sri Lanka & Bangladesh: Nandan Jha, Random House Publishers India Pte Ltd, New Delhi, India
New Zealand: Random House New Zealand Ltd, Auckland, New Zealand
South Africa: Random House (SA) Pty Ltd, Parktown, South Africa
Sweden, Iceland, Spain, France, Italy, Portugal, Cyprus, Greece, Malta, Middle East, Pakistan & Africa (excluding South Africa): Random House Group Ltd, London, UK
USA: Trafalgar Square Publishing / IPG, Chicago, IL, USA

Book Trade Association Membership:
Publishing Scotland; Booksellers Association

2457 ▬▬▬

*MANAGEMENT POCKETBOOKS LTD
Laurel House, Station Approach, Alresford, Hants SO24 9JH
Telephone: 01962 735573
Fax: 01962 733637
Email: sales@pocketbook.co.uk
Web Site: www.pocketbook.co.uk

Personnel:
Ros Baynes *(Managing Director)*
Adrian Hunt *(Director)*

Educational & Textbooks; Industry, Business & Management

Imprints, Series & ISBNs:
Management Pocketbooks: 978 1 870471, 978 1 903776, 978 1 906610
Teachers' Pocketbooks: 978 1 870471, 978 1 903776, 978 1 906610

Overseas Representation:
Australia: Training Solutions Group, Mudgeeraba, Qld, Australia
Caribbean: InterMedia Americana (IMA) Ltd, London, UK
Far East: Publishers International Marketing, Ferndown, Dorset, UK
India: Research Press, New Delhi, India
South Africa: Learning Resources Pty Ltd, Johannesburg, South Africa

Book Trade Association Membership:
Independent Publishers Guild

2458 ▬▬▬

MANCHESTER UNIVERSITY PRESS
Oxford Road, Manchester M13 9NR
Telephone: 0161 275 2310
Fax: 0161 274 3346
Email: mup@manchester.ac.uk
Web Site: manchesteruniversitypress.co.uk

Distribution (Trade Enquiries, Orders & Warehouse):
NBN International, Plymbridge House, Estover Road, Plymouth, Devon PL6 7PY
Telephone: 01752 202301
Fax: 01752 202333
Email: enquiries@nbninternational.com
Web Site: www.nbninternational.com

Sales Representation (UK):
Yale University Press, 47 Bedford Square, London WC1B 3DP
Telephone: 020 7079 4900
Fax: 020 7079 4901
Email: sales@yaleup.co.uk

Personnel:
David Rodgers *(Chief Executive)*
Emma Brennan *(Editorial Director)*
Simon Bell *(Director of Sales & Marketing)*

Academic & Scholarly; Architecture & Design; Cinema, Video, TV & Radio; Economics; Educational & Textbooks; Gay & Lesbian Studies; Gender Studies; History & Antiquarian; Illustrated & Fine Editions; Languages & Linguistics; Law; Literature & Criticism; Politics & World Affairs; Reference Books, Directories & Dictionaries; Sociology & Anthropology; Theatre, Drama & Dance; Transport

New Titles: 130 (2010) , 130 (2011)
No of Employees: 18

Imprints, Series & ISBNs:
Manchester University Press: 978 0 7190
Mandolin: 978 1 901341

Parent Company:
UK: The University of Manchester

Distributor for:
Netherlands: Amsterdam University Press
USA: Penn State University Press

Overseas Representation:
Asia & Middle East: Publishers International Marketing, Sutton St Nicholas, Herefordshire, UK
Australia & New Zealand: Footprint Books Pty Ltd, Warriewood, NSW, Australia
Canada: University of British Columbia Press, Vancouver, BC, Canada
Canada (Orders & Customer Service): cUPT Distribution, Toronto, Ont, Canada
Europe: Andrew Durnell Marketing Ltd, Tunbridge Wells, UK
India (Representation): Andrew White, The White Partnership, Tunbridge Wells, UK
India (Sales): Viva Books, New Delhi, India
Japan: United Publishers Services Ltd, Tokyo, Japan
Malaysia: Publishers Marketing Services, Petaling Jaya, Malaysia
Republic of Ireland: Robert Towers, Monkstown, Co Dublin, Republic of Ireland
Singapore: Publishers Marketing Services Pte Ltd, Singapore
USA: Palgrave, New York, NY, USA

Book Trade Association Membership:
Independent Publishers Guild; Association of Learned & Professional Society Publishers

2459 ▬▬▬

*MANDRAKE OF OXFORD
PO Box 250, Oxford OX1 1AP
Telephone: 01865 243671
Fax: 01865 432929
Email: mandrake@mandrake.uk.net
Web Site: www.mandrake.uk.net

Personnel:
Mogg Morgan *(Director)*
Kim Morgan *(Director)*

Children's Books; Crime; Fiction; Fine Art & Art History; Literature & Criticism; Magic & the Occult; Medical (incl. Self Help &

Alternative Medicine); Philosophy; Poetry; Religion & Theology; Sociology & Anthropology

Imprints, Series & ISBNs:
Golden Dawn: 978 1 869928
Mandrake of Oxford: 978 1 869928, 978 1 906958

Overseas Representation:
USA: Ingram Publisher Services, Nashville, TN, USA; New Leaf Distributing Co, Lithia Springs, GA, USA

Book Trade Association Membership:
Independent Publishers Guild

2460 ▬▬▬

MANEY PUBLISHING
Suite 1C, Joseph's Well, Hanover Walk, Leeds LS3 1AB
Telephone: 0113 243 2800
Fax: 0113 386 8178
Email: maney@maney.co.uk
Web Site: www.maney.co.uk

Also at:
1 Carlton House Terrace, London SW1Y 5AF
Telephone: 020 7451 7300
Fax: 020 7451 7307
Email: maney@maney.co.uk
Web Site: www.maney.co.uk

Personnel:
Michael Gallico *(Managing Director)*
Mark Simon *(Publishing Director)*
Shelly Lynds *(Sales & Marketing Director)*
Liz Rosindale *(Managing Editor)*
Mark Hull *(Managing Editor)*
Lynne Medhurst *(Head of Corporate Marketing & Communications)*
Emily Simpson *(Head of Marketing)*
Gaynor Redvers-Mutton *(Business Development Manager)*
Kim Martin *(US Executive Publisher)*

Academic & Scholarly; Archaeology; Architecture & Design; Atlases & Maps; Bibliography & Library Science; Biography & Autobiography; Electronic (Professional & Academic); Engineering; Environment & Development Studies; Fashion & Costume; Fine Art & Art History; Geography & Geology; History & Antiquarian; Illustrated & Fine Editions; Languages & Linguistics; Literature & Criticism; Medical (incl. Self Help & Alternative Medicine); Military & War; Religion & Theology; Scientific & Technical; Transport; Travel & Topography

Imprints, Series & ISBNs:
Legenda
Maney Publishing: 978 0 901286, 978 1 902653
Northern Universities Press: 978 0 901286

Distributor for:
European Respiratory Society; Modern Humanities Research Association; Pasold Research Fund; Society for Italian Studies; Society for Medieval Archaeology

Overseas Representation:
USA: Publishers Communication Group, Boston, MA, USA

Book Trade Association Membership:
International Group of Scientific, Medical & Technical Publishers; Association of Learned & Professional Society Publishers

2461 ▬▬▬

MANSON PUBLISHING LTD
73 Corringham Road, London NW11 7DL
Telephone: 020 8905 5150
Fax: 020 8201 9233
Email: manson@mansonpublishing.com
Web Site: www.mansonpublishing.com

Distribution:
NBN International, 10 Estover Road, Plymouth, Devon PL6 7PY
Telephone: 01752 202300
Fax: 01752 802330
Email: cservs@nbninternational.com
Web Site: www.nbninternational.com

Personnel:
Michael Manson *(Managing Director)*

Agriculture; Animal Care & Breeding; Biology & Zoology; Geography & Geology; Medical (incl. Self Help & Alternative Medicine); Scientific & Technical; Veterinary Science

New Titles: 10 (2010) , 15 (2011)
No of Employees: 4

Imprints, Series & ISBNs:
978 1 84076, 978 1 874545

Associated Companies:
The Veterinary Press Ltd

Distributor for:
Germany: Schluetersche Publishers

Overseas Representation:
All other areas: NBN International, Plymouth, UK
Australia & New Zealand (Medical & Veterinary titles): Woodslane, Warriewood, NSW, Australia
Australia & New Zealand (Science titles): CSIRO Publishing, Collingwood, Vic, Australia
Japan (Medical & Veterinary titles): Nankodo Co Ltd, Tokyo, Japan
USA: Thieme Publishers, New York, NY, USA

Book Trade Association Membership:
Publishers Association; Independent Publishers Guild

2462 ▬▬▬

MARITIME BOOKS
Lodge Hill, Liskeard, Cornwall PL14 4EL
Telephone: 01579 343663
Fax: 01579 346747
Email: sales@navybooks.com
Web Site: www.navybooks.com

Personnel:
M. Critchley *(Managing Director)*
S. Bush *(Editor)*
P. Garnett *(Manager)*

Military & War; Transport

New Titles: 5 (2010) , 4 (2011)
No of Employees: 2

Imprints, Series & ISBNs:
978 0 907771, 978 1 904459

2463 ▬▬▬

MAVERICK HOUSE PUBLISHERS
Office 19, Dunboyne Business Park, Dunboyne, Co Meath, Republic of Ireland
Telephone: +353 (01) 825 5717
Fax: +353 (01) 686 5036
Email: info@maverickhouse.com
Web Site: www.maverickhouse.com

Personnel:
John Mooney *(Managing Director)*

Biography & Autobiography; Crime; Fiction; Humour; Military & War; Politics & World Affairs; Sports & Games

Imprints, Series & ISBNs:
Book Republic: 978 1 907221
Maverick House Publishers: 978 0 9548707, 978 0 9548708, 978 1 905379, 978 1 908518

Overseas Representation:
Australia: Tower Books Pty Ltd, Frenchs Forest, NSW, Australia
Far East: Ashton International Marketing Services, Sevenoaks, UK
Singapore & Malaysia: Paperclip, Singapore
UK: Turnaround Publisher Services Ltd, London, UK

Book Trade Association Membership:
Publishing Ireland (Foilsiú Éireann)

2464 ▬▬▬

MEADOWSIDE CHILDREN'S BOOKS & GULLANE CHILDREN'S BOOKS
185 Fleet Street, London EC4A 2HS
Telephone: 020 7400 1092
Fax: 020 7400 1037
Email: info@meadowsidebooks.com & info@gullanebooks.com
Web Site: www.meadowsidebooks.com & www.gullanebooks.com

Personnel:
Simon Rosenheim *(Publisher)*
Rupert Harbour *(Sales Director)*
Katherine Judge *(Rights Director)*

Children's Books

Imprints, Series & ISBNs:
Gullane: 978 1 86233
Meadowside: 978 1 84539

Parent Company:
UK: D. C. Thomson

2465 ▬▬▬

MEDIA EIGHT INTERNATIONAL PUBLISHING LTD
3 Linkside, New Malden, Surrey KT3 4LA
Telephone: 020 8605 1097
Fax: 020 8605 1098

Book Trade Association Membership:
Publishers Association

2466 ▬▬▬

MEDIKIDZ LTD
1st Floor, 6 Burnsall Street, London SW3 3ST
Telephone: 020 7376 6632
Email: info@medikidz.com
Web Site: www.medikiz.com

Personnel:
Dr Kim Chilman-Blair *(Chief Executive Officer)*
Dr Kate Hersov *(Deputy Chief Executive Officer)*
Jon Squires *(Chief Operations Officer)*
Amanda Langerak *(Editor-in-Chief)*
Agustin Larocca *(Finance Director)*

Children's Books; Educational & Textbooks; Medical (incl. Self Help & Alternative Medicine); Scientific & Technical

Imprints, Series & ISBNs:
978 1 906935

Overseas Representation:
Canada: New Leaf Media
Greece: Smart Stuff
USA: American Cancer Society, New York, USA; Future Horizons, Texas, USA; The Guidance Group, New York, NY, USA; Rosen, New York, NY, USA

Book Trade Association Membership:
Booksellers Association

2467 ▬▬▬

MELISENDE UK LTD
G8 Allen House, The Maltings, Station Road, Sawbridgeworth, Herts CM21 9JX
Telephone: 01279 721398

Email: info.melisende@btinternet.com
Web Site: www.melisende.com

Personnel:
Leonard Harrow *(Editorial)*
Alan Ball *(Sales & Marketing)*
Vicki Coombs *(Office Manager)*

Academic & Scholarly; Antiques & Collecting; Archaeology; Architecture & Design; Crafts & Hobbies; Fine Art & Art History; History & Antiquarian; Illustrated & Fine Editions; Politics & World Affairs; Religion & Theology; Travel & Topography

New Titles: 3 (2010) , 3 (2011)
No of Employees: 3

Imprints, Series & ISBNs:
Atelier: 978 1 901360
Melisende: 978 1 901764

Distributor for:
India: East & West Publishing; Orientblackswan/Universities Press; Social Science Press; Visva-Bharati
UK: Sangam Books Ltd

Overseas Representation:
Middle East: Rimal Publications, Cyprus

2468 ▬▬▬

*MENTOR BOOKS
43 Furze Road, Sandyford Industrial Estate, Dublin 18, Republic of Ireland
Telephone: +353 (0)1 295 2112/3
Fax: +353 (0)1 295 2114
Email: all@mentorbooks.ie
Web Site: www.mentorbooks.ie

Personnel:
Daniel C. McCarthy *(General Manager)*

Academic & Scholarly; Biography & Autobiography; Biology & Zoology; Cinema, Video, TV & Radio; Crime; Economics; Educational & Textbooks; Fiction; Geography & Geology; Guide Books; Health & Beauty; History & Antiquarian; Humour; Industry, Business & Management; Languages & Linguistics; Mathematics & Statistics; Photography; Poetry; Politics & World Affairs; Reference Books, Directories & Dictionaries; Scientific & Technical; Sports & Games; Travel & Topography

Imprints, Series & ISBNs:
978 0 947548, 978 1 902586, 978 1 84210

Book Trade Association Membership:
Publishing Ireland (Foilsiú Éireann)

2469 ▬▬▬

MERCIER PRESS LTD
Unit 3b, Oak House, Bessboro Road, Blackrock, Cork, Republic of Ireland
Telephone: +353 (0)21 461 4700
Fax: +353 (0)21 461 4802
Email: info@mercierpress.ie
Web Site: www.mercierpress.ie

Personnel:
Clodagh Feehan *(Managing Director)*
Mary Feehan *(Commissioning Editor)*
Sharon O'Donovan *(Rights & Permissions)*
Wendy Logue *(Managing Editor)*
Niamh Hatton *(Sales Executive)*
Patrick Crowley *(Marketing Co-ordinator)*
Catherine Twibill *(Design)*

Academic & Scholarly; Biography & Autobiography; Children's Books; Cookery, Wines & Spirits; Crafts & Hobbies; Crime; Fiction; History & Antiquarian; Humour; Literature & Criticism; Military & War; Poetry; Politics & World Affairs; Religion & Theology; Sports & Games; Theatre, Drama & Dance

New Titles: 35 (2010) , 35 (2011)

Imprints, Series & ISBNs:
Marino Books: 978 1 86023
Mercier Press: 978 0 85342, 978 1 85635

Overseas Representation:
USA: Dufour, Chester Springs, PA, USA; James Trading Group, Nanuet, NY, USA

Book Trade Association Membership:
Publishing Ireland (Foilsiú Éireann); Independent Publishers Guild

2470 ▬▬▬

*MERCURY BOOKS
20 Bloomsbury Street, London WC1B 3JH
Telephone: 020 7636 7171
Fax: 020 7636 1922

Personnel:
Finbarr McCabe *(Managing Director)*
James Birney *(Sales Director)*

Archaeology; Atlases & Maps; Geography & Geology; History & Antiquarian; Literature & Criticism; Military & War; Reference Books, Directories & Dictionaries

Imprints, Series & ISBNs:
978 1 84560, 978 1 904668

Parent Company:
Caxton Publishing Group

Overseas Representation:
Australia & New Zealand: Bookwise International, Wingfield, SA, Australia
Europe: Bill Bailey Publishers Representatives, Newton Abbot, UK
Far East: Bookwise Asia, Singapore, Singapore
South Africa: Peter Matthews Agencies, Alberton, South Africa
USA & Canada: International Publishers Marketing Inc, Herndon, VA, USA

2471 ▬▬▬

*MERCURY JUNIOR
20 Bloomsbury Street, London WC1B 3JH
Telephone: 020 7636 7171
Fax: 020 7636 1922

Personnel:
Finbarr McCabe *(Managing Director)*
James Birney *(Sales Director)*

Children's Books; Fashion & Costume

Imprints, Series & ISBNs:
978 1 84560, 978 1 904668

Parent Company:
Caxton Publishing Group

Overseas Representation:
Australia & New Zealand: Bookwise International, Wingfield, SA, Australia
Europe: Bill Bailey Publishers Representatives, Newton Abbot, UK
Far East: Bookwise Asia, Singapore, Singapore
South Africa: Peter Matthews Agencies, Alberton, South Africa
USA & Canada: International Publishers Marketing Inc, Herndon, VA, USA

2472 ▬▬▬

THE MERLIN PRESS LTD
99b Wallis Road, London E9 5LN
Telephone: 020 8533 5800
Email: info@merlinpress.co.uk
Web Site: www.merlinpress.co.uk

Distribution:
Central Books Ltd, 99 Wallis Road, London E9 5LN
Telephone: 020 8986 4854

Fax: 020 8533 5821
Email: orders@centralbooks.com

Personnel:
Anthony Zurbrugg *(Managing Director)*
Adrian Howe *(Manager)*

Academic & Scholarly; Biography & Autobiography; Economics; Gender Studies; History & Antiquarian; Politics & World Affairs; Sociology & Anthropology

Imprints, Series & ISBNs:
Green Print: 978 1 85284
The Merlin Press Ltd: 978 0 85036

Overseas Representation:
Australia: Eleanor Brasch Enterprises, Artarmon, NSW, Australia
Canada: Brunswick Books, Toronto, Ont, Canada
South Africa: Blue Weaver Marketing, Tokai, South Africa
USA: Independent Publishers Group (IPG), Chicago, IL, USA

2473 ▬▬▬

*MERLIN PUBLISHING/ WOLFHOUND PRESS
Newmarket Hall, Cork Street, Dublin 8, Republic of Ireland
Telephone: +353 (0)1 453 5866
Fax: +353 (0)1 453 5930
Web Site: www.merlinwolfhound.com

Distribution:
Gill & Macmillan, Hume Avenue, Park West, Dublin 12, Republic of Ireland
Telephone: +353 (0)1 500 9500
Fax: +353 (0)1 500 9599
Email: info@gillmacmillan.ie
Web Site: www.gillmacmillan.ie

Personnel:
Chenile Keogh *(Publisher & Managing Director)*
Robert Doran *(Publishing Manager)*

Biography & Autobiography; Cinema, Video, TV & Radio; Cookery, Wines & Spirits; Crafts & Hobbies; Crime; Fashion & Costume; Fine Art & Art History; Guide Books; Health & Beauty; Humour; Music; Photography; Politics & World Affairs; Reference Books, Directories & Dictionaries; Sports & Games; Travel & Topography

Imprints, Series & ISBNs:
Merlin Publishing: 978 1 903582, 978 1 907162
Wolfhound Press: 978 0 86327

Parent Company:
Republic of Ireland: Merlin Media Ltd

Overseas Representation:
UK: Bounce! Sales & Marketing Ltd, London, UK
USA (Wolfhound & Merlin): Interlink Publishing Group Inc, Northampton, MA, USA

Book Trade Association Membership:
Publishing Ireland (Foilsiú Éireann)

2474 ▬▬▬

MERRELL PUBLISHERS LTD
81 Southwark Street, London SE1 0HX
Telephone: 020 7928 8880
Fax: 020 7928 1199
Web Site: www.merrellpublishers.com

Trade & Credit Orders, Returns:
Marston Book Services, PO Box 269, Abingdon, Oxon OX14 4YN
Telephone: 01235 465500
Fax: 01235 465555
Email: trade.order@marston.co.uk

Personnel:
Hugh Merrell *(Publisher)*
Claire Chandler *(Head of Editorial)*
Nicola Bailey *(Creative Director)*
Mark Scott *(Sales & Marketing Manager)*
Alenka Oblak *(Production Manager)*
Elizabeth Richards *(Foreign Rights Manager)*

Antiques & Collecting; Architecture & Design; Cinema, Video, TV & Radio; Cookery, Wines & Spirits; Crafts & Hobbies; Fashion & Costume; Fine Art & Art History; Gardening; Guide Books; History & Antiquarian; Humour; Illustrated & Fine Editions; Natural History; Photography; Transport; Travel & Topography

Imprints, Series & ISBNs:
978 1 85894

Overseas Representation:
All other territories: Mark Scott, Merrell Publishers, London, UK
Canada: Canadian Manda Group, Toronto, Ont, Canada
Central America & Caribbean: Chris Humphrys, Humphrys Roberts Associates, London, UK
Eastern Europe: Adriana Juncu, Voluntari, Jud. Ilfov, Romania
Estonia, Latvia, Lithuania & Ukraine: Tony Moggach, InterMedia Americana (IMA) Ltd, London, UK
France: Critiques Livres Distribution, Bagnolet, France
Germany, Austria & Switzerland: Gabriele Kern Publishers Services, Frankfurt-am-Main, Germany
Hong Kong, Taiwan, China, Korea, Japan, Indonesia, Philippines & Thailand: Julian Ashton, Ashton International Marketing Services, Sevenoaks, Kent, UK
India, Bangladesh, Nepal, Bhutan & Sri Lanka: Surit Mitra, Maya Publishers Pvt Ltd, New Delhi, India
Italy, Greece, Spain & Portugal: Padovani Books Ltd, London, UK; Padovani Books Ltd, Montanare di Cortona, Italy
Malaysia, Singapore & Brunei: Pansing Distribution Pte Ltd, Singapore
Middle East, Turkey, Israel, Cyprus & Malta: Peter Ward Book Exports, London, UK
Netherlands, Belgium & Luxembourg: Nilsson & Lamm BV, Weesp, Netherlands
Republic of Ireland & Northern Ireland: Robert Towers, Monkstown, Co Dublin, Republic of Ireland
Scandinavia: Elisabeth Harder-Kreimann, Hamburg, Germany
South America: Terry Roberts, Humphrys Roberts Associates, Cotia SP, Brazil
Southern Africa: Giulietta Campanelli, SG Distributors, Johannesburg, South Africa
Sub-Saharan Africa & Russian Federation: Tony Moggach, InterMedia Africa, London, UK
USA: Continental Sales (CSI) Inc, Barrington, IL, USA; Perseus Group, Jackson, TN, USA

2475

MERTON PRIORY PRESS LTD
9 Owen Falls Avenue, Chesterfield S41 0FR
Telephone: 01246 554026
Email: mertonpriory@btinternet.com
Web Site: www.mertonpriory.co.uk

Personnel:
Philip Riden *(Controlling Director)*

Academic & Scholarly; Archaeology; Biography & Autobiography; History & Antiquarian; Transport

New Titles: 4 (2010) , 4 (2011)
No of Employees: 3
Annual Turnover: £15,000

Imprints, Series & ISBNs:
978 1 898937

2476

MICHELIN MAPS & GUIDES
Hannay House, 39 Clarendon Road, Watford WD17 1JA
Telephone: 01923 205240
Fax: 01923 205241
Web Site: www.michelin.co.uk/travel

Warehouse/Returns:
Michelin Tyre Plc, Maps & Guides, Building 82 Campbell Road, Stoke on Trent, Staffs ST4 4EY
Telephone: 01923 205242
Fax: 01923 205241

Personnel:
I. Murray *(Commercial Director, Head of Travel Publications)*
C. Lemonnier *(Trade Marketing Manager)*

Atlases & Maps; Guide Books; Travel & Topography

Imprints, Series & ISBNs:
The Green Guide Series
Local Map Series: 978 2 06
National Map Series: 978 2 06
The Red Guide Series: 978 2 06
Regional Map Series: 978 2 06
Zoom Map Series: 978 2 06

Parent Company:
France: Manufacture Française des Pneumatiques Michelin

Overseas Representation:
Belgium & Luxembourg: Michelin Belux, Brussels, Belgium
Italy: Michelin Italiana SPA, Milan, Italy
Spain: Michelin Espana Portugal SA, Madrid, Spain
USA: Michelin Travel Publications, Greenville, SC, USA

Book Trade Association Membership:
Booksellers Association

2477

MICROFORM ACADEMIC PUBLISHERS
Main Street, East Ardsley, Wakefield, West Yorkshire WF3 2AP
Telephone: 01924 825700
Fax: 01924 871005
Email: map@microform.co.uk
Web Site: www.britishonlinearchives.co.uk

Personnel:
Nigel Le Page *(Managing Director)*
David Sarsfield *(Head of Publishing)*

Academic & Scholarly; Biography & Autobiography; Economics; Electronic (Professional & Academic); History & Antiquarian; Literature & Criticism; Military & War; Politics & World Affairs; Religion & Theology; Sociology & Anthropology

Imprints, Series & ISBNs:
British Records on the Atlantic World, 1700–1850: 978 1 85117
British Records Relating to America in Microform (BRRAM) (series)
Communist Party of Great Britain
Records of the Raj (series)

Associated Companies:
UK: Microform Imaging Ltd

Overseas Representation:
Japan: Far Eastern Booksellers, Tokyo, Japan
USA & Canada: Bludeau Partners International, New York, NY, USA; PraXess, New York, NY, USA

2478

MIDDLETON PRESS
Easebourne Lane, Midhurst, Sussex GU29 9AZ

Telephone: 01730 813169
Fax: 01730 812601
Email: sales@middletonpress.co.uk
Web Site: www.middletonpress.co.uk

Personnel:
Dr J. C. V. Mitchell *(Author & Proprietor)*
Mrs B Mitchell *(Partner)*
Mrs D Esher *(Partner)*

Military & War; Nautical; Transport

New Titles: 24 (2010) , 23 (2011)
No of Employees: 3
Annual Turnover: £350,000

Imprints, Series & ISBNs:
978 0 906520, 978 1 873793, 978 1 901706, 978 1 904474, 978 1 906008, 978 1 908174

2479

MILESTONE PUBLICATIONS
62 Murray Road, Horndean, Waterlooville, Hants PO8 9JL
Telephone: 023 9259 7440
Fax: 023 9259 1975
Email: info@gosschinaclub.co.uk
Web Site: www.gosschinaclub.co.uk

Personnel:
Lynda Pine *(Managing Director)*
Debbie Webb *(Manageress)*

Antiques & Collecting

Imprints, Series & ISBNs:
978 1 85265, 978 1 903852

Parent Company:
Goss & Crested China Ltd

2480

J. GARNET MILLER
10 Station Road Industrial Estate, Colwall, Malvern, Worcs WR13 6RN
Telephone: 01684 540154
Email: simon@cressrelles.co.uk
Web Site: www.cressrelles.co.uk

Personnel:
Leslie Smith *(Manager)*
Simon Smith *(Manager)*

Theatre, Drama & Dance

New Titles: 6 (2010) , 6 (2011)
No of Employees: 2

Imprints, Series & ISBNs:
Garnet Miller: 978 0 85343

Parent Company:
Cressrelles Publishing Co Ltd

Overseas Representation:
Australia: Origin Theatrical, Sydney, NSW, Australia
New Zealand: Play Bureau of New Zealand Ltd, New Plymouth, New Zealand
Republic of Ireland: Drama League of Ireland, Dublin, Republic of Ireland
South Africa: Dalro (Pty) Ltd, Braamfontein, South Africa
USA: Bakers Plays, Quincy, MA, USA

2481

MILLER'S
Endeavour House,
189 Shaftesbury Avenue, London WC2H 8JY
Telephone: 020 7632 5400
Email: info@octopus-publishing.co.uk
Web Site: www.octopusbooks.co.uk

Distribution:
Littlehampton Book Services Ltd, Faraday Close, Durrington, Worthing, West Sussex BN13 3RB

Telephone: 01903 828500
Fax: 01903 828625

Personnel:
Judith Miller *(Publisher/Managing Director)*

Antiques & Collecting

Parent Company:
Hachette UK

Overseas Representation:
See: Octopus Publishing Group, London, UK

Book Trade Association Membership:
Booksellers Association

2482

THE MIT PRESS LTD
Suite 2, 1 Duchess Street, London W1W 6AN
Telephone: 020 7306 0603
Email: info@mitpress.org.uk
Web Site: www.mitpress.mit.edu

Trade & Warehouse:
Wiley Distribution Services, New Era Estate, Oldlands Way, Bognor Regis, West Sussex PO22 9NQ
Telephone: 01243 779777
Fax: 01243 843296
Email: cs-books@wiley.com

European Sales Office:
University Press Group, 1st Floor Office, New Era Estate, Oldlands Way, Bognor Regis PO22 9NQ
Telephone: 01243 842165
Fax: 01243 842167
Email: lois@upguk.com

Personnel:
Judith Bullent *(Promotion Manager)*
Ann Twiselton *(Publicity Manager)*

Academic & Scholarly; Architecture & Design; Bibliography & Library Science; Biography & Autobiography; Biology & Zoology; Computer Science; Economics; Engineering; Environment & Development Studies; Fine Art & Art History; Gay & Lesbian Studies; Gender Studies; Industry, Business & Management; Languages & Linguistics; Music; Natural History; Philosophy; Photography; Politics & World Affairs; Psychology & Psychiatry; Reference Books, Directories & Dictionaries; Scientific & Technical

Parent Company:
USA: MIT Press

Distributor for:
USA: Afterall; Semiotext(e); Zone Books (Urzone Publishing Ltd)

Overseas Representation:
Africa: Cameroon, Ethiopia, Gambia, Ghana, Kenya, Malawi, Mauritius, Nigeria, Rwanda, Tanzania, Uganda, Zambia: Tony Moggach (IMA), London, UK
Australia & New Zealand: Footprint Books Pty Ltd, Warriewood, NSW, Australia
Brazil: Renata Zanzini, São Paulo, SP, Brazil
Canada: Patricia Nelson, Santa Fe, NM, USA (British Columbia only), John Eklund, Milwaukee, WI, USA
Caribbean: John Atkin, Norwalk, CT, USA
Central America, Northern South America: Jose Rios, Guatemala
China: Wei Zhao, Everest International Publishing Services, Beijing, P. R. of China
France, Belgium, Scandinavia, Switzerland, Italy, Poland: Peter Jacques, London, UK
Hong Kong: Jane Lam, Aromix Books Company, Hong Kong
India, Bangladesh, Sri Lanka: S. Janakiraman, Book Marketing Services, Chennai, India

Israel: Rodney Franklin Agency, Tel Aviv, Israel
Japan: Akiko Iwamoto, Tokyo, Japan
Malaysia, Brunei: Liang Hoe, Selangor, Malaysia
Mexico: Cynthia Zimpfer, Morelos, Mexico
Middle East (excluding Greece & Israel): Avicenna Partnership, Oxford, UK
Netherlands, Germany, Austria, Spain, Portugal, Greece, Hungary, Czech Republic, Croatia, Slovenia: Dominique Bartshukoff, Paris, France
Puerto Rico: David Rivera, San Juan, Puerto Rico
Republic of Ireland: Ben Mitchell, London, UK
South Africa: Cory Voigt, Palgrave, Johanesburg, South Africa
South Korea: Se-Yung Jun & Min-Hwa Yoo, Seoul, Republic of Korea
Taiwan: Chiafeng Peng, Taipei, Taiwan
Thailand: Suphaluck Sattabuz, Booknet Co., Bangkok, Thailand
Trinidad: Patrice Ammon-Jagdeo, Trinidad

2483

MITCHELL BEAZLEY
Endeavour House,
189 Shaftesbury Avenue, London
WC2H 8JY
Telephone: 020 7632 5400
Email: info@octopus-publishing.co.uk
Web Site: www.octopusbooks.co.uk

Distribution:
Littlehampton Book Services,
Faraday Close, Durrington, Worthing,
West Sussex BN13 3RB
Telephone: 01903 828801
Fax: 01903 828802
Web Site:
www.pubeasy.books.lbsltd.co.uk

Personnel:
Denise Bates *(Group Publishing Director)*
Tracey Smith *(Editorial Director)*

Antiques & Collecting; Archaeology; Architecture & Design; Cookery, Wines & Spirits; Crafts & Hobbies; Fashion & Costume; Fine Art & Art History; Gardening; Health & Beauty; History & Antiquarian; Illustrated & Fine Editions; Medical (incl. Self Help & Alternative Medicine); Music; Natural History; Photography; Reference Books, Directories & Dictionaries; Sports & Games; Travel & Topography

Imprints, Series & ISBNs:
978 1 84533

Parent Company:
Hachette UK

Overseas Representation:
See: Octopus Publishing Group, London, UK

Book Trade Association Membership:
Booksellers Association

2484

*M&K PUBLISHING
[an imprint of M&K Update Ltd]
The Old Bakery, St John's Street, Keswick,
Cumbria CA12 5AS
Telephone: 01768 773030
Fax: 01768 781099
Email: enquiries@mkupdate.co.uk
Web Site: www.mkupdate.co.uk

Personnel:
Mike Roberts *(Co-Director)*
Ken Russell *(Co-Director)*

Academic & Scholarly; Medical (incl. Self Help & Alternative Medicine); Psychology & Psychiatry

Imprints, Series & ISBNs:
978 1 905539

Parent Company:
UK: M&K Update Ltd

Overseas Representation:
Worldwide: IMR Agency Ltd, Lancaster, UK

Book Trade Association Membership:
Publishers Association

2485

*MOONLIGHT PUBLISHING LTD
The King's Manor, East Hendred, Oxon
OX12 8JY
Telephone: 01235 821821
Fax: 01235 821155
Email: johnclement@btconnect.com
Web Site:
www.moonlightpublishing.co.uk

Warehouse, Trade Enquiries & Orders:
BookSource, 50 Cambuslang Road,
Glasgow G32 8NB
Telephone: 0845 370 0067
Fax: 0845 370 0068
Email: moonlight@booksource.net
Web Site: www.booksource.net

Personnel:
John Clement *(Managing Director)*
Penny Clement *(Company Secretary)*

Atlases & Maps; Children's Books; English as a Foreign Language; Fine Art & Art History; Music; Natural History

Imprints, Series & ISBNs:
Close-Ups: 978 1 85103
First Discovery: 978 1 85103
My First Discoveries: 978 1 85103
Torchlight: 978 1 85103

Overseas Representation:
Australia: Era, Brooklyn Park, SA, Australia
Canada: Rainbow Books, Vancouver, BC, Canada
India: Rupa, New Delhi, India
Japan: First Discovery Japan, Tokyo, Japan
Korea: JY Books, Gyeonnggi-Do, Republic of Korea
Malaysia: BR Group, Kuching, Sarawak, Malaysia
South Africa: Wild Dog Press, Johannesburg, South Africa
Spain: Distribuidora Vicens Vives, Barcelona, Spain
Taiwan: Children's Publications Co Ltd, Taipei, Taiwan

Book Trade Association Membership:
Publishers Association; Publishing Scotland

2486

MOORLEY'S PRINT & PUBLISHING LTD
23 Park Road, Ilkeston, Derbyshire DE7 5DA
Telephone: 0115 932 0643
Fax: 0115 932 0643
Email: sales@moorleys.co.uk
Web Site: www.moorleys.co.uk

Personnel:
Peter R. Newberry *(Joint Managing, Financial)*
Patrick Mancini *(Joint Managing, Production)*

History & Antiquarian; Music; Poetry; Religion & Theology; Theatre, Drama & Dance

New Titles: 10 (2010) , 8 (2011)
No of Employees: 6
Annual Turnover: £360,000

Imprints, Series & ISBNs:
978 0 86071, 978 0 901495

Distributor for:
Cliff College Publishing; Darby Publications; Mainstream Baptists for Life & Growth; Met Specials; Nimbus Press; Social Work Christian Fellowship; Wesley Fellowship Publications
Malaysia: Pustaka Sufes Sdn Bhd

Book Trade Association Membership:
Publishing Licensing Society

2487

MOTOR RACING PUBLICATIONS LTD
PO Box 1318, Croydon, Surrey CR9 5YP
Telephone: 020 8654 2711
Fax: 020 8407 0339
Email: john@mrpbooks.co.uk
Web Site: www.mrpbooks.co.uk

Orders:
Vine House Distribution Ltd,
The Old Mill House, Mill Lane, Uckfield,
East Sussex TN22 5AA
Telephone: 01825 767396
Fax: 01825 765649
Email: sales@vinehouseuk.co.uk
Web Site: www.vinehouseuk.co.uk

Personnel:
John Blunsden *(Managing Director)*

Biography & Autobiography; Sports & Games; Transport

New Titles: 1 (2011)
No of Employees: 1
Annual Turnover: £52,000

Imprints, Series & ISBNs:
The Fitzjames Press: 978 0 948358
Motor Racing Publications: 978 0 900549, 978 0 947981, 978 1 899870
MRP Publishing: 978 0 900549, 978 0 947981, 978 1 899870

Overseas Representation:
All territories (excluding Australia, New Zealand, USA, Canada & Republic of Ireland): Gunnar Lie Associates, London, UK
USA & Canada: MBI Distribution Services, Osceola, WI, USA

2488

*MP PUBLISHING LTD
12 Strathallan Crescent, Douglas,
Isle of Man IM2 4NR
Telephone: 01624 618672
Fax: 01624 620798
Web Site: www.mppublishing.co.uk

Electronic (Entertainment); Fiction

2489

MPOWR LTD
Suite 11352, 2nd floor,
145–157 St John Street, London EC1V 4PY
Telephone: 020 8133 9783
Email: info@mpowrpublishing.com
Web Site: www.mpowrpublishing.com

Personnel:
Richard Hagen *(Contact)*

Children's Books

Book Trade Association Membership:
Publishers Association

2490

MURDOCH BOOKS UK LTD
6th Floor, Erico House,
93–99 Upper Richmond Road, London
SW15 2TG
Telephone: 020 8785 5995
Fax: 020 8785 5985
Email: info@murdochbooks.co.uk
Web Site: www.murdochbooks.co.uk

Distribution & Invoicing:
Macmillan Distribution Ltd, Brunel Road,
Houndmills, Basingstoke, Hants RG21 2XS
Telephone: 01256 329242
Fax: 01256 327961

Personnel:
Matt Handbury *(Group Chief Executive)*
Christine Jones *(UK Managing Director)*
John Sprinks *(UK Finance Director)*
Cathy Slater *(Foreign Rights Director)*

Biography & Autobiography; Cookery, Wines & Spirits; Crafts & Hobbies; Do-It-Yourself; Gardening; Health & Beauty; History & Antiquarian; Travel & Topography

No of Employees: 8

Imprints, Series & ISBNs:
Murdoch Books: 978 1 74045, 978 1 74196, 978 1 74266
Pier 9: 978 1 74045, 978 1 74196, 978 1 74266

Parent Company:
Australia: Murdoch Books Pty Ltd

Overseas Representation:
Africa: A–Z Africa Book Services, Rotterdam, Netherlands
Asia: Pan Macmillan Asia, Hong Kong
Australia, New Zealand & USA: Murdoch Books Pty Ltd, Sydney, NSW, Australia
Europe: Angell Eurosales, Berwick-on-Tweed, UK; Gabriele Kern Publishers' Services, Frankfurt-am-Main, Germany; Nilsson & Lamm, Sint-Niklaas, Belgium; Penny Padovani, London, UK
Middle East: Peter Ward Book Exports, London, UK

Book Trade Association Membership:
Independent Publishers Guild

2491

JOHN MURRAY PUBLISHERS
[a division of Hachette UK]
338 Euston Road, London NW1 3BH
Telephone: 020 7873 6000
Fax: 020 7873 6446
Web Site: www.johnmurray.co.uk

UK Orders & Invoicing, Payments & Credit Control & Warehouse:
Bookpoint, 130 Milton Park, Abingdon,
Oxon OX14 4SB
Telephone: 01235 400400
Fax: 01235 821511

Personnel:
Roland Philipps *(Managing Director)*
James Spackman *(Sales & Marketing Director)*
Nikki Barrow *(Publicity Director)*
Jason Bartholomew *(Rights Director)*
Eleanor Birne *(Publishing Director)*

Biography & Autobiography; Fiction; Fine Art & Art History; History & Antiquarian; Humour; Military & War; Travel & Topography

Imprints, Series & ISBNs:
978 0 7195

Parent Company:
Hachette UK

Overseas Representation:
Australia: Alliance Distribution Services Pty Ltd, Tuggerah, NSW, Australia; Hachette Livre Australia, Sydney, NSW, Australia
Canada: McArthur & Co Publishers Ltd, Toronto, Ont, Canada
Hong Kong: Asia Publishers Services Ltd, Hong Kong
India: Hachette Book Publishing India Pvt Ltd, Gurgaon, India
Netherlands (Hardbacks and Trade

Paperbacks): Nilsson & Lamm BV, Weesp, Netherlands
Netherlands (Paperbacks): Van Ditmar BV, Amsterdam, Netherlands
New Zealand: Hachette Livre New Zealand, Auckland, New Zealand
Pakistan: Oxford University Press Pakistan Branch, Karachi, Pakistan
Singapore & Malaysia: Pansing Distribution Sdn Bhd, Singapore
South Africa: Jonathan Ball Publishers (Pty) Ltd, Johannesburg, South Africa
USA: Trafalgar Square Publishing, North Pomfret, VT, USA

Book Trade Association Membership:
Publishers Association; Independent Publishers Guild

2492

MW EDUCATIONAL
Westcliff Drive, Leigh-on-Sea, Essex SS9 2LB
Telephone: 01702 715282
Fax: 01702 715172
Email: mweducational@yahoo.co.uk
Web Site: www.mweducational.co.uk

Distribution:
Gardners Books Ltd, 1 Whittle Drive, Eastbourne, East Sussex BN23 6QH
Telephone: 01323 521555

Personnel:
Mark Chatterton *(Chief Executive Officer)*

Children's Books; Educational & Textbooks; English as a Foreign Language; Mathematics & Statistics

New Titles: 6 (2011)

Imprints, Series & ISBNs:
The A Plus Series of 11+ Practice Papers: 978 1 901146
The Advantage Series of SATs Practice Papers: 978 1 901146
Primary Directories: 978 1 901146

2493

MYRIAD EDITIONS
59 Lansdowne Place, Brighton BN3 1FL
Telephone: 01273 720000
Email: info@MyriadEditions.com
Web Site: www.MyriadEditions.com

Personnel:
Candida Lacey *(Managing Director)*
Robert Benewick *(Director)*
Judith Mackay *(Director)*
Corinne Pearlman *(Creative Director)*
Isabelle Lewis *(Designer)*
Jannet King *(Editor)*
Vicky Blunden *(Fiction Editor)*
Emma Dowson *(Publicist)*
Adrian Weston *(Rights)*

Academic & Scholarly; Atlases & Maps; Electronic (Professional & Academic); Environment & Development Studies; Fiction; Gender Studies; Military & War; Politics & World Affairs

New Titles: 8 (2010) , 8 (2011)
No of Employees: 2

Imprints, Series & ISBNs:
978 0 9549309, 978 0 9565599, 978 0 9567926, 978 1 908434

Overseas Representation:
China & Taiwan: Big Apple Tuttle-Mori Agency Inc, Taipei, Taiwan
Japan: Tuttle-Mori Agency Inc, Tokyo, Japan
Spain, Portugal & South America: Ilustrata Empresariale SL, Barcelona, Spain

Book Trade Association Membership:
Independent Publishers Guild

2494

MYRMIDON BOOKS LTD
Rotterdam House, 116 Quayside, Newcastle upon Tyne NE1 3DY
Telephone: 0191 206 4005
Email: ed@myrmidonbooks.com
Web Site: www.myrmidonbooks.com

Distribution:
Littlehampton Book Services, Faraday Close, Durrington, Worthing, West Sussex TN13 3RB
Telephone: 01903 828500
Email: enquiries@lbsltd.co.uk
Web Site: www.lbsltd.co.uk

Personnel:
Edward Handyside *(Publishing Director)*

Fiction

Imprints, Series & ISBNs:
978 1 905802

Overseas Representation:
Australia & New Zealand: Bookwise International, Wingfield, SA, Australia
Singapore, Malaysia & neighbouring territories: Pansing Distribution Pte Ltd, Singapore
South Africa & neighbouring territories: Penguin Books, South Africa

Book Trade Association Membership:
Publishers Association; Independent Publishers Guild

2495

THE MYRTLE PRESS
Kemp House, 152–160 City Road, London EC1V 2NX
Telephone: 01604 890208
Web Site: www.themyrtlepress.com

New Titles: 3 (2010)

Book Trade Association Membership:
Publishers Association

2496

THE NATIONAL ACADEMIES PRESS
5 Victoria House, 138 Watling Street East, Towcester NN12 6BT
Telephone: 01327 357770
Fax: 01327 359572
Email: nap@oppuk.co.uk
Web Site: www.nap.edu

Warehouse & Distribution:
Marston Book Services, 160 Milton Park, PO Box 169, Abingdon, Oxon OX14 4YN
Telephone: 01235 465521
Email: direct.orders@marston.co.uk
Web Site: www.marston.co.uk

Personnel:
Gary Hall *(Marketing Manager)*

Academic & Scholarly; Agriculture; Animal Care & Breeding; Biology & Zoology; Chemistry; Educational & Textbooks; Engineering; Environment & Development Studies; Geography & Geology; Industry, Business & Management; Mathematics & Statistics; Medical (incl. Self Help & Alternative Medicine); Natural History; Nautical; Physics; Psychology & Psychiatry; Scientific & Technical; Veterinary Science

New Titles: 200 (2011)

Imprints, Series & ISBNs:
National Academies Press: 978 0 309

Parent Company:
USA: National Academies Press

2497

NATIONAL ARCHIVES OF SCOTLAND
HM General Register House, Edinburgh EH1 3YY
Telephone: 0131 535 1314
Fax: 0131 535 1360
Email: enquiries@nas.gov.uk
Web Site: www.nrscotland.gov.uk

Also at:
Ladywell House, Ladywell Road, Edinburgh EH12 7TF
Telephone: 0131 314 4299
Fax: 0131 314 4696
Email: customer@gro-scotland.gsi.gov.uk
Web Site: www.gro-scotland.gov.uk

Personnel:
George P. MacKenzie *(Registrar General for Scotland & Keeper of the Records of Scotland)*
Donna Hosie *(Head of Statistical Information Services)*

Academic & Scholarly; Electronic (Professional & Academic); History & Antiquarian; Mathematics & Statistics

New Titles: 2 (2011)
No of Employees: 350

Imprints, Series & ISBNs:
978 1 870874, 978 1 874451

Book Trade Association Membership:
Publishing Scotland

2498

THE NATIONAL ASSOCIATION FOR THE TEACHING OF ENGLISH (NATE)
50 Broadfield Road, Sheffield S8 0XJ
Telephone: 0114 255 5419
Fax: 0114 255 5296
Email: info@nate.org.uk
Web Site: www.nate.org.uk

Personnel:
A. Fairhall *(Publications Manager)*
R. Williams *(Senior Administrator)*
I. McNeilly *(Director)*

Academic & Scholarly; Educational & Textbooks

New Titles: 1 (2010) , 1 (2011)
No of Employees: 6

Imprints, Series & ISBNs:
978 0 901291, 978 1 904709

Distributor for:
Australia: Phoenix Education
UK: Routledge; Sage

Overseas Representation:
Australia: Phoenix Education, Putney, Australia

2499

*THE NATIONAL AUTISTIC SOCIETY (NAS)
393 City Road, London EC1V 1NG
Telephone: 020 7833 2299
Fax: 020 7833 9666
Email: nas@nas.org.uk
Web Site: www.autism.org.uk

Trade Enquiries & Orders:
Central Books, 99 Wallis Road, London E9 5LN
Telephone: 0845 458 9911
Fax: 0845 458 9912
Email: nas@centralbooks.com
Web Site: www.autism.org.uk/pubs

Personnel:
Alex Tyla *(Marketing Officer)*

Kathryn Quinton *(Communications)*
David Mason *(Publications Sales Officer)*

Children's Books; Educational & Textbooks; Psychology & Psychiatry

Imprints, Series & ISBNs:
978 1 899280, 978 1 905722

Book Trade Association Membership:
Publishers Form, NCVO

2500

NATIONAL CHILDREN'S BUREAU
NCB Publications, 8 Wakley Street, London EC1V 7QE
Telephone: 020 7843 6317
Fax: 020 7843 6087
Email: publications@ncb.org.uk
Web Site: www.ncb.org.uk/books

Distributor:
Central Books, 99 Wallis Road, London E9 5LN
Telephone: 0845 458 9912
Fax: 0845 458 9910
Email: ncb@centralbooks.com
Web Site: www.centralbooks.com

Personnel:
Paula McMahon *(Publishing Manager)*
Agnes Niciejewska *(Publishing Officer)*
Judith Sabah *(Marketing Officer)*

Academic & Scholarly; Educational & Textbooks; Electronic (Professional & Academic); Vocational Training & Careers

New Titles: 3 (2010) , 3 (2011)
No of Employees: 3
Annual Turnover: £150,000

Imprints, Series & ISBNs:
978 0 902817, 978 1 870985, 978 1 874579, 978 1 900990, 978 1 904787, 978 1 905818, 978 1 907969

Book Trade Association Membership:
Independent Publishers Guild

2501

*NATIONAL EXTENSION COLLEGE TRUST LTD
The Michael Young Centre, Purbeck Road, Cambridge CB2 8HN
Telephone: 01223 400200r2528
Fax: 01223 400399
Email: info@nec.ac.uk
Web Site: www.nec.ac.uk

Personnel:
Gavin Teasdale *(Chief Executive Director)*
Jorgen Clausen *(Finance Director)*
Tim Burton *(Education Director)*
Tony Hopwood *(Business Development Director)*

Economics; Educational & Textbooks; Electronic (Educational); Fine Art & Art History; Languages & Linguistics; Law; Mathematics & Statistics; Medical (incl. Self Help & Alternative Medicine); Physics; Psychology & Psychiatry; Religion & Theology; Sociology & Anthropology; Vocational Training & Careers

Imprints, Series & ISBNs:
978 0 86082, 978 1 85356

Book Trade Association Membership:
Independent Publishers Guild

2502

NATIONAL GALLERIES OF SCOTLAND
Belford Road, Edinburgh EH4 3DS
Telephone: 0131 624 6257 & 6261
Fax: 0131 623 7135
Email: publications@nationalgalleries.org

Web Site: www.nationalgalleries.org

Personnel:
Janis Adams (Head of Publishing)
Christine Thompson (Publishing Manager)
Olivia Sheppard (Editorial Assistant)

Fine Art & Art History; Photography

New Titles: 12 (2010) , 12 (2011)
No of Employees: 3

Imprints, Series & ISBNs:
978 0 903148, 978 0 903598, 978 1
903278

Overseas Representation:
North America: ACC, Easthampton, MA,
USA

Book Trade Association Membership:
Publishing Scotland

2503

*NATIONAL GALLERY CO LTD
St Vincent House, 30 Orange Street,
London WC2H 7HH
Telephone: 020 7747 5950
Fax: 020 7747 5951
Email: admin@nationalgallery.co.uk
Web Site: www.nationalgallery.co.uk

Distribution:
Yale University Press, 47 Bedford Square,
London WC1B 3DP
Telephone: 020 7079 4900
Fax: 020 7079 4901
Email: sales@yaleup.co.uk
Web Site: www.yalebooks.co.uk

Personnel:
Louise Rice (Publishing & Logistics Director)
J. Green (Senior Project Editor)
Giselle Osborne (Project Editor)
Claire Young (Project Editor)
Alex Glen (Publishing Administrator)
Jane Hyne (Production Manager)
Penny Le Tissier (Production Controller)
Suzanne Bosman (Senior Picture
Researcher)
Maria Ranauro (Picture Researcher)
Sara Purdy (Publishing Manager)

Academic & Scholarly; Children's Books;
Cookery, Wines & Spirits; Electronic
(Educational); Electronic (Professional &
Academic); Fine Art & Art History; Guide
Books

Imprints, Series & ISBNs:
978 0 901791, 978 0 947645, 978 1 85709

Parent Company:
The National Gallery Trust

Overseas Representation:
Africa (excluding Southern Africa & Nigeria):
Kelvin van Hasselt Publishing Services,
Briningham, Norfolk, UK
Austria, Germany, Italy & Switzerland: Uwe
Lüdemann, Berlin, Germany
Benelux, Denmark, Finland, France, Iceland,
Norway & Sweden: Fred Hermans,
Bovenkarspel, Netherlands
Hong Kong, China & Philippines: Ed
Summerson, Asia Publishers Services Ltd,
Hong Kong
India: S. Janakiraman, Book Marketing
Services, Chennai, India
Iran: Farhad Maftoon, Tehran, Iran
Middle East: International Publishers
Representatives (IPR) Ltd, Nicosia, Cyprus
Nigeria: Bounty Press Ltd, Ibadan, Nigeria
Pakistan: Anwer Iqbal, Book Bird Publishers
Representatives, Lahore, Pakistan
Poland, Czech Republic, Hungary &
Slovenia: Ewa Ledóchowicz, Konstancin-
Jeziorna, Poland
Republic of Ireland & Northern Ireland:
Robert Towers, Monkstown, Co Dublin,
Republic of Ireland

Singapore, Malaysia, Brunei & Indonesia:
APD Singapore Pte Ltd, Singapore
Southern Africa: Book Promotions Pty Ltd,
Diep River, South Africa
Spain & Portugal: Chris Humphrys,
Provincia de Malaga, Spain
USA, Canada, Mexico, Central & South
America, Australia, New Zealand, Japan,
Korea & Taiwan: Yale University Press,
New Haven, CT, USA

2504

NATIONAL HOUSING FEDERATION
Lion Court, 25 Procter Street, Holborn,
London WC1V 6NY
Telephone: 020 7067 1010
Fax: 020 7067 1011
Email: info@housing.org.uk
Web Site: www.housing.co.uk

Personnel:
Bev Markham (Head of Publications)
Fiona Shand (Production Editor)
Rick Lloyd (Publishing Coordinator)

Academic & Scholarly; Educational &
Textbooks; Industry, Business &
Management; Reference Books, Directories
& Dictionaries; Vocational Training &
Careers

Imprints, Series & ISBNs:
978 0 86297

2505

**NATIONAL PORTRAIT GALLERY
PUBLICATIONS**
National Portrait Gallery, St Martin's Place,
London WC2H 0HE
Telephone: 020 7306 0055 ext 266 & 020
7312 2482 (direct line)
Fax: 020 7321 6657
Email: pvadhia@npg.org.uk
Web Site: www.npg.org.uk/publications

Distribution:
Grantham Book Services, Trent Road,
Grantham, Lincs NG31 7XG
Telephone: 01476 541080
Fax: 01476 541061
Email: orders@gbs.tbs_ltd.co.uk (UK only)
Web Site:
www.granthambookservices.co.uk

Representation (UK):
Casemate Books, 17 Cheap Street,
Newbury, Berks RG14 5DD
Telephone: 01635 231091
Fax: 01635 41619
Web Site: www.casematepublishing.co.uk

Personnel:
Robert Carr-Archer (Head of Trading)
Tom Morgan (Head of Rights &
Reproduction)
Ruth Müller-Wirth (Production Manager)
Pallavi Vadhia (Sales & Marketing Manager)
Christopher Tinker (Managing Editor)
Sarah Ruddick (Editor)
Kate Tolley (Assistant Editor)
Alex Glen (Sales & Marketing Assistant)

Academic & Scholarly; Biography &
Autobiography; Fashion & Costume; Fine
Art & Art History; Guide Books; History &
Antiquarian; Illustrated & Fine Editions;
Photography; Reference Books, Directories
& Dictionaries

Imprints, Series & ISBNs:
978 0 904017, 978 1 85514

Overseas Representation:
Australia: Peribo Pty Ltd, Mount Kuring-Gai,
NSW, Australia
France: Casemate Books, Newbury, UK
Germany, Austria, Switzerland, Belgium &
Luxembourg: Exhibitions International,
Leuven, Belgium

Italy, Spain, Portugal & Greece: Penny
Padovani, London, UK
Netherlands: Amsterdam University Press,
Amsterdam, Netherlands
Republic of Ireland & Northern Ireland:
Robert Towers, Monkstown, Co Dublin,
Republic of Ireland
Scandinavia: Angell Eurosales
South America: David Williams, InterMedia
Americana (IMA) Ltd, London, UK
USA: Antique Collectors Club Ltd,
Easthampton, MA, USA

Book Trade Association Membership:
Booksellers Association; Independent
Publishers Guild

2506

THE NATIONAL TRUST
Heelis, Kemble Drive, Swindon, Wilts
SN2 2NA
Telephone: 01793 817400
Fax: 01793 817401
Email: grant.berry@nationaltrust.org.uk
Web Site: www.nationaltrust.org.uk

Also at:
Anova Books, 10 Southcombe Street,
London W14 0RA
Telephone: 020 7605 1400
Web Site: www.anovabooks.com

Personnel:
John Stachiewicz (Publisher & Commercial
Manager)
Grant Berry (Publishing Manager)
Oliver Garrett (Property Publisher)
Anna Groves (Editor)
Claire Forbes (Assistant Editor)

Academic & Scholarly; Agriculture;
Antiques & Collecting; Archaeology;
Architecture & Design; Biography &
Autobiography; Children's Books; Cookery,
Wines & Spirits; Fashion & Costume; Fine
Art & Art History; Gardening; Guide Books;
History & Antiquarian; Humour; Natural
History; Reference Books, Directories &
Dictionaries; Travel & Topography

Imprints, Series & ISBNs:
978 0 7078

Associated Companies:
Anova Books; Gardners Books; The History
Press

2507

**NATURAL HISTORY MUSEUM
PUBLISHING**
The Natural History Museum,
Cromwell Road, London SW7 5BD
Telephone: 020 7942 5060
Fax: 020 7942 5291
Email: publishing@nhm.ac.uk
Web Site: www.nhm.ac.uk/publishing

Warehouse & Distribution:
Bookpoint Ltd, 130 Milton Park, Abingdon,
Oxon OX14 4SB
Telephone: 01235 400400
Fax: 01235 400500
Email: mailorder@bookpoint.co.uk

Personnel:
Lynn Millhouse (Production Manager)
Trudy Brannan (Editorial Manager)
Colin Ziegler (Head of Publishing)
Howard Trent (Sales & Marketing Executive)

Academic & Scholarly; Biography &
Autobiography; Biology & Zoology;
Children's Books; Educational & Textbooks;
Fine Art & Art History; Geography &
Geology; Natural History; Reference Books,
Directories & Dictionaries; Scientific &
Technical

Imprints, Series & ISBNs:
978 0 565

2508

*NAXOS AUDIOBOOKS
40A High Street, Welwyn, Herts AL6 9EQ
Telephone: 01438 717808
Fax: 01438 717809
Email: info@naxosaudiobooks.com
Web Site: www.naxos.co.uk/audiobooks/

Distribution:
Select Music & Video, 3 Wells Place,
Redhill, Surrey RH1 3SL
Telephone: 01737 645600
Fax: 01737 645600

Personnel:
Nicolas Soames (Director)

Audio Books

Imprints, Series & ISBNs:
978 962 634

Parent Company:
Hong Kong: HNH International

Associated Companies:
Naxos Classical Music
Hong Kong: Naxos Classical Music

Overseas Representation:
Australia: Select, Sydney, Australia
Austria: Gramola Co, Vienna, Australia
Brazil: RKR Musical, São Paulo, Brazil
Canada: Naxos of Canada Ltd,
Scarborough, Ont, Canada
Czech Republic: Classic Music Distribution,
Prague, Czech Republic
Denmark: Olga Musik, Ry, Denmark
Finland: FG Distribution, Helsinki, Finland
France: Naxos of France, Paris, France
Germany: MVD, Munich, Germany; Naxos
Deutschland, Münster, Germany
Greece: Greek Record Club, Athens, Greece
Hungary: Phoenix Studio, Budapest,
Hungary
Iceland: JAPIS, Reykjavik, Iceland
Israel: MCI Records, Tel Aviv, Israel
Japan: Naxos Japan, Nagoya & Tokyo, Japan
Korea: Hae Dong Co Ltd, Seoul, Republic of
Korea
Malaysia: AV Masters Sdn Bhd, Kuala
Lumpur, Malaysia
Netherlands: Vanguard Classics,
Nieuwegein, Netherlands
New Zealand: Triton Music Ltd, Auckland,
New Zealand
Norway: Musikkdistribusjon AS, Oslo,
Norway
Philippines: Universal Records, Kalookan
City, Philippines
Republic of Ireland: Cosmic Sounds Ltd,
Dublin, Republic of Ireland
Singapore: Naxos Pte Ltd, Singapore
Slovak Republic: Slovart Music, Bratislava,
Slovakia
South Africa: Booktalk (Pty) Ltd, Craighall,
South Africa
Spain: FERYSA, Madrid, Spain
Sri Lanka: Titus Stores, Columbo, Sri Lanka
Sweden: Naxos Sweden, Orebro, Sweden
Switzerland: FAME, Meggen (Lucerne),
Switzerland
Taiwan: Rock Records & Tapes, Taipei,
Taiwan
Thailand: Media Plus & Broadcasting
Network Ltd, Bangkok, Thailand
Turkey: Haci Emin Elendi Sokak, Istanbul,
Turkey
USA: Naxos of America Inc, Pennsauken, NJ,
USA

Book Trade Association Membership:
Publishers Association; Spoken Word
Publishers' Association

2509

*NEED2KNOW
Remus House, Coltsfoot Drive, Woodston,
Peterborough PE2 9JX
Telephone: 01733 898103

Fax: 01733 313524
Email: sales@n2kbooks.com
Web Site: www.need2knowbooks.co.uk

Personnel:
Kate Gibbard (Imprint Manager)
Emma Gubb (Editorial Assistant)

Cookery, Wines & Spirits; Educational & Textbooks; Gardening; Health & Beauty; Medical (incl. Self Help & Alternative Medicine); Poetry; Vocational Training & Careers

Imprints, Series & ISBNs:
Need2Know: 978 1 86144
Triumph House

Parent Company:
Forward Press Ltd

Book Trade Association Membership:
Booksellers Association

2510

NELSON THORNES LTD
[formerly Stanley Thornes Ltd & Thomas Nelson & Sons Ltd]
Delta Place, 27 Bath Road, Cheltenham GL53 7TH
Telephone: 01242 267100
Fax: 01242 221914 (General) & 253695 (Orders)
Email: info@nelsonthornes.com
Web Site: www.nelsonthornes.com

Distribution:
Alexandra Way, Ashchurch, Tewkesbury, Glos GL20 8PE

Personnel:
Paul Howarth (Managing Director)
Wendy Rimmington (Sales & Marketing Director, UK & International)
Claire Varlet-Baker (Publishing Director)
Neil McQuillan (Operations Director)
Jennie Martin (Online Services Director)
Adrian Wheaton (Publishing Strategy Director)
Sarah Armstrong (HR Director)
Margot van de Weijer (Head of Customer Services & Distribution)
Caroline Blackburn (Head of Finance)

Accountancy & Taxation; Biology & Zoology; Chemistry; Children's Books; Computer Science; Economics; Educational & Textbooks; Electronic (Educational); Engineering; Environment & Development Studies; Fashion & Costume; Geography & Geology; Health & Beauty; History & Antiquarian; Industry, Business & Management; Languages & Linguistics; Law; Literature & Criticism; Mathematics & Statistics; Medical (incl. Self Help & Alternative Medicine); Music; Philosophy; Physics; Poetry; Politics & World Affairs; Psychology & Psychiatry; Religion & Theology; Scientific & Technical; Sociology & Anthropology; Sports & Games; Theatre, Drama & Dance; Vocational Training & Careers

Imprints, Series & ISBNs:
978 0 17, 978 0 7487, 978 1 4085

Parent Company:
UK: Infinitas Learning

Distributor for:
Australia: Cengage; Macmillan Library

Overseas Representation:
Argentina: Kel Ediciones SA (Agents), Buenos Aires, Argentina
Australia: Cengage (Australia), NSW, Australia
Barbados: Days Bookstore, Bridgetown, Barbados
Botswana, South Africa, Lesotho,

Swaziland, Mozambique & Namibia: Macmillan Education Ltd, Oxford, UK
Egypt: Galaxy Trade, Giza, Egypt
Gulf States, Iran, Syria, Libya, Jordan, Lebanon, Cyprus, Yemen, Tunis, Turkey, Morocco & Algeria (Further & Higher Education only): International Publishing Services (IPS) Middle East Ltd, Dubai, UAE
Guyana: Austin's Book Services, Georgetown, Guyana
Hong Kong & Macao: Transglobal Publishers Services Ltd, Hong Kong
India, Bangladesh, Sri Lanka, Nepal & Bhutan: Overleaf, New Delhi, India
Jamaica: Kingston Bookshop, Kingston, Jamaica
Kenya: Educate Yourself, Kenya
Malaysia: APD Kuala Lumpur Pte Ltd, Selangor, Malaysia
Malta: Miller Distributors Ltd, Luqa, Malta
Mauritius: Editions le Printemps, Vacoas, Mauritius
New Zealand: Cengage, New Zealand
Nigeria: Chelis Bookazine, Lagos, Nigeria
Pakistan: Publishers Marketing Associates, Karachi, Pakistan
Republic of Ireland (Primary, Secondary & Further Education): Carrol Educational Supplies, Dublin, Republic of Ireland
Singapore & Brunei: APD Singapore Pte Ltd, Singapore
St Vincent & The Grenadines: Gaymes Book Centre, St Vincent
Sweden, Denmark, Norway, Finland, Iceland, Estonia, Latvia & Lithuania (Health Science & Science & Engineering titles only): David Towle International, Stockholm, Sweden
Tajikistan, Uzbekistan, Kazakhstan, Kyrgyzstan & Turkmenistan: Silk Road Media, London, UK
Trinidad & Tobago: Books Etc, San Fernando, Trinidad
Uruguay: Opiciones en Educacion, Uruguay

Book Trade Association Membership:
Publishers Association

2511

NETWORK CONTINUUM EDUCATION LTD
see: Continuum International Publishing Group

2512

NEW ACADEMIC SCIENCE LTD
11a Little Mount Sion, Tunbridge Wells, Kent TN1 1YS
Telephone: 01892 557782
Fax: 01892 530358
Web Site:
www.newacademicscience.co.uk

Book Trade Association Membership:
Publishers Association

2513

*NEW INTERNATIONALIST PUBLICATIONS LTD
55 Rectory Road, Oxford OX4 1BW
Telephone: 01865 811400
Fax: 01865 793152
Email: ni@newint.org
Web Site: www.newint.org

Representation (UK):
Turnaround Publisher Services Ltd, Unit 3, Olympia Trading Estate, Coburg Road, London N22 6TZ
Telephone: 020 8829 3000
Fax: 020 8881 5088

Personnel:
Frank Syratt (Company Accountant)
Fran Harvey (Production Manager)
Dan Raymond-Barker (Publications Marketing Manager)
Troth Wells (Publications Editor)
Amanda Synnott (Magazine Marketing)

Atlases & Maps; Cookery, Wines & Spirits; Electronic (Educational); Environment & Development Studies; Fiction; Photography; Politics & World Affairs; Reference Books, Directories & Dictionaries

Imprints, Series & ISBNs:
No-Nonsense Series: 978 0 9540499, 978 1 869847, 978 1 904456, 978 1 906523
World Changing

Parent Company:
New Internationalist Trust Ltd

Overseas Representation:
Australia: Palgrave Macmillan, South Yarra, Vic, Australia
Australia & Papua New Guinea: New Internationalist Publications Ltd, Adelaide, SA, Australia
Canada: New Internationalist Publications Ltd, Toronto, Ont, Canada
New Zealand & Aotearoa: New Internationalist Publications Ltd, Christchurch, New Zealand
South Africa: Stephan Phillips (Pty) Ltd, Cape Town, South Africa
USA: Consortium Book Sales & Distribution Inc, St Paul, MN, USA

Book Trade Association Membership:
Independent Publishers Guild; Periodical Publishers Association

2514

NEW ISLAND BOOKS LTD
2 Brookside, Dundrum Road, Dublin 14, Republic of Ireland
Telephone: +353 (0)1 298 3411
Fax: +353 (0)1 298 2783
Email: sales@newisland.ie
Web Site: www.newisland.ie

Distribution:
Gill & Macmillan, Hume Avenue, Park West, Dublin 12, Republic of Ireland
Telephone: +353 (0)1 500 9555
Fax: +353 (0)1 500 9599
Email: sales@gillmacmillan.ie

Representation (Republic of Ireland & Northern Ireland):
Compass Ireland, 38 Kerdiff Avenue, Naas, Co Kildare, Republic of Ireland
Telephone: +353 (0)45 880805
Fax: +353 (0)45 880806
Email: alasdair@compassireland.ie

Personnel:
Edwin Higel (Publisher)
Deirdre O'Neill (Editorial Manager)
Inka Hagen (Production & Design Manager)
Aisling Glynn (Accounts Manager)
Karen O'Donoghue (Marketing, Publicity & Sales Manager)
Maria White (Rights Agent)
Elaina O'Neill (Editorial Assistant)

Biography & Autobiography; Children's Books; English as a Foreign Language; Fiction; Gender Studies; Guide Books; History & Antiquarian; Humour; Literature & Criticism; Poetry; Politics & World Affairs; Theatre, Drama & Dance

Imprints, Series & ISBNs:
Little Island: 978 1 84840
New Island: 978 1 84840, 978 1 874597, 978 1 902602, 978 1 904301, 978 1 905494

Overseas Representation:
UK: Compass DSA, Slough, UK
USA & Canada: Dufour Editions Inc, Chester Springs, PA, USA; ISBS, Portland, OR, USA

Book Trade Association Membership:
Publishing Ireland (Foilsiú Éireann)

2515

NEW PLAYWRIGHTS' NETWORK
10 Station Road Industrial Estate, Colwall, Malvern, Worcs WR13 6RN
Telephone: 01684 540154
Email: simon@cressrelles.co.uk
Web Site: www.cressrelles.co.uk

Personnel:
L. G. Smith (Managing Director)
S. R. Smith (Sales Director)

Theatre, Drama & Dance

New Titles: 5 (2010), 5 (2011)
No of Employees: 2

Imprints, Series & ISBNs:
978 0 86319, 978 0 903653, 978 0 906660

Parent Company:
Cressrelles Publishing Co Ltd

Overseas Representation:
Australia: Origin Theatrical, Sydney, NSW, Australia
New Zealand: Play Bureau of New Zealand Ltd, New Plymouth, New Zealand
Republic of Ireland: Drama League of Ireland, Dublin, Republic of Ireland
South Africa: Dalro (Pty) Ltd, Braamfontein, South Africa
USA: Bakers Plays, Quincy, MA, USA

2516

NHS IMMUNISATION INFORMATION
Department of Health, Wellington House, 133–155 Waterloo Road, London SE1 8UG
Telephone: 020 7972 4973
Fax: 020 7972 3989
Email: chris.owen@dh.gsi.gov.uk
Web Site: www.nhs.uk/vaccinations

Academic & Scholarly; Educational & Textbooks; Medical (incl. Self Help & Alternative Medicine)

2517

NIELSEN
3rd Floor, Midas House, 62 Goldsworth Road, Woking, Surrey GU21 6LQ
Telephone: 01483 712200
Fax: 01483 712201
Email: info.book@nielsen.com
Web Site: www.nielsenbook.co.uk

Editorial:
89–95 Queensway, Stevenage, Herts SG1 1EA
Telephone: 0845 450 0016
Fax: 01438 745578
Email: newtitles.book@nielsen.com & pubhelp.book@nielsen.com
Web Site: www.nielsenbook.co.uk

Personnel:
Jonathan Nowell (President)
Richard Knight (Product Development Director)
Ann Betts (Commercial Director)
Jon Windus (Operations Director)
Andrew Sugden (Financial Director)
Simon Skinner (Sales Director)
Mo Siewcharran (Head of Marketing)
Peter Mathews (Senior Manager, Publishing Services)
Howard Willows (Senior Manager, Data Development)
Gwyneth Morgan (Editorial Systems, Senior Manager)
Samantha Watson (Quality Assurance, Senior Manager)
Vesna Nall (Publisher Subscriptions Manager)
Paul Dibble (Head of Data Sales)
Stephen Long (Head of BookNet)
Christine Broadbent (HRBP)

Bibliography & Library Science

No of Employees: 120

Parent Company:
Nielsen Holdings N.V. (NYSE: NLSN)

Associated Companies:
BDS; ISTC Agency; Nielsen BookData; Nielsen BookData Asia Pacific; Nielsen BookNet; Nielsen BookScan; UK ISBN Agency; UK SAN Agency

Overseas Representation:
Germany & Western Balkans: Missing Link, Germany
South Africa: Publications Network (Pty) Ltd (trading as SAPNet), South Africa
Spain, Portugal and Gibraltar: Peter Prout, Spain

Book Trade Association Membership:
Publishing Scotland; Publishing Ireland (Foilsiú Éireann); Booksellers Association; Independent Publishers Guild

2518

*NIGHTINGALE PRESS
6 The Old Dairy, Melcombe Road, Bath BA2 3LR
Telephone: 01225 478444
Fax: 01225 478440
Email: sales@manning-partnership.co.uk
Web Site: www.manning-partnership.co.uk

Distribution:
Central Books, 99 Wallis Road, London E9 5LN
Telephone: 0845 458 9911
Fax: 0845 458 9912
Email: info@centralbooks.com
Web Site: www.centralbooks.com

Personnel:
Garry Manning *(Managing Director)*
Roger Hibbert *(Sales Director)*
Julie Pearson *(Finance Manager)*

Humour

Imprints, Series & ISBNs:
978 1 903222

Parent Company:
UK: The Manning Partnership

Distributor for:
Australia: Brimax; Five Mile Press
UK: Brown Dog Books; Carrol & Brown; Fanahan Books; Interpet Publishing; Search Press
USA: GPP; Sourcebooks

Overseas Representation:
USA: Richard Gay, Shepperton, Middlesex, UK

2519

NMS ENTERPRISES LIMITED - PUBLISHING
National Museums Scotland, Chambers Street, Edinburgh EH1 1JF
Telephone: 0131 247 4026
Fax: 0131 247 4012
Email: publishing@nms.ac.uk
Web Site: www.nms.ac.uk/books

Representation:
CPR, SPCK Head Office, 36 Causton Street, London SW1P 4ST
Telephone: 020 7592 3900
Email: sales@spck.org.uk

Distribution (UK):
BookSource, 50 Cambuslang Road, Glasgow G32 8NB
Telephone: 0845 370 0067
Fax: 0845 370 0068
Email: orders@booksource.net

Personnel:
Lesley A. Taylor *(Director of Publishing)*
Kate Blackadder *(Marketing Manager)*
Maggie Wilson *(Administration & Sales)*

Academic & Scholarly; Antiques & Collecting; Archaeology; Architecture & Design; Biography & Autobiography; Biology & Zoology; Children's Books; Cookery, Wines & Spirits; Educational & Textbooks; Fine Art & Art History; Geography & Geology; Guide Books; History & Antiquarian; Military & War; Natural History; Poetry; Scientific & Technical; Sociology & Anthropology; Transport

Imprints, Series & ISBNs:
978 0 948636, 978 1 901663, 978 1 905267

Parent Company:
National Museums Scotland

Overseas Representation:
USA: ACC Distributions, New York, NY, USA

Book Trade Association Membership:
Publishing Scotland

2520

NORTH YORK MOORS NATIONAL PARK AUTHORITY
The Old Vicarage, Bondgate, Helmsley, Yorks YO62 5BP
Telephone: 01439 770657
Fax: 01439 770691
Email: J.Renney@northyorkmoors-npa.gov.uk
Web Site: www.northyorkmoors.org.uk

Personnel:
Julie Lawrence *(Head of Information Service)*
Pat Waters-Marsh *(Finance Officer)*
Jill Renney *(Information & Interpretation Manager)*
Mark Lewis *(Interpretation Officer)*

Archaeology; Biology & Zoology; Children's Books; Educational & Textbooks; Environment & Development Studies; Geography & Geology; Guide Books; History & Antiquarian; Natural History

New Titles: 1 (2010) , 1 (2011)

Imprints, Series & ISBNs:
978 0 907480, 978 1 904622

2521

NORTHCOTE HOUSE PUBLISHERS LTD
Horndon House, Horndon, Tavistock, Devon PL19 9NQ
Telephone: 01822 810066
Fax: 01822 810034
Email: northcote.house@virgin.net
Web Site: www.northcotehouse.co.uk

Distributors:
Combined Book Services, Unit D, Paddock Wood Distribution Centre, Paddock Wood, Tonbridge, Kent TN12 6UU
Telephone: 01892 837171
Fax: 01892 837372
Email: orders@combook.co.uk
Web Site: www.combook.co.uk

Personnel:
Brian Hulme *(Managing Director & Publisher)*
Sarah Piper *(Marketing Manager)*

Academic & Scholarly; Educational & Textbooks; Literature & Criticism; Theatre, Drama & Dance

New Titles: 20 (2010) , 25 (2011)
No of Employees: 2

Annual Turnover: £100,000

Imprints, Series & ISBNs:
Northcote House: 978 0 7463
Resources in Education: 978 0 7463
Starting Out...: 978 0 7463
Writers and Their Work: 978 0 7463

Overseas Representation:
Africa (excluding South Africa) & Eastern Europe: Tony Moggach, IMA, London, UK
Australia & New Zealand: Book & Volume, Birregurra, Vic, Australia
Caribbean: Hugh Dunphy, Kingston, Jamaica
Germany, Austria, Switzerland, France, Japan, Italy & Benelux: Ted Dougherty, London, UK
India: Maya Publishers Pvt Ltd, New Delhi, India
Japan: Koro Komori, Eureka Press, Kyoto, Japan
Middle East: Hani Kreidieh, Beirut, Lebanon
Pakistan: Book Bird Publishers Representatives, Lahore, Pakistan
Scandinavia: David Towle International, Stockholm, Sweden
Spain & Portugal: Peter Prout Iberian Book Services, Madrid, Spain
USA, Canada & Mexico: David Brown Book Co, Oakville, CT, USA

Book Trade Association Membership:
Independent Publishers Guild

2522

*NORTHUMBRIA UNIVERSITY PRESS
Trinity Building, Northumbria University, Newcastle upon Tyne NE1 8ST
Telephone: 0191 227 3382
Fax: 0191 227 3387
Email: andrew.peden-smith@northumbria.ac.uk
Web Site: www.northumbriapress.co.uk

Orders::
Littlehampton Book Services, Faraday Close, Durrington, Worthing, West Sussex BN13 3RB
Telephone: 01903 828500
Fax: 01903 828511
Email: orders@lbsltd.co.uk
Web Site: www.lbsltd.co.uk

Personnel:
Andrew Peden Smith *(Head of Publishing)*
Mark Stafford *(Marketing/Publishing Assistant)*

Biography & Autobiography; Cookery, Wines & Spirits; Fine Art & Art History; Guide Books; History & Antiquarian; Music; Photography; Politics & World Affairs; Reference Books, Directories & Dictionaries; Theatre, Drama & Dance

Imprints, Series & ISBNs:
Northumbria Press: 978 0 85716
Northumbria University Press: 978 1 904794

Overseas Representation:
North America: Independent Publishers Group, Chicago, IL, USA

Book Trade Association Membership:
Publishers Association; Independent Publishers Guild

2523

W. W. NORTON & COMPANY LTD
Castle House, 75–76 Wells Street, London W1T 3QT
Telephone: 020 7323 1579
Fax: 020 7436 4553
Email: office@wwnorton.co.uk
Web Site: www.wwnorton.co.uk

Distribution:
John Wiley & Sons Ltd, 1 Oldlands Way, Shripney, Bognor Regis, West Sussex PO22 9SA
Telephone: 01243 779777
Fax: 01243 820250
Email: cs-books@wiley.co.uk

Personnel:
R. A. Cameron *(Chairman)*
S. King *(Director)*
W. D. McFeely *(USA Director)*
G. Luciano *(USA Director)*
P. Wright *(Director)*
R. Harrington *(USA Director)*
A. J. Llewellyn *(Director)*
J. Reidhead *(Director)*
E. Crutchley *(Managing Director)*

Academic & Scholarly; Architecture & Design; Biology & Zoology; Chemistry; Cinema, Video, TV & Radio; Computer Science; Cookery, Wines & Spirits; Economics; Educational & Textbooks; Fiction; Fine Art & Art History; Gardening; Gender Studies; Geography & Geology; History & Antiquarian; Literature & Criticism; Mathematics & Statistics; Military & War; Music; Natural History; Nautical; Philosophy; Physics; Poetry; Politics & World Affairs; Psychology & Psychiatry; Religion & Theology; Sociology & Anthropology; Sports & Games; Theatre, Drama & Dance

Imprints, Series & ISBNs:
The Countryman Press: 978 0 88150
Liveright: 978 0 87140
W.W. Norton: 978 0 393

Parent Company:
USA: W. W. Norton & Company

Distributor for:
USA: Dalkey Archive Press; New Directions Publishing Corporation

Overseas Representation:
Africa & Caribbean: Kelvin van Hasselt Publishing Services, Brininham, Norfolk, UK
India & Sri Lanka: Viva Group, New Delhi, India
Middle East & North Africa: International Publishers Representatives (IPR) Ltd, Nicosia, Cyprus
Pakistan: World Press, Lahore, Pakistan
Republic of Ireland: Andrew Russell Book Representation, Co Cork, Republic of Ireland
South Africa: Chris Reinders, The African Moon Press, Kelvin, South Africa
Spain & Portugal: Cristina de Lara Ruiz, Madrid, Spain

2524

THE NOSTALGIA COLLECTION
Silver Link Publishing Ltd, The Trundle, Ringstead Road, Great Addington, Kettering, Northants NN14 4BW
Telephone: 01536 330543 & 330588
Fax: 01536 330588
Email: sales@nostalgiacollection.com
Web Site: www.nostalgiacollection.com

Personnel:
Peter Townsend *(Managing Director, Publisher)*
Frances Townsend *(Company Secretary)*
David Walshaw *(Mail Order & Advertising Manager)*

Aviation; Crafts & Hobbies; Guide Books; History & Antiquarian; Military & War; Nautical; Transport

New Titles: 18 (2010) , 30 (2011)
No of Employees: 3
Annual Turnover: £350,000

Imprints, Series & ISBNs:
Past & Present Publishing Ltd: 978 1 85895

Silver Link Publishing Ltd: 978 0 947971, 978 1 85794

Associated Companies:
Past & Present Publishing Ltd; Silver Link Publishing Ltd

Distributor for:
UK: On Track Productions Ltd; Past & Present Publishing Ltd; Silver Link Publishing Ltd

Book Trade Association Membership:
Booksellers Association

2525

NOSY CROW
The Crow's Nest, 704 The Chandlery, 50 Westminster Bridge Road, London SE1 7QY
Telephone: 020 7953 7677

Book Trade Association Membership:
Publishers Association

2526

OAK TREE PRESS
19 Rutland Street, Cork, Republic of Ireland
Telephone: +353 (0)21 431 3855
Fax: +353 (0)21 431 3496
Email: info@oaktreepress.com
Web Site: www.oaktreepress.com

Personnel:
Brian O'Kane *(Managing Director)*
Rita O'Kane *(Sales Director)*
Anne Kennedy *(Office Manager)*

Academic & Scholarly; Accountancy & Taxation; Economics; Educational & Textbooks; Electronic (Professional & Academic); Industry, Business & Management; Law

New Titles: 5 (2010) , 6 (2011)
No of Employees: 3

Imprints, Series & ISBNs:
NuBooks: 978 1 84621
Oak Tree Press: 978 1 86076, 978 1 872853, 978 1 904887

Parent Company:
Republic of Ireland: Cork Publishing Ltd

Book Trade Association Membership:
Publishing Ireland (Foilsiú Éireann)

2527

THE O'BRIEN PRESS LTD
12 Terenure Road East, Rathgar, Dublin 6, Republic of Ireland
Telephone: +353 (0)1 492 3333
Fax: +353 (0)1 492 2777
Email: books@obrien.ie
Web Site: www.obrien.ie

Personnel:
Michael O'Brien *(Publisher)*
Ivan O'Brien *(Managing Director)*
Mary Webb *(Editorial Director)*
Kunak McGann *(Rights Manager)*
Erika McGann *(Production Manager)*
Ruth Heneghan *(Marketing Manager)*

Architecture & Design; Biography & Autobiography; Children's Books; Cookery, Wines & Spirits; Gardening; Guide Books; Humour; Politics & World Affairs; Sports & Games; Travel & Topography

Imprints, Series & ISBNs:
978 0 86278, 978 0 905140, 978 1 84717

Associated Companies:
Republic of Ireland: O'Brien Educational

Overseas Representation:
Britain: Francis Lincoln, UK

USA & Canada: James Trading Group, Nanuet, NY, USA

Book Trade Association Membership:
Independent Publishers Guild

2528

OCTOPUS PUBLISHING GROUP
Endeavour House, 189 Shaftesbury Avenue, London WC2H 8JY
Telephone: 020 7632 5400
Email: info@octopus-publishing.co.uk
Web Site: www.octopusbooks.co.uk

Distribution:
Littlehampton Book Services Ltd, Faraday Close, Durrington, Worthing, West Sussex BN13 3PB
Telephone: 01903 828500
Fax: 01903 828625
Email: orders@lbsltd.co.uk
Web Site: www.lbsltd.co.uk

Personnel:
Alison Goff *(Chief Executive)*
Andrew Welham *(Deputy Chief Executive Officer; Sales & Marketing Director)*
Angela Luxton *(Commercial Director)*
Fiona Smith *(Head of Publicity)*
Frances Johnson *(Group Operations Director)*
Henri Masurel *(Group Finance Director)*
Denise Bates *(Group Publishing Director)*

Animal Care & Breeding; Antiques & Collecting; Architecture & Design; Atlases & Maps; Cookery, Wines & Spirits; Crafts & Hobbies; Do-It-Yourself; Fine Art & Art History; Gardening; Health & Beauty; History & Antiquarian; Natural History; Sports & Games

Imprints, Series & ISBNs:
AWW AUS: 978 1 74245, 978 1 86396
AWW UK
Bounty: 978 0 7537
Cassell: 978 1 84403
Conran: 978 1 84091
Gaia: 978 1 84181
Godsfield Press: 978 1 85675
Hamlyn: 978 0 600
Mitchell Beazley: 978 1 84533
Philips: 978 1 84907
Spruce: 978 1 84601

Parent Company:
Hachette UK

Overseas Representation:
All Other Territories: Octopus Export Sales, Octopus Publishing Group, London, UK
Australia: Hachette Livre Australia, Sydney, NSW, Australia
Canada: Canadian Manda Group, Toronto, Ont, Canada
Caribbean: Chris Humphrys & Linda Hopkins, London, UK
Caribbean (for Philip's): David Williams, InterMedia Americana (IMA) Ltd, London, UK
Central America: Arturo Gutierrez Hernandez, Mexico
China, Hong Kong & Taiwan: Edward Summerson, Asia Publishers Services Ltd, Hong Kong
France, Belgium, Netherlands, Scandinavia, Iceland, Baltics, Eastern Europe & Russia: Bill Bailey Publishers Representatives, Newton Abbot, UK
Germany, Switzerland & Austria: Gabriele Kern Publishers Services, Frankfurt-am-Main, Germany
India, Bangladesh & Sri Lanka: Hachette Book Publishing India Pvt Ltd, Gurgaon, India
Italy & Greece: Penny Padovani, London, UK
Malaysia: APD Kuala Lumpur Pte Ltd, Selangor, Malaysia
Middle East, North Africa, Cyprus, Malta &

Israel: Ray Potts, Publishers International Marketing, Polfages, France
New Zealand: Hachette Livre New Zealand, Auckland, New Zealand
Philippines & Korea: Benjie Ocampo, Pasig City, Philippines
Singapore, Thailand, Indonesia, Vietnam, Brunei, Laos & Cambodia: APD Singapore Pte Ltd, Singapore
South Africa: Penguin Books South Africa (Pty) Ltd, Johannesburg, South Africa
South America: Terry Roberts, Humphrys Roberts Associates, Cotia SP, Brazil
Spain, Portugal & Gibraltar: Jenny Padovani, Barcelona, Spain
Sub-Saharan Africa: Anita Zih-De Haan, Rotterdam, Netherlands
USA: Octopus Books USA, c/o Hachette Book Group USA, Boston, MA, USA

2529

THE OLD STILE PRESS
Catchmays Court, Llandogo, Monmouthshire NP25 4TN
Telephone: 01291 689226
Email: oldstile@dircon.co.uk
Web Site: www.oldstilepress.com

Personnel:
Nicolas McDowall *(Partner)*
Frances McDowall *(Partner)*

Illustrated & Fine Editions; Literature & Criticism; Poetry; Theatre, Drama & Dance

Imprints, Series & ISBNs:
978 0 907664

Book Trade Association Membership:
Fine Press Book Association

2530

*THE OLEANDER PRESS
16 Orchard Street, Cambridge CB1 1JT
Telephone: 01638 500784
Email: editor@oleanderpress.com
Web Site: www.oleanderpress.com

Personnel:
Jon Gifford *(Managing Director & Publisher)*
Jane Doyle *(Sales Manager)*
Will Marston *(Rights Manager)*

Biography & Autobiography; History & Antiquarian; Humour; Languages & Linguistics; Literature & Criticism; Poetry; Reference Books, Directories & Dictionaries; Sports & Games; Travel & Topography

Imprints, Series & ISBNs:
978 0 900891, 978 0 902675, 978 0 906672

2531

OMNIBUS PRESS
14–15 Berners Street, London W1T 3LJ
Telephone: 020 7612 7400
Fax: 020 7612 7545
Email: music@musicsales.co.uk
Web Site: www.omnibuspress.co.uk

Warehouse:
Book Sales Ltd, Newmarket Road, Bury St Edmunds, Suffolk IP33 3YB
Telephone: 01284 702600
Fax: 01284 768301
Email: music@musicsales.co.uk
Web Site: www.musicsales.co.uk

Personnel:
Robert Wise *(Managing Director)*
Tony Latham *(Financial Director)*
Richard Hudson *(Sales Director)*
Mark Pickard *(Production Manager)*
Chris Charlesworth *(Editor)*
David Barraclough *(Commissioning Editor)*

Biography & Autobiography; Music

Imprints, Series & ISBNs:
Omnibus Press: 978 0 7119, 978 1 84449, 978 1 84609, 978 1 84772, 978 1 84938, 978 1 78038
Wise Publications: 978 0 7119, 978 1 84938, 978 1 78038

Parent Company:
Music Sales Ltd

Associated Companies:
Australia: Music Sales (Pty) Ltd
USA: Music Sales Corp

Distributor for:
Bobcat Books; Dover Books; Haymarket Publishing (Gramophone Guide); Parker Mead Ltd; Rogan House; Sanctuary; Schirmer Books; Vision On

Overseas Representation:
Australia: Macmillan Distribution, South Yarra, Vic, Australia
Australia (for Music Shops): Music Sales (Australia), Rosebery, NSW, Australia
Belgium: Exhibitions International, Leuven, Belgium
Canada: Login Canada, Winnipeg, Manitoba, Canada
Central America, Mexico & Caribbean: Humphrys Roberts Associates, London, UK
Eastern Europe: Tony Moggach, InterMedia Americana (IMA) Ltd, London, UK
France: Music Sales Ltd, UK
Germany, Austria & Switzerland: Gabriele Kern Publishers Services, Frankfurt-am-Main, Germany
Greece, Turkey, Cyprus, Malta & Middle East: Peter Ward Book Exports, London, UK
Indian Subcontinent: Publishers International Marketing, Storrington, UK
Netherlands & Luxembourg: Nilsson & Lamm BV, Weesp, Netherlands
New Zealand: Macmillan Publishers New Zealand Ltd, Auckland, New Zealand
Scandinavia: McNeish Publishing International, East Sussex, UK
South Africa: Trinity Books CC, Randburg, South Africa
South America: Humphrys Roberts Associates, Cotia SP, Brazil
South East & North Asia: Chris Ashdown Publishers International Marketing, London, UK
Spain, Portugal, Gibraltar & Italy: Penny Padovani, London, UK

Book Trade Association Membership:
BA (Associate Member)

2532

*ON STREAM PUBLICATIONS LTD
Currabaha, Cloghroe, Co Cork, Republic of Ireland
Telephone: +353 (0)21 438 5798
Email: info@onstream.ie
Web Site: www.onstream.ie

Personnel:
Roz Crowley *(Managing Director & Editor)*

Academic & Scholarly; Biography & Autobiography; Cookery, Wines & Spirits; Environment & Development Studies; Health & Beauty; Reference Books, Directories & Dictionaries

Imprints, Series & ISBNs:
978 1 897685

Book Trade Association Membership:
Publishing Ireland (Foilsiú Éireann)

2533

ONEWORLD CLASSICS
London House, 243–253 Lower Mortlake Road, Richmond, Surrey TW9 2LL

Telephone: 020 8948 9550
Fax: 020 8948 5599
Email: info@oneworldclassics.com
Web Site: www.oneworldclassics.com

Personnel:
Alessandro Gallenzi (*Publishing Director*)
Elisabetta Minervini (*Associate Publisher*)

Fiction; Literature & Criticism; Poetry

New Titles: 60 (2010) , 70 (2011)
Annual Turnover: £300,000

Imprints, Series & ISBNs:
Calder Publications: 978 0 7145
One World Classics: 978 1 84749

Associated Companies:
UK: Calder Publications Ltd

Overseas Representation:
Australia: Bloomsbury, Australia
South Africa: Jonathan Ball, South Africa
USA & Canada: Trafalgar Square Publishing / IPG, Chicago, IL, USA

Book Trade Association Membership:
Independent Publishers Guild

2534 ▬

ONLYWOMEN PRESS LTD
40 St Lawrence Terrace, London W10 5ST
Telephone: 020 8354 0796
Fax: 020 8960 2817
Email: onlywomenpress@btconnect.com
Web Site: www.onlywomenpress.com

Trade Distribution Central Books Ltd.:
Central Books Ltd, 99 Wallis Road, London E9 5LN
Telephone: 0845 458 9911
Fax: 0845 458 9912
Web Site: www.centralbooks.com

Personnel:
L. Mohin (*Managing Director*)
J. Traies (*Editorial Co-director*)
A. Lewis (*Illustrating Co-director*)

Academic & Scholarly; Biography & Autobiography; Children's Books; Crime; Fiction; Gay & Lesbian Studies; Gender Studies; Literature & Criticism

Imprints, Series & ISBNs:
978 0 9561053

Overseas Representation:
Australia: Bulldog Books, Beaconsfield, NSW, Australia
North America: Alamo Square Distribution, USA

Book Trade Association Membership:
Independent Publishers Guild

2535 ▬

THE OPEN BIBLE TRUST
Fordland Mount, Upper Basildon, Reading RG8 8LU
Telephone: 01491 671357
Email: admin@obt.org.uk
Web Site: www.obt.org.uk

Personnel:
Michael Penny (*Administrator, Editor*)
Sylvia Penny (*Treasurer*)

Religion & Theology

New Titles: 14 (2010) , 12 (2011)
No of Employees: 2

Imprints, Series & ISBNs:
978 0 947778, 978 1 902859

Associated Companies:
USA: Bible Search Publications Inc

Overseas Representation:
Australia: Berean Bible Fellowship of Australia, Glendale, NSW, Australia
Canada: Ron Moore, Bowmanville, Ont, Canada
New Zealand: Graeme Abbott, Hamilton, New Zealand
USA: Bible Search Publications, Brookfield, WI, USA

2536 ▬

*OPEN GATE PRESS
[incorporating Centaur Press (1954)]
51 Achilles Road, London NW6 1DZ
Telephone: 020 7431 4391
Fax: 020 7431 5129
Email: books@opengatepress.co.uk
Web Site: www.opengatepress.co.uk

Trade Enquiries & Orders:
Central Books Ltd, 99 Wallis Road, London E9 5LN
Telephone: 0845 458 9911
Fax: 0845 458 9912
Email: sales@centralbooks.com
Web Site: www.centralbooks.com

Personnel:
Jeannie Cohen (*Editorial*)
Elisabeth Petersdorff (*Production*)

Academic & Scholarly; Environment & Development Studies; Philosophy; Politics & World Affairs; Psychology & Psychiatry; Religion & Theology

Imprints, Series & ISBNs:
978 0 900001, 978 1 871871

Associated Companies:
Centaur Press; Linden Press (imprint of Centaur Press)

Book Trade Association Membership:
Publishers Association; Independent Publishers Guild

2537 ▬

OPEN UNIVERSITY WORLDWIDE
Michael Young Building, Walton Hall, Milton Keynes, Bucks MK7 6AA
Telephone: 01908 858785
Web Site: www.ouw.co.uk

Academic & Scholarly; Biology & Zoology; Chemistry; Computer Science; Economics; Educational & Textbooks; Electronic (Educational); Engineering; English as a Foreign Language; Environment & Development Studies; Fine Art & Art History; Geography & Geology; History & Antiquarian; Industry, Business & Management; Languages & Linguistics; Literature & Criticism; Mathematics & Statistics; Medical (incl. Self Help & Alternative Medicine); Natural History; Physics; Politics & World Affairs; Psychology & Psychiatry; Religion & Theology; Scientific & Technical; Sociology & Anthropology; Theatre, Drama & Dance

Imprints, Series & ISBNs:
978 0 7492, 978 1 84873

Book Trade Association Membership:
Independent Publishers Guild

2538 ▬

OPTIMUS PROFESSIONAL PUBLISHING
[A division of Electric Word Plc]
33–41 Dallington Street, London EC1V 0BB
Telephone: 0845 450 6400
Fax: 0845 450 6410
Email: info@optimus-education.com
Web Site: www.optimus-education.com

Personnel:
Russell Lawson (*Managing Director*)

Jenny Lee (*Content Manager*)
Margaret Garrard (*Head of Conferences*)
Jon Pyser (*Head of Sales*)
Sarah Kearney (*Head of Education Marketing*)

Academic & Scholarly; Educational & Textbooks; Electronic (Educational); Geography & Geology; Vocational Training & Careers

Imprints, Series & ISBNs:
Kington Publishing: 978 1 899857
Optimus Education: 978 1 907927, 978 1 905538, 978 1 908294
Teach to Inspire: 978 1 906517

Parent Company:
Electric Word PLC

Associated Companies:
IGaming Business; Incentive Plus; Peak Performance; Radcliffe Publishing; Speechmark Ltd; SportBusiness Group

Book Trade Association Membership:
Publishers Association; Educational Publishers Council

2539 ▬

*O'REILLY UK LTD
4 Castle Street, Farnham, Surrey GU9 7HS
Telephone: 01252 711776
Fax: 01252 734211
Email: information@oreilly.co.uk
Web Site: www.oreilly.com

Distributors:
John Wiley, 1 Oldlands Way, Bognor Regis PO22 9SA
Telephone: 01243 779777
Fax: 01243 843303
Email: cs-books@wiley.co.uk

Personnel:
Graham Cameron (*Managing Director*)
Josette Garcia (*Public Relations Manager*)
Simon Chappell (*Sales Director*)

Computer Science

Parent Company:
USA: O'Reilly Media Inc

Distributor for:
UK: microsoft press; pragmatic bookshelf; rocky nook

Book Trade Association Membership:
Independent Publishers Guild

2540 ▬

ORION BOOKS LTD
[Hachette UK]
Orion House, 5 Upper St Martins Lane, London WC2H 9EA
Telephone: 020 7240 3444
Fax: 020 7240 4822

Trade Counter & Warehouse:
Littlehampton Book Services Ltd, Faraday Close, Durrington, Worthing, West Sussex BN13 3RB
Telephone: 01903 828500
Fax: 01903 828625
Web Site: www.orionbooks.co.uk

Personnel:
Lisa Milton (*Trade Managing Director*)
Susan Lamb (*Managing Director Paperback Division*)
Jon Wood (*Publishing Director – Fiction*)
Fiona Kennedy (*Children's Publisher & Rights Director*)

Biography & Autobiography; Children's Books; Fiction; Science Fiction

Imprints, Series & ISBNs:
Gollancz: 978 1 85798

Orion: 978 1 85797
Orion Children's: 978 1 84255, 978 1 85881
Orion Paperbacks: 978 1 85797
Phoenix: 978 1 85799
Phoenix House

Parent Company:
The Orion Publishing Group Ltd

Overseas Representation:
see: The Orion Publishing Group Ltd, London, UK

2541 ▬

THE ORION PUBLISHING GROUP LTD
[Hachette UK]
Orion House, 5 Upper St Martins Lane, London WC2H 9EA
Telephone: 020 7240 3444
Fax: 020 7240 4822

Trade Counter & Warehouse:
Littlehampton Book Services Ltd, Faraday Close, Durrington, Worthing, West Sussex BN13 3RB
Telephone: 01903 828500
Fax: 01903 828625
Email: ...@lbsltd.co.uk
Web Site: www.lbsltd.co.uk

Personnel:
Arnaud Nourry (*Chairman*)
Peter Roche (*Chief Executive*)
Malcolm Edwards (*Deputy Chief Executive & Publisher*)
Susan Lamb (*Managing Director – Mass Market*)
Lisa Milton (*Managing Director – Orion Books*)
Dallas Manderson (*Group Sales Director*)
Dominic Smith (*Home Sales Director*)
Mark Streatfeild (*Export Sales Director*)
Fiona McIntosh (*Production Director*)
Clare Jarvis (*Finance Director*)
Chris Emerson (*Director*)
Lord George Weidenfeld (*Director*)
Susan Howe (*Group Rights Director*)
Tim Hely Hutchinson (*Director*)
Pierre de Cacqueray (*Director*)
Richard Kitson (*Director*)

Antiques & Collecting; Archaeology; Audio Books; Biography & Autobiography; Children's Books; Cinema, Video, TV & Radio; Cookery, Wines & Spirits; Crafts & Hobbies; Crime; Fashion & Costume; Fiction; Fine Art & Art History; Gardening; Guide Books; Health & Beauty; History & Antiquarian; Humour; Illustrated & Fine Editions; Military & War; Natural History; Nautical; Philosophy; Politics & World Affairs; Reference Books, Directories & Dictionaries; Science Fiction; Sports & Games; Travel & Topography

Imprints, Series & ISBNs:
Cassell: 978 0 304
J M Dent: 978 0 460
Everyman Paperbacks: 978 0 460
First Time Authors Fiction
Gollancz: 978 0 575, 978 1 85797, 978 1 85798
Oriel
Orion: 978 1 85797
Orion Children's: 978 1 84255, 978 1 85881
Orion Fiction: 978 0 7528
Orion Media: 978 0 7528
Orion Paperbacks: 978 0 460, 978 0 7528, 978 1 85797
Phoenix House
Phoenix Mass Market: 978 0 7538
Phoenix Press: 978 1 84212
W & N Illustrated: 978 0 297
Weidenfeld & Nicolson: 978 0 297

Parent Company:
France: Hachette Livre

Associated Companies:
Cassell plc; J M Dent Ltd; Victor Gollancz;
Littlehampton Book Services Ltd; Orion
Books Ltd; George Weidenfeld &
Nicolson Ltd

Distributor for:
Peter Halban Publishers

Overseas Representation:
Australia: Hachette Livre Australia (Orion
Division), Sydney, NSW, Australia
*Austria, Belgium, Cyprus, France, Germany,
Greece, Italy, Luxembourg, Netherlands,
Portugal, Spain & Switzerland:* Kim Else,
The Orion Publishing Group Ltd, London,
UK
Canada: Hachette Book Group, Toronto,
Ont, Canada
Caribbean: Chris Humphrys, Humphrys
Roberts Associates, London, UK
Eastern Europe: Csaba & Jackie Lengyel de
Bagota, Budapest, Hungary
India: Hachette India, New Delhi, India
*India, Pakistan, South America, Singapore,
Hong Kong, Thailand, Japan, Indonesia &
Malaysia:* Michael Goff, The Orion
Publishing Group Ltd, London, UK
New Zealand: Hachette New Zealand (Orion
Division), Auckland, New Zealand
Philippines, Korea & Taiwan: Ralph & Sheila
Summers, Woodford Green, Essex, UK
*Scandinavia, Middle East, Turkey, Malta,
Russia, North Africa & Baltic States:* Suzie
Jenner, The Orion Publishing Group Ltd,
London, UK
South Africa: Jonathan Ball Publishers (Pty)
Ltd, Johannesburg, South Africa

2542 ■■■■■■■■

ORPEN PRESS
Lonsdale House, Avoca Avenue, Blackrock,
Co Dublin, Republic of Ireland
Telephone: +353 (0)1 278 5090
Fax: +353 (0)1 278 4800
Email: info@orpenpress.com
Web Site: www.orpenpress.com

Send trade orders to::
Gill & Macmillan, Hume Avenue,
Park West, Dublin 12, Republic of Ireland
Telephone: +353 (0)1 500 9500
Fax: +353 (0)1 500 9599
Email: sales@gillmacmillan.ie
Web Site: www.gillmacmillan.ie

Personnel:
Gerard O'Connor *(Managing Director)*
Elizabeth Brennan *(Commissioning Editor)*
Conor O'Mahony *(Financial Controller)*
Eileen O'Brien *(Editor)*
Zoe Faulder *(Sales and Marketing)*
Benil Shah *(Typesetting Manager)*
Ciaran MacGlinchey *(Online Editor)*
Ailbhe O'Reilly *(Commissioning Editor)*

*Academic & Scholarly; Accountancy &
Taxation; Economics; Industry, Business &
Management; Law; Medical (incl. Self Help
& Alternative Medicine); Politics & World
Affairs; Psychology & Psychiatry; Sociology
& Anthropology*

New Titles: 22 (2011)
No of Employees: 6

Imprints, Series & ISBNs:
Blackhall Publishing: 978 1 84218, 978 1
901657
Kite Books: 978 1 84218
Lonsdale Law Publishing: 978 1 907325
Orpen Press: 978 1 871305

Associated Companies:
Blackhall Publishing; Kite Books; Lonsdale
Law Publishing

Overseas Representation:
UK: Gill & Macmillan, Dublin, Republic of
Ireland
USA: Gaunt Inc, Holmes Beach, Florida, USA

Book Trade Association Membership:
Publishing Ireland (Foilsiú Éireann)

2543 ■■■■■■■■

OSPREY PUBLISHING LTD
Midland House, West Way, Botley, Oxford
OX2 0PH
Telephone: 01865 727022
Fax: 01865 727017
Email: info@ospreypublishing.com
Web Site: www.ospreypublishing.com

Distribution:
Grantham Book Services, Trent Road,
Grantham, Lincs NG31 7XQ
Telephone: 01476 541080
Fax: 01476 541061
Email: orders@gbs-tbs-ltd.co.uk

Personnel:
Rebecca Smart *(Managing Director)*
Chris Tinsley *(Finance Director)*
Joanna Sharland *(Rights Director)*
Kate Moore *(Publisher)*

*Aviation; History & Antiquarian; Military &
War*

New Titles: 140 (2010) , 143 (2011)
No of Employees: 40
Annual Turnover: £6.1M

Imprints, Series & ISBNs:
978 0 85045, 978 1 84176, 978 1 84603,
978 1 84908, 978 1 85532

Overseas Representation:
Australia: Capricorn Link (Australia) Pty Ltd,
Windsor, NSW, Australia
Belgium, Netherlands & Switzerland:
Robbert J. Pleysier, Heerde, Netherlands
Central & Eastern Europe: Tony Moggach,
London, UK
Far East: Ashton International Marketing
Services, Sevenoaks, Kent, UK
France: Ted Dougherty, London, UK
Germany & Austria: Gabriele Kern, PS
Publishers Services, Frankfurt, Germany
Greece & Italy: Sandro Salucci, Florence,
Italy
Middle East: Peter Ward Book Exports,
London, UK
New Zealand: Nationwide Book
Distributors, New Zealand
Scandinavia: Katie McNeish, East Sussex,
UK
Spain, Portugal & Gibraltar: Peter Prout,
Iberian Book Services, Madrid, Spain
Turkey: Ayse Lale Colakoglu, Istanbul,
Turkey
USA, Caribbean & Latin America: Random
House Publishing Services, New York, NY,
USA

2544 ■■■■■■■■

OUTSELL (UK) LTD
25 Floral Street, London WC2E 9DS
Telephone: 020 8090 6590
Fax: 020 7031 8101

Book Trade Association Membership:
Publishers Association

2545 ■■■■■■■■

*PETER OWEN PUBLISHERS
73 Kenway Road, London SW5 0RE
Telephone: 020 7373 5628 & 7370 6093
Fax: 020 7373 6760
Email: admin@peterowen.com
Web Site: www.peterowen.com

Trade Counter & Warehouse:
Central Books, 99 Wallis Road, London
E9 5LN
Telephone: 020 8986 4854
Fax: 020 8533 5821
Email: orders@centralbooks.com
Web Site: www.centralbooks.com

Personnel:
Peter Owen *(Managing Director)*
Antonia Owen *(Editorial Director)*
Nick Pearson *(Production Manager)*
Michael O'Connell *(Sales & Publicity
Manager)*
Simon Smith *(Rights & Editorial Manager)*

*Biography & Autobiography; Cinema,
Video, TV & Radio; Fashion & Costume;
Fiction; Gay & Lesbian Studies; History &
Antiquarian; Literature & Criticism; Music;
Theatre, Drama & Dance*

Imprints, Series & ISBNs:
Peter Owen Modern Classics: 978 0 7206

Overseas Representation:
Australia: Peribo Pty Ltd, Mount Kuring-Gai,
NSW, Australia
Canada: Scholarly Book Services Inc,
Toronto, Canada
Europe, Scandinavia & Iceland: Books for
Europe, Massagno, Switzerland
New Zealand: Addenda Ltd, Grey Lynn,
New Zealand
South Africa: Stephan Phillips (Pty) Ltd,
Cape Town, South Africa
USA: Dufour Editions Inc, Chester Springs,
PA, USA

Book Trade Association Membership:
Independent Publishers Guild

2546 ■■■■■■■■

OXFAM PUBLISHING
Oxfam House, John Smith Drive, Cowley,
Oxford OX4 2JY
Telephone: 01865 472188
Fax: 01865 472393
Email: publish@oxfam.org.uk
Web Site: www.oxfam.org.uk/
policyandpractice

Personnel:
Robert Cornford *(Communications
Manager: Content Promotion)*
Claire Harvey *(Communications Manager:
Content Creation)*
Helen Moreno *(Digital Communications
Lead: Policy, Practice & Research)*

*Academic & Scholarly; Agriculture;
Economics; Environment & Development
Studies; Gender Studies; Politics & World
Affairs*

New Titles: 100 (2010) , 100 (2011)
No of Employees: 11

Imprints, Series & ISBNs:

Oxfam Online: 978 1 78077, 978 1 81814
Oxfam Publications: 978 0 85598

Associated Companies:
UK: Practical Action Publishing

Book Trade Association Membership:
Independent Publishers Guild; Association
of Learned & Professional Society Publishers

2547 ■■■■■■■■

OXFORD UNIVERSITY PRESS
Great Clarendon Street, Oxford OX2 6DP
Telephone: 01865 556767
Fax: 01865 556646
Web Site: www.oup.com

Personnel:
Nigel Portwood *(Chief Executive)*
David Gillard *(Finance Director)*
Kate Harris *(Managing Director: Educational
Division)*
Peter Marshall *(Managing Director: ELT)*
Tim Barton *(Managing Director: Academic
& Journals and President OUP USA)*
Neil Tomkins *(Managing Director:
International Division)*
Jesus Lezcano *(Director General: OUP Spain)*

*Academic & Scholarly; Biology & Zoology;
Children's Books; Economics; Educational &
Textbooks; Electronic (Professional &
Academic); English as a Foreign Language;
Industry, Business & Management;
Languages & Linguistics; Law; Mathematics
& Statistics; Medical (incl. Self Help &
Alternative Medicine); Music; Philosophy;
Physics; Politics & World Affairs; Psychology
& Psychiatry; Reference Books, Directories &
Dictionaries; Religion & Theology*

Book Trade Association Membership:
Publishers Association

2548 ■■■■■■■■

PACKARD PUBLISHING LTD
Forum House, Stirling Road, Chichester,
West Sussex PO19 7DN
Telephone: 01243 537977
Fax: 01243 537977
Email: packardpublishing@googlemail.com
Web Site: www.packardpublishing.com

Personnel:
Michael Packard *(Managing Director, Sales,
Rights & Permissions)*

*Academic & Scholarly; Agriculture;
Architecture & Design; Biology & Zoology;
Educational & Textbooks; Environment &
Development Studies; Gardening;
Geography & Geology; Languages &
Linguistics; Natural History; Reference
Books, Directories & Dictionaries; Scientific
& Technical*

New Titles: 2 (2010) , 5 (2011)
No of Employees: 1
Annual Turnover: £30,000

Imprints, Series & ISBNs:
978 0 906527, 978 1 85341

Distributor for:
USA: Carolina Biological Supply Co Inc
(Biology Readers only); Stipes Publishing
LLC

Overseas Representation:
North America: Stipes Publishing LLC,
Champaign, IL, USA

2549 ■■■■■■■■

PAGODA TREE PRESS
4 Malvern Buildings, Fairfield Park, Bath
BA1 6JX
Telephone: 01225 463552
Fax: 01225 463552
Email: enquiries@pagodatreepress.com
Web Site: www.pagodatreepress.com

Personnel:
Hugh Rayner *(Managing Director)*
Jane Murphy *(Creative Director)*

*Academic & Scholarly; Atlases & Maps;
Geography & Geology; Guide Books;
Photography; Politics & World Affairs;
Reference Books, Directories &
Dictionaries; Travel & Topography*

New Titles: 4 (2010) , 3 (2011)
No of Employees: 2

Imprints, Series & ISBNs:
978 0 9529782, 978 1 904289

Distributor for:
India: Library of Numismatic Studies
USA: Amur Maple Books
Zimbabwe: CBC Publishing

2550 ■■■■■■■■

PALAZZO EDITIONS LTD
2 Wood Street, Bath BA1 2JQ
Telephone: 01225 326444
Fax: 01225 330209
Email: info@palazzoeditions.com

Web Site: www.palazzoeditions.com

Send orders to:
ORCA Book Services, Unit A3,
Fleets Corner, Poole BH17 OHL
Telephone: 01202 665432
Email: orders@orcabookservices.co.uk

Personnel:
Miss Stephanie Bramwell-Lawes (Editorial Assistant)
Miss Chloe Pew Latter (PR & Marketing Assistant)

Architecture & Design; Children's Books; Cinema, Video, TV & Radio; History & Antiquarian; Music

2551 ▬▬▬▬▬

PALGRAVE MACMILLAN
Houndmills, Basingstoke, Hants RG21 6XS
Telephone: 01256 329242
Fax: 01256 479476
Web Site: www.palgrave.com

Warehouse, Trade Enquiries & Orders:
Macmillan Distribution (MDL), Brunel Road, Houndmills, Basingstoke, Hants RG21 6XS
Telephone: 01256 329242 & 302692
Email: mdl@macmillan.co.uk

Personnel:
Annette Thomas (Chief Executive Officer)
D. J. G. Knight (Managing Director)
S. Burridge (Publishing Director, Scholarly & Reference)
M. Hewinson (Publishing Director, College)
D. Bull (Publishing Director, Journals)
L. Keelan (Sales Director)
V. Capstick (Marketing Director)
A. J. Jones (Digital Development Director)
R. A. Mathias (Finance Director)
A. Williams (Operations Director)

Academic & Scholarly; Accountancy & Taxation; Biology & Zoology; Chemistry; Computer Science; Economics; Educational & Textbooks; Electronic (Educational); Engineering; Environment & Development Studies; Gender Studies; Geography & Geology; History & Antiquarian; Industry, Business & Management; Languages & Linguistics; Law; Literature & Criticism; Mathematics & Statistics; Medical (incl. Self Help & Alternative Medicine); Philosophy; Physics; Politics & World Affairs; Psychology & Psychiatry; Reference Books, Directories & Dictionaries; Religion & Theology; Scientific & Technical; Sociology & Anthropology; Theatre, Drama & Dance; Vocational Training & Careers

Imprints, Series & ISBNs:
978 0 333, 978 1 4039

Parent Company:
Macmillan Ltd

Associated Companies:
Macmillan Children's Books; Macmillan Education; Macmillan Publishers Ltd; Pan Macmillan Ltd; Stockton Press Ltd
USA: Stockton Press Inc

Distributor for:
Bedford; W. H. Freeman; Sinauer Associates; Spectrum; University Science Books; Worth Publishers

Overseas Representation:
Africa (excluding areas listed): Africa Dept, Palgrave Macmillan Ltd, Basingstoke, Hants, UK
Australia: Palgrave Macmillan, South Yarra, Vic, Australia
Austria & Germany: Dan Timmermanns, Frankfurt-am-Main, Germany
Central & Eastern Europe: Jacek Lewinson, Warsaw, Poland
China: Macmillan Publishers China Ltd, Kowloon, P. R. of China

Colombia: Grupo K-T-Dra Ltda, Santa Fe de Bogota, Colombia
Denmark, Norway, Finland, Sweden & Iceland: Ben Greig, Cambridge, UK
East Asia (including Hong Kong, Philippines, Thailand, Vietnam & Indonesia): Palgrave Macmillan, Hong Kong
Europe (excluding areas listed): Jo Waller, Palgrave Macmillan Ltd, Basingstoke, Hants, UK
Greece & Cyprus: Zitsa Seraphimidi, P. Faliro, Greece
India: Ajit De, Calcutta, India; Anand Vithalkar, Mumbai, India; Kalpana Shukla, Sunil Sharma, Jagat Bahadur, Palgrave Macmillan, New Delhi, India; V. Ravi, Palgrave Macmillan, Chennai, India
Iran: Sepehr Bookshop, Tehran, Iran
Italy & France: David Pickering, Mare Nostrum Publishing Consultants, Rome, Italy
Japan: Palgrave Macmillan Ltd, Basingstoke, Hants, UK
Korea: Macmillan Publishers, Jongro-Gu, Seoul, Republic of Korea
Latin America & Caribbean: Palgrave Macmillan Ltd, Basingstoke, Hants, UK
Malaysia: UBSD Distribution Sdn Bhd, Selangor, Malaysia
Middle East (all areas not listed): Jan Rylewicz, Middle Eastern Dept, Palgrave Macmillan Ltd, Basingstoke, Hants, UK
Netherlands, Belgium, Luxembourg, France & Switzerland: Daan Timmermans, Amsterdam, Netherlands
New Zealand: Macmillan Publishers New Zealand Ltd, Auckland, New Zealand

Book Trade Association Membership:
Publishers Association; BDPA; STM

2552 ▬▬▬▬▬

PAN MACMILLAN
20 New Wharf Road, London N1 9RR
Telephone: 020 7014 6000
Fax: 020 7014 6001
Email: books@macmillan.co.uk
Web Site: www.panmacmillan.com

Warehouse, Trade Enquiries & Orders:
Macmillan Distribution (MDL), Houndmills, Basingstoke, Hants RG21 6XS
Telephone: 01256 329242
Fax: 01256 840154
Email: mdl@macmillan.co.uk

Personnel:
Anthony Forbes Watson (Managing Director)
Annette Thomas (Chief Executive Officer, Macmillan Publishers Ltd)
Jane Carlin (Financial Director)
Anna Bond (UK Sales Director)
Aimee Roche (International Sales Director)
Ian Mitchell (Production Director)
Geoff Duffield (Sales & Marketing Director)
Camilla Elworthy (Publicity Director)
Paul Baggaley (Publisher – Picador)
Maria Rejt (Publisher – Mantle)
Jeremy Trevathan (Publisher, Fiction – Macmillan, Pan)
Georgina Morley (Editorial Director, Non-Fiction)
Harriet Sanders (Rights Director)
Jon Butler (Publisher, Non-Fiction)
Sara Lloyd (Digital Director)

Biography & Autobiography; Children's Books; Cinema, Video, TV & Radio; Fiction; Gardening; Guide Books; Health & Beauty; History & Antiquarian; Literature & Criticism; Poetry; Science Fiction; Sports & Games; Travel & Topography

New Titles: 754 (2010) , 728 (2011)
No of Employees: 170

Imprints, Series & ISBNs:
Boxtree
Campbell: 978 0 333
Macmillan: 978 0 230

Macmillan Children's Books: 978 0 230
Mantle
Pan: 978 0 330
Picador: 978 0 330
Sidgwick & Jackson: 978 0 283
Tor: 978 0 230

Parent Company:
Macmillan Ltd

Associated Companies:
Boxtree Ltd; Macmillan Children's Books; Macmillan Education; Macmillan Publishers Ltd; Palgrave Macmillan; Pan Books Ltd; Sidgwick & Jackson Ltd

Overseas Representation:
All other areas – send orders to: International Department, Pan Macmillan, Basingstoke, UK
Australia: Pan Macmillan (Australia) Pty Ltd, Sydney, NSW, Australia
Hong Kong: Publishers' Associates Ltd, Hong Kong
India: Pan Macmillan, New Delhi, India
Japan: Shino Yasuda, Tokyo, Japan
New Zealand: Macmillan Publishers New Zealand Ltd, Auckland, New Zealand
Republic of Ireland: David Adamson, Dublin, Republic of Ireland
South Africa, Botswana, Lesotho, Swaziland, Namibia & Zimbabwe: Pan Macmillan SA Pty Ltd, Hyde Park, South Africa
South East Asia: Pansing Distribution Sdn Bhd, Singapore
West Indies & Caribbean: Macmillan Education Ltd, Oxford, UK

Book Trade Association Membership:
Publishers Association

2553 ▬▬▬▬▬

PAPADAKIS PUBLISHER
[a member of New Architecture Group Ltd]
Kimber Studio, Winterbourne, Newbury, Berkshire RG20 8AN
Telephone: 01635 248833
Email: info@papadakis.net
Web Site: www.papadakis.net

Personnel:
Alexandra Papadakis (Publishing Director)
Stefano Rosignoli (Production and Rights Assistant)

Architecture & Design; Fashion & Costume; Fine Art & Art History; Illustrated & Fine Editions; Natural History; Photography; Scientific & Technical

New Titles: 10 (2010) , 10 (2011)
No of Employees: 4

Imprints, Series & ISBNs:
Papadakis [new ISBN]: 978 1 906506
Papadakis [old ISBN]: 978 1 901092

Parent Company:
New Architecture Group Ltd

Book Trade Association Membership:
Publishers Association

2554 ▬▬▬▬▬

PATRICKGEORGE
46 Vale Square, Ramsgate, Kent CT11 9DA
Telephone: 07773 096080
Web Site: www.patrickgeorge.biz

Annual Turnover: £25,000

Book Trade Association Membership:
Publishers Association

2555 ▬▬▬▬▬

PAUPERS' PRESS
37 Quayside Close, Trent Bridge, Nottingham NG2 3BP

Telephone: 0115 986 3334
Fax: 0115 986 3334
Email: books@pauperspress.com
Web Site: www.pauperspress.com

Personnel:
Colin Stanley (Managing Editor)

Academic & Scholarly; Literature & Criticism; Philosophy

New Titles: 3 (2010) , 3 (2011)
No of Employees: 0

Imprints, Series & ISBNs:
978 0 946650, 978 0 9568663

2556 ▬▬▬▬▬

*PC PUBLISHING
Keeper's House, Merton, Thetford, Norfolk IP25 6QH
Telephone: 01953 889900
Email: info@pc-publishing.com
Web Site: www.pc-publishing.com

Distribution:
Littlehampton Book Services, Faraday Close, Durrington, Worthing, West Sussex BN13 3RB
Telephone: 01903 828500
Fax: 01903 828625

Personnel:
Philip Chapman (Director & Publisher)

Music; Scientific & Technical

Imprints, Series & ISBNs:
978 1 870775, 978 1 906005

Parent Company:
UK: Music Technology Books Ltd

Overseas Representation:
Australia: Woodslane Pty Ltd, Warriewood, NSW, Australia
USA: O'Reilly Associates, Sebastopol, CA, USA

2557 ▬▬▬▬▬

PCCS BOOKS LTD
2 Cropper Row, Alton Road, Ross-on-Wye HR9 5LA
Telephone: 01989 763900
Fax: 01989 763901
Email: contact@pccs-books.co.uk
Web Site: www.pccs-books.co.uk

Personnel:
Maggie Taylor-Sanders (Director)
Peter J. Sanders (Director)

Academic & Scholarly; Gender Studies; Medical (incl. Self Help & Alternative Medicine); Psychology & Psychiatry; Religion & Theology

New Titles: 15 (2010) , 15 (2011)
No of Employees: 6
Annual Turnover: £330,000

Imprints, Series & ISBNs:
Critical Psychology Division (Series): 978 1 898059
PCCS Books: 978 1 898059
Person-Centred Approach & Client-Centred Therapy Essential Readers (Series): 978 1 898059
Primers Series: 978 1 898059
Rogers' Therapeutic Conditions Series (Vols 1–4): 978 1 898059
Steps in Counselling Series: 978 1 898059
Straight Talking Introductions Series: 978 1 906254

Overseas Representation:
Australasia: Footprint Books, Sydney, Australia

Book Trade Association Membership:
Independent Publishers Guild

2558 ▬▬▬

*PEARSON EDUCATION
Edinburgh Gate, Harlow, Essex CM20 2JE
Telephone: 01279 623623
Fax: 01279 431059
Web Site: www.pearson.com

*Academic & Scholarly; Educational &
Textbooks; Electronic (Professional &
Academic); Law*

Parent Company:
UK: Pearson Group

Book Trade Association Membership:
Publishers Association

2559 ▬▬▬

*THE PENGUIN GROUP (UK) LTD
80 Strand, London WC2R 0RL
Telephone: 020 7010 3000
Fax: 020 7010 6060
Web Site: www.penguin.co.uk

Distribution Centre:
Penguin UK, Central Park, Rugby,
Warwickshire CV23 0WB
Telephone: 01788 514300

Also at:
Pearson Shared Services/Pearson Education,
Edinburgh Gate, Harlow, Essex CM20 2JE
Telephone: 01279 623102
Fax: 0870 850 5255
Email: veronica.reeve@pearsontc.co.uk

Personnel:
John Makinson *(Chairman & Chief
  Executive)*
Peter Field *(Penguin UK Chief Executive
  Officer & Dorling Kindersley Worldwide
  Chief Executive Officer)*
Tom Weldon *(Penguin Deputy Chief
  Executive Officer)*
John Duhigg *(Dorling Kindersley Deputy
  Chief Executive Officer)*
Stephanie Barton *(Managing Director,
  Penguin Children's)*
Francesca Dow *(Puffin Managing Director)*
Suzi Brennan *(Finance Director, Penguin)*
Sally Johnson *(Finance Director, Dorling
  Kindersley)*
Helena Peacock *(Legal & Human Resources
  Director)*
Chantal Noel *(Rights Director – Penguin)*
Mike Symons *(Group Sales Director)*
Deborah Wright *(Group Operations
  Director)*
Simon Prosser *(Publishing Director – Hamish
  Hamilton)*
Tony Lacey *(Publishing Director – Viking)*
Juliet Annan *(Publishing Director – Fig Tree)*
Louise Moore *(Publishing Director – Michael
  Joseph)*
Joanna Prior *(Managing Director, Penguin
  General)*

*Academic & Scholarly; Antiques &
Collecting; Archaeology; Atlases & Maps;
Audio Books; Biography & Autobiography;
Children's Books; Cinema, Video, TV &
Radio; Cookery, Wines & Spirits; Crafts &
Hobbies; Crime; Do-It-Yourself; Fiction;
Gardening; Guide Books; Health & Beauty;
History & Antiquarian; Humour; Industry,
Business & Management; Literature &
Criticism; Medical (incl. Self Help &
Alternative Medicine); Military & War;
Music; Natural History; Philosophy;
Photography; Poetry; Politics & World
Affairs; Psychology & Psychiatry; Reference
Books, Directories & Dictionaries; Religion &
Theology; Travel & Topography*

Imprints, Series & ISBNs:
Allen Lane: 978 0 14
Arkana: 978 0 14

Joint ventures with BBC Paperbacks
Hamish Hamilton: 978 0 241
Michael Joseph: 978 0 7181
Ladybird: 978 0 14
Penguin: 978 0 14
Penguin Audiobooks: 978 0 14
Penguin Classics: 978 0 14
Penguin Music Classics: 978 0 14
The Penguin Press: 978 0 14
Puffin: 978 0 14
Viking: 978 0 670
Frederick Warne: 978 0 14

Associated Companies:
Dorling Kindersley Ltd; Hamish
  Hamilton Ltd; Michael Joseph Ltd;
  Ladybird Books Ltd; Rough Guides;
  Ventura Publishing Ltd; Viking Ltd;
  Frederick Warne (& Co) Ltd
Australia: Penguin Books Australia Ltd
Canada: Penguin Books Canada Ltd
New Zealand: Penguin Books (NZ) Ltd
USA: Penguin Putnam Inc

Distributor for:
Which; Wisden

Overseas Representation:
All other areas: Penguin International Sales,
  London, UK
Australia: Penguin Books Australia Ltd,
  Camberwell, Vic, Australia
Canada: Penguin Group Canada, Toronto,
  Ont, Canada
France: Penguin France SA, Blagnac, France
Germany & Austria: Penguin Books
  Deutschland GmbH, Frankfurt am Main,
  Germany
India, Bangladesh, Sri Lanka & Nepal:
  Penguin Books India, New Delhi, India
Italy: Penguin Italia srl, Milan, Italy
Netherlands: Penguin Books BV,
  Amsterdam, Netherlands
New Zealand: Penguin Books (New
  Zealand) Ltd, Auckland, New Zealand
*Poland, Baltic States, Slovenia, Slovakia &
  Ukraine:* Grazyna Soszynska, Poznan-
  Baranowo, Poland
Singapore & Malaysia: Penguin Books
  Singapore & Malaysia, Singapore
South Africa: Penguin Group SA, Rosebank,
  South Africa
Spain & Portugal: Penguin Books SA,
  Madrid, Spain
USA: Penguin Group USA, New York, NY,
  USA

Book Trade Association Membership:
Publishers Association

2560 ▬▬▬

*PENTATHOL PUBLISHING
40 Gibson Street, Wrexham,
Wrexham County LL13 7NS

Personnel:
Athol E. Cowen *(Owner/Chief Executive)*

Poetry

Book Trade Association Membership:
Booksellers Association

2561 ▬▬▬

PETAL PEOPLE PUBLISHING LTD
151 Salwarpe Road, Bromsgrove, Worcs
B60 3HS
Telephone: 01527 579377

Book Trade Association Membership:
Publishers Association

2562 ▬▬▬

PHAIDON PRESS LTD
18 Regent's Wharf, All Saints Street,
London N1 9PA
Telephone: 020 7843 1000
Fax: 020 7843 1010
Web Site: www.phaidon.com

Orders:
Phaidon Customer Services
Telephone: 020 7843 1234
Fax: 020 7843 1111
Email: sales@phaidon.com
Web Site: www.phaidon.com

Warehouse:
Grove Lane, Marston Trading Estate, Frome,
Somerset BA11 4AT
Telephone: 01373 474710
Fax: 01373 474711
Web Site: www.phaidon.com

Personnel:
David Davies *(CEO)*
Andrew Price *(Chairman)*
Amanda Ridout *(Managing Director)*
Amanda Renshaw *(Editorial Director)*
Emilia Terragni *(Editorial Director)*
Elaine Ward *(Production Director)*
Claudia Smitherman *(Financial Director)*

*Academic & Scholarly; Architecture &
Design; Children's Books; Cinema, Video,
TV & Radio; Cookery, Wines & Spirits;
Fashion & Costume; Fine Art & Art History;
Illustrated & Fine Editions; Music;
Photography*

Imprints, Series & ISBNs:
978 0 7148

Associated Companies:
France: Phaidon Sarl
Germany: Phaidon Verlag
Japan: Phaidon KK
USA: Phaidon Press Inc

Overseas Representation:
Australia: United Book Distributors,
  Scoresby, Vic, Australia
France: Phaidon SARL, Paris, France
Germany: Phaidon Verlag GmbH, Berlin,
  Germany
Italy: Phaidon Srl, Milan, Italy
Other Territories: Phaidon Press Ltd,
  London, UK
South Africa: Book Promotions Pty Ltd,
  Cape Town, South Africa
Spain: Phaidon Press, Barcelona, Spain
USA: Phaidon Press Inc, New York, NY, USA

Book Trade Association Membership:
Independent Publishers Guild

2563 ▬▬▬

PHILIP'S
Endeavour House,
189 Shaftesbury Avenue, London
WC2H 8JY
Telephone: 020 7632 5400
Email: info@octopus-publishing.co.uk
Web Site: www.octopusbooks.co.uk

Distribution:
Littlehampton Book Services,
Faraday Close, Durrington, West Sussex
BN13 3RP
Telephone: 01903 828500
Fax: 01903 828625
Email: orders@lbsltd.co.uk
Web Site: www.lbsltd.co.uk

Personnel:
Stephen Mesquita *(Publisher)*

*Atlases & Maps; Educational & Textbooks;
Natural History; Reference Books,
Directories & Dictionaries*

Imprints, Series & ISBNs:
978 1 84907

Parent Company:
Octopus Publishing Group

Overseas Representation:
See: Octopus Publishing Group, London, UK

Book Trade Association Membership:
International Map Traders Association

2564 ▬▬▬

PIATKUS BOOKS
[a division of Little, Brown Book Group]
Little, Brown Book Group,
100 Victoria Embankment, London
EC4Y 0DY
Telephone: 020 7911 8030
Fax: 020 7911 8100
Web Site: www.littlebrown.co.uk &
  www.piatkus.co.uk

Distribution:
Littlehampton Book Services,
Faraday Close, Durrington, Worthing,
West Sussex BN13 3RB
Telephone: 01903 828511
Fax: 01903 828801
Email: orders@lbsltd.co.uk
Web Site: www.lbsltd.co.uk

Personnel:
Ursula Mackenzie *(Chief Executive Officer &
  Publisher)*
Gill Bailey *(Non-Fiction Editorial Director)*
Robert Manser *(UK Sales & Marketing
  Director)*
Nick Ross *(Production Director)*
Emma Beswetherick *(Fiction Director)*
Emily-Jane Taylor *(Finance Director)*
Diane Spivey *(Rights Director)*

*Biography & Autobiography; Cookery,
Wines & Spirits; Crime; Fiction; Gender
Studies; Health & Beauty; History &
Antiquarian; Humour; Industry, Business &
Management; Magic & the Occult; Medical
(incl. Self Help & Alternative Medicine);
Military & War; Music; Psychology &
Psychiatry; Sociology & Anthropology*

New Titles: 180 (2010) , 180 (2011)

Imprints, Series & ISBNs:
Piatkus Books: 978 0 7499

Parent Company:
France: Hachette Livre

Overseas Representation:
Australia: Hachette Livre Australia, Sydney,
  NSW, Australia
Canada: Hachette, Montreal, Canada
New Zealand: Hachette Livre New Zealand,
  Auckland, New Zealand
Singapore & Malaysia: Pansing Distribution
  Sdn Bhd, Singapore
South Africa: Penguin Books SA (Pty) Ltd,
  Denver Ext 4, South Africa

Book Trade Association Membership:
Booksellers Association

2565 ▬▬▬

PICCADILLY PRESS
5 Castle Road, London NW1 8PR
Telephone: 020 7267 4492
Fax: 020 7267 4493
Email: books@piccadillypress.co.uk
Web Site: www.piccadillypress.co.uk

Warehouse & Distribution:
Grantham Book Services, Trent Road,
Grantham, Lincs NG31 7XQ
Telephone: 01476 541080
Fax: 01476 541061

UK Sales & Key Accounts:
Bounce Sales & Marketing Ltd,
14 Greville Street, London EC1N 8SB
Telephone: 020 7138 3650
Fax: 020 7138 3658
Email: sales@bouncemarketing.co.uk
Web Site: www.bouncemarketing.co.uk

Personnel:
Brenda Gardner *(Publisher & Managing
  Director)*

Anne Clark *(Editorial/Commissioning)*
Ruth Williams *(Editorial/Commissioning)*
Melissa Hyder *(Assistant Editor)*
Margot Edwards *(Foreign Rights Consultant)*
Geoffrey Lill *(Financial Controller)*
Andrea Reece *(Publicity Consultant)*
Geoff Barlow *(Production Consultant)*
Vivien Tesseras *(Publishing Administration)*
Natasha Barnden *(Editorial Assistant)*
Robert Snuggs *(Sales Manager, Bounce)*

Children's Books

New Titles: 38 (2010) , 30 (2011)
No of Employees: 6
Annual Turnover: £1M

Imprints, Series & ISBNs:
978 1 84812, 978 1 85340

Overseas Representation:
All other Export enquiries: Bounce Sales & Marketing Ltd, London, UK
Australia: Peribo Pty Ltd, Mount Kuring-Gai, NSW, Australia
New Zealand: South Pacific Book Distributors, Auckland, New Zealand

Book Trade Association Membership:
Independent Publishers Guild

2566 ▬▬

PICKERING & CHATTO (PUBLISHERS) LTD
21 Bloomsbury Way, London WC1A 2TH
Telephone: 020 7405 1005
Fax: 020 7405 6216
Email: info@pickeringchatto.co.uk
Web Site: www.pickeringchatto.com

Distribution & Orders:
Turpin Distribution Ltd,
Stratton Business Park, Pegasus Drive,
Biggleswade, Beds SG18 8QT
Telephone: 01767 604800
Fax: 01767 601640
Web Site: www.turpin-distribution.com

Personnel:
James Powell *(Director)*
Lord Rees-Mogg *(Chairman)*
Mark Pollard *(Editorial, Rights & Production)*
Stephen Warren *(Finance)*

Academic & Scholarly; Economics; History & Antiquarian; Literature & Criticism; Religion & Theology; Scientific & Technical

New Titles: 56 (2010) , 77 (2011)
No of Employees: 11
Annual Turnover: £1.25M

Imprints, Series & ISBNs:
978 1 84893, 978 1 85196

Overseas Representation:
China: China Publisher Services, Beijing, P. R. of China
India: Applied Media, New Delhi, India
Japan: Japan Book Associates, Kyoto, Japan
Korea: Wise Book Solutions, Seoul, Republic of Korea
Spain & Portugal: Iberian Book Services, Madrid, Spain
Taiwan: Unifacmanu Trading Co Ltd, Taipei, Taiwan
USA: Ashgate Publishing Co, Burlington, VT, USA

Book Trade Association Membership:
Independent Publishers Guild

2567 ▬▬

*PIPERS' ASH LTD
Church Road, Christian Malford,
Chippenham, Wiltshire SN15 4BW
Telephone: 01249 720563
Fax: 0870 056 8916
Email: pipersash@supamasu.com

Web Site: www.supamasu.com

Personnel:
A. Tyson *(Managing Director)*
Mrs A. M. Tyson *(Secretary)*

Academic & Scholarly; Aviation; Biography & Autobiography; Children's Books; Fiction; Literature & Criticism; Philosophy; Poetry; Psychology & Psychiatry; Science Fiction; Sports & Games; Theatre, Drama & Dance

Imprints, Series & ISBNs:
Biographies: 978 1 902628, 978 1 904494, 978 1 906928
Children's Libraries: 978 1 902628, 978 1 904494, 978 1 906928
Cornucopia: 978 1 902628, 978 1 904494, 978 1 906928
Kickstarters: 978 1 902628, 978 1 904494, 978 1 906928
Stagecraft: 978 1 902628, 978 1 904494, 978 1 906928
Trinity Collections: 978 1 902628, 978 1 904494, 978 1 906928

Overseas Representation:
Australia: Meagan Tyson, Sydney, Australia
Indonesia: Stephen Tyson, Jakarta, Indonesia
New Zealand: Dr Yvonne Eve Walus, Auckland, New Zealand

2568 ▬▬

*PIQUANT EDITIONS
4 Thornton Road, Carlisle, Cumbria
CA3 9HZ
Telephone: 01228 525075
Fax: 01228 501051
Email: info@piquant.net
Web Site: www.piquant.net

Representation (UK):
IVP, Norton Street, Nottingham NG7 3HR
Telephone: 0115 978 1054
Email: sales@ivpbooks.com
Web Site: www.piquanteditions.com

Personnel:
Pieter Kwant *(Director)*
Mrs Elria Kwant *(Publisher)*
John Bell *(Editor)*
Joshua Thompson *(Marketing Manager)*

Fiction; Fine Art & Art History; Religion & Theology

Imprints, Series & ISBNs:
Piquant: 978 0 9535757
Piquant Editions: 978 1 903689

Overseas Representation:
USA & Canada: STL Inc, Waynesboro, GA, USA

Book Trade Association Membership:
Publishers Association

2569 ▬▬

THE PLAYWRIGHTS PUBLISHING CO
70 Nottingham Road, Burton Joyce, Notts
NG14 5AL
Telephone: 0115 931 3356
Email:
playwrightspublishingco@yahoo.com
Web Site:
www.playwrightspublishing.com

Personnel:
Liz Breeze *(Proprietor)*
Tony Breeze *(Consultant)*

Theatre, Drama & Dance

New Titles: 6 (2010) , 6 (2011)
No of Employees: 2

Imprints, Series & ISBNs:
Playwrights Publishing Co: 978 1 873130

Ventus Books: 978 1 872758

Associated Companies:
Ventus Books

Distributor for:
The Playwrights Publishing Co; Ventus Books

2570 ▬▬

*PLOWRIGHT PRESS
PO Box 66, Warwick CV34 4XE
Telephone: 01926 499433
Fax: 01926 499433
Web Site: www.plowrightpress.co.uk

Personnel:
Ruth Johns *(Director)*

Biography & Autobiography; Environment & Development Studies; Gender Studies; History & Antiquarian; Sociology & Anthropology

Imprints, Series & ISBNs:
'Ordinary' Lives Series: 978 0 9516960, 978 0 9543127
Plowright Press: 978 0 9543127, 978 0 9550940

Distributor for:
Family First Ltd; Ruth's Archive

Book Trade Association Membership:
Independent Publishers Guild; Society of Authors

2571 ▬▬

PLUTO BOOKS LTD
345 Archway Road, London N6 5AA
Telephone: 020 8374 2193
Fax: 020 8348 9133
Email: pluto@plutobooks.com
Web Site: www.plutobooks.com

Trade Enquiries & Orders:
Marston Book Services, Unit 160,
Milton Park, Abingdon, Oxon OX14 4SD
Telephone: 01235 465500
Fax: 01235 465555
Email: trade.orders@marston.co.uk
Web Site: www.marston.co.uk

Personnel:
Anne Beech *(Managing Director)*
Roger Van Zwanenberg *(Chair)*
Simon Liebesny *(Sales Director)*
Gilly Duff *(Rights & Permissions)*
Robert Webb *(Managing Editor)*
Alec Gregory *(Head of Marketing)*
Jon Wheatley *(Publicity Manager)*
Robin Virgin *(IT & Systems Manager)*
Jon Maunder *(Marketing Assistant)*
Conor Deery *(Publishing Assistant)*
Melanie Patrick *(Design & Cover Manager)*

Academic & Scholarly; Cinema, Video, TV & Radio; Economics; Environment & Development Studies; Gender Studies; Law; Literature & Criticism; Philosophy; Politics & World Affairs; Sociology & Anthropology

Imprints, Series & ISBNs:
Journeyman Press: 978 1 85172
Pluto Press: 978 0 7453, 978 0 86104, 978 1 84964

Distributor for:
Paradigm Publishers

Overseas Representation:
Australia: Palgrave Macmillan, Melbourne, Vic, Australia
Canada: Brunswick Books, Toronto, Ont, Canada
Germany (stock-holding distributor): Missing Link International Booksellers, Bremen, Germany
Germany, Austria, Switzerland, Scandinavia,

Benelux, France, Italy, Greece, Malta, Central Europe & Baltic States: Andrew Durnell Marketing Ltd, Tunbridge Wells, UK
India: Maya Publishers Pvt Ltd, New Delhi, India
Japan: Tim Burland
Middle East: International Publishers Representatives (IPR) Ltd, Nicosia, Cyprus
Republic of Ireland & Northern Ireland: Brookside Publishing Services, Dublin, Republic of Ireland
South Africa: Jacana Media, Aukland Park, Johannesburg, South Africa
South East Asia: Taylor & Francis Asia Pacific, Kowloon, Hong Kong; Taylor & Francis Asia Pacific, Petaling Jaya, Malaysia; Taylor & Francis Asia Pacific, Singapore; Taylor & Francis, Beijing, P. R. of China
Spain & Portugal: Iberian Book Services, Madrid, Spain
USA: Palgrave Macmillan, New York, NY, USA
USA (Orders): MPS Distribution Center, Gordonsville, VA, USA

Book Trade Association Membership:
Independent Publishers Guild

2572 ▬▬

THE POLICY PRESS
University of Bristol, Fourth Floor,
Beacon House, Queen's Road, Bristol
BS8 1QU
Telephone: 0117 331 4054
Fax: 0117 331 4093
Email: tpp-info@bris.ac.uk
Web Site: www.policypress.co.uk

Distribution:
Marston Book Services, PO Box 269,
Abingdon, Oxon OX14 4YN
Telephone: 01235 465500
Fax: 01235 465556
Email: direct.orders@marston.co.uk
Web Site: www.marston.co.uk/

UK Representation:
Compass Academic Ltd,
13 Progress Business Centre,
Whittle Parkway, Slough SL1 6DQ
Telephone: 01628 559500
Fax: 01628 663876
Email: ca@compass-academic.co.uk
Web Site: www.academic.compass-booksales.co.uk

Personnel:
Alison Shaw *(Director)*
Julia Mortimer *(Assistant Director)*

Academic & Scholarly; Educational & Textbooks; Gender Studies; Politics & World Affairs; Sociology & Anthropology

Imprints, Series & ISBNs:
978 1 84742, 978 1 86134

Parent Company:
University of Bristol

Overseas Representation:
Australia, New Zealand & Papua New Guinea: DA Information Services Pty Ltd, Mitcham, Vic, Australia
Europe (excluding UK): Durnell Marketing Ltd, Tunbridge Wells, UK
India, Sri Lanka, Nepal, Bangladesh & Bhutan: Surit Mitra, Maya Publishers Pvt Ltd, New Delhi, India
Japan: Kinokuniya Co Ltd, Tokyo, Japan; Maruzen Co Ltd, Tokyo, Japan
Malaysia & Brunei: UBSD Distribution Sdn Bhd, Selangor, Malaysia
Middle East & North Africa: Dar Kreidieh, Beirut, Lebanon
Pakistan: Tahir M. Lodhi, Lahore, Pakistan
South Africa: Blue Weaver Marketing, Tokai, South Africa

Taiwan: Unifacmanu Trading Co Ltd, Taipei, Taiwan
Thailand, Taiwan, Hong Kong, Korea, China, Singapore, Malaysia, Philippines & Vietnam: Tony Poh Leong Wah, Singapore
USA & Canada: University of Chicago Press, Chicago IL, USA

Book Trade Association Membership:
Independent Publishers Guild

2573

***POLITY PRESS**
65 Bridge Street, Cambridge CB2 1UR
Telephone: 01223 324315
Fax: 01223 461385
Email: polity@politybooks.com
Web Site: www.polity.co.uk

Distribution Warehouse:
John Wiley & Sons Ltd, 1 Oldlands Way, Bognor Regis, West Sussex PO22 9SA
Telephone: 01243 843294
Fax: 01243 843303
Email: cs-books@wiley.co.uk

Publicity:
Polity Press, 9600 Garsington Road, Oxford OX4 2DQ
Telephone: 01865 476711
Fax: 01865 471711
Email: boconnor@wiley.com
Web Site: www.polity.co.uk

Personnel:
David Held *(Editorial Director)*
John Thompson *(Editorial Director)*

Academic & Scholarly; Cinema, Video, TV & Radio; Educational & Textbooks; Gender Studies; History & Antiquarian; Literature & Criticism; Philosophy; Politics & World Affairs; Sociology & Anthropology

Imprints, Series & ISBNs:
978 0 7456

Overseas Representation:
Australia: John Wiley & Sons Australia Ltd, Milton, Qld, Australia
Canada: John Wiley & Sons Canada Ltd, Etobicoke, Ont, Canada
Europe, Middle East & Africa: Karen Wootton, John Wiley & Sons Ltd, Chichester, UK
Germany: Wiley-VCH, Weinheim, Germany
Japan: Wiley Japan, Tokyo, Japan
Singapore: John Wiley & Sons (Asia) Pte Ltd, Singapore
USA: John Wiley & Sons Inc, Hoboken, NJ, USA

Book Trade Association Membership:
Independent Publishers Guild

2574

POLPERRO HERITAGE PRESS
Clifton-upon-Teme, Worcestershire WR6 6EN
Telephone: 01886 812304
Email: polperro.press@virgin.net
Web Site: www.polperropress.co.uk

Personnel:
Jerry Johns *(Managing Editor)*

Biography & Autobiography; History & Antiquarian; Natural History; Nautical; Photography; Reference Books, Directories & Dictionaries

Imprints, Series & ISBNs:
978 0 9530012, 978 0 9544233, 978 0 9549137, 978 0 9553648, 978 0 9559541

Book Trade Association Membership:
Independent Publishers Guild

2575

PORTLAND PRESS LTD
[a wholly owned subsidiary of the Biochemical Society]
Commerce Way, Colchester CO2 8HP
Telephone: 01206 796351
Fax: 01206 799331
Email: editorial@portlandpress.com & sales@portland-services.com
Web Site: www.portlandpress.com & www.portland-services.com

Editorial Office:
Portland Press Limited, Charles Darwin House, 12 Roger Street, London WC1N 2JU
Telephone: 020 7685 2400
Fax: 020 7685 2469
Email: editorial@portlandpress.com

Send orders to:
Portland Customer Services, Commerce Way, Colchester, Essex CO2 8HP
Telephone: 01206 796351
Fax: 01206 799331
Email: sales@portland-services.com
Web Site: www.portlandpress.com/pcs/

Personnel:
Caroline Black *(Managing Director)*
John Misselbrook *(Financial Director)*
Adam Marshall *(Marketing & Sales Director)*
John Day *(IT Director)*

Academic & Scholarly; Biology & Zoology; Educational & Textbooks; Electronic (Professional & Academic); Medical (incl. Self Help & Alternative Medicine); Reference Books, Directories & Dictionaries; Scientific & Technical

New Titles: 2 (2011)
No of Employees: 70
Annual Turnover: £2.5M

Imprints, Series & ISBNs:
Biochemical Society: 978 0 904498
Portland Press: 978 1 85578

Parent Company:
The Biochemical Society

Associated Companies:
Portland Customer Services

Distributor for:
Antiquity Publications Ltd; Bioscientifica Ltd incorporating The Society for Endocrinology; Caspian Publishing; Earthscan; Energy Institute; Expert Information; International Water Association Publishing; The Policy Press; Practical Action Publishing; The Royal College of Surgeons of England; The Royal Society; Royal Society of Chemistry; Royal Society of Medicine; Vathek Publishing; Water Environment Federation; WEF Publishing

Overseas Representation:
Australia: DA Information Services Pty Ltd, Mitcham, Vic, Australia
India: Affiliated East-West Press Pvt Ltd, New Delhi, India
Japan: USACO Corporation, Tokyo, Japan

Book Trade Association Membership:
International Group of Scientific, Medical & Technical Publishers; Independent Publishers Guild; Association of Learned & Professional Society Publishers; UK Serials Group

2576

***PORTOBELLO BOOKS LTD**
12 Addison Avenue, Holland Park, London W11 4QR
Telephone: 020 7605 1380
Fax: 020 7605 1361
Email: mail@portobellobooks.com

Web Site: www.portobellobooks.com

Personnel:
Laura Barber *(Editorial Director)*
Angela Rose *(Rights Director)*
Pru Rowlandson *(Publicity Director)*
Brigid Macleod *(Sales Director)*
Philip Gwyn Jones *(Publisher)*
Iain Chapple *(Marketing & Digital Director)*

Biography & Autobiography; Fiction; History & Antiquarian; Politics & World Affairs; Travel & Topography

Imprints, Series & ISBNs:
978 1 84627

Associated Companies:
UK: Granta

Overseas Representation:
Australia & New Zealand: Allen & Unwin Pty Ltd, Sydney, NSW, Australia
Canada: House of Anansi, Toronto, Ont, Canada
European Union: Faber & Faber, London, UK
Far East: Julian Ashton, Sevenoaks, Kent, UK
Netherlands: Nilsson & Lamm BV, Weesp, Netherlands
South Africa: Penguin Books South Africa (Pty) Ltd, Johannesburg, South Africa

Book Trade Association Membership:
Independent Publishers Guild; Independent Alliance

2577

***POSITIVE PRESS LTD**
28a Gloucester Road, Trowbridge, Wilts BA14 0AA
Telephone: 01225 719204
Fax: 01225 712187
Email: dankat@jennymosley.co.uk
Web Site: www.circle-time.co.uk

Personnel:
Jenny Mosley *(Managing Director)*
Danka Tadd *(Sales Account Manager)*

Children's Books; Educational & Textbooks

Imprints, Series & ISBNs:
978 0 09

Book Trade Association Membership:
Booksellers Association

2578

PP PUBLISHING
Suite 74, 17 Holywell Hill, St Albans, Herts AL1 1DT
Telephone: 01727 833866
Fax: 0845 456 6385
Email: sales@xplpublishing.com
Web Site: www.peerpractice.com

Personnel:
Andrew Griffin *(Managing Director)*

Academic & Scholarly; Accountancy & Taxation; Industry, Business & Management; Law; Medical (incl. Self Help & Alternative Medicine)

New Titles: 2 (2010) , 5 (2011)
No of Employees: 2

Imprints, Series & ISBNs:
978 1 85811

Parent Company:
Richard Griffin (1820) Ltd

Overseas Representation:
Hong Kong: Bloomsbury Books Ltd, Hong Kong

Book Trade Association Membership:
Independent Publishers Guild

2579

PRACTICAL PRE-SCHOOL BOOKS
[a division of MA Education Ltd]
St Jude's Church, Dulwich Road, Herne Hill, London SE24 0PB
Telephone: 020 7738 5454
Fax: 020 7733 2325
Email: orders@practicalpreschoolbooks.com
Web Site: www.practicalpreschoolbooks.com

Distributors:
Mark Allen Distribution, Jesses Farm, Dinton, Wilts SP3 5HN
Telephone: 01722 716935
Email: orders@practicalpreschoolbooks.com

Personnel:
Rebecca Linssen *(Group Editorial Director)*
Matt Govett *(Managing Director)*
Rebecca Haworth *(Associate Publisher)*
Tracey Mills *(Customer Services Manager)*

Educational & Textbooks; Vocational Training & Careers

Imprints, Series & ISBNs:
Practical Pre-School Books: 978 1 902438, 978 1 904575, 978 1 907241

Parent Company:
UK: MA Education Ltd.

Associated Companies:
UK: Mark Allen Group

Overseas Representation:
Malaysia: Extrazeal (M) Sdn Bhd, Petaling Jaya Selangor, Malaysia
Singapore, Brunei, Thailand: The Learning Needs Centre, Singapore
Southern Africa: Everybody's Books, South Africa
United Arab Emirates, Oman, Qatar, Kuwait, Egypt and Lebanon: Arif Abdullah Distribution, Dubai, UAE

Book Trade Association Membership:
British Educational Suppliers Association (BESA)

2580

PRESTEL PUBLISHING LTD
4 Bloomsbury Place, London WC1A 2QA
Telephone: 020 7323 5004
Fax: 020 7636 8004
Email: sales@prestel-uk.co.uk
Web Site: www.prestel.com

Warehouse, Trade Enquiries & Orders:
Macmillan Distribution Ltd, Brunel Road, Houndmills, Basingstoke, Hants RG21 6XS
Telephone: 01256 302692
Fax: 01256 812588
Email: orders@macmillan.co.uk
Web Site: www.macmillandistribution.co.uk

Personnel:
Andrew Hansen *(Managing Director)*
Ali Gitlow *(Commissioning Editor (London))*
Florence Andrew *(Marketing & Publicity Executive)*
Oliver Barter *(Sales Manager)*
Keira Parish *(Sales Executive)*

Antiques & Collecting; Archaeology; Architecture & Design; Children's Books; Fashion & Costume; Fine Art & Art History; Photography

Imprints, Series & ISBNs:
13 Children Should Know: 978 3 7913
50 You Should Know: 978 3 7913
Adventures in Art Series: 978 3 7913

Parent Company:
Germany: Verlagsgruppe Random House Bertelsmann

Associated Companies:
USA: Prestel Publishing

Distributor for:
Canada: Douglas & McIntyre Publishers
Switzerland: Lars Müller Publishers
USA: Periscope Publishing Ltd

Overseas Representation:
Africa (excluding South Africa): Tony Moggach, InterMedia Americana (IMA) Ltd, London, UK
Asia (including China, Hong Kong, Korea, Philippines & Taiwan): Ed Summerson, Asia Publishers Services Ltd, Hong Kong
Australia: Peribo Pty Ltd, Mount Kuring-Gai, NSW, Australia
Canada: Canadian Manda Group, Toronto, Ont, Canada
France: Interart SARL, Paris, France
Israel: Lonnie Kahn & Co Ltd, Rishon Lezion, Israel
Italy & Greece: Sandro Salucci, Italy
Japan: Andrew Hansen, Prestel, London, UK
Malta, Cyprus, Turkey, Middle East & North Africa: Peter Ward Book Exports, London, UK
Netherlands & Belgium: Nilsson & Lamm BV, Weesp, Netherlands
Scandinavia: Elisabeth Harder-Kreimann, Hamburg, Germany
South & Central America: David Williams, InterMedia Americana (IMA) Ltd, London, UK
South Africa: Zytek Publishing, Germiston, South Africa
South East Asia: Peter Couzens, Sales East, Bangkok, Thailand
Spain & Portugal: Christopher Humphrys, UK
Switzerland: Buchzentrum AG, Hägendorf, Switzerland
USA: Prestel Publishing, New York, NY, USA

2581

PRINCETON UNIVERSITY PRESS
6 Oxford Street, Woodstock, Oxon
OX20 1TW
Telephone: 01993 814500
Fax: 01993 814504
Email: admin@pupress.co.uk
Web Site: press.princeton.edu

Personnel:
Al Bertrand *(Publishing Director, Europe)*
Caroline Priday *(European Director of Publicity)*
Benjamin Tate *(Editor and Director of Foreign Rights)*
Kimberley Williams *(International Rights Manager)*

Academic & Scholarly; Biology & Zoology; Economics; Educational & Textbooks; Electronic (Professional & Academic); Environment & Development Studies; History & Antiquarian; Industry, Business & Management; Law; Mathematics & Statistics; Natural History; Philosophy; Politics & World Affairs; Reference Books, Directories & Dictionaries; Scientific & Technical; Sociology & Anthropology

Imprints, Series & ISBNs:
978 0 691

Parent Company:
USA: Princeton University Press

Overseas Representation:
All other countries: Export Department, Princeton University Press, Ewing, NJ, USA
Continental Europe & Israel: Customer Service Operations, Princeton University Press, c/o John Wiley & Sons Ltd, Bognor Regis, UK

Book Trade Association Membership:
Independent Publishers Guild

2582

PROFILE BOOKS
3A Exmouth House, Pine Street, London
EC1R 0JH
Telephone: 020 7841 6300
Fax: 020 7841 3969
Email: info@profilebooks.com
Web Site: www.profilebooks.com

Personnel:
Andrew Franklin *(Managing Director)*
Stephen Brough *(Commercial Director)*
Diana Broccardo *(Sales and Marketing Director)*
Ruth Killick *(Publicity Director)*
Claire Beaumont *(Sales Director)*
Sam Humphreys *(Publisher, Serpent's Tail)*
Daniel Crewe *(Publisher)*
Mark Ellingham *(Publisher)*
Rebecca Gray *(Publicity Director, Serpent's Tail)*
Penny Daniel *(Rights Director)*
Michael Bhaskar *(Digital Publishing Director)*
Geoff Mulligan *(Publisher, The Clerkenwell Press)*
Niamh Murray *(Marketing Director)*

Biography & Autobiography; Crime; Economics; Fiction; History & Antiquarian; Industry, Business & Management; Politics & World Affairs

New Titles: 120 (2011)
No of Employees: 28

Imprints, Series & ISBNs:
The Clerkenwell Press
The Economist Books
Profile Books
Serpent's Tail

Overseas Representation:
Australia & New Zealand: Allen & Unwin Pty Ltd, Sydney, NSW, Australia
Europe, Hong Kong, China, Japan, Korea, Taiwan, Middle East, North Africa & Turkey: Faber & Faber, London, UK
India & Pakistan: Viva Books, New Delhi, India
Philippines: Sarah Ward, Profile Books, Philippines
Singapore, Malaysia, Thailand & Vietnam: APD Singapore Pte Ltd, Singapore
South Africa: Book Promotions Pty Ltd, Cape Town, South Africa
USA & Canada: Consortium Book Sales & Distribution, Minneapolis, MN, USA

Book Trade Association Membership:
Publishers Association; Independent Publishers Guild

2583

PROQUEST
International Office, The Quorum, Barnwell Road, Cambridge CB5 8SW
Telephone: 01223 215512
Fax: 01223 215513
Email: marketing@proquest.co.uk
Web Site: www.proquest.co.uk

Personnel:
T. Robinson *(Sales)*
J. Taylor *(General Manager & Vice-President Technology & Operations)*
S. Tilley *(Marketing)*

Academic & Scholarly; Accountancy & Taxation; Agriculture; Architecture & Design; Bibliography & Library Science; Biology & Zoology; Cinema, Video, TV & Radio; Computer Science; Economics; Electronic (Educational); Electronic (Professional & Academic); Engineering; Fashion & Costume; Fine Art & Art History; History & Antiquarian; Industry, Business &
Management; Literature & Criticism; Mathematics & Statistics; Medical (incl. Self Help & Alternative Medicine); Music; Natural History; Physics; Poetry; Politics & World Affairs; Psychology & Psychiatry; Reference Books, Directories & Dictionaries; Religion & Theology; Scientific & Technical; Sociology & Anthropology; Theatre, Drama & Dance

Imprints, Series & ISBNs:
978 0 85964

Parent Company:
USA: ProQuest

Overseas Representation:
Australia & New Zealand: ProQuest, Melbourne, Vic, Australia
Canada: ProQuest, Toronto, Ont, Canada
China: ProQuest, Beijing, P. R. of China
Europe: ProQuest, Cambridge, UK
Germany: ProQuest, Berlin, Germany
Hong Kong, Macau & Taiwan: ProQuest, Wanchai, Hong Kong
Japan: ProQuest, Kanagawa, Japan
Korea: ProQuest, Seoul, Republic of Korea
Latin America: ProQuest, Rio de Janeiro, Brazil
North America: ProQuest, Ann Arbor, MI, USA
South East Asia & Far East: ProQuest, Petaling Jaya, Malaysia
Spain: ProQuest España, Madrid, Spain
United Arab Emirates: ProQuest, Dubai Media City, UAE

2584

PROSPECT BOOKS
Allaleigh House, Blackawton, Totnes, Devon
TQ9 7DL
Telephone: 01803 712269
Fax: 01803 712311
Email: tom.jaine@prospectbooks.co.uk
Web Site: www.prospectbooks.co.uk

Distribution:
Central Books, 99 Wallis Road, London
E9 5LN
Telephone: 020 8986 4854

Personnel:
Tom Jaine *(Owner)*

Cookery, Wines & Spirits

New Titles: 8 (2010) , 8 (2011)

2585

*PROSPERA PUBLISHING
Longreach, 36 Ashley Road, Berkhamsted, Herts HP4 3BL
Telephone: 020 7935 7750
Fax: 020 7935 7793
Email: suzybrownlee@prospera.co.uk
Web Site: www.prosperapublishing.co.uk

Children's Books; Fiction; Travel & Topography

2586

PSYCHOLOGY PRESS
Palmeira Mansions, 27 Church Road, Hove
BN3 2FA
Telephone: 01273 207411
Fax: 01273 205612
Web Site: www.psypress.co.uk

Book Trade Association Membership:
Publishers Association

2587

*PUNK PUBLISHING LTD
3 The Yard, Pegasus Place, London
SE11 5SD
Telephone: 020 7820 9333
Email: sophie@punkpublishing.co.uk

Web Site: www.punkpublishing.com & www.coolcamping.co.uk

Personnel:
Jonathan Knight *(Publisher)*
Shelley Bowdler *(Marketing Manager)*

Travel & Topography

Imprints, Series & ISBNs:
978 0 9552036, 978 1 906889

Book Trade Association Membership:
Independent Publishers Guild

2588

*PUSHKIN PRESS
12 Chester Terrace, London NW1 4ND
Telephone: 020 7730 0750
Email: books@pushkinpress.com
Web Site: www.pushkinpress.com

Personnel:
Melissa Ulfane *(Executive)*

Fiction

Imprints, Series & ISBNs:
978 1 901285, 978 1 906548

2589

QUADRILLE PUBLISHING LTD
5th Floor, Alhambra House,
27–31 Charing Cross Road, London
WC2H 0LS
Telephone: 020 7839 7117
Fax: 020 7839 7118
Email: enquiries@quadrille.co.uk

Personnel:
Alison Cathie *(Managing Director)*
Jane O'Shea *(Publishing Director)*
Vincent Smith *(Deputy Managing Director)*
Helen Lewis *(Creative Director)*
Melanie Gray *(Sales Director)*
Margaux Dungon *(International Sales Director)*
Clare Lattin *(Head of Publicity)*

Architecture & Design; Biography & Autobiography; Cookery, Wines & Spirits; Crafts & Hobbies; Do-It-Yourself; Fashion & Costume; Gardening; Health & Beauty; Humour; Magic & the Occult; Medical (incl. Self Help & Alternative Medicine); Photography; Travel & Topography

Imprints, Series & ISBNs:
978 1 84400, 978 1 84949, 978 1 899988, 978 1 902757, 978 1 903845

Book Trade Association Membership:
Booksellers Association

2590

QUARTET BOOKS
27 Goodge Street, London W1T 2LD
Telephone: 020 7636 3992
Fax: 020 7637 1866
Email: info@quartetbooks.co.uk
Web Site: www.quartetbooks.co.uk

Warehouse:
NBN International, Estover Road, Plymouth
PL6 7PZ
Telephone: 01752 202300
Fax: 01752 202330
Web Site: www.nbninternational.com

Personnel:
David Elliott *(Director)*
Chimene Pae *(Editorial)*
Anna Stothard *(Editorial)*
Gavin Bower *(Editorial / Digital)*

Biography & Autobiography; Fashion & Costume; Fiction; Fine Art & Art History; History & Antiquarian; Illustrated & Fine

Editions; Literature & Criticism; Music;
Politics & World Affairs; Theatre, Drama &
Dance

New Titles: 33 (2010) , 18 (2011)
No of Employees: 4

Imprints, Series & ISBNs:
Robin Clark: 978 0 86072

Parent Company:
Namara Group

Associated Companies:
Robin Clark; The Women's Press

Overseas Representation:
Australia: The Scribo Group, Frenchs Forest,
NSW, Australia
France, Belgium, Germany, Austria,
Switzerland, Italy & Greece: Ted
Dougherty, London, UK
India, Denmark, Finland, Norway & Sweden:
Quartet Books Ltd, London, UK
USA: Interlink Publishing Group Inc,
Northampton, MA, USA

2591 ━━━━━━━━━━━━━

QUILLER PUBLISHING LTD
Wykey House, Wykey, Shrewsbury SY4 1JA
Telephone: 01939 261616
Fax: 01939 261606
Email: admin@quillerbooks.com
Web Site: www.countrybooksdirect.com

**Warehouse, Distribution, Orders &
Sales Enquiries:**
Grantham Book Services, Trent Road,
Grantham, Lincolnshire NG31 7XQ
Telephone: 01476 541080
Fax: 01476 541061
Email: orders@gbs.tbs-ltd.co.uk

Personnel:
Andrew Johnston (Managing Director)
John Beaton (Editorial Director)
Julie Ward (Marketing Manager)
Jonathan Heath (Sales Manager)
Rob Dixon (Production Manager)

Animal Care & Breeding; Antiques &
Collecting; Biography & Autobiography;
Cookery, Wines & Spirits; Crafts & Hobbies;
Fine Art & Art History; Gardening;
Humour; Illustrated & Fine Editions; Military
& War; Natural History; Nautical; Reference
Books, Directories & Dictionaries; Sports &
Games; Transport; Travel & Topography;
Veterinary Science

New Titles: 30 (2010) , 30 (2011)

Imprints, Series & ISBNs:
Kenilworth Press: 978 0 901366, 978 1
872082, 978 1 872119, 978 1 905693
Quiller Press: 978 0 907621, 978 1 84689,
978 1 904057
The Sportsman's Press: 978 0 948253
Swan Hill Press: 978 1 84037, 978 1 85310

Distributor for:
South Africa: Rowland Ward
UK: JJG Publishing; The Pony Club
USA: Half Halt Press; Stackpole Books

Overseas Representation:
Australia: Peribo Pty Ltd, Mount Kuring-Gai,
NSW, Australia
Europe & Scandinavia: Jonathan Heath,
Quiller Publishing Ltd, Shrewsbury, UK
South Africa: Trinity Books CC, Randburg,
South Africa
USA & Canada: Half Halt Press, Boonsboro,
MD, USA; Stackpole Books Inc,
Mechanicsburg, PA, USA

Book Trade Association Membership:
Independent Publishers Guild

2592 ━━━━━━━━━━━━━

***RACEFORM LTD / RACING POST
BOOKS**
RFM House, High Street, Compton,
Newbury, Berks RG20 6NL
Telephone: 01933 304858
Fax: 01635 578101
Email: shop@racingpost.com
Web Site: www.racingpost.com/shop

Fulfilment House:
Raceform, Sanders Road, Wellingborough,
Northamptonshire NN8 4BX
Telephone: 01933 304858
Fax: 01933 270300
Email: shop@racingpost.com
Web Site: www.racingpost.com/shop

Personnel:
Julian Brown (Publishing Director)
James de Wesselow (Managing Director)
Liz Ampairee (Sales & Marketing Director)

Sports & Games

Imprints, Series & ISBNs:
Highdown Books / Racing Post: 978 1
905156
Raceform: 978 1 904317, 978 1 905153,
978 1 906820

Parent Company:
Racing Post

Book Trade Association Membership:
Independent Publishers Guild

2593 ━━━━━━━━━━━━━

THE RADCLIFFE PRESS
6 Salem Road, London W2 4BU
Telephone: 020 7243 1225
Fax: 020 7243 1226

Distributor:
Macmillan Distribution Ltd, Brunel Road,
Houndmills, Basingstoke, Hants RG21 6XS

Personnel:
Dr Lester Crook (Publisher)
Liz Stuckey (Finance Manager)
Stuart Weir (Production Director)
Anne Nicholson (Rights Manager)
Paul Davighi (Sales & Marketing Director)
Antonia Leslie (Publicity Officer)

Biography & Autobiography; History &
Antiquarian; Military & War; Politics &
World Affairs; Travel & Topography

Imprints, Series & ISBNs:
978 1 78076, 978 1 84511, 978 1 85043,
978 1 86064, 978 1 84885

Overseas Representation:
Australia: Palgrave Macmillan, South Yarra,
Vic, Australia
USA: Palgrave Macmillan, New York, NY,
USA

2594 ━━━━━━━━━━━━━

*RADCLIFFE PUBLISHING LTD
18 Marcham Road, Abingdon, Oxon
OX14 1AA
Telephone: 01235 528820
Fax: 01235 528830
Email: contact.us@radcliffepublishing.com
Web Site: www.radcliffepublishing.com

Personnel:
Gregory Moxon (Managing Director)
Gillian Nineham (Editorial Director)
Margaret McKeown (Financial Director)
Jamie Etherington (Editorial Manager)
Steve Bonner (Production Manager)
Dan Allen (Marketing Executive)
Carlos Sejournant (Sales Executive)

Educational & Textbooks; Electronic
(Educational); Electronic (Professional &

Academic); Industry, Business &
Management; Medical (incl. Self Help &
Alternative Medicine); Reference Books,
Directories & Dictionaries; Scientific &
Technical; Vocational Training & Careers

Imprints, Series & ISBNs:
978 1 84619, 978 1 85775, 978 1 870905

Overseas Representation:
Australia: Elsevier Australia, Marrickville,
NSW, Australia
India, Bangladesh, Sri Lanka, Nepal &
Pakistan: Jaypee Brothers Medical
Publishers (Pte) Ltd, New Delhi, India
Middle East: International Publishing
Services (IPS) Middle East Ltd, Dubai, UAE
Scandinavia: David Towle International,
Stockholm, Sweden
Singapore, Malaysia, Thailand, Vietnam,
Cambodia, Laos, Myanmar, Brunei,
Indonesia, Philippines & Taiwan: Alkem
Co (S) Pte Ltd, Singapore
USA: Martin P. Hill Consulting, New York,
NY, USA

Book Trade Association Membership:
Independent Publishers Guild

2595 ━━━━━━━━━━━━━

RAND PUBLICATIONS
5 Victoria House, 138 Watling Street East,
Towcester NN12 6BT
Telephone: 01327 357770
Fax: 01327 359572
Email: rand@oppuk.co.uk
Web Site: www.rand.org

Warehouse & Distribution:
NBN International, 10 Thornbuy Road,
Plymouth PL6 7PP
Telephone: 01752 202301
Fax: 01752 202331
Email: orders@nbninternational.com
Web Site: www.nbninternational.com

Personnel:
Gary Hall (Manager)

Academic & Scholarly; Economics;
Educational & Textbooks; Military & War;
Politics & World Affairs

New Titles: 140 (2011)

Imprints, Series & ISBNs:
978 0 8330

Parent Company:
USA: Rand Publications

2596 ━━━━━━━━━━━━━

***RANDOM HOUSE CHILDREN'S
BOOKS**
61–63 Uxbridge Road, London W5 5SA
Telephone: 020 8579 2652
Fax: 020 8231 6767
Web Site: www.kidsatrandomhouse.co.uk

Personnel:
Philippa Dickinson (Managing Director)
Helen Randles (Sales Director)
Barry O'Donovan (Marketing Director)
Jane Seery (Production Director)
Bronwen Bennie (Rights Director)
Annie Eaton (Fiction Publisher)
Fiona Macmillan (Colour & Custom
Publishing)

Children's Books

Parent Company:
UK: Random House Group Ltd

Associated Companies:
UK: Bodley Head; Jonathan Cape; Corgi;
Doubleday; David Fickling Books;
Hutchinson; Red Fox; Tamarind

Book Trade Association Membership:
Publishers Association

2597 ━━━━━━━━━━━━━

*RANDOM HOUSE UK LTD
20 Vauxhall Bridge Road, London
SW1V 2SA
Telephone: 020 7840 8400
Fax: 020 7233 8791
Web Site: www.randomhouse.co.uk

Personnel:
Gail Rebuck (Chair & Chief Executive
Officer)
Ian Hudson (Deputy Chief Executive Officer)
Mark Gardiner (Group Finance Director)
Garry Prior (Group Sales Director)
Stephen Esson (Group Production Director)
Maureen Corish (Group Communications
Director)

Architecture & Design; Children's Books;
Cookery, Wines & Spirits; Crafts & Hobbies;
Crime; Do-It-Yourself; Economics; Fiction;
Fine Art & Art History; Gardening; Guide
Books; Health & Beauty; History &
Antiquarian; Humour; Illustrated & Fine
Editions; Literature & Criticism; Military &
War; Music; Natural History; Philosophy;
Photography; Poetry; Politics & World
Affairs; Science Fiction; Sports & Games;
Transport

Parent Company:
UK: Random House Group Ltd

Associated Companies:
UK: Arrow; BBC Books; Black Lace; Bodley
Head; Jonathan Cape; Century; Chatto
& Windus; Ebury; Everyman; Fodor;
Harvill Secker; William Heinemann;
Hutchinson; Mainstream; Pimlico;
Preface; Random House Books; Rider;
Time Out; Vermilion; Vintage; Virgin
Books; Yellow Jersey

Book Trade Association Membership:
Publishers Association

2598 ━━━━━━━━━━━━━

RANSOM PUBLISHING LTD
Radley House, 8 St Cross Road, Winchester,
Hampshire SO23 9HX
Telephone: 01962 862307
Email: ransom@ransom.co.uk
Web Site: www.ransom.co.uk

Personnel:
Jenny Ertle (Managing Director/Marketing)
Stephen Rickard (Creative Director)

Audio Books; Children's Books; Educational
& Textbooks; Electronic (Educational)

Imprints, Series & ISBNs:
321 Go!: 978 1 84167, 978 1 900127
Boffin Boy: 978 1 84167, 978 1 900127
Cutting Edge: 978 1 84167, 978 1 900127
Dark Man: 978 1 84167, 978 1 900127
Goal!: 978 1 84167, 978 1 900127
Siti's Sisters: 978 1 84167, 978 1 900127
Starchasers: 978 1 84167, 978 1 900127
Trailblazers: 978 1 84167, 978 1 900127
Zone 13: 978 1 84167, 978 1 900127

Book Trade Association Membership:
Independent Publishers Guild

2599 ━━━━━━━━━━━━━

RAVEN'S QUILL LTD
63 High Street, Billingshurst, West Sussex
RH14 9QP
Telephone: 01403 782489
Email: info@ravensquill.com
Web Site: www.ravensquill.com

Personnel:
Mrs Emily Henderson (Director)
Alan Gilliland (Director)

Children's Books; Fiction

Imprints, Series & ISBNs:
Raven's Quill Ltd: 978 0 9555486
Shabby Tattler Press: 978 0 9555486

Overseas Representation:
Far East: Big Apple Tuttle-Mori, Shanghai, P. R. of China
Korea: Amo Agency, Seoul, Republic of Korea
Spain, Portugal & Latin America: Ilustrata, Barcelona, Spain

Book Trade Association Membership:
Publishers Association; Independent Publishers Guild

2600

RAVETTE PUBLISHING LTD
PO Box 876, Horsham, West Sussex RH12 9GH
Telephone: 01403 711443
Fax: 01403 711554
Email: ravettepub@aol.com

Warehouse, Invoicing & Accounts:
Orca Book Services, 160 Milton Park, Abingdon, Oxon OX14 4SD
Telephone: 01202 665432
Fax: 01235 465555
Email:
tradeorders@orcabookservices.co.uk
Web Site: www.orcabookservices.co.uk

Personnel:
Mrs M. Lamb *(Managing Director)*
Miss I. Parris *(Company Secretary)*

Children's Books; Humour; Military & War

New Titles: 9 (2010) , 12 (2011)
No of Employees: 2

Imprints, Series & ISBNs:
Born to Shop: 978 1 84161
Garfield: 978 1 84161
Hackman: 978 1 84161
Juicy Lucy: 978 1 84161
The Odd Squad: 978 1 84161, 978 1 85304
Odd Streak: 978 1 84161
Peanuts: 978 1 84161
Their Finest Hour: 978 1 84161
Yoga Cats/Dogs: 978 1 84161

Overseas Representation:
Australia: Peribo Pty Ltd, Mount Kuring-Gai, NSW, Australia
Denmark, Sweden, Norway & Finland: Angell Eurosales, UK
Eastern Europe: Inter Media Americana, UK
France, Belgium, Germany, Switzerland & Austria: Anselm Robinson, UK
Hong Kong, Philippines, Korea, Taiwan, Thailand & Indonesia: Ashton International Marketing Services, Sevenoaks, Kent, UK
Japan: Yasmy International Marketing, Ageo, Japan
Middle East: Peter Ward Book Exports, London, UK
Singapore & Malaysia: Pansing Distribution Sdn Bhd, Singapore
South Africa: Bag of Books, Park Town, South Africa
Spain, Portugal, Italy & Malta: Bookport Associates, Italy

Book Trade Association Membership:
Independent Publishers Guild

2601

*REARDON PUBLISHING
[also known as Reardon & Son Publishers]
PO Box 919, Cheltenham, Glos GL50 9AN
Telephone: 01242 231800
Email: reardon@bigfoot.com
Web Site: www.reardon.co.uk &
www.cotswoldbookshop.com

Personnel:
Nicholas Reardon *(Director)*

Archaeology; Atlases & Maps; Audio Books; Children's Books; Cinema, Video, TV & Radio; Guide Books; History & Antiquarian; Humour; Magic & the Occult; Military & War; Natural History; Nautical; Travel & Topography

Imprints, Series & ISBNs:
Driveabout Series: 978 1 874192
Rideabout Series: 978 0 9508674
Walkabout Series: 978 1 873877
Walkcards (series)

Distributor for:
Cheltenham Tourism; Cicerone Press; Cordee; Corinium Publications; Estate Publications; Flukes UK; Harvey Maps; OS Maps; Philips Maps; Rambler Association; Video Ex

Book Trade Association Membership:
Outdoor Writers Guild

2602

REDCLIFFE PRESS LTD
81g Pembroke Road, Bristol BS8 3EA
Telephone: 0117 973 7207
Fax: 0117 923 8991
Email: info@redcliffepress.co.uk
Web Site: www.redcliffepress.co.uk

Trade Orders:
Orca Book Services Ltd, Unit A3, Fleets Corner, Poole, Dorset BH17 0HL
Telephone: 01202 665432
Fax: 01202 666219
Email: orders@orcabookservices.co.uk

Personnel:
A. N. Sansom *(Sales Director)*
John Sansom *(Publishing Director)*
Clara Sansom *(Production Director)*

Architecture & Design; Fine Art & Art History; History & Antiquarian; Literature & Criticism; Poetry

Imprints, Series & ISBNs:
978 1 900178, 978 1 904537, 978 1 906593

Associated Companies:
Art Dictionaries Ltd; Sansom & Co Ltd; Westcliffe Books

Overseas Representation:
USA: Antique Collectors Club Ltd, Easthampton, MA, USA

2603

*REDEMPTORIST PUBLICATIONS
Alphonsus House, Chawton, Hants GU34 3HQ
Telephone: 01420 88222
Fax: 01420 88805
Email: rp@rpbooks.co.uk
Web Site: www.rpbooks.co.uk

Personnel:
Rev Denis McBride *(Publishing Director)*
Andrew Lane *(Head of Operations)*
Michael Roberts *(Sales & Service Manager)*
Christine Thirkell *(Financial Controller)*
Patricia Wilson *(Marketing Manager)*
Andrew Lyon *(Editorial Manager)*

Religion & Theology

Imprints, Series & ISBNs:
978 0 85231

Distributor for:
USA: Abbey Press; Creative Communications; Dimension Books; HarperCollins; ICS Publications; Liguori/ Triumph; Loyola Press; Peter Pauper Press; RCL (Resources for Christian Living); Regina Press (Malhame); Resurrection Press; Servant Publications; Sophia Institute; St Anthony Messenger Press/Franciscan Catholic Book Publishing Co

Book Trade Association Membership:
Booksellers Association

2604

REFLECTIONS OF A BYGONE AGE
15 Debdale Lane, Keyworth, Notts NG12 5HT
Telephone: 0115 937 4079
Fax: 0115 937 6197
Email:
reflections@postcardcollecting.co.uk

Personnel:
Brian Lund *(Contact)*
F. Mary Lund *(Contact)*

History & Antiquarian; Sports & Games; Transport

Imprints, Series & ISBNs:
978 0 946245, 978 1 900138, 978 1 905408

2605

RIPLEY PUBLISHING LTD
22 The Causeway, Bishop's Stortford, Herts CM23 2EJ
Telephone: 01279 502910
Web Site: www.ripleybooks.com

Personnel:
Anne Marshall *(Publisher)*
Becky Miles *(Editorial Director)*
Amanda Dula *(Foreign Rights Manager)*

Children's Books; Fiction; Reference Books, Directories & Dictionaries

New Titles: 6 (2010) , 14 (2011)

Parent Company:
Canada: The Jim Pattison Group

2606

*RISING STARS UK LTD
22 Grafton Street, London W1S 4EX
Telephone: 020 7495 6793
Fax: 020 7495 6796
Email: info@risingstars-uk.com
Web Site: www.risingstars-uk.com

Customer Service, Trade Enquiries & Warehouse:
Grantham Book Services, Trent Road, Grantham, Lincs NG31 7XQ

Personnel:
Andrea Carr *(Managing Director)*
Tim Pearce *(Production Director)*
Camilla Erskine *(Publishing Director)*

Children's Books; Educational & Textbooks; Electronic (Educational); Fiction

Imprints, Series & ISBNs:
978 1 84680, 978 1 905056

Overseas Representation:
Contact: English Language International, Dunstable, UK

Book Trade Association Membership:
Educational Publishers Council; Independent Publishers Guild

2607

RNIB
105 Judd Street, London WC1H 9NE
Telephone: 020 7388 1266
Fax: 020 7388 2034
Web Site: www.rnib.org.uk

Book Trade Association Membership:
Publishers Association

2608

ROADMASTER PUBLISHING
PO Box 176, Chatham, Kent ME5 9AQ
Telephone: 01634 862843
Fax: 01634 862843
Email:
roadmasterpublishing@blueyonder.co.uk

Personnel:
Malcolm Wright *(Sales Director)*

Geography & Geology; Guide Books; Nautical; Transport; Travel & Topography

Imprints, Series & ISBNs:
978 1 871814

2609

ROBINSWOOD PRESS LTD
30 South Avenue, Stourbridge, West Midlands DY8 3XY
Telephone: 01384 397475
Fax: 01384 440443
Email: publishing@robinswoodpress.com
Web Site: www.robinswoodpress.com

Personnel:
Christopher Marshall *(Managing Director)*
Susan Marshall *(Director / Author)*
George Marshall *(Company Secretary)*
Henry Marshall *(Non-Executive Director)*

Children's Books; Educational & Textbooks; Electronic (Educational); English as a Foreign Language; Fiction; Poetry

New Titles: 2 (2010) , 20 (2011)
No of Employees: 4
Annual Turnover: £100,000

Imprints, Series & ISBNs:
978 1 869981, 978 1 906053

Overseas Representation:
Australia: Lefty's, Sydney, Australia
Republic of Ireland: STA Ltd, Dublin, Republic of Ireland
Singapore: Knowledge Tree Resources

2610

ALAN ROGERS GUIDES LTD
[part of the Mark Hammerton Group]
Spelmonden Old Oast, Goudhurst, Cranbrook, Kent TN17 1HE
Telephone: 01580 214000
Email: russell@alanrogers.com
Web Site: www.alanrogers.com

Personnel:
Russell Wheldon *(Marketing Director)*

Travel & Topography

Parent Company:
Mark Hammerton Group

Book Trade Association Membership:
Booksellers Association

2611

ROTOVISION SA
Sheridan House, 112 Western Road, Hove, East Sussex BN3 1DD
Telephone: 01273 727268
Fax: 01273 727269
Email: sales@rotovision.com
Web Site: www.rotovision.com

Personnel:
David Breuer *(Managing Director)*
Nicole Kemble *(Rights Director)*
Mari Ahlfeld-Smith *(Financial Controller)*
April Sankey *(Publisher)*

Architecture & Design; Cinema, Video, TV &

Radio; Fashion & Costume; Fine Art & Art History; Music; Photography; Reference Books, Directories & Dictionaries; Theatre, Drama & Dance

Imprints, Series & ISBNs:
978 2 88046

Parent Company:
Quarto Group

Overseas Representation:
Australia: Thames & Hudson (Australia) Pty Ltd, Fishermans Bend, Vic, Australia
France: Interart SARL, Paris, France
Germany, Switzerland & Austria: Michael Klein, Vilsbiburg, Germany
Middle East: International Publishing Services (IPS) Middle East Ltd, Dubai, UAE
South East Asia: APD Singapore Pte Ltd, Singapore

Book Trade Association Membership:
Booksellers Association

2612 ▬▬▬▬

ROUND HALL
43 Fitzwilliam Place, Dublin 2, Republic of Ireland
Telephone: +353 (0)1 662 5301
Fax: +353 (0)1 662 5302
Email: rinfo@thomson.com
Web Site: www.roundhall.ie

Distribution:
Gill & Macmillan, Hume Avenue, Park West, Dublin 12, Republic of Ireland
Telephone: +353 (0)1 500 9500

Personnel:
Catherine Dolan *(Director)*
Martin McCann *(Editorial & Content Manager)*
Terri McDonnell *(Production Manager)*
Martin McCann *(Editorial Manager)*
Maura Smyth *(Marketing & Publishing Manager)*
Aengus McMorrow *(Online Account Manager)*
Pauline Ward *(Print Account Manager)*

Academic & Scholarly; Accountancy & Taxation; Educational & Textbooks; Electronic (Professional & Academic); Industry, Business & Management; Law; Medical (incl. Self Help & Alternative Medicine); Reference Books, Directories & Dictionaries

Imprints, Series & ISBNs:
Round Hall: 978 1 85800, 978 1 899738
Round Hall Professional: 978 1 86089

Parent Company:
USA: Thomson Reuters Corp

Associated Companies:
Australia: LBC
Canada: Carswell
New Zealand: Brookers
UK: Sweet & Maxwell
USA: West Group

2613 ▬▬▬▬

ROUNDHOUSE PUBLISHING LTD
Roundhouse Group, Unit B, 18 Marine Gardens, Brighton BN2 1AH
Telephone: 01273 603717
Fax: 01273 697494
Email: sales@roundhousegroup.co.uk
Web Site: www.roundhousegroup.co.uk

Warehouse & Distribution:
Orca Book Services, Unit A3, Fleets Corner, Poole BH17 0HL
Telephone: 01235 465521
Fax: 01235 465555
Email: orders@orca-book-services.co.uk
Web Site: www.orcabookservices.co.uk

Personnel:
Alan Goodworth *(Managing Director)*
Matt Goodworth *(Marketing Manager)*

Academic & Scholarly; Animal Care & Breeding; Archaeology; Architecture & Design; Atlases & Maps; Biography & Autobiography; Children's Books; Cinema, Video, TV & Radio; Cookery, Wines & Spirits; Crafts & Hobbies; Fine Art & Art History; Gardening; Guide Books; Health & Beauty; History & Antiquarian; Industry, Business & Management; Literature & Criticism; Medical (incl. Self Help & Alternative Medicine); Military & War; Philosophy; Photography; Politics & World Affairs; Psychology & Psychiatry; Reference Books, Directories & Dictionaries; Religion & Theology; Sports & Games; Travel & Topography

Imprints, Series & ISBNs:
Roundabout: 978 1 85710
Roundhouse Publishing: 978 1 85710

Associated Companies:
Roundabout Books; Roundhouse Arts; Roundtrip Travel; Windsor Books International

Distributor for:
Australia: Allen & Unwin
Canada: Crabtree Publishing
Italy: Charta Art Books; Giunti Editore
Republic of Ireland: Irish Museum of Modern Art
Spain: Santana Books
UK: Age UK
USA: ABC-Clio & Greenwood International; Allworth Press; C&T Publishing; Capstone Press; David Godine Publishers; Getty Publications; Gryphon House Publishers; Martingale & Co; Pelican Publishing Co; Prometheus Books; Quality Medical Publishing; J. Ross Publishing; University Press of Mississippi

Overseas Representation:
Europe (East) & Scandinavia: Bill Bailey Publishers Representatives, Totnes, UK
Europe (South): Bookport Associates, Milan, Italy
Europe (Spain & Portugal only): Iberian Book Services, Madrid, Spain
Europe (West) (excluding Scandinavia): Ted Dougherty, London, UK

2614 ▬▬▬▬

*ROUTE PUBLISHING LTD
PO Box 167, Pontefract WF8 4WW
Telephone: 01977 797695
Email: info@route-online.com
Web Site: www.route-online.com

Distribution:
Central Books, 99 Wallis Road, London E9 5LN
Telephone: 020 8986 4854
Fax: 020 8533 5821
Email: bill@centralbooks.com
Web Site: www.centralbooks.com

Personnel:
Ian Daley *(Editor)*
Isabel Galan *(Public Relations Director)*

Biography & Autobiography; Cinema, Video, TV & Radio; Fiction; Music; Poetry

Imprints, Series & ISBNs:
978 1 901927

Overseas Representation:
USA: Dufour Editions Inc, Chester Springs, PA, USA

Book Trade Association Membership:
Independent Publishers Guild

2615 ▬▬▬▬

JOSEPH ROWNTREE FOUNDATION
The Homestead, 40 Water End, York YO30 6WP
Telephone: 01904 629241
Fax: 01904 620072
Email: maria.beech@jrf.org.uk
Web Site: www.jrf.org.uk

Personnel:
Julia Unwin CBE *(Chief Executive)*
Julia Lewis *(Communications Director)*
Paul Dack *(Finance Director)*

Academic & Scholarly; Architecture & Design; Economics; Politics & World Affairs; Sociology & Anthropology

2616 ▬▬▬▬

ROYAL COLLECTION PUBLICATIONS
Stable Yard House, St James's Palace, London SW1A 1JR
Telephone: 020 7024 5584
Fax: 020 7839 8168
Email: publishing@royalcollection.org.uk
Web Site: www.royalcollection.org.uk

Distribution:
Thames & Hudson Ltd, 181a High Holborn, London WC1V 7QX
Telephone: 020 7845 5000
Fax: 020 7845 5055
Email: sales@thameshudson.co.uk
Web Site: www.thamesandhudson.com

Personnel:
Jacky Colliss Harvey *(Publisher)*
Kate Owen *(Commissioning Editor)*
Elizabeth Simpson *(Publishing & New Media Assistant)*
Nina Chang *(Publishing Assistant)*

Academic & Scholarly; Antiques & Collecting; Architecture & Design; Biography & Autobiography; Fashion & Costume; Fine Art & Art History; Guide Books; History & Antiquarian; Illustrated & Fine Editions; Natural History; Photography

Imprints, Series & ISBNs:
978 1 905686

Overseas Representation:
Rest of World: Thames & Hudson Ltd, London, UK
USA & Canada: University of Chicago Press, Chicago, IL, USA

2617 ▬▬▬▬

ROYAL COLLEGE OF GENERAL PRACTITIONERS
1 Bow Churchyard, London EC4M 9DQ
Telephone: 020 3188 7400
Fax: 020 3188 7401
Web Site: www.rcgp.org.uk

Personnel:
Ms Helen Farrelly *(Publishing Manager)*

Academic & Scholarly; Medical (incl. Self Help & Alternative Medicine)

Imprints, Series & ISBNs:
978 0 85084

Book Trade Association Membership:
Association of Learned & Professional Society Publishers

2618 ▬▬▬▬

THE ROYAL COLLEGE OF PSYCHIATRISTS
17 Belgrave Square, London SW1X 8PG
Telephone: 020 7235 2351
Fax: 020 7259 6507
Email: publications@rcpsych.ac.uk
Web Site: www.rcpsych.ac.uk

Warehouse:
Turpin Distribution, Customer Services, Pegasus Drive, Stratton Business Park, Biggleswade, Beds SG18 8TQ
Telephone: 01767 604951
Fax: 01767 601640
Email: custserv@turpin-distribution.com
Web Site: www.turpin-distribution.com

Personnel:
Dave Jago *(Director of Publications and Website)*
Daniel Tomkins *(Sales & Marketing Manager)*

Academic & Scholarly; Electronic (Professional & Academic); Medical (incl. Self Help & Alternative Medicine); Psychology & Psychiatry

New Titles: 7 (2010) , 10 (2011)
No of Employees: 11
Annual Turnover: £1.6M

Imprints, Series & ISBNs:
Gaskell: 978 0 902241, 978 1 901242
RCPsych Publications: 978 0 902241, 978 1 901242

Overseas Representation:
Australia & New Zealand: Footprint, Warriewood, NSW, Australia
Republic of Ireland: Compass Academic, London, UK
Scandinavia (including Iceland & Estonia): David Towle International, Stockholm, Sweden
USA & Canada: Princeton Selling Group Inc, Wayne, PA, USA

Book Trade Association Membership:
Independent Publishers Guild; Association of Learned & Professional Society Publishers

2619 ▬▬▬▬

ROYAL GEOGRAPHICAL SOCIETY
[with Institute of British Geographers]
1 Kensington Gore, London SW7 2AR
Telephone: 020 7591 3022
Fax: 020 7591 3001
Email: journals@rgs.org
Web Site: www.rgs.org

Personnel:
David Riviere *(Head of Finance & Services)*
Madeleine Hatfield *(Managing Editor: Journal)*

Academic & Scholarly; Electronic (Educational); Electronic (Professional & Academic); Environment & Development Studies; Geography & Geology

Imprints, Series & ISBNs:
RGS-IBG Book Series (academic/scholarly texts only)

2620 ▬▬▬▬

ROYAL IRISH ACADEMY
Academy House, 19 Dawson Street, Dublin 2, Republic of Ireland
Telephone: +353 (0)1 676 2570 & 676 4222
Fax: +353 (0)1 676 2346
Email: publications@ria.ie
Web Site: www.ria.ie/Publications

Trade Orders:
Gill & Macmillan Distribution, Hume Avenue, Park West Industrial Park, Dublin 12, Republic of Ireland
Telephone: +353 (0)1 500 9500
Fax: +353 (0)1 500 9599
Email: sales@gillmacmillan.ie
Web Site: www.gillmacmillan.ie

Personnel:
Ruth Hegarty *(Production & Sales, Managing Editor)*

Academic & Scholarly; Archaeology; Atlases & Maps; Biology & Zoology; History & Antiquarian; Languages & Linguistics; Mathematics & Statistics; Politics & World Affairs; Reference Books, Directories & Dictionaries

New Titles: 8 (2011)

Imprints, Series & ISBNs:
978 0 901714, 978 0 9543855, 978 1 874045, 978 1 904890
Prism: 978 1 904890

Overseas Representation:
North America: International Specialized Book Services Inc, Portland, OR, USA

Book Trade Association Membership:
Publishing Ireland (Foilsiú Éireann); Association of Learned & Professional Society Publishers; Cle is now called Publishing Ireland

2621

RSC PUBLISHING
[The publishing division of the Royal Society of Chemistry (RSC)]
Customer Care and Sales,
Thomas Graham House, Science Park, Milton Road, Cambridge CB4 0WF
Telephone: 01223 420066
Fax: 01223 423429
Email: sales@rsc.org
Web Site: www.rsc.org/publishing

Direct Orders for RSC Journals, Databases and Magazines:
RSC Distribution Services, c/
o Portland Customer Services, Commerce Way, Colchester CO2 8HP
Telephone: 01206 226050
Fax: 01206 226055
Email: sales@rscdistribution.org

Americas Sales Office, Royal Society of Chemistry:
University City Science Centre, 3711 Market Street, Suite 800, Philadelphia, PA 19104, USA
Telephone: +1 215 966 6206
Email: americas@rsc.org
Web Site: www.rsc.org/publishing

East Asia Pacific Sales Office, Royal Society of Chemistry:
Room 406, Building 2, No 345, Lingling Road, Shanghai 200032, P. R. of China
Telephone: +86 21 64047330
Email: sales@rsc.org
Web Site: www.rsc.org/publishing

Personnel:
Dr James Milne (*Acting Managing Director, Publishing*)
Mr Stephen Hawthorne (*Sales Director*)
Mr Richard Crouch (*Marketing Director*)
Mrs Jennifer Paterson (*Marketing Manager, Publishing*)
Miss Louise Peck (*Library Marketing Specialist*)
Mr Dan Dyer (*Head of Sales EMEAI*)

Academic & Scholarly; Chemistry; Educational & Textbooks; Electronic (Educational); Electronic (Professional & Academic); Reference Books, Directories & Dictionaries; Scientific & Technical

New Titles: 4 (2010) , 3 (2011)
No of Employees: 250

Imprints, Series & ISBNs:
978 0 85186, 978 0 85404, 978 1 84973

Parent Company:
UK: The Royal Society of Chemistry

Overseas Representation:
Brazil: EBSCO Brazil, Rio de Janeiro, Brazil

Brunei, Indonesia, Malaysia, Philippines, Singapore: Rosalinda Mohammed Razi, Singapore
Cambodia, Laos, Myanmar, Thailand and Vietnam: Wim Van der Putten, Bangkok, Thailand
Egypt: LIMS, Cairo, Egypt
India and Sri Lanka: Book Marketing Services, Chennai, India
Iran: Jahan Adib Publishing, Tehran, Iran
Israel: Inter View Information Resources, Ramat-Gan, Israel
Japan: Bureau Hosoya, Tokyo, Japan
Korea: EBSCO Korea, Seoul, Republic of Korea
Latin America (except Brazil): Accucoms, Lansdale, USA
Lebanon: Levant, Beirut, Lebanon
Middle East: Techknowledge, Dubai, UAE
Taiwan: Flysheet Information Services Co. Ltd, Taipei, Taiwan

Book Trade Association Membership:
Association of Learned Society Publishers; STM (European Group)

2622

*RUSSELL HOUSE PUBLISHING LTD
4 St George's House,
Uplyme Road Business Park, Lyme Regis DT7 3LS
Telephone: 01297 443948
Fax: 01297 442722
Email: help@russellhouse.co.uk
Web Site: www.russellhouse.co.uk

Personnel:
Geoffrey Mann (*Managing Director*)
Martin Jones (*Director*)
Terry Nemko (*Director*)

Academic & Scholarly; Educational & Textbooks; Electronic (Educational); Electronic (Professional & Academic); Gender Studies; Industry, Business & Management; Law; Medical (incl. Self Help & Alternative Medicine); Psychology & Psychiatry; Sociology & Anthropology; Sports & Games; Theatre, Drama & Dance; Vocational Training & Careers

Imprints, Series & ISBNs:
978 1 898924, 978 1 903855, 978 1 905541

Overseas Representation:
Australia: Psychoz, Vic, Australia
North America: International Specialized Book Services Inc, Portland, OR, USA

2623

*SAGE PUBLICATIONS LTD
1 Oliver's Yard, 55 City Road, London EC1Y 1SP
Telephone: 020 7324 8500
Fax: 020 7324 8600
Email: info@sagepub.co.uk
Web Site: www.sagepub.co.uk

Warehouse:
Unit 11, Keirbeck Business Centre, North Woolwich Road, Silvertown, London E16 2BG

Personnel:
Stephen Barr (*Managing Director*)
Katherine Jackson (*Financial & Deputy Managing Director*)
Ziyad Marar (*Deputy Managing Director*)
Clive Parry (*Marketing & Sales Director*)
Phil Denvir (*IT Director*)
Richard Fidczuk (*Production Director*)
Sara Miller McCune (*Director*)
Blaise Simqu (*Director*)
Paul Chapman (*Director*)
Tony Histed (*Associate Director, Sales*)
Anne Farlow (*Non-Executive Director*)
Brenda Gowley (*Non-Executive Director*)

Alison Browne (*Customer Service (Books) Manager*)
Huw Alexander (*Rights & Permissions Manager*)

Academic & Scholarly; Bibliography & Library Science; Economics; Educational & Textbooks; Electronic (Educational); Gender Studies; Industry, Business & Management; Mathematics & Statistics; Politics & World Affairs; Psychology & Psychiatry; Reference Books, Directories & Dictionaries; Religion & Theology; Scientific & Technical; Sociology & Anthropology

Imprints, Series & ISBNs:
978 0 7619, 978 0 8039, 978 1 4129

Parent Company:
USA: SAGE Publications Inc

Associated Companies:
Paul Chapman Publishing Ltd
India: SAGE Publications Pvt Ltd
USA: Corwin Press Inc; Pine Forge Press Inc; Sage Publications Inc

Overseas Representation:
Australia & New Zealand: Footprint Books Pty Ltd, Sydney, NSW, Australia
South Africa: Academic Marketing Services (Pty) Ltd, Craighall, South Africa

Book Trade Association Membership:
Publishers Association; Independent Publishers Guild

2624

SAINT ALBERT'S PRESS
[British Province of Carmelites (Carmelite Charitable Trust)]
Carmelite Projects & Publications Office, More House, Heslington, York YO10 5DX
Telephone: 01904 411521
Email: projects@carmelites.org.uk
Web Site: www.carmelite.org

Orders & Book Deposit:
Saint Albert's Press Book Distribution, Carmelite Friars, 34 Tanners Street, Faversham, Kent ME13 7JN
Telephone: 01795 537038
Fax: 01795 539511
Email: saintalbertspress@carmelites.org.uk
Web Site: www.carmelite.org

Personnel:
Johan Bergström-Allen (*Director*)
Kevin Bellman (*Sales*)
Brother Paul de Groot (*Bursar*)

Academic & Scholarly; History & Antiquarian; Poetry; Religion & Theology

New Titles: 2 (2010) , 2 (2011)
No of Employees: 2

Imprints, Series & ISBNs:
978 0 904849

Parent Company:
UK: Carmelite Charitable Trust

Associated Companies:
UK: The Carmelite Press; Whitefriars Press

Distributor for:
Italy: Edizioni Carmelitane
USA: Carmelite Institute Washington D.C.

Book Trade Association Membership:
Independent Publishers Guild

2625

ST JEROME PUBLISHING LTD
2 Maple Road West, Brooklands, Manchester M23 9HH
Telephone: 0161 973 9856
Fax: 0161 905 3498
Email: ken@stjeromepublishing.com

Web Site: www.stjerome.co.uk

Personnel:
Ken Baker (*Managing Director*)

Academic & Scholarly; Educational & Textbooks; Electronic (Professional & Academic); Gay & Lesbian Studies; Gender Studies; Languages & Linguistics; Reference Books, Directories & Dictionaries

New Titles: 14 (2010) , 11 (2011)

Imprints, Series & ISBNs:
978 1 900650, 978 1 905763

Book Trade Association Membership:
Publishers Association; Independent Publishers Guild

2626

SANDSTONE PRESS LTD
PO Box 5725, 1 High Street, Dingwall, Ross-shire IV15 9WJ
Telephone: 01349 862583
Fax: 01349 862583
Email: info@sandstonepress.com
Web Site: www.sandstonepress.com

Personnel:
Robert Davidson (*Managing Director*)
Iain Gordon (*Company Secretary*)
Moira Forsyth (*Director*)

Academic & Scholarly; Biography & Autobiography; Crime; English as a Foreign Language; Environment & Development Studies; Fiction; Humour; Illustrated & Fine Editions; Literature & Criticism; Politics & World Affairs; Science Fiction; Sports & Games

Imprints, Series & ISBNs:
Sandstone Meanmnach Series: 978 1 905207
Sandstone Vista Series: 978 1 905207

Overseas Representation:
USA & Canada: Silvermibe International Books Inc

Book Trade Association Membership:
Publishing Scotland

2627

SANSOM & CO LTD
81g Pembroke Road, Clifton, Bristol BS8 3EA
Telephone: 0117 973 7207
Fax: 0117 923 8991
Email: johnsansom@aol.com & info@sansomandcompany.co.uk
Web Site: www.sansomandcompany.co.uk

Trade Orders:
Orca Book Services, Unit A3, Fleets Corner, Poole, Dorset BH17 0HL
Telephone: 01202 665432
Fax: 01202 666219
Email: orders@orcabookservices.co.uk
Web Site: www.orcabookservices.co.uk

Personnel:
A. N. Sansom (*Sales Director*)
John Sansom (*Publishing Director*)
Clara Sansom (*Production Director*)

Architecture & Design; Fine Art & Art History; Literature & Criticism

Imprints, Series & ISBNs:
978 1 900178, 978 1 904537, 978 1 906593

Associated Companies:
Art Dictionaries Ltd; Redcliffe Press Ltd

Overseas Representation:
USA: Antique Collectors' Club, Woodbridge, Suffolk, UK

2628

SAQI BOOKS
26 Westbourne Grove, London W2 5RH
Telephone: 020 7221 9347
Fax: 020 7229 7492
Web Site: www.saqibooks.com

Distribution:
Marston Book Services, 160 Milton Park,
Abingdon, Oxon OX14 4SD
Telephone: 01235 465500
Fax: 01235 465555
Email: client.orders@marston.co.uk
Web Site: www.marston.co.uk

Personnel:
Lynn Gaspard (Publisher)
Dide Siemmond (Editorial and Rights
    Assistant)
Ashley Biles (Sales and Marketing Manager)
Charlotte Allen (Publicity Manager)
Will Brady (Production Manager)

Academic & Scholarly; Architecture &
Design; Biography & Autobiography;
Cookery, Wines & Spirits; Economics;
Educational & Textbooks; Environment &
Development Studies; Fashion & Costume;
Fiction; Fine Art & Art History; Gay &
Lesbian Studies; Gender Studies; History &
Antiquarian; Humour; Illustrated & Fine
Editions; Languages & Linguistics; Law;
Literature & Criticism; Mathematics &
Statistics; Music; Philosophy; Photography;
Poetry; Politics & World Affairs; Religion &
Theology; Sociology & Anthropology

Imprints, Series & ISBNs:
978 0 86356
Brief Introduction (series)
Saqi Essentials

Associated Companies:
Lebanon: Dar Al Saqi Sarl

Overseas Representation:
Australia: Palgrave Macmillan, South Yarra,
    Vic, Australia
USA: Consortium Publishers, St Paul, MN,
    USA

Book Trade Association Membership:
Booksellers Association; Independent
Publishers Guild

2629

S. B. PUBLICATIONS
14 Bishopstone Road, Seaford, East Sussex
BN25 2UB
Telephone: 01323 893498
Fax: 01323 893860
Email: sbpublications@tiscali.co.uk
Web Site: www.sbpublications.co.uk

Personnel:
Mrs L. S. Woods (Owner/Manager)
Mrs D. Quick (Finance)
Mr C. Howden (Proofreader)
Miss C. Gillett (Sales & Administration)

Guide Books; History & Antiquarian;
Natural History; Travel & Topography

New Titles: 10 (2010) , 8 (2011)
No of Employees: 1

Imprints, Series & ISBNs:
978 1 85770

2630

SCALA PUBLISHERS LTD
Northburgh House, 10 Northburgh Street,
London EC1V 0AT
Telephone: 020 7490 9900
Fax: 020 7336 6870
Email: jmckinley@scalapublishers.com
Web Site: www.scalapublishers.com

All orders (excluding Australia):
ACC Distribution, Sandy Lane,
Old Marlesham, Woodbridge, Suffolk
IP12 4SD
Telephone: 01394 389950
Fax: 01394 389999
Email: sales@antique-acc.com
Web Site: www.antiquecollectorsclub.com

Personnel:
David Campbell (Chairman)
Jennifer Wright (Museum Publications
    (USA) Director)
Jenny McKinley (Marketing & Publications
    (excl. USA) Director)
Oliver Craske (Editorial Director)
Tim Clarke (Production Director)
Mark Bicknell (Finance Director)

Antiques & Collecting; Architecture &
Design; Children's Books; Fine Art & Art
History; Guide Books; Illustrated & Fine
Editions; Sports & Games; Travel &
Topography

Imprints, Series & ISBNs:
978 1 85759

Overseas Representation:
Australia (Sales): In Books, NSW, Australia
Worldwide: ACC Distribution, Woodbridge,
    Suffolk, UK

2631

SCHOFIELD & SIMS
Dogley Mills, Penistone Road, Fenay Bridge,
Huddersfield, West Yorkshire HD8 0NQ
Telephone: 01325 467362
Web Site: www.schofieldandsims.co.uk

Book Trade Association Membership:
Publishers Association

2632

SCHOLASTIC UK LTD
Euston House, 24 Eversholt Street, London
NW1 1DB
Telephone: 020 7756 7756
Fax: 020 7756 7795
Web Site: www.scholastic.co.uk

Scholastic Book Clubs:
(as above)

Scholastic Children's Books:
(as above)

Scholastic Book Fairs:
(as above)

Scholastic Education:
Book End, Range Road, Witney, Oxon
OX29 0YD
Fax: 01993 893222

Personnel:
Hilary Murray Hill (Scholastic Children's
    Books – Managing Director)
Alan Hurcombe (Group Managing Director)
Nicola Dixon (Finance Director)
Steve Thompson (Managing Director, Fairs)
Julie Randles (Managing Director, Clubs)

Children's Books; Educational & Textbooks

Parent Company:
USA: Scholastic Inc

Associated Companies:
Australia: Scholastic Australia Pty Ltd
Canada: Scholastic Canada Ltd
New Zealand: Scholastic New Zealand Ltd
UK: Chicken House Publishing

Overseas Representation:
Australia: Scholastic Australia Ltd, Gosford,
    NSW, Australia
Canada: Scholastic Canada Ltd, Markham,
    Ont, Canada
Far East (excluding Singapore, Malaysia &

Indonesia): Scholastic Hong Kong, Hong
    Kong
New Zealand: Scholastic NZ, Auckland, New
    Zealand

Book Trade Association Membership:
Publishers Association; Educational
Publishers Council; Periodical Publishers
Association

2633

SCHOOLPLAY PRODUCTIONS LTD
15 Inglis Road, Colchester, Essex CO3 3HU
Telephone: 01206 540111
Fax: 01206 766944
Email: schoolplay@inglis-
house.demon.co.uk
Web Site:
www.schoolplayproductions.co.uk

Personnel:
J. R. Lucas (Managing Director)
W. Baker (Director)
Mrs C. S. Wenden (Administrator)

Educational & Textbooks; Music; Theatre,
Drama & Dance

Imprints, Series & ISBNs:
978 1 872475, 978 1 902472

Book Trade Association Membership:
Publishers Association

2634

SCHOTT MUSIC LTD
48 Great Marlborough Street, London
W1F 7BB
Telephone: 020 7534 0700
Fax: 020 7534 0719
Email: info@schott-music.com
Web Site: www.schott-music.com

Trade Enquiries & Orders:
MDS Service Centre,
5–6 Raywood Office Complex,
Leacon Lane, Charing, Ashford, Kent
TN27 0EN
Telephone: 01233 712233
Fax: 01233 714948
Email: orders.uk@mds-partner.com
Web Site: www.smdextranet.schott-
extranet.de

Personnel:
Judith Webb (Joint Managing Director)
Roberto Garcia (Sales & Marketing Director)
Guy Thomas (Buying Manager)
Wendy Lampa (Head of International
    Publishing)

Academic & Scholarly; Music

Imprints, Series & ISBNs:
Apollo-Verlag Paul Lincke GmbH: 978 3
    920030
Ars-Viva-Verlag: 978 3 920045
Atlantis Musikbuch-Verlag AG: 978 3 254
Anton J. Benjamin GmbH: 978 3 923051
Boosey & Hawkes Music Publishers Ltd: 978
    0 85162
Bote & Bock GmbH & Co KG: 978 3 7931,
    978 3 87090
Cranz GmbH: 978 3 920201
Matth. Hohner AG: 978 3 920468, 978 3
    937315
Schott London: 978 0 901938, 978 0
    946535, 978 1 902455
Schott Music & Media GmbH (Intuition):
    978 3 932398
Schott Music GmbH & Co KG: 978 3 7957
Schott USA: 978 0 930448
Richard Strauss GmbH & Co KG: 978 3
    901974

Parent Company:
Germany: Schott Music GmbH & Co KG

Associated Companies:
Ernst Eulenburg Ltd

Distributor for:
A piacere; Ars viva; Bardic Edition; Boosey &
    Hawkes Music Publishers Ltd; Delius
    Trust; Edition HH; Finzi Trust; Hyperion;
    Itchy Fingers Publications; Universal
    Edition Ltd
Austria: Amadeus; Apollo-Verlag Paul
    Lincke GmbH; Ars-Viva-Verlag; Atlantis-
    Musikbuch-Verlag; Anton J. Benjamin
    GmbH; Boosey & Hawkes GmbH; Bote &
    Bock GmbH & Co KG; Cranz GmbH; G.
    Henle Verlag; Matth. Hohner AG

Overseas Representation:
Europe: Schott Music GmbH & Co KG,
    Mainz, Germany
Japan: Schott Japan Co Ltd, Tokyo, Japan
USA: Hal Leonard Corporation, Milwaukee,
    WI, USA

2635

SCION PUBLISHING LTD
The Old Hayloft, Vantage Business Park,
Bloxham Road, Banbury, Oxon OX16 9UX
Telephone: 01295 258577
Fax: 01295 275624
Web Site: www.scionpublishing.com

Distribution:
NBN International, 10 Thornbury Road,
Plymouth PL6 7PP
Telephone: 01752 202301

Personnel:
Dr Jonathan Ray (Managing Director)
Simon Watkins (Sales & Marketing Director)

Academic & Scholarly; Biology & Zoology;
Chemistry; Medical (incl. Self Help &
Alternative Medicine); Scientific & Technical

New Titles: 6 (2010) , 10 (2011)
No of Employees: 3
Annual Turnover: £500,000

Imprints, Series & ISBNs:
978 1 904842

Distributor for:
Brazil: Artes Medicas
UK: Acheron Press; The Ray Society

Overseas Representation:
Australia & New Zealand: Macmillan
    Education Australia, South Yarra, Vic,
    Australia
Europe: Andrew Durnell Marketing Ltd,
    Tunbridge Wells, UK
Far East: The White Partnership, Tunbridge
    Wells, UK
South Africa: Mike Brightmore, Academic
    Marketing Services, Johannesburg, South
    Africa

Book Trade Association Membership:
International Group of Scientific, Medical &
Technical Publishers

2636

SCOTTISH CHILDREN'S PRESS
Unit 6, Newbattle Abbey Business Park,
Newbattle Road, Dalkeith EH22 3LJ
Telephone: 0131 660 4666
Fax: 0870 285 4846
Email: info@scottishbooks.com &
orders@scottishbooks.com
Web Site: www.scottishbooks.com

Personnel:
Brian Pugh (Company Secretary)
Avril Gray (Director)

Archaeology; Biography & Autobiography;
Children's Books; Cookery, Wines & Spirits;
Fiction; History & Antiquarian; Languages &
Linguistics; Natural History; Poetry; Religion
& Theology; Sports & Games

Imprints, Series & ISBNs:
978 1 899827

Associated Companies:
S. C. P. Publishers Ltd (trading as Scottish Cultural Press)

2637

SCOTTISH CULTURAL PRESS
Unit 6, Newbattle Abbey Business Park, Newbattle Road, Dalkeith EH22 3LJ
Telephone: 0131 660 4666
Fax: 0870 285 4846
Email: info@scottishbooks.com & orders@scottishbooks.com
Web Site: www.scottishbooks.com

Personnel:
Brian Pugh (Company Secretary)
Avril Gray (Director)

Archaeology; Audio Books; Biography & Autobiography; Cookery, Wines & Spirits; Environment & Development Studies; Geography & Geology; History & Antiquarian; Languages & Linguistics; Literature & Criticism; Military & War; Natural History; Nautical; Poetry; Reference Books, Directories & Dictionaries; Religion & Theology; Sociology & Anthropology; Theatre, Drama & Dance

Imprints, Series & ISBNs:
Scottish Children's Press: 978 1 899827
Scottish Cultural Press: 978 1 84017, 978 1 898218

Associated Companies:
S.C.P. Childrens Ltd (trading as Scottish Children's Press)

2638

SCOTTISH TEXT SOCIETY
School of English Studies, University of Nottingham, Nottingham NG7 2RD
Telephone: 0115 951 5922
Fax: 0115 951 5924
Email: editorialsecretary@scottishtextsociety.org
Web Site: www.scottishtextsociety.org

Registered Office:
25 Buccleuch Place, Edinburgh EH8 9LN

Personnel:
Sally Mapstone (President)
Nicola Royan (Editorial Secretary)
John Archer (Administrative Secretary)

Academic & Scholarly; History & Antiquarian; Literature & Criticism; Poetry

New Titles: 1 (2011)

Imprints, Series & ISBNs:
978 1 897976

Overseas Representation:
Worldwide: Boydell & Brewer Ltd, Woodbridge, Suffolk, UK

Book Trade Association Membership:
Publishing Scotland

2639

SCRIPTURE UNION PUBLISHING
Scripture Union, 207–209 Queensway, Bletchley, Milton Keynes, Bucks MK2 2EB
Telephone: 01908 856000
Fax: 01908 856111
Email: info@scriptureunion.org.uk
Web Site: www.scripture.org.uk/

Warehouse:
Marston Book Services
Telephone: 01235 465579
Fax: 01235 465518
Email: christian.orders@marston.co.uk

Mail Order:
PO Box 5148, Milton Keynes MLO MK2 2YX
Telephone: 01908 856006
Fax: 01908 856020
Email: subs@scriptureunion.org.uk

Personnel:
Alan Charter (Acting Publishing Team Leader)
Dave Parsons (Publishing Accounts Manager)
Rosemary North (Rights Manager)
Clive Cornelius (Production Manager)

Children's Books; Educational & Textbooks; Music; Religion & Theology

No of Employees: 85
Annual Turnover: £6.6M

Imprints, Series & ISBNs:
978 0 85421, 978 0 86201

Overseas Representation:
Australasia, East Asia & Pacific: Resources for Ministry, Gosford, NSW, Australia
Canada: Scripture Union, Pickering, Canada
New Zealand: Scripture Union Wholesale, Wellington, New Zealand
USA: Scripture Union, Wayne, PA, USA

Book Trade Association Membership:
Booksellers Association; Educational Publishers Council

2640

*SEASQUIRT PUBLICATIONS
18d Church Gate, Loughborough, Leics LE11 1UD
Telephone: 01509 219633
Fax: 01509 264441
Web Site: www.jimjazzmouse.com & www.infestedwaters.co.uk

Personnel:
David Hughes (Executive)

Children's Books

Book Trade Association Membership:
Booksellers Association; Independent Publishers Guild

2641

SEDA PUBLICATIONS
[Staff & Educational Development Association]
Woburn House, 20–24 Tavistock Square, London WC1H 9HF
Telephone: 020 7380 6767
Fax: 020 7387 2655
Email: office@seda.ac.uk
Web Site: www.seda.ac.uk

Personnel:
Julie Hall (Co-chair of SEDA)

Academic & Scholarly

Book Trade Association Membership:
Association of Learned & Professional Society Publishers

2642

SEREN
57 Nolton Street, Bridgend CF31 3AE
Telephone: 01656 663018
Web Site: www.serenbooks.com

Distribution:
Central Books, 99 Wallis Road, London E9 5LN
Telephone: 020 8986 4854
Fax: 020 8533 5821
Email: orders@centralbooks.com
Web Site: www.centralbooks.com

Personnel:
Mick Felton (Managing Director)
Simon Hicks (Sales and Marketing Manager)
Victoria Humphreys (Marketing Officer)
Amy Wack (Poetry Editor)
Penny Thomas (Fiction Editor)

Biography & Autobiography; Fiction; Fine Art & Art History; Literature & Criticism; Photography; Poetry

New Titles: 25 (2010) , 25 (2011)
No of Employees: 5

Imprints, Series & ISBNs:
978 0 907476, 978 1 85411

Parent Company:
Poetry Wales Press Ltd

Overseas Representation:
Australia: Eleanor Brasch Enterprises, Artarmon, NSW, Australia
USA & Canada: Independent Publishers Group (IPG), Chicago, IL, USA

Book Trade Association Membership:
Independent Publishers Guild

2643

*SHARON HOUSE PUBLISHING
152 Wakefield Road, Ossett, West Yorkshire WF5 9AQ
Telephone: 01924 279966
Fax: 01924 279966
Email: books@sharonhousepublishing.com
Web Site: www.sharonhousepublishing.com

Personnel:
Anna McKann (Director)
Tim Wicks (Director)

Children's Books

Imprints, Series & ISBNs:
978 0 9554438

Book Trade Association Membership:
Publishers Association

2644

SHEAF PUBLISHING
Beehive Works, Milton Street, Sheffield S3 7WL
Telephone: 0114 273 9067
Fax: 0114 270 6888
Email: sheafgraphics@btconnect.com

Personnel:
T. Cooper (Manager)

History & Antiquarian; Transport

No of Employees: 3

Imprints, Series & ISBNs:
978 0 9505458, 978 1 85048

2645

SHELDON PRESS
36 Causton Street, London SW1P 4ST
Telephone: 020 7592 3900
Fax: 020 7592 3939
Email: director@sheldonpress.co.uk
Web Site: www.sheldonpress.co.uk

Personnel:
Joanna Moriarty (Publishing Director)
Alan Mordue (Sales & Marketing Director)
Fiona Marshall (Editor)
Alexandra MacDonald (Rights Manager)

Gender Studies; Health & Beauty; Medical (incl. Self Help & Alternative Medicine); Psychology & Psychiatry

New Titles: 23 (2011)

Imprints, Series & ISBNs:
Azure Books: 978 1 902694
Sheldon Press: 978 0 85969

Parent Company:
The Society for Promoting Christian Knowledge (SPCK)

Book Trade Association Membership:
Independent Publishers Guild

2646

SHELDRAKE PRESS
188 Cavendish Road, London SW12 0DA
Telephone: 020 8675 1767
Fax: 020 8675 7736
Email: enquiries@sheldrakepress.co.uk
Web Site: www.sheldrakepress.co.uk

Distribution:
NBN International Ltd, 10 Thornbury Road, Plymouth PL6 7PP
Telephone: 01752 202300
Fax: 01752 202330
Email: enquiries@nbninternational.com
Web Site: www.nbninternational.com

Personnel:
Simon Rigge (Publisher Director)
Roger Rigge (Company Secretary)

Architecture & Design; Children's Books; Cookery, Wines & Spirits; Guide Books; History & Antiquarian; Humour; Music; Natural History; Photography; Transport; Travel & Topography

New Titles: 1 (2010) , 1 (2011)
No of Employees: 5
Annual Turnover: £100,000

Imprints, Series & ISBNs:
978 1 873329

Parent Company:
Sheldrake Holdings Ltd

Overseas Representation:
Australia: John Reed Book Distribution, Tea Gardens, NSW, Australia
USA: Interlink Publishing Group Inc, Northampton, MA, USA

2647

SHEPHEARD-WALWYN (PUBLISHERS) LTD
107 Parkway House, Sheen Lane, London SW14 8LS
Telephone: 020 8241 5927
Email: books@shepheard-walwyn.co.uk
Web Site: www.shepheard-walwyn.co.uk

Orders:
NBN International, Plymbridge House, Estover Road, Plymouth PL6 7PY
Telephone: 01752 202301
Fax: 01752 202330
Email: orders@nbninternational.com
Web Site: www.nbninternational.com

Personnel:
Anthony R. A. Werner (Managing Director)

Academic & Scholarly; Biography & Autobiography; Economics; History & Antiquarian; Illustrated & Fine Editions; Philosophy; Politics & World Affairs; Religion & Theology

New Titles: 9 (2010) , 1 (2011)
No of Employees: 2
Annual Turnover: £85,000

Imprints, Series & ISBNs:
978 0 85683
The Letters of Marsilio Ficino
Marsilio Ficino's Commentaries on Plato's Writings
Who's Who in British History series

Overseas Representation:
Australia & New Zealand: John Reed Book Distribution, Brookvale, NSW, Australia
USA & Canada: Independent Publishers Group (IPG), Chicago, IL, USA

2648

SHERWOOD PUBLISHING
Wildhill, Broadoak End, Hertford SG14 2JA
Telephone: 01992 550246
Fax: 01992 535283
Email: sherwood@adinternational.com
Web Site: www.sherwoodpublishing.com

Personnel:
Mrs Julie Hay *(Chief Executive)*

Industry, Business & Management; Psychology & Psychiatry

New Titles: 2 (2010) , 1 (2011)

Imprints, Series & ISBNs:
978 0 9521964, 978 0 9539852

Parent Company:
UK: Psychological Intelligence Ltd

Book Trade Association Membership:
Independent Publishers Guild

2649

*THE SHETLAND TIMES LTD
Gremista, Lerwick, Shetland ZE1 0PX
Telephone: 01595 693622
Fax: 01595 694637
Email: publishing@shetland-times.co.uk
Web Site: www.shetland-books.co.uk

Scottish Agent:
BookSource, 50 Cambuslang Road, Glasgow G32 8NB

Personnel:
Charlotte Black *(Publications Manager)*

Biography & Autobiography; Guide Books; Music; Natural History

Imprints, Series & ISBNs:
978 0 900662, 978 1 898852, 978 1 904746

Book Trade Association Membership:
Booksellers Association

2650

SHIRE PUBLICATIONS LTD
[A division of the Osprey Group.]
Midland House, West Way, Botley, Oxford OX2 0PH
Telephone: 01865 727022
Fax: 01865 727017
Email: shire@shirebooks.co.uk
Web Site: www.shirebooks.co.uk

Personnel:
Rebecca Smart *(Managing Director)*
Sue Ross *(Sales Manager)*
Nicholas Wright *(Publisher)*

Antiques & Collecting; Archaeology; Architecture & Design; Biography & Autobiography; Gardening; Guide Books; History & Antiquarian; Military & War; Natural History; Sociology & Anthropology; Transport; Travel & Topography

New Titles: 70 (2010) , 75 (2011)
No of Employees: 5
Annual Turnover: £690,000

Imprints, Series & ISBNs:
978 0 7478, 978 0 85263

Parent Company:
UK: Osprey Group

2651

SHORT BOOKS LTD
3A Exmouth House, Pine Street, London EC1R 0JH
Telephone: 020 7833 9429
Fax: 020 7833 9500
Email: info@shortbooks.co.uk
Web Site: www.shortbooks.co.uk

Distribution:
TBS, Colchester Road, Frating Green, Colchester CO7 7DW
Telephone: 01206 255678
Fax: 01206 255930

Personnel:
Rebecca Nicolson *(Publisher)*
Catherine Gibbs *(Managing Director)*
Aurea Carpenter *(Publisher/Editor)*

Biography & Autobiography; Children's Books; Fiction; History & Antiquarian; Humour; Natural History; Philosophy; Sports & Games

New Titles: 15 (2011)
No of Employees: 6

Imprints, Series & ISBNs:
978 0 904095, 978 0 904977, 978 0 906021, 978 0 907595

Overseas Representation:
Australasia: Allen & Unwin, Sydney, NSW, Australia
Rest of World: Intercontinental Literature Agency, London, UK
USA: Inkwell Management, New York, NY, USA

Book Trade Association Membership:
Independent Publishers Guild

2652

*SHU PUBLICATIONS LTD
437A Sandygate Road, Sheffield S10 5UD
Telephone: 0114 230 5104

Academic & Scholarly; Educational & Textbooks

Book Trade Association Membership:
Publishers Association

2653

*SIGEL PRESS
51A Victoria Road, Cambridge CB4 3BW
Telephone: 01223 303303
Fax: 01223 303303
Email: info@sigelpress.com
Web Site: www.sigelpress.com

Also at:
4403 Belmont Court, Medina, OH 44256, USA
Telephone: +1 (330) 722 2541
Fax: +1 (330) 722 2541
Email: info@sigelpress.com
Web Site: www.sigelpress.com

Personnel:
Thomas Sigel *(Managing & Publisher Director)*
Andrew Hogbin *(Operations Director)*

Academic & Scholarly; Accountancy & Taxation; Audio Books; Children's Books; Educational & Textbooks; Environment & Development Studies; Fiction; Industry, Business & Management; Military & War; Science Fiction

Imprints, Series & ISBNs:
978 1 905941

Associated Companies:
USA: Sigel Press

Book Trade Association Membership:
Independent Publishers Guild

2654

SIGMA PRESS
Stobart House, Pontyclerc, Penybanc Road, Ammanford, Carmarthenshire SA18 3HP
Telephone: 01269 593100
Fax: 01269 596116
Email: info@sigmapress.co.uk
Web Site: www.sigmapress.co.uk

Personnel:
Nigel Evans *(Managing Director)*
Jane Evans *(Managing Editor)*

Cookery, Wines & Spirits; Crafts & Hobbies; Guide Books; Sports & Games; Travel & Topography

Imprints, Series & ISBNs:
Sigma Leisure: 978 0 905104, 978 1 85058
Sigma Press: 978 0 905104, 978 1 85058

Parent Company:
UK: Stobart Davies Ltd

Overseas Representation:
Australia & New Zealand: Footprint Books Pty Ltd, Warriwood, NSW, Australia
Europe & Far East: Saltway Publishing Ltd, Cirencester, UK
USA: David Brown Book Co, Oakville, CT, USA

Book Trade Association Membership:
Booksellers Association; Independent Publishers Guild

2655

SILVER MOON BOOKS
108c Goldhurst Terrace, London NW6 3HR
Telephone: 020 7625 7592

Trade Enquiries & Orders:
Turnaround Publisher Services, Unit 3, Olympia Trading Estate, Coburg Road, London N22 6TZ
Telephone: 020 8829 3000
Fax: 020 8881 5088

Personnel:
Jane Cholmeley *(Director)*

Fiction; Gay & Lesbian Studies

Imprints, Series & ISBNs:
978 1 872642

2656

SIMON & SCHUSTER (UK) LTD
1st Floor, 222 Gray's Inn Road, London WC1X 8HB
Telephone: 020 7316 1900
Fax: 020 7316 0331
Web Site: www.simonandschuster.co.uk

Customer Services & Distribution Centre:
HarperCollins, Customer Service Centre, Westerhill Road, Bishopbriggs, Glasgow G64 2QT
Telephone: 0141 306 3100
Fax: 0141 306 3767

Personnel:
Ian Stewart Chapman *(Managing Director)*
Suzanne Baboneau *(Adult Publishing Director)*
Kerr MacRae *(Executive Director)*
Mike Jones *(Editorial – Non-Fiction Director)*
Ingrid Selberg *(Children's Publishing Director)*
Maxine Hitchcock *(Editorial – Fiction Director)*
Hannah Corbett *(Publicity – Adult Trade Director)*
David Hyde *(Production Director)*
Sarah Birdsey *(Rights Director)*

Nick Hayward *(Export Sales Director)*
Julian Shaw *(Finance & Operations Director)*
Dawn Burnett *(Marketing Director)*
James Horobin *(Group Sales & Marketing Director)*

Audio Books; Biography & Autobiography; Children's Books; Cinema, Video, TV & Radio; Cookery, Wines & Spirits; Crime; Fiction; Guide Books; Health & Beauty; Humour; Industry, Business & Management; Medical (incl. Self Help & Alternative Medicine); Military & War; Music; Politics & World Affairs; Religion & Theology; Science Fiction; Sports & Games; Travel & Topography

New Titles: 450 (2010) , 450 (2011)
No of Employees: 85

Imprints, Series & ISBNs:
Free Press: 978 0 671, 978 0 684, 978 0 7432, 978 1 4165
Pocket: 978 0 671, 978 0 7434, 978 1 4165, 978 1 84739, 978 1 84983
Scribner: 978 0 671, 978 0 684, 978 0 7432, 978 1 4165
Simon & Schuster: 978 0 671, 978 0 684, 978 0 7432, 978 0 85720, 978 1 4165, 978 1 84737
Simon & Schuster Audio: 978 0 7435, 978 0 85720
Simon & Schuster Children's: 978 0 689, 978 0 85707, 978 1 4169, 978 1 84738

Parent Company:
USA: Simon & Schuster Inc

Distributor for:
UK: Duncan Baird; BL Publishing
USA: Andrews McMeel; Atria; Fireside; Free Press; Gallery; Pocket; Scribner; Simon & Schuster Audio; Simon & Schuster Inc; Touchstone; VIZ Media

Overseas Representation:
Australia: Simon & Schuster (Australia) Pty Ltd, Pymble, NSW, Australia
Canada: Simon & Schuster (Canada), Markham, Ont, Canada
India: Simon & Schuster Publishers India Pvt Ltd, New Delhi, India
New Zealand: HarperCollins (NZ) Ltd, Glenfield, Auckland, New Zealand
Singapore: Penguin Books Singapore, Jurong, Singapore
South Africa: Jonathan Ball Publishers (Pty) Ltd, Johannesburg, South Africa
USA: Trafalgar Square Publishing / IPG, Chicago, IL, USA

Book Trade Association Membership:
Publishers Association

2657

*CHARLES SKILTON LTD
2 Caversham Street, London SW3 4AH
Telephone: 020 7351 4995
Fax: 020 7351 4995
Email: leonard.holdsworth@btinternet.com

Personnel:
James Hughes *(Managing Director)*
Margaret Fletcher *(Sales Director)*
Leonard Holdsworth *(Editor)*

Cinema, Video, TV & Radio; Cookery, Wines & Spirits; Fashion & Costume; Fiction; Fine Art & Art History; Gay & Lesbian Studies; Guide Books; Illustrated & Fine Editions; Literature & Criticism; Military & War; Poetry; Theatre, Drama & Dance; Transport; Travel & Topography

Imprints, Series & ISBNs:
Christchurch: 978 1 901846
Skilton: 978 0 284

Parent Company:
Christchurch Publishers Ltd

Associated Companies:
Caversham Communications Ltd;
  Christchurch Publishers Ltd; Luxor Press

Book Trade Association Membership:
Independent Publishers Guild

2658

SLIGHTLY FOXED
67 Dickinson Court, 15 Brewhouse Yard,
London EC1V 4JX
Telephone: 020 7549 2121
Fax: 0870 199 1245
Email: all@foxedquarterly.com
Web Site: www.foxedquarterly.com

Personnel:
Gail Pirkis (Managing Director)
Hazel Wood (Co-Editor)
Stephanie Allen (Marketing Manager)
Jennie Paterson (Administrator)

Academic & Scholarly; Biography &
Autobiography; Children's Books; Fiction;
Gardening; History & Antiquarian;
Illustrated & Fine Editions; Travel &
Topography

New Titles: 8 (2010) , 9 (2011)
No of Employees: 3
Annual Turnover: £400,000

Imprints, Series & ISBNs:
978 1 906562

2659

SLP EDUCATION
23 West View, Chirk, Wrexham LL14 5HL
Telephone: 01691 774778
Fax: 01691 774849
Email: sales@slpeducation.co.uk
Web Site: www.slpeducation.co.uk

Personnel:
Phil Roberts (Marketing Director)

Educational & Textbooks; English as a
Foreign Language; Geography & Geology;
History & Antiquarian; Humour;
Mathematics & Statistics; Sports & Games;
Theatre, Drama & Dance

New Titles: 8 (2011)
No of Employees: 2
Annual Turnover: £12,000

Imprints, Series & ISBNs:
978 1 871585

Overseas Representation:
All other areas: Blackwell Publishing Ltd,
Oxford, UK
USA, Canada & Puerto Rico: Blackwell
Publishing Inc, Malden, MA, USA;
Blackwell Publishing Professional, Ames,
IA, USA

Book Trade Association Membership:
Educational Publishers Council

2660

*SLS LEGAL PUBLICATIONS (NI)
Lansdowne House, 50 Malone Road,
Belfast BT9 5BS
Telephone: 028 9066 7711
Fax: 028 9066 7733
Email: s.gamble@qub.ac.uk
Web Site: www.sls.qub.ac.uk

Personnel:
Miss M. Dudley (Director)
Mrs S. Gamble (Publications Editor)

Academic & Scholarly; Law

Imprints, Series & ISBNs:
978 0 85389

Book Trade Association Membership:
Publishers Association; Independent
Publishers Guild

2661

SMALLFISH BOOKS
5 Thalia Close, Greenwich, London
SE10 9NA
Telephone: 07810 310375
Web Site: www.smallfishbooks.com

Children's Books

New Titles: 8 (2010)
No of Employees: 2

Book Trade Association Membership:
Publishers Association

2662

SMART LEARNING LTD
Unit 9, 23–25 Gwydir Street, Cambridge
CB1 2LG
Telephone: 01223 477560
Fax: 01223 477551
Web Site: www.smart-learning.co.uk

Book Trade Association Membership:
Publishers Association

2663

**SMITH SETTLE PRINTING &
BOOKBINDING LTD**
Gateway Drive, Yeadon, West Yorkshire
LS19 7XY
Telephone: 0113 250 9201
Fax: 0113 250 9223
Email: sales@smithsettle.com
Web Site: www.smithsettle.com

Personnel:
Donald Walters (Managing Director)
Tracey Thorne (Finance Director)

Academic & Scholarly; Agriculture;
Archaeology; Biography & Autobiography;
History & Antiquarian; Illustrated & Fine
Editions; Sports & Games; Travel &
Topography

Imprints, Series & ISBNs:
978 1 84103

Associated Companies:
Westbury

Distributor for:
Woodstock Books Ltd

Book Trade Association Membership:
Independent Publishers Guild

2664

COLIN SMYTHE LTD
38 Mill Lane, Gerrards Cross, Bucks
SL9 8BA
Telephone: 01753 886000
Fax: 01753 886469
Email: sales@colinsmythe.co.uk
Web Site: www.colinsmythe.co.uk

Warehouse & Dispatch only:
Print on Demand, 9 Culley Court,
Bakewell Road, Orton Southgate,
Peterborough PE2 6WA
Telephone: 01733 237867
Fax: 01733 234309

Personnel:
Colin Smythe (Managing Director)
Leslie Hayward (Director)

Academic & Scholarly; Biography &
Autobiography; Literature & Criticism;
Theatre, Drama & Dance

Imprints, Series & ISBNs:
978 0 86140, 978 0 900675, 978 0 901072
Dolmen Press: 978 0 85105
Van Duren: 978 0 905715

Distributor for:
Republic of Ireland: Tir Eolas
USA: ELT Press

Overseas Representation:
USA & Canada: Dufour Editions Inc, Chester
  Springs, PA, USA
USA & Canada (recent academic titles):
  Oxford University Press Inc USA, New
  York, NY, USA

Book Trade Association Membership:
Publishers Association; Booksellers
Association; Independent Publishers Guild

2665

SNOWFLAKE BOOKS LTD
28a Old Marston Road, Marston, Oxford
OX3 0JP
Telephone: 07981 666006
Web Site: www.snowflakebooks.co.uk

Book Trade Association Membership:
Publishers Association

2666

SOCCER BOOKS LTD
72 St Peter's Avenue, Cleethorpes, Lincs
DN35 8HU
Telephone: 01472 696226
Fax: 01472 698546
Email: info@soccer-books.co.uk
Web Site: www.soccer-books.co.uk

Personnel:
John Robinson (Managing Director)
Michael Robinson (Director)
Petra Askew (Director)

Sports & Games; Transport

New Titles: 22 (2011)
No of Employees: 4

Imprints, Series & ISBNs:
Complete Results & Line-ups (Series): 978 1
  86223
Football In (Series): 978 1 86223
Supporters' Guide (Series): 978 1 86223

Book Trade Association Membership:
PBFA

2667

SOCIAL AFFAIRS UNIT
10/11 Morley House,
314–322 Regent Street, London W1B 5SA
Telephone: 020 7637 4356
Fax: 020 7436 8530
Email: mosbacher@socialaffairsunit.org.uk
Web Site: www.socialaffairsunit.org.uk

Personnel:
Michael Mosbacher (Director)

Academic & Scholarly; Crime; Economics;
Educational & Textbooks; Environment &
Development Studies; Industry, Business &
Management; Medical (incl. Self Help &
Alternative Medicine); Politics & World
Affairs; Reference Books, Directories &
Dictionaries; Sociology & Anthropology

Imprints, Series & ISBNs:
978 0 907631, 978 1 904863

2668

**THE SOCIETY FOR PROMOTING
CHRISTIAN KNOWLEDGE (SPCK)**
36 Causton Street, London SW1P 4ST
Telephone: 020 7592 3900
Fax: 020 7592 3939
Email: publishing@spck.org.uk

Web Site: www.spckpublishing.co.uk

Warehouse & Distribution:
Marston Book Services, Unit 160,
Milton Park, Abingdon, Oxon OX14 4SD
Telephone: 01235 465500
Fax: 01235 465555

Personnel:
Simon Kingston (Chief Executive Officer)
Joanna Moriarty (Publishing Director)
Alan Mordue (Sales Director)
Barry Finch (Production Director)
Alison Barr (Editor)
Fiona Marshall (Editor)
Ruth McCurry (Editor)
Alexandra McDonald (Rights Manager)
Cynthia Hamilton (Senior Marketing &
  Publicity Manager)

Academic & Scholarly; Religion & Theology

Imprints, Series & ISBNs:
Azure Books: 978 1 902694
Lynx Communication: 978 0 7459
Sheldon Press: 978 0 85969, 978 1 84709
SPCK: 978 0 281
Triangle Books: 978 0 281

Associated Companies:
UK: Sheldon Press

Distributor for:
USA: Baker Academic Publishing; Brazos
Press

Overseas Representation:
South Africa: Penguin Books South Africa
USA & Canada: Lightning Source UK Ltd,
  Milton Keynes, UK

Book Trade Association Membership:
Independent Publishers Guild; Christian
Suppliers Group

2669

***SOCIETY OF GENEALOGISTS
ENTERPRISES LTD**
14 Charterhouse Buildings, London
EC1M 7BA
Telephone: 020 7251 8799
Fax: 020 7250 1800
Email: sales@sog.org.uk
Web Site: www.sog.org.uk/

Personnel:
June Perrin (Chief Executive)
Anthony Mortimer (Retail Manager)

History & Antiquarian

Imprints, Series & ISBNs:
978 1 903462

Parent Company:
Society of Genealogists

Book Trade Association Membership:
Booksellers Association

2670

**THE SOCIETY OF METAPHYSICIANS
LTD**
Archers' Court, Stonestile Lane, Hastings,
East Sussex TN35 4PG
Telephone: 01424 751577
Fax: 01424 751577
Email: newmeta@btinternet.com
Web Site: www.metaphysicians.org.uk

Personnel:
Dr J. J. Williamson (Managing Director)
Ms C. Yuen (Secretary)
D. Cumberland (Scientific & Literary
  Research)
Miss D. Harris (Paranormal Research)
Mervin Gould (Tutor)
David Servera-Williamon (Web)

Academic & Scholarly; Educational &

Textbooks; Electronic (Educational); Environment & Development Studies; Magic & the Occult; Medical (incl. Self Help & Alternative Medicine); Philosophy; Scientific & Technical

Imprints, Series & ISBNs:
978 0 900680, 978 1 85228, 978 1 85810

Associated Companies:
Metaphysical Research Group
Nigeria: Society of Metaphysicians (Nigeria) Ltd

Distributor for:
USA: Ars Obscura; Health Research

Overseas Representation:
Australia: Magic Circle Bookshop, Perth, Australia
Belgium: Ignoramus, As, Belgium; L' Univers Particulier, Brussels, Belgium
Netherlands: Boekhandel Synthese, 's Gravenhage, Netherlands
New Zealand: Bennet's Bookshop, Palmerston North, New Zealand
Spain: Eyras Editorial, Madrid, Spain
Tenerife: Soluciones, Spain
USA: H.R., Pomeroy, WA, USA

2671

*SOLIDUS
Hope Springs, Far End, Sheepscombe, Stroud, Glos GL6 7RL
Telephone: 01452 758940
Email: info@soliduspress.com
Web Site: www.soliduspress.com

Personnel:
Helen Miles *(Proprietor)*

Children's Books; Fiction

Imprints, Series & ISBNs:
Back to Front: 978 1 904529
Solidus: 978 1 904529

2672

SOUTHGATE PUBLISHERS
The Square, Sandford, Crediton, Devon EX17 4LW
Telephone: 01363 776888
Fax: 01363 776889
Email: info@southgatepublishers.co.uk
Web Site: www.southgatepublishers.co.uk

Personnel:
Drummond Johnstone *(Managing Director)*
Marlene Buckland *(Production Manager)*

Educational & Textbooks; Environment & Development Studies; Vocational Training & Careers

No of Employees: 3

Imprints, Series & ISBNs:
978 1 85741

Associated Companies:
Mosaic Educational Publications

Distributor for:
Campaign for Learning; Learning Through Landscapes Trust

Book Trade Association Membership:
Independent Publishers Guild

2673

SOUVENIR PRESS LTD
43 Great Russell Street, London WC1B 3PD
Telephone: 020 7580 9307/8 & 7637 5711/2/3
Fax: 020 7580 5064

Distribution & Warehouse:
Bookpoint Ltd, 130 Milton Trading Estate, Abingdon, Oxon OX14 4SB

Telephone: 01235 400400
Fax: 01235 400413

Personnel:
Ernest Hecht *(Managing Director & Chairman)*

Academic & Scholarly; Animal Care & Breeding; Antiques & Collecting; Archaeology; Biography & Autobiography; Crafts & Hobbies; Gardening; Gender Studies; Health & Beauty; Humour; Industry, Business & Management; Literature & Criticism; Magic & the Occult; Medical (incl. Self Help & Alternative Medicine); Military & War; Music; Natural History; Philosophy; Psychology & Psychiatry; Religion & Theology; Sociology & Anthropology; Sports & Games; Theatre, Drama & Dance; Travel & Topography; Veterinary Science

Imprints, Series & ISBNs:
Condor Books: 978 0 285
Human Horizons: 978 0 285
Souvenir Press (Educational & Academic) Ltd: 978 0 285
Souvenir Press Ltd: 978 0 285

Associated Companies:
Pictorial Presentations Ltd; Pop Universal Ltd; Souvenir Press (Educational & Academic) Ltd

Overseas Representation:
Austria, Benelux, France, Germany, Switzerland, Greece & Italy: Ted Dougherty, London, UK
India: Rupa, Delhi, India
Middle East: Peter Ward Book Exports, London, UK
New Zealand: Addenda, Auckland, New Zealand
Scandinavia: John Edgeler, London, UK
South Africa: Trinity Books CC, Randburg, South Africa

2674

SPARTAN PRESS MUSIC PUBLISHERS LTD
Strathmashie House, Laggan, Inverness-shire PH20 1BU
Telephone: 01528 544770
Fax: 01528 544771
Email: sales@spartanpress.co.uk
Web Site: www.spartanpress.co.uk

Personnel:
Mark Goddard *(Managing Director)*
Pat Goddard *(Director)*
Glenn Robertson *(Sales Manager)*
Guang Yang *(IT Manager)*

Music

Imprints, Series & ISBNs:
ISMN: 57 999

Distributor for:
Netherlands: European Music Centre
UK: Camden Music; CelloLid; Colne Edition; G. S. Music; Hunt Edition; Múzicas Editions; Nova Music; Pan Educational Music; Queen's Temple Publications; Sunshine Music Co; Useful Music; Waveney Music Publishing Ltd; Yorke Edition

Overseas Representation:
Netherlands: European Music Centre, Huizen, Netherlands
USA & Canada: Theodore Presser Co, King of Prussia, PA, USA

2675

SPECIAL INTEREST MODEL BOOKS LTD
PO Box 327, Poole, Dorset BH15 2RG
Telephone: 01202 649930
Fax: 01202 649950

Email: chrlloyd@globalnet.co.uk
Web Site:
www.specialinterestmodelbooks.co.uk

Personnel:
Chris Lloyd *(Managing Director)*

Aviation; Cookery, Wines & Spirits; Crafts & Hobbies; Engineering; Nautical; Transport

Imprints, Series & ISBNs:
Amateur Winemaker Books: 978 0 900841
formerly Argus Books: 978 1 85486
formerly MAP (Model & Allied Publications): 978 1 85486
formerly Nexus Special Interest Books: 978 1 85486
Workshop Practice Series: 978 0 85242

Associated Companies:
UK: Amateur Winemaker Books Ltd

Overseas Representation:
Australia: Capricorn Link (Australia) Pty Ltd, Windsor, NSW, Australia
Eastern Europe, East & West Africa: Anthony Moggach, InterMedia Americana (IMA) Ltd, London, UK
New Zealand: South Pacific Books (Imports) Ltd, Auckland, New Zealand
Scandinavia (including Denmark, Sweden, Norway, Finland & Iceland) & Netherlands: Angell Eurosales, Berwick-on-Tweed, UK
South Africa: Everybody's Books, Kwa Zulu Natal, South Africa
South & Central America & Caribbean: David Williams, InterMedia Americana (IMA) Ltd, London, UK
South East Asia (including Singapore, Malaysia, Brunei, Indonesia, Hong Kong, Taiwan, China, Philippines, Thailand & Japan): Ashton International Marketing Services, Sevenoaks, Kent, UK
Southern Europe (including Spain, Portugal, Italy, Malta & Greece): Joe Portelli, Bookport Associates, Corsico (MI), Italy
Western Europe (including France, Belgium, Germany, Switzerland & Austria): Anselm Robinson, European Marketing Services, London, UK

Book Trade Association Membership:
Publishers Association

2676

*SPOKESMAN
Russell House, Bulwell Lane, Nottingham NG6 0BT
Telephone: 0115 978 4504 & 970 8318
Fax: 0115 942 0433
Email: elfeuro@compuserve.com
Web Site: www.spokesmanbooks.com

Personnel:
Ken Fleet *(General Manager)*
Tony Simpson *(Publisher)*
Ken Coates *(Editor)*

Economics; Fiction; History & Antiquarian; Military & War; Philosophy; Poetry; Politics & World Affairs; Sociology & Anthropology; Theatre, Drama & Dance

Imprints, Series & ISBNs:
Socialist Renewal: 978 0 85124
The Spokesman: 978 0 85124

Associated Companies:
Bertrand Russell Peace Foundation Ltd

2677

SPORTSBOOKS LTD
1 Evelyn Court, Malvern Road, Cheltenham GL50 2JR
Telephone: 01242 256755
Fax: 01242 254694
Email: randall@sportsbooks.ltd.uk
Web Site: www.sportsbooks.ltd.uk

Distribution:
Turnaround Publisher Services Ltd, Unit 3, Olympia Industrial Estate, Coburg Road, London N22 6TZ
Telephone: 020 8829 3000
Fax: 020 8881 5088
Email: orders@turnaround-uk.com
Web Site: www.turnaround-psl.com

Personnel:
Randall Northam *(Chairman)*
Veronica Northam *(Director)*

Fiction; History & Antiquarian; Sports & Games

New Titles: 12 (2011)
Annual Turnover: £200,000

Imprints, Series & ISBNs:
BMM: 978 0 9541544
Sportsbooks: 978 1 907524, 978 1 899807

Overseas Representation:
New Zealand: Bookreps, Auckland, New Zealand

Book Trade Association Membership:
Publishers Association; Independent Publishers Guild

2678

STACEY INTERNATIONAL
128 Kensington Church Street, London W8 4BH
Telephone: 020 7221 7166
Fax: 020 7792 9288
Email: info@stacey- international.co.uk
Web Site: www.stacey-international.co.uk

Distribution:
Central Books, 99 Wallis Road, Hackney Wick, London E9 5LN
Telephone: 0845 458 9911
Fax: 0845 458 9912
Email: orders@centralbooks.com
Web Site: www.centralbooks.com

Personnel:
T. C. G. Stacey *(Chairman)*
Patrick Kelly *(Director)*
Hannah Young *(Editor)*
David Birkett *(Sales & Marketing)*

Academic & Scholarly; Archaeology; Architecture & Design; Biography & Autobiography; Children's Books; Cookery, Wines & Spirits; Economics; Educational & Textbooks; Fine Art & Art History; Gardening; Geography & Geology; Guide Books; History & Antiquarian; Illustrated & Fine Editions; Languages & Linguistics; Magic & the Occult; Military & War; Natural History; Photography; Poetry; Politics & World Affairs; Reference Books, Directories & Dictionaries; Religion & Theology; Scientific & Technical; Travel & Topography

Parent Company:
Stacey Publishing Ltd

Associated Companies:
Capuchin Classics; Gorilla Guides; Rubicon Press

Overseas Representation:
Asia: PIM, London, UK
Australia: Peribo Pty Ltd, Mount Kuring-Gai, NSW, Australia
Europe: Durnell Marketing Ltd, Tunbridge Wells, UK
South Africa: Stephan Philips, Cape Town, South Africa
South America & Caribbean: Intermedia Americana, London, UK
USA: The David Brown Book Co, Oakville, CT, USA; Interlink Publishing Group Inc, Northampton, MA, USA

Book Trade Association Membership:
Independent Publishers Guild

2679 ▬▬▬

STAINER & BELL LTD
PO Box 110, 23 Gruneisen Road, London N3 1DZ
Telephone: 020 8343 3303
Fax: 020 8343 3024
Email: post@stainer.co.uk
Web Site: www.stainer.co.uk

Personnel:
Keith Wakefield *(Joint Managing Director, Marketing, Permissions, Accounts & Distribution)*
Carol Wakefield *(Joint Managing Director)*
Antony Kearns *(Deputy Managing Director)*
Nicholas Williams *(Publishing Director)*
Amanda Aknai *(Production Director)*

Academic & Scholarly; Biography & Autobiography; History & Antiquarian; Music; Reference Books, Directories & Dictionaries; Religion & Theology; Theatre, Drama & Dance

New Titles: 25 (2010) , 30 (2011)
No of Employees: 10
Annual Turnover: £813,000

Imprints, Series & ISBNs:
Augener: 978 0 85249
Early English Church Music: 978 0 85249
Galliard: 978 0 85249
Music for London Entertainment: 978 0 85249
Musica Britannica: 978 0 85249
Purcell Society Edition: 978 0 85249
Stainer & Bell: 978 0 85249
Weekes: 978 0 85249
Joseph Williams: 978 0 85249

Distributor for:
USA: ECS Publishing Co (Rental Library only)

Overseas Representation:
USA (hymn copyrights & selected titles): Hope Publishing, Carol Stream, IL, USA
USA (Rental Library): ECS Publishing Co, Boston, MA, USA

Book Trade Association Membership:
The Music Publishers Association Ltd

2680 ▬▬▬

RUDOLF STEINER PRESS LTD
Hillside House, The Square, Forest Row, East Sussex RH18 5ES
Telephone: 01342 824433
Fax: 01342 826437
Email: office@rudolfsteinerpress.com
Web Site: www.rudolfsteinerpress.com

Trade Enquiries & Orders:
BookSource, 50 Cambuslang Road, Glasgow G32 8NB
Telephone: 0845 370 0063
Fax: 0845 370 0064
Email: orders@booksource.net
Web Site: www.booksource.net

Personnel:
Sevak Gulbekian *(Chief Editor)*

Audio Books; Biography & Autobiography; Educational & Textbooks; Fine Art & Art History; Magic & the Occult; Medical (incl. Self Help & Alternative Medicine); Music; Philosophy; Politics & World Affairs; Religion & Theology; Sociology & Anthropology; Theatre, Drama & Dance

New Titles: 19 (2010) , 18 (2011)
No of Employees: 1
Annual Turnover: £196,000

Imprints, Series & ISBNs:
Anthroposophic Press: 978 0 88010
Rudolf Steiner Press: 978 0 85440, 978 1 85584
Sophia Books: 978 0 85440, 978 1 85584
Steiner Books: 978 0 88010, 978 0 09

Distributor for:
USA: Steinerbooks

Overseas Representation:
Australia: Rudolf Steiner Book Centre, Sydney, NSW, Australia
Canada: Tri-fold Books, Guelph, Ont, Canada
New Zealand: Ceres Books, Auckland, New Zealand
South Africa: Rudolf Steiner Publications, Johannesburg, South Africa
USA: Steiner Books Inc, Herndon, VA, USA

Book Trade Association Membership:
Independent Publishers Guild

2681 ▬▬▬

*STENLAKE PUBLISHING LTD
54–58 Mill Square, Catrine, Ayrshire KA5 6RD
Telephone: 01290 551122
Fax: 01290 551122
Email: enquiries@stenlake.co.uk
Web Site: www.stenlake.co.uk

Personnel:
David Pettigrew *(Editorial)*
Richard Stenlake *(Managing Director)*
Alex F. Young *(Sales)*

Aviation; Crafts & Hobbies; History & Antiquarian; Literature & Criticism; Nautical; Poetry; Transport

Imprints, Series & ISBNs:
Alloway Publishing: 978 0 907526
Stenlake Publishing: 978 1 84033, 978 1 872074

2682 ▬▬▬

STILLWATER PUBLISHING LTD
2 Tcheur Cottages, Lower Brailes, Banbury, Oxon OX15 5HX
Telephone: 01608 686289
Web Site: www.stillwaterspublishing.co.uk

Book Trade Association Membership:
Publishers Association

2683 ▬▬▬

*STOBART DAVIES LTD
Stobart House, Pontyclerc, Penybanc Road, Ammanford, Carmarthenshire SA18 3HP
Telephone: 01269 593100
Fax: 01269 596116
Email: sales@stobartdavies.com
Web Site: www.stobartdavies.com

Personnel:
Jane Evans *(Director)*
Nigel Evans *(Director)*

Archaeology; Cookery, Wines & Spirits; Crafts & Hobbies; Do-It-Yourself; Guide Books; Natural History; Scientific & Technical; Travel & Topography

Imprints, Series & ISBNs:
Sigma Leisure / Sigma Press: 978 1 85058
Stobart Davies Ltd: 978 0 85442

Parent Company:
Stobart Davis (2002) Ltd

Overseas Representation:
Australia & New Zealand: Footprint Books Pty Ltd, Warriewood, NSW, Australia
Europe & Far East: Saltway Publishing Ltd, Cirencester, UK
South Africa: Peter Hyde Associates (Pty) Ltd, Cape Town, South Africa
USA: David Brown Book Co, Oakville, CT, USA

Book Trade Association Membership:
Booksellers Association; Independent Publishers Guild

2684 ▬▬▬

*STOTT'S CORRESPONDENCE COLLEGE
PO Box 35488, St John's Wood, London NW8 6WD
Telephone: 020 7586 4499
Email: microworld@ndirect.co.uk
Web Site: www.microworld.uk.com

Personnel:
S. C. Albert *(Director)*

Academic & Scholarly; Crafts & Hobbies; Fashion & Costume; Health & Beauty

Distributor for:
Australia: Stott's Correspondence College

2685 ▬▬▬

*STRI (SPORTS TURF RESEARCH INSTITUTE)
St Ives Estate, Bingley, West Yorks BD16 1AU
Telephone: 01274 565131
Fax: 01274 561891
Email: info@stri.co.uk
Web Site: www.stri.co.uk

Personnel:
Dr Gordon McKillop *(Chief Executive)*
Mark Godfrey *(Financial Director)*
Richard Hayden *(Director of Operations)*
Carolyn Beadsmoore *(Head of Sales & Marketing)*

Educational & Textbooks; Environment & Development Studies; Reference Books, Directories & Dictionaries; Scientific & Technical; Sports & Games

Imprints, Series & ISBNs:
978 0 9503647, 978 1 873431

2686 ▬▬▬

STRONG OAK PRESS
PO Box 728, Crawley, West Sussex RH10 7WD
Telephone: 01293 552727
Email: strongoakpress@hotmail.com

Personnel:
Steven Apps *(Managing Director)*

Biography & Autobiography; Fine Art & Art History; History & Antiquarian; Military & War; Travel & Topography

Imprints, Series & ISBNs:
Spa Books: 978 0 907590
The Strong Oak Press: 978 1 871048

Distributor for:
South Africa: William Waterman Publications
UK: Spa Books Ltd; The Strong Oak Press Ltd

2687 ▬▬▬

*SUBBUTEO NATURAL HISTORY BOOKS
[a division of C J Wild Bird Foods Ltd]
The Rea, Upton Magna, Shrewsbury SY4 4UR
Telephone: 01743 708017
Fax: 01743 709504
Email: joy.enston@birdfood.co.uk
Web Site: www.wildlifebooks.com

Personnel:
Tony Cordery *(Senior Executive)*
Paul Humber *(Finance)*
Claire Smith *(Marketing Manager)*

Natural History

Parent Company:
UK: C. J. Wild Bird Foods Ltd

Distributor for:
South Africa: Avian Demography Unit
South America: Rainforest Expeditions SAC Publications; Thomas Velqui
Spain: Arts Grafiques Delmau; Nayade Editorial
UK: Arlequin Press; Dizzy Daisy Books; Hobby Publications; Osmia Publications; Wings Plants & Paws
USA: American Birding Association

Book Trade Association Membership:
Booksellers Association

2688 ▬▬▬

SUMMERSDALE PUBLISHERS LTD
46 West Street, Chichester, West Sussex PO19 1RP
Telephone: 01243 771107
Fax: 01243 786300
Email: enquiries@summersdale.com
Web Site: www.summersdale.com

Warehouse, Trade Enquiries & Orders:
Littlehampton Book Services, Faraday Close, Durrington, Worthing, West Sussex BN13 3RB
Telephone: 01903 828500
Fax: 01903 828625
Email: orders@lbsltd.co.uk
Web Site: www.lbsltd.co.uk

Personnel:
Alastair Williams *(Managing Director)*
Nicky Douglas *(Sales & Marketing Director)*
Abbie Headon *(Managing Editor)*
Claire Plimmer *(Executive Commissioning Editor)*
Elly Donovan *(PR Manager)*

Audio Books; Biography & Autobiography; Cookery, Wines & Spirits; Crafts & Hobbies; Crime; Electronic (Educational); Electronic (Entertainment); Electronic (Professional & Academic); Guide Books; Health & Beauty; History & Antiquarian; Humour; Sports & Games; Travel & Topography

Imprints, Series & ISBNs:
978 1 84024, 978 1 84953, 978 1 873475

Distributor for:
Protection Publications

Overseas Representation:
Australia & New Zealand: Peribo Pty Ltd, Mount Kuring-Gai, NSW, Australia
India: Surit Mitra, New Delhi, India
Northern Europe: Michael Geoghegan, London, UK
Scandinavia: McNeish Publishing International, East Sussex, UK
South East & North East Asia, Middle East & Africa: Chris Ashdown, Publishers International Marketing, Ferndown, Dorset, UK
Southern Africa: A G Distribution
Southern Europe: Bookport Associates, Milan, Italy

Book Trade Association Membership:
Independent Publishers Guild

2689 ▬▬▬

SUSSEX ACADEMIC PRESS
PO Box 139, Eastbourne, East Sussex BN24 9BP
Telephone: 01323 479220
Fax: 01323 478185
Email: edit@sussex-academic.co.uk
Web Site: www.sussex-academic.co.uk

Warehouse, Trade Enquiries & Orders:
Gazelle Book Services, White Cross Mills, Hightown, Lancaster LA1 4XS
Telephone: 01524 68765
Fax: 01524 63232

Personnel:
Anthony Grahame *(Editorial Director)*
Anita Grahame *(Finance Director)*

Academic & Scholarly; Archaeology; Bibliography & Library Science; Biography & Autobiography; Economics; Educational & Textbooks; Environment & Development Studies; Fine Art & Art History; Gender Studies; Geography & Geology; History & Antiquarian; Industry, Business & Management; Law; Literature & Criticism; Military & War; Music; Philosophy; Politics & World Affairs; Psychology & Psychiatry; Religion & Theology; Sociology & Anthropology; Sports & Games; Theatre, Drama & Dance

Imprints, Series & ISBNs:
The Alpha Press: 978 1 898595
Sussex Academic: 978 1 84519, 978 1
   898723, 978 1 902210, 978 1 903900

Parent Company:
UK: The Alpha Press

Associated Companies:
Canada: Sussex Academic Press (Canada)

Overseas Representation:
Canada: University of Toronto Distribution,
   Canada
Rest of the World (excluding USA & Canada): Gazelle Book Services Ltd,
   Lancaster, UK
USA: International Specialized Book
   Services Inc, Portland, OR, USA

2690

*SUSSEX PUBLICATIONS
World Microfilms, PO Box 35488,
St John's Wood, London NW8 6WD
Telephone: 020 7586 4499
Email: microworld@ndirect.co.uk
Web Site: www.microworld.uk.com

Personnel:
S. C. Albert *(Director)*

Academic & Scholarly; Audio Books; Cinema, Video, TV & Radio; Fine Art & Art History; History & Antiquarian; Literature & Criticism; Music

Imprints, Series & ISBNs:
978 0 905272, 978 1 86013

2691

THE SWEDENBORG SOCIETY
20–21 Bloomsbury Way, London
WC1A 2TH
Telephone: 020 7405 7986
Fax: 020 7831 5848
Email: richard@swedenborg.org.uk
Web Site: www.swedenborg.org.uk

Personnel:
Richard Lines *(Company Secretary)*
Stephen McNeilly *(Publications Manager)*
Eoin McMahon *(Property Manager)*
James Wilson *(Assistant Editor & Librarian)*
Nora Foster *(Sales & Marketing
   Representative)*

Academic & Scholarly; Literature & Criticism; Religion & Theology

New Titles: 3 (2010) , 5 (2011)
No of Employees: 6
Annual Turnover: £365,000

Imprints, Series & ISBNs:
978 0 85448

2692

**SYMPOSIUM PUBLICATIONS
LITERARY & ART**
37 Chepstow Road, London W2 5BP
Telephone: 020 7792 3762

Email: sympo@sympo.fsworld.co.uk
Web Site: www.sympo.co.uk

Personnel:
Mrs L. A. Melech *(Director)*
John Wheeler-Melech *(Editorial Consultant)*

Academic & Scholarly; Children's Books; Educational & Textbooks; English as a Foreign Language; Fine Art & Art History; Literature & Criticism; Poetry

Imprints, Series & ISBNs:
Sympo Sunrise (Children's Stories): 978 0
   9547757
Symposium Brush-Up Shakespeare Series:
   978 0 9524749
Symposium Gem Art Series: 978 0 9524749

Overseas Representation:
Spain: Débora Vázquez Padín, Pontevedra,
   Spain

2693

*TA HA PUBLISHERS LTD
Unit 4, The Windsor Centre,
Windsor Grove, West Norwood, London
SE27 9NT
Telephone: 020 8670 1888
Fax: 020 8670 1998
Email: sales@taha.co.uk
Web Site: www.taha.co.uk

Personnel:
A. Siddiqui *(Director)*
Dr Abia A. Siddiqui *(Editor & Director)*
Dr J. U. N. Rafai *(Rights)*

Children's Books; Languages & Linguistics; Religion & Theology

Imprints, Series & ISBNs:
978 0 907461, 978 1 84200, 978 1 897940

Associated Companies:
Diwan Press Ltd

Overseas Representation:
USA: Islamic Bookstore.com, Baltimore,
   MD, USA

2694

TABB HOUSE
7 Church Street, Padstow, Cornwall
PL28 8BG
Telephone: 01841 532316
Email: tabbhouse.books@btinternet.com
Web Site: tabbhousebooks.com

**Distributor (for West Country titles in
Cornwall, Devon & Somerset):**
Tor Mark Press, PO Box 4, Redruth,
Cornwall TR16 5YX
Telephone: 01209 822101
Fax: 01209 822035
Email: sales@tormarkpress.prestel.co.uk
Web Site: www.willowbooks.co.uk

Wholesaler:
Gardners Books Ltd, 1 Whittle Drive,
Willingdon Drove, Eastbourne, Sussex
BN23 6QH
Telephone: 01323 521555
Fax: 01323 521666
Email: sales@gardners.com
Web Site: www.gardners.com

Personnel:
Caroline White *(Editorial Director)*
Katharine Bickmore *(Promotion &
   Marketing Assistant)*

Biography & Autobiography; Children's Books; Fiction; Literature & Criticism; Medical (incl. Self Help & Alternative Medicine); Poetry; Religion & Theology

New Titles: 2 (2011)
No of Employees: 2

Imprints, Series & ISBNs:
Tabb House: 978 0 907018, 978 1 873951
Tabb House Originals

Book Trade Association Membership:
Independent Publishers Guild

2695

TAIGH NA TEUD MUSIC PUBLISHERS
13 Upper Breakish, Isle of Skye IV42 8PY
Telephone: 01471 822528
Fax: 01471 822811
Email: sales@scotlandsmusic.com
Web Site: www.scotlandsmusic.com &
   www.playscottishmusic.com

Personnel:
Alasdair Martin *(Sales Manager)*
Christine Martin *(Music Editor)*

Languages & Linguistics; Music

Imprints, Series & ISBNs:
978 1 871931, 978 1 906804

Overseas Representation:
North America: Music Sales Corporation,
   Chester, NY, USA

2696

TANGO BOOKS LTD
PO Box 32595, London W4 5YD
Telephone: 020 8996 9970
Fax: 020 8996 9977
Email: info@tangobooks.co.uk
Web Site: www.tangobooks.co.uk

Sales & Marketing:
Bounce!, 14 Greville Street, London
EC1N 8SB
Telephone: 020 7138 3650
Fax: 020 7138 3658
Email: sales@bouncemarketing.co.uk
Web Site: www.bouncemarketing.co.uk

Personnel:
Sheri Safran *(Director/Publisher)*
David Fielder *(Director/Publisher)*

Children's Books; Educational & Textbooks; Environment & Development Studies; Natural History

2697

TARQUIN PUBLICATIONS
Suite 74, 17 Holywell Hill, St Albans, Herts
AL1 1DT
Telephone: 01727 833866
Fax: 0845 456 6385
Email: sales@tarquinbooks.com
Web Site: www.tarquingroup.com

Personnel:
Andrew Griffin *(Editorial)*
Peter Watson *(Sales & Promotion)*

Atlases & Maps; Children's Books; Crafts & Hobbies; Educational & Textbooks; Mathematics & Statistics; Scientific & Technical

New Titles: 2 (2010) , 8 (2011)

Imprints, Series & ISBNs:
978 0 906212, 978 1 899618, 978 1
   907550

Parent Company:
Richard Griffin (1820) Ltd

Distributor for:
Australia: Dr Paul Brown
UK: The Maths Press
USA: Tessellations

Overseas Representation:
Australia: H. E. Wootton & Sons, Toorak,
   Vic, Australia; W & G Education Pty Ltd,
   Berwick, Vic, Australia

New Zealand: Eton Press (Auckland) Ltd,
   Auckland, New Zealand; Mahobe
   Resources (NZ), Newmarket, New
   Zealand
Portugal: Editôra Replicação, Lisbon,
   Portugal
Singapore: Nature Craft Pte Ltd, Singapore
South Africa: Creative Learning Systems
USA: Parkwest Publications Inc, Jersey City,
   NJ, USA

Book Trade Association Membership:
Independent Publishers Guild

2698

TATE PUBLISHING
[a division of Tate Enterprises Ltd]
Millbank, London SW1P 4RG
Telephone: 020 7887 8869/70/71
Fax: 020 7887 8878
Email: tgpl@tate.org.uk

Warehouse, Trade Enquiries & Orders:
Telephone: 020 7887 8869 (5 lines)
Fax: 020 7887 8878
Email: tgpl@tate.org.uk
Web Site: www.tate.org.uk

Personnel:
Laura Wright *(Chief Executive)*
James Attlee *(Sales & Marketing Director)*
Sarah Rogers *(Head of Finance)*
Roger Thorp *(Publishing Director)*
Emma Woodiwiss *(Production Manager)*

Children's Books; Fine Art & Art History; Photography

Imprints, Series & ISBNs:
British Artists Series
Essential Artists Series: 978 0 905005, 978 0
   946590, 978 1 85437
Modern Artists Series: 978 1 85437
Movements in Modern Art Series
St Ives Artists Series

Parent Company:
Tate Enterprises Ltd

Overseas Representation:
*Asia (including Hong Kong, Taiwan, China,
   Korea & Philippines):* Asia Publishers
   Services Ltd, Hong Kong
Australia: Thames & Hudson (Australia) Pty
   Ltd, Fishermans Bend, Vic, Australia
*Austria, Belgium, Germany, Netherlands &
   Switzerland:* Exhibitions International,
   Leuven, Belgium
*Denmark, Finland, Iceland, Norway &
   Sweden:* Elisabeth Harder-Kreimann,
   Hamburg, Germany
Eastern Europe: Phil Tyers, Athens, Greece
*Far East (including Japan, Vietnam,
   Singapore, Malaysia, Indonesia &
   Thailand):* Andrew Hansen, London, UK
France: Interart SARL, Paris, France
Italy, Greece, Spain & Portugal: Penny
   Padovani, London, UK
Mexico, Central America & Caribbean:
   Chris Humphrys, Humphrys Roberts
   Associates, London, UK
Middle East: Ray Potts, Villanton, France
North & South America & Canada: Harry N.
   Abrams Inc, New York, NY, USA
Republic of Ireland & Northern Ireland:
   Gabrielle Redmond, Dublin, Republic of
   Ireland
South Africa: David Krut Publishing,
   Johannesburg, South Africa
South America: David Williams, InterMedia
   Americana (IMA) Ltd, London, UK

Book Trade Association Membership:
Booksellers Association

2699

I. B. TAURIS & CO LTD
6 Salem Road, London W2 4BU
Telephone: 020 7243 1225
Fax: 020 7243 1226

Email: mail@ibtauris.com
Web Site: www.ibtauris.com

Distribution:
Macmillan Distribution Ltd, Brunel Road,
Houndmills, Basingstoke, Hants RG21 6XS

Personnel:
Iradj Bagherzade (Chairman & Publisher)
Jonathan McDonnell (Managing Director)
Stuart Weir (Production Director)
Liz Stuckey (Company Secretary)
Paul Davighi (Sales & Marketing Director)
Antonia Leslie (Publicity Officer)

Academic & Scholarly; Archaeology;
Architecture & Design; Biography &
Autobiography; Cinema, Video, TV &
Radio; Fine Art & Art History; Gender
Studies; Geography & Geology; Guide
Books; History & Antiquarian; Military &
War; Philosophy; Politics & World Affairs;
Reference Books, Directories &
Dictionaries; Religion & Theology; Sociology
& Anthropology

Imprints, Series & ISBNs:
978 1 78076, 978 1 84511, 978 1 85043,
978 1 86064, 978 1 84885
International Library of African Studies: 978
1 84511, 978 1 85043, 978 1 86064
International Library of Historical Studies:
978 1 84511, 978 1 85043, 978 1 86064
International Library of Human Geography:
978 1 84511, 978 1 85043, 978 1 86064
International Library of Political Studies: 978
1 84511, 978 1 85043, 978 1 86064
Isma'ili Heritage Series: 978 1 84511, 978 1
85043, 978 1 86064
Library of International Relations: 978 1
84511, 978 1 85043, 978 1 86064
Library of Middle East History: 978 1 84511,
978 1 85043, 978 1 86064
Library of Modern Middle East Studies: 978
1 84511, 978 1 85043, 978 1 86064
Library of Ottoman Studies: 978 1 84511,
978 1 85043, 978 1 86064
Tauris Parke Paperbacks: 978 1 84511, 978
1 85043, 978 1 86064

Associated Companies:
Philip Wilson Publishers Ltd; The Radcliffe
Press

Distributor for:
UAE: Emirates Center for Strategic Studies
& Research
UK: Federal Trust; Libri Publications

Overseas Representation:
Africa (excluding South Africa &
Zimbabwe): InterMedia Americana (IMA)
Ltd, London, UK
Australia: Palgrave Macmillan, South Yarra,
Vic, Australia
Continental Europe & Russia: Andrew
Durnell Marketing Ltd, Tunbridge Wells,
UK
India: Viva Group, New Delhi, India
Iran: Behruz Neirami, Tehran, Iran
Japan: United Publishers Services Ltd,
Tokyo, Japan
New Zealand: Macmillan Publishers New
Zealand Ltd, Auckland, New Zealand
South Africa: Stephan Phillips (Pty) Ltd,
Cape Town, South Africa
South America & Caribbean: Palgrave
Macmillan, London, UK
Southeast Asia and East Asia: Taylor &
Francis Asia Pacific, Singapore
USA & Canada: Palgrave Macmillan, New
York, NY, USA

2700 ■■■■■■■■■■

TAYLOR & FRANCIS
[a divison of Informa]
2 & 4 Park Square, Milton Park, Abingdon,
Oxford OX14 4RN
Telephone: 020 7017 6000
Fax: 020 7017 6336

Email: jackie.benoist@tandf.co.uk
Web Site: www.taylorandfrancis.com

Warehouse, Trade Enquiries & Orders:
Bookpoint, 130 Milton Park, Abingdon,
Oxon OX14 4SB
Telephone: 01235 400400

Personnel:
Roger Horton (Chief Executive)
Jeremy North (Managing Director – Books)
Christoph Chesher (Sales Director)
Stuart Dawson (Finance Director)
Ian Bannerman (Managing Director –
Journals)
Mark Majurey (Digital Development
Director – Books)
David Green (Publishing Director – Journals)
Catriona Hauer (Global Marketing &
Customer Services Director – Journals)
Genevieve Early (Production Director –
Journals)
Claire L'Infant (Director: Humanities –
Books)
Alan Jarvis (Director: Social Sciences –
Books)
Nigel Eyre (Director: Production – Books)
Jackie Harbor (Global Marketing Director –
Books)
Adele Parker (Rights Manager – Books)
Paulette Dooler (Rights Manager – Journals)

Academic & Scholarly; Archaeology;
Architecture & Design; Biology & Zoology;
Chemistry; Economics; Educational &
Textbooks; Electronic (Professional &
Academic); Engineering; Environment &
Development Studies; Gay & Lesbian
Studies; Gender Studies; Geography &
Geology; History & Antiquarian; Industry,
Business & Management; Languages &
Linguistics; Law; Literature & Criticism;
Mathematics & Statistics; Medical (incl. Self
Help & Alternative Medicine); Military &
War; Music; Philosophy; Physics; Politics &
World Affairs; Psychology & Psychiatry;
Reference Books, Directories &
Dictionaries; Religion & Theology; Scientific
& Technical; Sociology & Anthropology;
Sports & Games; Theatre, Drama & Dance

New Titles: 3300 (2010) , 3500 (2011)
No of Employees: 800

Imprints, Series & ISBNs:
CRC: 978 0 8493
Dekker: 978 0 8247
Earthscan: 978 1 84407
Lawrence Erlbaum Associates: 978 0 8058
Garland: 978 0 8153
AK Peters: 978 1 56881
Psychology Press: 978 0 415
Routledge: 978 0 415
Routledge-Cavendish: 978 0 415
Taylor & Francis: 978 0 415
Willan: 978 1 84392

Parent Company:
Informa Plc

Associated Companies:
India: Routledge India Office
Norway: Taylor & Francis AS
P. R. of China: Taylor & Francis Beijing
Singapore: Taylor & Francis Asia Pacific
Sweden: Taylor & Francis AB
USA: Taylor & Francis Group LLC

Distributor for:
Guildford Press; Swedish Pharmaceutical
Press

Overseas Representation:
Australia: Palgrave Macmillan, South Yarra,
Vic, Australia
Austria, Switzerland & Germany: Gabriela
Mauch, Area Sales Manager, Central
Europe, Stuttgart, Germany
Belgium, Netherlands, France &
Luxembourg: Liza Walraven, Area Sales
Manager, Amsterdam, Netherlands

Botswana: Arthur Oageng, Book
Promotions/Horizon Books, Botswana
China: Taylor & Francis, Beijing, P. R. of
China
Eastern Europe: Marek Lewinson, Warsaw,
Poland
Greece: Ryan Cooper, Taylor & Francis
Group, Abingdon, UK
India: Taylor & Francis Books India Pvt Ltd,
New Delhi, India
Israel: Franklins International, Tel Aviv, Israel
Japan: Hans Van Ess, Sales & Marketing
Executive, Tokyo, Japan
Korea: Information & Culture Korea (ICK),
Seoul, Republic of Korea
Malaysia & Brunei: David Yeong, General
Manager, Petaling Jaya, Malaysia
Mexico, Central & South America:
Cranbury International LLC, Montpelier,
VT, USA
Middle East & North Africa: International
Publishing Services (IPS) Middle East Ltd,
Dubai, UAE
New Zealand: Victoria Johnson, Macmillan
Publishers New Zealand Ltd, Auckland,
New Zealand
Nigeria: Publisher Support Services Ltd,
Ikeja, Nigeria
Nordic Countries: Eva Nyika, Sales
Representative, Stockholm, Sweden
North America: Taylor & Francis Group LLC,
Boca Raton, FL, USA
Pakistan: M. Anwer Iqbal, Book Bird
Publishers Representatives, Lahore,
Pakistan
Republic of Ireland: Brookside Publishing
Services, Dublin, Republic of Ireland
Singapore, Hong Kong, Vietnam,
Philippines, Indonesia, Taiwan &
Thailand: Taylor & Francis Asia Pacific,
Singapore
South Africa, Namibia, Lesotho &
Swaziland: Book Promotions Pty Ltd,
Diep River, South Africa
Spain, Portugal & Italy: Philip Veysey, Area
Sales Manager, Madrid, Spain
West Indies & Caribbean: Jasmina Basic,
Taylor & Francis Group, Abingdon, UK

Book Trade Association Membership:
Publishers Association; International Group
of Scientific, Medical & Technical Publishers

2701 ■■■■■■■■■■

TEACHIT (UK) LTD
Queen Anne House, 11 Charlotte Street,
Bath BA1 2NE
Telephone: 01225 788850
Fax: 01225 430233
Email: membership@teachit.co.uk
Web Site: www.teachit.co.uk

Educational & Textbooks; Electronic
(Educational); Electronic (Professional &
Academic)

Parent Company:
UK: AQA

Book Trade Association Membership:
Publishers Association; Educational
Publishers Council

2702 ■■■■■■■■■■

TEE PUBLISHING LTD
The Fosse, Fosse Way, Leamington Spa,
Warks CV31 1XN
Telephone: 01926 614101

Book Trade Association Membership:
Publishers Association

2703 ■■■■■■■■■■

TELEGRAM BOOKS
26 Westbourne Grove, London W2 5RH
Telephone: 020 7229 2911
Fax: 020 7229 7492
Email: lynn@telegrambooks.com

Web Site: www.telegrambooks.com

Distribution (UK):
Marston Book Services Ltd,
160 Milton Park, Abingdon, Oxon
OX14 4SD
Telephone: 01235 465500
Fax: 01235 465555
Web Site: www.marston.co.uk

Sales (UK):
Compass, The Barley Mow Centre,
10 Barley Mow Passage, Chiswick, London
W4 4PH
Telephone: 020 8994 6477
Fax: 020 8400 6132
Web Site: www.compass-booksales.co.uk

Personnel:
Lynn Gaspard (Publisher)
Dide Siemmond (Editorial and Rights
Assistant)
Will Brady (Production Manager)
Ashley Biles (Sales Manager)
Charlotte Allen (Publicity Manager)

Fiction

New Titles: 2 (2010)
No of Employees: 5

Imprints, Series & ISBNs:
978 1 84659

Parent Company:
Saqi Books

Overseas Representation:
Australia & New Zealand: Palgrave
Macmillan, South Yarra, Vic, Australia
Europe: Andrew Durnell, Andrew Durnell
Marketing Ltd, Tunbridge Wells, UK
India: Pradeep Kumar, Viva Marketing, New
Delhi, India
Italy: Agnese Incisa, Letteraria Agnese
Incisa, Turin, Italy
Middle East: Dar al Saqi SARL, Beirut,
Lebanon
Pakistan: Mohammad Eusoph, Mr Books,
Islamabad, Pakistan
Singapore: Nelson Koh, Horizon Books Pte
Ltd, Singapore
South Africa: Stephan Phillips (Pty) Ltd,
Cape Town, South Africa
Spain, Portugal & Germany: Anna Soler-
Pont, Pontas Literary & Film Agency,
Barcelona, Spain
USA & Canada: Consortium Publishers, St
Paul, MN, USA

Book Trade Association Membership:
Independent Publishers Guild

2704 ■■■■■■■■■■

TELOS PUBLISHING LTD
17 Pendre Avenue, Prestatyn, Denbighshire
LL19 9SH
Telephone: 07905 311733
Email: david@telos.co.uk
Web Site: www.telos.co.uk

Business/Accounts:
5a Church Road, Shortlands, Bromley, Kent
BR2 0HP
Telephone: 020 8466 1115
Email: stephen@telos.co.uk

Personnel:
David J. Howe (Publisher)
Stephen James Walker (Publisher)

Cinema, Video, TV & Radio; Crime; Fiction

Imprints, Series & ISBNs:
978 1 84583, 978 1 903889

Overseas Representation:
USA & Canada: Fitzhenry & Whiteside Ltd,
Markham, Ont, Canada

2705

TEMPLAR PUBLISHING
The Granary, North Street, Dorking, Surrey
RH4 1DN
Telephone: 01306 876361
Fax: 01306 889097
Web Site: www.templarco.co.uk

Sales & Marketing:
Bounce Sales & Marketing,
14 Greville Street, London EC1N 8SB

Distribution:
Grantham Book Services, Trent Road,
Grantham, Lincs NG31 7XG

Personnel:
Amanda Wood (Managing Director)
Karen Ellison (Production Director)
Odile Louis-Sidney (Foreign Rights Director)

Children's Books; Fiction

Imprints, Series & ISBNs:
978 1 84011, 978 1 898784
Amazing Baby: 978 1 904513

Parent Company:
Bonnier Publishing Ltd

Book Trade Association Membership:
Booksellers Association; Independent
Publishers Guild

2706

TEMPLE LODGE PUBLISHING
Hillside House, The Square, Forest Row,
East Sussex RH18 5ES
Telephone: 01342 824000
Fax: 01342 826437
Email: office@templelodge.com
Web Site: www.templelodge.com

Distribution:
BookSource, 50 Cambuslang Road,
Glasgow G32 8NB
Telephone: 0141 643 3955
Fax: 0845 370 0068
Email: orders@booksource.net
Web Site: www.booksource.net

Personnel:
S. E. Gulbekian (Chief Editor)

Health & Beauty; Magic & the Occult;
Medical (incl. Self Help & Alternative
Medicine); Philosophy; Politics & World
Affairs; Religion & Theology

New Titles: 13 (2010) , 8 (2011)
No of Employees: 1
Annual Turnover: £65,000

Imprints, Series & ISBNs:
978 0 904693, 978 1 902636, 978 1
906999

Overseas Representation:
Australia: Rudolf Steiner Book Centre,
Sydney, NSW, Australia
Canada: Tri-fold Books, Guelph, Ont,
Canada
New Zealand: Steinerbooks, Auckland, New
Zealand
South Africa: Rudolf Steiner Publications,
Bryanston, South Africa
USA: Steiner Books Inc, Herndon, VA, USA

Book Trade Association Membership:
Independent Publishers Guild

2707

TENEUES PUBLISHING UK LTD
21 Marlowe Court, Lymer Avenue, London
SE19 1LP
Telephone: 020 8670 7522
Fax: 020 8670 7523
Email: bclark@teneues.co.uk
Web Site: www.teneues.com

Trade Enquiries & Orders:
Combined Book Services, Unit D,
Paddock Wood Distribution Centre,
Tonbridge, Kent TN12 6UU
Telephone: 01892 835599
Fax: 01892 837272
Email: orders@combook.co.uk

Personnel:
Hendrik teNeues (Chairman)
Bridget Clark (Director of Sales &
Marketing)
Claire Trigger (Sales Coordinator)

Architecture & Design; Fashion & Costume;
Illustrated & Fine Editions; Photography;
Travel & Topography

New Titles: 270 (2010) , 270 (2011)
No of Employees: 3
Annual Turnover: £2.1M

Imprints, Series & ISBNs:
Stern Portfolios: 978 3 570
teNeues: 978 1 60160, 978 3 8238, 978 3
8327

Book Trade Association Membership:
Booksellers Association

2708

***TFM PUBLISHING LTD**
Castle Hill Barns, Harley, Shrewsbury,
Shropshire SY5 6LX
Telephone: 01952 510061
Fax: 01952 510192
Email: nikki@tfmpublishing.com
Web Site: www.tfmpublishing.com

Representation (UK):
Gazelle, Lancaster

Personnel:
Nikki Bramhill (Director)
Paul Lawrence (Director)

Academic & Scholarly; Medical (incl. Self
Help & Alternative Medicine)

Imprints, Series & ISBNs:
978 1 903378

Overseas Representation:
Australia & New Zealand: Elsevier Australia,
Chatswood, NSW, Australia
Europe: Gazelle, Lancaster, UK
Hong Kong: MacBarron Book Co, Kowloon,
Hong Kong
India & Sri Lanka: Thieme Medical &
Scientific Publishers Pte Ltd, Noida, India
Japan: Igaku-Shoin Ltd, Tokyo, Japan;
Nankodo Co Ltd, Tokyo, Japan
Middle East & North Africa: International
Publishing Services, Dubai, UAE
South Africa: Academic Marketing Services
(Pty) Ltd, Johannesburg, South Africa
South East Asia: Elsevier (Singapore) Pte
Ltd, Singapore
Taiwan: Unifacmanu Trading Co Ltd, Taipei,
Taiwan
USA, Canada & South America: Martin P
Hill Consulting, New York, NY, USA

Book Trade Association Membership:
Booksellers Association

2709

THAMES & HUDSON LTD
181A High Holborn, London WC1V 7QX
Telephone: 020 7845 5000
Fax: 020 7845 5050
Email: l.willis@thameshudson.co.uk
Web Site: www.thamesandhudson.com

Warehouse, Accounts & Returns:
Thames & Hudson (Distributors) Ltd,
44 Clockhouse Road, Farnborough, Hants
GU14 7QZ
Telephone: 01252 541602

Fax: 01252 377380
Email:
customerservices@thameshudson.co.uk

Personnel:
Thomas Neurath (Chairman)
Constance Kaine (Deputy Chairman)
Jamie Camplin (Managing Director)
Sarah Forster (Financial Director)
Christopher Ferguson (Operations Director)
Neil Palfreyman (Production Director)
Brian Meek (Company Secretary)
Johanna Neurath (Design Director)
Christian Frederking (Sales & Marketing
Director)
Stephen Embrey (Export Area Manager)
Sara Ticci (Export Area Manager)
Scipio Stringer (Export Area Manager)
Laura Willis (Head of Marketing)
Melanie Stacey (UK Sales Manager)
Collette Hutchinson (Senior Publicist)
Andrew Stanley (Deputy Sales & Marketing
Director)
Ian Bartley (Export Sales)
Christian Gotsch (Head of Foreign Rights)

Academic & Scholarly; Antiques &
Collecting; Archaeology; Architecture &
Design; Biography & Autobiography;
Children's Books; Crafts & Hobbies;
Educational & Textbooks; Environment &
Development Studies; Fashion & Costume;
Fine Art & Art History; Gardening; Gay &
Lesbian Studies; Guide Books; History &
Antiquarian; Illustrated & Fine Editions;
Literature & Criticism; Magic & the Occult;
Military & War; Music; Natural History;
Philosophy; Photography; Reference Books,
Directories & Dictionaries; Religion &
Theology; Sociology & Anthropology;
Theatre, Drama & Dance; Travel &
Topography

Imprints, Series & ISBNs:
Aperture: 978 0 89381, 978 1 59711, 978 1
931788
Art Gallery of NSW: 978 0 7847
Ava Publishing: 978 2 88479, 978 2 940373
Mark Batty Publisher
Chris Boot: 978 0 9542813, 978 0
9546894, 978 1 905712
Booth-Clibborn: 978 1 86154
Braun Verlagshaus: 978 3 938780
British Museum Press: 978 0 7141
Dakini
Flammarion SA, France: 978 2 08
Frieze
Guggenheim Museum Publications: 978 0
89207
Ilex Press: 978 1 904705
Institute for Archaeo-Metallurgical Studies:
978 0 906183
Laurence King: 978 1 85669
Museum of Modern Art, New York: 978 0
87070
National Gallery of Australia: 978 0 642
River Books
The Royal Academy of Arts: 978 0 900946,
978 1 903973
The Royal Collection: 978 1 902163
Scriptum: 978 1 900826, 978 1 902686
Skira Editore: 978 3 87624, 978 88 8118,
978 88 8491
Steidl: 978 3 86521, 978 3 88243, 978 3
905509, 978 3 931141
Thames & Hudson: 978 0 500

Parent Company:
T & H Holdings Ltd

Associated Companies:
Thames & Hudson (Distributors) Ltd
Australia: Thames & Hudson (Australia) Pty
Ltd
France: Editions Thames & Hudson sarl
P. R. of China: Thames & Hudson China Ltd
Singapore: Thames & Hudson (S) Pte Ltd
USA: Thames & Hudson Inc

Distributor for:
British Museum Press; Laurence King
Australia: National Gallery of Australia

France: Flammarion SA
Germany: Braun Verlagshaus
Israel: Institute for Archaeo-Metallurgical
Studies
Italy: Skira Editore
USA: Mark Batty Publisher; Museum of
Modern Art, New York

Overseas Representation:
Africa, Caribbean, Central America, Eastern
Europe, Eastern Mediterranean,
Germany (South), Italy, Japan, Mexico,
Middle East, Portugal & Spain: Export
Sales Department, Thames & Hudson
Ltd, London, UK
Australia, New Zealand, Papua New Guinea
& Pacific Islands: Thames & Hudson
(Australia) Pty Ltd, Fishermans Bend, Vic,
Australia
Austria, Switzerland & Germany (excluding
South): Michael Klein, Vilsbiburg,
Germany
Bangladesh: Zeenat Book Supply Ltd,
Dhaka, Bangladesh
Brazil & South America: Terry Roberts, Cotia
SP, Brazil
China, Hong Kong & Macau: Thames &
Hudson China Ltd, Aberdeen, Hong
Kong
France: Interart SARL, Paris, France
India, Pakistan & Sri Lanka: Raj Rupam Bora,
New Delhi, India
Iran: Book City, Tehran, Iran
Israel: Lonnie Kahn & Co Ltd, Rishon Lezion,
Israel
Korea & Taiwan: Asia Publishers Services
Ltd, Hong Kong
Lebanon: Levant Distributors, Beirut,
Lebanon
Malaysia: Thames & Hudson (S) Pte Ltd,
Petaling Jaya, Malaysia
Netherlands: Sebastian van der Zee,
Amsterdam, Netherlands
Republic of Ireland: UK Sales Department,
Thames & Hudson Ltd, London, UK
Scandinavia & Baltic States: Per Burell,
Stocksund, Sweden
Singapore & South East Asia: Thames &
Hudson (S) Pte Ltd, Singapore
Thailand: Asia Book Co Ltd, Bangkok,
Thailand

Book Trade Association Membership:
Publishers Association

2710

***THARPA PUBLICATIONS**
Conishead Priory, Ulverston, Cumbria
LA12 9QQ
Telephone: 01229 588599
Fax: 01229 483919
Email: sales.uk@tharpa.com
Web Site: www.tharpa.com

Personnel:
Murdo McNab (Distribution Manager)
Manuel Rivero-Demartine (Production
Manager)
Steph Atkinson (Finance Director; Sales &
Marketing Manager)
Jim Bliether (Editorial)

Philosophy; Religion & Theology

Imprints, Series & ISBNs:
978 0 948006, 978 0 9548790

Parent Company:
New Kadampa Tradition

Overseas Representation:
Australia: Gary Allen Pty Ltd, Smithfield,
NSW, Australia
Canada: Tharpa Canada, Toronto, Ont,
Canada
Singapore & Malaysia: Tharpa Asia, Hong
Kong
South Africa: Bacchus Books, Gauteng,
South Africa
USA (Office): Tharpa Publications, New
York, NY, USA

Book Trade Association Membership:
Booksellers Association; Independent
Publishers Guild

2711

***THIRD MILLENNIUM PUBLISHING
LTD**
2–5 Benjamin Street, London EC1M 5QL
Telephone: 020 7336 0144
Fax: 020 7608 1188
Email: info@tmiltd.com
Web Site: www.tmiltd.com

Personnel:
Julian Platt *(Chairman)*
Christopher Fagg *(Publisher)*
Joel Burden *(Business Development
   Director)*
David Burt *(Director)*
Michael D. Jackson *(Marketing Manager)*
Bonnie Murray *(Production Manager)*

*Antiques & Collecting; Educational &
Textbooks; Fine Art & Art History; Guide
Books; Illustrated & Fine Editions; Military &
War; Photography*

Imprints, Series & ISBNs:
978 1 906507

Distributor for:
UK: Pardoe Blacker Design

Overseas Representation:
USA & Canada: John Bramcati, Antique
   Collectors Club Ltd, Easthampton, MA,
   USA

2712

**THOMSON REUTERS –
PROFESSIONAL DIVISION**
100 Avenue Road, Swiss Cottage, London
NW3 3PF
Telephone: 020 7393 7000
Fax: 020 7393 7010
Email:
   sweetandmaxwell.orders@thomson.com
Web Site: www.sweetandmaxwell.co.uk

Law

Parent Company:
Thomson Reuters

Associated Companies:
Republic of Ireland: Roundhall
UK: Current Law Publishers; Flosuite; IDS;
Lawtel; Localaw; Solcara; Sweet &
Maxwell; W Green & Son; Westlaw UK

2713

THOROGOOD PUBLISHING LTD
10–12 Rivington Street, London EC2A 3DU
Telephone: 020 7749 4739
Fax: 020 7720 6110
Email: info@thorogoodpublishing.co.uk
Web Site:
   www.thorogoodpublishing.co.uk

Trade Orders:
Marston Book Services, 160 Milton Park,
Abingdon, Oxon OX14 4SD
Telephone: 01235 465500
Fax: 01235 465655
Email: trade.enq@marston.co.uk
Web Site: www.marston.co.uk

Personnel:
Neil Thomas *(Chairman)*
Nina Rossey *(Finance Director)*
Angela Spall *(General, Editorial, Production
   Manager)*
Matthew Harris *(Marketing Manager)*
Elizabeth Hall *(Marketing Executive)*

*Accountancy & Taxation; Audio Books;
Biography & Autobiography; Electronic
(Entertainment); Electronic (Professional &
Academic); Fiction; Industry, Business &*

*Management; Law; Military & War; Travel &
Topography*

Imprints, Series & ISBNs:
978 1 85418

Associated Companies:
UK: Falconbury Ltd

Overseas Representation:
Australia & New Zealand: Woodslane Pty
   Ltd, Warriewood, NSW, Australia
Hong Kong, Taiwan, China & Korea: Asia
   Publishers Services Ltd, Hong Kong
India: Viva Group, New Delhi, India
Latin America: InterMedia Americana (IMA)
   Ltd, London, UK
Middle East, Greece & Cyprus: Ray Potts,
   Publishers International Marketing,
   Polfages, France
Singapore, Malaysia & South East Asia: APD
   Singapore Pte Ltd, Singapore

2714

F. A. THORPE PUBLISHING
The Green, Bradgate Road, Anstey,
Leicester LE7 7FU
Telephone: 0116 236 4325
Fax: 0116 234 0205
Email: enquiries@ulverscroft.co.uk
Web Site: www.ulverscroft.com

Personnel:
Robert Thirlby *(Chief Executive)*

*Biography & Autobiography; Crime;
Fiction; Travel & Topography*

Imprints, Series & ISBNs:
Charnwood Hardback Series: 978 0 7089,
   978 1 84395, 978 1 84617, 978 1 84782
Charnwood/Ulverscroft/Linford: 978 1 4448
Linford Softcover Series: 978 0 7089, 978 1
   84395, 978 1 84617, 978 1 84782
Ulverscroft Hardcover Series: 978 0 7089,
   978 1 84395, 978 1 84617, 978 1 84782

Parent Company:
Ulverscroft Large Print Books Ltd

Associated Companies:
Isis Publishing; Magna Large Print Books

Overseas Representation:
Australia: Sandra Lavender, Crows Nest,
   Australia
Canada: Charlene Kessel, Ulverscroft, West
   Seneca, NY, USA
New Zealand: John Gregory, Feilding, New
   Zealand
USA: Jan McGowan, Ulverscroft Large Print
   (USA) Inc, West Seneca, NY, USA

2715

THOTH PUBLICATIONS
64 Leopold Street, Loughborough, Leics
LE11 5DN
Telephone: 01509 210626
Fax: 0709 209 1129
Email: sales@thoth.co.uk
Web Site: www.thoth.co.uk

Personnel:
Tom Clarke *(Senior Partner)*
Susan Attwood *(Partner)*

*Biography & Autobiography; Magic & the
Occult; Religion & Theology*

Imprints, Series & ISBNs:
978 1 870450

Book Trade Association Membership:
Booksellers Association

2716

THRASS (UK) LTD
The Willows, 18 Long Lane, Upton, Chester
CH2 2PD

Telephone: 01244 373079
Fax: 0872 111 4327
Email: office@thrass.co.uk
Web Site: www.thrass.co.uk

Personnel:
Alan Davies *(Director)*
Hilary Davies *(Company Secretary)*

*Educational & Textbooks; Electronic
(Educational)*

New Titles: 6 (2010) , 6 (2011)
No of Employees: 2

Imprints, Series & ISBNs:
978 1 904912, 978 1 906295

2717

TINDAL STREET PRESS
217 The Custard Factory, Gibb Street,
Birmingham B9 4AA
Telephone: 0121 773 8157
Email: alan@tindalstreet.co.uk
Web Site: www.tindalstreet.co.uk

Distribution (UK):
TBS, Colchester Road, Colchester
CO7 7DW
Telephone: 01206 255678
Fax: 01206 255930
Email: sales@tbs-ltd.co.uk
Web Site: www.thebookservice.co.uk

Personnel:
Alan Mahar *(Publishing Director)*
Luke Brown *(Senior Editor/Publicist)*

Fiction

Imprints, Series & ISBNs:
978 0 9556476, 978 1 906994

Overseas Representation:
Australia: Allen & Unwin, 83 Alexander
   Street, Crows Nest, NSW 2065, Australia
India: Penguin Books India, 11 Community
   Centre, Panchsheel Park, New Delhi,
   110017, India
New Zealand: Allen & Unwin, Office 3, Level
   3, HB Building, 228 Queen Street,
   Auckland, New Zealand
South Africa: Penguin Books South Africa,
   24 Sturdee Avenue, Rosebank,
   Johannesburg 2196, South Africa
USA & Canada: Trafalgar Square,
   Independent Publishers Group, USA

Book Trade Association Membership:
Independent Publishers Guild

2718

TOP THAT! PUBLISHING PLC
Marine House, Tide Mill Way, Woodbridge,
Suffolk IP12 1AP
Telephone: 01394 386651
Fax: 01394 386011
Email: info@topthatpublishing.com
Web Site: www.topthatpublishing.com

Personnel:
David Henderson *(Managing Director)*
Dave Greggor *(Sales Director)*
Simon Couchman *(Creative Director)*
Douglas Eadie *(Finance Director)*
Daniel Graham *(Editorial Director)*
Stuart Buck *(Production Director)*
Barrie Henderson *(Chairman)*

*Children's Books; Crafts & Hobbies; Fiction;
Humour; Natural History; Reference Books,
Directories & Dictionaries; Sports & Games*

New Titles: 80 (2011)
No of Employees: 35
Annual Turnover: £9M

Imprints, Series & ISBNs:
Kudos: 978 1 84229
Pocket Money Press: 978 1 84956

Quest: 978 1 84956
Tide Mill Press: 978 1 84956
Top That! Kids: 978 1 84956

Book Trade Association Membership:
Independent Publishers Guild

2719

TOPICAL RESOURCES
Jumps Farm, Durton Lane, Broughton,
Preston, Lancs PR3 5LE
Telephone: 01772 863158
Fax: 01772 866153
Email: sales@topical-resources.co.uk
Web Site: www.topical-resources.co.uk

Personnel:
Peter Bell *(Partner)*
Heather Bell *(Partner)*
Kath Cope *(Sales Assistant)*

*Audio Books; Children's Books; Educational
& Textbooks*

Imprints, Series & ISBNs:
978 1 872977, 978 1 905509, 978 1
   907269

Overseas Representation:
Australia: Ian Harding, Farr Books, Wilston,
   Qld, Australia
Republic of Ireland: Martin Pender, Primary
   Educational Resources, Enniscorthy, Co
   Wexford, Republic of Ireland

2720

*TOTAL-E-NTWINED LTD
Think Tank, Ruston Way, Lincoln LN6 7FL
Telephone: 01522 668916
Web Site: www.total-e-bound.com

Fiction

Book Trade Association Membership:
Publishers Association

2721

TRANSWORLD PUBLISHERS LTD
[a company of the Random House Group
Ltd]
61–63 Uxbridge Road, London W5 5SA
Telephone: 020 8579 2652
Fax: 020 8579 5479
Email: info@transworld-publishers.co.uk
Web Site: www.booksattransworld.co.uk

Personnel:
Larry Finlay *(Managing Director)*
Bill Scott-Kerr *(Publisher & Director)*
Sally Gaminara *(Publishing Director –
   Bantam Press)*
Marianne Velmans *(Publishing Director –
   Doubleday)*
Leon Romero Montalvo *(Head of
   Commercial Affairs)*
Ed Christie *(Sales & Marketing Director)*
Martin Higgins *(UK Sales Director)*
Janine Giovanni *(UK Marketing Director)*
Eleanor Wood *(International Sales Director)*
Alison Martin *(Production Director)*
Patsy Irwin *(Publicity Director)*
Claire Ward *(Art Director)*
Helen Edwards *(Rights Director)*

*Audio Books; Biography & Autobiography;
Cinema, Video, TV & Radio; Cookery, Wines
& Spirits; Crime; Fiction; Gardening; History
& Antiquarian; Humour; Military & War;
Music; Politics & World Affairs; Science
Fiction; Sports & Games; Travel &
Topography*

Imprints, Series & ISBNs:
Bantam: 978 0 553
Bantam Press: 978 0 593
Black Swan: 978 0 552
Channel 4 Books
Corgi: 978 0 552
Doubleday: 978 0 385

Eden Project: 978 0 593
Expert Gardening Books
Transworld Ireland

Parent Company:
USA: Random House Inc

Associated Companies:
Random House Children's Books; Random
House UK Ltd
Australia: Random House Australia Pty Ltd
Canada: Random House of Canada Ltd
New Zealand: Random House New Zealand
Ltd
South Africa: Random House (Pty) Ltd

Overseas Representation:
Australia: Random House Australia Pty Ltd,
Sydney, NSW, Australia
Canada: Random House of Canada Ltd,
Toronto, Ont, Canada
New Zealand: Random House New Zealand
Ltd, Auckland, New Zealand
South Africa: Random House Struik Pty Ltd,
Parktown, South Africa

Book Trade Association Membership:
Publishers Association; BA (Associate
Member)

2722 ▬▬▬▬▬

*TRAVEL PUBLISHING LTD
Airport Business Centre,
10 Thornbury Road, Estover, Plymouth
PL6 7PP
Telephone: 01752 697280
Fax: 01752 697299
Email: info@travelpublishing.co.uk
Web Site: www.travelpublishing.co.uk

Sales & Distribution:
Portfolio, Suite 3 & 4, Great West House,
Great West Road, Brentford, Middx
TW8 9DF
Telephone: 020 8326 5620
Fax: 020 8326 5621
Email: e-mail@portfoliobooks.com

Personnel:
Peter Robinson *(Director & Chairman)*
Chris Day *(Director & Company Secretary)*

Guide Books; Travel & Topography

Imprints, Series & ISBNs:
Country Living Garden Centres & Nurseries
of Britain: 978 1 904434
Country Living Rural Guides: 978 1 902007,
978 1 904434
Country Pubs & Inns: 978 1 904434
Golfers Guides: 978 1 902007, 978 1
904434
Hidden Inns: 978 1 902007, 978 1 904434
Hidden Places: 978 1 902007, 978 1
904434
Off the Motorway: 978 1 902007, 978 1
904434

Overseas Representation:
USA & Canada: Casemate Publishers &
Book Distributors LLC, Havertown, PA,
USA

Book Trade Association Membership:
Independent Publishers Guild

2723 ▬▬▬▬▬

TRENTHAM BOOKS
Westview House, 734 London Road,
Oakhill, Stoke-on-Trent ST4 5NP
Telephone: 01782 745567 & 844699
Fax: 01782 745553
Email: tb@trentham-books.co.uk
Web Site: www.trentham-books.co.uk

Editorial:
28 Hillside Gardens, Highgate, London
N6 5ST
Telephone: 020 8348 2174
Email: gillian@trentham-books.co.uk

Representation (UK):
Compass Academic Ltd, Edinburgh
EH9 1QS

Personnel:
Gillian Klein *(Chairman, Rights &
Permissions, Editor)*
Barbara Wiggins *(Business Manager)*

*Academic & Scholarly; Educational &
Textbooks; Gender Studies; Law; Politics &
World Affairs; Theatre, Drama & Dance*

New Titles: 22 (2010) , 27 (2011)
No of Employees: 7

Imprints, Series & ISBNs:
978 0 948080, 978 0 9507735, 978 1
85856

Distributor for:
Commission for Racial Equality; Design and
Technology Association; Open University
France: European Institute of Education &
Social Policy; UNESCO Institute for
Educational Planning

Overseas Representation:
Australia, New Zealand & South East Asia:
DA Information Services Pty Ltd,
Mitcham, Vic, Australia
Canada: Bacon & Hughes Ltd, Ottawa, Ont,
Canada
*China, Taiwan, Hong Kong & South East
Asia:* Tony Poh Leong Wah, Singapore
Malaysia: UBSD Distribution Sdn Bhd,
Selangor, Malaysia
Philippines: Megatexts Phil Inc, Cebu City,
Philippines
Spain & Portugal: Iberian Book Services,
Madrid, Spain
Taiwan: Unifacmanu Trading Co Ltd, Taipei,
Taiwan
USA: Stylus Publishing Inc, Sterling, VA, USA

Book Trade Association Membership:
Independent Publishers Guild

2724 ▬▬▬▬▬

TRINITARIAN BIBLE SOCIETY
Tyndale House, Dorset Road, London
SW19 3NN
Telephone: 020 8543 7857
Fax: 020 8543 6370
Email: TBS@tbsbibles.org
Web Site: www.tbsbibles.org

Personnel:
D. P. Rowland *(General Secretary)*
D. Larlham *(Operations Director)*
D. J. Broome *(Resources Director)*
J. M. Wilson *(Finance & Supporter Manager)*
P. J. D. Hopkins *(Editorial Director)*
A. P. Clarke *(Sales Development & Grants
Manager)*

Religion & Theology

No of Employees: 60 (world)
Annual Turnover: £2.5M

Imprints, Series & ISBNs:
978 0 907861, 978 1 86228

Overseas Representation:
Australia: Trinitarian Bible Society
(Australia), Grafton, NSW, Australia
Brazil: Sociedade Bíblica Trinitariana do
Brasil, São Paulo, Brazil
Canada: Trinitarian Bible Society, Chilliwack,
BC, Canada
New Zealand: Trinitarian Bible Society (New
Zealand), Gisborne, New Zealand
USA: Trinitarian Bible Society (USA), Grand
Rapids, MI, USA

2725 ▬▬▬▬▬

TROG ASSOCIATES LTD
PO Box 243, South Croydon, Surrey
CR2 6NZ

Telephone: 020 8681 3301
Fax: 020 8681 3301
Email:
ericsutherland@writerofbooks.plus.com
Web Site: www.trogassociatesltd.biz

Personnel:
Eric Sutherland *(Contact)*

*Accountancy & Taxation; Health & Beauty;
Industry, Business & Management;
Literature & Criticism; Scientific & Technical*

Imprints, Series & ISBNs:
978 1 906440

Associated Companies:
UK: www.lulu.com/uk

2726 ▬▬▬▬▬

TROTMAN PUBLISHING
[an imprint of Crimson Publishing Ltd]
Crimson Publishing Ltd,
Westminster House, Kew Road, Richmond
TW9 2ND
Telephone: 020 8334 1788
Fax: 020 8334 1601
Email: GemmaS@crimsonpublishing.co.uk
Web Site: www.trotman.co.uk

Warehouse:
Grantham Book Services (GBS) Trent Road
Grantham Lincolnshire NG31 7XQ
Telephone: 01476 541080
Fax: 01476 541061

Personnel:
David Lester *(Managing Director)*
Beth Bishop *(Commissioning Editor)*
Holly Ivins *(Commissioning Editor)*

*Educational & Textbooks; Industry, Business
& Management; Reference Books,
Directories & Dictionaries; Vocational
Training & Careers*

Imprints, Series & ISBNs:
Trotman: 978 0 85660, 978 1 84455
Trotman Education: 978 0 85660, 978 1
84455

Parent Company:
UK: Crimson Publishing Ltd

Book Trade Association Membership:
Independent Publishers Guild; Data
Publishers Association

2727 ▬▬▬▬▬

TROUBADOR PUBLISHING LTD
9 Priory Business Park, Wistow Road,
Kibworth Beauchamp, Leics LE8 0RX
Telephone: 0116 279 2299
Fax: 0116 279 2277
Email: books@troubador.co.uk
Web Site: www.troubador.co.uk

Personnel:
Jeremy Thompson *(Managing Director)*
Jane Rowland *(Marketing Director)*
Sarah Taylor *(Marketing Assistant)*
Terry Compton *(Assistant Publisher)*
Amy Cooke *(Production Assistant)*
Amy Chadwick *(Production Assistant)*
Lauren Lewis *(Production Assistant)*
Sam Copson *(Distribution Manager)*
Jennifer Liptrot *(Production Assistant)*

*Academic & Scholarly; Accountancy &
Taxation; Biography & Autobiography;
Children's Books; Cookery, Wines & Spirits;
Crime; Economics; Fiction; Guide Books;
History & Antiquarian; Humour; Industry,
Business & Management; Languages &
Linguistics; Literature & Criticism; Magic &
the Occult; Medical (incl. Self Help &
Alternative Medicine); Military & War;
Music; Natural History; Philosophy; Poetry;
Politics & World Affairs; Psychology &
Psychiatry; Science Fiction; Sociology &*

*Anthropology; Sports & Games; Theatre,
Drama & Dance; Transport; Travel &
Topography*

New Titles: 220 (2010) , 240 (2011)
No of Employees: 9
Annual Turnover: £1.2M

Imprints, Series & ISBNs:
Italian Studies: 978 1 905237
Matador: 978 1 84876, 978 1 899293, 978
1 905886, 978 1 906221, 978 1 906510
T2: 978 1 904744

Book Trade Association Membership:
Independent Publishers Guild

2728 ▬▬▬▬▬

*TRURAN
Goonance, Water Lane, St Agnes, Cornwall
TR5 0RA
Telephone: 01872 553821
Email: info@truranbooks.co.uk
Web Site: www.truranbooks.co.uk

Trade Enquiries:
Tor Mark Press,
United Downs Industrial Estate, St Day,
Redruth, Cornwall TR16 5HY
Telephone: 01209 822101
Fax: 01209 822035
Email: sales@tormarkpress.prestel.co.uk

Personnel:
Ivan Corbett *(Director)*
Heather Corbett *(Director)*

*Aviation; Biography & Autobiography;
Cookery, Wines & Spirits; Crime; Fiction;
Fine Art & Art History; Gardening;
Geography & Geology; Guide Books;
History & Antiquarian; Languages &
Linguistics; Military & War; Natural History;
Nautical; Photography; Reference Books,
Directories & Dictionaries*

Imprints, Series & ISBNs:
978 0 9506431, 978 0 907566, 978 1
85022
Cornish Classics
Truran

2729 ▬▬▬▬▬

***TSO (THE STATIONERY OFFICE
LTD)**
St Crispins, Duke Street, Norwich NR3 1PD
Telephone: 01603 622211
Fax: 01603 696506
Email: tsoservices@tso.co.uk
Web Site: www.tso.co.uk

Press & Offices:
Mandela Way, London SE1 5SS
Telephone: 020 7394 4200
Email: tsoservices@tso.co.uk
Web Site: www.tso.co.uk

Personnel:
Richard Dell *(Chief Executive Officer)*
Richard South *(Official Publishing Director)*
Richard Coward *(Finance Director)*
Gordon Samson *(Operations Director)*
Lisa Hallett *(Sales & Marketing Director)*
Ashley Dampier *(Head of Sales)*
David Howell *(Client Services Director)*
Terry Blake *(Technology Services Director)*

*Academic & Scholarly; Accountancy &
Taxation; Aviation; Computer Science;
Economics; Educational & Textbooks;
Electronic (Professional & Academic);
Engineering; Geography & Geology;
Industry, Business & Management; Law;
Mathematics & Statistics; Medical (incl. Self
Help & Alternative Medicine); Nautical;
Politics & World Affairs; Reference Books,
Directories & Dictionaries; Scientific &
Technical; Transport; Veterinary Science*

Imprints, Series & ISBNs:
Non-Parliamentary Publications: 978 0 11
Northern Ireland Publications: 978 0 337
Parliamentary Publications: 978 0 10

Parent Company:
Williams Lea

Distributor for:
Construction Industry Publications; English
Heritage; International Labour
Organisation
France: Council of Europe; European
Pharmacopoeia Commission;
Organisation for Economic Co-operation
and Development; United Nations
Educational, Scientific and Cultural
Organisation
Germany: Deutscher Apotheker Verlag
Italy: Food and Agriculture Organisation of
the United Nations
Japan: Japanese Pharmacopoeia
Luxembourg: European Communities/
Union
Spain: World Tourism Organisation
Switzerland: United Nations; World Health
Organisation; World Trade Organisation
USA: Bernan Press; International Monetary
Fund; United Nations; US
Pharmacopoeia Convention; World Bank

Overseas Representation:
Australia: DA Information Services Pty Ltd,
Mitcham, Vic, Australia
Belgium & Luxembourg: Jean de Lannoy,
Brussels, Belgium
Brazil: Livraria Cultura Editora Ltda, São
Paulo, Brazil; Livraria LMC LTDA, Brazil
Canada: Renouf Publishing Co Ltd, Ottawa,
Ont, Canada
Croatia: VBZ d.o.o., Zagreb, Croatia
Denmark: Arnold Busck, Copenhagen,
Denmark
Egypt: MERIC, Cairo, Egypt
France: Bureau D'etudes Et De, France
Germany: Deutscher Apotheker, Germany
Greece: Athenian Science, Athens, Greece
Hong Kong: Swindon Book Co Ltd, Hong
Kong
Hungary: SpeedUp Ltd, Budapest, Hungary
India: Apple Books, New Delhi, India
Italy: Licosa SPA, Florence, Italy
Japan: Maruzen Co Ltd, Tokyo, Japan
Jordan: Jordan Book Centre, Amman,
Jordan
Kuwait: The Kuwait Bookshop Co Ltd,
Safat, Kuwait
Malaysia: Yuha Associates, Selangor Darul
Ehsan, Malaysia
Mexico: Libreria Arroyave, Mexico, Mexico
Netherlands: selexyz zakelijk, Netherlands;
Technische Boekhandel Waltman, Delft,
Netherlands
Norway: Academic Book Centre, Oslo,
Norway
Poland: Ars Plona, Poland

Book Trade Association Membership:
Booksellers Association; Educational
Publishers Council; Data Publishers
Association

2730

*TTS GROUP
Park Lane Business Park, Kirkby-in-Ashfield,
Nottinghamshire NG17 9GU
Telephone: 0800 318686
Fax: 0800 137525
Web Site: www.tts-group.co.uk

*Children's Books; Educational & Textbooks;
Electronic (Educational); Music*

2731

TWELVEHEADS PRESS
PO Box 59, Chacewater, Truro, Cornwall
TR4 8ZJ
Email: enquiries@twelveheads.com
Web Site: www.twelveheads.com

Personnel:
Alan Kittridge *(Partner)*
Michael Messenger *(Partner)*
John Stengelhofen *(Partner)*

*Archaeology; Guide Books; History &
Antiquarian; Nautical; Transport*

Imprints, Series & ISBNs:
978 0 906294

2732

TYNE BRIDGE PUBLISHING
Newcastle Libraries, PO Box 88,
Newcastle upon Tyne NE99 1DX
Telephone: 0191 277 4174
Fax: 0191 277 4137
Email: anna.flowers@newcastle.gov.uk
Web Site: www.newcastle.gov.uk/
tynebridgepublishing

Personnel:
Anna Flowers *(Publications Manager)*
Vanessa Histon *(Marketing Officer)*

*Archaeology; Biography & Autobiography;
History & Antiquarian*

New Titles: 4 (2010) , 4 (2011)
No of Employees: 2
Annual Turnover: £150,000

Imprints, Series & ISBNs:
Newcastle City Libraries: 978 0 902653
Newcastle Libraries and Information Service:
978 1 85795
Tyne Bridge Publishing: 978 1 85795

Parent Company:
City & Council of Newcastle upon Tyne

2733

UCAS
Rosehill, New Barn Lane, Cheltenham, Glos
GL52 3LZ
Telephone: 01242 222444
Fax: 01242 544806
Email: publicationservices@ucas.ac.uk
Web Site: www.ucas.com

Trade Enquiries & Orders:
Publication Services, UCAS, PO Box 130,
Cheltenham, Glos GL52 3ZF
Telephone: 01242 544610
Fax: 01242 544806
Email: publicationservices@ucas.ac.uk
Web Site: www.ucasbooks.com

Personnel:
Graham Bond *(Head of Publishing)*
Sona Waddy *(Publications Officer)*
Amruta Hiremath *(Senior Management
Accountant)*
Paul Bird *(Publications Logistics Manager)*

*Academic & Scholarly; Educational &
Textbooks; Reference Books, Directories &
Dictionaries; Vocational Training & Careers*

New Titles: 15 (2010) , 15 (2011)

Imprints, Series & ISBNs:
978 1 84361, 978 1 908077

2734

UNICORN PRESS
47 Earlham Road, Norwich NR2 3AD
Telephone: 01603 886151
Email: hugh.tradford@btconnect.com
Web Site: www.unicornpress.org

Trade Distributor:
Marston Book Services, 160 Milton Park,
PO Box 269, Abingdon, Oxford OX14 4YN
Telephone: 01235 465604
Fax: 01235 465655
Email: tammy.belcher@marston.co.uk

Personnel:
Hugh Tempest-Radford *(Proprietor)*
Emma Farrell *(Sales & Marketing)*

*Antiques & Collecting; Architecture &
Design; Biography & Autobiography; Crafts
& Hobbies; Fashion & Costume; Fine Art &
Art History; History & Antiquarian; Military
& War; Nautical; Photography; Reference
Books, Directories & Dictionaries; Travel &
Topography*

Imprints, Series & ISBNs:
978 0 906290, 978 1 906509

Overseas Representation:
All other areas: Unicorn Press, London, UK
*Germany, France, Benelux, Italy, Austria,
Switzerland, Malta & Greece:* Ted
Dougherty, London, UK
Spain, Portugal & Gibraltar: Chris
Humphrys, London, UK
USA: Antique Collectors Club Ltd,
Easthampton, MA, USA

2735

**UNITED WRITERS PUBLICATIONS
LTD**
Ailsa, Castle Gate, Penzance, Cornwall
TR20 8BG
Telephone: 01736 365954
Fax: 01736 365954
Email: sales@unitedwriters.co.uk
Web Site: www.unitedwriters.co.uk

Personnel:
M. Sheppard *(Editorial & Sales)*
T. Sully *(Production)*

*Biography & Autobiography; Children's
Books; Cinema, Video, TV & Radio;
Educational & Textbooks; Fiction; Humour;
Industry, Business & Management; Military
& War; Nautical; Psychology & Psychiatry;
Science Fiction; Sports & Games; Travel &
Topography*

New Titles: 6 (2010) , 6 (2011)
No of Employees: 5

Imprints, Series & ISBNs:
978 0 901976, 978 1 85200

2736

**UNIVERSITY COLLEGE OF DUBLIN
PRESS**
Newman House, 86 St Stephen's Green,
Dublin 2, Republic of Ireland
Telephone: +353 (0)1 477 9812 & 9813
Fax: +353 (0)1 477 9821
Email: ucdpress@ucd.ie
Web Site: www.ucdpress.ie

Distribution (Republic of Ireland):
Irish Book Distribution, Unit 12, North Park,
North Road, Finglas, Dublin 11,
Republic of Ireland
Telephone: +353 (0)1 923 9580
Fax: +353 (0)1 823 9599
Email: sales@irishbookdistribution.ie

Representation (Republic of Ireland):
Hibernian Book Services,
93 Longwood Park, Rathfarnham,
Dublin 14, Republic of Ireland
Telephone: +353 (0)1 493 6043
Fax: +353 (0)1 493 7833

Distributor UK:
Central Books, 99 Wallis Road, London
E9 5LN
Telephone: 020 8986 4854
Fax: 020 8533 5821
Email: orders@centralbooks.com

Personnel:
Noelle Moran *(Executive Editor)*

Academic & Scholarly

New Titles: 18 (2011)

Imprints, Series & ISBNs:
978 1 900621, 978 1 904558, 978 1
906359

Overseas Representation:
Australia & New Zealand: Eleanor Brasch
Enterprises, Artarmon, NSW, Australia
Germany, Austria & Switzerland: SHS
Publishers' Consultants and
Representatives, Oranienberg, Germany
North America: Dufour Editions Inc, Chester
Springs, PA, USA
Spain & Portugal: Iberian Book Services,
Madrid, Spain
UK & Benelux: Theo Van de Bilt Sales and
Marketing, Sawbridgeworth, UK
*UK, Europe & all other countries
(distribution):* Central Books Ltd, London,
UK

Book Trade Association Membership:
Publishing Ireland (Foilsiú Éireann)

2737

*UNIVERSITY OF EXETER PRESS
Reed Hall, Streatham Drive, Exeter EX4 4QR
Telephone: 01392 263066
Fax: 01392 263064
Email: uep@exeter.ac.uk
Web Site: www.exeterpress.co.uk

Distribution:
NBN International, Estover Road, Plymouth
PL6 7PY
Telephone: 01752 202301
Fax: 01752 202331
Email: cservs@nbninternational.com
Web Site: www.nbninternational.com

Personnel:
Simon Baker *(Publisher)*
Helen Gannon *(Sales)*

*Academic & Scholarly; Archaeology;
Cinema, Video, TV & Radio; History &
Antiquarian; Literature & Criticism; Theatre,
Drama & Dance*

Imprints, Series & ISBNs:
Bristol Phoenix Press: 978 1 904675
The Exeter Press: 978 1 905816
University of Exeter Press: 978 0 85989

Parent Company:
The Exeter Press Ltd

Overseas Representation:
Australia & New Zealand: Footprint Books
Pty, Mona Vale, NSW, Australia
*China, Hong Kong, Taiwan & South East
Asia:* Tony Poh, Singapore
France & Italy: Flavio Marcello Publishers'
Agents & Consultants, Padua, Italy
Germany, Austria & Switzerland: SHS
Publishers' Consultants and
Representatives, Oranienberg, Germany
Greece: Charles Gibbes Associates,
Louslitges, France
India: Viva Books Pvt Ltd, New Delhi, India
Japan & Korea: United Publishers Services
Ltd, Tokyo, Japan
Middle East: The Avicenna Partnership,
Oxford, UK
Republic of Ireland: Quantum Publishing
Solutions Ltd, Paisley, UK
Scandinavia: Jan Norbye, Ølstykke,
Denmark
Spain & Portugal: Iberian Book Services,
Madrid, Spain
USA & Canada, Central & South America:
University of Chicago Press, Chicago, IL,
USA

Book Trade Association Membership:
Independent Publishers Guild

2738

UNIVERSITY OF HERTFORDSHIRE PRESS

College Lane, Hatfield, Hertfordshire
AL10 9AB
Telephone: 01707 284654
Fax: 01707 284666
Email: UHPress@herts.ac.uk
Web Site: www.herts.ac.uk/UHPress

Trade Enquiries & Orders:
Central Books Ltd, 99 Wallis Road, London
E9 5LN
Telephone: 0845 458 9911
Fax: 0845 458 9912
Email: info@centralbooks.com
Web Site: www.centralbooks.com

Personnel:
Jane Housham (Press Manager)
Gill Cook (Administration Assistant)
Sarah Elvins (Production Editor)

Academic & Scholarly; Educational &
Textbooks; Environment & Development
Studies; Geography & Geology; History &
Antiquarian; Law; Literature & Criticism;
Magic & the Occult; Mathematics &
Statistics; Psychology & Psychiatry;
Sociology & Anthropology; Theatre, Drama
& Dance

Imprints, Series & ISBNs:
Guidelines for Research in Parapsychology:
    978 0 900458, 978 1 905313
Hertfordshire Publications: 978 0 9542189,
    978 1 905313, 978 1 907396
The Interface Collection: 978 0 900458,
    978 1 905313, 978 1 907396
Regional and Local History: 978 0 900458,
    978 1 905313, 978 1 907396
University of Hertfordshire (Faculties): 978 1
    898543, 978 1 905313, 978 1 907396
University of Hertfordshire Press: 978 1
    902806, 978 1 905313, 978 1 907396

Parent Company:
University of Hertfordshire

Overseas Representation:
Benelux: Netwerk Academic Book Agency,
    Rotterdam, Netherlands
Spain & Portugal: Iberian Book Services,
    Madrid, Spain
USA: Independent Publishers Group (IPG),
    Chicago, IL, USA

Book Trade Association Membership:
Independent Publishers Guild

2739

UNIVERSITY OF OTTAWA PRESS

5 Victoria House, 138 Watling Street,
Towcester NN12 6BT
Telephone: 01327 357770
Fax: 01327 359572
Email: uop@oppuk.co.uk
Web Site: www.press.uottawa.ca

Warehouse & Distribution:
Marston Book Services, 160 Milton Park,
PO Box 169, Abingdon, Oxon OX14 4YN
Telephone: 01235 465521
Email: direct.orders@marston.co.uk
Web Site: www.marston.co.uk

Personnel:
Gary Hall (Marketing Manager)

Academic & Scholarly; Cinema, Video, TV &
Radio; Economics; Educational &
Textbooks; Gender Studies; Industry,
Business & Management; Languages &
Linguistics; Literature & Criticism; Politics &
World Affairs; Reference Books, Directories
& Dictionaries; Sociology & Anthropology;
Theatre, Drama & Dance

New Titles: 10 (2011)

Imprints, Series & ISBNs:
978 1 4426, 978 0 8020

Parent Company:
Canada: University of Ottawa Press

2740

UNIVERSITY OF TORONTO PRESS

5 Victoria House, 138 Watling Street East,
Towcester NN12 6BT
Telephone: 01327 357770
Fax: 01327 359572
Email: toronto@oppuk.co.uk
Web Site: utppublishing.com

Warehouse & Distribution:
NBN International, 10 Thornbury Road,
Plymouth PL6 7PP
Telephone: 01752 202301
Fax: 01752 202331
Email: orders@nbninternational.com
Web Site: www.nbninternational.com

Personnel:
Gary Hall (Manager)

Academic & Scholarly; Cinema, Video, TV &
Radio; Economics; Gender Studies; History
& Antiquarian; Law; Literature & Criticism;
Medical (incl. Self Help & Alternative
Medicine); Military & War; Philosophy;
Politics & World Affairs; Reference Books,
Directories & Dictionaries; Sociology &
Anthropology; Theatre, Drama & Dance

New Titles: 200 (2011)

Imprints, Series & ISBNs:
978 0 8020, 978 1 4426

2741

UNIVERSITY OF WALES PRESS

10 Columbus Walk, Brigantine Place,
Cardiff CF10 4UP
Telephone: 029 2049 6899
Fax: 029 2049 6108
Email: press@press.wales.ac.uk
Web Site: uwp.co.uk

Distribution (UK):
NBN International Ltd, Estover Road,
Plymouth PL6 7PY
Telephone: 01752 202300
Fax: 01752 202330

Personnel:
Helgard Krause (Head of the Press)
Eleri Lloyd-Cresci (Sales & Marketing
    Manager)
Sarah Lewis (Commissioning Editor)
Catrin Harries (Marketing Assistant)
Sian Chapman (Production Manager)

Academic & Scholarly; Archaeology;
Biography & Autobiography; Educational &
Textbooks; Gender Studies; History &
Antiquarian; Illustrated & Fine Editions;
Languages & Linguistics; Literature &
Criticism; Military & War; Music;
Philosophy; Poetry; Politics & World Affairs;
Reference Books, Directories &
Dictionaries; Religion & Theology; Sociology
& Anthropology; Sports & Games

Imprints, Series & ISBNs:
GPC Books: 978 0 7083, 978 0 900768
Gwasg Prifysgol Cymru: 978 0 7083, 978 0
    900768
University of Wales Press: 978 0 7083, 978 0
    900768

Parent Company:
University of Wales

Distributor for:
The Glamorgan County History Trust; Zena
    Publications

Overseas Representation:
India: Maya Publishers Pvt Ltd, New Delhi,
    India
Japan: United Publishers Services Ltd,
    Tokyo, Japan
South East Asia: STM Publisher Services Pte
    Ltd, Singapore
USA, Canada & Australia: Chicago
    University Press, Chicago, IL, USA

Book Trade Association Membership:
Independent Publishers Guild; Literary
Publishers (Wales) Ltd

2742

MERLIN UNWIN BOOKS LTD

Palmers House, 7 Corve Street, Ludlow,
Shropshire SY8 1DB
Telephone: 01584 877456
Fax: 01584 877457
Email: books@merlinunwin.co.uk
Web Site: www.merlinunwin.co.uk

Warehouse & Returns:
Merlin Unwin Books Warehouse, c/
o Wow Distribution, The Yard,
Woofferton Grange, Brimfield, Ludlow
SY8 4NP

Personnel:
Merlin Unwin (Design Director)
Karen McCall (Managing Director, Editorial)
Joanne Potter (Marketing & Production)
Sue Bradley (Finance)

Biography & Autobiography; Cookery,
Wines & Spirits; Humour; Medical (incl. Self
Help & Alternative Medicine); Natural
History; Reference Books, Directories &
Dictionaries; Sports & Games

New Titles: 10 (2010) , 12 (2011)
No of Employees: 4

Imprints, Series & ISBNs:
978 1 873674, 978 1 906122

Book Trade Association Membership:
Independent Publishers Guild

2743

USBORNE PUBLISHING LTD

Usborne House, 83–85 Saffron Hill, London
EC1N 8RT
Telephone: 020 7430 2800
Fax: 020 7242 0974 & 7430 1562
Email: mail@usborne.co.uk
Web Site: www.usborne.com

Warehouse:
HarperCollins, Westerhill Road,
Bishopsbriggs, Glasgow G64 2QT
Telephone: 0141 306 3100
Fax: 0141 306 3767

Personnel:
T. P. Usborne (Managing Director)
R. Jones (General Manager)
J. Tyler (Editorial Director)
D. Harte (Director)
L. Hunt (Director)
K. M. Ball (Company Secretary)
P. Ziedna (Rights Controller)
C. Herisson (UK Marketing)
M. Larkin (Fiction)
G. Lewis (Production)

Children's Books; Computer Science; Crafts
& Hobbies; Fiction; Geography & Geology;
Languages & Linguistics; Music; Natural
History; Reference Books, Directories &
Dictionaries; Scientific & Technical; Sports &
Games

Imprints, Series & ISBNs:
978 0 7460, 978 0 86020

2744

V&A PUBLISHING

Victoria & Albert Museum,
South Kensington, London SW7 2RL
Telephone: 020 7942 2966
Fax: 020 7942 2967
Web Site: www.vandabooks.com

Distribution:
Macmillan Distribution (MDL), Houndmills,
Basingstoke RG21 6XS
Telephone: 01256 302692
Fax: 01256 812558 (UK orders) & 842084
(Export orders)
Email: mdl@macmillan.co.uk
Web Site:
www.macmillandistribution.co.uk

Personnel:
Mark Eastment (Head of Publishing)
Anjali Bulley (Managing Editor)
Nina Jacobson (Rights Manager)
Julie Chan (PR & Marketing Manager)
Clare Davis (Production Manager)
Clare Faulkner (Marketing Manager)
Tom Windross (Senior Editor)

Academic & Scholarly; Antiques &
Collecting; Architecture & Design;
Biography & Autobiography; Children's
Books; Crafts & Hobbies; Fashion &
Costume; Fine Art & Art History; Guide
Books; Photography; Theatre, Drama &
Dance

Imprints, Series & ISBNs:
978 0 905209, 978 0 948107, 978 1 85177

Parent Company:
Victoria & Albert Museum

Overseas Representation:
Australia & New Zealand: Allen & Unwin Pty
    Ltd, Sydney, NSW, Australia
Central & Eastern Europe: Grazyna
    Soszynska, Poznan-Baranowo, Poland
France: Critiques Livres Distribution,
    Bagnolet, France
Germany & Austria: Penguin Books
    Deutschland GmbH, Frankfurt-am-Main,
    Germany
India: Maya Publishers Pvt Ltd, New Delhi,
    India
Italy: Penguin Italia srl, Milan, Italy
Netherlands, Belgium & Luxembourg:
    Penguin Books BV, Amsterdam,
    Netherlands
Singapore, Indonesia & Thailand: APD
    Singapore Pte Ltd, Singapore
South America & Central America: David
    Williams, InterMedia Americana (IMA)
    Ltd, London, UK
Southern Africa: Book Promotions Pty Ltd,
    Cape Town, South Africa
Spain & Portugal: Penguin Books SA,
    Madrid, Spain
Turkey, Africa, Middle East, Japan, Hong
    Kong, Taiwan, Korea, Scandinavia,
    Switzerland, Malta, Greece, Cyprus,
    Israel, China & Philippines: International
    Sales Department, Penguin Books Ltd,
    London, UK
USA: Harry N. Abrams Inc, New York, NY,
    USA

Book Trade Association Membership:
Independent Publishers Guild; International
Association of Museum Publishers

2745

VALLENTINE MITCHELL PUBLISHERS

29–45 High Street, Edgware, Middx
HA8 7UU
Telephone: 020 8952 9526
Fax: 020 8952 9242
Email: info@vmbooks.com
Web Site: www.vmbooks.com

Trade Distribution:
NBN International, 10 Thornbury Road,
Plymouth PL6 7PP
Telephone: 01752 202301
Fax: 01752 202331
Email: orders@nbninternational.com
Web Site: www.nbninternational.com

Personnel:
Stewart Cass *(Managing Director)*
Jenni Tinson *(Production)*
Mariel Deegan *(Sales & Marketing, Publicity)*
Heather Marchant *(Editor)*
Deborah Mulqueen *(Accounts)*

*Academic & Scholarly; Biography &
Autobiography; History & Antiquarian;
Military & War; Politics & World Affairs;
Religion & Theology*

Imprints, Series & ISBNs:
978 0 85303

Overseas Representation:
North America: ISBS, Portland, OR, USA

Book Trade Association Membership:
Independent Publishers Guild

2746

*VELOCE PUBLISHING LTD
Veloce House,
Parkway Farm Business Estate,
Middle Farm Way, Poundbury, Dorchester
DT1 3AR
Telephone: 01305 260068
Fax: 01305 268864
Email: veloce@veloce.co.uk
Web Site: www.veloce.co.uk

Personnel:
Rod Grainger *(Publisher)*
Judith Brooks *(Company Secretary)*

*Animal Care & Breeding; Biography &
Autobiography; Illustrated & Fine Editions;
Military & War; Reference Books,
Directories & Dictionaries; Sports & Games;
Transport*

Imprints, Series & ISBNs:
978 1 84584, 978 1 874105, 978 1
901295, 978 1 903706, 978 1 904788

Overseas Representation:
Australia & New Zealand: Capricorn Link
(Australia) Pty Ltd, Windsor, NSW,
Australia
France: Editions du Palmier, Nîmes, France;
Librairie du Collectionneur, Paris, France
Germany: Heel-Verlag, Konigswinter,
Germany
Germany, Austria & Benelux: Anselm
Robinson, London, UK
Japan: Shimada & Co Inc, Tokyo, Japan;
Takahara Bookstore Co Ltd, Aichi-ken,
Japan
New Zealand: South Pacific Books (Imports)
Ltd, Auckland, New Zealand; TechBooks,
Auckland, New Zealand
Scandinavia: Angell Eurosales, Berwick-on-
Tweed, UK; MarGie Bookshop,
Stockholm, Sweden
South Africa: Motor Books, Johannesburg,
South Africa
South East Asia: Ashton International
Marketing Services, Sevenoaks, Kent, UK
Spain & Italy: Bookport Associates, Corsico
(MI), Italy; Libro Motor SI, Madrid, Spain
USA: Motorbooks International Inc,
Osceola, WI, USA

2747

VERITAS PUBLICATIONS
Veritas House, 7–8 Lower Abbey Street,
Dublin 1, Republic of Ireland
Telephone: +353 (0)1 878 8177
Fax: +353 (0)1 878 6507
Email: publications@veritas.ie
Web Site: www.veritas.ie

Send Orders to:
Veritas Warehouse, Veritas Distribution,
14 Rosemount Business Park, Ballycoolin,
Dublin 11, Republic of Ireland
Email: warehouse@veritas.ie
Web Site: www.veritas.ie

Personnel:
Maura Hyland *(Director)*
Aidan Chester *(Commercial Manager)*
Caitriona Clarke *(Manager of Publications)*
Eamonn Connelly *(Financial Controller)*
Donna Doherty *(Commissioning Editor)*
Derek Byrne *(Publicity & Marketing)*
Liam McCabe *(Sales Agent)*

*Academic & Scholarly; Biography &
Autobiography; Children's Books;
Educational & Textbooks; Philosophy;
Religion & Theology*

Imprints, Series & ISBNs:
978 0 85390, 978 0 86217, 978 1 84730,
978 1 85390

Parent Company:
Republic of Ireland: Veritas
Communications

Distributor for:
USA: Abbey Press; Abingdon Press; ACTA;
Augsburg Press; Ave Maria Press;
Bantam Press; Baronius Press; Candle
Books; Catholic Truth Society; Catholic
Word; Crossroad Publishing; Darton,
Longman and Todd; Doubleday;
Eerdman; HarperCollins; HarperOne;
Ignatius Press; Liturgy Training
Publications; Orbis Books; Our Sunday
Visitor / Oxford University Press / Piatkus /
Sheldon Press / SPCK

Overseas Representation:
Australia: John Garrett Publishing,
Mulgrave, Vic, Australia
Malta: Libreria Taghlim Nisrani, Sliema,
Malta
New Zealand: Catholic Supplies (NZ) Ltd,
Wellington, New Zealand
South Africa: The Catholic Bookshop, Cape
Town, South Africa; St Augustine's
Catholic Bookshop, Port Elizabeth, South
Africa
USA: Acta, Chicago, IL, USA; Dufour
Editions Inc, Chester Springs, PA, USA;
Ignatius Press, San Francisco, CA, USA

Book Trade Association Membership:
Publishing Ireland (Foilsiú Éireann)

2748

VERTICAL EDITIONS
Unit 4a, Snaygill Industrial Estate, Skipton,
North Yorkshire BD23 2QR
Telephone: 01756 790362
Fax: 01756 798618
Email: custserv@verticaleditions.com
Web Site: www.verticaleditions.com

Personnel:
Karl Waddicor *(Publisher)*
Diane Evans *(Editor)*

*Biography & Autobiography; Cinema,
Video, TV & Radio; History & Antiquarian;
Sports & Games*

New Titles: 10 (2011)

Imprints, Series & ISBNs:
978 1 904091

Book Trade Association Membership:
Independent Publishers Guild

2749

*VOLTAIRE FOUNDATION LTD
University of Oxford, 99 Banbury Road,
Oxford OX2 6JX

Telephone: 01865 284600
Fax: 01865 284610
Email: email@voltaire.ox.ac.uk
Web Site: www.voltaire.ox.ac.uk

Distribution:
Marston Book Services, 160 Milton Park,
Abingdon, Oxon OX14 4YN
Telephone: 01235 465521 (Trade) &
465500 (Direct Sales)
Fax: 01235 465555 (Trade) & 465556
(Direct Sales)
Email: trade.orders@marston.co.uk &
direct.orders@marston.co.uk
Web Site: www.marston.co.uk

Personnel:
Prof Nicholas Cronk *(Director)*
Clare Fletcher *(Sales, Marketing, Publisher)*
Janet Godden *(Editorial Manager)*
Lyn Roberts *(Senior Publishing, SVEC
Manager)*
Liz Hancock *(Sales, Marketing, Rights &
Permissions, Admin Support)*

*Academic & Scholarly; Bibliography &
Library Science; Biography &
Autobiography; Electronic (Professional &
Academic); Fiction; History & Antiquarian;
Languages & Linguistics; Literature &
Criticism; Philosophy; Reference Books,
Directories & Dictionaries; Religion &
Theology*

Imprints, Series & ISBNs:
Correspondance complète de Françoise de
Graffigny: 978 0 7294
Correspondance complète de Jean Jacques
Rousseau: 978 0 7294
Correspondance complète de Pierre Bayle:
978 0 7294
Correspondance générale de La Beaumelle:
978 0 7294
Œuvres complètes de Montesquieu: 978 0
7294
Œuvres complètes de Voltaire: 978 0 7294
SVEC (Studies on Voltaire and the
Eighteenth Century): 978 0 7294
Vif Une nouvelle collection en livre de
poche: 978 0 7294

Parent Company:
University of Oxford

Overseas Representation:
France: Aux Amateurs de Livres, Paris,
France

2750

WARBURG INSTITUTE
University of London, Woburn Square,
London WC1H 0AB
Telephone: 020 7862 8949
Fax: 020 7862 8955
Email: warburg.books@sas.ac.uk
Web Site: warburg.sas.ac.uk

*Academic & Scholarly; Archaeology;
Architecture & Design; Bibliography &
Library Science; Biography &
Autobiography; Fine Art & Art History;
History & Antiquarian; Magic & the Occult;
Philosophy; Religion & Theology*

New Titles: 4 (2011)

Imprints, Series & ISBNs:
Special Publications (Warburg): 978 0
85481
Studies of the Warburg Institute: 978 0
85481
Warburg Institute Colloquia: 978 0 85481
Warburg Institute Surveys and Texts: 978 0
85481
Warburg Studies and Texts: 978 0 85481

Overseas Representation:
Italy: Nino Aragno Editore, Savigliano, Italy

2751

WARD LOCK EDUCATIONAL CO LTD
Bic Ling Kee House, 1 Christopher Road,
East Grinstead, West Sussex RH19 3BT
Telephone: 01342 318980
Fax: 01342 410980
Web Site: www.wardlockeducational.com

Personnel:
Au Bak Ling *(Chairman – Hong Kong)*
Eileen Parsons *(Company Secretary & Sales,
Rights & Permissions)*

*Biology & Zoology; Chemistry; Educational
& Textbooks; Geography & Geology;
Mathematics & Statistics; Music; Physics;
Religion & Theology*

Imprints, Series & ISBNs:
978 0 7062

Parent Company:
Ling Kee (UK) Ltd

Associated Companies:
BLA Publishing Ltd

Overseas Representation:
Australia (KMP only): Concept Mathematics
Pty Ltd, Frankston, Vic, Australia
Canada: Bacon & Hughes Ltd, Ottawa, Ont,
Canada
Republic of Ireland: International
Educational Services, Leixlip, Republic of
Ireland

2752

WATERSIDE PRESS
Sherfield Gables, Reading Road,
Sherfield-on-Loddon, Hook, Hants
RG27 0JG
Telephone: 0845 2300 733
Fax: 01256 883987
Email: enquiries@watersidepress.co.uk
Web Site: www.WatersidePress.co.uk

Personnel:
Bryan Gibson *(Proprietor)*

*Academic & Scholarly; Biography &
Autobiography; Crime; Educational &
Textbooks; Electronic (Educational);
Electronic (Professional & Academic);
History & Antiquarian; Law; Reference
Books, Directories & Dictionaries; Sociology
& Anthropology*

New Titles: 15 (2010) , 22 (2011)

Imprints, Series & ISBNs:
978 1 872870, 978 1 904380, 978 1
906534, 978 1 908162

Overseas Representation:
USA: International Specialized Book
Services Inc, Portland, OR, USA

2753

PAUL WATKINS PUBLISHING
1 High Street, Donington, Lincs PE11 4TA
Telephone: 01775 821542
Email: pwatkins@
pwatkinspublishing.fsnet.co.uk

Personnel:
Dr Shaun Tyas *(Proprietor)*

*Academic & Scholarly; Architecture &
Design; Fine Art & Art History; History &
Antiquarian; Languages & Linguistics;
Nautical*

New Titles: 10 (2011)

Imprints, Series & ISBNs:
Shaun Tyas: 978 1 900289
Paul Watkins: 978 1 871615

Distributor for:
Caedmon of Whitby; English Place-Name Society; Richard III and Yorkist History Trust; Society for Name Studies in Britain and Ireland

Book Trade Association Membership:
Small Press Centre

2754 ▬▬▬▬

WAVERLEY BOOKS
144 Port Dundas Road, Glasgow G4 0HZ
Telephone: 0141 567 2830
Fax: 0141 567 2831
Email: liz@waverley-books.co.uk
Web Site: www.waverley-books.co.uk

Warehouse:
Booksource, 50 Cambuslang Road,
Glasgow G32 8NB
Telephone: 0845 370 0067
Fax: 0845 370 0068

Personnel:
Ron Grosset (*Publisher*)
Liz Small (*Sales & Marketing*)

Atlases & Maps; Children's Books; Cookery, Wines & Spirits; History & Antiquarian; Magic & the Occult; Medical (incl. Self Help & Alternative Medicine); Reference Books, Directories & Dictionaries

New Titles: 40 (2011)
No of Employees: 7
Annual Turnover: £1M

Imprints, Series & ISBNs:
978 1 84934, 978 1 85534, 978 1 902407

Parent Company:
D. C. Thomson & Co Ltd

Associated Companies:
Waverley Books Ltd

Overseas Representation:
Philippines: WS Pacific, Philippines
Russia: Alexander Korzhenevski, Alex Agency, Moscow, Russia
South Africa: Peter Matthews, Zambia

Book Trade Association Membership:
Publishing Scotland

2755 ▬▬▬▬

WEIDENFELD & NICOLSON
[imprint of The Orion Publishing Group Ltd]
Orion House, 5 Upper St Martin's Lane,
London WC2H 9EA
Telephone: 020 7240 3444
Fax: 020 7240 4822

Trade Counter & Warehouse:
Littlehampton Book Services Ltd,
Faraday Close, Durrington, Worthing,
West Sussex BN13 3RB
Telephone: 01903 828500
Fax: 01903 828802

Personnel:
Lisa Milton (*Managing Director*)
Alan Samson (*Publisher – Non-Fiction*)
Kirsty Dunseath (*Publishing Director – Fiction*)
Michael Dover (*Editor-in-Chief*)
Rowland White (*Publisher – Non-Fiction*)

Biography & Autobiography; Fiction; Humour; Illustrated & Fine Editions; Industry, Business & Management; Law; Philosophy; Photography; Politics & World Affairs; Sports & Games; Travel & Topography

Imprints, Series & ISBNs:
978 0 297

Parent Company:
The Orion Publishing Group Ltd

Overseas Representation:
see: The Orion Publishing Group Ltd,
London, UK

2756 ▬▬▬▬

*JOSEPH WEINBERGER LTD
12–14 Mortimer Street, London W1T 3JJ
Telephone: 020 7580 2827
Fax: 020 7436 9616
Email: general.info@jwmail.co.uk
Web Site: www.josef-weinberger.com

Personnel:
Sean Gray (*Managing Director*)
Robert Heath (*Financial Director*)
Michael Callahan (*Plays Division Manager*)

Theatre, Drama & Dance

Imprints, Series & ISBNs:
Dramatists Play Service Inc: 978 0 8222
Josef Weinberger Plays: 978 0 85676

Distributor for:
USA: Dramatists Play Service Inc

Overseas Representation:
Australia: Hal Leonard (Australia),
Melbourne, Vic, Australia
New Zealand: Play Bureau of New Zealand
Ltd, New Plymouth, New Zealand
Republic of Ireland & Northern Ireland:
Drama League of Ireland, Dublin,
Republic of Ireland
South Africa: Dalro (Pty) Ltd, Braamfontein,
South Africa
USA: Dramatists Play Service Inc, New York,
NY, USA

2757 ▬▬▬▬

WHICH? LTD
2 Marylebone Road, London NW1 4DF
Telephone: 020 7770 7000
Fax: 020 7770 7600
Email: which@which.co.uk
Web Site: www.which.co.uk

Send orders to:
Littlehampton Book Services Ltd,
Faraday Close, Durrington, Worthing,
West Sussex BN13 3RB
Telephone: 01903 828500

Personnel:
Angela Newton (*Head of Book Publishing*)

Accountancy & Taxation; Computer Science; Gardening; Law; Photography; Reference Books, Directories & Dictionaries; Vocational Training & Careers

New Titles: 8 (2010) , 8 (2011)

Imprints, Series & ISBNs:
978 1 84490

2758 ▬▬▬▬

THE WHITE ROW PRESS
135 Cumberland Road, Dundonald, Belfast
BT16 2BB
Telephone: 028 9087 4861
Email: info@whiterowpress.com
Web Site: www.whiterowpress.com

Imprints, Series & ISBNs:
978 1 870132

2759 ▬▬▬▬

WHITING & BIRCH LTD
90 Dartmouth Road, London SE23 3HZ
Telephone: 020 8244 2421
Fax: 020 8244 2448
Email: enquiries@whitingbirch.net
Web Site: www.whitingbirch.net

Personnel:
David Whiting (*Director*)
Diana Birch (*Director*)

Academic & Scholarly; Medical (incl. Self Help & Alternative Medicine); Psychology & Psychiatry; Sociology & Anthropology

New Titles: 2 (2010) , 14 (2011)
No of Employees: 4

Imprints, Series & ISBNs:
978 1 86177, 978 1 871177

Overseas Representation:
Australia: Lightning Source AU Pty Ltd,
Scoresby, Vic, Australia
USA: Ingram Publisher Services Inc,
Chambersburg, PA, USA; Lightning
Source Inc (US), Lavergne, TN, USA

2760 ▬▬▬▬

WHITTET BOOKS LTD
1, St John's Lane, Stansted, Essex
CM24 8JU
Telephone: 01279 815871
Fax: 01279 647564
Email: mail@whittetbooks.com
Web Site: www.whittetbooks.com

Sales Office:
Book Systems Plus, 1st Floor, 8 Hill Street,
Saffron Walden, Essex CB10 1JD
Telephone: 01799 524458
Fax: 01799 524459
Email: mail@booksystemsplus.com
Web Site: www.booksystemsplus.com

Personnel:
George Papa (*Managing Director*)
Shirley Greenall (*Publisher*)

Animal Care & Breeding; Biology & Zoology; Gardening; Natural History; Veterinary Science

Imprints, Series & ISBNs:
978 0 905483, 978 1 873580

Parent Company:
Book Systems Plus Ltd

Overseas Representation:
USA & Canada: Diamond Farm Book
Publishers, Brighton, Canada

2761 ▬▬▬▬

WHITTLES PUBLISHING
Dunbeath Mill, Dunbeath, Caithness
KW6 6EG
Telephone: 01593 731333
Fax: 01593 731400
Email: info@whittlespublishing.com
Web Site: www.whittlespublishing.com

Warehouse/Distributor:
BookSource, 50 Cambuslang Road,
Glasgow G32 8NB
Telephone: 0845 370 0063
Fax: 0845 370 0064
Email: customerservice@booksource.net
Web Site: www.booksource.net

Personnel:
Dr Keith Whittles (*Publisher*)
Mrs Sue Steven (*Sales & Promotions Manager*)
Ms Shelley Teasdale (*Production Editor*)

Academic & Scholarly; Biography & Autobiography; Educational & Textbooks; Engineering; Geography & Geology; Military & War; Natural History; Nautical; Reference Books, Directories & Dictionaries; Scientific & Technical

Imprints, Series & ISBNs:
978 1 84995, 978 1 870325, 978 1 904445

Distributor for:
Talisman Publishing

Overseas Representation:
Australia, New Zealand & Papua New

Guinea: James Bennett Pty Ltd, Belrose,
NSW, Australia
Germany, Austria & Switzerland: Missing
Link International Booksellers, Bremen,
Germany
Hong Kong, China, Taiwan & Korea: Asia
Publishers Services Ltd, Hong Kong
India: Sara Books Pvt Ltd, New Delhi, India
*Latin America, Caribbean & Sub-Saharan
Africa:* InterMedia Americana (IMA) Ltd,
London, UK
*Singapore, Malaysia, Brunei, Philippines,
Indonesia, Thailand, Laos, Cambodia &
Vietnam:* APD Singapore Pte Ltd,
Singapore
South Africa: Book Promotions (Pty) Ltd,
South Africa

Book Trade Association Membership:
Publishing Scotland

2762 ▬▬▬▬

WILD GOOSE PUBLICATIONS
4th Floor, Savoy House,
140 Sauchiehall Street, Glasgow G2 3DH
Telephone: 0141 332 6292
Fax: 0141 332 1090
Email: admin@ionabooks.com
Web Site: www.ionabooks.com

Trade Orders:
BookSource, 50 Cambuslang Road,
Glasgow G32 8NB
Email: orders@booksource.net
Web Site: www.booksource.net

Personnel:
Sandra Kramer (*Publishing Manager*)
Alex O'Neill (*Assistant Publishing Manager (Marketing)*)
Jane Riley (*Production*)
Lorna Rae Sutton (*Publishing Officer (Marketing)*)
Neil Paynter (*Project Editor*)

Music; Religion & Theology

No of Employees: 5

Imprints, Series & ISBNs:
978 0 947988, 978 1 901557, 978 1
905010

Parent Company:
The Iona Community

Overseas Representation:
Australia & New Zealand: Willow
Connection Pty Ltd, Brookvale, NSW,
Australia
Canada: Novalis Inc, Toronto, Ont, Canada
New Zealand: Pleroma Christian Supplies,
Otane, Central Hawkes Bay, New Zealand

Book Trade Association Membership:
Independent Publishers Guild

2763 ▬▬▬▬

JOHN WILEY & SONS LTD
The Atrium, Southern Gate, Chichester,
West Sussex PO19 8SQ
Telephone: 01243 779777
Fax: 01243 775878
Web Site: www.wiley.com

Send Orders to:
John Wiley & Sons Ltd,
European Distribution Centre,
New Era Estate, Oldlands Way,
Bognor Regis, West Sussex PO22 9NQ
Telephone: 01243 779777
Fax: 01243 843123
Email: customer@wiley.com
Web Site: www.wiley.com

Also at:
John Wiley & Sons Ltd,
9600 Garsington Road, Oxford OX4 2DQ
Telephone: 01865 776868
Web Site: www.wiley.com

Personnel:
C. J. Dicks *(Managing Director, International Finance & Operations)*
P. Kisray *(Vice-President, International Development)*
C. Nobbs *(Vice-President, Distribution & Customer Service, Europe, Middle East & Africa)*
D. Bova *(Vice-President & Director, HR, Europe)*
S. Joshua *(Director of Legal Affairs, Europe)*
M. Davis *(Vice-President & Managing Director, Life Sciences Editorial)*
A. Robinson *(Vice-President & Managing Director, Health Sciences Editorial)*
P. Carpenter *(Vice-President & Managing Director, SSH Journals Editorial)*
J. Walmsley *(Vice-President & Managing Director, Physical Sciences Editorial)*
S. Stevens *(Vice-President, HE Development, EMEA & Asia)*
C. Hall *(Vice-President & Director, Finance, STMS)*
U. D'Arcy *(Financial Director, Corporate Finance)*
M. Leete *(Vice-President & Consumer & Technology Publishing Director)*
K Wootton *(Sales Director EMEA)*

Academic & Scholarly; Accountancy & Taxation; Agriculture; Animal Care & Breeding; Archaeology; Architecture & Design; Atlases & Maps; Aviation; Biography & Autobiography; Biology & Zoology; Chemistry; Computer Science; Cookery, Wines & Spirits; Crafts & Hobbies; Do-It-Yourself; Economics; Educational & Textbooks; Electronic (Educational); Electronic (Professional & Academic); Engineering; Environment & Development Studies; Fashion & Costume; Fiction; Gardening; Geography & Geology; Guide Books; Health & Beauty; History & Antiquarian; Industry, Business & Management; Languages & Linguistics; Literature & Criticism; Mathematics & Statistics; Medical (incl. Self Help & Alternative Medicine); Military & War; Music; Natural History; Nautical; Philosophy; Photography; Physics; Poetry; Politics & World Affairs; Psychology & Psychiatry; Reference Books, Directories & Dictionaries; Religion & Theology; Scientific & Technical; Sociology & Anthropology; Sports & Games; Travel & Topography; Veterinary Science

Imprints, Series & ISBNs:
978 0 470, 978 0 471

Parent Company:
USA: John Wiley & Sons Inc

Associated Companies:
Blackwell Publishing (Holdings) Ltd;
Blackwell Publishing Ltd; Blackwell
Science (Overseas Holding); Blackwell
Science Ltd; Capstone Publishing Ltd;
Inpharm-Internet Services Ltd; John
Wiley & Sons Ltd; John Wiley & Sons UK
LLP; Whurr Publishers Ltd; Wiley
Distribution Services Ltd; Wiley Europe
Investment Holdings Ltd.; Wiley Europe
Ltd; Wiley Heyden Ltd; Wiley Interface
Ltd; Wiley Pharmafile Ltd; Wiley U.K.
(Unlimited Co.); Wiley-Blackwell Ltd
Germany: Wiley-VCH Verlag GmbH

Distributor for:
USA: California University Press; Columbia
University Press; Harvard University
Press; Johns Hopkins University Press;
Loeb Classical Library; O'Reilly UK Ltd;
Princeton University Press; Sybex
International Corp; The MIT Press; The
University of Chicago Press; W. W.
Norton & Co Ltd; Yale University Press

Book Trade Association Membership:
Publishers Association; Booksellers
Association; Educational Publishers

Council; International Group of Scientific,
Medical & Technical Publishers

2764 ▬▬▬

WILLOW ISLAND EDITIONS
41 Water Lane, Middlestown, Wakefield,
West Yorkshire WF4 4PX
Telephone: 01924 270723
Email: richard@willowisland.co.uk
Web Site: www.willowisland.co.uk

Personnel:
Richard Bell *(Contact)*

Crafts & Hobbies; Gardening; Guide Books; Natural History; Travel & Topography

Imprints, Series & ISBNs:
978 1 902467

2765 ▬▬▬

NEIL WILSON PUBLISHING LTD
O/2 19 Netherton Avenue, Glasgow
G13 1BQ
Telephone: 0141 954 8007
Fax: 0560 150 4806
Email: info@nwp.co.uk
Web Site: www.nwp.co.uk

**Distribution, Sales Ledger & Trade
Orders:**
BookSource, 50 Cambuslang Road,
Glasgow G32 5NB
Telephone: 0845 370 0067
Fax: 0845 370 0068
Email: orders@booksource.net
Web Site: www.booksource.net

Personnel:
Neil Wilson *(Managing Director, Sales, Rights & Permissions)*

Biography & Autobiography; Cookery, Wines & Spirits; Crime; Guide Books; History & Antiquarian; Humour; Military & War; Music; Nautical; Travel & Topography

New Titles: 12 (2010) , 6 (2011)
No of Employees: 1
Annual Turnover: £100,000

Imprints, Series & ISBNs:
978 1 897784, 978 1 903238, 978 1
    906476
11:9
The Angel's Share
The In Pinn
The Vital Spark

Overseas Representation:
Republic of Ireland: Geoff Bryan, Dublin,
    Republic of Ireland
Scotland: Don Morrison
USA: Interlink Publishing Group Inc,
    Northampton, MA, USA

Book Trade Association Membership:
Publishing Scotland

2766 ▬▬▬

PHILIP WILSON PUBLISHERS
6 Salem Road, London W2 4BU
Telephone: 020 7243 1225
Fax: 020 7243 1226
Email: sales@philip-wilson.co.uk
Web Site: www.philip-wilson.co.uk

Personnel:
Jonathan McDonnell *(Managing Director)*
Philip Wilson *(Publisher)*
Anne Jackson *(Commissioning Editor)*
Liz Stuckey *(Company Secretary)*

Academic & Scholarly; Antiques & Collecting; Architecture & Design; Fine Art & Art History; History & Antiquarian; Illustrated & Fine Editions; Photography

Imprints, Series & ISBNs:
978 0 85667

Parent Company:
UK: I.B. Tauris & Co Ltd

Distributor for:
India: Niyogi Books

Overseas Representation:
USA: Palgrave Macmillan, New York, NY,
    USA
Worldwide: I. B. Tauris & Co Ltd, London,
    UK

2767 ▬▬▬

WINDHORSE PUBLICATIONS
169 Mill Road, Cambridge CB1 3AN
Telephone: 01223 213300
Email: info@windhorsepublications.com
Web Site:
    www.windhorsepublications.com

UK Trade Orders:
BookSource, 50 Cambuslang Road,
Cambuslang, Glasgow G32 8NB
Telephone: 0845 370 0063
Fax: 0845 370 0064
Email: customerservice@booksource.net
Web Site: www.booksource.net

Personnel:
Peter Joseph *(Publishing Director)*
Lee Smith *(Publishing Assistant)*
Lee Walford *(Accountant)*

Biography & Autobiography; Medical (incl. Self Help & Alternative Medicine); Philosophy; Religion & Theology

New Titles: 5 (2010) , 5 (2011)
No of Employees: 3
Annual Turnover: £120,000

Imprints, Series & ISBNs:
978 0 904766, 978 1 899579, 978 1
    907314

Overseas Representation:
Asia: Horizon Books Pte Ltd, Singapore
Australia & New Zealand: Windhorse
    Books, Newtown, NSW, Australia
South Africa: Stephan Phillips (Pty) Ltd,
    Cape Town, South Africa
USA: Consortium Book Sales & Distribution
    Inc, St Paul, MN, USA

2768 ▬▬▬

WIT PRESS
Ashurst Lodge, Ashurst, Southampton,
Hampshire SO40 7AA
Telephone: 023 8029 3223
Fax: 023 8029 2853
Email: witpress@witpress.com
Web Site: www.witpress.com

Personnel:
Prof C. A. Brebbia *(Chairman)*
David Anderson *(Chief Executive Officer)*
B. S. Privett *(Production Manager)*
Ms Lorraine Carter *(Sales Co-ordinator)*

Academic & Scholarly; Archaeology; Architecture & Design; Biology & Zoology; Computer Science; Electronic (Professional & Academic); Engineering; Environment & Development Studies; Geography & Geology; Industry, Business & Management; Mathematics & Statistics; Medical (incl. Self Help & Alternative Medicine); Scientific & Technical; Transport

New Titles: 48 (2010) , 48 (2011)
No of Employees: 10
Annual Turnover: £500,000

Imprints, Series & ISBNs:
978 0 905451, 978 1 84564, 978 1 85312

Associated Companies:
USA: Computational Mechanics
    International Ltd

Book Trade Association Membership:
LAPSLD

2769 ▬▬▬

WITHERBY PUBLISHING GROUP
4 Dunlop Square, Deans, Livingston,
West Lothian EH54 8SB
Telephone: 01506 463227
Fax: 01506 468999
Email: info@emailws.com
Web Site: www.witherbyseamanship.com

Personnel:
Iain Macneil *(Managing Director)*
Kat Heathcote *(Director)*
Stewart Heney *(General Manager)*
Alison Hunter Gordon *(Personal Assistant to Director)*

Law; Nautical; Reference Books, Directories & Dictionaries; Transport; Travel & Topography

New Titles: 50 (2010) , 60 (2011)
No of Employees: 30
Annual Turnover: £3M

Imprints, Series & ISBNs:
978 0 900886, 978 0 948691, 978 1 85609

Distributor for:
Chartered Institute of Loss Adjustors;
    Chemical Distribution Institute; Institute
    of Chartered Shipbrokers; Institute of
    Risk Management; Intercargo;
    International Association of Classification
    Societies; International Institute of
    Marine Surveying; International Marine
    Pilots Association; International Maritime
    Organization; International Tanker
    Owners' Pollution Federation;
    INTERTANKO; Nautical Institute; Oil
    Companies International Marine Forum;
    Skuld; Society of International Gas
    Tanker & Terminal Operators

Overseas Representation:
Australia: Boat Books, St Kilda, Vic,
    Australia
Belgium: Bogerd Martin NV
Canada: Marine Press of Canada
Denmark: Iver Weilbach & Co A/S
Greece: Vanos SA
Hong Kong: Hong Kong Ships Supplies Co,
    Hong Kong
India: C & C Marine Combine
Italy: C.A.I.M. ARL
Japan: Cornes & Co, Tokyo, Japan
Norway: Nautisk Forlag A/S
Singapore: DPM Singapore Pte Ltd; E W
    Liner Charts And Publications; Motion
    Smith; Nautisk Forlag AS (Singapore)
South Korea: Korea Ocean Development
Taiwan: Hong Yunn Sea Professional Co Ltd
USA: New York Nautical, New York, USA

Book Trade Association Membership:
Publishing Scotland; Independent
Publishers Guild

2770 ▬▬▬

***WOLTERS KLUWER HEALTH (P & E)
LTD**
250 Waterloo Road, London SE1 8RD
Telephone: 020 7981 0500
Fax: 020 7981 0565
Email: enquiry@lww.co.uk
Web Site: www.lww.co.uk

Orders to:
NBN International, Estover Road, Plymouth
PL6 7PY
Telephone: 01752 202301
Fax: 01752 202331
Email: lww.orders@nbninternational.com
Web Site: www.nbninternational.com

Personnel:
Mrs Linda Albin (*Regional Director, Europe*)
Mr Andrew Davis (*Marketing Services Director*)
Mr Carlos Davis (*Vice-President & General Manager, International*)
Ms Sharon Zinner (*Senior International Director of Marketing & Business Development*)
Mr John Youens (*Sales Director: Middle East, Africa & Latin America*)
Ms Rachel Hendrick (*Acquisitions Editor*)
Ms Gemma Gillen (*Senior Sales Co-ordinator*)
Ms Alison Major (*Marketing Executive-Medical Education, Health Professions, Anatomical Charts & Nursing*)
Mr Daniel Raphael (*Marketing Executive-Clinical*)
Ms Jessica Buckingham (*Marketing Executive- Exhibitions*)

Academic & Scholarly; Educational & Textbooks; Electronic (Professional & Academic); Medical (incl. Self Help & Alternative Medicine); Psychology & Psychiatry; Reference Books, Directories & Dictionaries; Scientific & Technical

Imprints, Series & ISBNs:
AmirSys: 978 1 931884
Blackwell's (transferred list): 978 1 4051
Facts & Comparisons: 978 1 5121, 978 1 57439
Lippincott Raven: 978 0 316, 978 0 397
Lippincott Williams & Wilkins: 978 0 7817, 978 1 4051, 978 1 4511, 978 1 58255, 978 1 60547, 978 1 60831, 978 1 60913
Lippincott Williams & Wilkins – Spanish Language: 978 84 96921
Springhouse: 978 0 7817, 978 1 58255
Williams & Wilkins: 978 0 316, 978 0 683

Parent Company:
Netherlands: Wolters Kluwer

Associated Companies:
USA: Lippincott Williams & Wilkins / Wolters Kluwer Health (Professional & Education); Ovid / Wolter Kluwer Health (Market Research); Wolters Kluwer Health

Distributor for:
USA: AmirSys

Overseas Representation:
Eastern Europe: Jacek Lewinson, Publisher's Agents, Warsaw, Poland
Scandinavia: Colin Flint Ltd, Cambridge, UK
Spain: Lippincott Williams & Wilkins / Wolters Kluwer Health (Professional & Education), Barcelona, Spain

Book Trade Association Membership:
Publishers Association

2771 ━━━━━━

*THE WOMEN'S PRESS
27 Goodge Street, London W1T 2LD
Telephone: 020 7636 3992
Fax: 020 7637 1866
Email: david@the-womens-press.com
Web Site: www.the-womens-press.com

Warehouse:
NBN International Ltd, Estover Road, Plymouth PL6 7PY
Telephone: 01752 202300
Fax: 01752 202330
Email: control@nbninternational.com
Web Site: www.nbninternational.com

Personnel:
David Elliott (*Director*)

Biography & Autobiography; Crime; Fiction; Gay & Lesbian Studies; Gender Studies; Health & Beauty; Literature &

Criticism; Politics & World Affairs; Psychology & Psychiatry; Reference Books, Directories & Dictionaries

Overseas Representation:
Africa, Eastern Europe, Caribbean & South America: InterMedia Americana (IMA) Ltd, London, UK
Australia: The Scribo Group, Frenchs Forest, NSW, Australia
Europe: Ted Dougherty, London, UK
USA: Interlink Publishing Group Inc, Northampton, MA, USA

2772 ━━━━━━

*WOODHEAD PUBLISHING LTD
[incorporating Chandos Publishing]
Abington Hall, Granta Park,
Great Abington, Cambridge CB21 6AH
Telephone: 01223 891358
Fax: 01223 893694
Email: custserv@woodhead-publishing.com
Web Site: www.woodheadpublishing.com

Warehouse & Distribution:
Combined Book Services, Units I/K,
Paddock Wood Distribution Centre,
Paddock Wood, Tonbridge, Kent TN12 6UU
Telephone: 01892 837171
Fax: 01892 837272
Email: (as above)

Personnel:
Martin Woodhead (*Managing Director*)
R. Burleigh (*Finance Director*)
Francis Dodds (*Editorial Director*)
Neil MacLeod (*Marketing Manager*)
Mary Campbell (*Production Manager*)
Sarah Whitworth (*Commissioning Editor*)
Kathryn Picking (*Commissioning Editor*)
Jess Rowley (*Commissioning Editor*)
Sheril Leich (*Commissioning Editor*)
Cliff Elwell (*Commissioning Editor*)
Laura Bunney (*Commissioning Editor*)
Ian Borthwick (*Commissioning Editor*)
Glyn Jones (*Publisher, Chandos Publishing*)

Bibliography & Library Science; Electronic (Professional & Academic); Engineering; Environment & Development Studies; Industry, Business & Management; Law; Mathematics & Statistics; Scientific & Technical

Imprints, Series & ISBNs:
Abington Publishing: 978 1 85573
Chandos Publishing: 978 1 84334
Gresham Books: 978 1 85573
Woodhead Publishing: 978 1 84569, 978 1 85573

Distributor for:
Germany: Beuth (The German Standards Institute); Stahleisen (The German Iron & Steel Institute); VDI (The Association of German Engineers)

Overseas Representation:
China: Ian Taylor & Associates, Beijing, P. R. of China
Eastern Europe & Russia: Dr László Horváth Publishers Representative, Budapest, Hungary
Germany, Austria & Switzerland: Bernd Feldmann, Oranienburg, Germany
Greece, Middle East, Turkey, Cyprus & Malta: Avicenna Partnership, Oxford, UK
India: Sara Books Pvt Ltd, New Delhi, India
Iran: Farhad Maftoon, Tehran, Iran
Italy, Spain, Portugal & France: Flavio Marcello Publishers' Agents & Consultants, Padua, Italy
Japan: Ben Kato, Tokyo, Japan; United Publishers Services Ltd, Tokyo, Japan
Korea: Information & Culture Korea (ICK), Seoul, Republic of Korea
Mexico, Central & South America: Cranbury International LLC, Montpelier, VT, USA

Netherlands, Belgium & Luxembourg: Netwerk Academic Book Agency, Rotterdam, Netherlands
Nigeria: Bounty Books, Ibadan, Nigeria
Pakistan: Tahir M. Lodhi, Lahore, Pakistan
Scandinavia: Jan Norbye, Ølstykke, Denmark
South Africa: Academic Marketing Services, Johannesburg, South Africa
South East Asia: APAC Publishers Services Pte Ltd, Singapore

Book Trade Association Membership:
International Group of Scientific, Medical & Technical Publishers; Independent Publishers Guild

2773 ━━━━━━

WORDSWORTH EDITIONS LTD
8b East Street, Ware, Herts SG12 9HJ
Telephone: 01920 465167
Fax: 01920 462267
Email: enquiries@wordsworth-editions.com
Web Site: www.wordsworth-editions.com

Personnel:
Helen Trayler (*Managing Director*)
Derek Wright (*Finance Director*)

Children's Books; Fiction; Literature & Criticism; Philosophy; Poetry; Reference Books, Directories & Dictionaries

New Titles: 18 (2010) , 18 (2011)
No of Employees: 5
Annual Turnover: £2.4M

Imprints, Series & ISBNs:
978 1 84022, 978 1 85326

Overseas Representation:
Australia & Papua New Guinea: Peribo Pty Ltd, Mount Kuring-Gai, NSW, Australia
India: OM Book Services, Delhi, India
New Zealand: Nationwide Book Distributors Ltd, Oxford, New Zealand
Poland: Top Mark Centre, Warsaw, Poland
Spain: Ribera Libros, SL, Arrigorriaga, Spain
USA: L. B. May & Associates, Knoxville, TN, USA

Book Trade Association Membership:
Booksellers Association

2774 ━━━━━━

*WORLD MICROFILMS
PO Box 35488, St John's Wood, London NW8 6WD
Telephone: 020 7586 4499
Email: microworld@ndirect.co.uk
Web Site: www.microworld.uk.com, www.pidgeondigital.com

Personnel:
S. C. Albert (*Director*)

Academic & Scholarly; Architecture & Design; Cinema, Video, TV & Radio; History & Antiquarian

Imprints, Series & ISBNs:
978 1 85035

Distributor for:
UK: Masters of Architecture; Pidgeon Digital at www.pidgeondigital.com

2775 ━━━━━━

WORTH PRESS LTD
34 South End, Bassingbourn,
S Cambridgeshire SG8 5NJ
Telephone: 01763 248075
Fax: 01763 248155
Email: info@worthpress.co.uk
Web Site: www.worthpress.co.uk

Warehouse:
Antony Rowe Ltd, Units 3 & 4,
Pegasus Way, Bowerhill, Melksham
SN12 6TR
Telephone: 01225 703691
Fax: 01225 704518

Personnel:
Ken Webb (*Chairman*)
Rupert Webb (*Managing Director*)

Architecture & Design; Aviation; Crime; Fiction; Literature & Criticism; Military & War; Natural History; Religion & Theology

New Titles: 10 (2010) , 10 (2011)
No of Employees: 4
Annual Turnover: £650,000

Imprints, Series & ISBNs:
Worth Press Ltd: 978 1 84931, 978 1 903025

Overseas Representation:
Asia: John Beaufoy, Oxford, UK
Europe: Cristina Galimberti, Bristol, UK
Scandinavia: Anglo-Nordic Books, Godalming, UK

2776 ━━━━━━

Y LOLFA CYF
Hen Swyddfa'r Heddlu, Talybont,
Ceredigion SY24 5HE
Telephone: 01970 832304
Fax: 01970 832782
Email: ylolfa@ylolfa.com
Web Site: www.ylolfa.com

Personnel:
Garmon Gruffudd (*Director*)
Sonia Hughes (*Administrator*)
Lefi Gruffudd (*Editor*)
Morgan Tomos (*Marketing*)
Paul Williams (*Production*)

Biography & Autobiography; Children's Books; Cookery, Wines & Spirits; Crafts & Hobbies; Fiction; Guide Books; Humour; Languages & Linguistics; Music; Poetry; Politics & World Affairs; Sports & Games

Imprints, Series & ISBNs:
Dinas
Y Lolfa: 978 0 86243, 978 0 904864

Book Trade Association Membership:
Union of Welsh Publishers & Booksellers

2777 ━━━━━━

YALE UNIVERSITY PRESS LONDON
47 Bedford Square, London WC1B 3DP
Telephone: 020 7079 4900
Fax: 020 7079 4901
Web Site: www.yalebooks.co.uk

Warehouse & Fulfilment:
John Wiley & Sons Ltd, Distribution Centre,
Shripney Road, Bognor Regis, West Sussex
PO22 9SA
Telephone: 01243 829121
Fax: 01243 820250

Personnel:
Robert Baldock (*Managing Director*)
Kate Pocock (*Sales & Marketing Director*)
Gillian Malpass (*Art & Architecture Publisher*)
Sally Salvesen (*Decorative Arts Publisher*)
Heather McCallum (*Trade Books Publisher*)
Katie Harris (*Publicity Manager*)
Charlotte Stafford (*Promotion & Direct Mail Manager*)
Anne Bihan (*Head of Rights*)
Andrew Jarmain (*Sales Manager*)
Stephen Kent (*Production & Design Manager*)
Donal Burke (*Accountant*)
Phoebe Clapham (*Politics, Economics & Current Affairs Editor*)

Academic & Scholarly; Archaeology;
Architecture & Design; Biography &
Autobiography; Economics; Fashion &
Costume; Fine Art & Art History; Gender
Studies; History & Antiquarian; Illustrated &
Fine Editions; Languages & Linguistics;
Military & War; Music; Natural History;
Philosophy; Photography; Politics & World
Affairs; Religion & Theology; Theatre,
Drama & Dance

Imprints, Series & ISBNs:
978 0 300

Parent Company:
USA: Yale University Press

Associated Companies:
Yale Representation Ltd

Overseas Representation:
Africa (excluding Southern Africa & Nigeria):
Kelvin van Hasselt Publishing Services,
Norfolk, UK
*Australia, New Zealand, Fiji & Papua New
Guinea:* Inbooks, NSW, Australia
*Austria, Germany, Italy, Switzerland, Spain
& Portugal:* Uwe Lüdemann, Berlin,
Germany
*Benelux, Denmark, Finland, France, Iceland,
Norway & Sweden:* Fred Hermans,
Bovenkarspel, Netherlands
Central Europe: Ewa Ledóchowicz,
Konstancin-Jeziorna, Poland
China, Hong Kong & Philippines: Ed
Summerson, Asia Publishers Services Ltd,
Hong Kong
India: S. Janakiraman, Book Marketing
Services, Chennai, India
Iran: Farhad Maftoon, Tehran, Iran
Israel: International Publishers
Representatives, Nicosia, Cyprus
Malaysia: APD Malaysia Pte Ltd, Malaysia
Middle East: Claire de Grucy & Bill Kennedy,
Avicenna Partnership, Oxford, UK
Nigeria: Bounty Books, Ibadan, Nigeria
Pakistan: Anwer Iqbal, Book Bird Publishers
Representatives, Lahore, Pakistan
Republic of Ireland & Northern Ireland:
Robert Towers, Monkstown, Co Dublin,
Republic of Ireland
*Singapore, Thailand, Vietnam, Cambodia,
Indonesia & Brunei:* APD Singapore Pte
Ltd, Singapore
Southern Africa: Book Promotions Pty Ltd,
Diep River, South Africa
USA, Central & South America, Mexico,

Canada, Japan, Korea & Taiwan: Yale
University Press, New Haven, CT, USA

Book Trade Association Membership:
Independent Publishers Guild

2778

YORE PUBLICATIONS
12 The Furrows, Harefield, Middx UB9 6AT
Telephone: 01895 823404
Fax: 01895 823404
Email: fay.twydell@blueyonder.co.uk
Web Site: www.yore.demon.co.uk/
index.html

Personnel:
Dave Twydell *(Partner)*
Fay Twydell *(Partner)*
Kara Matthews *(Typist/Secretary)*

Sports & Games

New Titles: 8 (2010) , 7 (2011)
No of Employees: 1

Imprints, Series & ISBNs:
978 1 874427

2779

ZAMBEZI PUBLISHING LTD
22 Second Avenue, Camels Head,
Plymouth, Devon PL2 2EQ
Telephone: 01752 367300
Fax: 01752 350453
Email: info@zampub.com
Web Site: www.zampub.com

Business:
PO Box 221, Plymouth, Devon PL2 2YJ
Telephone: 01752 367300
Fax: 01752 350453
Email: (as above)
Web Site: (as above)

Personnel:
Mrs Sasha Fenton *(Chief Executive Officer)*
Jan Budkowski *(Managing Director)*

*Industry, Business & Management; Magic &
the Occult; Medical (incl. Self Help &
Alternative Medicine)*

New Titles: 8 (2010) , 7 (2011)
No of Employees: 2

Imprints, Series & ISBNs:
978 0 9533478, 978 1 903065

Overseas Representation:
Europe: Publishers Guild, Enfield, UK
USA & Rest of the World: Sterling
Publishing Co Inc, New York, NY, USA

2780

ZED BOOKS LTD
7 Cynthia Street, London N1 9JF
Telephone: 020 7837 4014 & 8466
Fax: 020 7833 3960
Email: sales@zedbooks.net
Web Site: www.zedbooks.co.uk

Distribution:
NBN International Ltd, 10 Thornbury Road,
Plymouth PL6 7PP
Telephone: 01752 202301
Fax: 01752 202331
Email: orders@nbninternational.com

**Trade Representation – UK & Republic
of Ireland:**
Compass Academic
Telephone: 020 8994 6477
Email: ca@compass-academic.co.uk
Web Site: www.academic.compass-
booksales.co.uk/academic

Personnel:
Julian Hosie *(Marketing Director)*
Margaret Ling *(Finance & Company
Secretary)*
Tamsine O'Riordan *(Senior Commissioning
Editor)*
Ken Barlow *(Commissioning Editor)*
Ruvani de Silva *(Publicity Officer)*
Ruben Mootoosamy *(Sales Executive)*
Jakob Horstmann *(Commissioning Editor)*
Anneberth Lux *(Sales Manager)*
Dan Och *(Production Manager)*
Federico Campagna *(Rights Manager)*
Kika Sroka-Miller *(Editorial Assistant)*

*Academic & Scholarly; Economics;
Environment & Development Studies;
Gender Studies; Politics & World Affairs;
Sociology & Anthropology*

New Titles: 46 (2010) , 47 (2011)
No of Employees: 11
Annual Turnover: £1.16M

Imprints, Series & ISBNs:
978 0 86232, 978 0 905762, 978 1 84277,
978 1 84813, 978 1 85649, 978 1 78032

Overseas Representation:
Australia & New Zealand: Inbooks, Frenchs
Forest, NSW, Australia
Canada: Brunswick Books Ltd, Toronto, ON,
Canada
Europe: Durnell Marketing, Tunbridge
Wells, UK
India: Maya Publishers, New Delhi, India
Ireland: Geoff Bryan Publishers Agent,
Dublin, Republic of Ireland
Middle East: Avicenna Partnership, Witney,
UK
*South Africa, Botswana, Namibia, Lesotho,
Swaziland:* Blue Weaver, Cape Town,
South Africa
South America & Caribbean: David
Williams, IntermediaAmericana, London,
UK
*Sub-Saharan Africa (excluding South Africa,
Botswana, Namibia, Lesotho, Swaziland):*
Tony Moggach, IntermediaAfricana,
London, UK
USA: Palgrave Macmillan, New York, USA

Book Trade Association Membership:
Independent Publishers Guild

2781

ZYMURGY PUBLISHING
Hoults Estate, Walker Road,
Newcastle upon Tyne NE6 2HL
Telephone: 0191 276 2425
Fax: 0191 276 2425
Email:
ZymurgyPublishing@googlemail.com
Web Site: Zymurgypublishing.co.uk

Personnel:
Martin Ellis *(Publisher)*

*Biography & Autobiography; Children's
Books; Gardening; Health & Beauty;
Humour; Illustrated & Fine Editions; Music;
Natural History; Photography*

Imprints, Series & ISBNs:
978 1 903506

Book Trade Association Membership:
Independent Publishers Guild; Publishers
Publicity Circle

3   Packagers

3001

ALBION PRESS LTD
Spring Hill, Idbury, Oxon OX7 6RU
Telephone: 01993 831094

Personnel:
Emma Bradford (*Managing Director*)
Neil Philip (*Editorial Director*)

Children's Books

3002

AMOLIBROS
Loundshay Manor Cottage,
Preston Bowyer, Milverton, Taunton,
Somerset TA4 1QF
Telephone: 01823 401527
Fax: 01823 401527
Email: amolibros@aol.com
Web Site: www.amolibros.co.uk

Trade Enquiries & Orders:
Gardners Books, 1 Whittle Drive,
Eastbourne BN23 6QH
Telephone: 01323 521555
Fax: 01323 521666

Personnel:
Jane Tatam (*Managing Consultant*)

Academic & Scholarly; Biography & Autobiography; Biology & Zoology; Chemistry; Children's Books; Cookery, Wines & Spirits; Fiction; Fine Art & Art History; Gardening; Geography & Geology; History & Antiquarian; Magic & the Occult; Medical (incl. Self Help & Alternative Medicine); Music; Nautical; Philosophy; Physics; Poetry; Politics & World Affairs; Sports & Games; Theatre, Drama & Dance; Travel & Topography; Vocational Training & Careers

3003

*ANNO DOMINI PUBLISHING (ADPS)
Book House, Orchard Mews,
18 High Street, Tring, Herts HP23 5AH
Telephone: 0845 868 1333
Email: info@ad-publishing.com
Web Site: www.ad-publishing.com

Children's Books; Religion & Theology

3004

*NICOLA BAXTER LTD
PO Box 215, The Brew House,
Framingham Earl Road, Yelverton, Norwich
NR14 7UR
Telephone: 01508 491111
Email: nb@nicolabaxter.co.uk
Web Site: www.nicolabaxter.co.uk

Personnel:
Nicola Baxter (*Proprietor*)

Children's Books; Educational & Textbooks

3005

*BENDER RICHARDSON WHITE
PO Box 266, Uxbridge UB9 5NX
Telephone: 01895 832444
Fax: 01895 835213
Email: brw@brw.co.uk
Web Site: www.brw.co.uk

Personnel:
Lionel Bender (*Editorial Director*)
Kim Richardson (*Sales & Production Director*)
Ben White (*Art & Design Director*)

Biology & Zoology; Children's Books; Educational & Textbooks; Natural History; Reference Books, Directories & Dictionaries; Religion & Theology

3006

BLA PUBLISHING LTD
1 Christopher Road, East Grinstead,
West Sussex RH19 3BT
Telephone: 01342 318980
Fax: 01342 410980
Email: eileen@wleducat.freeserve.co.uk

Personnel:
Au Bak Ling (*Chairman*)
Eileen Parsons (*Company Secretary, Sales, Rights & Permissions*)

Antiques & Collecting; Aviation; Biology & Zoology; Chemistry; Children's Books; Computer Science; Gardening; Medical (incl. Self Help & Alternative Medicine); Military & War; Music; Natural History; Nautical; Physics; Reference Books, Directories & Dictionaries; Religion & Theology

Imprints, Series & ISBNs:
Thames Head

Parent Company:
Ling Kee (UK) Ltd

Associated Companies:
Ward Lock Educational Co Ltd

3007

BLUE BEYOND BOOKS
4 Paget Road, Ipswich IP1 3RP
Telephone: 01473 423247
Fax: 01473 214096
Email: martin.spettigue@virgin.net

Personnel:
Martin Spettigue (*Manager*)
Mark Thomas (*Sales Representative*)
Nelly Coudoa (*Sales Representative*)
Hita Hirons (*Sales Representative*)

Magic & the Occult; Music; Philosophy; Poetry; Religion & Theology

Associated Companies:
USA: Aum Publications; McKeever Publishing

Distributor for:
USA: Aum Publications; McKeever Publishing

Overseas Representation:
Australia: Wisdom's Delight, Brisbane, Qld, Australia
Canada: Peace Publishing, Ottawa, Ont, Canada
France: Editions Sri Chinmey, Paris, France
Germany: The Golden Shore, Nurnberg, Germany
USA: Heart-Light Distributors, Seattle, WA, USA

3008

*BROWN WELLS & JACOBS LTD
2 Vermont Road, London SE19 3SR
Telephone: 020 8653 7670
Fax: 020 8653 7774
Email: graham@bwj-ltd.com
Web Site: www.bwj.org

Personnel:
Graham Brown (*Managing Director, Design, Sales & Production*)

Children's Books; Crafts & Hobbies

Imprints, Series & ISBNs:
978 1 873829

Distributor for:
Brown Wells & Jacobs Ltd (Packaging)

3009

CAMBRIDGE PUBLISHING MANAGEMENT LTD
Burr Elm Court, Main Street, Caldecote,
Cambs CB23 7NU
Telephone: 01954 214006
Fax: 01954 214001
Email: j.dobbyne@cambridgepm.co.uk
Web Site: www.cambridgepm.co.uk

Personnel:
Jackie Dobbyne (*Managing Director*)
Tim Newton (*Production Director*)
Catherine Burch (*Editorial Manager*)
Sharmeela Pydiah (*Business Development Manager*)

Academic & Scholarly; Archaeology; Architecture & Design; Biography & Autobiography; Cookery, Wines & Spirits; Crafts & Hobbies; Economics; Educational & Textbooks; English as a Foreign Language; Fine Art & Art History; Gardening; Illustrated & Fine Editions; Industry, Business & Management; Medical (incl. Self Help & Alternative Medicine); Military & War; Natural History; Reference Books, Directories & Dictionaries; Religion & Theology; Travel & Topography; Vocational Training & Careers

No of Employees: 13

Book Trade Association Membership:
Independent Publishers Guild

3010

*COWLEY ROBINSON PUBLISHING LTD
8 Belmont, Bath BA1 5DZ
Telephone: 01225 339999
Fax: 01225 339995
Email:
stewart.cowley@cowleyrobinson.com

Personnel:
Stewart Cowley (*Director*)
D. Hawcock (*Director*)
P. Fleming (*Director*)
Leanne Down (*Production Manager*)
Anna Sainaghi (*Senior Sales Manager*)

Children's Books

Parent Company:
Allcloud Ltd

3011

DIAGRAM VISUAL INFORMATION LTD
34 Elaine Grove, London NW5 4QH
Telephone: 020 7485 5941
Fax: 020 7485 5941
Email: info@diagramgroup.com
Web Site: www.diagramgroup.com

Personnel:
Bruce Robertson (*Managing Director*)
Patricia Robertson (*Director*)

Children's Books; Educational & Textbooks; Geography & Geology; Health & Beauty; Reference Books, Directories & Dictionaries; Sports & Games

Overseas Representation:
Bulgaria: Nika Literary Agency, Sofia, Bulgaria
Eastern Europe: DS Druck- und Verlags Service, London, UK

Hungary: DS Budapest Kft, Budapest, Hungary
Japan: Tuttle-Mori Agency Inc, Tokyo, Japan
Korea: KCC, Seoul, Republic of Korea
Lithuania: Musa Knyga, Vilnius, Lithuania
Netherlands & Scandinavia: Kolar Rights and Translation, Feidamsee, Austria
Poland: DS Druck Warszawa, Warsaw, Poland
Romania: Mast Publishing, Bucharest, Romania
Russia: DS, Moscow, Russia
Thailand: Big Apple Tuttle-Mori Agency (Thailand) Co Ltd, Bangkok, Thailand

3012

D & N PUBLISHING
8 Fiveways, Baydon, Wilts SN8 2LH
Telephone: 01672 540556
Email: d@dnpublishing.co.uk

Personnel:
David Price-Goodfellow *(Manager/Owner)*
Namrita Price-Goodfellow *(Designer/Owner)*

Animal Care & Breeding; Antiques & Collecting; Aviation; Biology & Zoology; Crafts & Hobbies; Do-It-Yourself; Fine Art & Art History; Guide Books; History & Antiquarian; Medical (incl. Self Help & Alternative Medicine); Military & War; Natural History; Photography; Reference Books, Directories & Dictionaries; Sports & Games; Theatre, Drama & Dance; Transport; Travel & Topography

3013

*EDDISON SADD EDITIONS LTD
St Chad's House, 148 King's Cross Road, London WC1X 9DH
Telephone: 020 7837 1968
Fax: 020 7837 2025
Email: info@eddisonsadd.co.uk
Web Site: www.eddisonsadd.com

Accounts:
Facts & Figures
Telephone: 01280 813111
Fax: 01280 817229

Personnel:
Nick Eddison *(Managing Director)*
Ian Jackson *(Editorial Director)*
Susan Cole *(Rights Director)*
David Owen *(Financial Director)*
Sarah Rooney *(Production Director)*

Children's Books; Cookery, Wines & Spirits; Health & Beauty; Magic & the Occult; Medical (incl. Self Help & Alternative Medicine)

Imprints, Series & ISBNs:
Bookinabox

Associated Companies:
Connections Book Publishing

Overseas Representation:
Worldwide: Melia Publishing Services for Connections Book Services, UK

3014

*ESSENTIAL WORKS LTD
The Green, 29 Clerkenwell Green, London EC1R 0DU
Telephone: 020 7017 0890
Email: info@essentialworks.co.uk
Web Site: www.essentialworks.co.uk

Personnel:
John Conway *(Managing Director)*
Mal Peachey *(Publishing Director)*
Jackie Strachan *(Rights & Co-Editions)*
Jane Moseley *(Rights & Co-Editions)*

Biography & Autobiography; Cinema,

Video, TV & Radio; Fashion & Costume; Health & Beauty; Humour; Illustrated & Fine Editions; Military & War; Music; Photography; Sports & Games; Transport

3015

FREELANCE MARKET NEWS
8–10 Dutton Street, Manchester M3 1LE
Telephone: 0161 819 9919
Fax: 0161 819 2842
Email: fmn@writersbureau.com
Web Site: www.freelancemarketnews.com

Personnel:
Miss Angela Cox *(Editorial & Circulation)*

Educational & Textbooks; Fiction; Literature & Criticism; Photography; Poetry

Parent Company:
The Writers Bureau Ltd

3016

GRAHAM-CAMERON PUBLISHING & ILLUSTRATION
The Studio, 23 Holt Road, Sheringham, Norfolk NR26 8NB
Telephone: 01263 821333
Fax: 01263 821334
Email: enquiry@gciforillustration.com
Web Site: www.gciforillustration.com

Marketing & Sales:
Duncan Graham-Cameron,
59 Hertford Road, Brighton BN1 7GG
Telephone: 01273 385890
Email: duncan@gciforillustration.com
Web Site: www.gciforillustration.com

Personnel:
Duncan Graham-Cameron *(Managing & Marketing Partner)*
Helen Graham-Cameron *(Art & Editorial Partner)*

Architecture & Design; Children's Books; Educational & Textbooks; English as a Foreign Language; Military & War; Natural History; Reference Books, Directories & Dictionaries; Religion & Theology

Imprints, Series & ISBNs:
978 0 947672

Associated Companies:
Graham-Cameron Illustration

Book Trade Association Membership:
Independent Publishers Guild; Cambridge Book Association; CAMPUS; The Paternosters

3017

HART McLEOD LTD
14A Greenside, Waterbeach, Cambridge CB25 9HP
Telephone: 01223 861495
Fax: 01223 862902
Email: inhouse@hartmcleod.co.uk
Web Site: www.hartmcleod.co.uk

Personnel:
Graham Hart *(Editorial Director)*
Joanne Barker *(Design Director)*

Academic & Scholarly; Educational & Textbooks; Electronic (Educational); Sports & Games

3018

*THE IVY PRESS LTD
210 High Street, Lewes, East Sussex BN7 2NS
Telephone: 01273 487440
Fax: 01273 487441
Web Site: www.ivy-group.co.uk

Personnel:
Stephen Paul *(Managing Director)*
Nikki Tilbury *(Rights Director)*
Peter Bridgewater *(Creative Director)*

Crafts & Hobbies; Fashion & Costume; Health & Beauty; Illustrated & Fine Editions

3019

LITTLE PEOPLE BOOKS
The Home of BookBod, Knighton, Radnorshire LD7 1UP
Telephone: 01547 520925
Email: littlepeoplebooks@thehobb.tv
Web Site: www.thehobb.tv/lpb

Personnel:
Grant Jessé *(Production Director, Managing Editor)*
Helen Wallis *(Rights, Finance Director)*

Audio Books; Children's Books; Educational & Textbooks

Imprints, Series & ISBNs:
978 1 899573

Parent Company:
Grant Jessé

Associated Companies:
Karavadra: Multimedia

Book Trade Association Membership:
Independent Publishers Guild; Book Packagers Association

3020

MARKET HOUSE BOOKS LTD
Suite B, Elsinore House,
43 Buckingham Street, Aylesbury, Bucks HP20 2NQ
Telephone: 01296 484911
Fax: 01296 338934
Email: books@mhbref.com
Web Site: www.markethousebooks.com

Personnel:
Elizabeth Martin *(Chief Editor)*
Anne Stibbs/Kerr *(Director (Production))*
Jonathan Law *(Director (Editorial))*

Computer Science; Industry, Business & Management; Law; Medical (incl. Self Help & Alternative Medicine); Music; Psychology & Psychiatry; Reference Books, Directories & Dictionaries; Scientific & Technical; Theatre, Drama & Dance

3021

*METHODIST PUBLISHING
17 Tresham Road, Orton Southgate, Peterborough PE2 6SG
Telephone: 01733 235962
Fax: 01733 390325
Web Site:
www.methodistpublishing.org.uk

Personnel:
Jane McClean *(Manager of Commercial Services)*

Imprints, Series & ISBNs:
Methodist Publishing House: 978 1 85852

Parent Company:
The Methodist Church

3022

NEW CARAMEL LONDON LTD
[a division of Editions Caramel SA]
12–13 Ship Street, Brighton, East Sussex BN1 1AD
Web Site: www.caramel.be

Contact:
Jean-Luc Dubois, Otto de Mentockplein 19, 1853 Strombeek-Bever, Belgium

Telephone: +32 2 263 20 51
Fax: +32 2 263 20 50
Email: jeanluc.dubois@caramel.be
Web Site: www.caramel.be

Personnel:
Jean-Michel d'Oultremont *(Joint Managing Director)*
Jean-Luc Dubois *(Joint Managing Director)*

Children's Books

Parent Company:
Belgium: Editions Caramel SA

Book Trade Association Membership:
Publishers Association

3023

*ORPHEUS BOOKS LTD
6 Church Green, Witney, Oxon OX28 4AW
Telephone: 01993 774949
Fax: 01993 700330
Email: nicholas@orpheusbooks.com
Web Site: www.orpheusbooks.com

Personnel:
Nicholas Harris *(Director)*
Sarah Hartley *(Director)*

Children's Books

Imprints, Series & ISBNs:
978 1 901323, 978 1 905473

3024

PARAGON PUBLISHING
4 North Street, Rothersthorpe, Northants NN7 3JB
Telephone: 01604 832149
Email: mark.webb@tesco.net
Web Site: www.intoprint.net

Personnel:
Mark Webb *(Proprietor)*

Academic & Scholarly; Architecture & Design; Biography & Autobiography; Children's Books; Computer Science; Cookery, Wines & Spirits; Crime; Educational & Textbooks; Electronic (Educational); Electronic (Professional & Academic); English as a Foreign Language; Environment & Development Studies; Fiction; Fine Art & Art History; Gay & Lesbian Studies; Geography & Geology; Guide Books; Humour; Industry, Business & Management; Languages & Linguistics; Magic & the Occult; Medical (incl. Self Help & Alternative Medicine); Military & War; Natural History; Nautical; Poetry; Religion & Theology; Science Fiction; Scientific & Technical; Sports & Games; Theatre, Drama & Dance; Travel & Topography

New Titles: 55 (2010) , 70 (2011)

Imprints, Series & ISBNs:
KinderKlub
Paragon Publishing: 978 1 899820, 978 1 907611, 978 1 908341
Primary Modern Language
Stadium & Arena
Venue Safety and Security

Overseas Representation:
Europe: Ingram Lightning Source
USA, Canada: Ingram Lightning Source

3025

QUANTUM PUBLISHING
6 Blundell Street, London N7 9BH
Telephone: 020 7700 6700
Fax: 020 7700 4191
Email: sarah.bloxham@quarto.com
Web Site: www.quarto.com

Personnel:
Sarah Bloxham *(Publisher)*
Valerie Saint-Pierre *(Foreign Rights Director)*

*Animal Care & Breeding; Antiques &
Collecting; Architecture & Design; Atlases &
Maps; Aviation; Children's Books; Cookery,
Wines & Spirits; Crafts & Hobbies; Crime;
Do-It-Yourself; Fashion & Costume; Fine Art
& Art History; Gardening; Health & Beauty;
History & Antiquarian; Humour; Industry,
Business & Management; Magic & the
Occult; Medical (incl. Self Help & Alternative
Medicine); Military & War; Music; Natural
History; Nautical; Photography; Religion &
Theology; Sports & Games; Transport*

Imprints, Series & ISBNs:
Cartographica Press
Oceana
Quantum

Parent Company:
Quarto Publishing Plc

3026 ▬▬▬▬

**READER'S DIGEST CHILDREN'S
PUBLISHING LTD**
The Ice House, 124–126 Walcot Street,
Bath BA1 5BG
Telephone: 01225 473200
Fax: 01225 460942

Personnel:
Paul E. Stuart *(Commercial Director)*
Jennifer Fifield *(International Sales Director)*

Children's Books

No of Employees: 12

Imprints, Series & ISBNs:
978 1 84880, 978 1 85724

Parent Company:
USA: The Reader's Digest Association Inc

Associated Companies:
USA: Reader's Digest Children's Publishing
Inc

3027 ▬▬▬▬

*REGENCY HOUSE PUBLISHING LTD
The Red House, 84 High Street,
Buntingford, Herts SG9 9AJ
Telephone: 01763 274666
Fax: 01763 273501
Email: regency-house@btconnect.com

Personnel:
Miss N. Trodd *(Managing Director)*
B. H. Trodd *(Manager)*
Annabel Trodd *(Manager)*

*Animal Care & Breeding; Architecture &
Design; Aviation; Children's Books; Crafts &
Hobbies; Magic & the Occult; Military &
War*

Imprints, Series & ISBNs:
978 1 85361

3028 ▬▬▬▬

*TANGERINE DESIGNS LTD
1 Limpley Mill, Lower Stoke, Bath BA2 7JF
Telephone: 01225 720001
Web Site: www.tangerinedesigns.co.uk

Personnel:
Christine Swift *(Managing Director)*
Trish Pugsley *(Co-edition Sales Agent)*
Rachel Pidcock *(Co-edition Sales Agent)*
Catherine Lyn Jones *(Rights Manager)*

Children's Books

Distributor for:
Alligator Books Ltd; Pinwheel

3029 ▬▬▬▬

*TOUCAN BOOKS LTD
Third Floor, 89 Charterhouse Street,
London EC1M 6PE
Telephone: 020 7250 3388
Fax: 020 7250 3123
Email: ellen@toucanbooks.co.uk

Personnel:
Ellen Dupont *(Managing Director)*
Robert Sackville-West *(Director)*

*Animal Care & Breeding; Architecture &
Design; Atlases & Maps; Children's Books;
Cookery, Wines & Spirits; Crafts & Hobbies;
Fine Art & Art History; Gardening; History &
Antiquarian; Illustrated & Fine Editions;
Military & War; Natural History; Reference
Books, Directories & Dictionaries; Travel &
Topography*

Book Trade Association Membership:
Book Packagers Association

3030 ▬▬▬▬

TUCKER SLINGSBY LTD
Fifth Floor, Regal House, 70 London Road,
Twickenham TW1 3QS
Telephone: 020 8744 1007
Fax: 020 8744 0041
Email: info@tuckerslingsby.co.uk
Web Site: www.tuckerslingsby.co.uk

Personnel:
Del Tucker *(Director)*
Janet Slingsby *(Director)*

*Children's Books; Crafts & Hobbies; Health
& Beauty*

Imprints, Series & ISBNs:
978 1 902272, 978 1 905844, 978 1
907358

Overseas Representation:
Spain, Portugal & Latin America: I E Ilustrata
SL, Barcelona, Spain

3031 ▬▬▬▬

DAVID WEST CHILDREN'S BOOKS
7 Princeton Court, 55 Felsham Road,
London SW15 1AZ
Telephone: 020 8780 3836
Fax: 020 8780 9313
Email: dww@btinternet.com
Web Site:
www.davidwestchildrensbooks.com

Personnel:
David West *(Proprietor/Publisher)*
Lynn Lockett *(Publisher)*

*Architecture & Design; Children's Books;
Cinema, Video, TV & Radio; Crafts &
Hobbies; Fashion & Costume; Geography &
Geology; History & Antiquarian; Military &
War; Music; Natural History; Scientific &
Technical; Sports & Games; Transport*

3032 ▬▬▬▬

*YOUNG PEOPLE IN FOCUS
23 New Road, Brighton, East Sussex
BN1 1WZ
Telephone: 01273 693311 & 647325
Fax: 01273 647322
Email:
publications@youngpeopleinfocus.org.u
k
Web Site:
www.youngpeopleinfocus.org.uk

Personnel:
Kevin Lane *(Co-Director)*
Debi Roker *(Co-Director)*

Educational & Textbooks

Imprints, Series & ISBNs:
978 1 871504

4 Authors' Agents

4001 ▬▬▬

AITKEN ALEXANDER ASSOCIATES
18–21 Cavaye Place, London SW10 9PT
Telephone: 020 7373 8672
Fax: 020 7373 6002
Email: reception@aitkenalexander.co.uk
Web Site: www.aitkenalexander.co.uk

Personnel:
Gillon Aitken (*Chairman*)
Clare Alexander (*Joint Managing Director*)
Sally Riley (*Joint Managing Director/Foreign Rights*)
Andrew Kidd (*Director*)
Lesley Thorne (*Director/Film & TV*)
Joaquim Fernandes (*Company Secretary*)

All MSS except plays, illustrated children's books, film & TV scripts, short stories & articles if not by existing clients.

Specialization: quality full-length fiction & non-fiction.

Overseas Representation:
America: Aitken Alexander Associates LLC, New York, NY, USA
Indian Subcontinent: Aitken Alexander Associates Pvt Ltd, New Delhi, India

4002 ▬▬▬

THE AMPERSAND AGENCY LTD
Ryman's Cottages, Little Tew, Oxon OX7 4JJ
Telephone: 01608 683677 & 683898
Fax: 01608 683449
Email: info@theampersandagency.co.uk
Web Site:
www.theampersandagency.co.uk

Personnel:
Peter Buckman (*Managing Director*)
Peter Janson-Smith (*Consultant*)
Anne-Marie Doulton (*Editor & Director*)

All MSS except poetry, science fiction, horror, fantasy or illustrated children's books.

Specialization: literary and commercial fiction and non-fiction for all markets. A full range of services including foreign and media rights is offered. Member of the Association of Authors' Agents.

Overseas Representation:
Worldwide: The Buckman Agency, Oxford, UK

4003 ▬▬▬

DARLEY ANDERSON LITERARY, TV & FILM AGENCY
Estelle House, 11 Eustace Road, London SW6 1JB
Telephone: 020 7386 2674
Fax: 020 7386 5571
Email: enquiries@darleyanderson.com
Web Site: www.darleyanderson.com

Personnel:
Darley Anderson (*Sole Proprietor*)
Madeleine Buston (*Women's & General Fiction Agent, Deputy MD Children's Books*)
Camilla Bolton (*Crime/Thriller Agent*)
Steve Fisher (*Film & TV*)
Rosanna Bellingham (*Financial Controller*)
Sophie Gordon (*Assistant to Darley Anderson, Illustrator's Agent*)
Clare Wallace (*Rights Manager*)

All MSS except short stories, academic or poetry.

Specialization: fiction: all types of thrillers & all types of fiction including contemporary, romantic comedy, bonkbusters, women in jeopardy, accessible literary, historical, exotic sagas, psychological suspense, paranormal, supernatural and cross-over fiction; also crime (cosy/hard-boiled/historical), horror, comedy & Irish novels; popular culture; children's, young adult and picture books; non-fiction: celebrity autobiographies, biographies, 'true life' women in jeopardy, popular psychology, self-improvement, diet, health, beauty & fashion, gardening, cookery, inspirational & religious.

Overseas Representation:
Bulgaria: Anthea Literary Agency, Sofia, Bulgaria
China & Taiwan: The Grayhawk Agency, Taipei, Taiwan
Czech & Slovak Republics: Andrew Nurnberg Associates, Prague, Czech Republic
Germany: Thomas Schlück Literary Agency, Garbsen, Germany
Greece: O A Literary Agency, Markopoulo, Athens, Greece
Hungary: Kàtai & Bolza Literary Agents, Budapest, Hungary
Israel: I. Pikarski Literary Agency, Tel Aviv, Israel
Italy: Natoli, Stefan & Oliva Agenzia Letteraria, Milan, Italy
Japan: Japan Uni Agency, Tokyo, Japan; Tuttle-Mori Agency Inc, Tokyo, Japan
Korea: Danny Hony Agency, Republic of Korea
Poland: Graal Ltd, Warsaw, Poland
Romania: International Copyright Agency, Bucharest, Romania
Russia: Synopsis Literary Agency, Moscow, Russia
Serbia: PLIMA Literary Agency, Belgrade, Serbia
Turkey: Akcali Copyright Agency, Istanbul, Turkey

USA: Darley Anderson Books, London, UK

4004 ▬▬▬

ARTELLUS LTD
30 Dorset House, Gloucester Place, London NW1 5AD
Telephone: 020 7935 6972
Fax: 020 7487 5957
Web Site: www.artellusltd.co.uk

Personnel:
Leslie Gardner (*Director*)
Darryl Samaraweera (*Company Secretary*)
Gabriele Pantucci (*Chair*)

All MSS except film scripts.

Specialization: speculative fiction, thrillers, fiction – commercial and literary, self-help, history, science, art history, politics, economics.

4005 ▬▬▬

TASSY BARHAM ASSOCIATES
231 Westbourne Park Road, London W11 1EB
Telephone: 020 7792 5899
Email: tassy@tassybarham.com

Personnel:
Tassy Barham (*Agent*)

Specialization: Brazil. Representing European and American agencies and publishers in Brazil, and Portuguese-language writers into the UK. No unsolicited MSS.

4006 ▬▬▬

LORELLA BELLI LITERARY AGENCY (LBLA)
54 Hartford House, 35 Tavistock Crescent, Notting Hill, London W11 1AY
Telephone: 020 7727 8547
Fax: 0870 787 4194
Email: info@lorellabelliagency.com
Web Site: www.lorellabelliagency.com

Personnel:
Lorella Belli (*Proprietor*)

All MSS except children's books, science fiction, fantasy, academic, poetry, original scripts. No reading fee. May suggest revision. Approach by query letter or email in the first instance.

Specialization: general fiction and non-fiction (particularly interested in first-time writers, commercial women's fiction, crime, thrillers, historical, international and multicultural writing, journalists with original book ideas, books on/about Italy,

current affairs, pop history, pop science, pop music, lifestyle, memoirs, biography, autobiography, MBS, cookery, fashion, personal finance, business, travel). The agency represents a number of international bestselling and award-winning authors of fiction and non-fiction. Also represents leading American agencies in the UK. Commission: 15% home; 20% overseas and dramatic rights. Works with co-agents abroad; film & TV rights handled by an associate agency. Member of the Association of Authors' Agents.

Rights Representative in UK for:
USA: Creative Culture Agency, New York, NY, USA; Fine Print Agency, New York, NY, USA; Mildred Marmur Associates, Larchmont, NY, USA; Paula Balzer Literary Agency, New York, NY, USA; Sarah Lazin Books, New York, NY, USA; Susan Schulman Agency, New York, NY, USA

4007 ▬▬▬

BLAKE FRIEDMANN LITERARY AGENCY LTD
122 Arlington Road, London NW1 7HP
Telephone: 020 7284 0408
Fax: 020 7284 0442
Email: 'firstname'@blakefriedmann.co.uk
Web Site: www.blakefriedmann.co.uk

Personnel:
Carole Blake (*Book Sales Director & Agent*)
Julian Friedmann (*Film & TV Director & Agent*)
Isobel Dixon (*Book Sales Director & Agent*)
Conrad Williams (*Film, TV & Radio Sales*)
Adrian Clark (*Accounts Manager*)
Oli Munson (*Book Sales Agent*)
Katie Williams (*Film & TV Agent*)

All MSS except science fiction, fantasy, children's books, plays, poetry & short stories (excluding those from existing clients).

Specialization: placing book rights internationally; film, television & radio rights.

Overseas Representation:
Bulgaria: Anthea Literary Agency, Sofia, Bulgaria
China: Andrew Nurnberg Associates, Beijing, P. R. of China
Czech Republic: Kristin Olson Literary Agency, Prague, Czech Republic
France: La Nouvelle Agence, Paris, France
Germany: Liepman AG, Zurich, Switzerland
Hungary: Kàtai & Bolza, Literary Agents, Budapest, Hungary
Italy: Natoli, Stefan & Oliva Agenzia Letteraria, Milan, Italy

Japan: The English Agency Japan Ltd, Tokyo, Japan
Korea: KCC International Ltd, Seoul, Republic of Korea
Poland: Graal Ltd, Warsaw, Poland
Romania: S. Kessler International Copyright Agency, Bucharest, Romania
Russia: Andrew Nurnberg Associates, Moscow, Russia
Scandinavia: Leonhardt & Hoier Literary Agency, Copenhagen, Denmark
Spain, Brazil & Portugal: The Foreign Office, Spain
Taiwan: Andrew Nurnberg Literary Agency, Taipei, Taiwan
Turkey: Amy Spangler, Anatolialit Agency, Turkey
USA, Canada, the Balkans & Greece: Blake Friedmann Literary Agency, London, UK

4008

LUIGI BONOMI ASSOCIATES LTD
91 Great Russell Street, London WC1B 3PS
Telephone: 020 7637 1234
Fax: 020 7637 2111
Email: info@bonomiassociates.co.uk
Web Site: www.bonomiassociates.co.uk

Personnel:
Luigi Bonomi *(Director)*
Amanda Preston *(Director)*
Ajda Vucicevic *(Administration Assistant)*
Thomas Stofer *(Literary Agent)*

All MSS except poetry, children's stories or adult science fiction/fantasy.

Specialization: fiction: commercial and literary fiction, thrillers, crime, women's fiction. Non-fiction: history, science, parenting, lifestyle, diet, health, TV tie-ins. Keen to find new authors and help them develop their careers. Send preliminary letter, synopsis and first three chapters. No reading fee. Will suggest revision. Works with foreign agencies and has links with TV presenters' agencies and production companies. Authors include Will Adams, James Barrington, James Becker, Jason Bradbury, Fern Britton, Jo Carnegie, Sam Christer, Gennaro Contaldo, Josephine Cox, Dean Crawford, Matthew Dunn, David Gibbins, Andrew Hammond, Richard Hammond, Matt Hilton, John Humphrys, Graham Joyce, Simon Kernick, Colin McDowell, Richard Madeley and Judy Finnigan, James May, Mike Morley, Sue Palmer, Andrew Pepper, Melanie Phillips, Gervase Phinn, Alice Roberts, Mike Rossiter, Catherine Sampson, Karen Swan, Prof Bryan Sykes, Alan Titchmarsh, Phil Vickery, Sir Terry Wogan. Founded 2005. Fiction and non-fiction (home 15%, overseas 20%).

Overseas Representation:
Worldwide: Intercontinental Literary Agency, London, UK, UK

4009

JENNY BROWN ASSOCIATES
33 Argyle Place, Edinburgh EH9 1JT
Telephone: 0131 229 5334
Email: jenny@jennybrownassociates.com
Web Site:
www.jennybrownassociates.com

Personnel:
Jenny Brown *(Agent)*
Mark Stanton *(Agent)*
Lucy Juckes *(Children's Agent)*
Allan Guthrie *(Agent)*
Kevin Pocklington *(Agent & Foreign Rights)*

All MSS except academic, poetry, science fiction, horror & fantasy. Submissions: see website for submission information.

Specialization: non-fiction (including sport & music), literary fiction (including crime &

thrillers) *and writing for children. Many of the agency's clients are based in Scotland, but the company represents writers from all over the UK, and sells their work worldwide.*

4010

FELICITY BRYAN
2a North Parade, Banbury Road, Oxford OX2 6LX
Telephone: 01865 513816
Fax: 01865 310055
Email: agency@felicitybryan.com
Web Site: www.felicitybryan.com

Personnel:
Felicity Bryan *(Director)*
Caroline Wood *(Director)*
Catherine Clarke *(Director)*

All MSS except science fiction, fantasy, romance, gardening, memoirs, self-help, picture/illustrated books, film, TV and play scripts or poetry.

Specialization: adult fiction & general non-fiction, history & popular science, children 8–12 upwards.

Overseas Representation:
China: Andrew Nurnberg Associates, Beijing, P. R. of China; Big Apple Tuttle-Mori Agency Inc, Shanghai, P. R. of China
Europe, Russia & China: Andrew Nurnberg Associates, London, UK
Japan: Japan Uni Agency, Tokyo, Japan; Tuttle-Mori Agency Inc, Tokyo, Japan
Korea: EYA, Seoul, Republic of Korea

4011

THE BUCKMAN AGENCY
Ryman's Cottage, Little Tew, Oxford OX7 4JJ
Telephone: 01608 683677
Fax: 01608 683449
Email: r.buckman@talk21.com

Also at:
Jessica Buckman, 118 Effra Road, Wimbledon, London SW19 8PR
Telephone: 020 8544 2674
Fax: 020 8543 9653
Email: j.buckman@talk21.com

Personnel:
Rosemarie Buckman *(Partner)*
Jessica Buckman *(Partner)*

Specialization: handling of translation rights in all foreign rights markets for fiction and non-fiction, working on behalf of UK and US agencies.

4012

BRIE BURKEMAN & SERAFINA CLARKE LTD
14 Neville Court, Abbey Road, London NW8 9DD
Telephone: 0870 199 5002
Fax: 0870 199 1029
Email: info@burkemanandclarke.com
Web Site: www.burkemanandclarke.com

Personnel:
Brie Burkeman *(Proprietor)*

All MSS except academic, text, poetry, short stories, musicals or short films. No reading fee but return postage essential. Unsolicited e-mail attachments will be deleted without opening. Please see website for full submission guidelines and whether we are currently accepting submissions.

Specialization: commercial and literary full-length fiction and non-fiction books, as well as full-length scripts for film and theatre. Worldwide representation, works with sub-agents where necessary. Also independent

film and TV consultant to literary agents and publishers. Commission: 15% home, 20% overseas. Member of AAA and PMA.*

Overseas Representation:
Worldwide – contact: Brie Burkeman & Serafina Clarke Ltd, London, UK

4013

CAMPBELL THOMSON & McLAUGHLIN LTD
see: The Marsh Agency Ltd

4014

CASAROTTO RAMSAY & ASSOCIATES LTD
Waverley House, 7–12 Noel Street, London W1F 8GQ
Telephone: 020 7287 4450
Fax: 020 7287 9128
Email: info@casarotto.co.uk
Web Site: www.casarotto..co.uk

Personnel:
Giorgio Casarotto *(Director)*
Tom Erhardt *(Director)*
Jenne Casarotto *(Director)*
Mel Kenyon *(Director)*
Jodi Shields *(Director)*
Rachel Holroyd *(Director)*

Specialization: film scripts, TV scripts, play scripts, radio scripts only after preliminary letter. No books.

4015

*CHAPMAN & VINCENT
7 Dilke Street, London SW3 4JE
Telephone: 020 7352 5582
Email: chapmanvincent@hotmail.co.uk

Personnel:
Jennifer Chapman *(Director)*
Gilly Vincent *(Director)*

All MSS except fiction of any kind, writing for children, poetry, scripts, domestic tragedies or academic work.

Specialization: non-fiction illustrated work in the areas of interiors, gardening, cookery, heritage and fashion. Write with two sample chapters and SAE. E-mail submissions without attachments can be considered. A small agency whose clients come mainly from personal recommendation. The agency is not actively seeking clients but is happy to consider really original work. Clients include George Carter, Leslie Geddes-Brown, Lucinda Lambton, Rowley Leigh and Eve Pollard. Commission: Home 15%; US & Europe 20%. Member of the Association of Authors' Agents.

Overseas Representation:
USA: Elaine Markson Literary Agency, New York, NY, USA

4016

MARY CLEMMEY LITERARY AGENCY
6 Dunollie Road, London NW5 2XP
Telephone: 020 7267 1290
Fax: 020 7813 9757
Email: mcwords@googlemail.com

Personnel:
Mary Clemmey *(Literary Agent)*

All MSS except science fiction, horror, fantasy, poetry, children's books. No unsolicited e-mail submissions.

Specialization: fiction and non-fiction, high-quality work with an international market.

TV, film, radio and theatre scripts from existing clients only. Please approach only by preliminary letter and synopsis (SAE essential for response).*

Rights Representative in UK for:
USA: Lynn C. Franklin Associates Ltd, New York, NY, USA; The Miller Agency, New York, NY, USA; Roslyn Targ Literary Agency Inc, New York, NY, USA; The Weingel Fidel Agency, New York, NY, USA

Overseas Representation:
USA: Elaine Markson Literary Agency, New York, NY, USA

4017

JANE CONWAY-GORDON LTD
38 Cromwell Grove, London W6 7RG
Telephone: 020 7371 6939
Email: jane@conway-gordon.co.uk

Personnel:
Jane Conway-Gordon *(Company Director)*

All MSS except science fiction, poetry, children's, short pieces; return postage essential.

Specialization: commercial and literary fiction, crime fiction, some biography.

Overseas Representation:
Europe (excluding Germany & France): Intercontinental Literary Agency, London, UK
Germany: Liepman AG, Zurich, Switzerland
USA: Lyons Literary LLC, New York, NY, USA

4018

COOMBS MOYLETT LITERARY AGENCY
120 New Kings Road, London SW6 4LZ
Telephone: 020 8740 0454
Email: lisa@coombsmoylett.com
Web Site: www.coombsmoylett.com

Personnel:
Lisa Moylett *(Proprietor)*
Juliet van Oss *(Editor)*
Laura Power *(Submissions)*

All MSS except science fiction, poetry or children's.

Specialization: commercial and literary fiction and non-fiction. Special interests in fiction are thrillers, crime/mystery; women's literary and contemporary and in non-fiction: biography; history and current affairs. The agency is particularly interested in finding and developing new talent. Services include the selling of subsidiary rights such as film & TV and translation. The agency has good relations with US publishers and is represented in both Japan by Tuttle Mori and in Germany by the Michael Meller Literary Agency. Guidelines for submission: first three chapters, a short synopsis and SAE (essential for the return of material). No e-mail or disc submissions.

Overseas Representation:
Germany: Michael Meller Literary Agency, Munich, Germany
Japan: Tuttle-Mori Agency Inc, Tokyo, Japan

4019

RUPERT CREW LTD
[International Literary Representation]
6 Windsor Road, London N3 3SS
Telephone: 020 8346 3000
Fax: 020 8346 3009
Email: info@rupertcrew.co.uk
Web Site: www.rupertcrew.co.uk

Personnel:
Doreen Montgomery (*Chairman & Joint Managing Director*)
Caroline Montgomery (*Company Secretary & Joint Managing Director*)

All MSS except science fiction, fantasy, short stories, poetry, film & TV scripts (although at the present time we are unable to accept unsolicited MSS of any kind).

Specialization: international business management for authors desiring world representation. Preliminary letter with SAE required. Also acts as publishers' consultants.

Overseas Representation:
China: Big Apple Agency Inc, Shanghai, P. R. of China
Eastern Europe: Andrew Nurnberg Associates, London, UK
France: Eliane Benisti, Paris, France
Germany: Paul & Peter Fritz AG Literary Agency, Zurich, Switzerland
Hungary: Kàtai & Bolza Literary Agents, Budapest, Hungary
Israel: The Deborah Harris Agency, Israel
Italy: Agenzia Letteraria Internazionale srl, Milan, Italy
Japan: The English Agency Japan Ltd, Tokyo, Japan; Tuttle-Mori Agency Inc, Tokyo, Japan
Scandinavia & Spain: Sane Töregård Agency, Karlshamn, Sweden
Taiwan: Big Apple Tuttle-Mori Associates, Shin-Juang, Taiwan
Turkey: The Kayi Literary Agency, Turkey
USA: The Martell Agency, New York, NY, USA
Worldwide (Film/TV): The Ki Agency Ltd, London, UK

4020

*CURTIS BROWN
Haymarket House, 28–29 Haymarket, London SW1Y 4SP
Telephone: 020 7393 4400
Fax: 020 7393 4401/2
Email: cb@curtisbrown.co.uk
Web Site: www.curtisbrown.co.uk

Personnel:
Jonathan Lloyd (*Chief Executive Officer*)
Jonny Geller (*Managing Director – Book Department*)
Nick Marston (*Managing Director – Theatre, Film & TV Department*)
Vivienne Schuster (*Literary Agent*)
Ben Hall (*Chief Operating Officer*)
Jacquie Drewe (*Director*)
Carol Jackson (*Rights Agent*)
Elizabeth Scheinkman (*Literary Agent*)
Sarah Spear (*Director*)
Craig Dickson (*Head of Legal and Business Affairs*)
Emma Bailey (*Operations Manager*)
Felicity Blunt (*Literary Agent*)
Sheila Crowley (*Literary Agent*)
Karolina Sutton (*Literary Agent*)
Stephanie Thwaites (*Literary Agent*)
Kate Cooper (*Joint Head of Foreign Rights*)
Betsy Robbins (*Joint Head of Foreign Rights*)
Daisy Meyrick (*Rights Agent*)
Katie McGowan (*Rights Agent*)
Helen Manders (*Rights Agent*)
Elizabeth Iveson (*Rights Agent*)

All MSS except short stories & poetry.

Specialization: negotiation in all publishing markets; and television, film & dramatic writing, directing, presenting & acting.

Rights Representative in UK for:
USA: Gelfman Schneider Literary Agents Inc, New York, NY, USA; ICM, New York, NY, USA

4021

ROBERT DUDLEY AGENCY
50 Rannoch Road, London W6 9SR
Telephone: 07879 426574
Email: info@robertdudleyagency.co.uk
Web Site: www.robertdudleyagency.co.uk

Personnel:
Robert Dudley (*Agent*)

All MSS except film scripts.

Specialization: Robert Dudley Agency is a non-fiction agency specializing in management, history, militaria, politics, health and well-being, travel, biography, film and archaeology.

Parent Company:
Bowerdean Publishing Co Ltd

Associated Companies:
Bowerdean Publishing Co Ltd

4022

EDWARDS FUGLEWICZ
49 Great Ormond Street, London WC1N 3HZ
Telephone: 020 7405 6725
Fax: 020 7405 6726
Email: ros@efla.co.uk

Personnel:
Ros Edwards (*Partner*)
Helenka Fuglewicz (*Partner*)

All MSS except children's books, science fiction, fantasy or horror. No unsolicited MSS.

Specialization: fiction and non-fiction: biography, history, and popular culture. Founded in 1996.

Rights Representative in UK for:
Republic of Ireland: Poolbeg Press, Dublin, Republic of Ireland
UK: The Bodleian Library, Oxford, UK

4023

*FAITH EVANS ASSOCIATES
27 Park Avenue North, London N8 7RU
Telephone: 020 8340 9920
Email: faith@faith-evans.co.uk

Specialization: Small agency. No phone calls or unsolicited MSS. Submissions will not be acknowledged.

4024

FOX & HOWARD LITERARY AGENCY
39 Eland Road, London SW11 5JX
Telephone: 020 7223 9452 & 01824 790817
Fax: 01824 790745
Email: fandhagency@googlemail.com

Personnel:
Chelsey Fox (*Agent*)
Charlotte Howard (*Agent*)

Specialization: general non-fiction: biography, history and popular culture, reference, business, mind, body and spirit, health (home 15%, overseas 20%). No reading fee, but preliminary letter and synopsis with SAE essential. No unsolicited submissions by email. Founded 1992.

4025

FRASER ROSS ASSOCIATES
6 Wellington Place, Edinburgh EH6 7EQ
Telephone: 0131 657 4412
Email: kjross@tiscali.co.uk
Web Site: www.fraserross.co.uk

Personnel:
Lindsey Fraser (*Partner*)
Kathryn Ross (*Partner*)

All MSS except poetry and short stories.

Specialization: representing writers and illustrators for children's books, and writers for adults (home 10–15%, overseas 20%). Send the first three chapters (or equivalent), a synopsis, CV and covering letter. Return postage is essential. Submissions from overseas will not be returned – senders should include an email contact address. Current clients include Barry Hutchison, Ella Burfoot, Sorrel Anderson, Joan Lingard, Tanya Landman, Vivian French, Lynne Rickards, Dugald Steer and Jamie Rix.

4026

JÜRI GABRIEL
35 Camberwell Grove, London SE5 8JA
Telephone: 020 7703 6186
Email: Juri@JuriGabriel.com

Personnel:
Jüri Gabriel (*Proprietor*)

All MSS except screenplays, tele or radio scripts (only handles performance rights in existing works for existing clients); science fantasy; children's books, poetry, short stories or articles.

Specialization: literary fiction, popular academic and anything that combines intellect, originality and wit. In first instance please send a two-page synopsis, three sample chapters, a brief c.v. and return postage if you want the material back. No submissions by fax or e-mail. Clients include, Tom Clempson, Diana Constance, Clare Druce, Miriam Dunne, Matt Fox, Paul Genney, Pat Gray, Mikka Haugaard, Robert Irwin, Andrew Killeen, John Lucas, David Madsen, Richard Mankiewicz, David Miller, Andy Oakes, John Outram, Phil Roberts, Roger Storey, Dr Stefan Szymanski, Jeremy Weingard, Dr Terence White. Commission: home 10%, US & translation 20%.

4027

DAVID GODWIN ASSOCIATES
55 Monmouth Street, London WC2H 9DG
Telephone: 020 7240 9992
Fax: 020 7395 6110
Web Site: www.davidgodwinassociates.co.uk

Personnel:
David Godwin (*Literary Agent*)
Heather Godwin (*Company Secretary*)
Kirsty McLachlan (*Film & TV Rights Manager*)
Anna Watkins (*Assistant*)

All MSS except science fiction & children's.

Specialization: UK, US and translation rights, TV & film.

4028

GRAHAM MAW CHRISTIE
19 Thornhill Crescent, London N1 1BJ
Telephone: 020 7609 1326
Email: enquiries@grahammawchristie.com
Web Site: www.grahammawchristie.com

Personnel:
Jane Graham Maw (*Director*)
Jennifer Christie (*Director*)

All MSS except fiction, children's or poetry.

Specialization: literary agents for general non-fiction: autobiography/memoir, humour and gift, business, history for the general market, web-to-book, food and drink, health, lifestyle, parenting, personal development, popular culture, popular science and popular philosophy, reference, TV tie-in. No reading fee. Will suggest revision. See website for guidance on submissions.

4029

LOUISE GREENBERG BOOKS LTD
The End House, Church Crescent, London N3 1BG
Telephone: 020 8349 1179
Fax: 020 8343 4559
Email: louisegreenberg@msn.com

All MSS except sport, leisure, poetry, children's. No telephone approaches from authors.

Specialization: full length literary fiction and serious non-fiction. Screen work for book clients only.

Rights Representative in UK for:
USA: Rosalie Siegel International Literary Agent, Penington, NJ, USA

4030

GREGORY AND CO
3 Barb Mews, London W6 7PA
Telephone: 020 7610 4676
Fax: 020 7610 4686
Email: info@gregoryandcompany.co.uk
Web Site: www.gregoryandcompany.co.uk

Personnel:
Jane Gregory (*Proprietor*)
Stephanie Glencross (*Editorial*)
Claire Morris (*Rights*)
Terry Bland (*Accounts*)
Linden Sherriff (*Rights Assistant*)
Mary Jones (*Submissions*)

All MSS except children's, juvenile, academic & technical books, poetry & plays, TV & film scripts, science fiction, short stories. Preliminary letter with synopsis, in the first instance either to maryjones@gregoryandcompany.co.uk or to the company address above.

Specialization: fiction: commercial, crime, literary, suspense and thrillers. Editorial advice given to own authors. Film & TV rights for own published authors only, no original scripts.

Overseas Representation:
Brazil: Tassy Barham Associates, London, UK
Bulgaria: Interrights Literary & Translation Agency, Sofia, Bulgaria
China: Big Apple Associates, Zhonghe City, Taiwan
Czech Republic & Slovakia: Andrew Nurnberg Associates, Prague, Czech Republic
France: La Nouvelle Agence, Paris, France
Hungary: Lex Copyright, Budapest, Hungary
Israel: Pikarski Agency, Tel Aviv, Israel
Japan: Japan Uni Agency Inc, Tokyo, Japan; Tuttle-Mori Agency Inc, Tokyo, Japan
Korea: EYA, Seoul, Republic of Korea
Poland: Andrew Nurnberg Associates, Warsaw, Poland
Romania: Simona Kessler International Copyright Agency Ltd, Bucharest, Romania
Russia: Andrew Nurnberg Associates, Moscow, Russia
Scandinavia: Leonhardt & Hoier Literary Agency, Copenhagen, Denmark
Spain: Carmen Balcells Agencia Literaria SA, Barcelona, Spain
Thailand: Tuttle Mori Thailand, Bangkok, Thailand

4031

THE HANBURY AGENCY LTD
28 Moreton Street, London SW1V 2PE
Telephone: 020 7630 6768

Email: enquiries@hanburyagency.com
Web Site: www.hanburyagency.com

Personnel:
Margaret Hanbury (*Managing Director*)
Henry de Rougemont (*Media Manager*)

Specialization: commercial fiction and quality non-fiction (home 15%, overseas 20%). See website for submission details. Authors include George Alagiah, Simon Callow, Jimmy Connors, Imran Khan, Judith Lennox, Katie Price. Founded in 1983.

Overseas Representation:
All translation rights: Intercontinental Literary Agency, London, UK
USA: The Hanbury Agency Ltd, London, UK

4032

ANTONY HARWOOD LTD
103 Walton Street, Oxford OX2 6EB
Telephone: 01865 559615
Fax: 01865 310660
Email: mail@antonyharwood.com
Web Site: www.antonyharwood.com

Personnel:
Antony Harwood (*Agent*)
James Macdonald Lockhart (*Agent*)

All MSS except screenwriting, poetry.

Specialization: fiction and non-fiction. Founded 2000.

4033

*A. M. HEATH & CO LTD
6 Warwick Court, London WC1R 5DJ
Telephone: 020 7242 2811
Fax: 020 7242 2711
Web Site: www.amheath.com

Personnel:
William Hamilton (*Managing Director*)
Euan Thorneycroft (*Director / Company Secretary*)
Victoria Hobbs (*Director*)
Jennifer Custer (*Foreign Rights Director*)
Sarah Molloy (*Children's Agent*)

All MSS except plays, scripts, poetry, scientific, technical for the layman only.

Rights Representative in UK for:
USA: Anne Edelstein Literary Agency, New York, NY, USA; Brandt & Hochman Inc, New York, NY, USA; Gina Maccoby Literary Agency, New York, NY, USA; Jane Chelius Literary Agency, Brooklyn, NY, USA; Lescher & Lescher Ltd, New York, NY, USA; Miriam Altshuler Literary Agency, Red Hook, NY, USA

Overseas Representation:
Brazil: Tassy Barham, London, UK
Bulgaria & Serbia: Andrew Nurnberg Literary Agency, Sofia, Bulgaria
China & Taiwan: Andrew Nurnberg Literary Agency, Shanghai, P. R. of China; Andrew Nurnberg Literary Agency, Taipei, Taiwan
Czech & Slovak Republics & Slovenia: Andrew Nurnberg Associates, Prague, Czech Republic
France: La Nouvelle Agence, Paris, France
Germany, Switzerland & Austria: Mohrbooks Literary Agency, Zurich, Switzerland
Hungary & Croatia: Andrew Nurnberg Ltd, Budapest, Hungary
Israel: Deborah Harris Agency, Jerusalem, Israel
Italy: Luigi Bernabó Associates Srl, Milan, Italy
Japan (fiction): The English Agency Japan Ltd, Tokyo, Japan
Japan (non-fiction): Tuttle-Mori Agency Inc, Tokyo, Japan
Korea: EYA, Seoul, Republic of Korea

Poland: ANAW Literary Agency, Warsaw, Poland
Romania: Simona Kessler International Copyright Agency Ltd, Bucharest, Romania
Russia: Andrew Nurnberg Associates, Moscow, Russia
Scandinavia: Licht & Burr Literary Agency, Copenhagen, Denmark
Turkey, Greece, Indonesia, Portugal, Latvia, Lithuania, Estonia, Spain & Netherlands: A. M. Heath & Co Ltd, London, UK

4034

DAVID HIGHAM ASSOCIATES
5–8 Lower John Street, Golden Square, London W1F 9HA
Telephone: 020 7434 5900
Fax: 020 7437 1072
Email: dha@davidhigham.co.uk
Web Site: www.davidhigham.co.uk

Specialization: agents for the negotiation of all rights in fiction, general non-fiction, children's fiction and picture books, plays, film and TV scripts. Represented in all foreign markets. Please see website for submissions guidelines. No reading fee. Founded 1935.

4035

KATE HORDERN LITERARY AGENCY
18 Mortimer Road, Clifton, Bristol BS8 4EY
Telephone: 0117 923 9368
Email: katehordern@blueyonder.co.uk & annewilliamskhla@googlemail.com
Web Site: www.katehordern.co.uk

Personnel:
Kate Hordern (*Proprietor*)
Anne Williams (*Associate Agent*)

Specialization: Quality literary and commercial fiction, including women's fiction, crime and thrillers, and general non-fiction, and children's/YA. Clients include Lyn Andrews, Richard Bassett, Jeff Dawson, Kylie Fitzpatrick, Sven Hassel, Duncan Hewitt, Julian Lees, Will Randall, Dave Roberts, John Sadler.

4036

VALERIE HOSKINS ASSOCIATES LTD
20 Charlotte Street, London W1T 2NA
Telephone: 020 7637 4490
Fax: 020 7637 4493
Email: vha@vhassociates.co.uk

Personnel:
Valerie Hoskins (*Managing Director*)
Rebecca Watson (*Associate*)
Sara Moore (*PA/ Manager*)

Specialization: film & television rights for published work. The company is not a publishing agency.

4037

IMG UK LTD
McCormack House, Burlington Lane, London W4 2TH
Telephone: 020 8233 5300
Fax: 020 8233 5268
Email: sarah.wooldridge@imgworld.com
Web Site: www.imgworld.com

Personnel:
Sarah Wooldridge (*Consultant*)
Sally Matthews (*Accountant*)

All MSS except science fiction, fiction, children's, short stories and poetry.

Specialization: non-fiction. No reading fee. Please send synopsis with sample chapter and SAE. Also handle IMG speakers. 20% commission.

4038

THE INSPIRA GROUP
5 Bradley Road, Enfield, Middx EN3 6ES
Telephone: 020 8292 5163
Fax: 0870 139 3057
Email: darin@theinspiragroup.com
Web Site: www.theinspiragroup.com

Personnel:
Darin Jewell (*Managing Director*)
Shaun Ebelthite (*Rights*)
Charlene Webber (*Administration*)

Specialization: children's books, fantasy/sci-fi, and general fiction. Manuscripts in all genres are considered. Clients include Michael Tolkien, Simon Hall, John Wilson and Simon Brown. Authors should e-mail their full MSS, synopsis and short literary CV (with their postal address and landline tel. no.) to darin@theinspiragroup.com

4039

INTERCONTINENTAL LITERARY AGENCY LTD
Centric House, 390 Strand, London WC2R 0LT
Telephone: 020 7379 6611
Fax: 020 7240 4724
Email: ila@ila-agency.co.uk
Web Site: www.ila-agency.co.uk

Personnel:
Nicki Kennedy (*Agent*)
Sam Edenborough (*Agent*)
Mary Esdaile (*Agent*)
Tessa Girvan (*Agent*)
Katherine West (*Agent*)
Jenny Robson (*Agent*)

Specialization: translation rights exclusively.

Rights Representative in UK for:
see website at:: Intercontinental Literary Agency, London, UK

4040

JANKLOW & NESBIT (UK) LTD
13a Hillgate Street, London W8 7SP
Telephone: 020 7243 2975
Fax: 020 7376 2915
Email: queries@janklow.co.uk
Web Site: www.janklowandnesbit.co.uk

Personnel:
Claire Paterson (*Literary Agent*)
Will Francis (*Literary Agent*)
Tim Glister (*Literary Agent*)
Rebecca Folland (*Foreign Rights Director*)
Jessie Botterill (*Office Manager*)

All MSS except poetry, plays, film & TV scripts.

Specialization: fiction and non-fiction; commercial and literary. Send full outline (non-fiction), synopsis and first three sample chapters (fiction) plus informative covering letter and return postage.

Parent Company:
USA: Janklow & Nesbit Associates

Associated Companies:
USA: Janklow & Nesbit Associates

Overseas Representation:
USA: Janklow & Nesbit Associates, New York, NY, USA

4041

JOHNSON & ALCOCK LTD
Clerkenwell House,
45–47 Clerkenwell Green, London EC1R 0HT
Telephone: 020 7251 0125
Fax: 020 7251 2172

Email: info@johnsonandalcock.co.uk
Web Site: www.johnsonandalcock.co.uk

Personnel:
Andrew Hewson (*Director*)
Michael Alcock (*Director*)
Anna Power (*Agent*)
Ed Wilson (*Agent*)
Fran Barrie (*Agent*)

All MSS except technical or academic material, poetry, plays. No unsolicited manuscripts; please send synopsis, full CV, sample opening chapters and SAE in the first instance. No reading fee.

Specialization: fiction and non-fiction. General non-fiction, biography, history, current affairs, health and lifestyle; literary and commercial fiction; sci-fi and graphic novels; 9+ children's and young adult.

Rights Representative in UK for:
USA: Vendome Press, New York, NY, USA

Overseas Representation:
Worldwide: Johnson & Alcock Ltd, London, UK

4042

JANE JUDD LITERARY AGENCY
18 Belitha Villas, London N1 1PD
Telephone: 020 7607 0273
Fax: 020 7607 0623
Web Site: www.janejudd.com

Personnel:
Jane C. Judd (*Proprietor*)

All MSS except plays, poetry and short stories.

Specialization: general non-fiction & fiction.

Rights Representative in UK for:
USA: Marian Young, New York, NY, USA; Mercury House, San Francisco, CA, USA; Permanent Press, Sag Harbor, NY, USA; RLR Associates, New York, NY, USA

Overseas Representation:
Eastern Europe: Prava i Prevodi Agency, Belgrade, Serbia
France: La Nouvelle Agence, Paris, France
Germany: Thomas Schlück Literary Agency, Garbsen, Germany
Italy: Stefania Fietta ALI, Milan, Italy
Netherlands & Scandinavia: Jan Michael, Amsterdam, Netherlands
Spain & Portugal: Julio F Yañez Literary Agency, Barcelona, Spain
USA: The Unter Agency, New York, NY, USA

4043

*MICHELLE KASS ASSOCIATES
85 Charing Cross Road, London WC2H 0AA
Telephone: 020 7439 1624
Fax: 020 7734 3394
Email: office@michellekass.co.uk

Personnel:
Michelle Kass (*Agent*)
Andrew Mills (*Agent*)

Specialization: an agency representing novelists, writers and directors for film, TV and theatre. No unsolicited MSS without preliminary phone call.

4044

THE FRANCES KELLY AGENCY
111 Clifton Road, Kingston-upon-Thames, Surrey KT2 6PL
Telephone: 020 8549 7830
Fax: 020 8547 0051

Personnel:
Frances Kelly (*Proprietor*)

Specialization: general non-fiction, all academic & professional disciplines; return postage & preliminary letter requested.

4045

*KNIGHT FEATURES LTD
20 Crescent Grove, London SW4 7AH
Telephone: 020 7622 1467
Fax: 020 7622 1522
Email: info@knightfeatures.co.uk
Web Site: www.knightfeatures.co.uk

Personnel:
Peter Knight (Proprietor)
Gaby Martin (Associate)
Andrew Knight (Associate)
Samantha Ferris (Associate)

All MSS except short stories, poetry & unsolicited MSS (reading fee). No e-mail submissions.

Specialization: worldwide selling of strip cartoons, major features and serializations. Exclusive syndication agent in UK & Irish Republic for United Feature Syndicate (Peanuts, Dilbert, etc.) & Newspaper Enterprise Association (Frank & Ernest, Born Loser, King Baloo, etc.), also Paws Inc (Garfield), Creators Syndicate (The Far Side).

Rights Representative in UK for:
New Zealand: The Puzzle Co, New Zealand
USA: Paws Inc, USA; United Media Inc, New York, NY, USA

4046

LENZ-MULLIGAN RIGHTS & CO-EDITIONS
15 Sandbourne Avenue, London SW19 3EW
Telephone: 020 8543 7846
Email: lenzmulligan@btinternet.com

Personnel:
Gundhild Lenz-Mulligan (Rights Manager)

All MSS except poetry and film scripts.

Specialization: sale of co-editions and rights in the Nordic countries and Dutch, English and German-speaking markets. Particularly interested in children's books. Also offers proofreading and translation services of German language material. Represents European, American and Australian publishers, packagers and authors.

Rights Representative in UK for:
Australia: Tracy Marsh Publications, West Beach, SA, Australia
Germany: Ars Edition, Germany
UK: Best Publishing Ever, UK

4047

BARBARA LEVY LITERARY AGENCY
64 Greenhill, Hampstead High Street, London NW3 5TZ
Telephone: 020 7435 9046
Fax: 020 7431 2063

Personnel:
John F. Selby (Solicitor Associate)

Specialization: general fiction & non-fiction, and TV presenters.

Rights Representative in UK for:
USA: Arcadia, Danbury, CT, USA; Richard Parks, New York, NY, USA

Overseas Representation:
Foreign Language Markets: The Buckman Agency, London, UK
USA: Marshall Rights, London, UK

4048

LIMELIGHT CELEBRITY MANAGEMENT LTD
10 Filmer Mews, 75 Filmer Road, London SW6 7JF
Telephone: 020 7384 9950
Fax: 020 7384 9955
Email: mail@limelightmanagement.com
Web Site: www.limelightmanagement.com

Personnel:
Fiona Lindsay (Managing Director, Owner/ Founder)
Mary Bekhait (Agent)
Maclean Lindsay (Operations Manager)
Alison Lindsay

Specialization: full-length book MSS. Commercial fiction and non-fiction. Food, wine, health, crafts, gardening, biography/ memoirs, popular culture, travel, women's interest (home 15%, overseas 20%), TV and radio rights (15–20%); will suggest revision where appropriate. No reading fee.

4049

CHRISTOPHER LITTLE LITERARY AGENCY
10 Eel Brook Studios,
125 Moore Park Road, London SW6 4PS
Telephone: 020 7736 4455
Fax: 020 7736 4490
Email: info@christopherlittle.net
Web Site: www.christopherlittle.net

Personnel:
Christopher Little (Agent Proprietor)
Caroline Hardman (Agent)

All MSS except poetry, plays, science fiction, fantasy, textbooks, illustrated children's, short stories. Film scripts for established clients only.

Specialization: full-length commercial fiction and non-fiction. No reading fee. Send detailed letter plus synopsis and three sample chapters, and SAE in first instance.

4050

LONDON INDEPENDENT BOOKS
26 Chalcot Crescent, London NW1 8YD
Telephone: 020 7706 0486
Fax: 020 7724 3122

Personnel:
Carolyn Whitaker (Literary Agent)

All MSS except computers & young children's.

Specialization: fiction & non-fiction, particularly travel & fantasy.

4051

ANDREW LOWNIE LITERARY AGENCY LTD
36 Great Smith Street, London SW1P 3BU
Telephone: 020 7222 7574
Fax: 020 7222 7576
Email: lownie@globalnet.co.uk
Web Site: www.andrew.lownie.co.uk

Personnel:
Andrew Lownie (Proprietor)

Specialization: history, biography, packaging celebrities for book market and representing book projects for journalists. Titles agented include Norma Major's books on Joan Sutherland and Chequers, Juliet Barker, Duncan Falconer, Laurence Gardner, Lawrence James, Christopher Lloyd, Sian Rees, David Stafford, Christian Wolmar, Sir John Mills, authorized lives of Sir Henry Cooper and Dick Emery, Desmond Seward, Daniel Tammet, Cathy Glass, Joyce Cary and

Julian Maclaren – Ross Estates, numerous books about the SAS. Return postage essential. No reading fee. Commission 15% worldwide.

Overseas Representation:
Worldwide (excluding USA & Japan): The Marsh Agency, London, UK

4052

LUTYENS & RUBINSTEIN LITERARY AGENCY
21 Kensington Park Road, London W11 2EU
Telephone: 020 7792 4855
Fax: n/a
Email: info@lutyensrubinstein.co.uk
Web Site: www.lutyensrubinstein.co.uk

Personnel:
Felicity Rubinstein (Partner)
Sarah Lutyens (Partner)
Jane Finigan (Agent and Rights Manager)
Anna Steadman (General Assistant)

All MSS except poetry, screenplays, scripts for theatre and/or TV and radio.

Specialization: general adult non-fiction and fiction.

Overseas Representation:
France: La Nouvelle Agence, Paris, France
Germany: Eggers & Landwehr, Berlin, Germany
Italy: Grandi & Associates, Milan, Italy
USA: Inkwell Management, New York, NY, USA

4053

DUNCAN McARA LITERARY AGENCY
28 Beresford Gardens, Edinburgh EH5 3ES
Telephone: 0131 552 1558
Email: duncanmcara@mac.com

All MSS except 'genre' fiction, educational & children's.

Specialization: literary fiction; non-fiction: art, architecture, archaeology, biography, history, military, Scottish. Home: 15%; Overseas: 20%. Preliminary email or letter with SAE essential. No reading fee. Also acts as editorial consultant on all aspects of general trade publishing. Editing, re-writing, copy-editing, proof correction for wide range of UK publishers.

4054

*THE McKERNAN LITERARY AGENCY & CONSULTANCY
5 Gayfield Square, Edinburgh EH1 3NW
Telephone: 0131 557 1771
Email: maggie@mckernanagency.co.uk
Web Site: www.mckernanagency.co.uk

Personnel:
Maggie McKernan (Agent)

All MSS except film scripts, screenplays, picture books for children.

Specialization: assisting and developing writers, as well as representing their interests in their dealings with publishers, selling rights and handling negotiations of contracts. Handle fiction and non-fiction (commercial and literary novels of all kinds, including crime, historical, contemporary). Consideration will be given to novels for children over the age of 10, but not picture books.

Overseas Representation:
USA & Worldwide (translation rights): Capel & Land Ltd, London, UK

4055

EUNICE McMULLEN LTD
Low Ibbotsholme Cottage, off Bridge Lane, Troutbeck Bridge, Windermere, Cumbria LA23 1HU
Telephone: 01539 448551
Email: eunicemcmullen@totalise.co.uk
Web Site: www.eunicemcmullen.co.uk

Specialization: Children's books (fiction only) for all ages – from picture books for toddlers to YA. No unsolicited MSS.

4056

*ANDREW MANN LTD
1 Old Compton Street, London W1D 5JA
Telephone: 020 7734 4751
Fax: 020 3441 0988
Email: info@andrewmann.co.uk
Web Site: www.andrewmann.co.uk

Personnel:
Anne Dewe (Director)
Tina Betts (Director)
Louise Burns (Agent)

All MSS except poetry.

Specialization: fiction, general non-fiction & radio, television scripts. No unsolicited MSS. Preliminary letter, synopsis – first 30 pages and SAE essential. No reading fee. No e-mail submissions.

Rights Representative in UK for:
USA: Richard McDonough, Irvine, CA, USA

Overseas Representation:
China (Mainland): Big Apple Tuttle-Mori Agency Inc, Shanghai, P. R. of China
Czech Republic, Slovakia, Poland & Bulgaria': Andrew Nurnberg Associates, London, UK
France: Lora Fountain Associates, Paris, France
Germany: Thomas Schlück Literary Agency, Garbsen, Germany
Hungary: Kàtai & Bolza Literary Agents, Budapest, Hungary
Israel: Deborah Harris Agency, Jerusalem, Israel
Italy: Living Literary Agency, Milan, Italy
Japan: Tuttle-Mori Agency Inc, Tokyo, Japan
Romania: Simona Kessler International Copyright Agency Ltd, Bucharest, Romania
Scandinavia, Netherlands, Spain & Portugal: Lennart Sane Agency, Karlshamn, Sweden
Taiwan: Big Apple Tuttle-Mori Associates, Shin-Juang, Taiwan
Thailand: Silk Road Agency, Bangkok, Thailand
Turkey: Asli Karasuil Agency, Istanbul, Turkey
USA: Jonathan Lyons, New York, NY, USA

4057

SARAH MANSON LITERARY AGENT
6 Totnes Walk, London N2 0AD
Telephone: 020 8442 0396
Email: info@sarahmanson.com
Web Site: www.sarahmanson.com

Personnel:
Sarah Manson (Proprietor)

All MSS except poetry and picture books.

Specialization: fiction for children and young adults. List of clients includes both well-established writers and promising new talent.

4058

MARJACQ SCRIPTS
34 Devonshire Place, London W1G 6JW
Telephone: 020 7935 9499

Fax: 020 7935 9115
Email: enquiries@marjacq.com
Web Site: www.marjacq.com

Personnel:
Philip Patterson (Literary Agent)
Luke Speed (Film Agent)
Isabella Floris (Literary Agent)

All MSS except poetry or stage plays.

Specialization: literary and commercial fiction, crime, thrillers, science fiction and women's fiction, and general non-fiction. Please submit three sample chapters and synopsis in first instance. SAE essential for return of MS.

Overseas Representation:
Austria, Germany, Switzerland & parts of Eastern Europe: Transnet Contracts Ltd, Vienna, Austria
Hungary: Kátai & Bolza Literary Agents, Budapest, Hungary
Israel: Ilana Pikarski Literary Agency, Tel Aviv, Israel
Italy: Agenzia Piergiorgio Nicolazzini, Milan, Italy
Japan: The English Agency Japan Ltd, Tokyo, Japan
Poland: Graal Ltd, Warsaw, Poland
Scandinavia, Netherlands, Spain & Portugal: Lennart Sane Agency, Karlshamn, Sweden
Turkey: Kayi Literary & Merchandising Agency, Istanbul, Turkey

4059

THE MARSH AGENCY LTD
[incorporating Paterson Marsh Ltd and Campbell Thomson & McLaughlin Ltd]
50 Albemarle Street, London W1S 4BD
Telephone: 020 7493 4361
Fax: 020 7495 8961
Email: see website
Web Site: www.marsh-agency.co.uk

Personnel:
Camilla Ferrier (Foreign Rights Director)
Jessica Woollard (Agent)
Stephanie Ebdon (Agent)

All MSS except children's, poetry, drama, TV, film & radio scripts.

Specialization: selling of rights in the work of English-language writers throughout the world, representing a number of UK authors as well as British and American agencies and publishers.

Rights Representative in UK for:
Worldwide: see Website for full list

4060

BLANCHE MARVIN
21a St Johns Wood High Street, London NW8 7NG
Telephone: 020 7722 2313
Fax: 020 7722 2313

Personnel:
Blanche Marvin (Director)

Specialization: theatre, film, TV, radio & publishing for UK & USA. MSS from published authors only.

4061

MBA LITERARY AGENTS
62 Grafton Way, London W1T 5DW
Telephone: 020 7387 2076
Fax: 020 7387 2042
Web Site: www.mbalit.co.uk

Personnel:
Diana Tyler (Joint Managing Director)
Laura Longrigg (Joint Managing Director)
Timothy Webb (Financial Director)

David Riding (Director)
Susan Smith (Director)
Jean Kitson (Agent)
Sophie Gorell Barnes (Agent)
Stella Kane (Foreign Rights Manager)

All MSS except poetry, short stories.

Specialization: fiction and non-fiction. Also scripts for film, TV, radio & theatre.

Rights Representative in UK for:
USA: Donald Maass Agency, New York, NY, USA

Overseas Representation:
Brazil: Tassy Barham, London, UK
Eastern Europe & Greece: Prava i Prevodi, Belgrade, Serbia
France: Lora Fountain Associates, Paris, France
Germany: Mohrbooks Literary Agency, Zurich, Switzerland; Thomas Schlück Literary Agency, Garbsen, Germany
Israel: I. Pikarski Literary Agency, Tel Aviv, Israel
Italy: Vicki Satlow Literary Agency, Milan, Italy
Japan: Tuttle-Mori Agency Inc, Tokyo, Japan
Netherlands: Caroline Van Gelderen Literary Agency, Hilversum, Netherlands
Russia: Prava i Prevodi RAO, Moscow, Russia
Scandinavia: Licht & Burr Literary Agency, Copenhagen, Denmark
Spain: Carmen Balcells Agencia Literaria SA, Barcelona, Spain

4062

THE CATHY MILLER FOREIGN RIGHTS AGENCY
29A The Quadrangle, 49 Atalanta Street, London SW6 6TU
Telephone: 020 7386 5473
Fax: 020 7385 1774
Email: cathy@millerrightsagency.com

Personnel:
Mrs Cathy Miller (Principal/Managing Director)

All MSS except poetry & educational.

Specialization: foreign rights; acting as consultants to publishers on sales of foreign rights of non-fiction titles (psychoanalysis, medical, business & management, esoteric, health & general trade books); handling market research for lists or one-off projects; helping to set up rights departments; advising on all matters concerning translation rights and negotiations with foreign publishers.

Rights Representative in UK for:
Canada: Fletcher Peacock, Canada; Golden Globe Publishing, Notre Dame-de-l'Ile Perrot, PQ, Canada; Mark Fisher, Canada
UK: Ann Henning-Jocelyn, Countess of Roden, UK; Artemis Music Publishing, UK; Foulsham Publishers, UK; Free Association Books, UK; Karnac Books, UK; Phantom Genius Ltd, UK; Shepheard-Walwyn, UK; Thorogood Publishing Ltd, UK

Overseas Representation:
China: Mei Yao, New York, NY, USA
Greece: Read n Right Agency, Cahlkida, Greece
Japan: The English Agency Japan Ltd, Tokyo, Japan
Korea: EYA, Seoul, Republic of Korea
Poland: Graal Ltd, Warsaw, Poland
Russia: Alexander Korzhenevski Literary Agency, Moscow, Russia
Spain: Julio F Yañez Literary Agency, Barcelona, Spain

4063

NEW WRITING SOUTH
9 Jew Street, Brighton BN1 1UT
Telephone: 01273 735353
Email: admin@newwritingsouth.com
Web Site: www.newwritingsouth.com

Personnel:
Chris Taylor (Director)
Mark Bryant (Operations Manager)
Anna Jefferson (Creative Learning)

Specialization: New Writing South is the new writing development agency for the south-east region. We find and enable new creative writing talent to flourish, support emerging and mid-career writers, bring the work of professional writers to new audiences and create new paid work for writers.

4064

*THE MAGGIE NOACH LITERARY AGENCY
7 Peacock Yard, Iliffe Street, London SE17 3LH
Telephone: 020 7708 3073
Email: info@mnla.co.uk

All MSS except short stories, poetry, plays, screenplays, cookery, gardening, mind/body/spirit, illustrated children's, scientific/academic/specialist non-fiction. Absolutely no illustrated books.

Specialization: fiction, general non-fiction and children's books. No unsolicited manuscripts – submissions by arrangements only. Home 15%, USA & translation 20%.

Overseas Representation:
Worldwide: Jill Hughes, Aubourn, Lincs, UK

4065

ANDREW NURNBERG ASSOCIATES LTD
20–23 Greville Street, London EC1N 8SS
Telephone: 020 3327 0400
Fax: 020 7430 0801
Email: contact@andrewnurnberg.com
Web Site: www.andrewnurnberg.com

Personnel:
Andrew Nurnberg (Managing Director)
Sarah Nundy (Deputy Managing Director)
Vicky Mark (Director)

Specialization: representing leading British & American agents & authors throughout the world.

4066

PATERSON MARSH LTD
see: The Marsh Agency

4067

JOHN PAWSEY
8 Snowshill Court, Giffard Park, Milton Keynes, Bucks MK14 5QG
Telephone: 01908 217179

Personnel:
John Pawsey (Sole Proprietor)

All MSS except fiction, poetry, short stories, journalism, children's, original film & stage scripts.

Specialization: sport, popular culture.

Rights Representative in UK for:
USA: Alison J. Picard, Cotuit, MA, USA; Bobbe Siegel, New York, NY, USA

Overseas Representation:
France: Lora Fountain Associates, Paris, France

Germany: Thomas Schlück Literary Agency, Garbsen, Germany
Hungary: Lex Copyright, Budapest, Hungary
Italy: Living Literary Agency, Milan, Italy
Japan: The English Agency Japan Ltd, Tokyo, Japan
Korea: Korea Copyright Center, Seoul, Republic of Korea
Netherlands: International Literatur Bureau BV, Hilversum, Netherlands
Russia: Prava i Prevodi RAO, Moscow, Russia
Scandinavia: Sane Töregård Agency, Karlshamn, Sweden
Spain & South America: International Editors Co, Barcelona, Spain
USA: Alison J. Picard, Cotuit, MA, USA
Yugoslav States: Prava i Prevodi, Belgrade, Serbia

4068

POLLINGER LIMITED
9 Staple Inn, Holborn, London WC1V 7QH
Telephone: 020 7404 0342
Fax: 020 7242 5737
Email: info@pollingerltd.com
Web Site: www.pollingerltd.com

Personnel:
Lesley Pollinger (Managing Director)
Leigh Pollinger (Director)
Joanna Devereux (Literary Agent)
Tim Bates (Literary Agent)
Hayley Yeeles (Literary Agent)

All MSS except poetry & articles – see website for submission details.

Specialization: adult fiction and non-fiction, children's and literary estates.

Rights Representative in UK for:
UK: Wallflower Press, London, UK
UK (dramatic rights): Summersdale, UK
USA: New Directions Publishing Corporation, New York, NY, USA

Overseas Representation:
China: Big Apple Tuttle-Mori Agency, Taipei, Taiwan
Denmark, Finland, Norway & Sweden: Licht & Burr Literary Agency, Copenhagen, Denmark
Eastern Europe & Russia: Prava i Prevodi, Belgrade, Serbia
France: Michelle Lapautre Agency, Paris, France
Germany & Switzerland: Mohrbooks Literary Agency, Zurich, Switzerland
Greece: Read n Right Agency, Cahlkida, Greece
Hungary: Lex Copyright, Budapest, Hungary
Israel: The Book Publishers Association of Israel, Tel Aviv, Israel
Japan: Tuttle-Mori Agency Inc, Tokyo, Japan
Korea: The Eric Yang Agency, Seoul, Republic of Korea
Portugal & Brazil: Ilidio da Fonseca Matos, Lisbon, Portugal
Spain & South America: Carmen Balcells Agencia Literaria SA, Barcelona, Spain
Turkey: ONK Agency Ltd, Istanbul, Turkey

4069

SHELLEY POWER LITERARY AGENCY LTD
13 rue du Pré Saint Gervais, 75019 Paris, France
Telephone: +33 1 42 38 36 49
Email: shelley.power@wanadoo.fr

Personnel:
Shelley Power (Director, Literary Agent)

All MSS except children's books, poetry, plays or film/tv scripts. No horror, science fiction or fantasy.

Specialization: literary agency.

Overseas Representation:
China: Big Apple Tuttle-Mori Agency Inc, Shanghai, P. R. of China; Big Apple Tuttle-Mori Agency, Taipei, Taiwan
Czech Republic: Transnet Contracts, Czech Republic
France: Lora Fountain Associates, Paris, France
Germany: Liepman AG, Germany
Greece: JLM Literary Agency, Athens, Greece
Hungary: Kàtai & Bolza Literary Agents, Budapest, Hungary
Israel: Ilana Pikarski Literary Agency, Tel Aviv, Israel
Italy: Natoli, Stefan & Oliva Agenzia Letteraria, Milan, Italy
Japan: The English Agency Japan Ltd, Tokyo, Japan
Korea: The Eric Yang Agency, Seoul, Republic of Korea
Poland: Graal Ltd, Warsaw, Poland
Romania: Simona Kessler International Copyright Agency Ltd, Bucharest, Romania
Spain: Julio F Yañez Literary Agency, Barcelona, Spain

4070

REAL CREATIVES WORLDWIDE (RCW)
www.realcreatives.com
Telephone: 0788 422 8835
Email: malcolm.rasala@realcreatives.com
Web Site: www.realcreatives.com

Specialization: literary agency for books (factual & fiction); film agent for motion pictures; TV agent for TV programmes worldwide; advertiser – supply TV programme agents; agent representing 700 professionals (creatives, etc.) in the advertising, motion picture, TV and digital industries,

4071

THE SAYLE LITERARY AGENCY
1 Petersfield, Cambridge CB1 1BB
Telephone: 01223 303035
Web Site: www.sayleliteraryagency.com

Personnel:
Rachel Calder (*Proprietor*)

All MSS except children's, poetry, technical, science fiction.

Specialization: fiction (literary & crime), biography, history, current affairs, travel, social issues.

Rights Representative in UK for:
USA: Darhansoff Verrill Feldman Literary Agency, New York, NY, USA

Overseas Representation:
Europe & Rest of the World: The Marsh Agency, London, UK
USA: Dunow, Carlson & Lerner Agency, New York, NY, USA

4072

CAROLINE SHELDON LITERARY AGENCY LTD
71 Hillgate Place, London W8 7SS
Telephone: 020 7727 9102
Email:
carolinesheldon@carolinesheldon.co.uk & pennyholroyde@carolinesheldon.co.uk
Web Site: www.carolinesheldon.co.uk & www.carolinesheldonillustrators.co.uk

Personnel:
Caroline Sheldon (*Literary Agent*)
Penny Holroyde (*Literary Agent*)

All MSS except short stories.

Specialization: fiction, women's fiction & children's books, human interest non-fiction.

4073

DORIE SIMMONDS AGENCY LTD
Riverbank House,
1 Putney Bridge Approach, London
SW6 3JD
Telephone: 020 7736 0002
Email: dorie@doriesimmonds.com

Personnel:
Dorie Simmonds (*Proprietor*)
Frances Lubbe (*Rights Executive*)

All MSS except plays, poetry,short stories.

Specialization: commercial fiction and non-fiction in both the adult and children's markets.

4074

JEFFREY SIMMONS
15 Penn House, Mallory Street, London
NW8 8SX
Telephone: 020 7224 8917
Email: jasimmons@unicombox.co.uk

All MSS except children's books, cookery, science fiction, romances & some specialist subjects.

Specialization: biography & memoirs; cinema, drama & the arts; general fiction; history; law & crime; literature; politics & world affairs.

Overseas Representation:
Japan: The English Agency Japan Ltd, Tokyo, Japan
Spain: Julio F Yañez Literary Agency, Barcelona, Spain

4075

*SINCLAIR-STEVENSON
3 South Terrace, London SW7 2TB
Telephone: 020 7581 2550
Fax: 020 7581 2550

Translation Rights:
c/o David Higham Associates Ltd,
5–8 Lower John Street, Golden Square,
London W1F 9HA

All MSS except children's books, science fiction, science, fantasy, film or play scripts.

Specialization: non-fiction – biography and autobiography, the arts, politics and current affairs, travel, history; and fiction.

Rights Representative in UK for:
USA: T. C. Wallace Ltd, New York, NY, USA

Overseas Representation:
USA: T. C. Wallace Ltd, New York, NY, USA

4076

ROBERT SMITH LITERARY AGENCY LTD
12 Bridge Wharf, 156 Caledonian Road,
London N1 9UU
Telephone: 020 7278 2444
Fax: 020 7833 5680
Email:
robertsmith.literaryagency@virgin.net

Personnel:
Robert Smith (*Managing Director*)
Anne Smith (*Director*)

All MSS except fiction, poetry, children's books or reference. Writers may submit synopses but no unsolicited manuscripts.

Specialization: the agency sells books, series and articles to book publishers, newspapers and magazines across the world. It operates only in non-fiction. Main areas are autobiography and biography, show business, hot topics, history, health, lifestyle and true crime.

Overseas Representation:
Germany: Thomas Schlück Literary Agency, Garbsen, Germany
Italy: Natoli, Stefan & Oliva Agenzia Letteraria, Milan, Italy
Spain: RDC Agencia Literaria, Madrid, Spain
USA: Renee Zuckerbrot Literary Agency, New York, USA

4077

*SHIRLEY STEWART LITERARY AGENCY
3rd Floor, 4a Nelson Road, London
SE10 9JB
Telephone: 020 8293 3000

Personnel:
Shirley Stewart (*Director*)

All MSS except children's books, poetry, plays, science fiction and fantasy.

Specialization: full-length MSS only. Fiction and non-fiction (home 10–15%, overseas 20%). No reading fee but preliminary letter and return postage essential.

Rights Representative in UK for:
USA: Curtis Brown Ltd, New York, NY, USA

4078

THE SUSIJN AGENCY LTD
3rd Floor, 64 Great Titchfield Street,
London W1W 7QH
Telephone: 020 7580 6341
Fax: 020 7580 8626
Email: info@thesusijnagency.com
Web Site: www.thesusijnagency.com

Personnel:
Laura Susijn (*Literary Agent*)

All MSS except children's books, sci-fi, romantic fiction, fantasy, sagas, self-help, business, military and computer books.

Specialization: selling rights world-wide in literary fiction and non-fiction. Also represents non-English language publishers and authors for UK, US and translation rights world-wide. Deals direct, using sub-agent in Eastern Europe, Israel and the Far East. Preliminary letter, synopsis and first two chapters preferred. No reading fee.

4079

THE TENNYSON AGENCY
10 Cleveland Avenue, London SW20 9EW
Telephone: 020 8543 5939
Email: submissions@tenagy.co.uk
Web Site: www.tenagy.co.uk

Personnel:
Adam Sheldon (*Partner*)

All MSS except poetry, short stories, science fiction, popular romantic and historical fiction, children's books and non-fiction unrelated to the arts.

Specialization: writing for the theatre, TV, radio and film. Related subjects and literary fiction are considered on an ad hoc basis. Commission rates: literature: 12.5%, drama: 15%, overseas: 20%. Submissions by post, on invitation, following introductory letter. Full details on the agency's website.

4080

*J. M. THURLEY MANAGEMENT
Archery House, 33 Archery Square, Walmer, Deal, Kent CT14 7AY
Telephone: 01304 371721
Email: jmthurley@aol.com
Web Site: www.thecuttingedge.biz

Personnel:
Jon Thurley (*Contact*)
Patricia Preece (*Contact*)

All MSS except short stories & poetry.

Specialization: will give editorial help by arrangement on all types of projects.

4081

LAVINIA TREVOR
29 Addison Place, London W11 4RJ
Telephone: 020 7603 5254
Fax: 0870 129 0838
Email: info@laviniatrevor.co.uk
Web Site: www.laviniatrevor.co.uk

Personnel:
Lavinia Trevor (*Agent*)

Specialization: fiction and non-fiction for the general trade market (see website). Sorry, no unsolicited material.

4082

*JANE TURNBULL AGENCY
58 Elgin Crescent, London W11 2JJ
Telephone: 020 7727 9409
Email: jane@janeturnbull.co.uk
Web Site: www.janeturnbull.co.uk

Mailing Address:
Barn Cottage, Veryan, Truro, Cornwall
TR2 5QA
Telephone: 01872 501317

Personnel:
Jane Turnbull (*Proprietor*)

All MSS except science or romantic fiction, children's fiction, poetry or plays.

Specialization: literary fiction, current affairs, biography, design, lifestyle, health, TV tie-ins, humour, natural history. Initial letter essential; no unsolicited MSS. Commission 15% home sales, 20% US, 20% translation, 15% radio/TV/film. Founded 1986, member of the Association of Authors' Agents.

Overseas Representation:
Worldwide: Aitken Alexander Associates, London, UK

4083

UNITED AGENTS LTD
12–26 Lexington Street, London W1F 0LE
Telephone: 020 3214 0800
Fax: 020 3214 0801
Web Site: www.unitedagents.co.uk

Personnel:
Simon Trewin (*Head, Books Department*)
Caroline Dawnay (*Agent*)
Sarah Ballard (*Agent*)
Carol MacArthur (*Agent*)
James Gill (*Agent*)
Robert Kirby (*Agent*)
Rosemary Scoular (*Agent*)
Charles Walker (*Agent*)
Anna Webber (*Agent*)
Jodie Marsh (*Agent*)

Specialization: literary and talent agency, operating across books, theatre, film, TV and commercials. Offers a full service to its client base and is always interested in new clients. Please consult website at www.unitedagents.co.uk for full submission guidelines.

4084

*ED VICTOR LTD
6 Bayley Street, Bedford Square, London WC1B 3HE
Telephone: 020 7304 4100
Fax: 020 7304 4111
Email: mary@edvictor.com

Personnel:
Ed Victor *(Executive Chairman)*
Margaret Phillips *(Joint Managing Director)*
Sophie Hicks *(Foreign Rights & Joint Managing Director)*
Leon Morgan *(Director)*
Carol Ryan *(Director)*
Graham Greene *(Director)*
Hitesh Shah *(Finance Director)*

All MSS except unsolicited manuscripts.

Specialization: fiction, non-fiction, biography, children's books.

4085

WADE & DOHERTY LITERARY AGENCY LTD
33 Cormorant Lodge, Thomas More Street, London E1W 1AU
Telephone: 020 7488 4171
Fax: 020 7488 4172
Email: rw@rwla.com
Web Site: www.rwla.com

Personnel:
Broo Doherty *(Partner)*

All MSS except scripts, poetry, plays, children's books including picture books or short stories.

Specialization: handles general fiction and non-fiction excluding children's books. Send detailed synopsis and first 10,000 words by e-mail. No reading fee. Commission: home 10%; film, TV and translation 20% (fees negotiable if a contract has already been offered). Founded 2001. Please see our website for detailed email submission guidelines.

4086

WATSON, LITTLE LTD
48–56 Bayham Place, London NW1 0EU
Telephone: 020 7388 7529
Fax: 020 7388 8501

Email: office@watsonlittle.com
Web Site: www.watsonlittle.com

Personnel:
Mandy Little *(Managing Director)*
James Wills *(Director)*
Sallyanne Sweeney *(Literary Agent)*

All MSS except short stories, plays, poetry, works for very small children & articles (except by established columnists).

Specialization: literary and commercial fiction, serious non-fiction, psychology, self-help, popular culture, health, sport, humour, children's.

Rights Representative in UK for:
USA (children's): The Chudney Agency, New York, NY, USA

Overseas Representation:
USA (adult): Howard Morhaim Literary Agency, New York, NY, USA
USA (children's): The Chudney Agency, New York, NY, USA
Worldwide: The Marsh Agency, London, UK
Worldwide (film & TV associates): MBA Literary Agents, London, UK; The Sharland Organisation, Raunds, Northants, UK

4087

A. P. WATT LTD
20 John Street, London WC1N 2DR
Telephone: 020 7405 6774
Fax: 020 7831 2154
Email: apw@apwatt.co.uk
Web Site: www.apwatt.co.uk

Personnel:
Caradoc King *(Director)*
Linda Shaughnessy *(Director)*
Georgia Garrett *(Director)*
Derek Johns *(Director)*
Natasha Fairweather *(Director)*

All MSS except poetry.

Specialization: general fiction and non-fiction. No unsolicited manuscripts.

4088

JOSEF WEINBERGER PLAYS LTD
[formerly Warner/Chappell Plays Ltd]
12–14 Mortimer Street, London W1T 3JJ
Telephone: 020 7580 2827
Fax: 020 7436 9616

Email: general.info@jwmail.co.uk
Web Site: www.josef-weinberger.com

Personnel:
Michael Callahan *(Manager)*
Fiona Staples *(Licensing)*

Specialization: stage plays. Works in conjunction with overseas agents. No unsolicited manuscripts, preliminary letter essential.

Parent Company:
UK: Josef Weinberger Ltd

Associated Companies:
UK: Josef Weinberger Ltd

Rights Representative in UK for:
USA: Dramatists Play Service Inc, New York, NY, USA

Overseas Representation:
Australia: Hal Leonard (Australia) Ltd, Melbourne, Vic, Australia
Canada & USA: Dramatists Play Service Inc, New York, NY, USA
New Zealand: Play Bureau (NZ) Ltd, New Plymouth, New Zealand
South Africa: Dalro (Pty) Ltd, Johannesburg, South Africa

4089

EVE WHITE LITERARY AGENT
54 Gloucester Street, London SW1V 4EG
Telephone: 020 7630 1155
Email: eve@evewhite.co.uk
Web Site: www.evewhite.co.uk

Personnel:
Eve White *(Director)*

All MSS except poetry, picture books, plays, screenplays.

Specialization: UK agency representing internationally published authors of commercial and literary fiction and non-fiction, children's fiction and picture books. Foreign rights handled in conjunction with Diana Mackay at Melcombe International Ltd and Caroline Hill-Trevor. Film rights in conjunction with Rod Hall. Clients include: Rae Earl, Chris Pascoe, Alexander Stobbs, Ruth Saberton, Fergus McNeill, Yvette Edwards. Children's authors: Andy Stanton, Ivan Brett, Rae Earl, Ruth Warburton, Michaela Morgan, Jimmy Docherty, Susannah Corbett, Gillian Rogerson, Kate Maryon, Rachael Mortimer, Tracey

Corderoy, Ciaran Murtagh, Miriam Halahmy & Abie Longstaff. *Authors wishing to submit work must consult the submission page of our website.*

Overseas Representation:
Commonwealth countries & USA: Eve White, London, UK
Worldwide (children's books): Caroline Hill-Trevor, Gloucestershire, UK
Worldwide (excluding Commonwealth countries & USA): Melcombe International, Somerset, UK

4090

DINAH WIENER LTD
12 Cornwall Grove, London W4 2LB
Telephone: 020 8994 6011
Fax: 020 8994 6044

Personnel:
Dinah Wiener *(Director)*
D. P. Wiener *(Director)*
B. M. Wiener *(Director)*

All MSS except juvenile, plays, film scripts, poetry & short stories.

Specialization: general fiction and non-fiction.

4091

JONATHAN WILLIAMS LITERARY AGENCY
Rosney Mews, Upper Glenageary Road, Glenageary, Co Dublin, Republic of Ireland
Telephone: +353 (0)1 280 3482
Fax: +353 (0)1 280 3482

Personnel:
Jonathan Williams *(Director)*

All MSS except plays or film scripts. Return postage and packing is appreciated. Irish postage stamps or international postal coupons, please.

Specialization: typescripts of Irish interest.

Overseas Representation:
Italy: Agenzia Piergiorgio Nicolazzini, Milan, Italy
Japan: Tuttle-Mori Agency Inc, Tokyo, Japan
Netherlands & Germany: International Literatuur Bureau, Amsterdam, Netherlands
Spain & Spanish-speaking Latin America: Antonia Kerrigan Literary Agency, Barcelona, Spain

5 Trade & Allied Associations

5.1 INTERNATIONAL

5001

EDITEUR LTD
United House, North Road, London N7 9DP
Telephone: 020 7503 6148
Fax: 020 7503 6418
Email: info@editeur.org
Web Site: www.editeur.org

Personnel:
Mark Bide (*Executive Director*)
Stella Griffiths (*Associate Director*)
Sarah Hilderley (*Accessibility Project Lead*)
Graham Bell (*Chief Data Architect*)
Tim Devenport (*Lead Consultant to ICEDIS*)
Nick Woods (*Operations Manager*)
Michael Hopwood (*Linked Heritage, Project Lead*)

EDItEUR is the international group co-ordinating development of the standards infrastructure for electronic commerce in the book and serials sectors.
  EDItEUR provides its membership with research, standards and guidance in such diverse areas as:
  – EDI and other e-commerce standards for book and serial transactions
    – Bibliographic and product information
    – The standards infrastructure for digital publishing
    – Rights management and trading
    – Radio frequency identification tags.
  Established in 1991, EDItEUR is a truly international organisation with 90 members from 17 countries, including Australia, Canada, Japan, South Africa, United States and most of the European countries.
  A leader in global standards for the exchange of bibliographic information (particularly the ONIX for Books Product Information standard) and of e-commerce messages in the book and journal supply chains, EDItEUR is also engaged in shaping key national and international projects aimed at developing rights and permissions expressions.

5002

*FEDERATION OF EUROPEAN PUBLISHERS
31 rue Montoyer, Box 8, 1000 Brussels, Belgium
Telephone: +32 (02) 770 11 10
Fax: +32 (02) 771 20 71
Email: info@fep-fee.eu
Web Site: www.fep-fee.eu

Personnel:
Ms Anne Bergman-Tahon (*Director*)

Lobbying European institutions on behalf of the European publishing community.

5003

INTERNATIONAL BOARD ON BOOKS FOR YOUNG PEOPLE – IBBY
Nonnenweg 12, Postfach, 4003 Basel, Switzerland
Telephone: +41 (0)61 272 29 17
Fax: +41 (0)61 272 27 57

Email: luzmaria.stauffenegger@ibby.org
Web Site: www.ibby.org

Personnel:
Elizabeth Page (*Executive Director*)
Ahmad Redza Ahmad Khairuddin (*President of the Executive Committee*)
Luzmaria Stauffenegger (*Administrative Assistant*)

Promotion of children's books and reading worldwide.

5004

THE INTERNATIONAL ISBN AGENCY
United House, North Road, London N7 9DP
Telephone: 020 7503 6418
Fax: 020 7503 6418
Email: info@isbn-international.org
Web Site: www.isbn-international.org

Personnel:
Nick Woods (*Operations Manager*)
Stella Griffiths (*Executive Director*)

The International ISBN Agency is the registration authority for the ISBN system globally. The administration of the ISBN system is carried out on three levels:
    – International agency
    – Group agencies
    – Publisher level.
  The main functions of the International ISBN Agency are:
  – To promote, co-ordinate and supervise the world-wide use of the ISBN system
  – To approve the definition and structure of group agencies
  – To allocate group identifiers to group agencies
  – To advise on the establishment and functioning of group agencies
  – To advise group agencies on the allocation of international publisher identifiers
  – To publish the assigned group numbers and publishers' prefixes.
  There are over 160 local ISBN agencies covering 200 countries. Publishers apply to their local ISBN agency to obtain ISBNs.

5005

PRIVATE LIBRARIES ASSOCIATION
Ravelston, South View Road, Pinner, Middx HA5 3YD
Email: dchambrs@aol.com
Web Site: www.plabooks.org

Personnel:
Keith Fletcher (*Hon President*)
Dean A. Sewell (*Hon Secretary*)
David Chambers (*Hon Publications Secretary*)
Robert Hirst (*Hon Treasurer*)

An international society of book collectors, run on a voluntary basis. Publications include a quarterly journal and *The Exchange List*, which circulate among member collectors throughout the world, an annual bibliography, and other books concerned with book collecting.

5.2 UNITED KINGDOM & REPUBLIC OF IRELAND

5006

*YR ACADEMI GYMREIG
Mount Stuart House, Mount Stuart Square, Cardiff CF10 5FQ
Telephone: 029 2047 2266
Fax: 029 2049 2930
Email: post@academi.org
Web Site: www.academi.org

Glyn Jones Centre for Writers:
Wales Millennium Centre, Bute Place, Cardiff CF10 5AL
Telephone: (as above)
Fax: 029 2047 0691
Email: (as above)
Web Site: (as above)

Personnel:
Peter Finch (*Chief Executive*)
Lleucu Siencyn (*Deputy*)

Founded in 1959, Yr Academi Gymreig / The Welsh Academy is the national society which promotes the writers and literatures of Wales. The Academi runs courses, competitions (including the Cardiff International Poetry Competition), conferences, tours by authors, international exchanges, events for schools, readings, literary performances and festivals. The Academi also offers advice to authors, a writers' critical and mentoring service and financial bursaries, and runs the annual Book of the Year Award. It works in partnership with Tŷ Newydd, the Criciəth-based residential writers' centre.
  Publications include *A470*; *Taliesin*, a quarterly literary journal in the Welsh language; *The Oxford Companion to the Literature of Wales*; *The Welsh Academy English-Welsh Dictionary*; *The Welsh Academy Encyclopaedia of Wales* published with the support of the Lottery, and a variety of translated works.
  In 2004 Academi became a resident at the Wales Millennium Centre. The Glyn Jones Centre for Writers opened in 2005.

5007

THE ACADEMIC AND PROFESSIONAL DIVISION OF THE PUBLISHERS ASSOCIATION
29B Montague Street, London WC1B 5BW
Telephone: 020 7691 9191
Fax: 020 7691 9199
Email: gtaylor@publishers.org.uk
Web Site: www.publishers.org.uk

Personnel:
Graham Taylor (*Director*)

Parent Company:
UK: The Publishers Association

The Academic and Professional Division of The Publishers Association represents the interests of publishers serving higher education, scholarly communication and the professional and commercial market. Collective activities are organized on their behalf. Membership is open to any publisher in membership of the Publishers Association which produces books, journals or similar published material for these markets.

5008

ALLIANCE OF LITERARY SOCIETIES (ALS)
59 Bryony Road, Selly Oak, Birmingham B29 4BY
Telephone: 0121 475 1805
Email: l.j.curry@bham.ac.uk
Web Site: www.allianceofliterarysocieties.org.uk

Personnel:
Linda J. Curry (Chair)
Julie Shorland (Hon Treasurer / Membership Secretary)
Anita Fernandez-Young (Secretary)

The ALS is an umbrella organization for literary societies/groups within the UK. The AGM is hosted by different member societies each year, with accompanying talks etc covering a weekend (usually in April or May). Members of affiliated societies are welcome to attend but only the delegate of the affiliated society may have a vote. Details are on the website – including subscription rates. An annual journal (ALSo...) is also produced. This is freely available to member societies but can be purchased by non-members.

5009

ARCHIVES AND RECORDS ASSOCIATION (UK & IRELAND)
Prioryfield House, 20 Canon Street, Taunton, Somerset TA1 1SW
Telephone: 01823 327030 & 327077
Fax: 01823 271719
Email: ara@archives.org.uk
Web Site: www.archives.org.uk

Personnel:
John Chambers (Chief Executive)
Lorraine Logan (Membership & Office Administrator)
Marie Owens (Head of Public Affairs)

Publication of texts/periodicals on archives and records management. Conferences and training courses.

5010

ASSOCIATION OF AUTHORS' AGENTS
10 Iron Bridge House, Bridge Approach, London NW1 8BD
Email: olivia@jonathanclowes.co.uk
Web Site: www.agentsassoc.co.uk

Personnel:
Anthony Goff (President)
Peter Straus (Vice-President)
Sarah Ballard (Treasurer)
Olivia Guest (Secretary)

Founded in 1974 to institute and maintain a code of professional behaviour, to discuss matters of common professional interest and to provide a vehicle for representing the view of authors' agents in discussions on matters of common interest with other professional bodies.

5011

ASSOCIATION OF FREELANCE EDITORS, PROOFREADERS & INDEXERS (IRELAND)
11 Clonard Road, Sandyford, Dublin 16, Republic of Ireland
Telephone: +353 (0)1 295 2194 and +3531 8395345
Email: Brenda@ohanlonmedia.com and
tesstattersall@gmail.com
Web Site: www.afepi.ie

Personnel:
Tess Tattersall (Joint Chair)
Brenda O'Hanlon (Joint Chair)

The AFEPI was established to provide information to publishers on Irish freelancers working in this field, and to protect the interests of those freelancers. Membership is restricted to freelancers with experience and/or references, but skills of members are not tested or evaluated.

5012

ASSOCIATION OF ILLUSTRATORS
2nd Floor Back Building, 150 Curtain Road, London EC2A 3AT

Telephone: 020 7613 4328
Fax: 020 7613 4417
Email: info@theaoi.com
Web Site: www.theaoi.com

Personnel:
Ramon Blomfield (Managing Director)
Derek Brazell (Special Projects Manager)
Ian Veacock (Finance Officer Manager)
Becky Brown (Events & Marketing Co-ordinator Manager)
Paul Ryding (Membership Co-ordinator)

Established in 1973 to advance and protect illustrators' rights, the AOI is a non-profit-making trade association dedicated to its members' professional interest and the promotion of illustration.
    Corporate members (agents and clients) receive a free copy of the Images Annual, discounts on events, publications and our Images competition entry, plus Varoom – the journal of illustration and made images, published three times per year.

5013

ASSOCIATION OF LEARNED & PROFESSIONAL SOCIETY PUBLISHERS
Email: sarah.durrant@alpsp.org
Web Site: www.alpsp.org

Executive Director, UK:
Audrey McCulloch, 15 Windmill Way, Tring, Herts HP23 4HQ
Telephone: 01442 828928
Fax: 01442 311328
Email: audrey.mcculloch@alpsp.org
Web Site: www.alpsp.org

Personnel:
Sarah Durrant (Chief Executive)
Audrey McCulloch (Executive Director, UK)
Isabel Czech (Executive Director, North America)
Ian Hunter (Finance & Administration Manager)
Lesley Ogg (Events Manager)
Amanda Whiting (Training Manager)
Dee French (Administrator)
Barbara Holmes (Training Administrator)
Melanie Goinden (Events Administrator)
Alan Singleton (Editor-in-Chief, Learned Publishing Editor)

ALPSP is an international trade association for the community of not-for-profit publishers and those who work with them to disseminate academic and professional information; it was founded in 1972, and currently has over 350 members in more than 40 countries. ALPSP carries out research and other projects, monitors national and international issues and represents members' interests to the wider world. The Association provides co-operative services such as the ALPSP Learned Journals Collection. It also offers an extensive programme of courses and seminars, an informative website (www.alpsp.org), a quarterly journal and a monthly electronic newsletter.

5014

*ASSOCIATION OF SUBSCRIPTION AGENTS AND INTERMEDIARIES
Field Cottage, School Lane, Benhall, Suffolk IP17 1HE
Telephone: 01728 633196
Email: info@subscription-agents.org
Web Site: www.subscription-agents.org

Personnel:
Sarah Durrant (Secretary General)

The ASA is the international trade association serving subscription agents, sales agents and other intermediaries providing products and services within the professional and scholarly information supply chain. The ASA exists to provide information to its members from all areas of the information industry, to create a forum for exchange amongst these groups and to represent members' common interests to publishers, customers, representative and governmental organizations and associations.

5015

*AUTHORS' FOUNDATION
84 Drayton Gardens, London SW10 9SB
Telephone: 020 7373 6642
Fax: 020 7373 5768
Email: info@societyofauthors.org
Web Site: www.societyofauthors.org

Personnel:
Mark Le Fanu (General Secretary)

Founded in 1984 to mark the centenary of the Society of Authors, the Foundation offers grants to published writers who need additional funding for research, travel, etc. Open to fiction, poetry and non-fiction. The Foundation incorporates the Phoenix Trust. Closing dates for applications: 30 April and 30 September.

5016

AUTHORS' LICENSING & COLLECTING SOCIETY (ALCS)
The Writers' House, 13 Haydon Street, London EC3N 1DB
Telephone: 020 7264 5700
Fax: 020 7264 5755
Email: alcs@alcs.co.uk
Web Site: www.alcs.co.uk

Personnel:
Owen Atkinson (Chief Executive)
Barbara Hayes (Deputy Chief Executive)
Alison Baxter (Communications Manager)

The Authors' Licensing & Collecting Society is the UK collective rights management society for writers of all genres. Members grant to the Society the right to administer on their behalf those rights which an author is unable to exercise as an individual or which are best handled on a collective basis. These include photocopying, rental and lending right, off-air and private recording, electronic rights, cable retransmission and rights for the public reception of broadcasts. Membership costs a one-off lifetime fee of £25. Please contact the Society for further information. The ALCS administers these rights in the UK and Northern Ireland. Under reciprocal arrangements with foreign collecting societies other territories are also covered. Distributions to members are made bi-annually. For advice and further information please contact the ALCS office or click www.alcs.co.uk.

5017

BAPLA (BRITISH ASSOCIATION OF PICTURE LIBRARIES AND AGENCIES)
59 Tranquil Vale, Blackheath, London SE3 0BS
Email: enquiries@bapla.org.uk
Web Site: www.bapla.org.uk

Personnel:
Simon Cliffe (Executive Director)
Damalie Nakalema (Association Administrator)
Susanne Kittlinger (Membership & Communications Manager)

The British Association of Picture Libraries and Agencies, or BAPLA, is the trade association for picture libraries in the UK, and has been a trade body since 1975. Members include the major news, stock and production agencies as well as Sole Traders and Cultural Heritage Institutions.
    Please see the website for details: www.bapla.org.uk

5018

THE BIBLIOGRAPHICAL SOCIETY
c/o Institute of English Studies, Senate House, Malet Street, London WC1E 7HU
Telephone: 020 7862 8679
Fax: 020 7862 8720
Email: admin@bibsoc.org.uk
Web Site: www.bibsoc.org.uk

Personnel:
Margaret Ford (Hon Secretary)

The Bibliographical Society promotes the study of historical, analytical, descriptive and textual bibliography. It publishes its own journal, The Library, and supports a publishing programme of books and monographs on bibliographical subjects.

5019

BOOK AID INTERNATIONAL
39–41 Coldharbour Lane, Camberwell, London SE5 9NR
Telephone: 020 7733 3577
Fax: 020 7978 8006
Email: info@bookaid.org
Web Site: www.bookaid.org

Personnel:
HRH The Duke of Edinburgh KG, KT, OM *(Patron)*
Nigel Newton *(President)*
Philip Walters *(Chair)*
Clive Nettleton *(Director)*

Every year, Book Aid International sends over half a million books to sub-Saharan Africa. Almost 90% of these are donated to us new by UK publishers from returned, obsolete or excess stock. These books reach public and community libraries, and libraries in schools, universities, slums, refugee centres and prisons.

We are always in need of suitable books: especially children's; education; EFL; teacher training; vocational; medical; law; fiction; library and information management; computing.

Without the books we send, many of the libraries we support would have nothing on their shelves. Please get in touch if you can help.

5020

BOOK INDUSTRY COMMUNICATION
7 Ridgmount Street, London WC1E 7AE
Telephone: 020 7255 0500
Email: info@bic.org.uk
Web Site: www.bic.org.uk

Personnel:
Peter Kilborn *(Executive Director)*

Book Industry Communication (BIC) is an independent organization set up and sponsored by the Publishers Association, Booksellers Association, the Chartered Institute of Library and Information Professionals and the British Library to promote supply chain efficiency in all sectors of the book world through e-commerce and the application of standard processes and procedures. Its subscribers include most of the UK's major publishers, booksellers and service providers.

5021

THE BOOK TRADE CHARITY (BTBS)
The Foyle Centre, The Retreat, Kings Langley, Herts WD4 8LT
Telephone: 01923 263128
Fax: 01923 270732
Email: david@btbs.org
Web Site: www.booktradecharity.org

Personnel:
David Hicks *(Chief Executive)*
Glenda Barnard *(Care Services Housing)*
Nigel Batt *(Treasurer)*
Carole Blake *(President)*

The welfare charity of the book trade, offering support to colleagues in difficult personal circumstances. The Book Trade Charity gives direct financial support, regular and one-off, to individuals, to help with a wide range of problems. Accommodation at The Retreat, Kings Langley, offers pre-retirement and retirement housing. The book trade Helpline (freephone 0808 100 2304) provides sympathetic, confidential help. Anyone who has worked in the book trade (publishing, distribution, bookselling, etc. for more than one year, employed, self-employed or freelance) is eligible to apply for assistance.

5022

BOOKSELLERS ASSOCIATION OF THE UNITED KINGDOM & IRELAND LTD
Minster House, 272 Vauxhall Bridge Road, London SW1V 1BA
Telephone: 020 7802 0802
Fax: 020 7802 0803
Email: mail@booksellers.org.uk
Web Site: www.booksellers.org.uk

Personnel:
Jane Streeter *(President)*
Tim Godfray *(Chief Executive)*

Associated Companies:
UK: Batch.co.uk Ltd; Book Industry Communication Ltd; Book Tokens Ltd; Word Book Day Ltd

Founded in 1895. Represents over 4400 outlets. Promotes and looks after the interests of booksellers, helps them become more efficient and fights for better distribution in the trade. It also helps booksellers increase sales and reduce

costs and gives advice on opening and running a bookshop. Among other services, the Association produces catalogues for distribution throughout the retail trade at Christmas, and directories of members, publishers and services.

5023

BOOKTRUST
Book House, 45 East Hill, London SW18 2QZ
Telephone: 020 8516 2977
Fax: 020 8516 2978
Email: query@booktrust.org.uk
Web Site: www.booktrust.org.uk

Personnel:
Viv Bird *(Chief Executive)*

Booktrust is an independent charity dedicated to encouraging people of all ages and cultures to engage with books. The written word underpins all our activity and enables us to fulfil our vision of inspiring a lifelong love of books for all.

5024

*BRITISH CENTRE FOR LITERARY TRANSLATION (BCLT)
University of East Anglia, Norwich NR4 7TJ
Telephone: 01603 592785
Fax: 01603 592737
Email: bclt@uea.ac.uk
Web Site: www.bclt.org.uk

Personnel:
Valerie Henitiuk *(Associate Director)*
Catherine Fuller *(Co-ordinator)*

Parent Company:
UK: University of East Anglia

Raises the profile of literary translation and the professional development of literary translators. Organizes events, readings, workshops aimed at translators, professionals in arts and publishing and the general public.

5025

BRITISH FANTASY SOCIETY
17 Pendre Avenue, Prestatyn LL19 9SH
Telephone: 07905 311 733
Email: secretary@britishfantasysociety.org
Web Site: www.britishfantasysociety.org

Personnel:
David Howe *(Chair)*
Debbie Bennett *(Secretary)*

Formed for devotees of fantasy, horror and related fields in literature, art and the cinema. Publications are a quarterly Journal containing fiction and non-fiction. There is an annual convention, 'FantasyCon', which features the British Fantasy Awards sponsored by the Society. Please visit our website for full information. www.britishfantasysociety.org

5026

THE BRITISH GUILD OF TRAVEL WRITERS
335 Lordship Road, London N16 5HG
Telephone: 020 8144 8713
Web Site: www.bgtw.org

Personnel:
Robert Ellison *(Secretariat)*

The Guild has a membership of around 270, all professional journalists, broadcasters and photographers who derive the majority of their earnings from travel writing or broadcasting. Monthly meetings are devoted to discussion of travel topics, usually with outside speakers, and take place at a variety of venues. There is a monthly *Newsletter* for members. An annual year book giving full details of all members together with comprehensive lists of PRs and other contacts in the travel trade is available for purchase.

5027

*BSI GROUP
389 Chiswick High Road, London W4 4AL
Telephone: 020 8996 9000
Fax: 020 8996 7400
Email: info@bsigroup.com
Web Site: www.bsigroup.com

Personnel:
Sir David John *(Chairman)*
Howard Kerr *(Chief Executive Officer)*

BSI Group:
 – develops private, national and international standards
 – certifies management systems and products
 – provides testing and certification of products and services
 – provides training and information on standards and international trade and
 – provides performance management and supply chain management software solutions.

5028

CHARTERED INSTITUTE OF JOURNALISTS
2 Dock Offices, Surrey Quays Road, London SE16 2XU
Telephone: 020 7252 1187
Fax: 020 7232 2302
Email: memberservices@cioj.co.uk
Web Site: www.cioj.co.uk

Personnel:
Liz Justice *(President)*
Norman Bartlett *(Treasurer)*
Dominic Cooper *(General Secretary)*

The senior professional society of journalists worldwide. Incorporated by Royal Charter in 1890, it had its origin in the National Association of Journalists, which was founded in 1884 and converted into the Institute in 1889. Its primary object is 'the promotion by all reasonable means of the interests of journalists and journalism'. Representing the profession as a whole, it is a completely independent body free of political partiality. It gives equal rights of membership to all members of the profession, including radio and television journalists, press photographers and public relations officers with journalistic qualifications. Trade union representation is provided by the IOJ (TU), an independent certificated trade union.

5029

CHILDREN'S BOOKS IRELAND
17 North Great George's Street, Dublin 1, Republic of Ireland
Telephone: +353 (0)1 872 7475
Fax: +353 (0)1 872 7476
Email: info@childrensbooksireland.com
Web Site: www.childrensbooksireland.com

Personnel:
Mags Walsh *(Director)*
Aoife Murray *(Programme Officer)*
Jenny Murray *(Administrator, Communications & Production)*
Patricia Kennon *(Editor – Inis Magazine)*
Marion Keyes *(Editor – Inis Magazine)*

Associated Companies:
Republic of Ireland: Children's Book Festival; Inis Magazine

Children's Books Ireland is the national children's book organization of Ireland. The aim of Children's Books Ireland is to promote quality children's books and reading. CBI runs an annual nationwide Children's Book Festival, the Bisto/CBI Book of the Year awards, publishes *Inis*, a quarterly magazine, which carries a wide range of articles about children's books in Ireland and abroad as well as an extensive review section, and hosts an annual Children's Books conference.

CBI is a resource and support organization for teachers, pupils, writers, publishers, booksellers and librarians as well as an imaginative programmer of events for young readers.

5030

CHILDREN'S WRITERS & ILLUSTRATORS GROUP
The Society of Authors, 84 Drayton Gardens, London SW10 9SB
Telephone: 020 7373 6642
Fax: 020 7373 5768
Email: ldowdeswell@societyofauthors.org
Web Site: www.societyofauthors.org

Personnel:
Jo McCrum *(Secretary)*

Parent Company:
UK: The Society of Authors

The Children's Writers and Illustrators Group is an organization, founded in 1963, for writers and illustrators of children's books, who are members of The Society of Authors. Meetings are held regularly, with opportunities for members to meet each other, as well as to hear talks or discussions on various aspects of their work.

5031

COMHAIRLE NAN LEABHRAICHEAN / THE GAELIC BOOKS COUNCIL
32 Mansfield Street, Glasgow G11 5QP
Telephone: 0141 337 6211
Email: brath@gaelicbooks.net
Web Site: www.gaelicbooks.org

Personnel:
Donald-Ian Brown (Chair)
Rosemary Ward (Manager)

The Council was set up in 1968 to administer the Gaelic Books Grant awarded by the Scottish Education Department, and its purpose is to stimulate Gaelic publishing. It normally has about ten members as its board, and a paid staff of four. In April 1983 the Scottish Arts Council became its main funding body, and its Assessor attends meetings. The Council became a charitable company in July 1996.

It provides financial assistance in the form of publication grants (paid to the publisher) for individual Gaelic books, and also commission grants for authors. Editorial advice is available, and a word-processing and proof-reading service. In 2003 it launched the highly successful Ùr-Sgeul imprint for prose work in Gaelic, with the associated books, CDs and DVDs being issued by the publisher Clàr.

As a retailer, the Council stocks all Gaelic and Gaelic-related works in print, regular lists of these being published in its catalogue, , and on its website. It has its own shop at the address above, and also does mail order and mobile selling at selected events, as well as running a book club (A' Chiste Leabhraichean).

5032

COMPASS DSA LTD
13 Progress Business Park, Whittle Parkway, Slough SL1 6DQ
Telephone: 01628 559500
Fax: 01628 663876
Email: alan@compass-dsa.co.uk
Web Site: www.compass-dsa.co.uk

Personnel:
Alan Jessop (Joint Managing Director)
Derek Searle (Joint Managing Director)
June Searle (Director)

Associated Companies:
Republic of Ireland: Compass Ireland Ltd
UK: Compass Academic Ltd

Client publishers:
Republic of Ireland: Collins Press; New Island Books Ltd
UK: Absolute Press; Accent Press; Assouline; Benefactum; Birlinn Ltd; Biteback Publishing; Black & White Publishing; Carcanet Press; Carnegie Publishing; Comma Press; Enitharmon Press; Gibson Square; Good Hotel Guide; Hay House Publishers; Heritage House; Hesperus Press; How to Books / Springhill; Little Books; Magnum; Malavan Media; Myrmidon Books; Oldie Publications; Oxygen Books; Parthian; Peter Owen; Plexus; Polygon Ltd; Pomona Books; Pushkin Press; Radio Times; Robson Press; Ryland, Peter & Small / Cico; Summersdale; Telegram; Thorogood; TMI; Warboys; Which?

Compass DSA is one of the leading independent sales companies, providing sales and marketing services for publishers to both the traditional and non-traditional markets across the UK and Ireland.

5033

COPYRIGHT TRIBUNAL
2nd Floor, 21 Bloomsbury Street, London WC1B 3HB
Telephone: 020 7034 2836
Fax: 020 7034 2826
Email: catherine.worley@ipo.gov.uk
Web Site: www.ipo.gov.uk/ctribunal.htm

Personnel:
Judge Fysh QC (Chairman)
Catherine Worley (Secretary/Head)

The main function of the Tribunal is to decide, where the parties cannot agree between themselves, the terms and conditions of licences offered by, or licensing schemes operated by, collective licensing bodies in the copyright and related rights area. It has the statutory task of conclusively establishing the facts of a case and of coming to a decision that is reasonable in the light of those facts. Its decisions are appealable to the High Court only on points of law. (Appeals on a point of law against decisions of the Tribunal in Scotland are to the Court of Session.)

Broadly, the Tribunal's jurisdiction is such that anyone who has unreasonably been refused a licence by a collecting society or considers the terms of an offered licence to be unreasonable may refer the matter to the Tribunal. The Tribunal also has the power to decide some matters even though collecting societies are not involved. For example, it can settle disputes over the royalties payable by publishers of TV programme listings to broadcasting organizations.

5034

THE CRITICS' CIRCLE
PO Box 59382, London NW8 1HG
Telephone: 020 7483 1181
Web Site: www.criticscircle.org.uk

Personnel:
Tom Sutcliffe (President)
William Russell (Honorary General Secretary)

Founded in 1913 by J. T. Grein, S. R. Littlewood and John Parker. Aims to promote the art of criticism and to uphold its integrity in practice, to foster and safeguard the professional interests of its members and to provide opportunities for social intercourse among them, and to support the advancement of the arts. Membership is only by invitation of the Council and is confined to persons engaged professionally, regularly and substantially in the writing or broadcasting of criticism of theatre, music, film, dance, and art and architecture. There is no literary section per se.

5035

*DATA PUBLISHERS ASSOCIATION (DPA)
Queen's House, 28 Kingsway, London WC2B 6JR
Telephone: 020 7405 0836
Fax: 020 7404 4167
Email: sarah.gooch@dpa.org.uk
Web Site: www.dpa.org.uk

Personnel:
Jerry Gosney (Executive Director)
Sarah Gooch (Marketing Co-ordinator)

The Data Publishers Association (DPA) is the industry body representing data and directory publishers in the UK. Its role is to protect and promote the interests of the industry, both in print and online.

5036

DESIGN AND ARTISTS COPYRIGHT SOCIETY
33 Great Sutton Street, London EC1V 0DX
Telephone: 020 7336 8811
Fax: 020 7336 8822
Email: info@dacs.org.uk
Web Site: www.dacs.org.uk

Personnel:
Gilane Tawadros (Chief Executive)
John Robinson (Legal & International Director)
Tania Spriggens (Communications Director)
Jane Sandeman (Finance Director)
Jeremy Stein (Services Director)

Established by artists for artists, DACS is a not-for-profit visual arts rights management organisation.

DACS translates rights into revenues and recognition for a wide spectrum of visual artists and their beneficiaries. It provides three rights management services: Payback, Artist's Resale Right and Copyright Licensing, as well as lobbying, advocacy, and legal advice for artists.

DACS represents 60,000 artists worldwide through its international network of rights management organisations.

Any publisher wishing to reproduce works of art in copyright should contact DACS in the first instance to obtain clearance prior to publication.

5037

THE EDUCATIONAL PUBLISHERS COUNCIL
[Schools Division of The Publishers Association]

The Publishers Association, 29B Montague Street, London WC1B 5BW
Telephone: 020 7691 9191
Fax: 020 7691 9199
Email: gtaylor@publishers.org.uk
Web Site: www.publishers.org.uk

Personnel:
Graham Taylor (Director)

Parent Company:
UK: The Publishers Association

The Educational Publishers Council is the division within the PA which looks after the interests of educational publishers. It promotes the nature and importance of educational publishers' work both to the educational system and to the general public, and organizes collective activities on their behalf. Membership is open to any publisher in membership of The Publishers Association which produces books or other published resources for use in schools.

5038

EDUCATIONAL WRITERS GROUP
The Society of Authors, 84 Drayton Gardens, London SW10 9SB
Telephone: 020 7373 6642
Fax: 020 7244 0743
Email: info@societyofauthors.org
Web Site: www.societyofauthors.org

Personnel:
Elizabeth Haylett Clark (Secretary)

Parent Company:
UK: The Society of Authors

The Educational Writers Group is a subsidiary group of The Society of Authors. Its purpose is to advise members on their publishing problems etc, to study the conditions peculiar to the market at home and overseas, to watch developments in teaching as they affect the educational writer, and to hold meetings at which experience can be pooled, and matters of mutual interest discussed.

5039

ENGLISH ASSOCIATION
University of Leicester, University Road, Leicester LE1 7RH
Telephone: 0116 229 7622
Fax: 0116 229 7623
Email: engassoc@le.ac.uk
Web Site: www.le.ac.uk/engassoc

Personnel:
Helen Lucas (Chief Executive)
Julia Hughes (Assistant)

Founded in 1906 to promote the knowledge, enjoyment and study of the English language and its literatures.

The Year's Work in English Studies is the annual qualitative narrative bibliographical overview of scholarly work on English language and literature written in English. Published annually in December.

The Year's Work in Critical and Cultural Theory, companion volume to YWES, provides a narrative bibliography of work in the field of critical and cultural theory.

Other journals also published. See website on www.le.ac.uk/engassoc Order from: Julia Hughes, engassoc@le.ac.uk or tel 0116 229 7622

5040

FACET PUBLISHING
7 Ridgmount Street, London WC1E 7AE
Telephone: 020 7255 0500 & (020) 7255 0505 (textphone)
Fax: 020 7255 0501
Email: info@facetpublishing.co.uk
Web Site: www.facetpublishing.co.uk

Facet Publishing, the commercial publishing and bookselling arm of CILIP: the Chartered Institute of Library and Information Professionals, is the leading publisher of books for library and information professionals worldwide.

Previously known as Library Association Publishing, Facet Publishing has an internationally established list of over 200 specialist titles in print.

Together these products cover all the major aspects of professional LIS activity.

Facet Publishing sells its books in virtually every country in the world. It has customers in the public and private sectors and publishes books for library, museum, archive, records management and publishing communities, as well as students on information, media, business and communications courses.

5041

*THE FEDERATION OF CHILDREN'S BOOK GROUPS
2 Bridge Wood View, Horsforth, Leeds LS18 5PE
Telephone: 0113 258 8910
Email: info@fcbg.org.uk
Web Site: www.fcbg.org.uk

A national, voluntary organization concerned with children and their books. The Federation's aim is to promote enjoyment and interest in children's books and reading, and to encourage the availability of a range of literature for all ages, from pre-school to teenage. The Federation liaises with schools, playgroups, publishers, libraries and other official bodies.
National activities include:
– organizes, annually, The Red House Children's Book Award
– promotes National Share-a-Story Month in May
– organizes an annual conference each spring.
Members are able to receive Federation publications, including the *Federation Newsletter*, the annual *Red House Children's Book Award 'Pick of the Year' Top Fifty Booklist*, and information about National Share-a-Story Month.

5042

GAY AUTHORS WORKSHOP
BM Box 5700, London WC1N 3XX
Email: eandk2@btinternet.com

Personnel:
Kathryn Bell *(Secretary)*

Associated Companies:
UK: Gay Authors Self-Publishing Society

Gay Authors Workshop is an association of lesbians, gay men and bisexuals who are creative writers – poets, dramatists, fiction writers. Its aim is to raise the standard of gay literature by providing opportunities for gay writers to meet, read, discuss and criticize their work in a constructive way. Monthly meetings are held at different places in the London area (and occasionally elsewhere) for that purpose, and to share information about publishing outlets and competitions. Although London-based, it is a national organization. The quarterly newsletter (print and tape) keeps members in touch with activities. Membership is open to all gay writers, beginners as well as published authors. The subscription is £7 a year, £3 unwaged, currently under review.

5043

GIBB MEMORIAL TRUST
2 Penarth Place, Cambridge CB3 9LU
Telephone: 01223 566630
Email: Secretary@gibbtrust.org
Web Site: www.gibbtrust.org

Book Distribution:
Oxbow Books Ltd, 10 Hythe Bridge Street, Oxford OX1 2BW
Telephone: 01865 241249
Fax: 01865 794449
Email: oxbow@oxbowbooks.com
Web Site: www.oxbowbooks.com

Personnel:
P. R. Bligh *(Secretary to the Trustees)*

The Trust is a registered charity whose aim is to support the publication of works of scholarly research within the areas of the history, literature, philosophy and religion of the Persians, Turks and Arabs. Its activities are in financing and organizing the production and publication of books, and in marketing the published works. The books are distributed by Oxbow Books in Oxford, UK, and Oakville, USA.

5044

GUILD OF FOOD WRITERS
255 Kent House Road, Beckenham, Kent BR3 1JQ
Telephone: 020 8659 0422
Email: gfw@gfw.co.uk
Web Site: www.gfw.co.uk

Personnel:
Mr Jonathan Woods *(Administrator)*

The Guild of Food Writers is the professional association of food writers and broadcasters in the UK. Established in 1984, it now has 400 authors, columnists, freelance journalists and broadcasters amongst its members.
The objectives of the Guild as set out in its constitution are as
follows:
– To bring together professional food writers, to print and issue an annual list of members, to extend the range of members' knowledge and experience, and to encourage the development of new writers by every means including competitions and awards.
– To contribute to the growth of public interest in, and knowledge of, the subject of food and to campaign for improvements in the quality of food.
The Guild is a self-supporting body that offers its members a busy calendar that includes an annual lecture dinner and AGM, annual awards, monthly workshops and occasional professional and social events. It also publishes a monthly newsletter and comprehensive and detailed annual directory of members.
The Guild offers professional support and guidance to its members. In the public forum it campaigns with authority for improvements in the awareness and quality of food in every sector of society.

5045

INDEPENDENT PUBLISHERS GUILD (IPG)
PO Box 12, Llain, Whitland SA34 0WU
Telephone: 01437 563335
Fax: 01437 562071
Email: info@ipg.uk.com
Web Site: www.ipg.uk.com

Personnel:
Bridget Shine *(Chief Executive)*

The Independent Publishers Guild (IPG) actively represents the interests of independent publishers in the UK and is represented on many committees and forums, which form the strategy for the UK book trade. The IPG helps publishers to do better business and is somewhere they can find advice, ideas and information.
With more than 520 members and steadily growing with combined revenues of more than £500M, the IPG provides a vibrant networking base. Members receive regular e-newsletters, training courses and seminars covering important areas. The IPG Conference is a must attend event in the publishing calendar.
The IPG runs a collective stand for members at leading international book fairs including Frankfurt and London.

5046

*INFORMATION COMMISSIONER'S OFFICE
Wycliffe House, Water Lane, Wilmslow, Cheshire SK9 5AF
Telephone: 01625 545745
Fax: 01625 524510
Email: mail@ico.gsi.gov.uk
Web Site: www.ico.gov.uk

Personnel:
Christopher Graham *(Information Commissioner)*

The Information Commissioner's Office is the UK's independent public body set up to promote access to official information and to protect personal information.
It regulates and enforces the Data Protection Act, the Freedom of Information Act, the Privacy and Electronic Communications Regulations and the Environmental Information Regulations.
The ICO provides guidance to organizations and individuals. It rules on eligible complaints and can take action when the law is broken.
Reporting directly to Parliament, the Commissioner's powers include the ability to order compliance, using enforcement and decision notices, and prosecution.

5047

INSTITUTE OF INTERNAL COMMUNICATION
Suite GA2, Oak House, Woodlands Business Park, Breckland, Milton Keynes MK14 6EY
Telephone: 01908 313755
Fax: 01908 313661
Email: enquiries@ioic.org.uk
Web Site: www.ioic.org.uk

Personnel:
Steve Doswell *(Chief Executive)*

The Institute of Internal Communication (IoIC) (formerly CiB) is the UK's professional body for internal communication, with members working in-house, agency or freelance roles in all sectors of the economy in the UK and Ireland.
Whatever your responsibility – strategy, planning and delivery, consultancy, change management, writing, design, online, print, measurement, brand management – if internal communication is your focus, the Institute exists to support you.

Major activities include the annual IoIC and Icon Awards competitions, annual conference and a regular programme of regional educational and training events as well as our ongoing professional qualifications in internal communications.

5048

INSTITUTE OF SCIENTIFIC AND TECHNICAL COMMUNICATORS (ISTC)
Airport House, Purley Way, Croydon CR0 0XZ
Telephone: 020 8253 4506
Fax: 020 8253 4510
Email: istc@istc.org.uk
Web Site: www.istc.org.uk

Personnel:
Paul Ballard *(President)*
Peter Fountain *(Treasurer)*
Katherine Judge *(Communicator – ISTC Journal Editor)*
Elaine Cole *(Administration)*
Rachel Potts *(Marketing)*

Formed in 1972 as a result of the amalgamation of the Presentation of Technical Information Group (1948), the Institution of Technical Authors and Illustrators (originally the Technical Publications Association), formed in 1953, and the Institute of Technical Publicity and Publications (1963).
The Institute aims to establish and maintain professional codes of practice for those employed in all branches of scientific and technical communication. It provides a forum for the exchange of views between its members, and aims to further their expectations and interests. The membership embodies a wide range of specialist knowledge of the principles and modern practices of effective communication of scientific and technical information. Through its publications and meetings, the Institute disseminates this experience to a growing profession and to those who employ the services of its members.
The Institute represents Great Britain on the International Council for
Technical Communication (INTECOM). Publications: (UK subscription: £37 per year).

5049

INSTITUTE OF TRANSLATION & INTERPRETING
Fortuna House, South Fifth Street, Milton Keynes MK9 2PQ
Telephone: 01908 325250
Fax: 01908 325259
Email: info@iti.org.uk
Web Site: www.iti.org.uk

Personnel:
Mr Nick Rosenthal *(Chair)*

The Institute of Translation and Interpreting (ITI) is the UK's main professional association for translators and interpreters and aims to promote the highest standards in translating and interpreting. It has a strong corporate membership and runs professional development courses and conferences, sometimes in conjunction with its language, regional and subject networks. Membership is open to those with a genuine and proven involvement in translation and interpreting. As a full and active member of the International Federation of Translators, it maintains good contacts with translators and interpreters worldwide. ITI's bi-monthly Bulletin is available on subscription through the ITI office in Milton Keynes.
ITI's directory of translators and interpreters may be accessed from the website at www.iti.org.uk.

5050

IP3 (INSTITUTE OF PAPER, PRINTING & PUBLISHING)
Claremont House, 70–72 Alma Road, Windsor, Berks SL4 3EZ
Telephone: 0870 330 8625
Fax: 0870 330 8615

Email: info@ip3.org.uk
Web Site: www.ip3.org.uk

Personnel:
David Pryke *(Director)*
Lynda King *(Administration Manager)*

Fostering excellence in publishing through:
– the promotion, support and endorsement of a programme of educational training, research and development
– the introduction of a code of practice
– the development of standards of occupational compe-
tence
– the publication of bulletins, handbooks, reports and
research designed to assist in the improvement of individual
performance
– the development of professional publishing qualifications
– meetings, seminars and conferences.
The Institute will offer individuals:
– membership of an active community of people working
in publishing
– the opportunity to participate in and influence the direction of a body that has their best interests at heart
– a community that can raise professional standards and,
as a consequence, individual and collective status
– opportunities to network, seek advice, guidance and
career counselling
– access to career, education and training information
– a range of cost-saving services and activities.
IP3 will be a forum providing opportunities for individuals
in publishing to develop themselves and progress in their
careers and to meet the challenges of an increasingly competitive business.

5051

*ISSN UK CENTRE
The British Library, Boston Spa, Wetherby, West Yorkshire
LS23 7BQ
Telephone: 01937 546959
Fax: 01937 546562
Email: issn-uk@bl.uk
Web Site: www.bl.uk/issn

Assigns ISSN (International Standard Serial Numbers) to
serial titles published in the UK.

5052

MEDICAL WRITERS GROUP
The Society of Authors, 84 Drayton Gardens, London
SW10 9SB
Telephone: 020 7373 6642
Fax: 020 7373 5768
Email: info@societyofauthors.org &
sbaxter@societyofauthors.org
Web Site: www.societyofauthors.org

Personnel:
Sarah Baxter *(Secretary)*

The Medical Writers Group is a group within The Society of
Authors. Its principal objects are to represent its members in
all matters affecting their interests as medical writers; to
hold meetings from time to time for the discussion of matters of common interest; and to provide, through the Society, advice to members on the special problems of medical
authorship. Authors who have had a book accepted for publication, but not yet published, can join the Society and
obtain advice.

5053

MUSIC PUBLISHERS ASSOCIATION
6th Floor, British Music House, 26 Berners Street, London
W1T 3LR
Telephone: 020 7580 0126
Fax: 020 7637 3929
Email: info@mpaonline.org.uk
Web Site: www.mpaonline.org.uk

Personnel:
Stephen Navin *(Chief Executive)*

Associated Companies:
UK: MCPS Ltd

The Music Publishers Association (MPA) was established in
1881 and is governed by an elected Board. The MPA exists
to safeguard the interests of music publishers and the writers signed to them. It provides them with a forum and a col-

lective voice, and aims to inform and to educate the wider
public in the importance and value of copyright.
The MPA offers a range of services and publications to
those interested in music publishing (including training) and
participates in education and information initiatives across
the music industry.

5054

NATIONAL ACQUISITIONS GROUP
12–14 King Street, Wakefield WF1 2SQ
Telephone: 01924 383010
Fax: 01924 383010
Web Site: www.nag.org.uk

Personnel:
Heather Sherman *(Chair)*
Karen Carden *(Vice Chair)*
Regina Ferguson *(Hon. Treasurer)*
Judith Rhodes *(Administrator)*

Established in 1986, NAG is a broadly based organization
which stimulates, co-ordinates and publicizes developments
in library acquisitions and the book trade. The membership
includes individuals and organizations within publishing,
bookselling and systems supply, as well as librarians responsible for choosing and buying books for academic, public,
national, government and special institutions.
NAG has two main aims:
– to bring together all those in any way concerned with
library acquisitions, to assist them in exchanging information
and comment and to promote understanding and good
practice between them;
– to seek to influence other organizations and individuals
to adopt its opinions and standards.
NAG's objectives are to:
– provide a forum for discussion and the exchange of
information;
– extend knowledge and understanding of technological
developments;
– promote the dissemination of information about library
acquisitions;
– develop the awareness of producers, suppliers and
librarians;
– act as a channel of communication with Government
and other bodies.

5055

***NATIONAL ASSOCIATION FOR THE TEACHING
OF ENGLISH**
50 Broadfield Road, Sheffield S8 0XJ
Telephone: 0114 555 419
Fax: 0114 555 296
Email: info@nate.org.uk
Web Site: www.nate.org.uk

Personnel:
Ian McNeilly *(Director)*
Anne Fairhall *(Publications Manager)*
Julia Elliott *(Senior Office Administrator)*

NATE is the UK subject association for all aspects of English
teaching from pre-school to university. NATE publishes its
own and distributes other titles covering:
– *classroom resources:* primary, secondary, post 16
– *teaching English:* theoretical titles including: language,
literacy, literature, speaking and listening, media, drama,
information and communications technologies, assessment,
theory, equal opportunities
– *management & staff development:* curriculum, planning, managing the English department, whole school
issues relating to English teaching.
The Association publishes four periodicals: *English in Education, NATE News, English Drama Media* and *Classroom.*

5056

*NATIONAL LITERACY TRUST
68 South Lambeth Road, London SW8 1RL
Telephone: 020 7587 1842
Fax: 020 7587 1411
Email: contact@literacytrust.org.uk
Web Site: www.literacytrust.org.uk

The National Literacy Trust is an independent charity that
believes that literacy transforms lives, and that with better
literacy, everyone can succeed in life.
The National Literacy Trust campaigns to improve public
understanding of the vital importance and impact of literacy.
It uses careful, targeted communication to encourage individuals in most need of support to understand the impor-

tance of literacy in their lives and to inspire them to
overcome their own anxieties or prejudices about literacy.
It also supports those trying to improve their literacy
through projects, networks and communities across the UK
and it delivers projects and programmes. It investigates and
innovates, conducting research to improve and measure the
effectiveness of services and support for people who need
help with literacy. It also works in partnership, bringing
together key organizations to lead literacy promotion in the
UK, and it shares its knowledge as widely as possible.
For more information see www.literacytrust.org.uk

5057

NEW WRITING NORTH
Holy Jesus Hospital, City Road, Newcastle upon Tyne
NE1 2AS
Telephone: 0191 233 3850
Email: olivia@newwritingnorth.com
Web Site: www.newwritingnorth.com

Personnel:
Cath Robson *(Finance Director)*
Anna Disley *(Deputy, Theatre & Education Director)*
Olivia Chapman *(Communications Manager)*

New Writing North is the literature development agency for
the north-east of England.

5058

NIELSEN BOOKDATA
3rd Floor, Midas House, 62 Goldsworth Road, Woking,
Surrey GU21 6LQ
Telephone: 01483 712200
Fax: 01483 712201
Email: info.bookdata@nielsen.com
Web Site: www.nielsenbookdata.co.uk

Personnel:
Ann Betts *(Commercial Director)*
Simon Skinner *(Sales Director)*
Mo Siewcharran *(Head of Marketing)*
Paul Dibble *(Head of Data Sales)*
Vesna Nall *(Publisher & Subscriptions Manager)*
Lucy Huddlestone *(Business Development Manager)*
Melanie Brassington *(Export Sales Manager)*
Helen Anderson *(Key Account Manager)*
David Kennedy *(Key Account Manager)*
Richard Merrick *(Customer Services Manager)*

Parent Company:
UK: Nielsen

Associated Companies:
Nielsen Registration Agencies (ISBN, SAN & ISTC)
UK: Nielsen BookNet; Nielsen BookScan

Nielsen BookData is an information provider worldwide. The
company has a range of products and services which provide
content-rich, accurate and timely book information for English-language titles published internationally. These services
are sold to booksellers, libraries and publishers in over 100
countries, including the UK, Ireland, Europe, Australia, New
Zealand, South Africa and the USA.

5059

NIELSEN ISBN AGENCY
3rd Floor, Midas House, 62 Goldsworth Road, Woking,
Surrey GU21 6LQ
Telephone: 01483 712215
Fax: 01483 712214
Email: isbn.agency@nielsen.com
Web Site: www.isbn.nielsenbook.co.uk

Personnel:
Julian Sowa *(Senior Manager)*
Diana Williams *(Manager)*

Parent Company:
Nielsen

Associated Companies:
Nielsen BookData
UK: Nielsen ISTC Agency; Nielsen SAN Agency

The UK International Standard Book Numbering Agency is
responsible for assigning ISBN prefixes to publishers based in
the UK or the Irish Republic. The UK ISBN Agency cannot
assign ISBNs to publishers based in other countries.
The Agency:

– allocates ISBN publisher prefixes to eligible publishers based on the information provided by the publisher;

– advises publishers on the correct and proper implementation of the ISBN system;

– maintains a database of publishers and their prefixes for inclusion in the *Publishers' International ISBN Directory*;

– encourages and promotes the use of the Bookland EAN bar code format;

– encourages and promotes the importance of the ISBN for a proper listing of titles with bibliographical agencies;

– provides technical advice and assistance to publishers and the booktrade on all aspects of ISBN usage.

Any new publishers wishing to apply for an allocation of ISBNs

should contact the ISBN Agency for an application pack. A registration fee is payable.

5060

NIELSEN ISTC AGENCY
3rd Floor, Midas House, 62 Goldsworth Road, Woking, Surrey GU21 6LQ
Telephone: 01483 712215
Fax: 01483 712714
Email: istc.agency@nielsen.com
Web Site: www.istc.nielsenbook.co.uk

Personnel:
Julian Sowa (*Senior Manager*)
Diana Williams (*Manager*)

Parent Company:
UK: Nielsen

Associated Companies:
Nielsen BookData
UK: Nielsen ISBN Agency; Nielsen SAN Agency

The International Standard Text Code (ISTC) is a global identification system for textual works, i.e. the content in text-based publications. Nielsen operates one of the first ISTC registration agencies, enabling authors, publishers and other authorized representatives to register textual works with an ISTC. It also provides advice and guidance on how to make the most of this important new system. Nielsen also runs the ISBN and SAN agencies.

5061

NIELSEN SAN AGENCY
3rd Floor, Midas House, 62 Goldsworth Road, Woking, Surrey GU21 6LQ
Telephone: 01483 712215
Fax: 01483 712214
Email: san.agency@nielsen.com
Web Site: www.san.nielsenbook.co.uk

Personnel:
Julian Sowa (*Senior Manager*)
Diana Williams (*Manager*)

Parent Company:
UK: Nielsen

Associated Companies:
Nielsen BookData
UK: Nielsen ISBN Agency; Nielsen ISTC Agency

SANs, Standard Address Numbers, are unique for geographical locations and can be assigned to the addresses of organizations involved in the bookselling and publishing industries. The SAN Agency is responsible for managing the scheme on behalf of Book Industry Communication in any country except the USA, Canada, Australia and New Zealand. Nielsen also runs the ISBN and ISTC agencies.

5062

THE POETRY SOCIETY
22 Betterton Street, London WC2H 9BX
Telephone: 020 7420 9880
Fax: 020 7240 4818
Email: info@poetrysociety.org.uk
Web Site: www.poetrysociety.org.uk

The Society's principal activities include: the quarterly publication of the UK's world-class poetry magazine, and the Society's newsletter, *Poetry News*; the National Poetry Competition which awards over £8000 in prizes each year and has brought many poets to national attention; the annual Foyle Young Poets of the Year Award (for 11–17 year olds); the Poet Laureate funded Ted Hughes Award for New Work

in Poetry. The Poetry Society also produces a range of publications including as well as posters. Other resources include , an invaluable teacher-training resource for both primary and secondary school teachers and the Young Poets Network, a resource for young people with an interest in the artform.

5063

PROFESSIONAL PUBLISHERS ASSOCIATION
Queens House, 28 Kingsway, London WC2B 6JR
Telephone: 020 7404 4166
Fax: 020 7404 4167
Web Site: www.ppa.co.uk

Personnel:
Barry McIlheney (*Chief Executive*)

Associated Companies:
UK: Periodical Publishers Association Scotland; Periodicals Training Council

Trade association representing publishers of consumer, business-to-business and customer magazines.

5064

PUBLIC LENDING RIGHT
Richard House, Sorbonne Close, Stockton-on-Tees TS17 6DA
Telephone: 01642 604699
Fax: 01642 615641
Email: authorservices@plr.uk.com
Web Site: www.plr.uk.com

Personnel:
Jim Parker (*Registrar*)

Public Lending Right (PLR) exists to make payments to authors for the borrowing of their books from public libraries. PLR is funded by the Department for Culture, Media and Sport, and is headed by a Registrar. To qualify, authors must register their books with the PLR office. Payment calculations are based on book loans from a representative sample of public libraries. Payments are made annually. No author may receive more than £6600.

5065

THE PUBLISHERS ASSOCIATION
29B Montague Street, London WC1B 5BW
Telephone: 020 7691 9191
Fax: 020 7691 9199
Email: mail@publishers.org.uk
Web Site: www.publishers.org.uk

Personnel:
Richard Mallet (*Chief Executive*)
Graham Taylor (*Educational, Academic & Professional Publishing Director*)
Emma House (*Trade & International Director*)
Mark Wharton (*Operations Director*)

The Publishers Association is a trade organization serving book, journal and electronic publishers in the UK. It brings publishers together to discuss the main issues facing the industry and to define the practical policies that will take the industry forward. The aim of The Publishers Association is to serve and promote by all lawful means the interest of book, journal and electronic publishers and to protect their interests.

5066

PUBLISHERS LICENSING SOCIETY LTD
37–41 Gower Street, London WC1E 6HH
Telephone: 020 7299 7730
Fax: 020 7299 7780
Email: pls@pls.org.uk
Web Site: www.pls.org.uk

Personnel:
Mark Millar (*Chairman*)
Tom West (*Operations Manager*)
Lydia Murray (*Finance Manager*)
David Bishop (*Licensing & Communications Manager*)
Mark Bide (*Consultant*)
Sarah Faulder (*Chief Executive*)

The Publishers Licensing Society (PLS) obtains mandates from publishers which grant PLS the authority to license

photocopying and digitization of pages from published works. PLS also consults with publishers on the development of licences.

PLS aims to maximize revenue from licences for mandating publishers and to expand the range and repertoire of mandated publishers available to licence holders. It supports the Copyright Licensing Agency (CLA) in its efforts to increase the number of legitimate users through the issuing of licences and pursues any infringements of copyright works belonging to rights holders.

5067

PUBLISHERS PUBLICITY CIRCLE
65 Airedale Avenue, London W4 2NN
Telephone: 020 8994 1881
Email: ppc@lineone.net
Web Site: www.publisherspublicitycircle.co.uk

Personnel:
Heather White (*Secretary/Treasurer*)

For over 50 years, the Publishers Publicity Circle has enabled book publicists – both from publishing houses and freelance PR agencies – to meet and share information regularly. Representatives of the media are invited to speak about the ways in which they can feature authors and their books, and how book publicists can provide most effectively the information and material needed.

Annual prizes are awarded for the best publicity campaigns of the year.

A directory of the PPC membership is published each year and distributed to over 2500 media contacts, providing the names of publicity staff, their fax and telephone numbers, and email addresses.

5068

PUBLISHING IRELAND (FOILSIÚ ÉIREANN)
Guinness Enterprise Centre, Taylor's Lane, Dublin 8, Republic of Ireland
Telephone: +353 (0)1 415 1210
Email: info@publishingireland.com
Web Site: www.publishingireland.com

Personnel:
Jean Harrington (*President Publishing Ireland*)
Jolly Ronan (*Project Manager*)
Karen Kenny (*Administrator*)
Clara Schuessler (*Admin Assistant*)

Publishing Ireland promotes the publication, distribution, sale and publicity of books at home and abroad. There are over 100 members of the association. Publishing Ireland is a member of the Federation of European Publishers and of the International Publishers Association.

5069

PUBLISHING SCOTLAND
Scottish Book Centre, 137 Dundee Street, Edinburgh EH11 1BG
Telephone: 0131 228 6866
Fax: 0131 228 3220
Email: enquiries@publishingscotland.org
Web Site: www.publishingscotland.org

Personnel:
Marion Sinclair (*Chief Executive*)
Lucy Feather (*Member Services Manager*)
Joan Lyle (*Training and Information Manager*)
Liam Davison (*BooksfromScotland.com Editor*)

Associated Companies:
UK: BookSource Ltd

Publishing Scotland is an organization with responsibility for the support and development of the book publishing sector in Scotland. The remit is to work with companies, organizations and individuals in the industry, and to co-ordinate joint initiatives and partnerships.

Publishing Scotland represents its members' interests in a number of capacities, in training, co-operative promotion and marketing of their books, attendance at international book fairs, joint catalogue mailings and export services.

Publishing Scotland has been in existence for over 30 years, representing over 60 book publishers. It also offers network membership to those individuals, organizations and companies who work with or within the publishing industry.

5070

*ROMANTIC NOVELISTS' ASSOCIATION

(contact by email only)
Email: RNAHonSec@o2.co.uk
Web Site: www.rna-uk.org

Personnel:
E. M. Ryle (Secretary)

The Romantic Novelists' Association aims to raise the prestige of romantic authorship and generally to encourage and foster the writing of romantic works. The RNA makes annual awards for the Romantic Novel of the Year, and for the Love Story of the Year (for Category Romance). The RNA runs a critique scheme for unpublished writers who may join the Association as New Writers' Scheme (non-voting) members. The Joan Hessayon Award is made annually for the best published novel to have gone through the NWS critique scheme. The RNA's annual residential conference takes place over a weekend in early July. Regional chapters, around the country, organize their own meetings and events. In addition, there are members' meetings in London, with guest speakers, and summer and winter parties where published and unpublished writers network with agents, editors and publishers. The RNA's magazine, *Romance Matters*, is published four times a year and distributed free to members.

5071

ROYAL SOCIETY OF LITERATURE

Somerset House, Strand, London WC2R 1LA
Telephone: 020 7845 4676
Fax: 020 7845 4679
Email: info@rslit.org
Web Site: www.rslit.org

Personnel:
Colin Thubron FRSL (President)
Anne Chisholm FRSL (Chair)
Maggie Fergusson FRSL (Secretary)

The Royal Society of Literature nurtures, celebrates and defends all that is best in British literature, past and present. The RSL organizes talks, discussions and readings, runs a series of creative writing Masterclasses in collaboration with the Booker Prize Foundation, and campaigns in the interest of writers. The Society administers a number of awards including the V. S. Pritchett Memorial Prize for a previously unpublished short story, and the Royal Society of Literature Ondaatje Prize, a £10,000 prize awarded annually to the book of the highest literary merit, fiction or non-fiction, which evokes the spirit of a place. At the heart of the Society is its Fellowship, which has always encompassed the most distinguished writers in the English language.

5072

*RSA (THE ROYAL SOCIETY FOR THE ENCOURAGEMENT OF ARTS, MANUFACTURES AND COMMERCE)

8 John Adam Street, London WC2N 6EZ
Telephone: 020 7451 6902
Fax: 020 7839 5805
Email: editor@rsa.org.uk
Web Site: www.theRSA.org

Publisher:
Wardour Publishing & Design, Elsley Court,
20–22 Great Titchfield Street, London W1W 8BE
Telephone: 020 7016 2555
Web Site: www.wardour.co.uk

Personnel:
Luke Johnson (Chairman)
Matthew Taylor (Chief Executive)
Stephen King (Chief Operating Officer)
Nina Bolognesi (External Affairs Director)
Belinda Lester (Fellowship Director)
Julian Thompson (Projects Director)
Carrie Walsh (Commercial Director)
Frances Hedges (Editor)

Publishes quarterly *RSA Journal* and reports, conference papers and occasional books.

5073

SAN AGENCY

36 Mackenzie Road, Beckenham, Kent BR3 4RU
Telephone: 020 8249 9716

Email: ra@britishscbwi.org
Web Site: www.britishscbwi.org

Personnel:
Natascha Biebow (Regional Advisor (Chair))
Benjamin Scott (Assistant Regional Advisor)
Anne-Marie Perks (Illustrator Co-ordinator)
Sue Hyams (Membership Co-ordinator)
Nick Cross (Website Co-ordinator)

Parent Company:
USA: SCBWI

The SCBWI is an international professional organization for writers and illustrators of children's books. It is a network for the exchange of knowledge between writers, illustrators, editors, publishers, agents, librarians, educators, booksellers and others involved with literature for young people. There are currently more than 18,000 members worldwide, in over 70 regions.

The SCBWI International sponsors three annual conferences on writing and illustrating books and multimedia, one in New York in February, one in Bologna, Italy, and one in Los Angeles in August, as well as dozens of regional conferences and events throughout the world. It also publishers a bi-monthly newsletter, *The Bulletin*, awards grants for works in progress, and provides many informational publications on the art and business of writing and selling written, illustrated and electronic material. The SCBWI also presents numerous grants and awards, including the Golden Kite Award for the best fiction and non-fiction books.

The SCBWI British Isles (SCBWI-BI) region meets bi-monthly, usually in London, for a speaker or workshop event. It also sponsors local critique groups, master classes and regional networks events, and publishes a quarterly newsletter, *Words and Pictures*, which includes up-to-date events and marketing information, and articles on the craft of children's writing and illustrating. It also runs a yearly Writers' and Illustrators' Conference with hands-on workshops on improving your craft and the opportunity to meet publishing professionals and find out what they are looking for. SCBWI-BI runs a listserve and social networking site where writers and illustrators can set up their own promotional website.

SCBWI is open to both published and unpublished writers and illustrators. Full membership is open to those whose work for children's books, illustrations or photographs, films, electronic media, articles, poems or stories has been published or produced. Associate membership is open to all those with an interest in children's literature or media, whether or not they have published. To join, see our web site www.britishscbwi.org

5074

*SCHOOL LIBRARY ASSOCIATION

Unit 2, Lotmead Business Village, Lotmead Farm,
Wanborough, Swindon SN4 0UY
Telephone: 01793 791787
Fax: 01793 791786
Email: info@SLA.org.uk
Web Site: www.SLA.org.uk

Personnel:
Steve Hird (Editor)
Chris Brown (Review Editor)
Richard Leveridge (Production Editor)

The School Library Association is an independent organization working to promote the development of school libraries, primary and secondary. Services to members include advice and information, publications at reduced prices, *The School Librarian*, a quarterly journal of articles and reviews, training courses and a network of area branches. Membership includes schools, colleges, local education authorities, public libraries, publishers and individuals in the United Kingdom and overseas. Membership costs £79.50 p.a.

5075

*SCOTTISH BOOK TRUST

Sandeman House, Trunks Close, 55 High Street, Edinburgh EH1 1SR
Telephone: 0131 524 0160
Fax: 0131 524 0161
Email: info@scottishbooktrust.com
Web Site: www.scottishbooktrust.com

Personnel:
Marc Lambert (Chief Executive Officer)
Jeanette Harris (General Manager)

Sophie Moxon (Head of Programme)
Marion Bourbouze (Head of Marketing & Audience Development)

Scottish Book Trust is a leading agency for the promotion of literature in Scotland, developing innovative projects to encourage adults and children to read, write and be inspired by books.

It promotes children's literature and the joys of reading and writing by organizing book awards, author tours and talks, and writing competitions, and by developing interactive online projects. It supports writers with a range of projects including skills development and bursaries, the funding of literature events, book awards and the promotion of Scottish writing to over 10 million people worldwide. It fosters readers and writers by offering a variety of events, advice and online information on books and authors. It works with learning professionals all over Scotland to create innovative and effective resources and events which inspire people through literature.

5076

SOCIETY FOR EDITORS & PROOFREADERS

Erico House, 93–99 Upper Richmond Road, London SW15 2TG
Telephone: 020 8785 5617
Fax: 020 8785 5618
Email: admin@sfep.org.uk
Web Site: www.sfep.org.uk

Personnel:
Wendy Toole (Chair)
Justina Amenu (Executive Secretary)

Founded in 1988 with the twin aims of promoting high editorial standards and achieving recognition of its members' professional status, the Society works to disseminate information and training, foster good relations between members and their clients, and combat the isolation often experienced by freelances. It supports recognized standards of training and accreditation for editors and proofreaders, and is establishing recognized standards for its own members. Membership in 2011 was approximately 1500.

One of the major aims of the Society for Editors and Proofreaders is to help editorial freelances and staff to improve and update their skills. It is gradually building up a wide range of one-day courses, from 'Introduction to Proofreading' to 'Project Management' and 'On-Screen Editing', as well as more specialized courses. Most of its courses are run in London. About twice a year, two or three courses are run in Edinburgh, York and Bristol. Discounts are offered to members of the SFEP and to SI and NUJ members. Current details can be found on the SFEP website.

5077

*SOCIETY OF AUTHORS

84 Drayton Gardens, London SW10 9SB
Telephone: 020 7373 6642
Fax: 020 7373 5768
Email: info@societyofauthors.org
Web Site: www.societyofauthors.org

Personnel:
Tom Holland (Chairman)
Mark Le Fanu (General Secretary)

An independent trade union for authors. Its purpose is to further the interests of its 8500 members through individual advice and general campaigning. It is controlled by an elected Committee of Management and administered by a staff with long experience in the business and legal aspects of authorship. Members have access to a comprehensive advisory service and may seek advice on all forms of contracts. The Society also serves the interests of specialist writers through a number of subsidiary groups – viz the Broadcasting Group, the Translators Association, Children's Writers and Illustrators, Educational Writers, Academic Writers and Medical Writers Groups. It makes representations to government departments and promotes campaigns on behalf of the profession as a whole (eg public lending right, tax concessions for authors, etc). It also administers literary estates, publishes a quarterly journal, *The Author*, issues numerous *Quick Guides* to its members and manages a variety of awards and trust funds for authors.

5078

SOCIETY OF AUTHORS PENSION FUND

84 Drayton Gardens, London SW10 9SB
Telephone: 020 7373 6642

Fax: 020 7373 5768
Email: info@societyofauthors.org
Web Site: www.societyofauthors.org

Personnel:
Mark Le Fanu *(Secretary)*

A small number of pensions is granted by the Pension Fund Committee to authors over the age of 60 who have been members of the Society for 10 years. Pensions are normally £1700 per annum.

5079

SOCIETY OF EDITORS
University Centre, Granta Place, Cambridge CB2 1RU
Telephone: 01223 304080
Fax: 01223 304090
Email: office@societyofeditors.org
Web Site: www.societyofeditors.org

Personnel:
Bob Satchwell *(Executive Director)*

The Society of Editors has more than 400 members in national, regional and local newspapers, magazines, broadcasting and digital media, journalism, education and media law. It campaigns for media freedom, self-regulation, the public's right to know and the maintenance of standards in journalism.

5080

SOCIETY OF INDEXERS
Woodbourn Business Centre, 10 Jessell Street, Sheffield S9 3HY
Telephone: 0114 244 9561
Email: admin@indexers.org.uk
Web Site: www.indexers.org.uk

Personnel:
John Silvester *(Company Secretary)*

Founded in 1957 as an autonomous professional body to promote greater awareness of indexing and raise standards in all forms of indexing. The Society's well-established distance learning course (with CILIP seal of
recognition) now runs on a web-based platform and gives a thorough grounding in the principles (and pitfalls) of indexing. Workshops and an annual conference provide additional training opportunities. An online directory, *Indexers Available*, contains full details of qualified and experienced indexers with specialist subjects ranging from accountancy to zoology, together with advice on commissioning an indexer and guidelines on fees. The Society also publishes a quarterly international journal, *The Indexer*, plus occasional papers on specialized aspects of indexing and a newsletter for members. The Wheatley Medal is awarded annually for an outstanding index, conferring prestige on indexer, author and publisher. The Society wishes to impress on both publishers and authors the need for adequate and competent indexes in non-fiction works, whether in print or electronic format.

5081

SOCIETY OF MEDICAL WRITERS
Corner Croft, Lonsties, Keswick, Cumbria CA12 4TD
Telephone: 01768 774689
Email: dorothy@crowther.eu
Web Site: www.somw.org.uk

Personnel:
Dr Dorothy Crowther *(Chairman)*
Dr Richard Cutler *(Finance Officer)*
Dr Mary Anderson *(Acting Editor)*

Membership of the Society of Medical Writers is open to anyone who publishes or aspires to publish their work of whatever nature – medical or non-medical, fact or fiction, prose or poetry. It is intended that the association should be enjoyable, stimulating and educational so that writing from medical practice, including general practice, is improved and encouraged.
The aims of the Society are therefore to:
– improve standards of writing by medical practitioners;
– encourage literacy whether in scientific papers, review articles, or historical or anecdotal essays;

– provide meetings for practitioners interested in writing, for the exchange of views, skills and ideas;
– provide education on the preparation, presentation and submission of written material for publication;
– act as a means of introduction between practitioners and suitable publishers and editors;
– maintain a register of members of the SOMW, available to commissioning editors and others;
– advise on sources of assistance with regard to technical, legal and financial aspects of writing;
– consider questions of ethics relating to writing and publication;
– further developments in the art of writing and to facilitate access to educational opportunities for those motivated to become better writers.

5082

SOCIETY OF YOUNG PUBLISHERS
The Publishers Association, 29B Montague Street, London WC1B 5BW
Email: membersec@thesyp.org.uk
Web Site: www.thesyp.org.uk

Personnel:
Ella Kahn *(Chair)*
Naomi Holt *(Vice-Chair)*
Alex Higson *(Membership Secretary)*
Alice Herbert *(Treasurer and Secretary)*
Lizzie Jones *(Press and Publicity Officer)*
Konstantinos Vasdekis *(Marketing Officer)*
Francesca Brazzorotto *(Web Content Editor)*
Lucia Sandin *(Social Co-ordinator)*
Bhav Mehta *(Special Projects)*
Laura Givans *(InDigital Commissioning Editor)*

Established in 1949, the Society of Young Publishers is open to anyone in publishing or a related trade (in any capacity) – or who is hoping to be soon. Its aim is to assist, inform and enthuse anyone trying to break into the publishing industry or progress within it.
It organizes monthly speaker meetings which discuss different topics of relevance to the publishing industry. Guest speakers are drawn from a variety of backgrounds. The society also organizes a highly successful annual conference.
Members receive approximately four issues per year of its magazine, *InPrint*, to keep them up-to-date with the society and events and issues within the industry. The online magazine is available on the website. The SYP informs its members of jobs vacancies from across the UK through its weekly Jobs Bulletin.
Members are also entitled to discounts at Foyles book shop and on several publishing and related training courses.

5083

TRANSLATORS ASSOCIATION
84 Drayton Gardens, London SW10 9SB
Telephone: 020 7373 6642
Fax: 020 7373 5768
Email: info@societyofauthors.org
Web Site: www.societyofauthors.org

Personnel:
Sarah Burton *(Secretary)*

The Translators Association is a subsidiary of the Society of Authors and advises literary translators on such matters as contracts and fees. Publishers seeking book translators can search the online database.

5084

*TRAVELLING SCHOLARSHIP FUND
Society of Authors, 84 Drayton Gardens, London SW10 9SB
Telephone: 020 7373 6642
Fax: 020 7373 5768
Email: info@societyofauthors.org
Web Site: www.societyofauthors.org

Personnel:
Mark Le Fanu *(Secretary)*

Founded in 1944 by an anonymous donor, to enable British creative writers to travel and to keep in touch with their colleagues abroad. A special committee annually reviews the field of contemporary literature before making its awards, which are not for open candidature, and are normally made

to established writers of over 30 years of age. The Fund is administered by the Society of Authors.

5085

WATCH (WRITERS ARTISTS & THEIR COPYRIGHT HOLDERS)
The Library, University of Reading, PO Box 223, Whiteknights, Reading RG6 6AE
Telephone: 0118 378 8783
Fax: 0118 378 6636
Email: d.c.sutton@reading.ac.uk
Web Site: www.watch-file.com

Personnel:
Dr D. Sutton *(Director)*

WATCH provides a free online database of information about the copyright holders of literary authors, artists and prominent persons. The database is in the form of an open-access public website, jointly maintained by the Universities of Texas and Reading.

5086

WELSH BOOKS COUNCIL / CYNGOR LLYFRAU CYMRU
Castell Brychan, Aberystwyth, Ceredigion SY23 2JB
Telephone: 01970 624151
Fax: 01970 625385
Email: castellbrychan@cllc.org.uk
Web Site: www.cllc.org.uk & www.gwales.com

Personnel:
Elwyn Jones *(Chief Executive)*
Sion Ilar *(Design)*
Marian Beech Hughes *(Editorial)*
D. Philip Davies *(Information Services)*
Delyth Humphreys *(Children's Books)*
Neville Evans *(Distribution)*
Arwyn Roderick *(Finance)*
Moelwen Gwyndaf *(Administration)*
Tom Ferris *(Sales & Marketing)*
Richard Owen *(Grants)*

The Welsh Books Council is a national organization with charitable status funded by the Welsh Government. Established in 1961, it is responsible for promoting all sectors of the publishing industry in Wales, in both languages, in conjunction with publishers, booksellers, libraries and schools. The Council is also responsible for distributing publishing grants for Welsh-language publishing and Welsh writing in English. Its Wholesale Distribution Centre stocks the vast majority of Welsh-interest titles currently available. www.gwales.com, the Council's on-line information and ordering service, is a one-stop shop for titles of relevance to Wales.

5087

WORSHIPFUL COMPANY OF STATIONERS AND NEWSPAPER MAKERS
Stationers' Hall, Ave Maria Lane, London EC4M 7DD
Telephone: 020 7248 2934
Fax: 020 7489 1975
Email: admin@stationers.org
Web Site: www.stationers.org

Personnel:
N. J. Stapleton *(Master)*
W. J. Alden MBE DL *(Clerk)*

The Worshipful Company of Stationers had its beginnings in a Guild dating back at least to 1403; the original Charter was granted in 1557. The Company was expanded in modern times (1933) to include the Newspaper Makers. For nearly four centuries it was essential for the protection of copyright to register books at Stationers' Hall; since 1924 an extensively used system of voluntary registration has been in force. This was discontinued in February 2000.
The Company's object has always been to promote the interests of the printing and allied trades, among them publishing and bookbinding. Its activities at the present day include the binding of apprentices and the award of scholarships to young men and women in these trades and the provision of pensions and financial help for tradesmen and their widows. The Company also plays a full part in the life of the City of London.
The Stationers' Hall may be hired for functions.

6 Trade & Allied Services

6.1 EDITORIAL SERVICES

6001

ACUPUNCTUATION LTD
4 Harbidges Lane, Long Buckby, Northampton NN6 7QL
Telephone: 01327 844119
Email: acuedit@fireflyuk.net
Web Site: www.acuedit.co.uk

Personnel:
David Price (Contact)

Writing, rewriting, editing, proofreading.
Special interests:
– Fine Art (particularly Modern Art);
– Music (particularly operettas and musicals, pop and rock music);
– Travel Guides;
– Modern European History and Politics (particularly Eastern Europe and the former Soviet Union);
– Social and Cultural History.

6002

AESOP (ALL EDITORIAL SERVICES ONLINE FOR PUBLISHERS & AUTHORS)
28 Abberbury Road, Iffley, Oxford OX4 4ES
Telephone: 01865 429563
Fax: 08700 635449
Email: mart@copyedit.co.uk
Web Site: www.copyedit.co.uk & (for Ireland) www.aesop.co

Personnel:
Martin Noble (Owner/Editor)

AESOP provides the following editorial services to publishers, authors, academics and businesses: copy-editing; proof-reading; structural editing; rewriting; co-writing; ghost-writing; thesis and dissertation editing and printing; improving use of English of non-native English writers of academic reports and books; indexing; editorial reports and reviews; advice to publishers, authors and literary agents; novelization; research; fact-checking; bibliographical research; CRC (camera ready copy) in Word format; text capture; scanning/ OCR; e-book production on CD-ROM or online; keying in MSS; audio transcription; tagging. Specializes in fiction, literature, poetry, media, music, performing arts, humour, biography, memoirs, travel, education, economics, psychology, history, alternative health, new age, esoteric and spiritual subjects, special needs.

6003

ASGARD PUBLISHING SERVICES
75 Woodside View, Leeds LS4 2QS
Telephone: 0113 274 1037
Fax: 0113 274 1037
Email: andrew.shackleton@asgardpublishing.co.uk
Web Site: www.asgardpublishing.co.uk

Also at:
Allan Scott
Telephone: 01449 741747

Fax: 01449 740118
Email: allan.scott@asgardpublishing.co.uk

Personnel:
Philip Gardner (Personnel)
Michael Scott Rohan (Personnel)
Allan Scott (Personnel)
Andrew Shackleton (Personnel)

Established in 1984. Full editorial service, including writing and re-writing, translating, copy-editing, proof-reading, indexing, design and layout. Projects can be taken from manuscript to PDF or to Quark XPress files. Extensive experience with DTP, computer-based multimedia projects (including video production) and electronic publishing. Reference material is a speciality.

6004

*BLACK ACE BOOK PRODUCTION
PO Box 7547, Perth PH2 1AU
Telephone: 01821 642822
Fax: 01821 642101
Web Site: www.blackacebooks.com

Personnel:
Hunter Steele (Director)
Boo Wood (Director)

Book production and text processing, including text capture (or scanning), editing, proofing to camera-ready/film, printing and binding, jacket artwork and design. Delivery of finished books; can sometimes help with distribution.

6005

BLUE ELEPHANT STORYSHAPING
36 Mackenzie Road, Beckenham BR3 4RU
Telephone: 07951 604097
Email: hello@blueelephantstoryshaping.com
Web Site: www.blueelephantstoryshaping.com

Personnel:
Natascha Biebow (Editor, Coach and Mentor)

Parent Company:
UK: Blue Elephant Storyshaping

Blue Elephant Storyshaping offers a range of creative services to children's book authors, illustrators, agents and publishers. It also runs workshops and seminars. For children's book authors and illustrators, it offers supportive editorial reviews, creative brainstorming sessions, portfolio advice, ongoing project development and mentoring services to help you fine-tune work for submission. For publishers, it offers freelance editing, project management, storyshaping and creative brainstorming sessions. For agents, it offers manuscript reviews, fine-tune projects for submission and scout for new talent.

6006

BOOK CREATION LTD
20 Lochaline Street, London W6 9SH
Telephone: 020 8563 9982
Fax: 020 3355 0201

Email: info@librios.com
Web Site: www.bookcreation.com

Personnel:
Hal Robinson (Managing Director)

Associated Companies:
UK: Librios Ltd

Book Creation provides editorial, translation, design and packaging/repackaging services, using Mac and PC technology, to text and layouts or final film, primarily in illustrated non-fiction, partworks, dictionaries and general reference, often involving re-use of existing illustrative or text resources.
Its sister company, Librios, provides comprehensive, XML-based electronic publishing and content management services.
With the growing importance of digital delivery, Book Creation Ltd is working ever more closely with its sister company, Librios Ltd, to provide the full range of print, e-book, website and mobile media options that publishers require.

6007

*COPYTRAIN
Pitts, Great Milton, Oxford OX44 7NF
Telephone: 01844 279345
Fax: 01844 279345
Email: rbalkwill@aol.com

Personnel:
Richard Balkwill (Proprietor)

Copytrain provides a consultancy and advisory service to publishers in the training and copyright fields.
Training: Publishing Training Centre lecturer in editorial management, financial planning and copyright. Seminars in contracts, copyright and rights. Courses in all aspects of publishing and management.
Copyright: Advice to publishers on rights and copyright matters. Review of authors' and suppliers' contracts and agreements. Associate of Rightscom.
Clients include UNESCO, WIPO and the CfBT Education Trust.
Copytrain provides 'work-for-hire' writing commissions, especially in the children's reference area (non-fiction, history, railways).

6008

FIRST EDITION TRANSLATIONS LTD
6 Wellington Court, Wellington Street, Cambridge CB1 1HZ
Telephone: 01223 356733
Fax: 01223 316232
Email: info@firstedit.co.uk
Web Site: www.firstedit.co.uk

Personnel:
Sheila Waller (Director)
Melanie Greve (Head of Editorial)

First Edition offers complete and specialized editorial and translation services, including all necessary liaison: translation, research, editing, Americanization, proofreading, indexing, desktop publishing, print ready PDF or CD output. Assessment of foreign language books for the market.

6009

GEO GROUP & ASSOCIATES
4 Christian Fields, London SW16 3JZ
Telephone: 0115 981 9418
Fax: 0115 981 9418
Email: Nyala.publishing@geo-group.co.uk
Web Site: www.geo-group.co.uk

Also at:
Nyala Publishing, 97 Rivermead, West Bridgford,
Nottingham NG2 7RF, Republic of Ireland
Telephone: 0115 981 9418
Email: (as above)
Web Site: (as above)

Personnel:
John Douglas (Director)

Associated Companies:
UK: Nyala Publishing

Publishing services: pre-press, editing, design, proofreading, reading.

6010

ALEXANDRA NYE, LITERARY CONSULTANT
6 Kinnoull Avenue, Dunblane, Perthshire FK15 9JG
Telephone: 01786 825114

Personnel:
Alexandra Nye (Editorial Director / Literary Consultant)

Provides a consultancy service for all types of fiction, with special interest in literary fiction, Scottish history, upmarket thrillers. Children's fiction age range 9–12, teens and young adult. Will supply detailed 5-page report on MSS. Does not accept poetry, plays, TV scripts or biographies.

6011

CHRISTOPHER PICK
41 Chestnut Road, London SE27 9EZ
Telephone: 020 8761 2585
Fax: 020 8761 6388
Email: christopher@the-picks.co.uk

Personnel:
Christopher Pick (Publications Consultant)

Research, writing, editing and producing information materials for public- and voluntary-sector agencies and for the corporate sector. Specializing in producing documents (e.g. policy and research reports, annual reports, handbooks) that are accessible and clearly written and that meet the needs of the target audience/readership. Also writing and producing family memoirs and 'popular' histories of organizations, companies, etc.

6012

THE PUZZLE HOUSE
Ivy Cottage, Battlesea Green, Stradbroke, Suffolk IP21 5NE
Telephone: 01379 384656
Fax: 01379 384656
Email: puzzlehouse@btinternet.com
Web Site: www.thepuzzlehouse.co.uk

Personnel:
Roy Preston (Partner)
Sue Preston (Partner)

The Puzzle House supplies crossword, quiz and puzzle material for books and magazines. Full editorial service is offered on projects ranging from a one-off puzzle to a full CRC book. All subject areas and age ranges catered for. Specialist interest and experience in the children's activity market. Established 1988. Puzzles available for syndication.

6013

RONNE RANDALL
26 Oak Tree Avenue, Radcliffe-on-Trent, Nottingham NG12 1AD
Telephone: 0115 933 5804
Email: ronnerandall@aol.com
Web Site: www.freelancersintheuk.co.uk/ronne-randall-i430.html

Personnel:
Ronne Randall (Proprietor)

Accurate Americanization by a native of the USA, as well as editorial services including editing, copy-editing, writing, rewriting/adapting, and proofreading. More than 30 years of experience on both sides of the Atlantic. Special interest and experience in children's books. Recent clients include Ladybird, Quarto/QED, Parragon, Hamlyn And Boxer Books.

6014

*READING AND RIGHTING
[Robert Lambolle Services]
618b Finchley Road, London NW11 7RR
Telephone: 020 8455 4564
Email: lambhorn@gmail.com
Web Site: readingandrighting.netfirms.com

Personnel:
Robert Lambolle (Literary/Script Consultant & Managing Director)

Established in 1987, Reading & Righting is an independent script consultancy providing evaluation and editing services, based on wide-ranging agency and publishing experience. Detailed assessment, analysis of prospects and next-step guidelines for fiction, non-fiction, screenplays, plays and poetry, plus full editing service, one-to-one tutorials, mentoring, lectures, creative writing courses, and research. Prospective clients should consult website or request leaflet outlining procedure and terms.

Specialist interests include cinema, the performing arts, popular culture, psychotherapy and current affairs.

6015

SANDHURST EDITORIAL
36 Albion Road, Sandhurst, Berks GU47 9BP
Telephone: 01252 877645
Fax: 01252 877645
Email: lionel.browne@sfep.net
Web Site: www.sandhurst-editorial.co.uk

Personnel:
Lionel Browne (Proprietor)

Sandhurst Editorial provides a complete editorial service for clients inside and outside the UK, both private sector and public sector: academic and educational publishers, research associations, commercial clients, and government departments. The skills on offer include editorial development and consultancy, project management, writing, rewriting, copy-editing and proofreading.

The company specializes in science and technology, but has handled projects as diverse as bibles, biography, travel guides and corporate reports.

6016

SUNRISE SETTING LTD
12a Fore Street, St Marychurch, Torquay, Devon TQ1 4NE
Telephone: 01803 322635
Fax: 01803 323565
Email: enquiries@sunrise-setting.co.uk
Web Site: www.sunrise-setting.co.uk

Personnel:
Jessica Stock (Finance & Marketing Director)
Alistair Smith (Production Director)

Sunrise Setting Ltd has over 30 years' experience of providing a high-quality typesetting, editorial and project management service to STM and General publishers, including copy-editing, a full XML/mathML workflow, graphics manipulation, project management of conference proceedings, books and journals, and the writing of LaTex class files and author support.

6017

HANS ZELL PUBLISHING CONSULTANTS
Glais Bheinn, Lochcarron, Ross-shire IV54 8YB
Telephone: 01520 722951
Fax: 01520 722953
Email: hanszell@hanszell.co.uk
Web Site: www.hanszell.co.uk/

Personnel:
Hans M. Zell (Proprietor)

Associated Companies:
UK: Hans Zell Publishing

Consultancy service to publishers and academic institutions, in particular providing advisory services and individual project management for publishers, research institutes, and the book community in Africa and in other developing countries.
Specialization:
– scholarly publishing, especially university press publishing, and publishing by research institutions and NGOs, including editorial and financial management, administration, marketing and promotion, pricing and distribution, general publishing management, and dealing with author and publisher contracts
– journals publishing management, including subscription management and fulfilment, financial control, journals promotion, and market assessments
– reference book publishing, particularly for reference resources focusing on Africa and the developing world, including research, project evaluations, editorial services, and market assessments
– training – in-house or through workshops and seminars – in editorial and production management, financial planning, and all areas of marketing - marketing and distribution of books on African and development studies, and African literature and culture
– providing a range of specialist mailing list services in this area, full details available on request - Internet training for the book professions in developing countries.
Under the Hans Zell Publishing imprint we publish a number of reference resources (print and online) on Africa, African studies and African publishing.

6.2 DESIGN & PRODUCTION SERVICES

6018

BBR SOLUTIONS LTD
12 Cutthorpe Road, Chesterfield S42 7AE
Telephone: 01246 271662
Email: bbr@bbr-online.co.uk
Web Site: www.bbr-online.co.uk

Personnel:
Chris Reed (Director)
Amanda Thompson (Director)

Associated Companies:
UK: BBR Distribution

BBR provides editorial, design, typesetting and project management services for publishers. With over 25 years' experience in publishing, the company meticulously proofs and edits manuscripts for publication, and creates clean, typography-led designs for books and journals.
Please visit the company's website for more information and to view its portfolio.

6019

BOOK PRODUCTION CONSULTANTS LTD
25–27 High Street, Chesterton, Cambridge CB4 1ND
Telephone: 01223 352790
Fax: 01223 460718
Email: bpc@bpccam.co.uk
Web Site: www.bpccam.co.uk

Personnel:
Colin Walsh (Managing Director)
Jo Littlechild (Marketing Manager)
Susan Buck (Accounts Manager)

Associated Companies:
UK: Book Connections; Granta Editions

A totally comprehensive publishing service including editing, sub-editing, designing, technical mark-up, illustrating, technical drawing, estimating, paper buying, typesetting and origination. BPC arranges the printing and binding of black-and-white or colour publications in the UK or overseas and supervises quality control and delivery schedules; also computer software packs including design of packaging and manufacture of boxes, tapes and discs. Other specialities include the design and production of illustrated books, music and foreign language setting projects, academic journals and institutional publications, producing company-sponsored books and company histories. Electronic publishing and CD-ROM origination, particularly as joint ventures, form part of current expansion. Specialist divisions include business histories (providing authors, archivists and picture researchers), contract magazine production and company literature.

6020

BOOKCRAFT LTD
18 Kendrick Street, Stroud, Glos GL5 1AA
Telephone: 0870 1601900
Fax: 0870 1601901
Email: information@bookcraft.co.uk
Web Site: www.bookcraft.co.uk

Personnel:
John Button *(Publishing Director)*

Bookcraft provides publishers with a wide range of editorial, design, technical and training services.
 Main areas of activity are:
 – publishing consultancy
 – publishing software training
 – design services
 – editorial and proofreading services
 – project management.

6021

CHASE PUBLISHING SERVICES LTD
33 Livonia Road, Sidmouth, Devon EX10 9JB
Telephone: 01395 514709
Fax: 01395 514709
Email: r.addicott@chase-publishing.co.uk

Personnel:
Ray Addicott *(Director)*

Chase offers a complete editorial and production service to authors and publishers – from copy-editing of the author's typescript to finished books at the delivery point. It specializes in academic books.
 Founded in 1989.

6022

FOTOLIBRA
22 Mount View Road, London N4 4HX
Telephone: 020 8348 1234
Email: professionals@fotoLibra.com
Web Site: www.fotoLibra.com

Personnel:
Gwyn Headley *(Managing Director)*
Yvonne Seeley *(Marketing Director)*

Parent Company:
UK: VisConPro Ltd

Associated Companies:
USA: Idea Logical Company Inc

fotoLibra is a picture library set up by publishers for publishers. The company has 18,000+ photographers in over 150 countries ready and willing to take the required image if it is not already in the library – and there's no obligation to buy. Over 550,000 images on line.

6023

GRAHAM-CAMERON ILLUSTRATION
The Studio, 23 Holt Road, Sheringham, Norfolk NR26 8NB
Telephone: 01263 821333
Fax: 01263 821334
Email: enquiry@gciforillustration.com
Web Site: www.gciforillustration.com

Illustration commissions:
Duncan Graham-Cameron, 59 Hertford Road, Brighton BN1 7GG
Telephone: 01273 385890
Email: duncan@gciforillustration.com
Web Site: www.gciforillustration.com

Personnel:
Duncan Graham-Cameron *(Sales & Marketing Director)*
Helen Graham-Cameron *(Art Director)*

Parent Company:
UK: Graham-Cameron Publishing

Associated Companies:
UK: Helen Herbert, Fine Art

This agency represents some 37 qualified professional published illustrators who use a wide range of techniques and media. GCI specializes in supplying commissioned illustrations for educational and children's books, and for general information publications.

6024

*HOLBROOK DESIGN OXFORD LTD
Holbrook House, 105 Rose Hill, Oxford OX4 4HT
Telephone: 01865 459000
Email: info@holbrook-design.co.uk
Web Site: www.holbrook-design.co.uk

Personnel:
Peter Tucker *(Design Director)*

Holbrook Design Oxford Ltd was founded as PGT Design in 1974. It offers the following services: typography, editorial design and art direction, photography; from concept through dummies, mark-up and typesetting, page layouts to artwork, in consultation with photographers, illustrators and printers. Clients include many national and international publishers. Holbrook Design has particular experience in educational and general publishing; subject areas covered range from science to religion, cookery to history and first readers to A-level.

6025

*HOLBROOK HOSTING
Holbrook House, 105 Rose Hill, Oxford OX4 4HT
Telephone: 01865 459000
Email: info@holbrookhosting.com
Web Site: www.holbrookhosting.com

Personnel:
Peter Tucker *(Consultant)*

Design Systems is a consultancy providing both technical and design expertise in the implementation and use of both Macs and PCs in graphics and publishing industries. Agents include Adobe, Quark, Ventura Software, Monotype, Linotype and other associated companies. Affiliated to Holbrook Design Oxford Ltd, for many years designers in publishing and print.

6026

HYBERT DESIGN LTD
52 High Street, Eton, Berkshire SL4 6BL
Telephone: 01753 206723
Fax: 01753 206357
Email: info@hybertdesign.com
Web Site: www.hybertdesign.com

Also at:
Buterud P1 8722, 464 91 Dals Rostock, Sweden
Telephone: +46 (0)530 30084
Email: info@hybertdesign.com
Web Site: www.hybertdesign.com

Personnel:
Tom Hybert *(Director)*
Kate Hybert *(Company Secretary)*
Linda Elliott *(Senior Designer)*

We're a small, friendly, family-run studio with over 35 years experience. We design books, marketing, and corporate material for print & web. We specialise in design for publishers. We keep it simple, stylish, successful and speedy.

6027

IMAGO PUBLISHING LTD
Albury Court, Albury, Thame, Oxon OX9 2LP
Telephone: 01844 337000
Fax: 01844 339935
Email: debbiek@imago.co.uk
Web Site: www.imago.co.uk; www.imagocreate.co.uk

Personnel:
Colin Risk *(Managing Director)*
Jim Allpass *(Finance Director)*
Angela Young *(Director)*
Debbie Knight *(Marketing Director)*
Cherry Jaquet *(Production Director)*
Martina Scheible *(European Sales Director)*
Paolo Scaramuzza *(UK Sales Director)*

Imago offers production services including print management, sourcing, training & consultancy to the publishing and creative industries. With offices in the UK, Paris, Hong Kong, China, Singapore, Malaysia, India, Sydney, New York and California, the group is able to locate and control sources of manufacture on a worldwide basis. The group works with a wide range of clients, offering its extensive expertise in many ways, from running all the production needs for small publishers/packagers, to sourcing and arranging for the manufacture of individual projects on a competitive broking basis. All types of work are handled, including colour separation, children's books involving handwork, books plus, short- and long-run general books and magazines. Training courses in Digital Publishing, Colour, Product Safety, Paper, InDesign, Quark and Photoshop run regularly in the UK.

6028

MY WORD!
PO Box 4575, Rugby, Warwickshire CV21 9EH
Telephone: 01788 571294
Email: janet@myword.co.uk
Web Site: www.myword.co.uk

Personnel:
Roderick Grant *(Partner)*
Janet Grant *(Partner)*

My Word! is a family business which specializes in typesetting of materials for both printing and the Internet.
 Its range includes magazines, books, newsletters, newspapers, brochures, conference and sales materials, leaflets, posters and stationery.
 Clients come from both the charity and commercial sectors.

6029

ROYAL NATIONAL INSTITUTE OF BLIND PEOPLE (RNIB)
Bakewell Road, Orton Southgate, Peterborough PE2 6XU
Telephone: 0303 123 9999
Fax: 01733 375001
Email: helpline@rnib.org.uk
Web Site: rnib.org.uk

Royal National Institute of Blind People (RNIB) is one of the UK's leading charities offering information, support and advice to over two million people with sight loss.
 It produces accessible format editions of publications so that blind and partially sighted people can read them in a format such as braille, large print or audio – from textbooks supporting children in education to a Mills and Boon romance, and everything in between. It offers transcription services for businesses and publishers.
 It publishes a range of material about living with sight loss, such as eye condition leaflets and information on benefits.

6030

SMALL PRINT
The Old School House, 74 High Street, Swavesey, Cambridge CB24 4QU
Telephone: 01954 231713 (mobile: 07760 430206)
Email: info@smallprint.co.uk
Web Site: www.smallprint.co.uk

Personnel:
Naomi Laredo *(Proprietor)*

Flexible project management service specialising in multilingual and multimedia packages. Founded in 1986 and highly experienced in educational, vocational, academic and business publishing.
 Translation covering most European and Asian languages.
 Also copywriting, editing and proofreading, design and layout (for web or print), audio and video production.
 Clients include Association of Commonwealth Universities, BBC, Collins, Edco of Ireland, Historic Chapels Trust, Nelson Thornes, Palgrave Macmillan, Pearson Education, Teach Yourself (Hodder).

6031

TAMR TRANSLATIONS LTD
[sister company to American Pie (American Eyes Ltd)]
197 Kings Cross Road, London WC1X 9DB
Telephone: 020 7278 9490
Fax: 020 7278 2447
Email: bacon@langservice.com
Web Site: www.tamrtranslations.com

Also at:
215 West Red Oak #I, Sunnyvale, CA 94086–6632, USA
Email: DHenderson@aol.com
Web Site: www.americanization.com

Personnel:
Josephine Bacon (Director)
Dan Henderson (Director)
Azmi Jbeily (Director)

Parent Company:
UK: American Pie (American Eyes Ltd)

Tamr Translations Ltd specializes in translations for publication, into and from English, including highly illustrated books. Specialist languages are French, Arabic and Hebrew, specialist subjects cookery, art and architecture. American Pie, with offices in London and Sunnyvale, California, translates between British and American English.

The two companies have translated more than 100 books between them, and have also published three translations. Their work has won the Gourmand Prize for Cookery Translation.

We are experts on book translations from French, German, Hebrew, Russian, Polish, Italian and Spanish into English and translations to and from English and Arabic. We also offer Arabic and Hebrew typesetting.

6.3 ELECTRONIC PUBLISHING SERVICES

6032

*ATTWOOLL ASSOCIATES LTD
90 Divinity Road, Oxford OX4 1LN
Telephone: 01865 422230
Fax: 01865 791192
Email: david@attwoollassociates.com
Web Site: www.attwoollassociates.com

Personnel:
David Attwooll (Director)
Clare Painter (Associate)

Attwooll Associates Ltd is a publishing consultancy and licensing agency specializing in electronic and print media, in North American and UK markets. It was founded in April 2002.
Activities include:
– publishing and media strategy
– intellectual property exploitation and licensing
– project management and innovation
– market-driven content creation and acquisition
– information mapping and knowledge management
– mergers and acquisitions advice
– training seminars and lectures.
Please see www.attwoollassociates.com

6033

GLOBAL MAPPING
Units 2 & 3, Glebe Farm, Turweston, Brackley, Northants NN13 5JE
Telephone: 01280 840770
Fax: 01280 840816
Email: sales@globalmapping.uk.com
Web Site: www.globalmapping.uk.com

Personnel:
Alan Smith (Managing Director)

Publishes its own range of maps. Also creates bespoke map products for other publishers including interactive map-based websites. Online retailer of map-based products such as wall maps, postcode maps, Ordnance Survey data, atlases, globes and guides. Global Mapping aims to be a one-stop shop for all map-based requirements.

6034

KOALA PUBLISHING LTD
Downend House, 112 North Street, Downend, Bristol BS16 5SE
Telephone: 0117 910 9111
Fax: 0117 910 9222
Email: gordon.dennis@koalapub.co.uk
Web Site: www.koalapub.co.uk

Personnel:
Gordon Dennis (Commercial Director)
Vivienne Willoughby-Ellis (Managing Director)
Robin Shobbrook (Marketing Manager)

Koala helps suppliers of complex products and services who need to:
– create straightforward, easy to use documentation and get it to their customers in the most effective way possible – from PDAs to printer manuals;
– efficiently organize, write and deliver their technical manuals, policies and procedures;
– reduce the cost and time constraints on professional staff of providing information to their customers, and reduce the long-term risks of litigation caused by faulty documentation.
Koala provides software products for publishing technical documentation including manuals, training materials, catalogues, directories and listings. Services include project management and control; analysis and design; bespoke programming; data format conversion; and full training and support.

6035

LIGHTNING SOURCE UK LTD
Chapter House, Pitfield, Kiln Farm, Milton Keynes MK11 3LW
Telephone: 0845 121 4567
Fax: 0845 121 4594
Email: enquiries@lightningsource.co.uk
Web Site: www.lightningsource.com

Personnel:
David Taylor (Group Managing Director)
Dave Piper (Managing Director)
Terry Gridley (Operations Director)
Frank Devine (Finance Director)
Lawrence Felice (Marketing Manager)

Parent Company:
USA: Ingram Content Group, Inc.

Associated Companies:
USA: Lightning Source, Inc.

Lightning Source offers quality e-book and one-off book manufacturing and access to comprehensive distribution solutions in the publishing industry.

6036

*MMT
[trading as MMT Digital]
1A Uppingham Gate, Ayston Road, Uppingham, Rutland LE15 9NY
Telephone: 01572 822278
Fax: 01572 820213
Email: info@mmtdigital.co.uk
Web Site: www.mmtdigital.co.uk

London Office:
Suite 54–55, 88–90 Hatton Gardens, London EC1N 8PN
Telephone: 020 7242 5698
Fax: (as above)
Email: (as above)
Web Site: (as above)

Personnel:
Peter Cannings (Human Resources & Finance Director)
Ben Rudman (Joint Managing & Marketing Director)
James Cannings (Joint Managing & Production Director)

Currently working with Hodder on their e-titles.

6037

NIELSEN BOOKNET
3rd Floor, Midas House, 62 Goldsworth Road, Woking, Surrey GU21 6LQ
Telephone: 01483 712200
Fax: 01483 712201
Email: sales.booknet@nielsen.com
Web Site: www.nielsenbooknet.co.uk

Personnel:
Ann Betts (Commercial Director)
Stephen Long (Head of BookNet)
Mo Siewcharran (Head of Marketing)
Joanna De Courville (Business Development Manager)
Paul Dibble (Head of Data Sales)

Lucy Huddlestone (Business Development Manager)
Melanie Brassington (Export Sales Manager)
Richard Merrick (Customer Services Manager)

Parent Company:
UK: Nielsen

Associated Companies:
Nielsen Registration Agencies (ISBN, SAN & ISTC)
UK: Nielsen BookData; Nielsen BookScan

Nielsen BookNet provides a range of e-commerce services that allow electronic trading between booksellers, distributors, publishers, libraries and other suppliers, regardless of their size and location. Services include BookNet Transaction Services for booksellers and publishers/distributors, TeleOrdering and EDI. Nielsen BookNet is uniquely placed in the book trade to be the trading hub for orders, invoices, delivery notes and other EDI messaging.

6038

TRILOGY GROUP
Aries House, 43 Selkirk Street, Cheltenham, Glos GL52 2HJ
Telephone: 01242 222132
Fax: 01242 235103
Web Site: www.trilogygroup.com

Personnel:
Alex Dare (Managing Director)
Simon Gough (IT Director)
Mike Ribbins (Group Chairman)

The Trilogy Group specializes in software for the specialist publisher, especially those requiring a totally integrated business solution to handle publishing management, administration, direct and distribution sales together with active marketing. Our software, which uses Microsoft SQL Server technology, offers:
– title management
– customer management with profiles and buying history
– active marketing facilities
– direct mail management with optional integration to MailSort
– subscriptions management
– royalties
– integration to accounting systems
– vast range of 'real-time' management reports
– real-time stock management
– warehouse and despatch management
– integrated on-line shopping facilities with web hosting
– multi-site management
– EPOS
– production control, scheduling and job costing.

6.4 TRANSLATION SERVICES

6039

FIRST EDITION TRANSLATIONS LTD
6 Wellington Court, Wellington Street, Cambridge CB1 1HZ
Telephone: 01223 356733
Fax: 01223 316232
Email: info@firstedit.co.uk
Web Site: www.firstedit.co.uk

Personnel:
Sheila Waller (Director)
Melanie Greve (Head of Editorial)
Ana Grilo (Commercial Translations Manager)

Translations – commercial, technical, academic and of any length – undertaken in any language according to publisher's requirements. Editing, proofreading, Americanization, indexing, typesetting/desktop publishing.
Output to print ready PDF or CD. Quotations given without obligation.

6040

SATRAP PUBLISHING & TRANSLATION
Suite 21, London House, 271 King Street, Hammersmith, London W6 9LZ
Telephone: 020 8748 9397
Fax: 020 8748 9394
Email: satrap@btconnect.com
Web Site: www.satrap.co.uk

Personnel:
Alex Vahdat *(Managing Director)*
Mrs Homa Lohrasb *(Technical Manager)*

Satrap Publishing is a UK-based international company, specializing in the fields of translation, typesetting and print services in Oriental and East European languages.

The company produces promotional literature, exhibition catalogues, information pamphlets, books, reports, manuals, business stationery, product labels, diaries, etc for Western European companies, trade centres and various organizations which have foreign language requirements for their overseas trade links.

The human resources and advanced technical facilities available are ideal for those clients who wish to target ethnic minorities for their social, cultural and educational programmes. Satrap Publishing offers a complete package of expert translation, typesetting, professional graphic design as well as printing. Production of exclusive greeting cards and wedding stationery in non-European languages are among other services from Satrap Publishing.

6041

SWEDISH-ENGLISH LITERARY TRANSLATORS ASSOCIATION (SELTA)
89 Grove Road, Rayleigh SS6 8RA
Telephone: 01268 747877
Web Site: www.selta.org.uk &
www.swedishbookreview.com

Personnel:
Martin Murrell *(Hon Secretary)*
Sarah Death *(Editor, Swedish Book Review)*

SELTA aims to promote the publication of Swedish literature in English and to represent the interests of those involved in its translation. Publishes *Swedish Book Review* (ISSN: 0265 8119): biannual, £15 p.a.

6042

UPS TRANSLATIONS
[the language division of United Publicity Services Plc]
111 Baker Street, London W1U 6RR
Telephone: 020 7224 1220
Fax: 020 7486 3272
Email: info@upstranslations.com
Web Site: www.upstranslations.com

Personnel:
Justin Silver *(Chairman & Managing Director)*
Denise McKenzie *(Company Secretary)*
Katya Silver *(Director)*

Parent Company:
UK: United Publicity Services Plc

UPS Translations provide full translation, DTP and proofreading services for all kinds of publications.

The company's clients include leading publishing houses; it works on some of the world's best known books and magazines. For ongoing work volume discounts are offered: these tend to work in blocks of 50,000 words or more in a 12 month period. The company has considerable experience in providing translation services for international publications, whether highly technical or creative. Most of UPS's publishing, newspaper or ad agency clients use the company as a one-stop-shop for all their foreign language requirements.

The company's editing and proofreading service is of special note. Many clients trust UPS to take their project through production to final film or digital file ready for printing or publishing on-line. The company's expertise extends from books to CDs, periodicals, magazines, house journals, national newspapers and websites.

6043

*SALLY WALKER LANGUAGE SERVICES
43 St Nicholas Street, Bristol BS1 1TP
Telephone: 0117 929 1594
Fax: 0117 929 0633
Email: translations@sallywalker.co.uk
Web Site: www.sallywalker.co.uk

Also at:
Perch Buildings, 9 Mount Stuart Square, Cardiff CF10 5EE
Telephone: 029 2048 0747
Fax: 029 2048 8736
Email: languages@sallywalker.co.uk
Web Site: www.sallywalker.co.uk

Personnel:
Sally Walker *(Director)*
Richard Smith *(General Manager)*

Established in 1969 Sally Walker Language Services provides a 70 language capability. Languages include all European and major Middle Eastern and Far Eastern. Additionally most Indian and African languages are offered.

6044

WESSEX TRANSLATIONS LTD
Barn 500, The Grange, Romsey Road, Michelmersh, Romsey, Hants SO51 0AE
Telephone: 0870 1669 300
Fax: 0870 1669 299
Email: sales@wt-lm.com
Web Site: www.wt-lm.com

Personnel:
Jonathan Nater *(Director)*
Robin Weber *(Director)*
Paul Stewart *(Director)*

Associated Companies:
France: Wessex Traductions

In addition to translation our services include face to face and telephone interpreting, typesetting, DTP and artwork, editing and proofreading, copywriting, software localization, language training, audio and video transcription, voiceovers and website translations.

These are available in all languages, and covering all sectors, including technical, defence, medical/pharmaceutical, legal, etc.

Translators always work into their mother tongue, and all translations

are double-checked, and then re-worked, DTPed if required and checked again before despatch. The final text is sent by email with hard copy if required to meet clients' individual software requirements, ready to print wherever possible.

A special urgent Tender Translation Service is also offered, where exceptionally fast turnaround is required.

6.5 SALES & MARKETING SERVICES

6045

*BERTOLI MITCHELL LLP
53 Chandos Place, Covent Garden, London WC2N 4HS
Telephone: 020 7812 6416
Fax: 020 7812 6677
Email: nb@bertolimitchell.co.uk
Web Site: www.bertolimitchell.co.uk

Personnel:
William Mitchell *(Managing Partner)*
Natalina Bertoli *(Partner)*
Paul Mitton *(Senior Associate)*

Bertoli Mitchell LLP is a specialist mergers and acquisitions advisory firm in the publishing and information industries.

The partnership offers corporate finance services for mergers, acquisitions and divestitures including:
– sell-side advisory representation to sellers of privately held businesses and corporate clients seeking to divest business units or assets
– buy-side advisory services and representation
– commercial and contracts due diligence
– valuations
Since Bertoli Mitchell was founded in 1994 it has advised successfully on over 80 transactions.
Bertoli Mitchell also undertakes strategic research and consultancy. Activities include:
– profiling, analysis, forecasting and recommendations for clients considering entry into specific markets or sectors
– benchmarking, cost audits and development of financial targets
– development of business plans
Clients range from large fully listed international companies to shareholders of small and medium-sized private businesses.

6046

*BEST MAILING SERVICES LTD
Merlin Way, North Weald, Epping, Essex CM16 6HR

Telephone: 01992 524343
Fax: 01992 524552
Email: sales@bestmailing.co.uk
Web Site: www.bestmailing.co.uk

Personnel:
Mrs Lyn Reed *(Managing Director)*
Peter Cook *(Client Services Director)*

BMS offers a complete direct mail production facility.

Comprehensive services include database management, data capture, laser printing, mail order fulfilment, subscription management, machine and hand enclosing, bulk despatch, overseas and UK postal discounts.

BMS also provides high volume digital printing and on demand publishing, backed up with a professional finishing service which includes booklet making and collating.

6047

BOOKLINK
42 Reigate Road, Ewell, Epsom, Surrey KT17 1PX
Telephone: 020 8394 1578
Email: info@booklink.co.uk
Web Site: www.booklink.co.uk

Also at:
15 Bd Ralli – 13008 Marseille, France
Telephone: +33 (0)4 91 77 76 38
Email: info@booklink.co.uk
Web Site: www.booklink.co.uk

Personnel:
Evelyne Duval *(Managing Director)*
Maria White *(Agent)*

An international connection for foreign rights sales and consultancy. Representing French, English and American publishers/packagers.

6048

BOOKS ON MUSIC
3 Kendal Green, Kendal, Cumbria LA9 5PN
Telephone: 01539 740049
Fax: 01539 737744
Web Site: www.booksonmusic.co.uk

Personnel:
Rosemary Dooley *(Manager)*

Books on Music runs collaborative publishers' exhibitions at academic music conferences. Specialization in music.

6049

BROOKSIDE PUBLISHING SERVICES LTD
2 Brookside, Dundrum Road, Dublin 14, Republic of Ireland
Telephone: +353 (0)1 298 3411
Fax: +353 (0)1 298 2783
Email: sales@brookside.ie

Personnel:
Edwin Higel *(Managing Director)*
Conor Graham *(Sales & Marketing Manager)*
Michael Darcy *(Academic Sales)*

Agents for various imprints in Ireland including:
A & A Farmar; Bloomsbury Professional Publishing; Cambridge University Press; Chartered Accountants Ireland; Clarus Press; Continuum; Irish Academic Press; Irish Theatre Handbook; Jessica Kingsley; Jones & Bartlett; Learning Matters; Nick Hern Books; Pharmaceutical Press; Pluto Press; Radcliffe Medical; Routledge / Taylor & Francis; Taxation Advice Bureau Guide

Represents both trade and academic publishers.

6050

BROOMFIELD BOOKS LTD
36 De La Warr Road, East Grinstead, West Sussex RH19 3BP
Telephone: 01342 313237
Fax: 01342 322525
Email: nic@broomfieldbooks.co.uk
Web Site: www.broomfieldbooks.co.uk

Personnel:
Nic Webb *(Director)*
Mrs Andrea Grant-Webb *(Director)*

Broomfield Books is a publishing consultancy and sales agency for small and medium publishers of non-fiction and fiction. The sales agency covers London and the south-east of England, together with UK key accounts and the export market. We also deal in quality overstocks and remainder books.

6051

THE CENTRE FOR INTERFIRM COMPARISON
32 St Thomas Street, Winchester, Hants SO23 9HJ
Telephone: 01962 844144
Fax: 01962 843180
Email: mikebayliss@cifc.co.uk
Web Site: www.cifc.co.uk

Personnel:
Mr M. J. Bayliss (Director)

An independent organization established in 1959 by the British Institute of Management and the British Productivity Council specifically to meet the demand for a neutral specialist body to conduct interfirm comparisons (IFCs) and benchmarking projects on a confidential basis as a service to management.

The Centre has run a series of confidential IFCs specifically designed for book publishers in conjunction with the Publishers Association. These provided participants with measures for assessing how their overall performance compared, where and why it differed, and lines of action for improvement. More recently the Centre carried out projects for learned journal and magazine publishers. It has become a specialist in conducting in-depth and carefully defined benchmarking projects for firms and organizations of all kinds, based on information supplied confidentially by participants.

6052

COLMAN GETTY CONSULTANCY
28 Windmill Street, London W1T 2JJ
Telephone: 020 7631 2666
Fax: 020 7631 2699
Email: info@colmangetty.co.uk
Web Site: www.colmangetty.co.uk

Personnel:
Dotti Irving (Chief Executive)
Liz Sich (Managing Director)
Amy Maclaren (Associate Director)
Truda Spruyt (Associate Director)
Jane Acton (Associate Director)
Ruth Cairns (Associate Director)

Colman Getty is a London-based PR and communications consultancy, founded in 1987 and headed by Dotti Irving, formerly publicity director of Penguin Books. The agency specializes in book publishing, cultural and campaigning PR and event management, and has established a reputation for handling complex, high-profile campaigns, individual promotions, literary prizes and anniversaries and longer-term consultancies. As well as offering a wide-based expertise in PR and publicity, Colman Getty offers bespoke marketing services – from copywriting and print production to sales promotion, advertising and digital and social media campaigns. Its client list includes The Man Booker Prize for Fiction, the BBC Samuel Johnson Prize for Non Fiction, Cheltenham Literature Festival, World Book Day, award-winning bookseller Foyles and a number of individual writers such as Jeffrey Archer, Charlie Higson, Val McDermid and Patricia Cornwell. Other clients include the Association of Graduate Recruiters.

6053

THE COLUMBA BOOKSERVICE
55A Spruce Avenue, Stillorgan Industrial Park, Blackrock, Co Dublin, Republic of Ireland
Telephone: +353 (0)1 294 2556
Fax: +353 (0)1 294 2564
Email: info@columba.ie
Web Site: www.columba.ie

Personnel:
Séan O Boyle (Managing Director)

UK distributor/representative for:
Canada: Novalis
Republic of Ireland: The Columba Press
USA: Michael Glazier Books; The Liturgical Press; Loyola Press; Paraclete Press; Paulist Press; Pueblo Books; Resource Publications; Twenty-third Publications

The Columba Bookservice provides trade representation, sales and marketing services for a number of religious publishers.

6054

DAVENPORT PUBLISHING SERVICES
11 Silbury Rise, Keynsham, Bristol BS31 1JP
Telephone: 0117 986 2914
Fax: 0117 986 2074
Email: anne@annedavenport.demon.co.uk

Personnel:
Anne Davenport (Proprietor & Consultant)

Davenport Publishing Services offers consultancy in marketing, promotion, sales and distribution for academic, STM and society publishers.

Projects successfully completed include marketing planning and market research, promotion planning, copywriting for print and electronic media, sales advice, sourcing of overseas agents, representatives and distributors, and lapsed subscriber chasing.

Davenport Publishing Services offers a full service from consultancy to implementation of marketing campaigns. Long-term or short-term projects are welcome.

Clients include society publishers, university presses and independent institutions with publishing interests.

6055

DURNELL MARKETING LTD
2 Linden Close, Tunbridge Wells, Kent TN4 8HH
Telephone: 01892 544272
Fax: 01892 511152
Email: admin@durnell.co.uk & orders@durnell.co.uk
Web Site: www.durnell.co.uk

Personnel:
Andrew Durnell (Managing Proprietor/Director)
Julia Lippiatt (Finance Proprietor/Director)

Durnell Marketing provides a solution for publishers wishing to maximize their sales – via a single sales force – to all of Central, Eastern and Western Europe's diverse markets, including Ireland (but excluding the UK). A team of multilingual sales representatives ensures maximum, effective and personal coverage of publishers' potential customers, be they library suppliers, general wholesalers, bookshop chains, specialist independents, campus bookshops, non-trade, museum or institutional accounts. Travelling representatives are supported by office-based multilingual sales specialists who provide extra sales backup by promoting trade books, potential textbooks and major reference works to the trade, individual academics and institutions. In addition, Durnell Marketing organizes specific promotions, exhibitions, mailings, author signings and more.

6056

*GAZELLE ACADEMIC
White Cross Mills, Hightown, Lancaster LA1 4XS
Telephone: 01524 68765
Fax: 01524 63232
Email: sales@gazellebooks.co.uk
Web Site: www.gazellebookservices.co.uk

Personnel:
Trevor Witcher (Managing Director)
Brian Haywood (Finance Director)
Mark Trotter (Sales & Distribution Director)

Parent Company:
UK: Gazelle Book Services Ltd

Clients:
Australia: FHA Publishing & Communication
Belgium: EuroComment
Canada: Calgary University Press; Canadian Humanist Publications; Wilfrid Laurier University Press; Museum of New Mexico Press; New Society Publishers
Denmark: Aarhus University Press; Museum Tusculanum Press
Finland: Finnish Literature Society; PG-Team Oy; Sophi Academic Press
Germany: Ontos-verlag.de
Israel: Yad Ben Zvi
Netherlands: Aspekt Uitgeverij BV; Nova Vista Publishing; VU University Press
Norway: Tapir Academic Press
Sweden: International Idea; Nordic Academic Press; Student Litteratur

Switzerland: INU Press
UK: Arabian Publishing; Boulevard Books; Clinical Press – Europe; Elector Electronics; William Harvey Press Ltd; Institute of Economic Affairs; Merit Publishing (Medical); Sponsorship Unit; Sussex Academic Press; TFM Publishing Ltd (Medical); World Council of Churches
USA: Ariadne Press; Colorado University Press; Current Clinical Strategies Publishing; Darwin Press; Duquesne University Press; Encounter Books; Feminist Press; Hackett Publishing Co; Harlan Davidson Inc; Ibex Publishers; J & S Publishing Co Inc; Liberty Fund; Mage Publishers; MediPress; Nova Science Publishers Inc; Scientific Publishing Co; Truman State University Press; University of Alberta Press; University of New Mexico Press; Woodbine House Inc

Gazelle Academic is now a division of Gazelle Book Services.

6057

GLOBAL BOOK MARKETING LTD
99b Wallis Road, London E9 5LN
Telephone: 020 8533 5800
Fax: 020 8533 5800
Email: info@globalbookmarketing.co.uk

Personnel:
A. Zurbrugg (Managing Director)
A. Howe (Sales Manager)
A. Hanson (IT Manager)

European agents for:
Canada: Between the Lines; Fernwood Publishing
France: Cacimbo Editions
Germany: Bayreuth African Studies; Barbara Budrich; LIT Verlag
Jamaica: Ian Randle Publishers; Universities of the Caribbean Press
Netherlands: International Books (Utrecht); Techne
Nigeria: Kachifo
South Africa: Blue Weaver Marketing; Briza Publications; Human & Rousseau; Jacana Education; Kwela Books; Pharos; David Philip / Spearhead / New Africa Books Consortium; Protea; Tafelberg
Switzerland: Basler Afrika Bibliografien
Tanzania: Blue Mango Publishing
UK: Battlebridge; Eastern Arts / Saffron; Horniman Museum Publications
USA: International Publishers (New York)

Agents and representatives. Many publishers are distributed by Central Books Ltd.

6058

HAWKINS PUBLISHING SERVICES
12 Parkview Cottages, Crowhurst Lane End, Oxted, Surrey RH8 9NT
Telephone: 01342 893029
Fax: 01342 893316
Email: gill.hawkins@virgin.net

Personnel:
Gillian Hawkins (Director)

Distributor for:
Australia: Sibling Press
UK: Dynasty Press; Full Circle Editions; Gullane; Inside Pocket; Meadowside; Shepheard Walwyn

Sales, marketing, publicity, rights and distribution.

6059

HUMPHRYS ROBERTS ASSOCIATES
5 Voluntary Place, Wanstead, London E11 2RP
Telephone: 020 8530 5028
Fax: 020 8530 7870
Email: humph4hra@aol.com

Also at:
Terry Roberts, Humphrys Roberts Associates, Caixa Postal 801, Agencia Jardim da Gloria, 06700–990 Cotia SP, Brazil
Telephone: +55 (11) 4702 4496 & 4702 6997
Fax: +55 (11) 4702 6896
Email: hrabrasil@intercall.com.br

Personnel:
Christopher Humphrys (Joint Managing Director)
Terry Roberts (Joint Managing Director)

Publishers' agents and representatives, representing UK and US publishers in South America, Central America, Mexico, the Caribbean, Spain, Portugal and Gibraltar.

6060

BRIAN INNS BOOKSALES & SERVICES
9 Ashley Crescent, Warwick CV34 6QH
Telephone: 01926 498428
Fax: 01926 498428
Email: brian.inns@btinternet.com

Personnel:
Brian Inns (Managing Director)

Specialization: general non-fiction and technical books.
Services: consultancy and solutions for publishers. Development of business with multiple bookselling groups and key accounts handled personally by Brian Inns. Specialist at improving market penetration.
Representation in UK. Distribution arranged.

6061

JEM EDUCATION DIRECT
Staplehurst Road, Sittingbourne, Kent ME10 2NH
Telephone: 01795 415115
Fax: 01795 439551
Email: info@jem.co.uk
Web Site: www.jem.co.uk

Personnel:
Andre Kleinman (Managing Director)
David Edwards (Sales and Client Services Director)
Chris Gray (Marketing Director)
Karen Neal (Account Manager)
Gemma Wyatt (Account manager)
Joanna Pope (Account Manager)
Stuart Butterfield (Account Manager)

Parent Company:
Orbital Marketing Services Group

Fulfilment and Distribution Services:
UK: BP Education Services; Cross Academe; English and Media Centre; Robert Powell Publications; Smart Learning

Education Direct and JEM Education Marketing Services joined forces in late 2010 to form Jem Education Direct and provide their clients with superior mailing and marketing support services.

JEM Education Direct offers a most comprehensive range of data, marketing services and direct marketing solutions to a wide range of clients who market their products and services to the UK education sector, enabling them to communicate with and promote to schools, colleges, universities and other educational establishments in the most effective, cost efficient way.
The company has production facilities in Sittingbourne, Kent, while our client services team operates from both Sittingbourne and the group's head office in Ashford, Kent.
Core services are complemented by additional services that are available either from within the Orbital Marketing Services Group or from carefully selected partners with whom we have developed close working relationships. These services include Education Market Research, Design & Print, Response & Fulfilment and Marketing Consultancy.
For more information call our Client Services Team on 01795 415115 for more information, or e-mail sales@jem.co.uk

6062

KUPERARD PUBLISHERS
59 Hutton Grove, London N12 8DS
Telephone: 020 8446 2440
Fax: 020 8446 2441
Email: office@kuperard.co.uk
Web Site: www.kuperard.co.uk

Personnel:
Joshua Kuperard (Chief Executive)
Martin Kaye (Sales & Marketing Manager)
Linda Tenenbaum (Special Sales Manager)

Distributor for:
Israel: Koren Publishers; Maggid Books; Toby Press
UK: Cade's Camping Guides; Caravan Club of Great Britain; Culture Smart! Guides; Customs & Etiquette; FHG

Guides; Kuperard Books; Monjeune Publishers; Simple Guides
USA: HarperCollins; Lerner Books; Living Language (Random House); The Modern Library (Random House); Penguin US; Schocken Books / Random House; Smithsonian Institute

Kuperard, a division and imprint of Bravo Ltd, acts as publishers, co-publishers and distributors, handling marketing and representation. Kuperard handle over 30 UK and overseas publishers. Stocklists, catalogues and brochures are available upon request.
Travel subjects include leisure guides covering a wide variety of destinations and markets. Kuperard publishes cross-cultural guides helping a wide range of people, from businessmen to travellers, gain an understanding of different cultures. Religion subjects covered include Art, Cookery, the Holy Land, Bible, History, Language, Mysticism, Holocaust, Faith, Prayer and Spirituality.

6063

CHRIS LLOYD SALES & MARKETING SERVICES
50a Willis Way, Poole, Dorset BH15 3SY
Telephone: 01202 649930
Fax: 01202 649950
Email: chrlloyd@globalnet.co.uk
Web Site: www.chrislloydsales.co.uk

Distribution:
Orca Book Services
Telephone: 01202 665432

Personnel:
Christopher Lloyd (Proprietor)

Publishers & Imprints represented include:
Australia: Jane Curry Publishing
Belgium: Tectum; Versant Sud
Canada: Annick Press; Boston Mills Press; Firefly Books; Master Point Press; Robert Rose
France: Herrisey Editions
New Zealand: Ventura Publications
Spain: Loft Publications
UK: Amateur Winemaker Books; Argus Books; Book Guild Publishing; Bromley Books; Centenar Publishing; D & B Publishing; Everyman Mindsports; Fighting High; Full Back Media; Galago Books; Herridge & Sons; Jaguar Daimler Heritage Trust; Key Books; LDA (Learning Development Aids); Mushroom Model Publications; Panther Publishing; Plane Essentials; Ravette; Special Interest Model Books (SIMB) (formerly Nexus Special Interests); Veloce Publishing
USA: Cycle Publishing / van der Plas Publications; Meadowbrook Press; Mikaya; Potomac Books (formerly Brassey Inc)

An independent sales and marketing agency for small and medium-sized publishers.

6064

*THE MANNING PARTNERSHIP LTD
6 The Old Dairy, Melcombe Road, Oldfield Park, Bath BA2 3LR
Telephone: 01225 478444
Fax: 01225 478440
Email: karen@manning-partnership.co.uk
Web Site: www.manning-partnership.co.uk

Personnel:
Garry Manning (Joint Managing Director)
Roger Hibbert (Joint Managing Director)
James Wheeler (Sales Manager)
Karen Twissell (Office Manager)

Associated Companies:
UK: Brown Dog Books; Nightingale Press

UK Distributor for:
UK: Brimax; Carroll & Brown; Five Mile Press; G2; Globe Pequot Press; Interpet Publishing; Ivy Press; Oval Books; Tony Potter; Mathew Price; Search Press; Selectabook; Source Books

The Manning Partnership Ltd offers a total sales, marketing and distribution solution for publishers both in the UK and in English-language export markets. Formed in March 1997. Traditional and non-traditional markets are serviced.

6065

MARKETABILITY (UK) LTD
12 Sandy Lane, Teddington, Middx TW11 0DR
Telephone: 020 8977 2741
Fax: 020 8977 2741
Email: rachel@marketability.info
Web Site: www.marketability.info

Personnel:
Rachel Maund (Director)

Current and recent clients include:
Australia: Australian Publishers Association
Canada: B. C. Decker
China: Elsevier; Higher Education Press
Mexico: CANIEM (Mexican Publishers Association)
Republic of Ireland: CLÉ (Irish Publishers Association); New Island
Russia: Guild of Book Dealers
Singapore: National Book Development Council; Singapore Book Publishers' Association; Taylor & Francis; Wiley Asia; World Scientific
UK: ALPSP; Ashgate Publishing; BBC Active; A. & C. Black; Bradt Travel Guides; Brilliant Publications; Cambridge University Press; Centre for Alternative Technology; Continuum; Dundee University Press; Elsevier; European Database of Libraries; HarperCollins Publishers; Hodder Education; Hymns Ancient and Modern; Institute of Physics; Kogan Page Ltd; Learning Matters; Little, Brown Book Group; Lonely Planet; Macmillan; McGraw-Hill; Natural History Museum Publications; NBN International; NCVO (National Council for Voluntary Organisations); Oxford University Press; Palgrave Macmillan; Paperless Proofs; Pearson Education; Pen and Sword Books; Pluto Press; ProQuest; Publishing Scotland; Publishing Training Centre; Random House Group; Roots for Churches; Royal Society; Sage Publications; Specialist Schools & Academies Trust; Taylor & Francis Group; University College London; University of Wales Press; John Wiley & Sons; World Scientific

Marketability is a group of experienced publishing consultants, all ex-publishers, providing complete support to publishers' marketing departments, from campaigns to consultancy. It supplies resources when needed: to manage catalogue or direct marketing campaigns, devise and conduct market research, or provide consultancy and advice on strategic and practical issues. Its experience is across all publishing sectors, and with both small and large organizations.
Also provides in-company and external training courses – see our separate entry under Training.

6066

MIDAS PUBLIC RELATIONS LTD
10 Old Court Place, Kensington, London W8 4PL
Telephone: 020 7361 7860
Fax: 020 7938 1268
Email: info@midaspr.co.uk
Web Site: www.midaspr.co.uk

Personnel:
Tony Mulliken (Chairman)
Steven Williams (Chief Executive Officer)
Jacks Thomas (Chief Executive Officer)
Fiona Marsh (Executive Director, New Business)

Midas Public Relations, a PR Week Top 50 consumer agency and a fully accredited member of the PRCA, has established a reputation as one of the leading PR agencies for the book, magazine and publishing industry, through its work with major publishing houses, high-profile authors, corporate communications, trade and consumer events and awards, and the Direct Marketing Industry. Originally formed in 1990 to service the publishing industry, its areas of expertise now span related sectors including the arts, awards, events, media, entertainment, online, music and children's. Specialists in creative, original and award-winning PR campaigns – traditional and online – and named in The Bookseller Magazine's Top 100 'most influential in publishing', Midas Public Relations has a strong reputation for understanding the commercial reality of the arts and publishing world with numerous contacts in the industry.

6067

*MOMENTA PUBLISHING LTD
2 Moorlands Close, Hindhead, Surrey GU26 6SY
Telephone: 01428 606339
Fax: 01428 606339
Email: roblmomenta@compuserve.com

Personnel:
Robert Leech (*Director*)
Mahara Collier (*Company Secretary*)

Founded 1972. Momenta represents various publishing houses, mainly specializing in academic, scholastic, technical, architectural, scientific and medical books, located in continental Europe and the USA as well as the UK.
Momenta offers the following services:
– full sales representation in the UK and Western Europe;
– visits to bookshops, sci-tech, academic and medical centres, universities, libraries;
– medical and sci-tech lecturers and personnel;
– participation in book fairs, congresses and exhibitions;
– detailed visit reports containing comments, impressions and recommendations;
– market research;
– contact with overdue debtors;
– book distribution if required.
Momenta is a dynamic company with a wide experience in book sale and promotion.

6068

NIELSEN BOOKSCAN
3rd Floor, Midas House, 62 Goldsworth Road, Woking, Surrey GU21 6LQ
Telephone: 01483 712222
Fax: 01483 712220
Email: info.bookscan@nielsen.com
Web Site: www.nielsenbookscan.co.uk

Personnel:
Mo Siewcharran (*Head of Marketing*)
Ann Betts (*Commercial Director*)
Reeta Windsor (*Business Development Manager*)
Carol Brownlee (*Deputy Director*)
Paul Dibble (*Head of Data Services*)
Andre Breedt (*Head of Publisher Account Management*)
David Walter (*Research and Development Analyst*)
Lucy Huddlestone (*Business Development Manager*)
Melanie Brassington (*Export Sales Manager*)

Parent Company:
UK: Nielsen

Associated Companies:
Nielsen Registration Agencies (ISBN, SAN & ISTC)
UK: Nielsen BookData; Nielsen BookNet

Nielsen BookScan is a continuous book sales tracking service operating in the UK, Ireland, Australia, the USA, South Africa, Italy, New Zealand, Denmark, Spain and India. BookScan collects total transaction data at the point of sale directly from tills and dispatch systems of all major book retailers. This ensures that detailed and highly accurate sales information on what books are selling, and at what price, is available to the book trade. LibScan measures book borrowings in public libraries.

6069

OXFORD CREATIVE MARKETING LTD
48 Appleton Road, Cumnor, Oxford OX2 9QH
Telephone: 01865 861669
Email: sue.miller@oxfordcreative.com
Web Site: www.oxfordcreative.com

Personnel:
Sue Miller (*Managing Director*)

Oxford Creative Marketing provides wide-ranging marketing, publicity and consultancy services for academic, educational, professional and trade publishers.
Services include:
– marketing planning and new strategy advice;
– copywriting for corporate material, catalogues, fliers, newsletters, etc;
– direct mail campaigns;
– publicity campaigns for trade and academic books, and any work that is usually handled by an in-house marketing department.
As well as handling one-off projects, OCM can provide ongoing marketing support for publishers looking for more regular help.

6070

THE OXFORD PUBLICITY PARTNERSHIP LTD
5 Victoria House, 138 Watling Street East, Towcester NN12 6BT
Telephone: 01327 357770

Fax: 01327 359572
Email: info@oppuk.co.uk
Web Site: www.oppuk.co.uk

Personnel:
Gary Hall (*Director*)

Launched in 1989, the Oxford Publicity Partnership provides a comprehensive range of sales and marketing services for general non-fiction, academic and professional publishers on an on-going or freelance basis.
OPP acts as the UK and European sales and marketing office for a number of British and North American publishers and its focus is on the development of their presence in these markets to achieve wider recognition and enhanced sales.
OPP's team of experienced marketing staff work with clients to achieve the best combination of publicity and PR, direct mail, electronic marketing, advertising, and exhibition participation. It also has close links with reps, distributors, and the book trade.

6071

*JOHN RULE, PUBLISHERS SALES AGENT
40 Voltaire Road, London SW4 6DH
Telephone: 020 7498 0115
Email: johnrule@johnrule.co.uk

Personnel:
John Rule (*Manager*)

Sales and distribution services for small publishers into UK and export markets.

6072

*SALT WAY PUBLISHING (TORPEDO GLOBAL SALES NETWORK) LTD
33 Hatherop Nr Cirencester Gloucestershire GL7 3NA
Telephone: 01285 750212
Email: chris.mclaren@saltwaypublishing.co.uk
Web Site: http://torpedo-global.com

Personnel:
Mr Chris McLaren (*Managing Director*)
Mr Peter Couzens (*Manager South East Asia*)
Mr Peter Matthews (*Manager South Africa*)
Mr Tom McGorry (*Manager North America*)

Parent Company:
Salt Way Publishing Ltd

Associated Companies:
Gunpowder Press; Torpedo Global Sales Network; Watling Street Publishers

Salt Way Publishing Ltd provides highly professional sales representation, for Adult and Children's Trade lists, in the UK and Ireland.
The company has seven highly experienced sales personnel covering all areas of retailer and wholesale and works very closely with its publishing clients. Salt Way Publishing also publishes its own lists under the Watling Street imprint and (in joint venture with Bookcraft Ltd) the Gunpowder Press imprint.
Salt Way also acts as managing partner for Torpedo Global Sales Network, which is a federation of long-established and experienced independent publishers' sales agencies, operating in all the major English Language markets across the world.
In addition Torpedo has strong working relationships with other agents in key foreign language territories.
Torpedo Global Sales Network can also offer assistance in regard to shipping, printing, book production and distribution.
The aim of Salt Way and Torpedo is to provide bespoke international sales solutions to client publishers whose lists are appropriate to our experience, customer base and overall offer.

6073

SEOL LTD
West Newington House, 10 Newington Road, Edinburgh EH9 1QS
Telephone: 0131 668 1456
Fax: 0131 668 4466

Personnel:
Hugh Andrew (*Joint Managing Director*)
Carol Crawford (*Joint Managing Director*)

Harry Ward (*Joint Managing Director*)
Carole Hamilton (*Joint Managing Director*)
Rona Stewart (*Financial Manager*)

Clients include:
UK: Appletree Press Ltd; Argyll Publishing; Atelier; Colin Baxter; Birlinn Ltd; Clan Books; John Donald; Fort Publishing; Goblinshead; Hallewell Publications; House of Lochar; Glen Murray Publishing; Polygon; RCAHMS (Royal Commission on the Ancient & Historical Monuments of Scotland); Rucksack Readers; Saltire Society; Usborne

A sales representation agency to the trade and non-traditional outlets in Scotland.

6074

STAR BOOK SALES
PO Box 20, Whimple, Exeter EX5 2WY
Telephone: 0845 156 7082
Fax: 01404 823820
Email: enquiries@starbooksales.com
Web Site: www.starbooksales.com

Personnel:
Dennis Buckingham (*Sales Director*)

UK distributor for:
BELGIUM: Nova Vista Books
CHINA: Earnshaw Books; Make-Do Publishing
GERMANY: EditorailRM; Frechmann Kolon; Meyer
IT: Edit Vallard; Giorgio Nada
ITALY: Renzo Piano Foundation
MALTA: Portfolio Curtains
UK: Angela Patchell Books; Ashgrove Press; Choc Lit; Coastal Publishing; Contact Publishing; Dimensional Entertainment; Dynasty Press; Earlswood Press; Envisage Books; Evans Mitchell Books; John Beaufoy Publishing; Last Passage; Manchester Press; Methuen; Rickshaw Publishing; Sibling Press; Tonto Books; Troubador Publishing
USA: Changing Lives Press; Parker House Publishing

6075

UNIVERSITY PRESSES MARKETING
The Tobacco Factory, Raleigh Road, Southville, Bristol BS3 1TF
Telephone: 0117 902 0275
Fax: 0117 902 0294
Email: sales@universitypressesmarketing.co.uk
Web Site: www.universitypressesmarketing.co.uk

Personnel:
Andrew Gilman (*Chief Executive Officer*)
Paul Skinner (*Office Manager*)
Helena Svojsikova (*Area Manager*)

Sales agent for (mainly) American university presses in the UK and Europe.

6076

*THE UNIVERSITY PRESSES OF CALIFORNIA, COLUMBIA & PRINCETON LTD
John Wiley & Sons Ltd, Distribution Centre,
1 Oldlands Way, Bognor Regis, West Sussex PO22 9SA
Telephone: 01243 842165
Fax: 01243 842167
Email: lois@upccp.demon.co.uk

Personnel:
Andrew Brewer (*Managing Director*)
Lois Edwards (*Business Manager*)

6.6 DISTRIBUTORS

6077

AFRICAN BOOKS COLLECTIVE
PO Box 721, Oxford OX1 9EN
Telephone: 01869 349110
Fax: 01869 349110
Email: orders@africanbookscollective.com
Web Site: www.africanbookscollective.com

Personnel:
Mary Jay (*Chief Executive Officer*)
Justin Cox (*Marketing & Production Director*)

Participating publishers include:

Benin: Centre Panafricain de Prospective Sociale / Pan-African Social Prospects Centre

Botswana: Lightbooks Publishers; Pyramid Publishing

Cameroon: University of Buea

Eritrea: Hdri Publishers

Ethiopia: Development Policy Management Forum (DPMF); Forum for Social Studies; Organisation for Social Science Research in Eastern and Southern Africa (OSSREA)

Ghana: Afram Publications (Ghana) Ltd; Africa Christian Press; Association of African Universities Press; Blackmask; Freedom Publishers; Ghana Universities Press; Sedco Publishing; SEM Financial Training Centre Ltd; Sub-Saharan Publishers; Third World Network Africa; Woeli Publishing Services; Women's Health Action Research Centre

Kenya: Academy Science Publishers; East African Educational Publishers; Focus Books; Kwani Trust; LawAfrica; Nairobi University Press; Twaweza Communications

Lesotho: Institute of Southern African Studies, National University of Lesotho; Law Society of Lesotho

Liberia: Cotton Tree Press

Malawi: Central Africana; Chancellor College Publishers; Kachere Series

Mauritius: Editions Vivazi

Namibia: Reader in Namibian Sociology; University of Namibia Press

Nigeria: African Heritage Press; College Press Publishers; CSS Ltd; Enicrownfit Publishers; Fourth Dimension Publishing Co Ltd; Handel Books; Heinemann Educational Books (Nigeria); Ibadan Cultural Studies Group; Ibadan University Press; Kraft Books; Maiyati Chambers; Malthouse Press Ltd; New Horn Press Ltd; Obafemi Awolowo University Press; Onyoma Research Publications; Opon ifa Readers; Saros International Publishers; Spectrum Books Ltd; University of Lagos Press; University Press Ltd; Yintab Books

Senegal: African Renaissance; Council for the Development of Social Science Research in Africa (CODESRIA)

Sierra Leone: PenPoint Publishers

South Africa: Africa Institute of South Africa; Brenthurst Collection / Frank Horley Books; Ikhwezi Afrika Publishers; Mail and Guardian Books; Modjaji Books; Umsinsi Books; UNISA Press

Swaziland: JAN Publishing Centre

Tanzania: Centre for Energy, Environment, Science & Technology (CEEST); Dar es Salaam University Press; E & D Ltd; Mkuki na Nyota Publishers; Tanzania Publishing House

Uganda: Femrite (Uganda Women Writers' Association); Fountain Publishers

Zambia: Bookworld Publishers; Multimedia Zambia; University of Zambia; Zambia Women Writers' Association

Zimbabwe: Africa Community Publishing & Development Trust; Baobab Books; Kimaathi Publishing House; Mambo Press; Southern African Printing and Publishing House / SAPES Trust; University of Zimbabwe Publications; Weaver Press Ltd; Women and Law in South Africa Research Trust; Zimbabwe International Book Fair Trust; Zimbabwe Publishing House Ltd

African Books Collective is a major initiative to promote African-published books in Europe, North America, and in Commonwealth countries outside Africa. It is owned by the founding publishers, and is non-profit making on its own behalf. Centralized billing and shipping is provided from Oxford. Over 1700 titles are available, from 125 publishers in 21 African countries.

The greater part of the list is available print-on-demand, supplied from within the US for North America; from Australia for Australia and New Zealand; and from the UK for the rest of the world. Joint catalogues are available, and on the website for download. New title information is sent monthly to the e-subscriber list; RSS feeds are also available.

English-language material is stocked, with an emphasis on scholarly, literature and children's titles. A small number of titles in French and children's titles in Swahili are also stocked. Standing order / blanket order plans are available and can be geared to meet libraries' specific requirements or acquisitions profiles.

Trading started in May 1990.

6078

ANGLO-AMERICAN BOOKS
Crown Buildings, Bancyfelin, Carmarthen SA33 5ND
Telephone: 01267 211880
Fax: 01267 211882
Email: books@anglo-american.co.uk
Web Site: www.anglo-american.co.uk

Personnel:
Mr D. Bowman *(Managing Director)*
Mrs C. Lenton *(Marketing Director)*

UK Distributor/Representative for:

USA: Center Press; Milton H. Erickson Foundation Press; Free Spirit Publishing; Genesis II; International Society of Neuro-Semantics; Kagan & Kagan; Kendall/Hunt; Leading Edge Communications; Meta Publications; Network 3000 Publishing; NLP Comprehensive; Science and Behavior Books; Success Strategies; Teacher Created Materials; Transforming Press; Westwood Publishing

Anglo-American Books is a stockholding distributor of British and American books with particular expertise in the NLP, personal growth, hypnotherapy, accelerated learning and psychotherapy fields. Stock book orders received by 2.30 pm are dispatched the same day.

Order Department opening times: 9–5 Monday to Friday.

6079

BBR DISTRIBUTION
12 Cutthorpe Road, Chesterfield S42 7AE
Telephone: 01246 271662
Email: distribution@bbr-online.co.uk
Web Site: www.bbr-online.co.uk/catalogue

Personnel:
Chris Reed *(Director)*

Parent Company:
UK: BBR Solutions Ltd

UK distributor for:
Australia: Aurealis; Chimaera Publications
Canada: Tesseract Books
Republic of Ireland: Aeon Press; Albedo One
UK: Bowland Press; British Association for Korean Studies (BAKS); EAHMH Publications; Endcliffe Press; European Association for the History of Medicine and Health Publications; Hilltop Press
USA: Automatism Press; Cambrian Publications; Cyber-Psycho's A.O.D.; Dreams and Nightmares; Fairwood Press; Jazz Police Books; New York Review of S.F.; Not One of Us; Nova Express; Ocean View Books; Permeable Press; Space & Time; Talebones; Wordcraft of Oregon

BBR is a mail order distributor of independent literary, speculative fiction and fringe interest publications, serving customers throughout the world.

6080

BEBC DISTRIBUTION
Albion Close, Parkstone, Poole, Dorset BH12 3LL
Telephone: 01202 715555
Fax: 01202 715556
Web Site: www.bebcdistribution.co.uk

Personnel:
John Walsh *(Managing Director)*
Rosy Jones *(Operations Manager)*
Charles Kipping *(Marketing Manager)*
Karen Bickers *(Client Manager)*

Parent Company:
UK: The Bournemouth English Book Centre Ltd

UK Distributor/Representative for:

Australia: Actual Enterprises; Adams & Austen Press; Boyer Education; Insearch Publications; Language Australia (CELUSA)
Germany: Ernst Klett *(ELT Titles only)*
Netherlands: John Benjamins bv
New Zealand: Catt Publishing
UK: Academic Book Collection; Barrington Stoke *(School Orders)*; Bath Publishing; Brookemead ELT; Coat Meur Press; College of Law Publishing; Commonwealth Secretariat; The Dr Margaret Lowenfeld Trust; Ferard-Reeve Publishing; FunSongs Ltd; Gem Publishing; The Language Factory; Languages Out There Ltd; Learning Cycle Ltd t/a Priya Desai; Learning Matters; Listen & Speak Publications; North Star ELT; Redhead Music; Reflect Press; Roslin Publishing; Three Vee; TP Publications; York Associates

Distributors for educational publishers specializing in Business, Law, English Language Teaching, ICT books, Human Rights and Conservation. For further information or to order, please telephone
01202 715555.

6081

THE BOOK SERVICE LTD
Colchester Road, Frating Green, Colchester, Essex CO7 7DW
Telephone: 01206 256000 (orders: 255678)
Fax: 01206 255929 (orders: 255930)
Email: sales@tbs-ltd.co.uk
Web Site: www.TheBookService.co.uk

Personnel:
Mark Williams *(Managing Director)*
Colin James *(Deputy Managing Director)*
Justin Smith *(Finance & Commercial Director)*
Andy Willis *(Business Development Director)*

Parent Company:
UK: The Random House Group

Associated Companies:
UK: Grantham Book Services

Distributors for::
Andersen Press; Atlantic Books; AudioGo; Nicholas Brealey; Canongate Books; Constable & Robinson; Faber & Faber; Granta Books; Harlequin UK D2C; Icon Books; Kogan Page; Mainstream Publishing; Methuen Publishing; Profile Books; Quercus; Random House Group; Sort of Books; Transworld; Walker Books

The Book Service (TBS) is the UK's leading distributor. Distributing over 100 million books per year, TBS has high-tech fully automated handling systems and offers full electronic ordering and e-Commerce capabilities. TBS operates a full sales ledger, offers cash collection, debt and stock insurance policies, telesales, royalties and sub-rights services. Ancillary work such as mailing, shrink-wrapping, re-pricing, dump-bin and counter pack make-up is also offered.

6082

BOOK SYSTEMS PLUS LTD
BSP House, Station Road, Linton, Cambs CB21 4NW
Telephone: 01799 524458
Fax: 01799 524459
Email: bsp2b@aol.com
Web Site: www.booksystemsplus.com

Personnel:
George J. Papa *(Managing Director)*
Shirley Greenall *(Marketing & New Business)*

Parent Company:
UK: Whittet Books Ltd

Publishers represented:
Australia: A & B Publishers Pty Ltd; Bookbiz International
Canada: The Althouse Press; The Charlton Press; Detselig Enterprises Ltd; Greatest Escapes.com
Germany: Chateaux & Manoirs
Netherlands: Mo' Media
South Africa: Dreams 4 Africa
UK: Aardvark Publishing; Alice & Fred Books; Caister Academic Press; Chakula Press Ltd; Classic Locations; Cobwebs Brentwood; Cracking It; Delfryn Publications; EFL Ltd; Euro Impala; Fitzwarren Publishing; Focus Publications Ltd; Gudrun Publishing / Edda UK; Hiller Airguns; Hoopoe Books; Idlewild Publishers; Institute for Psychophysical Research; Oxford Forum; Pathfinder Audio; Porpoise Books; Raleo Publishing Ltd; RevengeInk Ltd; Tricorn; UK International Ceramics; Vista Consulting Team Ltd; Whittet Books Ltd; Wild Boar Trading
USA: John F. Blair, Publisher

Book Systems Plus provides full distribution, invoicing and customer services to publishers from the UK and overseas. It also offers bookshop representation and marketing support. It has particular marketing expertise with travel guides and books on antiques and collectables. It acts as the UK sole agent for publishers in North America, Australia, South Africa and Europe.

6083

BOOKPOINT LTD
130 Milton Park, Abingdon, Oxon OX14 4SB
Telephone: 01235 400400
Fax: 01235 832068
Web Site: www.bookpoint.co.uk

Personnel:
Chris Emerson *(Chief Operating Officer)*

Martyn Burchall *(Head of Operations)*
Ray Webb *(Head of Customer Services)*
Graham Money *(General Manager & Director)*
Lesley Morgan *(Group IT Director)*
Jon Swan *(Head of Credit Control)*

Parent Company:
UK: Hachette UK

Distributor for:
UK: Ashgate/Gower Publishing; Debretts; Facet Publishing *(formerly Library Association)*; Hachette Children's; Headline Book Publishing; Hodder & Stoughton; Hodder Education; Hodder Gibson; Hodder Religious; In Easy Steps; Frances Lincoln; John Murray; Plexus Publishing; Souvenir Press; Taylor & Francis

Bookpoint services encompass a number of industry-leading initiatives, plus a full suite of EDI applications, order processing, accounting, royalty maintenance, management reporting, warehousing, dispatch and ancillary functions. Bookpoint also operate a Premier Next Day Service, and offer PUBEASY to booksellers.

6084

BOOKSOURCE
50 Cambuslang Road, Cambuslang, Glasgow G32 8NB
Telephone: 0845 370 0063
Fax: 0845 370 0064
Email: info@booksource.net
Web Site: www.booksource.net

Personnel:
Davinder Bedi *(Managing Director)*
Lorraine Fannin *(Director)*
Mike Miller *(Director)*
Christian Maclean *(Director)*
Dr Keith Whittles *(Director)*
Marion Sinclair *(Director)*
Philip Walters *(Director)*
Kirsty O'Connor *(Credit Control Manager)*
Louise Morris *(Customer Service Director)*
Jim O'Donnell *(Operations Director)*
David Warnock *(Systems Manager)*

Parent Company:
Publishing Scotland

Distribution on behalf of:
UK: Acair Ltd; Appletree Press; APS *(for the Scottish Executive)*; Argyll Publishing; Association for Scottish Literary Studies; Atelier Books; Backpage Press; BILD Publications; Birlinn Ltd; Black & White Publishing; Books Noir; Carnegie Publishing; Cicerone Press; Clairview Books; Clan Publishers; Coolcanals Guide; Distilled Discourse; John Donald; Richard Drew Ltd; Dundee University Press; Floris Books; Fort Publishing; Freight Design; Geddes & Grosset Ltd; Gullane Children's Books; Hallewell Publications; Hawthorn Press; IPC Media; Islands Book Trust; Librario Publishing; Little Star Creations; Macdonald Media Publishing; Meadowside Children's Books; Mercat Press; Moonlight Publishing; Glen Murray Publishing; Myhobbystore.com; NMS Enterprises Ltd Publishing; Phoenix Yard Books; Polygon; Publishing Scotland; Real Reads; Rider French Publications; Roving Press; Royal Commission on the Ancient and Historical Monuments of Scotland; Rucksack Readers; Saltire Society; Sandstone Press; Steve Savage Publishing; Scottish Society for Northern Studies; Scottish Text Society; Sparkling Books; Starlet; Rudolf Steiner Press; Stone Country Press; Strident Publishing; Sunday Herald Books; Temple Lodge Publishing; Tuckwell Press; Two Ravens Press; Warners Group Publications; Waverley Press; Whittles Publishing; Wild Goose Publications; Neil Wilson Publishing; Windhorse Publications

Established in 1995, BookSource offers warehousing and worldwide distribution services to book trade publishers, charities and funded institutions, and other commercial enterprises.

6085

BUSHWOOD BOOKS LTD
6 Marksbury Avenue, Kew Gardens, Surrey TW9 4JF
Telephone: 020 8392 8585
Fax: 020 8392 9876
Email: info@bushwoodbooks.co.uk
Web Site: www.bushwoodbooks.co.uk

Personnel:
Richard Hansen *(Director)*
Victoria Hansen *(PA)*
Ian McLellan *(Sales)*

Exclusive distributor for:
USA: Schiffer *(Mind, Body, Spirit titles)*; Schiffer Collectibles Arts & Crafts; Schiffer Publishing Ltd *(Military Aviation)*

The company also carries in stock hundreds of titles on antiques and collectibles, predominantly horology, jewellery, ceramics and glass. It specializes in providing a service for UK customers to purchase from North American publishers.

Bushwood Books is one of the leading UK distributors of German World War II titles in English, and also carries the Schiffer Mind, Body, Spirit list.

6086

CENGAGE LEARNING EMEA
[a division of Cengage Learning]
Cheriton House, North Way, Andover, Hants SP10 5BE
Telephone: 01264 332424
Fax: 01264 342732
Web Site: www.cengage.co.uk

Personnel:
Jill Jones *(Chief Executive Officer)*
Chad Bonney *(Chief Financial Officer)*
Carrie Willicome *(Operations Director)*

Parent Company:
USA: Cengage Learning Inc

Distributors for:
UK: Cengage Learning *(selected imprints)*; Evans Publishing Group; Janes

6087

*CENTRAL BOOKS
99 Wallis Road, London E9 5LN
Telephone: 0845 458 9911 & 020 8986 4854
Fax: 0845 458 9912
Email: orders@centralbooks.com
Web Site: www.centralbooks.com

Personnel:
Bill Norris *(Managing Director)*
Mark Chilver *(Magazine Director)*
Bob Moheebob *(Accountant)*
Eric McCorkle *(Warehouse Manager)*
Indy Kaur Naura *(Trade Returns & Customer Services Manager)*
Graham Charnock *(Trade Customer Services Manager)*
Mike Drabble *(Mail Order Manager)*
Sasha Simic *(Magazine Sales Rep Manager)*
Regina Henrich *(Publisher Liaison Manager)*

Distribution for:
Australia: Fremantle Arts Centre Press
Canada: Black Rose Books; Fernwood Press
France: Zulma
Germany: European Photography
Italy: Giancarlo Politi Editore
Jamaica: Ian Randle
Kenya: Camerapix
Netherlands: Get Lost Publishing; International Books
Republic of Ireland: Dedalus Press; A & A Farmer; Galway University Press; The Lilliput Press; Oisin Publishing; Salmon Publishing Ltd; University College Dublin Press
South Africa: Fernwood Press; Kwela; Ravan Press
UK: 21; Absolute Press; Agraphia Press; Ambit Books; Amnesty International UK; Archetype; Aurora Metro Press; Auteur; Battlebridge; Blue Island Publishing; Bowerdean Publishing Co Ltd; Broadcast Books; Calouste Gulbenkian Foundation; Catalyst Press; Centre for Policy on Ageing; CILT; Comerford & Miller; Corvo Books; CPAG (Child Poverty Action Group); Dedalus; Demos; Directory of Social Change; Disability Alliance; English Heritage; Enitharmon Press; Five Leaves Publications; Flambard; Flowers East; Foreign Policy Centre; Format Publishing; Friction Press; Gambit; Golgonooza; Green Books; Greenprint; Greenwich Exchange; Harbord Publishing; Heretic Books Ltd *(formerly GMP Publishers Ltd)*; Holo Books; Hood Hood Books; Human Givens; Human Rights Watch; Imprint Academic; Latin America Bureau; Lawrence & Wishart; Libris Ltd; Loki Books; London Art & Artists; Lucas

Publications Ltd; Mares Nest; Menard Press; Merlin Press; Middlesex University Press; Minority Rights Group; Muslim Academic Trust; National Autistic Society (NAS); New Clarion Press; New European Publications Ltd; Northway; Open Gate Press; Peepal Tree Books; Pomona Books; Prospect Books; Quilliam; Redstone Press; Refugee Council; Right Angle Publishing; Route; Runnymede Trust; Seafarer; Seren; Serif; Smith / Doorstep; Smith Institute; Social Market Foundation; Stacey International; Totterdown Books; University of Hertfordshire Press; Vegan Society; Wallflower Press; Weston Publishing; Westworld International; Wooden Books; WorldView
USA: International Publishers NY; McPherson & Co; Monthly Review; Pamphleteer's Press

The main activity and purpose of Central Books is to assist independent publishers to reach the widest possible audience for their books. Central Books offer warehousing, distribution, representation and some help with marketing and promotion. It supplies booksellers and library suppliers throughout the world. The company is one of Europe's leading distributors of magazines and journals to the book trade.

6088

COMBINED ACADEMIC PUBLISHERS LTD
15a Lewins Yard, East Street, Chesham, Bucks HP5 1HQ
Telephone: 01494 581601
Fax: 01494 581602
Email: nickesson@combinedacademic.co.uk
Web Site: www.combinedacademic.co.uk

Personnel:
Nicholas Esson *(Managing Director)*
Ms Julia Monk *(Marketing Manager)*
Ms Denise Martin *(Accounts Manager)*
Keith Woods *(Representative)*

UK & European distributor for:
Canada: McGill-Queen's University Press
USA: Duke University Press; Indiana University Press; New York University Press; Temple University Press; University of Illinois Press; University of Nebraska Press; University of Texas Press; University of Washington Press

Combined Academic Publishers, in association with Marston Book Services, is a professional representation and distribution agency for academic and university presses.

UK and Republic of Ireland field sales are handled by our own representative and a team of experienced commission agents, while agents are active in five continental European territories – Scandinavia; the Netherlands and Belgium; Southern Europe; Germany, Austria and Switzerland; Central and Eastern Europe – as well as the Middle East and Africa.

CAP has a proactive marketing department offering direct mail campaigns, space advertising and review copy distribution.

6089

COMBINED BOOK SERVICES LTD
Unit D, Paddock Wood Distribution Centre, Paddock Wood, Tonbridge, Kent TN12 6UU
Telephone: 01892 837171
Fax: 01892 837272
Email: info@combook.co.uk
Web Site: www.combook.co.uk

Personnel:
Keith Neale *(Joint Managing Director)*
Allan Smith *(Joint Managing Director)*

Associated Companies:
Eddington Hook

Distributors for:
Germany: earBOOKS (edel)
India: Frontpage Publications; Roman Books
UK: A Jot Publishing; J. A. Allen *(Equestrian)*; Anshan Publishers; Cambridge House; Claerhout Publishing; Discovery Books; Encyclopaedia Britannica; Graffito Books; Robert Hale; Hammersmith Press; Hawkins Publishing Services; Hoberman Collection; Jonescat Publishing; Korero Books; Lotus Publishing; Management Books 2000; Momenta Publishing; NAG Publishers; New Academic Science; Northcote House Publishers; Phoenix Publishers; Pocket Issue; Pucci Books *(formerly Oblique)*; Pushkin Press; Thomas Telford Ltd *(Institute of Civil Engineers)*; teneues Publishing UK; Time Publishing; Woodhead Publishing

Combined Book Services provides full distribution services for publishers of trade, academic and professional books. The service includes invoicing and cash collection together with a comprehensive range of management reports. CBS also distributes calendars and stationery products.

6090

CONTOUR MANAGEMENT SERVICES (CMS)
PO Box 3042, New Milton, Hants BH25 7XG
Telephone: 01425 620532
Fax: 01425 620532
Email: mikecms@btinternet.com
Web Site: www.contourmanagementservices.com

Personnel:
Mike Cranidge (Managing Partner)
Sue Cranidge (Partner)

Agent and distributor for:
Australia: Meridian Maps
Portugal: Turinta
USA: Hedberg Maps Inc; Map Link

Importers and distributors of maps with a difference.

6091

CORNERHOUSE PUBLICATIONS
70 Oxford Street, Manchester M1 5NH
Telephone: 0161 200 1503
Fax: 0161 200 1504
Email: Publications@Cornerhouse.org
Web Site: www.Cornerhouse.org/books

Personnel:
Paul Daniels (Publications Director)
Debbie Fielding (Administrator)
Suzanne Davies (Publications Officer)
James Brady (Publications Officer)

Clients include:
Germany: DuMont Buchverlag; Kerber Verlag; Richter Verlag; Verlag für moderne Kunst Nurnberg; Walther König
Switzerland: JRPRingier
UK: British Council Visual Arts & Design; Haunch of Venison; Hayward Gallery; ICA; Ikon; Modern Art Oxford; Henry Moore Institute; Photoworks; Ridinghouse

Distributor of contemporary visual arts and photography books for publishers, museums and galleries worldwide. A full list of publishers to which we distribute is available in our catalogue or at our website: www.Cornerhouse.org/books.

6092

DEEP BOOKS LTD
Unit 3, Goose Green Trading Estate, 47 East Dulwich Road, London SE22 9BN
Telephone: 020 8693 0234
Fax: 020 8693 1400
Email: sales@deep-books.co.uk
Web Site: www.deep-books.co.uk

Personnel:
Chris Custance (Managing Director)
Alan Ritchie (Marketing Manager)
Paul Woodfield (Sales Manager)

Client Publishers include:
Australia: Michelle Anderson Publishing (formerly Hill of Content Publishing); Finch Publishing; Barry Long Books (Australia); Milne Books
Austria: Ennsthaler Publishing House
Italy: Lo Scarabeo
Monaco: Alpen Editions
Netherlands: Gottmer Publishing Group
UK: Camino Guides; Earthdancer; Findhorn Press; Gothic Image Publications; Khaniqahi Nimatullahi Publications (KNP); Barry Long Books (Britain); Polair Publishing
USA: Alpha Books / Penguin USA; Amber Lotus; ARE Press; Avery/Penguin USA; Basic Health Publications; Bear & Co; Bear Cub Books; Berkley Publishing Group; Best Life Media; Bindu Books; Blue Dolphin Publishing Inc; Bluestar Communications; Boys Town Press; Career Press; Celebra; Chamberlain Bros / Penguin USA; Chiron Publications; Crystal Clarity Publishers; Dawn Publications; Dawnhorse Publications; De Vorss & Co; Destiny Audio Books; Destiny Books; Destiny Recordings; Dragonhawk Publishing; Dutton / Penguin USA; Earth Magic Productions Inc; Freedom Press; Glorian

Publishing; Golden Sufi Center; Gotham Books / Penguin USA; Hampton Roads Publishing; Nicolas Hays; Healing Arts Press; Himalayan Institute Press; Hologram Books; Hudson Street / Penguin USA; Hunter House Inc; Ibis Press; Inner Traditions International; Inner Travel Books; Integral Yoga Publications; Jewish Light Publishing; JZK Publishing; Veronica Lane Books; Lantern Books; Music Design; New American Library; New Page Books; Original Publications; Park St Press; Penguin Group USA (selected imprints); Perigee/Penguin; Plume; Polair Publishing; Power Press; Red Wheel Weiser (selected imprints); Self-Realization Fellowship; Skylight Paths; Square One Publishing (Vital Health Publishing); Synergetic Press; Timeless Books; Veronica Lane Books; Witches Almanac; World Wisdom Books

Specialist mind body spirit distributors. Deep Books handles publishers lists from the UK, the USA and Australia. It provides sales and distribution for these publishers throughout the UK, Republic of Ireland, mainland Europe and Scandinavia and acts as their exclusive agents in those territories.

6093

EUROPEAN SCHOOLBOOKS LTD
Ashville Trading Estate, The Runnings, Cheltenham GL51 9PQ
Telephone: 01242 245252
Fax: 01242 224137
Email: direct@esb.co.uk
Web Site: www.eurobooks.co.uk

Personnel:
Frank Preiss (Managing Director)
Ruth Trippett (Marketing)

Associated Companies:
UK: The European Bookshop; The Italian Bookshop

Distributor for:
Brazil: Pontes Editores
Denmark: Grafisk Forlag
France: 10/18; Assimil; Bordas; Casterman; CLE International; Armand Colin; Didier; Ecole des loisirs; Editions du Fallois; Editions du Seuil; Flammarion; Folio; Foucher; Gallimard; Garnier Flammarion; Gault Millau; Hachette; Hatier; J'ai lu; Larousse; Livres de poche; Minuit; Nathan; Presses de la cité; Presses Pocket; Presses Universitaires de France; Presses Universitaires de Grenoble; Le Robert
Germany: Arena; Bibliographisches Institut Mannheim; Brockhaus; Carlsen; Cornelsen; Deutscher Taschenbuch Verlag; Diogenes; Duden; Fischer; Gilde Buchhandlung; Goldmann; Heyne; Max Hueber Verlag; Insel; Kiepenheuer & Witsch; Knaur; Langenscheidt; Luchterhand; Reclam; Rowohlt; Suhrkamp; Ullstein; Verlag Dürr & Kessler; Verlag für Deutsch; Verlag Moritz Diesterweg
Italy: Alma Edizioni; Bonacci Editore; Edilingua; Einaudi; European Language Institute; Fabbri-Bompiani; Feltrinelli; Garzanti; Giunti; Guerra; Mondadori; Le Monnier; Oscar; Piemme; Rizzoli; Rux; La Spiga; Zanichelli
Netherlands: Intertaal
Portugal: Dinapress; Lidel Edições Técnicas; Porto Editora Lda; Public. Europa-America
Spain: Alfaguara; Alianza; Anaya; Anaya ELE; Austral; Catedra; Colegio de España; Destino; Difusión; EDELSA; Ediciones Edhasa

Distributors of some 80,000 titles in the main European languages on behalf of over 100 publishers. Large-scale promotion in all sectors of the foreign languages educational market. Suppliers of foreign-published stock to academic and general bookshops. General wholesale service for non-stock titles.

6094

THE EUROSPAN GROUP
3 Henrietta Street, Covent Garden, London WC2E 8LU
Telephone: 020 7240 0856
Fax: 020 7379 0609
Email: info@eurospangroup.com
Web Site: www.eurospanbookstore.com

Send orders to::
Eurospan Group, c/o Turpin Distribution, Pegasus Drive, Stratton Business Park, Biggleswade SG18 8TQ
Telephone: 01767 604972
Fax: 01767 601640

Email: eurospan@turpin-distribution.com
Web Site: www.eurospanbookstore.com

Personnel:
Michael Geelan (Managing Director & Chairman)
Kate Fraser (Director of Operations)
Stephen Lustig (Marketing Director)

Marketing, Sales & Distribution for overseas publishers, including:
USA: American Academy of Ophthalmology; American Academy of Orthopaedic Surgeons; American Academy of Pediatrics; American Mathematical Society; American Psychological Association; American Society of Civil Engineers (ASCE); Autism Asperger Publishing Co; Broadview Press; Brookes Publishing; Facts on File; Future Horizons; Hazelden Publishing; IGI Global; Left Coast Press; Lynne Rienner Publishers; McFarland & Co; Northwestern University Press; PennWell Books; Rutgers University Press; M. E. Sharpe & Co; Slack Incorporated; Springer Publishing Company; Stanford University Press; Teachers College Press; Transaction Publishers; University of Hawai'i Press; The University of Michigan; University of North Carolina Press; University Press of New England; World Bank Publications

Eurospan Group is one of Europe's fastest-growing independent marketing, sales and distribution agencies for US book publishers seeking to expand sales in Europe, the Middle East, Africa, Asia and the Pacific. It provides a similar one-stop solution, in Europe and the Middle East only, for book publishers from South Africa, Asia and Australasia.
A complete list of publishers and subsidiary imprints distributed by Eurospan is available on request: see www.eurospangroup.com

6095

FREELANCE MARKET NEWS
8–10 Dutton Street, Manchester M3 1LE
Telephone: 0161 819 9919
Fax: 0161 819 2842
Email: fmn@writersbureau.com
Web Site: www.freelancemarketnews.com

Personnel:
Miss Angela Cox (Managing Editor)

Parent Company:
UK: The Writers Bureau Ltd

Distributor for:
USA: Writer's Digest Books (books on writing)

6096

GAZELLE BOOK SERVICES LTD
White Cross Mills, Hightown, Lancaster LA1 4XS
Telephone: 01524 68765
Fax: 01524 63232
Email: sales@gazellebooks.co.uk
Web Site: www.gazellebooks.co.uk

Personnel:
Trevor Witcher (Managing Director)
Brian Haywood (Company Secretary & Finance Director)
Mark Trotter (Distribution & Sales Director)
Kevin Dixon (Warehouse Manager)
Lee Hodgkiss (Marketing & Exhibitions Manager)
Gareth Hindson (Customer Service Manager)
Melanie Warren (Sales & Marketing Manager)
Analyn Dixon (Book-keeper)

Gazelle Book Services handles both trade and academic lists and covers the whole of the UK and Europe. It provides:
– fast order turn-round;
– comprehensive stock and regular stock replenishment;
– efficient reporting and information service to customers;
– regular sales calling and regular liaison with booksellers in connection with promotion, exhibitions, special events, etc;
– following through;
– friendly, helpful service;
– regular and adaptable reporting to publishers;
– flexibility and co-operation.
Complete list of client publishers is available on request.

6097

GMC PUBLICATIONS LTD
GMC Publications Ltd, 166 High Street, Lewes, East Sussex BN7 1XU

Telephone: 01273 402808
Fax: 01273 402866
Email: distribution@thegmcgroup.com
Web Site: www.gmcbooktrade.com

Personnel:
Mr Jonathan Phillips (*Joint Managing Director*)
Mr Michael Robb (*Sales Director*)
Mr Jonathan Bailey (*Publisher*)
Ms Melanie Arora (*Books Marketing Manager*)

Associated Companies:
Ammonite Press; The Guild of Master Craftsman
Publications; The Photographer's Institute Press

Book publisher and distributor (via Orca):
UK: Rowan
USA: Fox Chapel Publishing; Leisure Arts; Potter Craft (*The Crown Publishing Group*); Sterling Publishing Co Inc (*This includes their imprints*); The Taunton Press Inc; Watson-Guptill (*The Crown Publishing Group*)

GMC is one of the UK's leading publishers and distributors of craft & leisure books and magazines. GMC Publications produces approximately 50 illustrated books a year and has 8 magazines. Established in 2006, GMC Distribution carries 3000 books for other publishers, including Ammonite Press, Sterling Publishing, The Taunton Press, Watson-Guptill, Potter Craft, Leisure Arts and Fox Chapel.

6098

GRANTHAM BOOK SERVICES
Trent Road, Grantham, Lincs NG31 7XQ
Telephone: 01476 541000 (541080)
Fax: 01476 541060 (541061)
Email: orders@gbs.tbs-ltd.co.uk
Web Site: www.granthambookservices.co.uk

Personnel:
Mark Williams (*Managing Director*)
Colin James (*Deputy Managing Director*)
Justin Smith (*Finance & Commercial Director*)
Andy Willis (*Client Services Director*)

Parent Company:
UK: Random House Group

Associated Companies:
UK: The Book Service

Clients include::
France: Abrams and Chronicle Books
UK: AA Special Sales; Barrington Stoke; Bounce Sales & Marketing; Chronicle; Compass Maps; Thomas Cook; Crombie Jardine; Crown House; The Crowood Press; Gerald Duckworth & Co; Footprint Handbooks; FW Media; Hay House; Nick Hern Books; Hesperus Press; Horizon Press; How To Books; Lerner; Lonely Planet; Manchester United; Manning Partnership; Melia Publishing Services; National Archives; New Holland; Nosy Crow; Oneworld Publications; Osprey; Osprey Publishing; Oval; Perseus Books; PGUK; Piccadilly Press; Portfolio Books; Quarto Group; Quayside Publishing; Quiller Publishing; Reaktion Books; Rotovision; Running Press; Severn House Publishers; Templar Publishing; Timber Press; Titan Books
USA: Everyman; MBI; Rockport; Workman Publishing

Grantham Book Services (GBS) is the UK's Independent's Specialist.
Distributing over 26 million books per year, GBS offers a bespoke book distribution service with full electronic ordering and e-Commerce capabilities. GBS operates a full sales ledger, cash collection service, debt and stock insurance policies, telesales, royalties and sub-rights services.
Ancillary work such as mailing, shrink-wrapping, re-pricing, dump-bin and counter pack make-up is also offered.

6099

LITTLEHAMPTON BOOK SERVICES LTD
Faraday Close, Durrington, Worthing, West Sussex
BN13 3RB
Telephone: 01903 828500
Fax: 01903 828625
Email: enquiries@lbsltd.co.uk
Web Site: www.lbsltd.co.uk

Personnel:
Chris Emerson (*Chief Operating Officer*)
Matt Wright (*Finance Director*)

Lesley Morgan (*Group IT Director*)
Bridget Radnedge (*Publishing Services Director*)
Alan Rakes (*Inventory Director*)
Issy Harrash (*General Manager – Operations*)
Dave Nickless (*Quality Assurance Director*)

Parent Company:
UK: Hachette UK Publishing Group

Clients include:
Ian Allan; Aurum Press, Apple & JR Books; Automobile Association; Barefoot Books; John Blake Publishing; Bloodaxe; Blue Sky Publishing; Can of Worms Enterprises Ltd; DAAB; Express Newspapers; Eye Books Ltd; Gallic Books; Gibson Square Publishing; The Good Hotel Guide Ltd; Grub Street; Infinite Ideas Co; Kyle Cathie; LBBG; Make Believe Ideas Ltd; Max Press; Myrmidon Books; Michael O'Mara Books; Octopus Publishing Group; Old St Publishing; Oldie Publications; Orion Group; PC Publishing; Pitch Publishing Ltd; Private Eye; Raceform / Highdown Publishing; Radio Times; Summersdale; Taschen; Thames & Hudson; Transit Publishing; Which? The Consumer Association

Littlehampton Book Services provides publishers with full warehouse management and distribution services that include credit control and trust accounting, sophisticated management reporting, telesales, customer service and royalty accounting.

6100

B. McCALL BARBOUR
28 George IV Bridge, Edinburgh EH1 1ES
Telephone: 0131 225 4816
Fax: 0131 225 4816
Web Site: www.mccallbarbour.co.uk

Personnel:
Rev Dr T. C. Danson-Smith (*Managing Partner*)
Miss G. A. Danson-Smith (*Dispatch Manager*)

USA companies represented:
USA: AMG Publishers; Chick Publications; Dake Bible Sales; Discovery House; Harvest-House; Kirkbride Bible Co; Kregel Publishers; Living Stories Inc; Thomas Nelson & Sons; Oxford University Press (*Bibles*); John Peterson Music; Rainbow Study Bibles; Schoettle Publishing House; Singspiration Inc; Sword of the Lord Publishers; Zondervan Corporation

Distributor of Bibles, Christian books and greeting cards, also videos, DVDs, gifts.

6101

MACMILLAN DISTRIBUTION (MDL)
Brunel Road, Houndmills, Basingstoke, Hants RG21 6XS
Telephone: 01256 302840
Fax: 01256 841426
Email: www-mdl@macmillan.co.uk
Web Site: www.macmillandistribution.co.uk

Personnel:
Lawrence Jennings (*Chairman*)
David Smith (*Managing Director*)
Andrew May-Miller (*Information Services Director*)
Guy Browning (*Distribution Director*)

Parent Company:
UK: Macmillan Ltd

Distributor for:
Accent Press Ltd; Alma Books; Arcturus Publishing Ltd; Arden Shakespeare; Berg Publishers; A. & C. Black; Bloomsbury Academic; Bloomsbury Information; Bloomsbury Publishing Plc; Boxtree; Camra; Cico Books; Class Publishing (London) Ltd; CRW Publishing Ltd; Dennis Publishing; Edinburgh University Press; Elliott & Thompson Ltd; Fairchild; Featherstone; First Second Editions; W. Foulsham & Co Ltd; W. H. Freeman & Worth Publishers; Guinness World Records Ltd; Jones & Bartlett; Kingfisher; Jessica Kingsley Publishers; Little Tiger Press (Magi); Macmillan Children's Books; Macmillan Compass; Macmillan Digital Audio; Macmillan Education; Macmillan English Campus; Macmillan New Writing; Mantle; Methuen Drama; Murdoch Books (UK) Ltd; Nature Publishing Group; Office for National Statistics (ONS); One World Classics; Palgrave; Pan Macmillan; Panini Books; Pharmaceutical Press; Picador; Prestel

Publishing Ltd; Priddy Books; Quadrille Publishing Ltd; Rodale; Ryland Peters & Small; Sidgwick & Jackson; Sinauer Associates; I. B. Tauris; V & A Publications; John Wisden & Co Ltd

Macmillan Distribution (MDL) offers a full book distribution service to the Macmillan publishers as well as a wide range of third-party clients. It provides order fulfilment in a variety of electronic formats as well as more traditional forms, cash collection and information provision through its sophisticated sales analysis system. MDL was one of the first publisher's distribution companies to obtain ISO9000 certification, the internationally recognized standard for quality systems, and is fully accredited under BIC's 'Supply Chain Excellence' programme. It consciously looks for ways to expand and improve the services it offers, which include printing, catalogue despatch A.I. provision and links with reps using PDAs for order transfer and title and price availability. It recently invested in separate units of 120,000 sq feet and 60 000 sq feet of new state-of-the-art warehousing. Refinements of its warehousing and stock systems are ongoing.

6102

MARSTON BOOK SERVICES LTD
160 Milton Park, Abingdon, Oxon OX14 4SD
Telephone: 01235 465604
Fax: 01235 465655
Email: monica.harding@marston.co.uk
Web Site: www.marston.co.uk

Marston Digital Print:
Omega 2, Southmead Industrial Estate, Didcot, Oxon OX11 7WB
Telephone: 01235 515700
Web Site: www.marston.co.uk

Personnel:
John Holloran (*Chairman*)
Ross Clayton (*Managing Director*)
Graham Cooper (*Financial Director*)
Melanie Khosla (*Customer Service Manager*)
Donna Green (*Assistant Customer Service & Trade Manager*)
Monica Harding (*Client Development & Service Manager*)
Annemarie Cuddon (*Assistant Client Development & Service Manager*)
Simon Clayton (*Marston Print Client Service Manager*)

Associated Companies:
UK: Orca Book Services

Clients represented:
Belgium: Brepols Publishing; Harvey Miller Publishers
Denmark: Copenhagen Business School Press
Germany: Actar Birkhauser Dist; Boerm Bruckmeier Verlag GmbH; Fraunhofer Verlag; Hogrefe Publishing
Italy: Damiani Editore
Republic of Ireland: Cork University Press / Attic Press
Singapore: World Scientific Publishing
UK: Acumen Publishing; Adamson Publishing; Alban Books; Alpha International; Alpha Science International Ltd; Anthem Press; Arts Council of England; Assouline Publishing Inc; The Barbirolli Society; Bennett & Bloom; Bibles for Children; Biteback Publishing Ltd; Black Dog Publishing Ltd; Bloomsbury Professional; Burke Publishing; CIPAC; Clinical Publishing; Combined Academic Publishers Ltd; Compass – DSA; Edinburgh University Press; Edward Elgar Publishing Ltd; Equinox; Flame Tree Publishing; Gestalten UK; Hann Barton; Harriman House Ltd; The History Press; Hurst & Co (Publishers) Ltd; ICSA; Imaginative Minds; Island Press; Peter Lang Ltd; Lion Hudson Plc; Liverpool University Press; Manchester University Press; Manticore Books Ltd; Mapin; Marshall Cavendish; Merrell Publishers Ltd; Multilingual Matters Ltd / Channel View Publications; NGT Publishing; NIAS; Nova Law & Finance; Now Publishing; Oberon; Oxford Publicity Partnership; Papadakis; Permillion; Pluto Press; The Policy Press; Public Catalogue Foundation; Royal Botanic Gardens Kew; The Royal Society of Medicine Press Ltd; John Rule Sales & Marketing; Saqi Books; Scottish Council for Law Reporting; Scripture Union for England & Wales; Society for Promoting Christian Knowledge; Terra Publishing; Third Millennium Publishing Ltd; Thorogood Publishing; Turning Point; Unicorn Press; University of Buckingham; Vagabond Voices; Verso; The Voltaire Foundation; WARC
USA: ABC-CLIO; Enisen Publishing; National Academies Press; Omnigraphics; Rizzoli International Publications; University of Pennsylvania Press

Provides fulfilment services to the publishing world.

Services available include: order processing; customer service; credit control; management reporting; production of royalty statements; pick, pack and dispatch (automated warehouse management system); digital print facility; journal fulfilment; ancillary work; exhibition services; EDI; IT support and development.

6103

MDS BOOK SALES
128 Pikes Lane, Glossop, Derbys SK13 8EH
Telephone: 01457 861508
Fax: 01457 868332
Email: enquiries@mdsbooks.co.uk
Web Site: www.mdsbooks.co.uk

Personnel:
Mark Senior (*Proprietor*)

Associated Companies:
UK: Venture Publications Ltd

Distributor for:
UK: Birmingham Transport Historical Group; DTS Sales; Earlswood Press; John Hambley Books; Robin Hood Publishing; Senior Publications; Venture Publications Ltd; Peter Watts Publishing; Woodpecker Publications

Book wholesalers and distributors specialising in transport-related lists.

6104

MELIA PUBLISHING SERVICES LTD
ONE, St Peter's Road, Maidenhead, Berkshire SL6 7QU
Telephone: 01628 633673
Fax: 01628 635562
Email: melia@melia.co.uk
Web Site: www.melia.co.uk

Personnel:
Terry Melia (*Managing Director*)
Joanna Melia (*Deputy MD*)
Linda West (*Accounts Manager*)
Rob Richardson (*Key Accounts*)
Elaine McEwen (*Sales Administrator*)

Distributor for:
Oxmoor House; Splendid Books; The Experiment
UK: Connections; Snake River Press
USA: Algonquin; Artisan; Farrar, Straus & Giroux; Filipacchi; Forge; Griffin; Harcourt Trade Books; Henry Holt; Houghton Mifflin Harcourt; Kensington Publishing Corporation; Minotaur; Newmarket Press; Owl; Papercutz; Picador; Rodale; Seven Seas; St Martins Press; Storey Books; Time Inc Home Entertainment; Tor; Workman Publishing

Sales and distribution for English language publishers.

6105

METANOIA BOOK SERVICE
[Book service of the London Mennonite Trust]
14 Shepherds Hill, London N6 5AQ
Telephone: 0845 4500 214
Fax: 020 8341 6807
Email: metanoia@menno.org.uk
Web Site: www.metanoiabooks.org.uk

Personnel:
Will Newcomb (*Manager*)

Parent Company:
UK: London Mennonite Centre

Distributor for:

To raise awareness of Mennonite and Anabaptist distinctives through the selling of Mennonite/Anabaptist and radical discipleship literature/publications.

6106

MK BOOK SERVICE
7 East Street, Hartford Road, Huntingdon PE29 1WZ
Telephone: 01480 353710
Fax: 01480 431703
Email: mkbooks@tiscali.co.uk

Personnel:
M. R. King (*Owner*)

UK distributor/representative for clients including:
Argentina: Del Nuevo Extremo; Lola
Australia: Academic English Press; Gary Allen Pty Ltd NSW; Art Media; Ausmed; Australian Medical Publications; Blue Cat Books; E. J. Bowles; Coffee School Melbourne; Corkwood Press; Crossing Press; Ken Duncan Panographs; Eagles Nest Golf Guides; East Street Publications; Golden Point Press; Haese & Harris; Hobby Investment; IBID Press; Indo Lingo Surf; JB Books; Linford; Melting Pot Press; Mitchell Wordsmith; Parrot Books; Perfect Potion; Piscean Books; Slouch Hat Publications; Wizard Study Guides; Woodmore
Bangladesh: University Press Dhaka
Canada: Creative Newfoundland; Empty Mirror Press; Fitzhenry & Whiteside; St James Publishing BC
Estonia: Periodika
France: Editions Pelisser
Germany: ADAC
Iceland: Forglaid; Iceland Review; Mimir
India: Aditya Prakashan; Allied Publications; Anmol; Asa; Ashish/APH; Asia Bookclub; Atlantic Publishing; Authors Press; Best Books Kolkata; Biotech; Book Enclave; Concord Press; Daya; Deep & Deep; Diamond Pocket Books; DK Printworld Pty Ltd; Galaxy; Gene-Tech Books; India Research Press; Indus; Intellectual Book Corner; ISPCK; Kaushal; Low Price Publications; Mahaveer & Sons; Minerva Associates; Modern Publishers; National Book Trust; Papyrus; Prestige; Rajesh; Regency; South Asian Publications
Israel: Ben Zvi Press; Bible Lands Museum; Carta; Francisian Printing Press; Gefen; Israel Academy of Sciences; Israel Exploration Society; Magnes Press; Rubin Mass Publishing Jerusalem; Yad Vaschem
Italy: Biblico Pontificio
Latvia: Avots
New Zealand: Hyndmans
USA: Eisenbrauns; Kendall Hunt

Distributor for overseas publishers; importer from overseas, for whom we are not agents; distributor for selected UK publishers; library supply; booksearch for out-of-print UK books.

6107

MOTILAL (UK) – BOOKS OF INDIA
367 High Street, London Colney, St Albans, Herts AL2 1EA
Telephone: 01727 761677
Fax: 01727 761357
Email: info@mlbduk.com

Personnel:
R. J. McLennan (*Managing Director*)
Ms Ann Moister (*Finance*)
Richard Neil (*Customer Service*)
Barbara Doffman (*Customer Service*)

Parent Company:
UK: Moneysavers (Ldn) Ltd

Associated Companies:
UK: Ahimsa Books

Indian publishers represented include:
India: Abhinav Publications; Amexfel Publishers; Anmol Publications; Aravali Books International; Aryan Books International; Asian Educational Services; Asiatic Publishing House; Banjara Academy; Bihar School of Yoga; Bookwell Publications; Brijbasi Art Press; Centre for Studies in Civilizations; Commonwealth Youth Programme; Cosmo Publications; Crest Publishing House; Deep & Deep Publications; DK Printworld; Excel Books; Foundation Books; Full Circle Publishing Ltd; Gemini Books; Gulshan Publishers; Gyan Publishing House; HarperCollins India; Hind Pocket Books; Indian Book Centre; Indiana Publishing House; Indica Books; Indus Publishing; Institute for Human Development; Jaico Publishing House; Jaya Books; Jaypee Brothers Medical Publishers; Kalpaz Publications; Katha; Kitab Bhavan; Laxmi Publications; Low Price Publications; Malhotra Publishing; Manas Publications; Manohar Publishers; Motilal Banarsidass; New Age Books; Orient Paperbacks; Paljor Publications; Pentagon Press; Pragati Publications; Sandeep Prakashan; Prentice-Hall of India Pvt Ltd; Pustak

Mahal; Rawat; Readworthy Publications Pvt Ltd; Sahasrara Publications; Sanskrit Religious Institute; Sanskriti; Shubhi Publications; Spectrum Publications; Sura Books; Torchlight Publishing; Unisun Publications; Universal Law Publishing; Vanity Books International; Wordspeak; Worldview Publications; Zubaan

Distributor of books and other materials dealing with the philosophies, religions and cultures of India.

In November 1998 the company took over Motilal Books, which is the European distributor for Motilal Banarsidass Ltd (MLBD) of New Delhi. MLBD are the foremost publishers for the academic market on the topics of Hinduism, Buddhism, Jainism and all subjects unique to India. We supply all markets with titles in all fields, books from India in general, representing all major Indian publishers.

The company now represents over 300 Indian publishers as their UK distributor, with over 35,000 English titles listed on Nielsen BookData.

6108

*NMD TRADING CO
[trading as Mayfield Books & Gifts]
9 Orgreave Close, Sheffield S13 9NP
Telephone: 0114 288 9522
Fax: 0114 269 1499
Email: sales@mayfield-books.co.uk

Personnel:
David N. Smith (*Managing Director*)
Andrew Smith (*Sales Director*)

Supply bookshops and other trade outlets through the Midlands and Northern England with maps and guides and local book product. Specialize in walking and outdoor activity books. Four representatives call regularly throughout the year. Main suppliers are Ordnance Survey, George Philips, Collins and Geographers A-Z Map Co. Provide a service for small publishers into the multiple chains, e.g. W. H. Smith, Waterstone's. Distributor for Myriad Books and a growing range of nostalgia products from the Frith Collection.

Sole supplier of LAM-fold maps. Also supply laminated flat maps and other special product, such as library supply.

6109

OHL GLOBAL FREIGHT MANAGEMENT & LOGISTICS
Action Court, Ashford Road, Ashford, Middx TW15 1XS
Telephone: 01784 890005
Fax: 01784 890013
Email: pbarrett@ohl.com
Web Site: www.ohl.com

Oceanfreight Division:
OHL Global Freight Management & Logistics, Watkins Close, Burnt Mills Industrial Estate, Basildon, Essex SS13 1TL
Telephone: 01268 724400
Fax: 01268 728226
Email: mcaines@ohl.com
Web Site: www.ohl.com

Personnel:
Geoff Corpe (*President*)
Steve Lai (*Finance Director*)
Paul Barrett (*International Sales Director*)
Martin Caines (*Oceanfreight Director*)
Chris Packwood (*Managing Director*)
Steve Buckerfield (*VP Airfreight Sales*)

Parent Company:
USA: OHL Inc

Freight forwarder to the publishing industry, providing efficient cost-effective services specifically designed for the worldwide movement of trade and academic books. Services offered are by air, sea and road between publisher's warehouse and bookshop door. Sponsor of the British Book Awards.

6110

ORCA BOOK SERVICES LTD
Unit A3, Fleets Corner, Poole, Dorset BH17 0HL
Telephone: 01235 465521
Fax: 01235 465555
Email: tradeorders@orcabookservices.co.uk
Web Site: www.orcabookservices.co.uk

Orders to:
Orca Book Services, 160 Milton Park, Abingdon, Oxon
OX14 4SD

Personnel:
Martyn Chapman (*Commercial Director*)
Denise Shonfeld (*Publisher Services Manager*)
Ian Whyte (*Logistics Director*)
Trish Clapp (*Publisher Services Development Manager*)

Parent Company:
UK: Marston Book Services Ltd

UK distributor for:
Amberley Publishing; Ammo Books; Armchair Traveller;
Arris Publishing; Blue Ibex; Book Foundation; Book Guild;
Continuum International Publishing Group; Dimensional
Entertainment; Dynasty Press; Evans Mitchell Books;
Family Doctor Publications; Firefly Books; Global Oriental;
Guild of Master Craftsmen Publications; Heni Publishing;
Hirmen Verlag; John Hunt Publishing; Industrial Press;
Islamic Texts; JB Publishing; Kuperard Publishers; Lark
Books; Learning Development Aids; Lifetime Careers
Publishing; Management Briefs; Maverick Arts; O Books;
Palazzo Editions; Parkstone Press; Pepin Press; Potomac
Books; Ravette Publishing; Redcliffe Press; Roundhouse
Publishing; Special Interest Model Books; Sterling
Publishing; T & G Publishing; Taunton Press; Tonto;
Trolley Books; Troubador; Veloce Publishing; Vine House;
White Star Publishers

Orca Book Services provides a full distribution service to general, academic and specialist publishers. A comprehensive
package of management reports comes as standard, via
Vista. Royalty accounting is also available as well as representation through the various sales agencies with which we
have arrangements.

6111

*REARDON PUBLISHING
PO Box 919, Cheltenham, Glos GL50 9AN
Telephone: 01242 231800
Email: reardon@bigfoot.com
Web Site: www.reardon.co.uk &
www.cotswoldbookshop.com

Personnel:
Nicholas Reardon (*Director*)

UK distributor for:
UK: Cassell (*selected publications*); Cicerone (*selected
publications*); Cordee (*selected publications*); Corinium
Publications; Estate Publications; Flukes UK (*illustrated
maps*); The Gloucestershire Ramblers Association; Harvey
Maps (*all maps*); Ordnance Survey (*all maps*); Orion
(*selected publications*); Philips Maps; Video Ex (*selected
titles*)

Reardon Publishing offers a wide range of Costwold books,
maps, videos, CDs and postcards and prints mostly in the
specialized areas of walking, cycling, driving, folklore, leisure
and tourism in both the Cotswold and associated counties,
plus a new range of books on Antarctica and Antarctic
heroes.

6112

SCANDINAVIA CONNECTION
26 Woodsford Square, London W14 8DP
Telephone: 020 7602 0657
Email: books@scandinavia-connection.co.uk
Web Site: www.scandinavia-connection.co.uk

Personnel:
Max Morgan-Witts (*Chairman*)

Parent Company:
UK: Max Morgan-Witts Productions Ltd

UK distributor for:
Denmark: Aschehoug; Borgen; Nyt Nordisk
Iceland: JPV
Norway: Cappelen; KOM; Normann's; Wennergren-
Cappelen
Sweden: Atlantis; ICA; J-P Lahall
USA: Pelican (*for Norway B&B Book*)

Sole UK supplier for various Scandinavian publishers of non-
fiction English edition Scandinavian books, maps, videos and
CD-ROMs; UK book distributor for non-fiction English editions by Norwegian, Finnish, Icelandic, Danish and Swedish
publishers.

6113

TRADE COUNTER DISTRIBUTION LTD
Mendlesham Industrial Estate, Norwich Road, Mendlesham,
Norfolk IP14 5ND
Telephone: 01449 766629
Fax: 01449 767122
Email: patrick.curran@tradecounter.co.uk
Web Site: www.tradecounter.co.uk

Personnel:
Patrick Curran (*Managing Director*)
Martin Leigh (*General Manager*)
Alan Wagstaff (*Chairman*)

Distributor:
UK: Brilliant Publishing; Capital Transport; Miles Kelly; Rising
Stars Publishing; Transatlantic Press

Storage, packing and distribution of books for publishers.
Order processing and credit control. Operates both full
service and fulfilment.

6114

TRANSATLANTIC PUBLISHERS GROUP LTD
Unit 242, 235 Earls Court Road, London SW5 9FE
Telephone: 020 7373 2515
Fax: 020 7244 1018
Email: Richard@tpgltd.co.uk
Web Site: www.TransatlanticPublishers.com

Personnel:
Richard Williamson (*Managing Director*)
Mark Chaloner (*Sales & Marketing Director*)

UK distributor for:
Australia: Tilde University Press
India: Byword Books; I.K. International
USA: American Institute of Aeronautics & Astronautics;
American Institute of Mathematical Sciences; American
Pharmacists Association; American Society of Agronomy;
American Society of Health System Pharmacists (ASHP);
Apple Academic Press; Business Expert Press Inc; Crop
Science Society of America; Demos Medical Publishers;
Destech Publishers; Franklin Beedle & Associates;
Industrial Press; Joint Commission Resources; Lexicomp
Inc; Mercury Learning Inc; Momentum Press; Potomac
Books; Soil Science Society of America; Zero to Three
Press

Distributors and agents for scientific, technical and medical,
and academic publishers in the UK, Europe and the Middle
East.

6115

TURNAROUND PUBLISHER SERVICES LTD
Unit 3, Olympia Trading Estate, Coburg Road, London
N22 6TZ
Telephone: 020 8829 3000
Fax: 020 8881 5088
Email: sales@turnaround-uk.com
Web Site: www.turnaround-uk.com

Personnel:
Bill Godber (*Managing Director*)
Claire Thompson (*Marketing Director & Company Secretary*)
Sue Gregg (*Finance Director*)
Andy Webb (*Sales Director*)

Clients include:
Australia: Etram Publishing; Ocean Press; Outre Gallery &
Publishing; Power Publications (Australia)
Canada: McClelland & Stewart; Random House Canada;
Tradewind
Czech Republic: Magic Realist Press
France: JNF Productions; La Marelle; MonaGallery SARL
Germany: From Here to Fame Publishing; Bruno Gmunder
Verlag; Kehrer Verlag; Konkursbuch Verlag; Mix of Pix
Italy: Europa Editions
Jamaica: LMH Publishing Ltd
Japan: Kumon Publishing Group
Netherlands: De Harmonie
P. R. of China: Better Link
Philippines: Paddleless Press
Republic of Ireland: Maverick House; Mount Eagle
Publications

Sweden: Dokument Press; Nicotext; Premium Publishing
Thailand: Creation / Oneiros Books; Creation / Solar Books;
Creation / Wet Angel
UK: Adelita Ltd; AK Press; Allison & Busby; The Aquarium;
Arcadia Books; Artists' & Photographers' Press Ltd;
Ayebia Clarke Publishing Ltd; Beautiful Books; Black
Spring; Blackamber Books; Bliss; Bloody Books;
Bookmarks; Borderline Publications; Burning House;
Cinebook; Creative Essentials; Crocus Books; Cutting
Edge Press; Dalen Books; Dexter Haven Publishing;
Education Now Books; Emerald Publishing; Erotic Review
Books; Eurocrime; Facts, Figures & Fun; Fanfare; Guerilla
Books; Hansib Publications; Helter Skelter Publishing;
High Stakes Publishing; Honno Welsh Women's Press;
Inglis Publications; Kamera; Dewi Lewis Publishing;
Lifeguides; Little Roots; London Books; LVSC; Monday
Books; Myriad Editions; New Internationalist; Noir
Publishing; Rankin Photography Ltd; Susan Russell
Publishing; Salt Publishing; Satchel; Selfmadehero;
Sorted; Southbank Publishing; Sportsbooks;
Straightforward Publishing; Strange Attractor; Suitcase
Press; True Crime Library; Vice UK; Zidane Press; Ziji
Publishing
USA: Africa World Press; Angel City Press; Arcata Arts; Atlas
& Co; Atria Books; Barricade Books; Blood Moon
Productions; Bywater Books; Catbird Press; Checker
Publishing; Cleis Press; Counterpoint; Demo; DGN
Productions Inc; Disinformation Co Ltd; Dominion Press;
Drag City; Exact Change; Fantagraphics; Ferine Books
(*select stock holdings only*); Fulcrum; Green Candy Press;
Green Integer; Haymarket Books; IG Publishing; Last
Gasp; Leyland Publications; Majority Press; Manic D
Press; Mircocosm Publishing; NBM; The New Press;
Process; The Red Sea Press; Santa Monica Press; Speck
Press; Starbooks; Steerforth Press; Testify Books; Turtle
Point Press; Van Patten

Turnaround provides a sales, marketing and distribution
service for a range of UK, US and Irish publishers in the UK
and Europe. The above list is only a selection: contact
Turnaround for a complete list.

6116

TURPIN DISTRIBUTION SERVICES LTD
Pegasus Drive, Stratton Business Park, Biggleswade, Beds
SG18 8TQ
Telephone: 01767 604868
Fax: 01767 604949
Email: neil.castle@turpin-distribution.com
Web Site: www.turpin-distribution.com

Also at:
Turpin North America, The Bleachery, 143 West Street,
New Milford, CT 06778, USA
Telephone: +1 (860) 350 0041
Fax: +1 (860) 350 0039
Email: turpinna@turpin-distribution.com
Web Site: www.turpin-distribution.com

Personnel:
Lorna Summers (*Managing Director*)
Richard Stroud (*Company Accountant*)
Neil Castle (*Head of Customer Relations & Distribution*)
Alan Medd (*Head of IT*)
Elizabeth Just (*Head of Operations, Turpin USA*)
Julie Barnes (*Senior Manager: HR & Business Performance*)

Parent Company:
UK: Eurospan Group

Clients include:
France: Organisation for Economic Co-operation and
Development (OECD)
Greece: Adcotec
Japan: Japanese Society for Analytical Chemistry
Netherlands: Brill Academic Publishers; Hes en de Graaf;
Kluwer Law International; New in Chess
UK: Adcotec; Advanced Materials; Philip Allan Updates; The
Association of Learned and Professional Society
Publishers (ALPSP); The Association of Project Managers;
Beech Tree Publishing; Berg Publishing; Biohealthcare;
The Bodleian Library; The British Library; Dunedin
Academic Press; Euromoney PLC; Eurospan Group; Fiscal
Publications; John Harper Publishing; Hodder Education;
Intellect Journals; Internet Archaeology; IP Publishing;
Journal of Transport & Economic Policy; Modern
Humanities Research Association; Pickering & Chatto;
Pion Publishers; The Royal College of Psychiatrists;
Spiramus; The Way; White Horse Press; Zophorus Books
USA: American Association Cancer Research; American

School of Classical Studies; Aspen Publishers Inc; Berghahn Journals; The Freer Gallery of Art; United Nations

Turpin Distribution is an international fulfilment and distribution company providing services to the academic, scholarly and professional publishing industry. We provide solutions for book, journal and online publishers that include:
– Global fulfilment and distribution
– UK and US offices with multilingual customer care advisors
– Order and renewals processing
– Billing and account collection
– Comprehensive warehouse services with global distribution for books and journals
– Full subscription management for print and online journals with e-commerce ordering
– Online sales reporting with data manipulation for analysis and customer management.
Turpin can accommodate any business model and pricing policy, enabling publishers to retain control of their products, develop collections, set multiple pricing options, use a variety of routes to market; and manage its customers successfully.

6117

VINE HOUSE DISTRIBUTION LTD
The Old Mill House, Mill Lane, Uckfield, East Sussex TN22 5AA
Telephone: 01825 767396
Fax: 01825 765649
Email: sales@vinehouseuk.co.uk
Web Site: www.vinehouseuk.co.uk

Personnel:
Sarah Squibb *(Managing Director)*
Pauline Gosden *(Client & Customer Services Manager)*
Julie McCarron *(Sales & Marketing Manager)*
Tara Horwood *(Research & Marketing Manager)*

Book Publishers:
Australia: Inn Australia
Finland: Fine Publishing
France: ETAI; Vinipresse
Hong Kong: Wheel Away Disabled Travel
India: Spenta Multimedia
Italy: Mediane
Netherlands: Kavino Book Publishing
New Zealand: Wooden Dragon Press
Poland: Muza SA
South Africa: Cheviot Publishing; Medspice; Outstanding 100
Spain: Editorial Moll
Sweden: MagDig Media
Switzerland: Chronosports; Valais Guides
UK: Andrew Martin International; Bearmondsey Publishing; Biomedic; Brighton & Hove Libraries; British Institute of Radiology; Calder Walker Associates; Dance Books; Dove Publishing; Easy on the Eye; Fitzjames Press; Foresight Preconception; Haldane Mason; Honeyglen Publishing; Horse's Mouth Publications; Infrastructure Project Development; The International Institute for Islamic Thought; J W McKenzie; Jaspal Jandu Photography; Julian Richer Publishing; Legacy Publishing; Martin Holmes Rallying; Motor Racing Publications; Muze Media; Oval Publishing; Oxbridge Applications; Park Lane Books; Philip Kaplan; Picnic Publishing; Puck Books; Red Kite Books; Royal Academy of Dance; Saxon Books; R. D. & A. S. Shepherd Partnership; Silent But Deadly Publications; Superbrands; Sylph Editions; Tartarus Press; Tattered Flag Press; Tiger Books; Touchstone Books; Travelwise; Turn End Charitable Trust; Umbria Press; WildGuides; WSG Media
USA: Dance Horizons; Princeton Book Co; Wine Appreciation Guild
West Indies: Royards

Vine House Distribution provides a comprehensive range of services for small and medium sized book publishers, including representation, distribution, marketing, publicity and promotion, and mail order fulfilment.

6118

WINDSOR BOOKS
31 Furze Platt Road, Maidenhead, Berkshire SL6 7NE
Telephone: 01628 770542
Fax: 01628 770546
Email: geoffcowen@windsorbooks.co.uk
Web Site: www.windsorbooks.co.uk

Personnel:
Geoff Cowen *(Managing Director)*
Angela Prysor-Jones *(Publicity Manager)*

Associated Companies:
UK: Meyer & Meyer Sport (UK); Star Book Sales

UK Distributor/Representative for:
Germany: Meyer & Meyer Verlag

Windsor Books, provides full representation and distribution in the UK and Ireland for the English language division of the sports book publisher Meyer & Meyer. Its associated company, Star Book Sales, also provides sales representation, distribution and marketing in the UK and European markets for publishers, linked to order fulfillment by Orca Distribution Services Ltd.

6.7 REMAINDER MERCHANTS

6119

*BOOKMARK REMAINDERS LTD
Rivendell, Illand, Launceston, Cornwall PL15 7LS
Telephone: 01566 782728
Fax: 01566 782059
Email: andrew.rattray@book-bargains.co.uk
Web Site: www.book-bargains.co.uk

Personnel:
Andrew Rattray *(Director)*
Carol Rattray *(Director)*

A wide range of genuine remainders and bargain books. Prompt payment to publishers, authors for surplus stocks.

6120

FANSHAW BOOKS LTD
Unit 7, Lysander Mews, Lysander Grove, London N19 3QP
Telephone: 020 7281 9387
Fax: 020 7561 3502
Email: info@roybloom.com
Web Site: www.roybloom.com

Personnel:
Adam Bloom *(Managing Director)*
Roy Bloom *(Chairman)*

Remainder company specializing in real UK publishers' books, mainly non-fiction, art, military, history, etc. It also has a number of retail stores, so customers can buy from one to 50,000 copies of a book.

6121

OCTAGON BOOKS (WHOLESALE) LTD
The Old Exchange, New Pond Road, Holmer Green, High Wycombe, Bucks HP15 6SU
Telephone: 01494 711717 (mobile: 07718 364857)
Fax: 01494 711176
Email: info@octagonbooks.co.uk

Personnel:
Ron Ive *(Director)*
Bernard McDonnell *(Commercial Director)*

All types of remainders and promotional reprints.

6122

*JIM OLDROYD BOOKS
The Old Town Jail, 14–18 London Road, Sevenoaks, Kent TN13 1AJ
Telephone: 01732 463356
Fax: 01732 464486
Email: Stephen@oldroyd.co.uk
Web Site: www.oldroyd.co.uk

Personnel:
Jim Oldroyd *(Director)*
Stephen Bryan *(Manager)*
Niki Oldroyd *(Buyer Manager)*
Sally Millest *(Assistant)*
Tim Finch *(Sales)*
Colin Gower *(Sales)*
Margaret Walker *(Sales)*
Hugh Llewellyn-Jones *(Director)*

Remainders, bargain books and overstocks of adult and children's books. All ages and all interests.

6123

SANDPIPER BOOKS LTD
6 Battle Road, Heathfield Estate, Newton Abbot, Devon TQ12 6RY
Telephone: 01626 832225
Fax: 01626 834539
Email: enquiries@sandpiper.co.uk
Web Site: www.sandpiper.co.uk & www.psbooks.co.uk

Distribution:
Alton Logistics Ltd, 4 Battle Road, Heathfield Estate, Newton Abbot, Devon TQ12 6RY
Telephone: 01626 832225
Fax: 01626 832398
Email: enquiries@altonlogistics.co.uk

Personnel:
Robert Collie *(Managing Director)*
Simon Lang *(Mail Order (Postscript))*

Primarily a mail order company of remainders and overstocks, trading with a monthly catalogue and online sales, Sandpiper also wholesales to an extensive network of trade and non-trade outlets both in the UK and overseas. We buy from major publishers as well as university presses and small trade publishers. Subjects range across the visual arts, history, philosophy, reference, travel, STM and literature, and from general interest publications to scholarly works. We have been trading for 32 years, and are moving our offices which have been in Tooting Bec down to our distribution in Devon, as from September 2011.

6.8 MAIN WHOLESALERS

6124

ARGOSY LIBRARIES LTD
Unit 12, North Park, North Road, Finglas, Dublin 11, Republic of Ireland
Telephone: +353 (0)1 823 9500
Fax: +353 (0)1 823 9599
Email: info@argosybooks.ie
Web Site: www.argosybooks.ie

Personnel:
Fergal Stanley *(Managing Director)*
Eddie Walsh *(General Manager)*
Ronan Richmond *(Sales Manager)*
Mary Healy *(Buyer)*

Trade book wholesaler specializing in books of Irish interest and maps and guides to Ireland. Export service available.

6125

BERTRAMS
1 Broadland Business Park, Norwich NR7 0WF
Telephone: 0871 803 6666
Fax: 0871 803 6709 (customer services)
Email: sales@bertrams.com
Web Site: www.bertrams.com

Personnel:
Graeme Underhill *(Managing Director)*
Ian Hendrie *(Finance Director)*
Chris Rushby *(Sales & Marketing Director)*
Roger Miah *(Buying Director)*

Parent Company:
UK: Smiths News PLC

Bertrams is wholly owned by Smiths News PLC, the UK's leading wholesaler of newspapers and magazines. Bertrams celebrated 40 years of trading in
2008 with a stockholding of over 220,000 titles from over 18,000 publishers and can source over 5 million English language titles from both the UK and USA. With a customer base of over 5,000 it supplies books and other related products into independent booksellers, online retailers, chain booksellers, library suppliers and other multinationals/non-book trade outlets worldwide. Customers can access availability of stock, product information, ordering and shipping details in real time through www.bertrambooks.com, Bertrams' own stock management system as well as its Customer Services department. A proactive marketing program enables publishers to market their titles effectively

and efficiently through all sales channels, both business to business and to the end consumer. The warehouse works at 24/7 at peak season and provides a market leading customer service.

Bertram Library Services business provides stock and selection advice for public libraries throughout the country. Bertram Publisher Services, the distribution arm of the group, provides distribution facilities for a range of publishers and retailers.

Bertrams is a key industry player with membership of the BA and BIC, working towards improving the supply chain throughout the book industry.

6126

BOOKSPEED
16 Salamander Yards, Edinburgh EH6 7DD
Telephone: 0131 467 8100
Fax: 0131 467 8008
Email: sales@bookspeed.com
Web Site: www.bookspeed.com

Personnel:
Kingsley Dawson (Chairman)
Gary Weston (Managing Director)
Fiona Stout (Director of Sales)
Matthew Perren (Director of Operations)
Lewis Dawson (Director of Commercial Development)
Shona Rowan (Marketing & Bibliographic Manager)

Parent Company:
UK: Rhodawn Ltd

The company provides a wholesale bookselling and consultancy service to non-bookshop outlets in the UK and Republic of Ireland, most of whom operate in the Gift, Heritage and Tourist sectors. For publishers we provide an easy route to this difficult-to-reach market.

6127

BOOKWORLD WHOLESALE LTD
Unit 10, Hodfar Road, Sandy Lane Industrial Estate, Stourport-on-Severn, Worcs DY13 9QB
Telephone: 01299 823330
Fax: 01299 829970
Email: info@bookworldws.co.uk
Web Site: www.bookworldws.co.uk

Personnel:
Justin Gainham (Sales Director)
Andrea Gainham (Director)

Transport, military, aviation and modelling book wholesaler and distributor. Mail order department worldwide. Minimum order one book, full trade terms given but postage added to orders under £50 in value. Teleordering mnemonic BK WORLD. Range of distribution whole of UK. Number of publishers for whom we distribute is in excess of 70.

6128

GARDNERS BOOKS LTD
1 Whittle Drive, Eastbourne, East Sussex BN23 6QH
Telephone: 01323 521555
Fax: 01323 521666
Email: sales@gardners.com
Web Site: www.gardners.com

Personnel:
Alan Little (Chairman)
Jonathan Little (Managing Director)
Nicky Little (Finance Director)
Andrew Little (Technical Director)
Bob Jackson (Commercial Director)
Simon Morley (Buying Director)
David O'Reilly (Warehouse Director)
Gary Sheppard (Marketing Manager)
Phil Edwards (Senior Buying Manager)
David Brewster (Customer Care Manager)

Gardners Books is a leading independent book and entertainment product wholesaler, offering one of the largest stock catalogues available from any UK wholesaler, with in excess of 4.5 million titles available from over 5,000 publishers, 165,000+ eBook files, 50,000+ DVDs and Blu-ray discs and 130,000 Music CDs.

Gardners offers a comprehensive range of e-commerce solutions including bespoke data feeds and drop-ship fulfilment to meet retailers' business requirements. Orders can be placed 24 hours a day via its account holders' website,

Gardlink electronic ordering system, Gardcall automated telephone enquiry service, fax and EDI. Its experienced customer care team is available from Monday to Saturday between 9am and 6pm to take orders and assist customers.

Gardners Books trade website, www.gardners.com, is free to account holders and features data on over 2 million British books in print, as well as real-time stock figures, invoices, backorders and promotional offers. Information on additional services Gardners offers, such as B2B and B2C home delivery fulfilment, marketing materials, distribution services and print on demand can also be found on the site.

6129

*SHOGUN INTERNATIONAL LTD
87 Gayford Road, London W12 9BY
Telephone: 020 8749 2022
Fax: 020 8740 1086
Email: info@shoguninternational.com

Personnel:
G. Blanc (Manager)

Shogun International deals exclusively with wholesaling of martial arts goods and related sports books.

6.9 MAIN LIBRARY SUPPLIERS

6130

*THE HOLT JACKSON BOOK CO LTD
Park Mill, Great George Street, Preston PR1 1TJ
Telephone: 01772 798000
Email: info@holtjackson.co.uk
Web Site: www.holtjackson.co.uk

Personnel:
Yvette Stafford (Chairman)
Kathryn Pattinson (Managing Director)
J. Little (Director)
A. Little (Director)
Mrs J. Holborn (Director)

Parent Company:
UK: The Little Group Ltd

Booksellers.

6131

STEVEN SIMPSON BOOKS
5 Hardingham Road, Hingham, Norwich NR9 4LX
Telephone: 01953 850471
Fax: 01953 850471
Web Site: www.aquariumatlas.co.uk

Trade Webshop:
AquariumAtlas.EU, 5 Hardingham Road, Norwich NR9 4LX
Telephone: 01953 850471
Fax: 01953 850471
Email: info@aquariumatlas.eu
Web Site: www.aquariumatlas.eu

Personnel:
S. J. Simpson (Proprietor)

UK distributor for:
Germany: Hans A. Baenasch / Mergus Verlag GmbH (exclusive); Birgit Schmettkamp Verlag (exclusive); Verlag ACS Aqualog GmbH (exclusive); Verlag Eugen Ulmer KG (exclusive)
Italy: Aquapress Publishers (exclusive); FAO (Food & Agriculture Organization of the United Nations)
Mexico: El Colegio de la Frontera Sur (exclusive); Comisión Nacional para el Conocimiento y Uso de la Biodiversidad (exclusive); Sociedad Ictiológica Mexicana AC (exclusive)
Nepal: T. K. Shrestha (exclusive)
USA: Desert Fishes Council (exclusive)

Distributor to the trade for overseas publishers in the field of natural history.

6132

*STARKMANN LTD
6 Broadley Street, London NW8 8AE
Telephone: 020 7724 5335

Fax: 020 7724 9863
Email: orders@starkmann.co.uk
Web Site: www.starkmann.com

Delivery Address:
6 Plympton Place, London NW8 8AD

Personnel:
Dr Bernard Starkmann (Managing Director)
Sheikh Obarey (Accounts Manager)
Martin Illmann (Sales Manager)
Steven Wright (Operations Manager)
Rodney Latham (IT Manager)
Kerstin Peter (Customer Service Manager)

Suppliers of academic and scientific books and ebooks to university, college, industrial and research libraries in Europe. Customers and potential customers receive frequent and accurate new book information. Distribution of the main line publishers from UK, USA, Netherlands, Germany and Switzerland. Supplies made at publisher's list price. Fast airfreight service of US books. Comprehensive website featuring bibliographic database, online ordering, order tracking, new title alert service and special offers.

6133

ROY YATES BOOKS
Smallfields Cottage, Cox Green, Rudgwick, Horsham, West Sussex RH12 3DE
Telephone: 01403 822299
Fax: 01403 823012
Email: royyatesbooks@btconnect.com

Personnel:
Roy Yates (Managing Director)

Specialist supplier of children's books to schools and libraries; distributes multilingual books; distributes foreign-language books, especially bilingual dictionaries.

6.10 BOOK CLUBS

6134

BIBLIOPHILE BOOKS
Unit 5 Datapoint Business Centre, 6 South Crescent, London E16 4TL
Telephone: 020 7474 2474
Fax: 020 7474 8589
Email: orders@bibliophilebooks.com
Web Site: www.bibliophilebooks.com

Personnel:
Jackie McDaid (General Manager)
Steven Lee (Distribution)
Anne Quigley (Director)

Produces 10 catalogues a year, offering books at bargain prices to private buyers.
Range: general, eg biography, history, travel, handicrafts, humour, literature.

6135

LETTERBOX LIBRARY
71–73 Allen Road, Stoke Newington, London N16 8RY
Telephone: 020 7503 4801
Fax: 020 7503 4800
Email: info@letterboxlibrary.com
Web Site: www.letterboxlibrary.com

Personnel:
Kerry Mason (Contact)
Fen Coles (Contact)

Letterbox Library is a children's bookseller specializing in children's books which celebrate equality and diversity. Quarterly catalogues are produced with up to 70 new titles, offered at discounts to members. Books are multicultural and non-sexist, and also show groups of people traditionally under-represented in children's books, e.g. different faith groups, disabled children, refugees. All books are approved by an independent team of reviewers.

Subscription is £5 a year and entitles members to discounts. Non-members can buy books at the retail price. Letterbox Library also provides book displays for schools and libraries and attends exhibitions. Letterbox Library is a not-for-profit social enterprise.

6136 ▬▬▬

POETRY BOOK SOCIETY
Dutch House, 307–308 High Holborn, London WC1V 7LL
Telephone: 020 7831 7468
Fax: 020 7833 5990
Email: info@poetrybooks.co.uk
Web Site: www.poetrybooks.co.uk &
www.poetrybookshoponline.com

Personnel:
Chris Holifield *(Director)*

Publicly funded charity, membership organization, mail order book club promoting contemporary poetry titles to an international readership. Quarterly publication of *Bulletin* magazine featuring selected new poetry titles. Also has Children's Poetry Bookshelf, relaunched 2005 with new website (www.childrenspoetrybookshelf.co.uk) and parent and library memberships. The Society also acts as sole distributor for The Poetry Archive CDs, and awards the annual T. S. Eliot Prize for Poetry.
    Membership from £12 p.a.
    Also runs www.poetrybookshoponline.com, selling a wide range of poetry and SoundBlast performance poets' CDs.

6.11 LITERARY & TRADE EVENTS

6137 ▬▬▬

BOOKSELLERS ASSOCIATION ANNUAL CONFERENCE
Minster House, 272 Vauxhall Bridge Road, London SW1V 1BA
Telephone: 020 7802 0802
Fax: 020 7802 0803
Email: naomi.gane@booksellers.org.uk
Web Site: www.booksellers.org.uk

Personnel:
Tim Godfray *(Chief Executive)*
Naomi Gane *(Conference Organizer)*
Alan Staton *(Head of Marketing & Events)*

Major UK book trade event. The Conference provides an opportunity for those supplying or serving the retail book trade to meet trade customers and for both to learn from the business programme. Details from: above address.

6138 ▬▬▬

THE TIMES CHELTENHAM LITERATURE FESTIVAL
Cheltenham Festivals Ltd, 109 Bath Road, Cheltenham, Glos GL53 7LS
Telephone: 01242 775026
Fax: 01242 256457
Email: nicola.tuxworth@cheltenhamfestivals.com
Web Site: www.cheltenhamfestivals.com

Personnel:
Donna Renney *(Chief Executive)*
Sarah Smyth *(Artistic Director)*
Clair Greenaway *(Executive Director)*

Annual in October. Promoted by Cheltenham Festivals Ltd. Performances, poetry readings, talks and discussions by literary personalities. Includes Book It! Festival for Children, and Write Away creative writing workshops.
    Details from: Artistic Director: Sarah Smyth or Executive Director: Clair Greenaway.

6139 ▬▬▬

CHILDREN'S BOOK WEEK
Booktrust, Book House, 45 East Hill, Wandsworth, London SW18 2QZ
Telephone: 020 8516 2976
Fax: 020 8516 2992
Email: education@booktrust.org.uk
Web Site: www.booktrust.org.uk

Personnel:
HRH The Duchess of Cornwall *(Patron)*
Viv Bird *(Chief Executive)*
Sue Horner *(Chair)*

Children's Book Week is a national celebration of reading for pleasure for children of primary school age, which takes place each year in the first full week of October. During the week, a range of book-related events and activities take place in schools and libraries across England.

6140 ▬▬▬

CIANA LTD
24 Langroyd Road, London SW17 7PL
Telephone: 020 8682 1969
Fax: 020 8682 1997
Email: enquiries@ciana.co.uk
Web Site: www.ciana.co.uk

Personnel:
Robert Collie *(Director)*
Sarah Weedon *(Director)*

Organizers of two annual trade fairs for the remainder, overstock and promotional book market. Over 100,000 discounted books, stationery items, CDs and DVDs.
    The September Fair is held in London Islington. The January Fair is in the Barbican in the City of London.

6141 ▬▬▬

EDINBURGH INTERNATIONAL BOOK FESTIVAL
5A Charlotte Square, Edinburgh EH2 4DR
Telephone: 0131 718 5666
Email: admin@edbookfest.co.uk
Web Site: www.edbookfest.co.uk

Personnel:
Nick Barley *(Director)*
Sara Grady *(Children & Education Programme Director)*
Andrew Coulton *(Administrative Director)*
Amanda Barry *(Marketing & PR Manager)*
Lois Wolffe *(Sponsorship & Development Manager)*
James Shaw *(Book Sales Manager)*

The Edinburgh International Book Festival is a public celebration of the written word and takes place every August. Over 800 events feature writers from across the globe, bringing authors together with their readers to talk about books, discuss ideas and share the latest thinking on a range of subjects from the environment to poetry.
    The festival runs its own independent book sales operation on the site – a tented village in Edinburgh's Charlotte Square Gardens – offering three large retail outlets including a bookshop dedicated to children's books.

6142 ▬▬▬

*FRANKFURT BOOK FAIR
Reineckstrasse 3, 60313 Frankfurt am Main, Germany
Telephone: +49 (0)69 2102 0
Fax: +49 (0)69 2102 227 & 277
Email: info@book-fair.com
Web Site: www.book-fair.com

Personnel:
Juergen Boos *(Chief Executive Officer)*
Katja Böhne *(Director, Marketing & Communication)*

Parent Company:
Germany: Börsenverein des Deutschen Buchhandels

The Frankfurt Book Fair is one of the largest book fairs in the world with more than 7000 exhibitors from over 100 countries. Open exclusively to the trade for the first three days and to the public for the last two days it attracts publishers, booksellers, authors, agents, distributors and the whole range of multimedia companies.
    The Frankfurt Book Fair also organizes the participation of German publishers at more than 25 international book fairs and is associated with the Cape Town Book Fair in South Africa and the Abu Dhabi International Book Fair. The Frankfurt Book Fair is a subsidiary of the German Publishers & Booksellers Association.

6143 ▬▬▬

GENERAL DIRECTORATE OF INTERNATIONAL BOOK EXHIBITIONS & FAIRS
Malaya Dmitrovka Street 16, Moscow 127006, Russia
Telephone: +7 (495) 699 4034, 699 9790 & 699 3466
Fax: +7 (495) 699 2539 & 299 1110
Email: mibf@mibf.ru & vbelov@mibf.ru
Web Site: www.mibf.ru

Personnel:
Nikolay Ph. Ovsyannikov *(General Director)*
Nina Sudina *(Head of Foreign Relations Department)*
Valery Belov *(Project Manager)*

Organization of annual Moscow International and Russian National Book Fairs, as well as collective and national book stands of Russian publishers at the international book fairs.

6144 ▬▬▬

*GÖTEBORG BOOK FAIR
412 94 Göteborg, Sweden
Telephone: +46 (0)31 708 8400
Fax: +46 (0)31 209103
Email: info@goteborg-bookfair.com
Web Site: www.goteborg-bookfair.com

Personnel:
Birgitta Jacobsson Ekblom *(Public Relations Manager)*
Anna Falck *(Managing Director)*

Göteborg Book Fair is one of the biggest bookfairs in northern Europe; 100,000 visits in four days, 900 exhibitors, 450 seminars and more than 1000 journalists covering the fair.
    Göteborg Book Fair is arranged annually in September, and takes place at the Swedish Exhibition Centre located in the centre of the city of Göteborg.

6145 ▬▬▬

*LEIPZIG BOOK FAIR
Leipziger Messe GmbH, Messe-Allee 1, 04356 Leipzig, Germany
Telephone: +49 (0)341 678 8240
Fax: +49 (0)341 678 8242
Email: info@leipziger-buchmesse.de
Web Site: www.leipziger-buchmesse.de

Personnel:
Oliver Zille *(Exhibition Director)*

The Leipzig Book Fair is an independent, general book fair concentrating on the German-speaking countries of Europe (Germany, Austria and Switzerland, also the Central and Eastern European countries). It also features international book art and is additionally characterized by general themes (e.g. audio books, travelling, music) which change from year to year and which are highlighted by special events relating to these themes. The commercial aspect of the Leipzig Book Fair is accompanied by a wide range of fringe events, including a section for antique books and prints.
    Visitors to the Leipzig Book Fair are mainly made up of representatives from publishers, the book trade, libraries, the newer media, the printing industry, and all other areas connected with the production of books, including book illustrators and graphic designers.
    2011 dates: 17–20 March.

6146 ▬▬▬

*THE LONDON BOOK FAIR
Gateway House, 28 The Quadrant, Richmond, Surrey TW9 1DN
Telephone: 020 8271 2124
Fax: 020 8910 7930
Email: lbf.helpline@reedexpo.co.uk
Web Site: www.londonbookfair.co.uk

Personnel:
Alistair Burtenshaw *(Group Exhibition Director)*
Amy Webster *(International Key Accounts Manager)*
Emma Lowe *(Sales Manager)*
Matt Colgan *(Sales Manager)*
Barbara Davis *(International Sales Manager)*
Orna O'Brien *(Conference Manager)*
Rebecca Hearn *(Marketing Executive)*
Christine Dolan *(Exhibition Co-ordinator)*
Lucy Holland-Smith *(Marketing Manager)*

The London Book Fair is a global marketplace for rights negotiation and the sale and distribution of content across print, audio, TV, film and digital channels, bringing three days of focused access to customers content and emerging markets.
    2011 Fair: 11–13 April at Earls Court, London. For further information, please visit our website www.londonbookfair.co.uk

6147 ▬

*THE LONDON LITERARY MAFIA
618b Finchley Road, London NW11 7RR
Telephone: 020 8455 4564
Email: lambhorn@gmail.com
Web Site: www.phantomcaptain.netfirms.com

Personnel:
Neil Hornick (Artistic Director)

Parent Company:
UK: The Phantom Captain

'Are You Reading Me?' – Established in 1997, The London Literary Mafia (a.k.a. The Phantom Captain Literary Lions) is a performance company specializing in entertainments, talks and readings devised to brighten up literature festivals, conferences, book launches, award ceremonies, promotions, luncheons and dinners, book fairs, writing courses and related writer/reader-themed events. Activities draw on the extensive experience of Neil Hornick, artistic director of the company, as writer-director-actor and (under a pen-name) as a professional literary consultant. Events can be commissioned and designed for specific occasions.

6148 ▬

SALON DU LIVRE DE MONTRÉAL
300 rue St-Sacrement, Bureau 430, Montreal, PQ,
H2Y 1X4, Canada
Telephone: +1 (514) 845 2365
Fax: +1 (514) 845 7119
Email: slm.info@videotron.ca
Web Site: www.salondulivredemontreal.com

Personnel:
Francine Bois (General Manager)

The Salon du Livre de Montréal is a public book fair which aims to promote reading. 2011 dates: November 16 to 21.

6149 ▬

*TOKYO INTERNATIONAL BOOK FAIR
Reed Exhibitions Japan Ltd, 18F Shinjuku Nomura Building,
1-26-2 Nishi-Shinjuku, Shinjuku-ku, Tokyo 163-0570, Japan
Telephone: +81 3 3349 8507
Fax: +81 3 3345 7929
Email: tibf-eng@reedexpo.co.jp
Web Site: www.bookfair.jp/english

Personnel:
Kaoru Iwata (International Sales Director)
Janet Or (International Sales Manager)
Keisuke Amano (Show Director)

Parent Company:
UK: Reed Exhibition Companies

Tokyo International Book Fair (TIBF) represents the world's second largest single publishing market - Japan. TIBF has built its success upon the full support of its joint organization committee comprising the seven most influential Japanese publishing trade associations.
TIBF offers exhibitors opportunities to meet major book publishers, literary agents, distributors and booksellers from all over Japan and neighbouring countries such as Korea, Taiwan, Hong Kong and China, and develop extensive business opportunities including:
– international rights negotiation
– joint publishing projects
– direct book exports.
2011 Fair: 7–10 July at Tokyo Big Sight.
For more information, please contact Reed Exhibitions in Tokyo.

6150 ▬

*WOMEN IN PUBLISHING
London
Email: info@wipub.org.uk
Web Site: www.womeninpublishing.org.uk

Women in Publishing works to promote the status of women working in publishing and related areas by helping them to develop their careers.

6151 ▬

*WORLD BOOK DAY
c/o Booksellers' Association, 272 Vauxhall Bridge Road,
London SW1V 1BA
Telephone: 020 7802 0802
Email: cathy.schofield@blueyonder.co.uk
Web Site: www.worldbookday.com

Personnel:
Cathy Schofield (Word Book Day Co-ordinator)

One of the UK's biggest celebrations of books and reading, held on the first Thursday in March. It is a partnership of publishers, booksellers and interested parties who work together to promote books and reading for the personal enrichment and enjoyment of all. One of the main aims of World Book Day is to encourage children to explore the pleasures of reading by providing them with the opportunity to have a book of their own. Thanks to the generosity of National Book Tokens and participating booksellers, school-children are entitled to receive a World Book Day £1 book token, which can be exchanged for one of the specially published £1 books or is redeemable against a book or audio-book of their choice.

6.12 PUBLISHING REFERENCE BOOKS & PERIODICALS

6152 ▬

THE AUTHOR
84 Drayton Gardens, London SW10 9SB
Telephone: 020 7373 6642
Fax: 020 7373 5768
Email: TheAuthor@societyofauthors.org
Web Site: www.societyofauthors.org

Personnel:
Andrew Rosenheim (Editor)
Kate Pool (Manager)

Parent Company:
UK: The Society of Authors

Free to members. £12, post free, per copy for others. Annual subscription: £30, post free.
The quarterly journal of The Society of Authors. Articles on the legal, commercial and technical side of authorship.

6153 ▬

BOOKS FOR KEEPS
1 Effingham Road, London SE12 8NZ
Telephone: 020 8852 4953
Fax: 020 8318 7580
Email: enquiries@booksforkeeps.co.uk
Web Site: www.booksforkeeps.co.uk

Personnel:
Richard Hill (Managing Director)
Rosemary Stones (Editor)

ISSN: 0143-909X
Available to all via website.
Reviews all children's books and carries articles/features about authors, publishing, education, etc. Main readership - teachers, librarians and parents.

6154 ▬

*BOOKS IN PRINT 2.0
Bowker (UK) Ltd, St Andrew's House,
18–20 St Andrew Street, London EC4A 3AG
Telephone: 020 7832 1770
Fax: 020 7832 1710
Email: sales@bowker.co.uk
Web Site: www.bowker.com

Personnel:
Doug McMillan (Managing Director)
Pam Roud (Sales Director)
Jo Grange (Marketing Manager)

Associated Companies:
USA: R. R. Bowker LLC; Cambridge Information Group

Annual subscription: from £2290.
Books in Print 2.0 has a new search and discovery interface that gives a faster and more efficient way to build collections and help users find the books they need. It incorporates global data; users may choose to subscribe to the international or USA side.

6155 ▬

*BOOKS IN PRINT 2010–2011
Grey House Publishing, 4919 Route 22, PO Box 56,
Amenia, NY 12501, USA
Telephone: +1 (518) 789 8700
Fax: +1 (518) 789 0556
Email: books@greyhouse.com
Web Site: www.greyhouse.com

Personnel:
Richard Gottlieb (President)
Leslie Mackenzie (Publisher)
Jessica Moody (Vice-President, Marketing)

Associated Companies:
USA: R. R. Bowker LLC; Cambridge Information Group

ISBN: 978 1 59237 636 0
Published August 2010, 7 volumes, hbk, $1045.
Full bibliographic and ordering information for over two million titles published or distributed in the USA.

6156 ▬

*THE BOOKSELLER
5th Floor, Endeavour House, 189 Shaftesbury Avenue,
London WC2H 8TJ
Telephone: 020 7420 6006
Fax: 020 7420 6103
Email: firstname.surname@bookseller.co.uk
Web Site: www.theBookseller.com

Personnel:
Nigel Roby (Managing Director)
Nicola Chin (Advertising Manager)
Samantha Missingham (Head of Audience Marketing)
Neill Denny (Editor-in-Chief)
Marzia Ghiselli (Business Development Director)

Parent Company:
UK: Bookseller Media Group Ltd

ISSN: 0006-7539
Weekly £4.40. Annual subscription: £177 (UK: public libraries), £186 (UK: all other businesses), £192 (Europe – airmail), £264 (rest of world – airmail).
The weekly newspaper of the book trade, offering in the course of a year over 7000 pages of news, analysis, features, letters, advertising and lists of books published in the UK. Major national and international events reported, regular authoritative articles on matters of trade, special features, book features and rights, stock market, legal and financial pages. Twice a year a six-month special issue of over 700 pages provides the best reference source for British publishers' publishing plans. Regular supplements in specialist areas.

6157 ▬

*BOOKSELLER + PUBLISHER
Thorpe-Bowker, PO Box 6509, St Kilda Road Central,
Vic 8008, Australia
Telephone: +61 (03) 8517 8333
Fax: +61 (03) 8517 8399
Email: bookseller.publisher@thorpe.com.au
Web Site: www.booksellerandpublisher.com.au

Personnel:
Gary Pengelly (General Manager)
Tim Coronel (Publisher)
Xeverie Swee (Advertising Manager)
Silvana Paolini (Production & Design)
Matthia Dempsey (Editor in Chief)

Parent Company:
Australia: Thorpe-Bowker
USA: R. R. Bowker LLC

Published continuously since 1921, Bookseller + Publisher magazine (and its offshoots the Weekly Book Newsletter, WBN Media Extra and Australian Library News) is the trade publication of the book industry for Australia and the region.

6158

BRITISH COPYRIGHT COUNCIL
Copyright House, 29–33 Berners Street, London W1T 3AB
Telephone: 01986 788122
Email: info@britishcopyright.org
Web Site: www.britishcopyright.org

The BCC was founded in 1965 and incorporated in 2007. It is a national consultative and advisory body representing those who create, hold interests in or manage rights in literary, dramatic, musical and artistic works, films, sound recordings, broadcasts and other material in which there are rights of copyright or related rights; and those who perform such works.

6159

*CHILDREN'S BOOKS IN PRINT 2010
Grey House Publishing, 4919 Route 22, PO Box 56, Amenia, NY 12501, USA
Telephone: +1 (518) 789 8700
Fax: +1 (518) 789 0556
Email: books@greyhouse.com
Web Site: www.greyhouse.com

Personnel:
Richard Gottlieb (President)
Leslie Mackenzie (Publisher)
Jessica Moody (Vice-President, Marketing)

Associated Companies:
USA: R. R. Bowker LLC; Cambridge Information Group

ISBN: 978 0 8352 5025 2
Published December 2009, 2 volumes, $455.
Most complete list of currently available children's books published in the USA.

6160

*CHILDREN'S WRITERS' & ARTISTS' YEARBOOK
A. & C. Black Publishers Ltd, 36 Soho Square, London W1D 3QY
Telephone: 020 7758 0201
Fax: 020 7758 0222
Email: wayb@acblack.com
Web Site: www.acblack.com & www.writersandartists.co.uk

Personnel:
Jill Coleman (Managing Director)
Jonathan Glasspool (Deputy Managing Director)

Parent Company:
UK: Bloomsbury Publishing Plc

ISBN: 978 1 4081 28596
Annual. 2011 edition, published August 2010, £14.99.
A comprehensive guide to markets in all areas of children's media. Contains articles and information on a wide range of topics written by well-known authors and illustrators, best-selling publishers and editors, leading figures in TV and radio and other children's media experts. Also contains market contacts including book publishers and packagers, literary and art agents, magazines, TV and radio, festivals, courses and bookshops.

6161

*THE COMPLETE DIRECTORY OF LARGE PRINT BOOKS AND SERIALS 2010
Grey House Publishing, 4919 Route 22, PO Box 56, Amenia, NY 12501, USA
Telephone: +1 (518) 789 8700
Fax: +1 (518) 789 0556
Email: books@greyhouse.com
Web Site: www.greyhouse.com

Personnel:
Richard Gottlieb (President)
Leslie Mackenzie (Publisher)
Jessica Moody (Vice-President, Marketing)

Associated Companies:
USA: R. R. Bowker LLC; Cambridge Information Group

ISBN: 978 1 59237 612 4
Published January 2010, 1 volume, $415.
Bigger than ever, this invaluable guide covers the large print field like no other resource. Inside you'll discover cur-

rent, accurate bookfinding and ordering information on some 32,000 titles.

6162

DIRECTORY OF UK & IRISH BOOK PUBLISHERS
The Booksellers Association of UK & Ireland, 272 Vauxhall Bridge Road, London SW1V 1BA
Telephone: 020 7802 0802
Fax: 020 7802 0803
Email: mail@booksellers.org.uk
Web Site: www.booksellers.org.uk

Personnel:
Tim Godfray (Chief Executive)

BA online Directory of UK & Irish Book Publishers (www.ukpublishers.net)
£25 (BA members), £50 (non-members).
Contains addresses and comprehensive information (including personnel,
e-mail and www sites) about UK and Irish publishers, sales agents, remainder dealers, distributors and book wholesalers, including distribution arrangements in the UK for overseas publications. Also includes trade terms and returns information, details of product specialization such as audio books, electronic publishing and maps, plus a subject specialization index and ISBN prefixes.

6163

DIY: BOOKFINDING AND BOOKSELLING
Magna Graecia's Publishers, PO Box 342, Oxford OX2 7YF
Telephone: 01865 553653
Fax: 01865 553653
Email: info@magnagraeciaspublishers.co.uk
Web Site: www.magnagraeciaspublishers.co.uk

Personnel:
Luigi Gigliotti (Research Editor Director)

Single parts: £29.95 each, except Volume 5: £19.95. Complete set: £229.60 plus p&p.
List of titles reported wanted by our members, clients in the UK and worldwide. The Register is updated daily. It is available on-line or in print format.
Set of eight parts: Volume One (3 parts) by authors; Volume Two (2 parts) by titles; Volume Three (1 part) by categories; Volume Four (1 part) by subjects; Volume Five (1 part) by subjects.

6164

*NEW WELSH REVIEW
PO Box 170, Aberystwyth, Ceredigion SY23 1WZ
Telephone: 01970 628410
Email: admin@newwelshreview.com
Web Site: www.newwelshreview.com

Personnel:
Kathryn Gray (Editor)
Sue Fisher (Development Manager)

New Welsh Review is a quarterly magazine which brings its readers a selection of new writing from Wales and the UK. Each issue includes a range of critical articles, book reviews, fiction and poetry. While the magazine's focus is on Welsh writing in English, its outlook is deliberately eclectic, encompassing broader European and international literary contexts.

6165

PUBLISHING, BOOKS & READING IN SUB-SAHARAN AFRICA: A CRITICAL BIBLIOGRAPHY
Hans Zell Publishing, Glais Bheinn, Lochcarron, Ross-shire IV54 8YB
Telephone: 01520 722951
Email: hanszell@hanszell.co.uk
Web Site: www.hanszell.co.uk/pbrssa/index.shtml

Personnel:
Hans Zell (Editor & Publisher)

ISBN: 978 0 9541029 5 1
Published October 2008, 762 pp, cased, £130/195/$260. Print and online (online access bundled with print). Online only £65/€97.50/$130.
This is a new, completely revised and fully updated edition of a much acclaimed bibliography published over ten years ago. Covering both print and online resources, it charts the

growth of publishing and book development in the countries of Africa south of the Sahara, as well as including a very large number of entries on many other topics as they relate to books and reading in Africa. With over 2500 critically annotated citations, it is a detailed documentation resource on the current state of the book on the African continent. The annotations aim to provide informed commentary and critical analysis, and draw attention to particularly important contributions of the literature on publishing and the book in Africa.
The bibliography is arranged under five major parts: (1) Serials and reference; (2) General, comparative and regional studies; (3) Country studies; (4) Studies by topic, listing material by 30 topic headings;
(5) Book industry training/Self-publishing

6166

SHEPPARD'S WORLD
Richard Joseph Publishers Ltd, PO Box 15, Torrington, Devon EX38 8ZJ
Telephone: 01805 625750
Email: office@sheppardsconfidential.com
Web Site: www.sheppardsconfidential.com

Personnel:
Richard Joseph (Managing Director)

Sheppard's World is a central reference source for businesses in the secondhand and antiquarian book trades, and includes dealers in antique maps, prints and ephemera. Subscribers can search on line (and in printed directories as and when published) covering all the details previously found in our printed directories – full contact details, opening hours, size of stock, major subjects stocked, credit cards accepted, and membership of trade associations. Details are posted to www.sheppardsworld.co.uk
Dealers, collectors and members of the trade can receive our free trade newsletter Sheppard's Confidential, which carries the latest trade news, news about forthcoming fairs and auctions – and reviews of fairs and auctions. The website www.sheppardsconfidential.com includes dealers' catalogues, calendar of fairs and auctions, and books wanted.

6167

THE TIMES LITERARY SUPPLEMENT
3 Thomas More Square, London E98 1BS
Telephone: 020 7782 4985
Fax: 020 7782 4966
Email: letters@the-tls.co.uk
Web Site: www.the-tls.co.uk

Personnel:
Sir Peter Stothard (Editor)
Alan Jenkins (Deputy Editor)
Robert Potts (Managing Editor)

The TLS is a weekly literary review, which carries reviews by leading authorities on up to 3000 books a year on literature and language, history, politics, philosophy, the arts and music, social studies, economics, natural history and many other subjects. It also reviews exhibitions and performing arts, carries articles of general interest, publishes poetry and has a letters page which is the principal forum for literary debate. It is essential reading for librarians, booksellers and academics, and also for its broad, worldwide general readership.

6168

WRITERS' & ARTISTS' YEARBOOK
[owned by Select Publisher Services Ltd]
PO Box 6337, Bournemouth BH1 9EH
Telephone: 01202 586848
Email: www.selectps.com
Web Site: www.writers-forum.com

Advertisement & PR Manager:
Wendy O'Brien, 6 Wallace Avenue, Exeter EX4 8DB
Telephone: 01392 466099
Email: wendy.obrien99@googlemail.com

Personnel:
Tim Harris (Publisher)
Carl Styants (Editor)
Wendy O'Brien (Advertising & PR Manager)
Chris Wigg (Subscriptions Manager)

Parent Company:
UK: Select Publisher Services

Associated Companies:
UK: The Flower Press

12 issues a year. Subscription: UK £36; Europe £46; Rest of World £52.

Writers' Forum is a major resource for all writers; covering the who,

why, where, what and how on the craft and business of writing; it runs monthly story and poetry competitions featuring large cash prizes where the winners are printed in the magazine.

Welcomes articles on any aspect of the craft and business of writing. Length: 800–2000 words. Payment: by arrangement. Founded 1993.

6.13 TRAINING

6169

*CENTRE FOR PUBLISHING, UNIVERSITY COLLEGE LONDON
Department of Information Studies, UCL, Gower Street, London WC1E 6BT
Telephone: 020 7679 2473
Fax: 020 7383 0557
Email: ma-publishing@ucl.ac.uk
Web Site: www.publishing.ucl.ac.uk

Personnel:
Prof Iain Stevenson (*Teaching Director*)
Prof David Nicholas (*Director*)
Dr Ian Rowlands (*Research Director*)
Prof Anthony Watkinson (*Industry Liaison*)
Ms Kerstin Michaels (*Administrator*)
Ms Lucy Lyons (*Administration Secretary*)
Dr Claire Warwick (*Electronic Publishing*)

Research and education in publishing. Offers a taught MA in Publishing with pathways in Publishing, Electronic Publishing and Magazine Publishing (from 2010). Also Mphil and PhD research in publishing.

6170

CITY UNIVERSITY LONDON
Department of Creative Practice and Enterprise, Northampton Square, London EC1V 0HB
Telephone: 020 7040 8266
Fax: 020 7040 8594
Email: maryann.kernan.1@city.ac.uk
Web Site: http://www.city.ac.uk/courses/postgraduate/publishing-studies

Personnel:
Mary Ann Kernan (*Programme Director*)
Dr Richard Guthrie (*Lecturer in Publishing*)
Richard Balkwill (*Visiting Lecturer*)
Brenda Stones (*Visiting Lecturer*)
Dominic Vaughan (*Visiting Lecturer*)
Stephen Mesquita (*Visiting Lecturer*)
Max Adam (*Visiting Lecturer*)

The City publishing programme offers a full-time one-year Master's Degree (MA) in Publishing Studies to prepare entrants and re-entrants to the industry.

The MA consists of eight taught units, a 5–6 week industrial placement and a dissertation. The department directly involves its close industry links in module projects, industry visits and visitor presentations; and the module leaders include leading industry professionals, who actively encourage gains in industry-specific skills alongside MA-level knowledge gains through the year. The programme has a strong track record of student satisfaction, and of supporting its graduates in gaining employment in the industry. Candidates can study full-time or part-time.

The programme also offers the award of MA in International Publishing to candidates with publishing experience, following the same module structure with a module entitled International Publishing Case Studies in place of an assessed placement. In addition to gaining an applied understanding of the processes of global publishing, and informal publishing placements in London through the teaching year, candidates are encouraged to work directly with publishers in other countries to develop their market awareness as well as enhance their skills in business analysis.

The programme team also conducts research into publishing and supervises research students.

The MSc in Electronic Publishing offers a practical introduction to digital media, information management and

multi-media production. Please contact Dr Vesna Brujic-Okretic in the Department of Informatics: 020 7040 8551 or v.brujic-okretic@city.ac.uk.

6171

*EDINBURGH NAPIER UNIVERSITY, SCHOOL OF ARTS & CREATIVE INDUSTRIES
Craighouse Campus, Craighouse Road, Edinburgh EH10 5LG
Telephone: 0131 455 6133
Fax: 0131 455 6193
Email: de.allan@napier.ac.uk
Web Site: www.napier.ac.uk\sci

Personnel:
Avril Gray (*MSc Publishing full and part-time Programme Leader*)

BA and MSc Publishing. Higher education full and part-time qualifications.

6172

GERMAN TUITION – BARBARA CLASSEN
2 Blackall Street, London EC2A 4AD
Telephone: 020 7613 3177
Email: barbara@germantuition.com
Web Site: www.germantuition.com

Personnel:
Barbara Classen (*Director/Tutor*)
Nicole Nagel (*Co-Tutor*)
Itamar Groisman (*Co-Tutor*)
Eva Friedrich (*Co-Tutor*)
Marina de Quay (*Co-Tutor*)
Janka Troeber (*Co-Tutor*)

The company offers lively German tuition at all levels and specializes in German for the book trade. Students can choose between one-to-one tuition or small groups of 4–6. German Tuition also offers short-term tailor-made intensive courses.

Tutors are professional, experienced native speakers and offer free consultations with trial lesson. Students may work towards one of many recognized exams. Clients include publishers, booksellers, journalists and other professionals. Classes are held in the central London German Tuition office or in client's office/home 7 days a week.

German Tuition London has a small branch in Freiburg, Germany, offering tailor-made German language holidays and Business German courses for the book trade, usually over one week.

6173

*LONDON COLLEGE OF COMMUNICATION
Elephant & Castle, London SE1 6SB
Telephone: 020 7514 6569
Fax: 020 7514 2035
Email: info@lcc.arts.ac.uk
Web Site: www.lcc.arts.ac.uk

Personnel:
Sandra Kemp (*Head of College*)

Parent Company:
UK: University of the Arts, London

MA, BA Hons Publishing.

6174

MARKETABILITY (UK) LTD
12 Sandy Lane, Teddington, Middx TW11 0DR
Telephone: 020 8977 2741
Fax: 020 8977 2741
Email: rachel@marketability.info
Web Site: www.marketability.info

Personnel:
Rachel Maund (*Director*)

Marketability provides practical training to publishers, both through its small-group open workshop programme and through tailored in-house training. These flexible courses can be devised to cover a wide range of publishing issues. All tutors are actively working for publishers in the areas in which they are training. Our clients represent all areas of publishing, from large academic, STM and university presses, to small institutes, to large and small trade publish-

ers. We devise and deliver training programmes for publishers' associations internationally as well as in the UK. (See our client list in our other entry under section 6.5 of this directory for more details.)

The open course programme includes: academic marketing, e-marketing, email marketing, copywriting, SEO marketing, schools marketing, direct mail, marketing planning, marketing digital products, introduction to marketing in publishing, publicity, essential editorial skills, profitable commissioning and creative publishing for textbook markets. There are numerous in-house course options including market research, working with authors, grammar and proofreading.

Also provides marketing support and consultancy. See separate entry under 6.5 Sales and Marketing Services.

6175

OXFORD INTERNATIONAL CENTRE FOR PUBLISHING STUDIES
Oxford Brookes University, Buckley Building, Gipsy Lane, Headington, Oxford OX3 0BP
Telephone: 01865 484967
Fax: 01865 484082
Email: angus.phillips@brookes.ac.uk
Web Site: www.brookes.ac.uk/publishing

Personnel:
Angus Phillips (*Director*)

The Oxford International Centre for Publishing Studies is renowned for its degree programmes at both undergraduate and postgraduate level. It is also active in the areas of research, consultancy and professional development. It has excellent contacts throughout the industry and already works closely with industry organizations such as the Publishers Association, Independent Publishers Guild, and the London Book Fair.

Through organizations such as the Arts Council, British Council and UK Trade & Investment, it is well known for its work around the world.

Staff have published widely on the history and future of publishing. Its website has podcasts, the latest news about the Centre, and listings of job vacancies and work experience opportunities: www.brookes.ac.uk/publishing

6176

THE PUBLISHING TRAINING CENTRE AT BOOK HOUSE
45 East Hill, Wandsworth, London SW18 2QZ
Telephone: 020 8874 2718
Fax: 020 8870 8985
Email: publishing.training@bookhouse.co.uk
Web Site: www.train4publishing.co.uk

Personnel:
Peter McKay (*Chief Executive*)
Cassie Fox (*Course Administration Manager*)
Edelweiss Arnold (*Marketing Manager*)

The Publishing Training Centre was set up in 1979 as an educational charity for book and journal publishers.

It offers over 60 different courses, most of which are run several times a year. Courses are between one and five days long and cover a wide range of publishing and management skills.

Most courses are held at The Publishing Training Centre's London premises, though some are residential, and are based mainly in the Oxford area.

In addition, The Publishing Training Centre offers:
– in-company courses in the UK and overseas;
– distance learning courses in proofreading, editing, picture research, editorial project management and copywriting;
– consultancy service;
– training needs analysis;
– books.

The Publishing Training Centre is responsible for the development and updating of the industry-agreed standards for each job function specific to publishing.

6177

SOCIETY FOR EDITORS & PROOFREADERS
Erico House, 93–99 Upper Richmond Road, London SW15 2TG
Telephone: 020 8785 5617
Fax: 020 8785 5618
Email: admin@sfep.org.uk
Web Site: www.sfep.org.uk

Personnel:
Wendy Toole *(Chair)*
Justina Amenu *(Executive Secretary)*

Founded in 1988 with the twin aims of promoting high editorial standards and achieving recognition of its members' professional status, the Society works to disseminate information and training, foster good relations between members and their clients, and combat the isolation often experienced by freelances. It supports recognized standards of training and accreditation for editors and proofreaders, and is establishing recognized standards for its own members. Membership in 2011 was approximately 1500.

One of the major aims of the Society for Editors and Proofreaders is to help editorial freelances and staff to improve and update their skills. It is gradually building up a wide range of one-day courses, from 'Introduction to Proofreading' to 'Project Management' and 'On-Screen Editing', as well as more specialized courses. Most of its courses are run in London. About twice a year, two or three courses are run in Edinburgh, York and Bristol. Discounts are offered to members of the SFEP and to SI and NUJ members. Current details can be found on the SFEP website.

6178

STIRLING CENTRE FOR INTERNATIONAL PUBLISHING & COMMUNICATION
School of Arts and Humanities, Pathfoot Building, University of Stirling, Stirling FK9 4LA
Telephone: 01786 467510
Fax: 01786 466210
Email: alison.scott@stir.ac.uk
Web Site: www.publishing.stir.ac.uk

Personnel:
Prof Claire Squires *(Director)*
Dr Padmini Ray Murray *(Lecturer)*
Mrs Frances Sessford *(Teaching Fellow)*

The Stirling Centre for International Publishing and Communication at the University of Stirling was established in 1982, and has since developed a global reputation for its postgraduate degrees in publishing, its research activities, and its industry links. Focusing on book, magazine, journal and digital publishing, the Centre trains the publishers of the future, provides opportunities for those currently working in the industry to reflect on their professional practice and, through its research, critically analyses the past, present and future of publishing.

The Centre offers an Mlitt in Publishing Studies and an MSc in International Publishing Management (one year full time or two years part time), as well as an Mres in Publishing Studies and possibilities for research at PhD level.

7 Appendices

7.1 PUBLISHERS CLASSIFIED BY FIELDS OF ACTIVITY

The categories shown below are those in which the publishers listed have declared their interest. The list is intended to be neither exclusive nor comprehensive.

Packagers are shown in *italic* print.

ACADEMIC & SCHOLARLY

Acumen Publishing Ltd
Adam Matthew Digital Ltd
Alban Books Ltd
American Psychiatric Publishing Inc
Amolibros
Anglo-Saxon Books
Ann Arbor Publishers Ltd
Anshan Ltd
Anthem Press
Archetype Publications Ltd
Arena Books (Publishers)
Ashgate Publishing Ltd
Ashmolean Museum Publications
Association for Learning Technology
Association for Scottish Literary Studies
Audio-Forum – The Language Source
Aurora Metro Publications Ltd
Austin & Macauley Publishers Ltd
Authentic Media
Ruth Bean Publishers
Bedford Freeman Worth (BFW)
Berg Publishers
Berghahn Books
Joseph Biddulph Publisher
Biohealthcare Publishing (Oxford) Ltd
Black Ace Books
Blackstaff Press
Blue Ocean Publishing
Blueberry Press Ltd
BML
Bodleian Library Publishing
Borthwick Publications
Bowker (UK) Ltd
Boydell & Brewer Ltd
British Association for Adoption & Fostering
British Library
British Museum Press
CABI
Calypso Publications
Cambridge Archive Editions Ltd
Cambridge Publishing Management Ltd
Cambridge University Press
Capstone Global Library Ltd
Capuchin Classics
Carnegie Publishing Ltd
Jon Carpenter Publishing
Cengage Learning EMEA Ltd

Centre for Economic Policy Research
Centre for Policy on Ageing
Chalksoft Ltd
Channel View Publications Ltd
Chartered Institute of Personnel & Development
Christian Education
Church of Ireland Publishing
CILT, the National Centre for Languages
James Clarke & Co
Clear Answer Medical Publishing Ltd
Coachwise Ltd
Cois Life
Columba
Commonwealth Secretariat
The Continuum International Publishing Group Ltd
Cork University Press
Countyvise Ltd
Crossbow Education Ltd
Crown House Publishing Ltd
Dance Books Ltd
Darton, Longman & Todd Ltd
The Davenant Press
Richard Dennis Publications
Denor Press Ltd
J M Dent
Ditto International Ltd
Ashley Drake Publishing Ltd
Dunedin Academic Press
Earthscan
Edward Elgar Publishing Ltd
Elsevier Ltd
Emerald Group Publishing Ltd
Energy Institute
English Heritage
Equinox Publishing Ltd
The Erskine Press
Ethics International Press Ltd
Everyman's Library
Fabian Society
Facet Publishing
A. & A. Farmar
Filament Publishing Ltd
Five Leaves Publications
Floris Books Trust Ltd
Four Courts Press
Friends of the Earth
Geography Publications
The Geological Society
Gill & Macmillan
GLMP Ltd
Gracewing Publishing
Granta Editions
Greenleaf Publishing
Guildhall Press
Gwasg Gwenffrwd
John Harper Publishing Ltd
HarperCollins Publishers Ltd
Hart McLeod Ltd
Hart Publishing
Harvard University Press

Hawthorn Press
Roger Heavens
Helion & Co Ltd
Historical Publications Ltd
Hobnob Press
Hodder Education
Hodder Gibson
Holo Books
Human Kinetics Europe Ltd
C. Hurst & Co (Publishers) Ltd
Hymns Ancient & Modern Ltd
Hypatia Publications
Icon Books Ltd
Imperial College Press
Imprint Academic
Institute for Employment Studies
Institute of Acoustics
Institute of Education (Publications), University of London
Institute of Employment Rights
Institution of Engineering and Technology (IET)
Intellect Ltd
International Medical Press
International Network for the Availability of Scientific Publications (INASP)
Irish Academic Press
The Islamic Texts Society
Ithaca Press
IVP
IWA Publishing
James & James (Publishers) Ltd
Janus Publishing Co Ltd
Jarndyce Booksellers
Kew Publishing
Jessica Kingsley Publishers
Sean Kingston Publishing
Kogan Page Ltd
Kube Publishing Ltd
Peter Lang Ltd
Learning Matters Ltd
The Lilliput Press Ltd
The Littman Library of Jewish Civilization
Liverpool University Press
Living Time® Media International
Lund Humphries
The Lutterworth Press
McGraw-Hill Education
Macmillan Publishers Ltd
Manchester University Press
Maney Publishing
Melisende UK Ltd
Mentor Books
Mercier Press Ltd
The Merlin Press Ltd
Merton Priory Press Ltd
Microform Academic Publishers
The MIT Press Ltd
M&K Publishing
Myriad Editions
The National Academies Press
National Archives of Scotland

The National Association for the Teaching of English (NATE)
National Children's Bureau
National Gallery Co Ltd
National Housing Federation
National Portrait Gallery Publications
The National Trust
Natural History Museum Publishing
NHS Immunisation Information
NMS Enterprises Limited - Publishing
Northcote House Publishers Ltd
W. W. Norton & Company Ltd
Oak Tree Press
On Stream Publications Ltd
Onlywomen Press Ltd
Open Gate Press
Open University Worldwide
Optimus Professional Publishing
Orpen Press
Oxfam Publishing
Oxford University Press
Packard Publishing Ltd
Pagoda Tree Press
Palgrave Macmillan
Paragon Publishing
Paupers' Press
PCCS Books Ltd
Pearson Education
The Penguin Group (UK) Ltd
Phaidon Press Ltd
Pickering & Chatto (Publishers) Ltd
Pipers' Ash Ltd
Pluto Books Ltd
The Policy Press
Polity Press
Portland Press Ltd
PP Publishing
Princeton University Press
ProQuest
Rand Publications
Round Hall
Roundhouse Publishing Ltd
Joseph Rowntree Foundation
Royal Collection Publications
Royal College of General Practitioners
The Royal College of Psychiatrists
Royal Geographical Society
Royal Irish Academy
RSC Publishing
Russell House Publishing Ltd
Sage Publications Ltd
Saint Albert's Press
St Jerome Publishing Ltd
Sandstone Press Ltd
Saqi Books
Schott Music Ltd
Scion Publishing Ltd
Scottish Text Society
SEDA Publications
Shepheard-Walwyn (Publishers) Ltd
SHU Publications Ltd

Sigel Press
Slightly Foxed
SLS Legal Publications (NI)
Smith Settle Printing & Bookbinding Ltd
Colin Smythe Ltd
Social Affairs Unit
The Society for Promoting Christian Knowledge (SPCK)
The Society of Metaphysicians Ltd
Souvenir Press Ltd
Stacey International
Stainer & Bell Ltd
Stott's Correspondence College
Sussex Academic Press
Sussex Publications
The Swedenborg Society
Symposium Publications Literary & Art
I. B. Tauris & Co Ltd
Taylor & Francis
tfm publishing Ltd
Thames & Hudson Ltd
Trentham Books
Troubador Publishing Ltd
TSO (The Stationery Office Ltd)
UCAS
University College of Dublin Press
University of Exeter Press
University of Hertfordshire Press
University of Ottawa Press
University of Toronto Press
University of Wales Press
V&A Publishing
Vallentine Mitchell Publishers
Veritas Publications
Voltaire Foundation Ltd
Warburg Institute
Waterside Press
Paul Watkins Publishing
Whiting & Birch Ltd
Whittles Publishing
John Wiley & Sons Ltd
Philip Wilson Publishers
WIT Press
Wolters Kluwer Health (P & E) Ltd
World Microfilms
Yale University Press London
Zed Books Ltd

ACCOUNTANCY & TAXATION

Austin & Macauley Publishers Ltd
Cengage Learning EMEA Ltd
The Chartered Institute of Public Finance & Accountancy
Emerald Group Publishing Ltd
Filament Publishing Ltd
W. Foulsham & Co Ltd
Gower Publishing Co Ltd
Granta Editions
Harriman House
Hodder Education
In Easy Steps Ltd
Jordan Publishing Ltd
Kogan Page Ltd

McGraw-Hill Education
Nelson Thornes Ltd
Oak Tree Press
Orpen Press
Palgrave Macmillan
PP Publishing
ProQuest
Round Hall
Sigel Press
Thorogood Publishing Ltd
Trog Associates Ltd
Troubador Publishing Ltd
TSO (The Stationery Office Ltd)
Which? Ltd
John Wiley & Sons Ltd

AGRICULTURE

Austin & Macauley Publishers Ltd
Blackstaff Press
CABI
Clairview Books Ltd
Commonwealth Secretariat
The Crowood Press Ltd
Earthscan
Eco-logic Books
Edward Elgar Publishing Ltd
Food Trade Press Ltd
Granta Editions
Manson Publishing Ltd
The National Academies Press
The National Trust
Oxfam Publishing
Packard Publishing Ltd
ProQuest
Smith Settle Printing &
    Bookbinding Ltd
John Wiley & Sons Ltd

ANIMAL CARE & BREEDING

J. A. Allen
Amber Books Ltd
Anova Books
Austin & Macauley Publishers Ltd
CABI
Calypso Publications
Capall Bann Publishing
Carroll & Brown Ltd
Chalksoft Ltd
Collins & Brown
The Crowood Press Ltd
D & N Publishing
The Davenant Press
Findhorn Press Ltd
Robert Hale Ltd
HarperCollins Publishers Ltd
Haynes Publishing
Hodder Education
How To Books Ltd
Manson Publishing Ltd
The National Academies Press
Octopus Publishing Group
Quantum Publishing
Quiller Publishing Ltd
Regency House Publishing Ltd
Roundhouse Publishing Ltd
Souvenir Press Ltd
Toucan Books Ltd
Veloce Publishing Ltd
Whittet Books Ltd
John Wiley & Sons Ltd

ANTIQUES & COLLECTING

Antique Collectors' Club Ltd
Austin & Macauley Publishers Ltd
Ruth Bean Publishers
Bene Factum Publishing Ltd
BLA Publishing Ltd
Bodleian Library Publishing
British Museum Press
Cameron Books
Carlton Publishing Group
Caxton Publishing Group Ltd
The Crowood Press Ltd
D & N Publishing
Richard Dennis Publications
W. Foulsham & Co Ltd
Granta Editions
Robert Hale Ltd
HarperCollins Publishers Ltd

Hodder Education
The Horizon Press
How To Books Ltd
Lund Humphries
The Lutterworth Press
Melisende UK Ltd
Merrell Publishers Ltd
Milestone Publications
Miller's
Mitchell Beazley
The National Trust
NMS Enterprises Limited -
    Publishing
Octopus Publishing Group
The Orion Publishing Group Ltd
The Penguin Group (UK) Ltd
Prestel Publishing Ltd
Quantum Publishing
Quiller Publishing Ltd
Royal Collection Publications
Scala Publishers Ltd
Shire Publications Ltd
Souvenir Press Ltd
Thames & Hudson Ltd
Third Millennium Publishing Ltd
Unicorn Press
V&A Publishing
Philip Wilson Publishers

ARCHAEOLOGY

Archaeopress Ltd
Archetype Publications Ltd
Ashmolean Museum Publications
Batsford
Blackstaff Press
Borthwick Publications
Boydell & Brewer Ltd
British Museum Press
Brown & Whittaker Publishing
*Cambridge Publishing
    Management Ltd*
Cambridge University Press
Capall Bann Publishing
Capuchin Classics
Carnegie Publishing Ltd
Colour Heroes Ltd
Cork University Press
Cornwall Editions Ltd
Council for British Archaeology
The Davenant Press
The Dovecote Press
Emerald Group Publishing Ltd
English Heritage
Equinox Publishing Ltd
Ex Libris Press
Four Courts Press
Geography Publications
Granta Editions
Halsgrove
Heart of Albion Press
Hobnob Press
Hodder Education
Holo Books
The King's England Press
Logaston Press
Maney Publishing
Melisende UK Ltd
Mercury Books
Merton Priory Press Ltd
Mitchell Beazley
The National Trust
NMS Enterprises Limited -
    Publishing
North York Moors National Park
    Authority
The Orion Publishing Group Ltd
The Penguin Group (UK) Ltd
Prestel Publishing Ltd
Reardon Publishing
Roundhouse Publishing Ltd
Royal Irish Academy
Scottish Children's Press
Scottish Cultural Press
Shire Publications Ltd
Smith Settle Printing &
    Bookbinding Ltd
Souvenir Press Ltd
Stacey International
Stobart Davies Ltd
Sussex Academic Press
I. B. Tauris & Co Ltd

Taylor & Francis
Thames & Hudson Ltd
Twelveheads Press
Tyne Bridge Publishing
University of Exeter Press
University of Wales Press
Warburg Institute
John Wiley & Sons Ltd
WIT Press
Yale University Press London

ARCHITECTURE & DESIGN

Anova Books
Antique Collectors' Club Ltd
Architectural Association
    Publications
Ashgate Publishing Ltd
Aurum Press
AVA Publishing (UK) Ltd
Batsford
Berg Publishers
Joseph Biddulph Publisher
Black Dog Publishing Ltd
A. & C. Black (Publishers) Ltd
Bodleian Library Publishing
Boydell & Brewer Ltd
*Cambridge Publishing
    Management Ltd*
Cambridge University Press
Cameron Books
Carlton Publishing Group
Caxton Publishing Group Ltd
Centre for Alternative Technology
    Publications
Compendium Publishing Ltd
Conran Octopus
Cork University Press
Countryside Books
Richard Dennis Publications
Eric Dobby Publishing Ltd
Donhead Publishing Ltd
Gerald Duckworth & Co Ltd
Earthscan
Eco-logic Books
English Heritage
Fiell Publishing Ltd
Garnet Publishing Ltd
Gower Publishing Co Ltd
Gracewing Publishing
Graffeg
*Graham-Cameron Publishing &
    Illustration*
Granta Editions
Green Books
HarperCollins Publishers Ltd
Haynes Publishing
Hayward Publishing
The Herbert Press
Historical Publications Ltd
IHS BRE Press
Intellect Ltd
Laurence King Publishing Ltd
Dewi Lewis Publishing
Liberties Press
The Lilliput Press Ltd
Liverpool University Press
Logaston Press
Lund Humphries
The Lutterworth Press
McGraw-Hill Education
Macmillan Publishers Ltd
Manchester University Press
Maney Publishing
Melisende UK Ltd
Merrell Publishers Ltd
The MIT Press Ltd
Mitchell Beazley
The National Trust
NMS Enterprises Limited -
    Publishing
W. W. Norton & Company Ltd
The O'Brien Press Ltd
Octopus Publishing Group
Packard Publishing Ltd
Palazzo Editions Ltd
Papadakis Publisher
Paragon Publishing
Phaidon Press Ltd
Prestel Publishing Ltd
ProQuest
Quadrille Publishing Ltd

Quantum Publishing
Random House UK Ltd
Redcliffe Press Ltd
Regency House Publishing Ltd
RotoVision SA
Roundhouse Publishing Ltd
Joseph Rowntree Foundation
Royal Collection Publications
Sansom & Co Ltd
Saqi Books
Scala Publishers Ltd
Sheldrake Press
Shire Publications Ltd
Stacey International
I. B. Tauris & Co Ltd
Taylor & Francis
teNeues Publishing UK Ltd
Thames & Hudson Ltd
Toucan Books Ltd
Unicorn Press
V&A Publishing
Warburg Institute
Paul Watkins Publishing
David West Children's Books
John Wiley & Sons Ltd
Philip Wilson Publishers
WIT Press
World Microfilms
Worth Press Ltd
Yale University Press London

ATLASES & MAPS

AA Publishing
Ian Allan Publishing Ltd
Amber Books Ltd
Anthem Press
The Belmont Press
British Geological Survey
Carel Press Ltd
Caxton Publishing Group Ltd
Collins Geo
Cork University Press
G. L. Crowther
Discovery Walking Guides Ltd
Earthscan
Encyclopaedia Britannica (UK) Ltd
The Geographical Association
Geography Publications
Alan Godfrey Maps
Granta Editions
HarperCollins Publishers Ltd
Harvey Map Services Ltd
Haynes Publishing
Hodder Education
The Ilex Press Ltd
Instant-Books UK Ltd
Macmillan Education
Maney Publishing
Mercury Books
Michelin Maps & Guides
Moonlight Publishing Ltd
Myriad Editions
New Internationalist Publications
    Ltd
Octopus Publishing Group
Pagoda Tree Press
The Penguin Group (UK) Ltd
Philip's
Quantum Publishing
Reardon Publishing
Roundhouse Publishing Ltd
Royal Irish Academy
Tarquin Publications
Toucan Books Ltd
Waverley Books
John Wiley & Sons Ltd

AUDIO BOOKS

Ashgrove Publishing
AudioGO Ltd
Austin & Macauley Publishers Ltd
Barefoot Books
Beautiful Books Ltd
John Blake Publishing Ltd
Bloomsbury Publishing Plc
Canongate Books
Cló Iar-Chonnachta
Cois Life
CSA Word
Day One Publications

Dref Wen Cyf/Ltd
Filament Publishing Ltd
Gatehouse Media Ltd
GLMP Ltd
Hachette Children's Books
HarperCollins Publishers Ltd
Hodder Education
Hodder & Stoughton General
ISIS Publishing Ltd
Kube Publishing Ltd
Little, Brown Book Group
Little People Books
Macmillan Children's Books Ltd
Macmillan Publishers Ltd
Magna Large Print Books
Naxos Audiobooks
The Orion Publishing Group Ltd
The Penguin Group (UK) Ltd
Ransom Publishing Ltd
Reardon Publishing
Scottish Cultural Press
Sigel Press
Simon & Schuster (UK) Ltd
Rudolf Steiner Press Ltd
Summersdale Publishers Ltd
Sussex Publications
Thorogood Publishing Ltd
Topical Resources
Transworld Publishers Ltd

AVIATION

A. M. S. Educational Ltd
Air-Britain (Historians) Ltd
Ian Allan Publishing Ltd
Amber Books Ltd
Ashgate Publishing Ltd
Bene Factum Publishing Ltd
BLA Publishing Ltd
Bridge Books
Brooklands Books Ltd
Caxton Publishing Group Ltd
Countryside Books
Crécy Publishing Ltd
The Crowood Press Ltd
D & N Publishing
Energy Institute
Granta Editions
Greenhill Books / Lionel Leventhal
    Ltd
Grub Street
Halsgrove
Haynes Publishing
Hodder Education
The Horizon Press
Icon Books Ltd
IHS Jane's
McGraw-Hill Education
The Nostalgia Collection
Osprey Publishing Ltd
Pipers' Ash Ltd
Quantum Publishing
Regency House Publishing Ltd
Special Interest Model Books Ltd
Stenlake Publishing Ltd
Truran
TSO (The Stationery Office Ltd)
John Wiley & Sons Ltd
Worth Press Ltd

BIBLIOGRAPHY & LIBRARY
SCIENCE

Ashgate Publishing Ltd
Austin & Macauley Publishers Ltd
Bowker (UK) Ltd
British Library
James Clarke & Co
The Continuum International
    Publishing Group Ltd
Facet Publishing
Galactic Central Publications
Gwasg Gwenffrwd
Hypatia Publications
International Network for the
    Availability of Scientific
    Publications (INASP)
Jarndyce Booksellers
LISU
Maney Publishing
The MIT Press Ltd
Nielsen

ProQuest
Sage Publications Ltd
Sussex Academic Press
Voltaire Foundation Ltd
Warburg Institute
Woodhead Publishing Ltd

BIOGRAPHY & AUTOBIOGRAPHY

A. M. S. Educational Ltd
Accent Press Ltd
Acumen Publishing Ltd
Allison & Busby
Alma Books Ltd
Amolibros
Anshan Ltd
Arcadia Books Ltd
Ashgrove Publishing
Atlantic Books
Attic Press
Aureus Publishing Ltd
Aurum Press
Austin & Macauley Publishers Ltd
Authentic Media
Authorhouse UK Ltd
Barny Books
Beautiful Books Ltd
Bene Factum Publishing Ltd
Berghahn Books
Black Ace Books
Black Spring Press Ltd
Blackstaff Press
John Blake Publishing Ltd
Bloomsbury Publishing Plc
Bodleian Library Publishing
Book Castle Publishing Ltd
Marion Boyars Publishers Ltd
Nicholas Brealey Publishing
Brewin Books Ltd
British Library
Brown & Whittaker Publishing
Cambridge Publishing Management Ltd
Camra Books
Canongate Books
Capuchin Classics
Carlton Publishing Group
The Catholic Truth Society
Christian Focus Publications
James Clarke & Co
Cló Iar-Chonnachta
Colourpoint Books
Constable & Robinson Ltd
The Continuum International Publishing Group Ltd
David C. Cook (UK)
Cork University Press
Countyvise Ltd
Crimson Publishing
Cualann Press
Darton, Longman & Todd Ltd
The Davenant Press
Day One Publications
Dedalus Ltd
Richard Dennis Publications
Denor Press Ltd
J M Dent
The Derby Books Publishing Co Ltd
The Dovecote Press
Ashley Drake Publishing Ltd
Gerald Duckworth & Co Ltd
Elliott & Thompson
Equinox Publishing Ltd
The Erskine Press
Essential Works Ltd
Ex Libris Press
Faber & Faber Ltd
Family Publications
Fastprint
Filament Publishing Ltd
Flambard Press
Geography Publications
Gibson Square
Gill & Macmillan
Gomer
Gothic Image Publications
Gracewing Publishing
Granta Books
Granta Editions
Green Books

Guildhall Press
Gwasg Gwenffrwd
Gwasg Gwynedd
Hachette Scotland
Halban Publishers
Robert Hale Ltd
Halsgrove
HarperCollins Publishers Ltd
Harvard University Press
Haynes Publishing
Highland Books
Hodder Faith
Hodder & Stoughton General
Alison Hodge Publishers
Holo Books
Honno (Welsh Women's Press)
Hymns Ancient & Modern Ltd
Hypatia Publications
Icon Books Ltd
Independent Music Press
Indepenpress Publishing Ltd
Irish Academic Press
ISIS Publishing Ltd
IVP
Janus Publishing Co Ltd
The Lilliput Press Ltd
Lion Hudson Plc
Little, Brown Book Group
The Littman Library of Jewish Civilization
Living Time® Media International
Londubh Books
Luath Press Ltd
The Lutterworth Press
Macmillan Publishers Ltd
Mainstream Publishing Co (Edinburgh) Ltd
Maney Publishing
Maverick House Publishers
Mentor Books
Mercier Press Ltd
The Merlin Press Ltd
Merlin Publishing/Wolfhound Press
Merton Priory Press Ltd
Microform Academic Publishers
The MIT Press Ltd
Motor Racing Publications Ltd
Murdoch Books UK Ltd
John Murray Publishers
National Portrait Gallery Publications
The National Trust
Natural History Museum Publishing
New Island Books Ltd
NMS Enterprises Limited - Publishing
Northumbria University Press
The O'Brien Press Ltd
The Oleander Press
Omnibus Press
On Stream Publications Ltd
Onlywomen Press Ltd
Orion Books Ltd
The Orion Publishing Group Ltd
Peter Owen Publishers
Pan Macmillan
Paragon Publishing
The Penguin Group (UK) Ltd
Piatkus Books
Pipers' Ash Ltd
Plowright Press
Polperro Heritage Press
Portobello Books Ltd
Profile Books
Quadrille Publishing Ltd
Quartet Books
Quiller Publishing Ltd
The Radcliffe Press
Roundhouse Publishing Ltd
Route Publishing Ltd
Royal Collection Publications
Sandstone Press Ltd
Saqi Books
Scottish Children's Press
Scottish Cultural Press
Seren
Shepheard-Walwyn (Publishers) Ltd
The Shetland Times Ltd
Shire Publications Ltd

Short Books Ltd
Simon & Schuster (UK) Ltd
Slightly Foxed
Smith Settle Printing & Bookbinding Ltd
Colin Smythe Ltd
Souvenir Press Ltd
Stacey International
Stainer & Bell Ltd
Rudolf Steiner Press Ltd
Strong Oak Press
Summersdale Publishers Ltd
Sussex Academic Press
Tabb House
I. B. Tauris & Co Ltd
Thames & Hudson Ltd
Thorogood Publishing Ltd
F. A. Thorpe Publishing
Thoth Publications
Transworld Publishers Ltd
Troubador Publishing Ltd
Truran
Tyne Bridge Publishing
Unicorn Press
United Writers Publications Ltd
University of Wales Press
Merlin Unwin Books Ltd
V&A Publishing
Vallentine Mitchell Publishers
Veloce Publishing Ltd
Veritas Publications
Vertical Editions
Voltaire Foundation Ltd
Warburg Institute
Waterside Press
Weidenfeld & Nicolson
Whittles Publishing
John Wiley & Sons Ltd
Neil Wilson Publishing Ltd
Windhorse Publications
The Women's Press
Y Lolfa Cyf
Yale University Press London
Zymurgy Publishing

BIOLOGY & ZOOLOGY

Amolibros
Austin & Macauley Publishers Ltd
Bedford Freeman Worth (BFW)
Bender Richardson White
BLA Publishing Ltd
Brown & Whittaker Publishing
CABI
Calypso Publications
Cambridge University Press
Cengage Learning EMEA Ltd
Clear Answer Medical Publishing Ltd
D & N Publishing
Earthscan
GLMP Ltd
HarperCollins Publishers Ltd
Harvard University Press
Hodder Education
Imperial College Press
Jones & Bartlett International
Kew Publishing
McGraw-Hill Education
Macmillan Education
Macmillan Publishers Ltd
Manson Publishing Ltd
Mentor Books
The MIT Press Ltd
The National Academies Press
Natural History Museum Publishing
Nelson Thornes Ltd
NMS Enterprises Limited - Publishing
North York Moors National Park Authority
W. W. Norton & Company Ltd
Open University Worldwide
Oxford University Press
Packard Publishing Ltd
Palgrave Macmillan
Portland Press Ltd
Princeton University Press
ProQuest
Royal Irish Academy
Scion Publishing Ltd

Taylor & Francis
Ward Lock Educational Co Ltd
Whittet Books Ltd
John Wiley & Sons Ltd
WIT Press

CHEMISTRY

Amolibros
Anshan Ltd
Anthem Press
Atlantic Europe Publishing Co Ltd
Bedford Freeman Worth (BFW)
Biohealthcare Publishing (Oxford) Ltd
BLA Publishing Ltd
Cambridge University Press
Cengage Learning EMEA Ltd
Elsevier Ltd
Energy Institute
Food Trade Press Ltd
GLMP Ltd
HarperCollins Publishers Ltd
Hodder Education
Icon Books Ltd
Imperial College Press
Jones & Bartlett International
McGraw-Hill Education
Macmillan Education
Macmillan Publishers Ltd
The National Academies Press
Nelson Thornes Ltd
W. W. Norton & Company Ltd
Open University Worldwide
Palgrave Macmillan
RSC Publishing
Scion Publishing Ltd
Taylor & Francis
Ward Lock Educational Co Ltd
John Wiley & Sons Ltd

CHILDREN'S BOOKS

A. M. S. Educational Ltd
Acair Ltd
Accent Press Ltd
Alban Books Ltd
Albion Press Ltd
Allison & Busby
Amber Books Ltd
Amolibros
Andersen Press Ltd
Anno Domini Publishing (ADPS)
Anova Books
Antique Collectors' Club Ltd
Archive Publishing
Atlantic Europe Publishing Co Ltd
Aurora Metro Publications Ltd
Austin & Macauley Publishers Ltd
Authentic Media
Authorhouse UK Ltd
Award Publications Ltd
b small publishing ltd
Badger Publishing Ltd
Barefoot Books
Barny Books
Nicola Baxter Ltd
The Belmont Press
Bender Richardson White
Bene Factum Publishing Ltd
Bible Reading Fellowship
BLA Publishing Ltd
A. & C. Black (Publishers) Ltd
Bloomsbury Publishing Plc
Blue Ocean Publishing
Bodleian Library Publishing
Marion Boyars Publishers Ltd
British Association for Adoption & Fostering
British Museum Press
Brown Dog Books
Brown Wells & Jacobs Ltd
Capuchin Classics
Carlton Publishing Group
The Catholic Truth Society
Caxton Publishing Group Ltd
Chalksoft Ltd
Chicken House Publishing Ltd
Child's Play (International) Ltd
Christian Education
Christian Focus Publications
Church of Ireland Publishing

Cló Iar-Chonnachta
Coachwise Ltd
Cois Life
Cornwall Editions Ltd
Countyvise Ltd
Cowley Robinson Publishing Ltd
CRW Publishing Ltd
Cyhoeddiadau'r Gair
Day One Publications
Delancey Press Ltd
J M Dent
Diagram Visual Information Ltd
Ashley Drake Publishing Ltd
Dramatic Lines
Dref Wen Cyf/Ltd
Gerald Duckworth & Co Ltd
Eddison Sadd Editions Ltd
Egmont UK Ltd
Encyclopaedia Britannica (UK) Ltd
Evans Publishing Group
Everyman's Library
Faber & Faber Ltd
Five Leaves Publications
Floris Books Trust Ltd
Galore Park Publishing Ltd
Glowworm Books & Gifts Ltd
Gomer
Graham-Cameron Publishing & Illustration
W. F. Graham (Northampton) Ltd
Guildhall Press
Gwasg Gwenffrwd
Gwasg Gwynedd
Hachette Children's Books
Peter Haddock Publishing
Haldane Mason Ltd
HarperCollins Publishers Ltd
Hawthorn Press
Haynes Publishing
Highland Books
Holland Publishing Plc
John Hunt Publishing Ltd
Icon Books Ltd
Indepenpress Publishing Ltd
Janus Publishing Co Ltd
Kew Publishing
The King's England Press
Jessica Kingsley Publishers
Kube Publishing Ltd
Letterland International Ltd
Lexus Ltd
Lion Hudson Plc
Little People Books
Little Tiger Press
Living Time® Media International
Lomond Books Ltd
Luath Press Ltd
The Lutterworth Press
McCrimmon Publishing Co Ltd
Macmillan Children's Books Ltd
Macmillan Education
Macmillan Publishers Ltd
Mandrake of Oxford
Meadowside Children's Books & Gullane Children's Books
Medikidz Ltd
Mercier Press Ltd
Mercury Junior
Moonlight Publishing Ltd
mPowr Ltd
MW Educational
The National Autistic Society (NAS)
National Gallery Co Ltd
The National Trust
Natural History Museum Publishing
Nelson Thornes Ltd
New Caramel London Ltd
New Island Books Ltd
NMS Enterprises Limited - Publishing
North York Moors National Park Authority
The O'Brien Press Ltd
Onlywomen Press Ltd
Orion Books Ltd
The Orion Publishing Group Ltd
Orpheus Books Ltd
Oxford University Press
Palazzo Editions Ltd
Pan Macmillan

Paragon Publishing
The Penguin Group (UK) Ltd
Phaidon Press Ltd
Piccadilly Press
Pipers' Ash Ltd
Positive Press Ltd
Prestel Publishing Ltd
Prospera Publishing
Quantum Publishing
Random House Children's Books
Random House UK Ltd
Ransom Publishing Ltd
Raven's Quill Ltd
Ravette Publishing Ltd
Reader's Digest Children's Publishing Ltd
Reardon Publishing
Regency House Publishing Ltd
Ripley Publishing Ltd
Rising Stars UK Ltd
Robinswood Press Ltd
Roundhouse Publishing Ltd
Scala Publishers Ltd
Scholastic UK Ltd
Scottish Children's Press
Scripture Union Publishing
Seasquirt Publications
Sharon House Publishing
Sheldrake Press
Short Books Ltd
Sigel Press
Simon & Schuster (UK) Ltd
Slightly Foxed
Smallfish Books
Solidus
Stacey International
Symposium Publications Literary & Art
Ta Ha Publishers Ltd
Tabb House
Tangerine Designs Ltd
Tango Books Ltd
Tarquin Publications
Tate Publishing
Templar Publishing
Thames & Hudson Ltd
Top That! Publishing Plc
Topical Resources
Toucan Books Ltd
Troubador Publishing Ltd
TTS Group
Tucker Slingsby Ltd
United Writers Publications Ltd
Usborne Publishing Ltd
V&A Publishing
Veritas Publications
Waverley Books
David West Children's Books
Wordsworth Editions Ltd
Y Lolfa Cyf
Zymurgy Publishing

CINEMA, VIDEO, TV & RADIO

Anova Books
Aurora Metro Publications Ltd
Aurum Press
Austin & Macauley Publishers Ltd
AVA Publishing (UK) Ltd
Beautiful Books Ltd
Berg Publishers
Berghahn Books
Black Dog Publishing Ltd
Black Spring Press Ltd
Blackstaff Press
Bloomsbury Publishing Plc
Marion Boyars Publishers Ltd
Canongate Books
Carlton Publishing Group
The Continuum International Publishing Group Ltd
Cork University Press
Gerald Duckworth & Co Ltd
Essential Works Ltd
Faber & Faber Ltd
Gibson Square
Robert Hale Ltd
HarperCollins Publishers Ltd
Harvard University Press
Nick Hern Books
Hodder Education
Hodder & Stoughton General

Intellect Ltd
Living Time® Media International
Luath Press Ltd
Macmillan Publishers Ltd
Mainstream Publishing Co (Edinburgh) Ltd
Manchester University Press
Mentor Books
Merlin Publishing/Wolfhound Press
Merrell Publishers Ltd
W. W. Norton & Company Ltd
The Orion Publishing Group Ltd
Peter Owen Publishers
Palazzo Editions Ltd
Pan Macmillan
The Penguin Group (UK) Ltd
Phaidon Press Ltd
Pluto Books Ltd
Polity Press
ProQuest
Reardon Publishing
RotoVision SA
Roundhouse Publishing Ltd
Route Publishing Ltd
Simon & Schuster (UK) Ltd
Charles Skilton Ltd
Sussex Publications
I. B. Tauris & Co Ltd
Telos Publishing Ltd
Transworld Publishers Ltd
United Writers Publications Ltd
University of Exeter Press
University of Ottawa Press
University of Toronto Press
Vertical Editions
David West Children's Books
World Microfilms

COMPUTER SCIENCE

Anshan Ltd
Austin & Macauley Publishers Ltd
Bernard Babani (Publishing) Ltd
BLA Publishing Ltd
Cambridge University Press
Emerald Group Publishing Ltd
Haynes Publishing
Hodder Education
The Ilex Press Ltd
Imperial College Press
In Easy Steps Ltd
Institution of Engineering and Technology (IET)
Intellect Ltd
IOP Publishing
Jones & Bartlett International
McGraw-Hill Education
Macmillan Publishers Ltd
Market House Books Ltd
The MIT Press Ltd
Nelson Thornes Ltd
W. W. Norton & Company Ltd
Open University Worldwide
O'Reilly UK Ltd
Palgrave Macmillan
Paragon Publishing
ProQuest
TSO (The Stationery Office Ltd)
Usborne Publishing Ltd
Which? Ltd
John Wiley & Sons Ltd
WIT Press

COOKERY, WINES & SPIRITS

Accent Press Ltd
Amolibros
Anova Books
Antique Collectors' Club Ltd
Appletree Press Ltd
Ashgrove Publishing
Attic Press
Aurora Metro Publications Ltd
Aurum Press
Austin & Macauley Publishers Ltd
Authorhouse UK Ltd
Barny Books
Bene Factum Publishing Ltd
Blackstaff Press
John Blake Publishing Ltd
Bloomsbury Publishing Plc

Blue Ocean Publishing
Bossiney Books Ltd
Brown Dog Books
Brown & Whittaker Publishing
Cambridge Publishing Management Ltd
Camra Books
Capall Bann Publishing
Capuchin Classics
Carlton Publishing Group
Carnegie Publishing Ltd
Jon Carpenter Publishing
Carroll & Brown Ltd
Caxton Publishing Group Ltd
Clairview Books Ltd
Collins & Brown
Conran Octopus
Copper Beech Publishing Ltd
Cork University Press
Dedalus Ltd
Ashley Drake Publishing Ltd
Eddison Sadd Editions Ltd
Elliott & Thompson
Equinox Publishing Ltd
Ex Libris Press
F+W Media International, LTD (formerly David & Charles)
Faber & Faber Ltd
Findhorn Press Ltd
W. Foulsham & Co Ltd
Garnet Publishing Ltd
Gill & Macmillan
The Good Food Guide
Graffeg
Granta Editions
Green Books
Grub Street
Hachette Scotland
Haldane Mason Ltd
HarperCollins Publishers Ltd
Haynes Publishing
Ian Henry Publications Ltd
Hodder Education
Hodder & Stoughton General
Alison Hodge Publishers
How To Books Ltd
Indepenpress Publishing Ltd
Kyle Books
Liberties Press
Lomond Books Ltd
Luath Press Ltd
Macmillan Publishers Ltd
Mainstream Publishing Co (Edinburgh) Ltd
Mercier Press Ltd
Merlin Publishing/Wolfhound Press
Merrell Publishers Ltd
Mitchell Beazley
Murdoch Books UK Co Ltd
National Gallery Co Ltd
The National Trust
Need2Know
New Internationalist Publications Ltd
NMS Enterprises Limited - Publishing
Northumbria University Press
W. W. Norton & Company Ltd
The O'Brien Press Ltd
Octopus Publishing Group
On Stream Publications Ltd
The Orion Publishing Group Ltd
Paragon Publishing
The Penguin Group (UK) Ltd
Phaidon Press Ltd
Piatkus Books
Prospect Books
Quadrille Publishing Ltd
Quantum Publishing
Quiller Publishing Ltd
Random House UK Ltd
Roundhouse Publishing Ltd
Saqi Books
Scottish Children's Press
Scottish Cultural Press
Sheldrake Press
Sigma Press
Simon & Schuster (UK) Ltd
Charles Skilton Ltd
Special Interest Model Books Ltd
Stacey International

Stobart Davies Ltd
Summersdale Publishers Ltd
Toucan Books Ltd
Transworld Publishers Ltd
Troubador Publishing Ltd
Truran
Merlin Unwin Books Ltd
Waverley Books
John Wiley & Sons Ltd
Neil Wilson Publishing Ltd
Y Lolfa Cyf

CRAFTS & HOBBIES

Accent Press Ltd
Amber Books Ltd
Anova Books
Aurum Press
b small publishing ltd
Bernard Babani (Publishing) Ltd
Batsford
Ruth Bean Publishers
Black Dog Publishing Ltd
A. & C. Black (Publishers) Ltd
Blue Ocean Publishing
Brown Wells & Jacobs Ltd
Calypso Publications
Cambridge Publishing Management Ltd
Capall Bann Publishing
Carlton Publishing Group
Caxton Publishing Group Ltd
Collins & Brown
Conran Octopus
Crimson Publishing
The Crowood Press Ltd
D & N Publishing
Eco-logic Books
F+W Media International, LTD (formerly David & Charles)
Filament Publishing Ltd
Floris Books Trust Ltd
W. Foulsham & Co Ltd
Stanley Gibbons
Haldane Mason Ltd
Robert Hale Ltd
HarperCollins Publishers Ltd
Hawthorn Press
Haynes Publishing
Hodder Education
The Ilex Press Ltd
In Easy Steps Ltd
Indepenpress Publishing Ltd
Instant-Books UK Ltd
The Ivy Press Ltd
Kyle Books
Lomond Books Ltd
The Lutterworth Press
Macmillan Publishers Ltd
Melisende UK Ltd
Mercier Press Ltd
Merlin Publishing/Wolfhound Press
Merrell Publishers Ltd
Mitchell Beazley
Murdoch Books UK Ltd
The Nostalgia Collection
Octopus Publishing Group
The Orion Publishing Group Ltd
The Penguin Group (UK) Ltd
Quadrille Publishing Ltd
Quantum Publishing
Quiller Publishing Ltd
Random House UK Ltd
Regency House Publishing Ltd
Roundhouse Publishing Ltd
Sigma Press
Souvenir Press Ltd
Special Interest Model Books Ltd
Stenlake Publishing Ltd
Stobart Davies Ltd
Stott's Correspondence College
Summersdale Publishers Ltd
Tarquin Publications
Thames & Hudson Ltd
Top That! Publishing Plc
Toucan Books Ltd
Tucker Slingsby Ltd
Unicorn Press
Usborne Publishing Ltd
V&A Publishing
David West Children's Books

John Wiley & Sons Ltd
Willow Island Editions
Y Lolfa Cyf

CRIME

Accent Press Ltd
Allison & Busby
Alma Books Ltd
Amber Books Ltd
Arcadia Books Ltd
Atlantic Books
Austin & Macauley Publishers Ltd
Authorhouse UK Ltd
Bitter Lemon Press
Blackstaff Press
John Blake Publishing Ltd
Canongate Books
Carlton Publishing Group
Caxton Publishing Group Ltd
CBD Research Ltd
Countyvise Ltd
Eric Dobby Publishing Ltd
Gerald Duckworth & Co Ltd
The Erskine Press
Five Leaves Publications
Flambard Press
Gibson Square
Guildhall Press
Hachette Scotland
Robert Hale Ltd
HarperCollins Publishers Ltd
Haynes Publishing
Hodder & Stoughton General
Honno (Welsh Women's Press)
Icon Books Ltd
Indepenpress Publishing Ltd
ISIS Publishing Ltd
Janus Publishing Co Ltd
Jordan Publishing Ltd
Librario Publishers Ltd
Little, Brown Book Group
Living Time® Media International
Luath Press Ltd
Macmillan Publishers Ltd
Mainstream Publishing Co (Edinburgh) Ltd
Mandrake of Oxford
Maverick House Publishers
Mentor Books
Mercier Press Ltd
Merlin Publishing/Wolfhound Press
Onlywomen Press Ltd
The Orion Publishing Group Ltd
Paragon Publishing
The Penguin Group (UK) Ltd
Piatkus Books
Profile Books
Quantum Publishing
Random House UK Ltd
Sandstone Press Ltd
Simon & Schuster (UK) Ltd
Social Affairs Unit
Summersdale Publishers Ltd
Telos Publishing Ltd
F. A. Thorpe Publishing
Transworld Publishers Ltd
Troubador Publishing Ltd
Truran
Waterside Press
Neil Wilson Publishing Ltd
The Women's Press
Worth Press Ltd

DO-IT-YOURSELF

Anova Books
Austin & Macauley Publishers Ltd
Caxton Publishing Group Ltd
Centre for Alternative Technology Publications
Collins & Brown
The Crowood Press Ltd
D & N Publishing
W. Foulsham & Co Ltd
Granta Editions
Green Books
HarperCollins Publishers Ltd
Haynes Publishing
Hodder Education
How To Books Ltd

Indepenpress Publishing Ltd
Janus Publishing Co Ltd
Murdoch Books UK Ltd
Octopus Publishing Group
The Penguin Group (UK) Ltd
Quadrille Publishing Ltd
Quantum Publishing
Random House UK Ltd
Stobart Davies Ltd
John Wiley & Sons Ltd

ECONOMICS

Anthem Press
Arena Books (Publishers)
Ashgate Publishing Ltd
Atlantic Books
Austin & Macauley Publishers Ltd
Berghahn Books
Nicholas Brealey Publishing
Cambridge Publishing
  Management Ltd
Cambridge University Press
Jon Carpenter Publishing
Cengage Learning EMEA Ltd
Centre for Economic Policy
  Research
The Chartered Institute of Public
  Finance & Accountancy
Commonwealth Secretariat
The Continuum International
  Publishing Group Ltd
Cork University Press
Delta Alpha Publishing Ltd
J M Dent
DJØF
Gerald Duckworth & Co Ltd
Earthscan
Edward Elgar Publishing Ltd
Elliott & Thompson
Emerald Group Publishing Ltd
Euromonitor International
Fabian Society
Gibson Square
Gill & Macmillan
Gower Publishing Co Ltd
Granta Editions
Green Books
HarperCollins Publishers Ltd
Harriman House
Harvard University Press
Hodder Education
Icon Books Ltd
Imperial College Press
Institute of Employment Rights
Ithaca Press
Janus Publishing Co Ltd
Jarndyce Booksellers
Kogan Page Ltd
Kube Publishing Ltd
Luath Press Ltd
McGraw-Hill Education
Macmillan Publishers Ltd
Manchester University Press
Mentor Books
The Merlin Press Ltd
Microform Academic Publishers
The MIT Press Ltd
National Extension College Trust
  Ltd
Nelson Thornes Ltd
W. W. Norton & Company Ltd
Oak Tree Press
Open University Worldwide
Orpen Press
Oxfam Publishing
Oxford University Press
Palgrave Macmillan
Pickering & Chatto (Publishers) Ltd
Pluto Books Ltd
Princeton University Press
Profile Books
ProQuest
Rand Publications
Random House UK Ltd
Joseph Rowntree Foundation
Sage Publications Ltd
Saqi Books
Shepheard-Walwyn (Publishers)
  Ltd
Social Affairs Unit
Spokesman

Stacey International
Sussex Academic Press
Taylor & Francis
Troubador Publishing Ltd
TSO (The Stationery Office Ltd)
University of Ottawa Press
University of Toronto Press
John Wiley & Sons Ltd
Yale University Press London
Zed Books Ltd

EDUCATIONAL & TEXTBOOKS

A. M. S. Educational Ltd
Acair Ltd
Accent Press Ltd
Acumen Publishing Ltd
Adamson Publishing Ltd
Advance Materials
Alban Books Ltd
Philip Allan Publishers Ltd
American Psychiatric Publishing
  Inc
Anglo-Saxon Books
Ann Arbor Publishers Ltd
Anshan Ltd
Anthem Press
Ashgate Publishing Ltd
Association for Scottish Literary
  Studies
Atlantic Europe Publishing Co Ltd
Aurora Metro Publications Ltd
Austin & Macauley Publishers Ltd
AVA Publishing (UK) Ltd
Bernard Babani (Publishing) Ltd
Badger Publishing Ltd
Barefoot Books
Nicola Baxter Ltd
BEAM Education
Bender Richardson White
Berg Publishers
Bible Reading Fellowship
A. & C. Black (Publishers) Ltd
Blue Ocean Publishing
Blueberry Press Ltd
Borthwick Publications
Brilliant Publications
Butterfingers Books
Calypso Publications
Cambridge Publishing
  Management Ltd
Cambridge University Press
Capall Bann Publishing
Capstone Global Library Ltd
Carel Press Ltd
Cengage Learning EMEA Ltd
Centre for Alternative Technology
  Publications
Chalksoft Ltd
Channel View Publications Ltd
Chartered Institute of Personnel &
  Development
Chemcord Ltd
Christian Education
Christian Focus Publications
CILT, the National Centre for
  Languages
Claire Publications
Clear Answer Medical Publishing
  Ltd
Cló Iar-Chonnachta
Coachwise Ltd
Cois Life
Collins Geo
Colour Heroes Ltd
Colourpoint Books
The Continuum International
  Publishing Group Ltd
Coordination Group Publications
  Ltd (CGP Ltd)
Crimson Publishing
Crossbow Education Ltd
Darton, Longman & Todd Ltd
The Davenant Press
Delta ELT Publishing Ltd
Denor Press Ltd
Diagram Visual Information Ltd
Ditto International Ltd
Ashley Drake Publishing Ltd
Dramatic Lines
Dref Wen Cyf/Ltd
Earthscan

ECO Publishing International Ltd
Educational Planning Books Ltd
Egon Publishers Ltd
Edward Elgar Publishing Ltd
Elm Publications
Elsevier Ltd
Emerald Group Publishing Ltd
English Heritage
Equinox Publishing Ltd
Ethics International Press Ltd
Evans Publishing Group
Facet Publishing
Filament Publishing Ltd
First & Best in Education
The Fostering Network
Freelance Market News
Friends of the Earth
Galore Park Publishing Ltd
Gatehouse Media Ltd
The Geographical Association
Geography Publications
Gill & Macmillan
GLMP Ltd
Gower Publishing Co Ltd
Graham-Cameron Publishing &
  Illustration
Granada Learning
Granta Editions
Greenleaf Publishing
Guildhall Press
Gwasg Gwenffrwd
Hachette Children's Books
Haldane Mason Ltd
John Harper Publishing Ltd
HarperCollins Publishers Ltd
Hart McLeod Ltd
Hawthorn Press
Ian Henry Publications Ltd
Hinton House Publishers Ltd
Hodder Education
Hodder Gibson
Holland Publishing Plc
Hopscotch
How To Books Ltd
Human Kinetics Europe Ltd
Hymns Ancient & Modern Ltd
Hypatia Publications
Icon Books Ltd
ICSA Information & Training Ltd
In Easy Steps Ltd
Indepenpress Publishing Ltd
Institute of Education
  (Publications), University of
  London
Institution of Engineering and
  Technology (IET)
Intellect Ltd
International Network for the
  Availability of Scientific
  Publications (INASP)
IPS Educational Publishing
Janus Publishing Co Ltd
Jolly Learning Ltd
Jones & Bartlett International
Hilda King Educational
Jessica Kingsley Publishers
Kogan Page Ltd
Kube Publishing Ltd
Learning Matters Ltd
Learning Together
Letterland International Ltd
Lexus Ltd
Lion Hudson Plc
Little People Books
The Littman Library of Jewish
  Civilization
Liverpool University Press
Living Time® Media International
The Lutterworth Press
McCrimmon Publishing Co Ltd
McGraw-Hill Education
Macmillan Education
Macmillan Publishers Ltd
Management Pocketbooks Ltd
Manchester University Press
Medikidz Ltd
Mentor Books
MW Educational
The National Academies Press
The National Association for the
  Teaching of English (NATE)

The National Autistic Society
  (NAS)
National Children's Bureau
National Extension College Trust
  Ltd
National Housing Federation
Natural History Museum
  Publishing
Need2Know
Nelson Thornes Ltd
NHS Immunisation Information
NMS Enterprises Limited -
  Publishing
North York Moors National Park
  Authority
Northcote House Publishers Ltd
W. W. Norton & Company Ltd
Oak Tree Press
Open University Worldwide
Optimus Professional Publishing
Oxford University Press
Packard Publishing Ltd
Palgrave Macmillan
Paragon Publishing
Pearson Education
Philip's
The Policy Press
Polity Press
Portland Press Ltd
Positive Press Ltd
Practical Pre-School Books
Princeton University Press
Radcliffe Publishing Ltd
Rand Publications
Ransom Publishing Ltd
Rising Stars UK Ltd
Robinswood Press Ltd
Round Hall
RSC Publishing
Russell House Publishing Ltd
Sage Publications Ltd
St Jerome Publishing Ltd
Saqi Books
Scholastic UK Ltd
SchoolPlay Productions Ltd
Scripture Union Publishing
SHU Publications Ltd
Sigel Press
SLP Education
Social Affairs Unit
The Society of Metaphysicians Ltd
Southgate Publishers
Stacey International
Rudolf Steiner Press Ltd
STRI (Sports Turf Research
  Institute)
Sussex Academic Press
Symposium Publications Literary &
  Art
Tango Books Ltd
Tarquin Publications
Taylor & Francis
Teachit (UK) Ltd
Thames & Hudson Ltd
Third Millennium Publishing Ltd
THRASS (UK) Ltd
Topical Resources
Trentham Books
Trotman Publishing
TSO (The Stationery Office Ltd)
TTS Group
UCAS
United Writers Publications Ltd
University of Hertfordshire Press
University of Ottawa Press
University of Wales Press
Veritas Publications
Ward Lock Educational Co Ltd
Waterside Press
Whittles Publishing
John Wiley & Sons Ltd
Wolters Kluwer Health (P & E) Ltd
Young People in Focus

ELECTRONIC (EDUCATIONAL)

Adam Matthew Digital Ltd
Adamson Publishing Ltd
Anthem Press
Atlantic Europe Publishing Co Ltd
AVA Publishing (UK) Ltd
Bernard Babani (Publishing) Ltd

Bowker (UK) Ltd
Cambridge University Press
Carel Press Ltd
Chalksoft Ltd
Claire Publications
Coachwise Ltd
Collins Geo
Commonwealth Secretariat
The Continuum International
  Publishing Group Ltd
Crimson Publishing
Elm Publications
Emerald Group Publishing Ltd
Encyclopaedia Britannica (UK) Ltd
Ethics International Press Ltd
Evans Publishing Group
First & Best in Education
Galore Park Publishing Ltd
The Geographical Association
GLMP Ltd
HarperCollins Publishers Ltd
Hart McLeod Ltd
Heart of Albion Press
Hodder Education
Hodder Gibson
Holland Publishing Plc
Hopscotch
Human Kinetics Europe Ltd
Imperial College Press
Intellect Ltd
Jolly Learning Ltd
Kogan Page Ltd
Letterland International Ltd
Life of Riley Productions Ltd
Living Time® Media International
McCrimmon Publishing Co Ltd
McGraw-Hill Education
National Extension College Trust
  Ltd
National Gallery Co Ltd
Nelson Thornes Ltd
New Internationalist Publications
  Ltd
Open University Worldwide
Optimus Professional Publishing
Palgrave Macmillan
Paragon Publishing
ProQuest
Radcliffe Publishing Ltd
Ransom Publishing Ltd
Rising Stars UK Ltd
Robinswood Press Ltd
Royal Geographical Society
RSC Publishing
Russell House Publishing Ltd
Sage Publications Ltd
The Society of Metaphysicians Ltd
Summersdale Publishers Ltd
Teachit (UK) Ltd
THRASS (UK) Ltd
TTS Group
Waterside Press
John Wiley & Sons Ltd

ELECTRONIC (ENTERTAINMENT)

Amber Books Ltd
Bernard Babani (Publishing) Ltd
Carlton Publishing Group
HarperCollins Publishers Ltd
Haynes Publishing
Holland Publishing Plc
The Ilex Press Ltd
Living Time® Media International
MP Publishing Ltd
Summersdale Publishers Ltd
Thorogood Publishing Ltd

ELECTRONIC (PROFESSIONAL & ACADEMIC)

Adam Matthew Digital Ltd
Anthem Press
Ashgate Publishing Ltd
Bernard Babani (Publishing) Ltd
Berg Publishers
Berghahn Books
BML
Bowker (UK) Ltd
Cambridge University Press
Centre for Policy on Ageing

Christian Education
The Continuum International
  Publishing Group Ltd
Creative Content Ltd
Earthscan
Edward Elgar Publishing Ltd
Emerald Group Publishing Ltd
Energy Institute
Equinox Publishing Ltd
Ethics International Press Ltd
Facet Publishing
Filament Publishing Ltd
Gower Publishing Co Ltd
Gwasg Gwenffrwd
HarperCollins Publishers Ltd
Haynes Publishing
Hodder Education
Human Kinetics Europe Ltd
IHS Jane's
Imperial College Press
In Easy Steps Ltd
Institution of Engineering and
  Technology (IET)
Intellect Ltd
International Medical Press
International Network for the
  Availability of Scientific
  Publications (INASP)
IOP Publishing
IT Governance Publishing
IWA Publishing
Jordan Publishing Ltd
Kogan Page Ltd
Learning Matters Ltd
McGraw-Hill Education
Macmillan Publishers Ltd
Maney Publishing
Microform Academic Publishers
Myriad Editions
National Archives of Scotland
National Children's Bureau
National Gallery Co Ltd
Oak Tree Press
Oxford University Press
Paragon Publishing
Pearson Education
Portland Press Ltd
Princeton University Press
ProQuest
Radcliffe Publishing Ltd
Round Hall
The Royal College of Psychiatrists
Royal Geographical Society
RSC Publishing
Russell House Publishing Ltd
St Jerome Publishing Ltd
Summersdale Publishers Ltd
Taylor & Francis
Teachit (UK) Ltd
Thorogood Publishing Ltd
TSO (The Stationery Office Ltd)
Voltaire Foundation Ltd
Waterside Press
John Wiley & Sons Ltd
WIT Press
Wolters Kluwer Health (P & E) Ltd
Woodhead Publishing Ltd

ENGINEERING

Anshan Ltd
Anthem Press
Bernard Babani (Publishing) Ltd
Cambridge University Press
Cengage Learning EMEA Ltd
Earthscan
Emerald Group Publishing Ltd
Energy Institute
The Geological Society
Gower Publishing Co Ltd
Granta Editions
IChemE
Imperial College Press
Institute of Physics & Engineering
  in Medicine
Institution of Engineering and
  Technology (IET)
IWA Publishing
McGraw-Hill Education
Macmillan Publishers Ltd
Maney Publishing
The MIT Press Ltd

The National Academies Press
Nelson Thornes Ltd
Open University Worldwide
Palgrave Macmillan
ProQuest
Special Interest Model Books Ltd
Taylor & Francis
TSO (The Stationery Office Ltd)
Whittles Publishing
John Wiley & Sons Ltd
WIT Press
Woodhead Publishing Ltd

ENGLISH AS A FOREIGN
LANGUAGE

Austin & Macauley Publishers Ltd
b small publishing ltd
A. & C. Black (Publishers) Ltd
*Cambridge Publishing
  Management Ltd*
Cambridge University Press
Cengage Learning EMEA Ltd
Delta ELT Publishing Ltd
Gatehouse Media Ltd
GLMP Ltd
*Graham-Cameron Publishing &
  Illustration*
Gwasg Gwenffrwd
HarperCollins Publishers Ltd
Hodder Education
Letterland International Ltd
Living Time® Media International
McGraw-Hill Education
Macmillan Education
Macmillan Publishers Ltd
Moonlight Publishing Ltd
MW Educational
New Island Books Ltd
Open University Worldwide
Oxford University Press
Paragon Publishing
Robinswood Press Ltd
Sandstone Press Ltd
SLP Education
Symposium Publications Literary &
  Art

ENVIRONMENT &
DEVELOPMENT STUDIES

Anshan Ltd
Anthem Press
Ashgate Publishing Ltd
Atlantic Europe Publishing Co Ltd
Austin & Macauley Publishers Ltd
Berghahn Books
Black Dog Publishing Ltd
CABI
Cambridge University Press
Capall Bann Publishing
Jon Carpenter Publishing
Centre for Alternative Technology
  Publications
Channel View Publications Ltd
Clairview Books Ltd
Collins Geo
Commonwealth Secretariat
Cork University Press
Earthscan
Eco-logic Books
ECO Publishing International Ltd
Edward Elgar Publishing Ltd
Emerald Group Publishing Ltd
Energy Institute
Ethics International Press Ltd
Fabian Society
Friends of the Earth
The Geological Society
Granta Editions
Green Books
Greenleaf Publishing
HarperCollins Publishers Ltd
Hodder Education
IHS BRE Press
Imperial College Press
Instant-Books UK Ltd
Intellect Ltd
Macmillan Education
Macmillan Publishers Ltd
Maney Publishing
The MIT Press Ltd

Myriad Editions
The National Academies Press
Nelson Thornes Ltd
New Internationalist Publications
  Ltd
North York Moors National Park
  Authority
On Stream Publications Ltd
Open Gate Press
Open University Worldwide
Oxfam Publishing
Packard Publishing Ltd
Palgrave Macmillan
Paragon Publishing
Plowright Press
Pluto Books Ltd
Princeton University Press
Royal Geographical Society
Sandstone Press Ltd
Saqi Books
Scottish Cultural Press
Sigel Press
Social Affairs Unit
The Society of Metaphysicians Ltd
Southgate Publishers
STRI (Sports Turf Research
  Institute)
Sussex Academic Press
Tango Books Ltd
Taylor & Francis
Thames & Hudson Ltd
University of Hertfordshire Press
John Wiley & Sons Ltd
WIT Press
Woodhead Publishing Ltd
Zed Books Ltd

FASHION & COSTUME

Amber Books Ltd
Anova Books
Antique Collectors' Club Ltd
Aurum Press
Austin & Macauley Publishers Ltd
AVA Publishing (UK) Ltd
Batsford
Ruth Bean Publishers
Beautiful Books Ltd
Bene Factum Publishing Ltd
Berg Publishers
Black Dog Publishing Ltd
A. & C. Black (Publishers) Ltd
Carlton Publishing Group
Collins & Brown
Copper Beech Publishing Ltd
Eric Dobby Publishing Ltd
Gerald Duckworth & Co Ltd
Essential Works Ltd
Fiell Publishing Ltd
Granta Editions
The Herbert Press
Independent Music Press
The Ivy Press Ltd
Laurence King Publishing Ltd
Maney Publishing
Mercury Junior
Merlin Publishing/Wolfhound
  Press
Merrell Publishers Ltd
Mitchell Beazley
National Portrait Gallery
  Publications
The National Trust
Nelson Thornes Ltd
The Orion Publishing Group Ltd
Peter Owen Publishers
Papadakis Publisher
Phaidon Press Ltd
Prestel Publishing Ltd
ProQuest
Quadrille Publishing Ltd
Quantum Publishing
Quartet Books
RotoVision SA
Royal Collection Publications
Saqi Books
Charles Skilton Ltd
Stott's Correspondence College
teNeues Publishing UK Ltd
Thames & Hudson Ltd
Unicorn Press
V&A Publishing

David West Children's Books
John Wiley & Sons Ltd
Yale University Press London

FICTION

Acair Ltd
Accent Press Ltd
Alban Books Ltd
Albyn Press
Allison & Busby
Alma Books Ltd
Amolibros
Arcadia Books Ltd
Archive Publishing
Arena Books (Publishers)
Ashgrove Publishing
Association for Scottish Literary
  Studies
Atlantic Books
Aurora Metro Publications Ltd
Austin & Macauley Publishers Ltd
Authorhouse UK Ltd
Barny Books
Beautiful Books Ltd
Birlinn Ltd
Bitter Lemon Press
Black Ace Books
Black Spring Press Ltd
Blackstaff Press
Bloomsbury Publishing Plc
Blue Sky Press
Blueberry Press Ltd
Marion Boyars Publishers Ltd
Brewin Books Ltd
Canongate Books
Capuchin Classics
Caxton Publishing Group Ltd
Cló Iar-Chonnachta
Cois Life
Collins & Brown
Colour Heroes Ltd
Colourpoint Books
Constable & Robinson Ltd
Cornwall Editions Ltd
Countyvise Ltd
CRW Publishing Ltd
Dedalus Ltd
Delancey Press Ltd
Denor Press Ltd
J M Dent
Dref Wen Cyf/Ltd
Gerald Duckworth & Co Ltd
Enitharmon Press
Everyman's Library
Faber & Faber Ltd
Fastprint
Five Leaves Publications
Flambard Press
Freelance Market News
Garnet Publishing Ltd
Victor Gollancz Ltd
Granta Books
Guildhall Press
Hachette Children's Books
Hachette Scotland
Halban Publishers
Robert Hale Ltd
Harlequin Mills & Boon Ltd
HarperCollins Publishers Ltd
Ian Henry Publications Ltd
Highland Books
Hodder Faith
Hodder & Stoughton General
Honno (Welsh Women's Press)
John Hunt Publishing Ltd
Icon Books Ltd
Indepenpress Publishing Ltd
ISIS Publishing Ltd
Janus Publishing Co Ltd
Jarndyce Booksellers
Kube Publishing Ltd
Legend Press
Librario Publishers Ltd
The Lilliput Press Ltd
Lion Hudson Plc
Little, Brown Book Group
Living Time® Media International
Luath Press Ltd
Macmillan Publishers Ltd
Magna Large Print Books
Mandrake of Oxford

Maverick House Publishers
Mentor Books
Mercier Press Ltd
MP Publishing Ltd
John Murray Publishers
Myriad Editions
Myrmidon Books Ltd
New Internationalist Publications
  Ltd
New Island Books Ltd
W. W. Norton & Company Ltd
Oneworld Classics
Onlywomen Press Ltd
Orion Books Ltd
The Orion Publishing Group Ltd
Peter Owen Publishers
Pan Macmillan
Paragon Publishing
The Penguin Group (UK) Ltd
Piatkus Books
Pipers' Ash Ltd
Piquant Editions
Portobello Books Ltd
Profile Books
Prospera Publishing
Pushkin Press
Quartet Books
Random House UK Ltd
Raven's Quill Ltd
Ripley Publishing Ltd
Rising Stars UK Ltd
Robinswood Press Ltd
Route Publishing Ltd
Sandstone Press Ltd
Saqi Books
Scottish Children's Press
Seren
Short Books Ltd
Sigel Press
Silver Moon Books
Simon & Schuster (UK) Ltd
Charles Skilton Ltd
Slightly Foxed
Solidus
Spokesman
Sportsbooks Ltd
Tabb House
Telegram Books
Telos Publishing Ltd
Templar Publishing
Thorogood Publishing Ltd
F. A. Thorpe Publishing
Tindal Street Press
Top That! Publishing Plc
Total-E-Ntwined Ltd
Transworld Publishers Ltd
Troubador Publishing Ltd
Truran
United Writers Publications Ltd
Usborne Publishing Ltd
Voltaire Foundation Ltd
Weidenfeld & Nicolson
John Wiley & Sons Ltd
The Women's Press
Wordsworth Editions Ltd
Worth Press Ltd
Y Lolfa Cyf

FINE ART & ART HISTORY

Albyn Press
Amolibros
Anova Books
Antique Collectors' Club Ltd
Archetype Publications Ltd
Ashgate Publishing Ltd
Ashmolean Museum Publications
Aureus Publishing Ltd
Austin & Macauley Publishers Ltd
Bene Factum Publishing Ltd
Berg Publishers
Black Dog Publishing Ltd
A. & C. Black (Publishers) Ltd
Blackthorn Press
Bodleian Library Publishing
British Library
British Museum Press
*Cambridge Publishing
  Management Ltd*
Cambridge University Press
Cameron Books
Canongate Books

Carlton Publishing Group
Caxton Publishing Group Ltd
Cork University Press
D & N Publishing
Richard Dennis Publications
Gerald Duckworth & Co Ltd
Flambard Press
Four Courts Press
Gibson Square
Gothic Image Publications
Granta Editions
Green Books
Hachette Children's Books
Robert Hale Ltd
Halsgrove
HarperCollins Publishers Ltd
Harvard University Press
Hayward Publishing
The Herbert Press
Alison Hodge Publishers
Hypatia Publications
The Ilex Press Ltd
Janus Publishing Co Ltd
Kew Publishing
Laurence King Publishing Ltd
Dewi Lewis Publishing
The Lilliput Press Ltd
The Littman Library of Jewish
  Civilization
Liverpool University Press
Logaston Press
Lund Humphries
The Lutterworth Press
Macmillan Publishers Ltd
Mainstream Publishing Co
  (Edinburgh) Ltd
Mandrake of Oxford
Maney Publishing
Melisende UK Ltd
Merlin Publishing/Wolfhound
  Press
Merrell Publishers Ltd
The MIT Press Ltd
Mitchell Beazley
Moonlight Publishing Ltd
John Murray Publishers
National Extension College Trust
  Ltd
National Galleries of Scotland
National Gallery Co Ltd
National Portrait Gallery
  Publications
The National Trust
Natural History Museum
  Publishing
NMS Enterprises Limited -
  Publishing
Northumbria University Press
W. W. Norton & Company Ltd
Octopus Publishing Group
Open University Worldwide
The Orion Publishing Group Ltd
Papadakis Publisher
Paragon Publishing
Phaidon Press Ltd
Piquant Editions
Prestel Publishing Ltd
ProQuest
Quantum Publishing
Quartet Books
Quiller Publishing Ltd
Random House UK Ltd
Redcliffe Press Ltd
RotoVision SA
Roundhouse Publishing Ltd
Royal Collection Publications
Sansom & Co Ltd
Saqi Books
Scala Publishers Ltd
Seren
Charles Skilton Ltd
Stacey International
Rudolf Steiner Press Ltd
Strong Oak Press
Sussex Academic Press
Sussex Publications
Symposium Publications Literary &
  Art
Tate Publishing
I. B. Tauris & Co Ltd
Thames & Hudson Ltd
Third Millennium Publishing Ltd

Toucan Books Ltd
Truran
Unicorn Press
V&A Publishing
Warburg Institute
Paul Watkins Publishing
Philip Wilson Publishers
Yale University Press London

GARDENING

Amolibros
Anova Books
Antique Collectors' Club Ltd
Aurum Press
Austin & Macauley Publishers Ltd
Barny Books
Batsford
Bene Factum Publishing Ltd
BLA Publishing Ltd
Black Dog Publishing Ltd
Cambridge Publishing
  Management Ltd
Capall Bann Publishing
Capuchin Classics
Caxton Publishing Group Ltd
Centre for Alternative Technology
  Publications
Chalksoft Ltd
Conran Octopus
Constable & Robinson Ltd
Copper Beech Publishing Ltd
Cork University Press
The Crowood Press Ltd
Dedalus Ltd
J M Dent
Eco-logic Books
Ex Libris Press
Findhorn Press Ltd
Floris Books Trust Ltd
W. Foulsham & Co Ltd
Friends of the Earth
Graffeg
Green Books
Robert Hale Ltd
HarperCollins Publishers Ltd
Hawthorn Press
Haynes Publishing
Hodder Education
Alison Hodge Publishers
How To Books Ltd
Kew Publishing
Kyle Books
Luath Press Ltd
Macmillan Publishers Ltd
Merrell Publishers Ltd
Mitchell Beazley
Murdoch Books UK Ltd
The National Trust
Need2Know
W. W. Norton & Company Ltd
The O'Brien Press Ltd
Octopus Publishing Group
The Orion Publishing Group Ltd
Packard Publishing Ltd
Pan Macmillan
The Penguin Group (UK) Ltd
Quadrille Publishing Ltd
Quantum Publishing
Quiller Publishing Ltd
Random House UK Ltd
Roundhouse Publishing Ltd
Shire Publications Ltd
Slightly Foxed
Souvenir Press Ltd
Stacey International
Thames & Hudson Ltd
Toucan Books Ltd
Transworld Publishers Ltd
Truran
Which? Ltd
Whittet Books Ltd
John Wiley & Sons Ltd
Willow Island Editions
Zymurgy Publishing

GAY & LESBIAN STUDIES

Arcadia Books Ltd
Aurora Metro Publications Ltd
Austin & Macauley Publishers Ltd
Cló Iar-Chonnachta

Cork University Press
Findhorn Press Ltd
Gibson Square
Guildhall Press
Indepenpress Publishing Ltd
Manchester University Press
The MIT Press Ltd
Onlywomen Press Ltd
Peter Owen Publishers
Paragon Publishing
St Jerome Publishing Ltd
Saqi Books
Silver Moon Books
Charles Skilton Ltd
Taylor & Francis
Thames & Hudson Ltd
The Women's Press

GENDER STUDIES

Adam Matthew Digital Ltd
Anthem Press
Arcadia Books Ltd
Ashgate Publishing Ltd
Attic Press
Aurora Metro Publications Ltd
Berghahn Books
Cambridge University Press
Capall Bann Publishing
Commonwealth Secretariat
Cork University Press
Equinox Publishing Ltd
HarperCollins Publishers Ltd
Harvard University Press
Hawthorn Press
Hodder Education
Holo Books
C. Hurst & Co (Publishers) Ltd
Icon Books Ltd
Intellect Ltd
Irish Academic Press
Ithaca Press
Karnac Books Ltd
Macmillan Publishers Ltd
Manchester University Press
The Merlin Press Ltd
The MIT Press Ltd
Myriad Editions
New Island Books Ltd
W. W. Norton & Company Ltd
Onlywomen Press Ltd
Oxfam Publishing
Palgrave Macmillan
PCCS Books Ltd
Piatkus Books
Plowright Press
Pluto Books Ltd
The Policy Press
Polity Press
Russell House Publishing Ltd
Sage Publications Ltd
St Jerome Publishing Ltd
Saqi Books
Sheldon Press
Souvenir Press Ltd
Sussex Academic Press
I. B. Tauris & Co Ltd
Taylor & Francis
Trentham Books
University of Ottawa Press
University of Toronto Press
University of Wales Press
The Women's Press
Yale University Press London
Zed Books Ltd

GEOGRAPHY & GEOLOGY

Albyn Press
Amolibros
Anthem Press
Ashgate Publishing Ltd
Atlantic Europe Publishing Co Ltd
Bedford Freeman Worth (BFW)
Blackstaff Press
British Geological Survey
Cambridge University Press
Chalksoft Ltd
Coastal Publishing
Collins Geo
Cork University Press
G. L. Crowther

Diagram Visual Information Ltd
The Dovecote Press
Dunedin Academic Press
Earthscan
Ex Libris Press
The Geographical Association
Geography Publications
The Geological Society
Graffeg
HarperCollins Publishers Ltd
Hodder Education
Alison Hodge Publishers
Icon Books Ltd
Imray Laurie Norie & Wilson Ltd
Jones & Bartlett International
Luath Press Ltd
McGraw-Hill Education
Macmillan Education
Maney Publishing
Manson Publishing Ltd
Mentor Books
Mercury Books
The National Academies Press
Natural History Museum
  Publishing
Nelson Thornes Ltd
NMS Enterprises Limited -
  Publishing
North York Moors National Park
  Authority
W. W. Norton & Company Ltd
Open University Worldwide
Optimus Professional Publishing
Packard Publishing Ltd
Pagoda Tree Press
Palgrave Macmillan
Paragon Publishing
Roadmaster Publishing
Royal Geographical Society
Scottish Cultural Press
SLP Education
Stacey International
Sussex Academic Press
I. B. Tauris & Co Ltd
Taylor & Francis
Truran
TSO (The Stationery Office Ltd)
University of Hertfordshire Press
Usborne Publishing Ltd
Ward Lock Educational Co Ltd
David West Children's Books
Whittles Publishing
John Wiley & Sons Ltd
WIT Press

GUIDE BOOKS

AA Publishing
Accent Press Ltd
Albyn Press
Appletree Press Ltd
Birlinn Ltd
Blackstaff Press
Bossiney Books Ltd
Bradt Travel Guides Ltd
British Geological Survey
Brown & Whittaker Publishing
Camra Books
Capall Bann Publishing
Capuchin Classics
The Catholic Truth Society
Cicerone Press Ltd
Collins Geo
Colour Heroes Ltd
Countryside Books
Crimson Publishing
D & N Publishing
Day One Publications
The Derby Books Publishing Co
  Ltd
Discovery Walking Guides Ltd
The Dovecote Press
English Heritage
Everyman's Library
Ex Libris Press
FHG Guides Ltd
Findhorn Press Ltd
Footprint Travel Guides
W. Foulsham & Co Ltd
Garnet Publishing Ltd
The Geographical Association
Gill & Macmillan

The Good Food Guide
Gothic Image Publications
Gracewing Publishing
Graffeg
Granta Editions
Green Books
Guildhall Press
Halsgrove
Harden's Ltd
HarperCollins Publishers Ltd
Haynes Publishing
Heart of Albion Press
Hobnob Press
Alison Hodge Publishers
Holo Books
The Horizon Press
How To Books Ltd
Instant-Books UK Ltd
Logaston Press
Lomond Books Ltd
Luath Press Ltd
Macmillan Publishers Ltd
Mainstream Publishing Co
  (Edinburgh) Ltd
Mentor Books
Merlin Publishing/Wolfhound
  Press
Merrell Publishers Ltd
Michelin Maps & Guides
National Gallery Co Ltd
National Portrait Gallery
  Publications
The National Trust
New Island Books Ltd
NMS Enterprises Limited -
  Publishing
North York Moors National Park
  Authority
Northumbria University Press
The Nostalgia Collection
The O'Brien Press Ltd
The Orion Publishing Group Ltd
Pagoda Tree Press
Pan Macmillan
Paragon Publishing
The Penguin Group (UK) Ltd
Random House UK Ltd
Reardon Publishing
Roadmaster Publishing
Roundhouse Publishing Ltd
Royal Collection Publications
S. B. Publications
Scala Publishers Ltd
Sheldrake Press
The Shetland Times Ltd
Shire Publications Ltd
Sigma Press
Simon & Schuster (UK) Ltd
Charles Skilton Ltd
Stacey International
Stobart Davies Ltd
Summersdale Publishers Ltd
I. B. Tauris & Co Ltd
Thames & Hudson Ltd
Third Millennium Publishing Ltd
Travel Publishing Ltd
Troubador Publishing Ltd
Truran
Twelveneads Press
V&A Publishing
John Wiley & Sons Ltd
Willow Island Editions
Neil Wilson Publishing Ltd
Y Lolfa Cyf

HEALTH & BEAUTY

Amberwood Publishing Ltd
Ashgrove Publishing
Aurum Press
Austin & Macauley Publishers Ltd
A. & C. Black (Publishers) Ltd
Blackstaff Press
Bloomsbury Publishing Plc
Capall Bann Publishing
Carlton Publishing Group
Carroll & Brown Ltd
Cengage Learning EMEA Ltd
Clairview Books Ltd
Class Publishing
Collins & Brown
Crimson Publishing

Diagram Visual Information Ltd
Eddison Sadd Editions Ltd
Essential Works Ltd
Findhorn Press Ltd
Floris Books Trust Ltd
W. Foulsham & Co Ltd
Gibson Square
Granta Editions
Green Books
Haldane Mason Ltd
HarperCollins Publishers Ltd
Harvard University Press
Hawker Publications
Haynes Publishing
Hodder Education
How To Books Ltd
Human Kinetics Europe Ltd
Icon Books Ltd
Indepenpress Publishing Ltd
The Ivy Press Ltd
Jessica Kingsley Publishers
Kyle Books
Liberties Press
Londubh Books
Macmillan Publishers Ltd
Mainstream Publishing Co
   (Edinburgh) Ltd
Mentor Books
Merlin Publishing/Wolfhound
   Press
Mitchell Beazley
Murdoch Books UK Ltd
Need2Know
Nelson Thornes Ltd
Octopus Publishing Group
On Stream Publications Ltd
The Orion Publishing Group Ltd
Pan Macmillan
The Penguin Group (UK) Ltd
Piatkus Books
Quadrille Publishing Ltd
Quantum Publishing
Random House UK Ltd
Roundhouse Publishing Ltd
Sheldon Press
Simon & Schuster (UK) Ltd
Souvenir Press Ltd
Stott's Correspondence College
Summersdale Publishers Ltd
Temple Lodge Publishing
Trog Associates Ltd
Tucker Slingsby Ltd
John Wiley & Sons Ltd
The Women's Press
Zymurgy Publishing

HISTORY & ANTIQUARIAN

A. M. S. Educational Ltd
Acair Ltd
Acumen Publishing Ltd
Adam Matthew Digital Ltd
Albyn Press
Ian Allan Publishing Ltd
Amber Books Ltd
Amolibros
Anglo-Saxon Books
Anova Books
Appletree Press Ltd
Arena Books (Publishers)
Ashgate Publishing Ltd
Ashmolean Museum Publications
Atlantic Books
Atlantic Europe Publishing Co Ltd
Barny Books
Batsford
BBH Publishing Ltd
The Belmont Press
Bene Factum Publishing Ltd
Berghahn Books
Birlinn Ltd
Black Ace Books
Blackstaff Press
Blackthorn Press
Bloomsbury Publishing Plc
Blue Ocean Publishing
Bodleian Library Publishing
Book Castle Publishing Ltd
Borthwick Publications
Bossiney Books Ltd
Boydell & Brewer Ltd
Brewin Books Ltd

Bridge Books
British Library
British Museum Press
Brown & Whittaker Publishing
Cambridge Archive Editions Ltd
Cambridge University Press
Canongate Books
Capall Bann Publishing
Capuchin Classics
Carlton Publishing Group
Carnegie Publishing Ltd
Jon Carpenter Publishing
The Catholic Truth Society
Christian Focus Publications
Church of Ireland Publishing
James Clarke & Co
Cló Iar-Chonnachta
Colour Heroes Ltd
Colourpoint Books
Columba
Compendium Publishing Ltd
The Continuum International
   Publishing Group Ltd
Copper Beech Publishing Ltd
Cork University Press
Cornwall Editions Ltd
Countryside Books
Countyvise Ltd
Crécy Publishing Ltd
Cualann Press
D & N Publishing
The Davenant Press
Richard Dennis Publications
J M Dent
The Dovecote Press
Ashley Drake Publishing Ltd
Dramatic Lines
Gerald Duckworth & Co Ltd
Elliott & Thompson
English Heritage
Equinox Publishing Ltd
The Erskine Press
Ex Libris Press
F+W Media International, LTD
   (formerly David & Charles)
Family Publications
A. & A. Farmar
Five Leaves Publications
Four Courts Press
Garnet Publishing Ltd
Geography Publications
Gibson Square
Gill & Macmillan
GLMP Ltd
Alan Godfrey Maps
Gomer
Gracewing Publishing
Granta Editions
Greenhill Books / Lionel Leventhal
   Ltd
Gresham Books Ltd
Guildhall Press
Gwasg Gwenffrwd
Hachette Scotland
Halban Publishers
Robert Hale Ltd
Halsgrove
HarperCollins Publishers Ltd
Harvard University Press
Haynes Publishing
Heart of Albion Press
Helion & Co Ltd
Ian Henry Publications Ltd
Historical Publications Ltd
Hobnob Press
Hodder Education
Hodder Faith
Hodder & Stoughton General
Alison Hodge Publishers
Holo Books
The Horizon Press
Hypatia Publications
Icon Books Ltd
Intellect Ltd
Irish Academic Press
Ithaca Press
James & James (Publishers) Ltd
Janus Publishing Co Ltd
The King's England Press
Liberties Press
Librario Publishers Ltd
The Lilliput Press Ltd

Little, Brown Book Group
The Littman Library of Jewish
   Civilization
Liverpool University Press
Living Time® Media International
Logaston Press
Lomond Books Ltd
Londubh Books
Luath Press Ltd
The Lutterworth Press
Macmillan Education
Macmillan Publishers Ltd
Mainstream Publishing Co
   (Edinburgh) Ltd
Manchester University Press
Maney Publishing
Melisende UK Ltd
Mentor Books
Mercier Press Ltd
Mercury Books
The Merlin Press Ltd
Merrell Publishers Ltd
Merton Priory Press Ltd
Microform Academic Publishers
Mitchell Beazley
Moorley's Print & Publishing Ltd
Murdoch Books UK Ltd
John Murray Publishers
National Archives of Scotland
National Portrait Gallery
   Publications
The National Trust
Nelson Thornes Ltd
New Island Books Ltd
NMS Enterprises Limited -
   Publishing
North York Moors National Park
   Authority
Northumbria University Press
W. W. Norton & Company Ltd
The Nostalgia Collection
Octopus Publishing Group
The Oleander Press
Open University Worldwide
The Orion Publishing Group Ltd
Osprey Publishing Ltd
Peter Owen Publishers
Palazzo Editions Ltd
Palgrave Macmillan
Pan Macmillan
The Penguin Group (UK) Ltd
Piatkus Books
Pickering & Chatto (Publishers) Ltd
Plowright Press
Polity Press
Polperro Heritage Press
Portobello Books Ltd
Princeton University Press
Profile Books
ProQuest
Quantum Publishing
Quartet Books
The Radcliffe Press
Random House UK Ltd
Reardon Publishing
Redcliffe Press Ltd
Reflections of a Bygone Age
Roundhouse Publishing Ltd
Royal Collection Publications
Royal Irish Academy
S. B. Publications
Saint Albert's Press
Saqi Books
Scottish Children's Press
Scottish Cultural Press
Scottish Text Society
Sheaf Publishing
Sheldrake Press
Shepheard-Walwyn (Publishers)
   Ltd
Shire Publications Ltd
Short Books Ltd
Slightly Foxed
SLP Education
Smith Settle Printing &
   Bookbinding Ltd
Society of Genealogists
   Enterprises Ltd
Spokesman
Sportsbooks Ltd
Stacey International
Stainer & Bell Ltd

Stenlake Publishing Ltd
Strong Oak Press
Summersdale Publishers Ltd
Sussex Academic Press
Sussex Publications
I. B. Tauris & Co Ltd
Taylor & Francis
Thames & Hudson Ltd
Toucan Books Ltd
Transworld Publishers Ltd
Troubador Publishing Ltd
Truran
Twelveheads Press
Tyne Bridge Publishing
Unicorn Press
University of Exeter Press
University of Hertfordshire Press
University of Toronto Press
University of Wales Press
Vallentine Mitchell Publishers
Vertical Editions
Voltaire Foundation Ltd
Warburg Institute
Waterside Press
Paul Watkins Publishing
Waverley Books
David West Children's Books
John Wiley & Sons Ltd
Philip Wilson Publishers
Neil Wilson Publishing Ltd
World Microfilms
Yale University Press London

HUMOUR

Accent Press Ltd
Allison & Busby
Alma Books Ltd
Anova Books
Antique Collectors' Club Ltd
Appletree Press Ltd
Atlantic Books
Aurora Metro Publications Ltd
Aurum Press
Austin & Macauley Publishers Ltd
Authorhouse UK Ltd
Barny Books
Beautiful Books Ltd
Bene Factum Publishing Ltd
Birlinn Ltd
A. & C. Black (Publishers) Ltd
Blackstaff Press
John Blake Publishing Ltd
Bloomsbury Publishing Plc
Bodleian Library Publishing
Brown Dog Books
Canongate Books
Carlton Publishing Group
Constable & Robinson Ltd
Countryside Books
Countyvise Ltd
CRW Publishing Ltd
Delancey Press Ltd
Gerald Duckworth & Co Ltd
Essential Works Ltd
Exley Publications Ltd
F+W Media International, LTD
   (formerly David & Charles)
W. Foulsham & Co Ltd
Gibson Square
Gill & Macmillan
Guildhall Press
Hachette Scotland
Robert Hale Ltd
HarperCollins Publishers Ltd
Haynes Publishing
Ian Henry Publications Ltd
Hodder & Stoughton General
Holo Books
Icon Books Ltd
Indepenpress Publishing Ltd
ISIS Publishing Ltd
Janus Publishing Co Ltd
Little, Brown Book Group
Lomond Books Ltd
Luath Press Ltd
Macmillan Publishers Ltd
Mainstream Publishing Co
   (Edinburgh) Ltd
Maverick House Publishers
Mentor Books
Mercier Press Ltd

Merlin Publishing/Wolfhound
   Press
Merrell Publishers Ltd
John Murray Publishers
The National Trust
New Island Books Ltd
Nightingale Press
The O'Brien Press Ltd
The Oleander Press
The Orion Publishing Group Ltd
Paragon Publishing
The Penguin Group (UK) Ltd
Piatkus Books
Quadrille Publishing Ltd
Quantum Publishing
Quiller Publishing Ltd
Random House UK Ltd
Ravette Publishing Ltd
Reardon Publishing
Sandstone Press Ltd
Saqi Books
Sheldrake Press
Short Books Ltd
Simon & Schuster (UK) Ltd
SLP Education
Souvenir Press Ltd
Summersdale Publishers Ltd
Top That! Publishing Plc
Transworld Publishers Ltd
Troubador Publishing Ltd
United Writers Publications Ltd
Merlin Unwin Books Ltd
Weidenfeld & Nicolson
Neil Wilson Publishing Ltd
Y Lolfa Cyf
Zymurgy Publishing

ILLUSTRATED & FINE EDITIONS

Albyn Press
Amber Books Ltd
Ashgate Publishing Ltd
Bene Factum Publishing Ltd
Birlinn Ltd
Black Dog Publishing Ltd
Blackstaff Press
British Library
Cambridge Publishing
   Management Ltd
Canongate Books
Carlton Publishing Group
Constable & Robinson Ltd
Richard Dennis Publications
Gerald Duckworth & Co Ltd
Enitharmon Press
The Erskine Press
Essential Works Ltd
Everyman's Library
Granta Editions
Halsgrove
HarperCollins Publishers Ltd
The Herbert Press
The Ivy Press Ltd
Dewi Lewis Publishing
The Lilliput Press Ltd
Lomond Books Ltd
The Lutterworth Press
Mainstream Publishing Co
   (Edinburgh) Ltd
Manchester University Press
Maney Publishing
Melisende UK Ltd
Merrell Publishers Ltd
Mitchell Beazley
National Portrait Gallery
   Publications
The Old Stile Press
The Orion Publishing Group Ltd
Papadakis Publisher
Phaidon Press Ltd
Quartet Books
Quiller Publishing Ltd
Random House UK Ltd
Royal Collection Publications
Sandstone Press Ltd
Saqi Books
Scala Publishers Ltd
Shepheard-Walwyn (Publishers)
   Ltd
Charles Skilton Ltd
Slightly Foxed

Smith Settle Printing & Bookbinding Ltd
Stacey International
teNeues Publishing UK Ltd
Thames & Hudson Ltd
Third Millennium Publishing Ltd
Toucan Books Ltd
University of Wales Press
Veloce Publishing Ltd
Weidenfeld & Nicolson
Philip Wilson Publishers
Yale University Press London
Zymurgy Publishing

INDUSTRY, BUSINESS & MANAGEMENT

Accent Press Ltd
Anthem Press
Arena Books (Publishers)
Ashgate Publishing Ltd
Atlantic Books
Aurelian Information Ltd
Austin & Macauley Publishers Ltd
AVA Publishing (UK) Ltd
Barny Books
Bene Factum Publishing Ltd
Biohealthcare Publishing (Oxford) Ltd
Blue Ocean Publishing
Nicholas Brealey Publishing
Cambridge Publishing Management Ltd
Cambridge University Press
Carnegie Publishing Ltd
Cengage Learning EMEA Ltd
Centre for Economic Policy Research
Chartered Institute of Personnel & Development
Commonwealth Secretariat
Crimson Publishing
DJØF
Ashley Drake Publishing Ltd
Earthscan
Edward Elgar Publishing Ltd
Elliott & Thompson
Elm Publications
Emerald Group Publishing Ltd
Energy Institute
Ethics International Press Ltd
Euromonitor International
Executive Grapevine International Ltd
Filament Publishing Ltd
W. Foulsham & Co Ltd
GLMP Ltd
Gower Publishing Co Ltd
Granta Editions
Greenleaf Publishing
HarperCollins Publishers Ltd
Harriman House
Hawthorn Press
Hodder Education
How To Books Ltd
ICSA Information & Training Ltd
IHS Jane's
Imperial College Press
In Easy Steps Ltd
Indepenpress Publishing Ltd
Institute for Employment Studies
Institution of Engineering and Technology (IET)
IWA Publishing
James & James (Publishers) Ltd
Jordan Publishing Ltd
Kogan Page Ltd
McGraw-Hill Education
Management Pocketbooks Ltd
Market House Books Ltd
Mentor Books
The MIT Press Ltd
The National Academies Press
National Housing Federation
Nelson Thornes Ltd
Oak Tree Press
Open University Worldwide
Orpen Press
Oxford University Press
Palgrave Macmillan
Paragon Publishing
The Penguin Group (UK) Ltd

Piatkus Books
PP Publishing
Princeton University Press
Profile Books
ProQuest
Quantum Publishing
Radcliffe Publishing Ltd
Round Hall
Roundhouse Publishing Ltd
Russell House Publishing Ltd
Sage Publications Ltd
Sherwood Publishing
Sigel Press
Simon & Schuster (UK) Ltd
Social Affairs Unit
Souvenir Press Ltd
Sussex Academic Press
Taylor & Francis
Thorogood Publishing Ltd
Trog Associates Ltd
Trotman Publishing
Troubador Publishing Ltd
TSO (The Stationery Office Ltd)
United Writers Publications Ltd
University of Ottawa Press
Weidenfeld & Nicolson
John Wiley & Sons Ltd
WIT Press
Woodhead Publishing Ltd
Zambezi Publishing Ltd

LANGUAGES & LINGUISTICS

Advance Materials
Anglo-Saxon Books
Association for Scottish Literary Studies
Audio-Forum – The Language Source
b small publishing ltd
Berghahn Books
Joseph Biddulph Publisher
Brilliant Publications
Cambridge University Press
Carel Press Ltd
Channel View Publications Ltd
CILT, the National Centre for Languages
Claire Publications
Cló Iar-Chonnachta
Cois Life
The Continuum International Publishing Group Ltd
Delta ELT Publishing Ltd
Ashley Drake Publishing Ltd
Dunedin Academic Press
Emerald Group Publishing Ltd
Equinox Publishing Ltd
Geography Publications
GLMP Ltd
Gomer
Gwasg Gwenffrwd
HarperCollins Publishers Ltd
Hinton House Publishers Ltd
Hodder Education
Icon Books Ltd
Intellect Ltd
Ithaca Press
Jarndyce Booksellers
Lexus Ltd
Liverpool University Press
Luath Press Ltd
Macmillan Education
Macmillan Publishers Ltd
Manchester University Press
Maney Publishing
Mentor Books
The MIT Press Ltd
National Extension College Trust Ltd
Nelson Thornes Ltd
The Oleander Press
Open University Worldwide
Oxford University Press
Packard Publishing Ltd
Palgrave Macmillan
Paragon Publishing
Royal Irish Academy
St Jerome Publishing Ltd
Saqi Books
Scottish Children's Press
Scottish Cultural Press

Stacey International
Ta Ha Publishers Ltd
Taigh na Teud Music Publishers
Taylor & Francis
Troubador Publishing Ltd
Truran
University of Ottawa Press
University of Wales Press
Usborne Publishing Ltd
Voltaire Foundation Ltd
Paul Watkins Publishing
John Wiley & Sons Ltd
Y Lolfa Cyf
Yale University Press London

LAW

Anthem Press
Ashgate Publishing Ltd
Atlantic Books
Bene Factum Publishing Ltd
Borthwick Publications
Cambridge University Press
Class Publishing
Commonwealth Secretariat
Delta Alpha Publishing Ltd
J M Dent
DJØF
Earthscan
Edward Elgar Publishing Ltd
Ethics International Press Ltd
Four Courts Press
GLMP Ltd
Granta Editions
W. Green The Scottish Law Publisher
Hart Publishing
Harvard University Press
Hodder Education
Holo Books
Incorporated Council of Law Reporting for England and Wales
Institute of Employment Rights
The Islamic Texts Society
Ithaca Press
Jones & Bartlett International
Jordan Publishing Ltd
Jessica Kingsley Publishers
Kube Publishing Ltd
Law Reports International Ltd
Law Society Publishing
Leatherhead Food Research
Legal Action Group
McGraw-Hill Education
Macmillan Publishers Ltd
Manchester University Press
Market House Books Ltd
National Extension College Trust Ltd
Nelson Thornes Ltd
Oak Tree Press
Orpen Press
Oxford University Press
Palgrave Macmillan
Pearson Education
Pluto Books Ltd
PP Publishing
Princeton University Press
Round Hall
Russell House Publishing Ltd
Saqi Books
SLS Legal Publications (NI)
Sussex Academic Press
Taylor & Francis
Thomson Reuters – Professional Division
Thorogood Publishing Ltd
Trentham Books
TSO (The Stationery Office Ltd)
University of Hertfordshire Press
University of Toronto Press
Waterside Press
Weidenfeld & Nicolson
Which? Ltd
Witherby Publishing Group
Woodhead Publishing Ltd

LITERATURE & CRITICISM

Adam Matthew Digital Ltd
Albyn Press

Anthem Press
Arena Books (Publishers)
Ashgate Publishing Ltd
Association for Scottish Literary Studies
Atlantic Books
Austin & Macauley Publishers Ltd
Beautiful Books Ltd
Berghahn Books
Blackstaff Press
Blackthorn Press
Bloodaxe Books Ltd
Bloomsbury Publishing Plc
Blue Ocean Publishing
Bodleian Library Publishing
Marion Boyars Publishers Ltd
Boydell & Brewer Ltd
Cambridge University Press
Canongate Books
Carel Press Ltd
James Clarke & Co
Cló Iar-Chonnachta
Cois Life
The Continuum International Publishing Group Ltd
Cork University Press
The Davenant Press
Dedalus Ltd
J M Dent
Dionysia Press Ltd
Ashley Drake Publishing Ltd
Gerald Duckworth & Co Ltd
Enitharmon Press
Everyman's Library
Faber & Faber Ltd
Four Courts Press
Freelance Market News
Garnet Publishing Ltd
GLMP Ltd
Gomer
Green Books
Guildhall Press
Gwasg Gwenffrwd
Halban Publishers
HarperCollins Publishers Ltd
Harvard University Press
Hippopotamus Press
Hobnob Press
Hodder Education
How To Books Ltd
Icon Books Ltd
Indepenpress Publishing Ltd
Intellect Ltd
Irish Academic Press
Ithaca Press
Janus Publishing Co Ltd
Jarndyce Booksellers
Liberties Press
The Lilliput Press Ltd
Little, Brown Book Group
The Littman Library of Jewish Civilization
Liverpool University Press
Living Time® Media International
Luath Press Ltd
The Lutterworth Press
Macmillan Publishers Ltd
Mainstream Publishing Co (Edinburgh) Ltd
Manchester University Press
Mandrake of Oxford
Maney Publishing
Mercier Press Ltd
Mercury Books
Microform Academic Publishers
Nelson Thornes Ltd
New Island Books Ltd
Northcote House Publishers Ltd
W. W. Norton & Company Ltd
The Old Stile Press
The Oleander Press
Oneworld Classics
Onlywomen Press Ltd
Open University Worldwide
Peter Owen Publishers
Palgrave Macmillan
Pan Macmillan
Paupers' Press
The Penguin Group (UK) Ltd
Pickering & Chatto (Publishers) Ltd
Pipers' Ash Ltd
Pluto Books Ltd

Polity Press
ProQuest
Quartet Books
Random House UK Ltd
Redcliffe Press Ltd
Roundhouse Publishing Ltd
Sandstone Press Ltd
Sansom & Co Ltd
Saqi Books
Scottish Cultural Press
Scottish Text Society
Seren
Charles Skilton Ltd
Colin Smythe Ltd
Souvenir Press Ltd
Stenlake Publishing Ltd
Sussex Academic Press
Sussex Publications
The Swedenborg Society
Symposium Publications Literary & Art
Tabb House
Taylor & Francis
Thames & Hudson Ltd
Trog Associates Ltd
Troubador Publishing Ltd
University of Exeter Press
University of Hertfordshire Press
University of Ottawa Press
University of Toronto Press
University of Wales Press
Voltaire Foundation Ltd
John Wiley & Sons Ltd
The Women's Press
Wordsworth Editions Ltd
Worth Press Ltd

MAGIC & THE OCCULT

Aeon Books
Amolibros
Anglo-Saxon Books
Austin & Macauley Publishers Ltd
Blue Beyond Books
Bossiney Books Ltd
Capall Bann Publishing
Caxton Publishing Group Ltd
Collins & Brown
Gerald Duckworth & Co Ltd
Eddison Sadd Editions Ltd
W. Foulsham & Co Ltd
Godsfield Press Ltd
Gothic Image Publications
Robert Hale Ltd
HarperCollins Publishers Ltd
Heart of Albion Press
John Hunt Publishing Ltd
Indepenpress Publishing Ltd
Janus Publishing Co Ltd
Luath Press Ltd
Mandrake of Oxford
Paragon Publishing
Piatkus Books
Quadrille Publishing Ltd
Quantum Publishing
Reardon Publishing
Regency House Publishing Ltd
The Society of Metaphysicians Ltd
Souvenir Press Ltd
Stacey International
Rudolf Steiner Press Ltd
Temple Lodge Publishing
Thames & Hudson Ltd
Thoth Publications
Troubador Publishing Ltd
University of Hertfordshire Press
Warburg Institute
Waverley Books
Zambezi Publishing Ltd

MATHEMATICS & STATISTICS

Anshan Ltd
Anthem Press
Atlantic Books
Atlantic Europe Publishing Co Ltd
Austin & Macauley Publishers Ltd
Bernard Babani (Publishing) Ltd
BEAM Education
Bedford Freeman Worth (BFW)
Blackstaff Press
Cambridge University Press

Carel Press Ltd
Cengage Learning EMEA Ltd
Chalksoft Ltd
Claire Publications
GLMP Ltd
Hodder Education
Icon Books Ltd
Imperial College Press
Institute of Mathematics and its
  Applications
IOP Publishing
Jones & Bartlett International
S. Karger AG
McGraw-Hill Education
Macmillan Education
Macmillan Publishers Ltd
Mentor Books
MW Educational
The National Academies Press
National Archives of Scotland
National Extension College Trust
  Ltd
Nelson Thornes Ltd
W. W. Norton & Company Ltd
Open University Worldwide
Oxford University Press
Palgrave Macmillan
Princeton University Press
ProQuest
Royal Irish Academy
Sage Publications Ltd
Saqi Books
SLP Education
Tarquin Publications
Taylor & Francis
TSO (The Stationery Office Ltd)
University of Hertfordshire Press
Ward Lock Educational Co Ltd
John Wiley & Sons Ltd
WIT Press
Woodhead Publishing Ltd

**MEDICAL (INCL. SELF HELP &
ALTERNATIVE MEDICINE)**

Accent Press Ltd
Amberwood Publishing Ltd
American Psychiatric Publishing
  Inc
Amolibros
Anshan Ltd
Anthem Press
Archive Publishing
Ashgrove Publishing
Austin & Macauley Publishers Ltd
Barny Books
Bene Factum Publishing Ltd
Biohealthcare Publishing (Oxford)
  Ltd
BLA Publishing Ltd
Blackstaff Press
CABI
*Cambridge Publishing
  Management Ltd*
Cambridge University Press
Capall Bann Publishing
Jon Carpenter Publishing
Carroll & Brown Ltd
Caxton Publishing Group Ltd
Clairview Books Ltd
Class Publishing
Clear Answer Medical Publishing
  Ltd
Collins & Brown
Constable & Robinson Ltd
Crown House Publishing Ltd
D & N Publishing
Denor Press Ltd
Dunedin Academic Press
Eddison Sadd Editions Ltd
Elsevier Ltd
The Erskine Press
Filament Publishing Ltd
Findhorn Press Ltd
Floris Books Trust Ltd
W. Foulsham & Co Ltd
Gibson Square
GLMP Ltd
Godsfield Press Ltd
Granta Editions
Haldane Mason Ltd
HarperCollins Publishers Ltd

Hawker Publications
Hawthorn Press
Haynes Publishing
Ian Henry Publications Ltd
Hinton House Publishers Ltd
Hodder Education
How To Books Ltd
Human Kinetics Europe Ltd
John Hunt Publishing Ltd
Imperial College Press
Indepenpress Publishing Ltd
Institute of Physics & Engineering
  in Medicine
International Medical Press
Janus Publishing Co Ltd
Jones & Bartlett International
S. Karger AG
Jessica Kingsley Publishers
Librario Publishers Ltd
Londubh Books
Luath Press Ltd
McGraw-Hill Education
Macmillan Publishers Ltd
Mainstream Publishing Co
  (Edinburgh) Ltd
Mandrake of Oxford
Maney Publishing
Manson Publishing Ltd
Market House Books Ltd
Medikidz Ltd
Mitchell Beazley
M&K Publishing
The National Academies Press
National Extension College Trust
  Ltd
Need2Know
Nelson Thornes Ltd
NHS Immunisation Information
Open University Worldwide
Orpen Press
Oxford University Press
Palgrave Macmillan
Paragon Publishing
PCCS Books Ltd
The Penguin Group (UK) Ltd
Piatkus Books
Portland Press Ltd
PP Publishing
ProQuest
Quadrille Publishing Ltd
Quantum Publishing
Radcliffe Publishing Ltd
Round Hall
Roundhouse Publishing Ltd
Royal College of General
  Practitioners
The Royal College of Psychiatrists
Russell House Publishing Ltd
Scion Publishing Ltd
Sheldon Press
Simon & Schuster (UK) Ltd
Social Affairs Unit
The Society of Metaphysicians Ltd
Souvenir Press Ltd
Rudolf Steiner Press Ltd
Tabb House
Taylor & Francis
Temple Lodge Publishing
tfm publishing Ltd
Troubador Publishing Ltd
TSO (The Stationery Office Ltd)
University of Toronto Press
Merlin Unwin Books Ltd
Waverley Books
Whiting & Birch Ltd
John Wiley & Sons Ltd
Windhorse Publications
WIT Press
Wolters Kluwer Health (P & E) Ltd
Zambezi Publishing Ltd

MILITARY & WAR

A. M. S. Educational Ltd
Adam Matthew Digital Ltd
Air-Britain (Historians) Ltd
Ian Allan Publishing Ltd
Amber Books Ltd
Anglo-Saxon Books
Anova Books
Arena Books (Publishers)
Ashgate Publishing Ltd

Ashgrove Publishing
Atlantic Books
Aurum Press
Austin & Macauley Publishers Ltd
Barny Books
Bene Factum Publishing Ltd
Berghahn Books
Birlinn Ltd
BLA Publishing Ltd
Blackstaff Press
Bloomsbury Publishing Plc
Bodleian Library Publishing
Boydell & Brewer Ltd
Brewin Books Ltd
Bridge Books
Brooklands Books Ltd
*Cambridge Publishing
  Management Ltd*
Carlton Publishing Group
Carnegie Publishing Ltd
Caxton Publishing Group Ltd
Chatham Publishing
Clairview Books Ltd
Colour Heroes Ltd
Compendium Publishing Ltd
Constable & Robinson Ltd
Cork University Press
Countryside Books
Crécy Publishing Ltd
The Crowood Press Ltd
Cualann Press
D & N Publishing
Eric Dobby Publishing Ltd
The Dovecote Press
Ashley Drake Publishing Ltd
Gerald Duckworth & Co Ltd
Elliott & Thompson
English Heritage
The Erskine Press
Essential Works Ltd
Filament Publishing Ltd
W. Foulsham & Co Ltd
Four Courts Press
GLMP Ltd
*Graham-Cameron Publishing &
  Illustration*
Greenhill Books / Lionel Leventhal
  Ltd
Grub Street
Hachette Scotland
Robert Hale Ltd
Halsgrove
HarperCollins Publishers Ltd
Harvard University Press
Haynes Publishing
Helion & Co Ltd
Hodder & Stoughton General
C. Hurst & Co (Publishers) Ltd
Icon Books Ltd
IHS Jane's
Indepenpress Publishing Ltd
Irish Academic Press
ISIS Publishing Ltd
Janus Publishing Co Ltd
Librario Publishers Ltd
Little, Brown Book Group
Luath Press Ltd
The Lutterworth Press
Macmillan Publishers Ltd
Mainstream Publishing Co
  (Edinburgh) Ltd
Maney Publishing
Maritime Books
Maverick House Publishers
Mercier Press Ltd
Mercury Books
Microform Academic Publishers
Middleton Press
John Murray Publishers
Myriad Editions
NMS Enterprises Limited -
  Publishing
W. W. Norton & Company Ltd
The Nostalgia Collection
The Orion Publishing Group Ltd
Osprey Publishing Ltd
Paragon Publishing
The Penguin Group (UK) Ltd
Piatkus Books
Quantum Publishing
Quiller Publishing Ltd
The Radcliffe Press

Rand Publications
Random House UK Ltd
Ravette Publishing Ltd
Reardon Publishing
Regency House Publishing Ltd
Roundhouse Publishing Ltd
Scottish Cultural Press
Shire Publications Ltd
Sigel Press
Simon & Schuster (UK) Ltd
Charles Skilton Ltd
Souvenir Press Ltd
Spokesman
Stacey International
Strong Oak Press
Sussex Academic Press
I. B. Tauris & Co Ltd
Taylor & Francis
Thames & Hudson Ltd
Third Millennium Publishing Ltd
Thorogood Publishing Ltd
Toucan Books Ltd
Transworld Publishers Ltd
Troubador Publishing Ltd
Truran
Unicorn Press
United Writers Publications Ltd
University of Toronto Press
University of Wales Press
Vallentine Mitchell Publishers
Veloce Publishing Ltd
David West Children's Books
Whittles Publishing
John Wiley & Sons Ltd
Neil Wilson Publishing Ltd
Worth Press Ltd
Yale University Press London

MUSIC

Amolibros
Anova Books
Archive Publishing
Ashgate Publishing Ltd
Atlantic Books
Attic Press
Aureus Publishing Ltd
Aurum Press
Beautiful Books Ltd
BLA Publishing Ltd
Black Dog Publishing Ltd
A. & C. Black (Publishers) Ltd
Black Spring Press Ltd
Blackstaff Press
John Blake Publishing Ltd
Bloomsbury Publishing Plc
Blue Beyond Books
Blue Sky Press
Marion Boyars Publishers Ltd
Boydell & Brewer Ltd
Cambridge University Press
Canongate Books
Capall Bann Publishing
Carlton Publishing Group
Chalksoft Ltd
Cló Iar-Chonnachta
Collins & Brown
Compendium Publishing Ltd
The Continuum International
  Publishing Group Ltd
Cork University Press
Dance Books Ltd
Denor Press Ltd
J M Dent
Gerald Duckworth & Co Ltd
Elliott & Thompson
Equinox Publishing Ltd
Essential Works Ltd
Faber & Faber Ltd
Four Courts Press
Granta Editions
Gresham Books Ltd
Guildhall Press
Hachette Scotland
Robert Hale Ltd
HarperCollins Publishers Ltd
Harvard University Press
Hawthorn Press
Haynes Publishing
Helter Skelter Publishing Ltd
Hymns Ancient & Modern Ltd
Independent Music Press

Indepenpress Publishing Ltd
The Lilliput Press Ltd
Little, Brown Book Group
The Littman Library of Jewish
  Civilization
Luath Press Ltd
McCrimmon Publishing Co Ltd
Macmillan Publishers Ltd
Mainstream Publishing Co
  (Edinburgh) Ltd
Market House Books Ltd
Merlin Publishing/Wolfhound
  Press
The MIT Press Ltd
Mitchell Beazley
Moonlight Publishing Ltd
Moorley's Print & Publishing Ltd
Nelson Thornes Ltd
Northumbria University Press
W. W. Norton & Company Ltd
Omnibus Press
Peter Owen Publishers
Oxford University Press
Palazzo Editions Ltd
PC Publishing
The Penguin Group (UK) Ltd
Phaidon Press Ltd
Piatkus Books
ProQuest
Quantum Publishing
Quartet Books
Random House UK Ltd
RotoVision SA
Route Publishing Ltd
Saqi Books
SchoolPlay Productions Ltd
Schott Music Ltd
Scripture Union Publishing
Sheldrake Press
The Shetland Times Ltd
Simon & Schuster (UK) Ltd
Souvenir Press Ltd
Spartan Press Music Publishers Ltd
Stainer & Bell Ltd
Rudolf Steiner Press Ltd
Sussex Academic Press
Sussex Publications
Taigh na Teud Music Publishers
Taylor & Francis
Thames & Hudson Ltd
Transworld Publishers Ltd
Troubador Publishing Ltd
TTS Group
University of Wales Press
Usborne Publishing Ltd
Ward Lock Educational Co Ltd
David West Children's Books
Wild Goose Publishing
John Wiley & Sons Ltd
Neil Wilson Publishing Ltd
Y Lolfa Cyf
Yale University Press London
Zymurgy Publishing

NATURAL HISTORY

AA Publishing
Antique Collectors' Club Ltd
Atlantic Books
Aurum Press
Austin & Macauley Publishers Ltd
Bender Richardson White
BLA Publishing Ltd
A. & C. Black (Publishers) Ltd
Blackstaff Press
Bodleian Library Publishing
British Museum Press
Brown & Whittaker Publishing
Calypso Publications
*Cambridge Publishing
  Management Ltd*
Cambridge University Press
Cameron Books
Capall Bann Publishing
Capuchin Classics
Carlton Publishing Group
Carnegie Publishing Ltd
Caxton Publishing Group Ltd
Chalksoft Ltd
Colour Heroes Ltd
Cork University Press
Cornwall Editions Ltd

Countyvise Ltd
The Crowood Press Ltd
D & N Publishing
The Dovecote Press
Gerald Duckworth & Co Ltd
Earthscan
Elliott & Thompson
The Erskine Press
Ex Libris Press
Graffeg
Graham-Cameron Publishing & Illustration
Granta Editions
Green Books
Haldane Mason Ltd
Robert Hale Ltd
Halsgrove
HarperCollins Publishers Ltd
Harvard University Press
Hodder Education
Alison Hodge Publishers
Icon Books Ltd
Kew Publishing
Librario Publishers Ltd
Logaston Press
Lomond Books Ltd
Luath Press Ltd
The Lutterworth Press
Macmillan Publishers Ltd
Merrell Publishers Ltd
The MIT Press Ltd
Mitchell Beazley
Moonlight Publishing Ltd
The National Academies Press
The National Trust
Natural History Museum Publishing
NMS Enterprises Limited - Publishing
North York Moors National Park Authority
W. W. Norton & Company Ltd
Octopus Publishing Group
Open University Worldwide
The Orion Publishing Group Ltd
Packard Publishing Ltd
Papadakis Publisher
Paragon Publishing
The Penguin Group (UK) Ltd
Philip's
Polperro Heritage Press
Princeton University Press
ProQuest
Quantum Publishing
Quiller Publishing Ltd
Random House UK Ltd
Reardon Publishing
Royal Collection Publications
S. B. Publications
Scottish Children's Press
Scottish Cultural Press
Sheldrake Press
The Shetland Times Ltd
Shire Publications Ltd
Short Books Ltd
Souvenir Press Ltd
Stacey International
Stobart Davies Ltd
Subbuteo Natural History Books
Tango Books Ltd
Thames & Hudson Ltd
Top That! Publishing Plc
Toucan Books Ltd
Troubador Publishing Ltd
Truran
Merlin Unwin Books Ltd
Usborne Publishing Ltd
David West Children's Books
Whittet Books Ltd
Whittles Publishing
John Wiley & Sons Ltd
Willow Island Editions
Worth Press Ltd
Yale University Press London
Zymurgy Publishing

NAUTICAL

Adlard Coles Nautical
Ian Allan Publishing Ltd
Amber Books Ltd
Amolibros

Austin & Macauley Publishers Ltd
The Belmont Press
BLA Publishing Ltd
A. & C. Black (Publishers) Ltd
Brown, Son & Ferguson, Ltd
Chatham Publishing
Countyvise Ltd
Crécy Publishing Ltd
The Crowood Press Ltd
Ex Libris Press
Granta Editions
Haynes Publishing
The Horizon Press
IHS Jane's
Imray Laurie Norie & Wilson Ltd
Janus Publishing Co Ltd
Librario Publishers Ltd
Middleton Press
The National Academies Press
W. W. Norton & Company Ltd
The Nostalgia Collection
The Orion Publishing Group Ltd
Paragon Publishing
Polperro Heritage Press
Quantum Publishing
Quiller Publishing Ltd
Reardon Publishing
Roadmaster Publishing
Scottish Cultural Press
Special Interest Model Books Ltd
Stenlake Publishing Ltd
Truran
TSO (The Stationery Office Ltd)
Twelveheads Press
Unicorn Press
United Writers Publications Ltd
Paul Watkins Publishing
Whittles Publishing
John Wiley & Sons Ltd
Neil Wilson Publishing Ltd
Witherby Publishing Group

PHILOSOPHY

Acumen Publishing Ltd
Alban Books Ltd
Amolibros
Arena Books (Publishers)
Ashgate Publishing Ltd
Atlantic Books
Austin & Macauley Publishers Ltd
Black Ace Books
Blue Beyond Books
Marion Boyars Publishers Ltd
Boydell & Brewer Ltd
Cambridge University Press
Canongate Books
Capall Bann Publishing
Jon Carpenter Publishing
James Clarke & Co
Compendium Publishing Ltd
The Continuum International Publishing Group Ltd
Cork University Press
Darton, Longman & Todd Ltd
Gerald Duckworth & Co Ltd
Emerald Group Publishing Ltd
Equinox Publishing Ltd
Everyman's Library
Fabian Society
Filament Publishing Ltd
Floris Books Trust Ltd
Four Courts Press
Gibson Square
Gothic Image Publications
Gracewing Publishing
Green Books
Halban Publishers
Harvard University Press
Heart of Albion Press
Hodder Education
Hodder Faith
John Hunt Publishing Ltd
Hymns Ancient & Modern Ltd
Icon Books Ltd
Imprint Academic
Indepenpress Publishing Ltd
Intellect Ltd
Janus Publishing Co Ltd
The Littman Library of Jewish Civilization
Living Time® Media International

The Lutterworth Press
McGraw-Hill Education
Macmillan Publishers Ltd
Mandrake of Oxford
The MIT Press Ltd
Nelson Thornes Ltd
W. W. Norton & Company Ltd
Open Gate Press
The Orion Publishing Group Ltd
Oxford University Press
Palgrave Macmillan
Paupers' Press
The Penguin Group (UK) Ltd
Pipers' Ash Ltd
Pluto Books Ltd
Polity Press
Princeton University Press
Random House UK Ltd
Roundhouse Publishing Ltd
Saqi Books
Shepheard-Walwyn (Publishers) Ltd
Short Books Ltd
The Society of Metaphysicians Ltd
Souvenir Press Ltd
Spokesman
Rudolf Steiner Press Ltd
Sussex Academic Press
I. B. Tauris & Co Ltd
Taylor & Francis
Temple Lodge Publishing
Thames & Hudson Ltd
Tharpa Publications
Troubador Publishing Ltd
University of Toronto Press
University of Wales Press
Veritas Publications
Voltaire Foundation Ltd
Warburg Institute
Weidenfeld & Nicolson
John Wiley & Sons Ltd
Windhorse Publications
Wordsworth Editions Ltd
Yale University Press London

PHOTOGRAPHY

AA Publishing
Anova Books
Antique Collectors' Club Ltd
Arcadia Books Ltd
Aurum Press
AVA Publishing (UK) Ltd
BBH Publishing Ltd
Berg Publishers
Black Dog Publishing Ltd
Blackstaff Press
Carlton Publishing Group
Cló Iar-Chonnachta
Coastal Publishing
Collins & Brown
Compendium Publishing Ltd
Cork University Press
D & N Publishing
Delta Alpha Publishing Ltd
Essential Works Ltd
F+W Media International, LTD (formerly David & Charles)
Fiell Publishing Ltd
Flambard Press
Freelance Market News
Garnet Publishing Ltd
Gomer
Graffeg
Granta Editions
Guildhall Press
Robert Hale Ltd
HarperCollins Publishers Ltd
Haynes Publishing
Hayward Publishing
Alison Hodge Publishers
The Ilex Press Ltd
In Easy Steps Ltd
Dewi Lewis Publishing
The Lilliput Press Ltd
Luath Press Ltd
Lund Humphries
Mainstream Publishing Co (Edinburgh) Ltd
Mentor Books
Merlin Publishing/Wolfhound Press

Merrell Publishers Ltd
The MIT Press Ltd
Mitchell Beazley
National Galleries of Scotland
National Portrait Gallery Publications
New Internationalist Publications Ltd
Northumbria University Press
Pagoda Tree Press
Papadakis Publisher
The Penguin Group (UK) Ltd
Phaidon Press Ltd
Polperro Heritage Press
Prestel Publishing Ltd
Quadrille Publishing Ltd
Quantum Publishing
Random House UK Ltd
RotoVision SA
Roundhouse Publishing Ltd
Royal Collection Publications
Saqi Books
Seren
Sheldrake Press
Stacey International
Tate Publishing
teNeues Publishing UK Ltd
Thames & Hudson Ltd
Third Millennium Publishing Ltd
Truran
Unicorn Press
V&A Publishing
Weidenfeld & Nicolson
Which? Ltd
John Wiley & Sons Ltd
Philip Wilson Publishers
Yale University Press London
Zymurgy Publishing

PHYSICS

Amolibros
Anshan Ltd
Anthem Press
Atlantic Europe Publishing Co Ltd
Bedford Freeman Worth (BFW)
BLA Publishing Ltd
Cambridge University Press
Cengage Learning EMEA Ltd
Gerald Duckworth & Co Ltd
GLMP Ltd
Granta Editions
HarperCollins Publishers Ltd
Hodder Education
Icon Books Ltd
Imperial College Press
Institute of Physics & Engineering in Medicine
IOP Publishing
Jones & Bartlett International
McGraw-Hill Education
Macmillan Education
Macmillan Publishers Ltd
The National Academies Press
National Extension College Trust Ltd
Nelson Thornes Ltd
W. W. Norton & Company Ltd
Open University Worldwide
Oxford University Press
Palgrave Macmillan
ProQuest
Taylor & Francis
Ward Lock Educational Co Ltd
John Wiley & Sons Ltd

POETRY

A. M. S. Educational Ltd
Acair Ltd
Accent Press Ltd
Albyn Press
Alma Books Ltd
Amolibros
Anglo-Saxon Books
Anthem Press
Anvil Press Poetry Ltd
Association for Scottish Literary Studies
Atlantic Books
Austin & Macauley Publishers Ltd
Authorhouse UK Ltd

Barddas
Bene Factum Publishing Ltd
Joseph Biddulph Publisher
Birlinn Ltd
Blackstaff Press
Bloodaxe Books Ltd
Blue Beyond Books
Blue Ocean Publishing
Blue Sky Press
Bonacia Ltd
Brown & Whittaker Publishing
Canongate Books
Cló Iar-Chonnachta
Cois Life
Countyvise Ltd
Enitharmon Press
Everyman's Library
Ex Libris Press
Faber & Faber Ltd
Fastprint
Five Leaves Publications
Flambard Press
W. Foulsham & Co Ltd
Freelance Market News
The Gallery Press
GLMP Ltd
Gomer
Green Books
Guildhall Press
Gwasg Gwenffrwd
Hachette Children's Books
HarperCollins Publishers Ltd
Hippopotamus Press
Icon Books Ltd
Indepenpress Publishing Ltd
ISIS Publishing Ltd
Ithaca Press
Janus Publishing Co Ltd
Jarndyce Booksellers
The King's England Press
Lapwing Publications
Liverpool University Press
Living Time® Media International
Luath Press Ltd
Macmillan Children's Books Ltd
Macmillan Publishers Ltd
Mandrake of Oxford
Mentor Books
Mercier Press Ltd
Moorley's Print & Publishing Ltd
Need2Know
Nelson Thornes Ltd
New Island Books Ltd
NMS Enterprises Limited - Publishing
W. W. Norton & Company Ltd
The Old Stile Press
The Oleander Press
Oneworld Classics
Pan Macmillan
Paragon Publishing
The Penguin Group (UK) Ltd
Pentathol Publishing
Pipers' Ash Ltd
ProQuest
Random House UK Ltd
Redcliffe Press Ltd
Robinswood Press Ltd
Route Publishing Ltd
Saint Albert's Press
Saqi Books
Scottish Children's Press
Scottish Cultural Press
Scottish Text Society
Seren
Charles Skilton Ltd
Spokesman
Stacey International
Stenlake Publishing Ltd
Symposium Publications Literary & Art
Tabb House
Troubador Publishing Ltd
University of Wales Press
John Wiley & Sons Ltd
Wordsworth Editions Ltd
Y Lolfa Cyf

POLITICS & WORLD AFFAIRS

Acumen Publishing Ltd
Amolibros

Anthem Press
Arcadia Books Ltd
Arena Books (Publishers)
Ashgate Publishing Ltd
Atlantic Books
Attic Press
Austin & Macauley Publishers Ltd
Berghahn Books
Blackstaff Press
Bloomsbury Publishing Plc
Bodleian Library Publishing
Cambridge Archive Editions Ltd
Cambridge University Press
Canongate Books
Capuchin Classics
Jon Carpenter Publishing
Centre for Economic Policy
 Research
Clairview Books Ltd
Commonwealth Secretariat
The Continuum International
 Publishing Group Ltd
The Davenant Press
Ashley Drake Publishing Ltd
Gerald Duckworth & Co Ltd
Earthscan
Elliott & Thompson
Ethics International Press Ltd
Faber & Faber Ltd
Fabian Society
Five Leaves Publications
Garnet Publishing Ltd
Gibson Square
Gill & Macmillan
GLMP Ltd
Gothic Image Publications
Granta Books
Green Books
Guildhall Press
Gwasg Gwenffrwd
Halban Publishers
Robert Hale Ltd
John Harper Publishing Ltd
HarperCollins Publishers Ltd
Harvard University Press
Hawthorn Press
Hodder Education
Hodder & Stoughton General
C. Hurst & Co (Publishers) Ltd
Icon Books Ltd
IHS Jane's
Imprint Academic
Indepenpress Publishing Ltd
Institute of Employment Rights
Irish Academic Press
Ithaca Press
Janus Publishing Co Ltd
Liberties Press
Little, Brown Book Group
The Littman Library of Jewish
 Civilization
Liverpool University Press
Luath Press Ltd
The Lutterworth Press
McGraw-Hill Education
Macmillan Publishers Ltd
Mainstream Publishing Co
 (Edinburgh) Ltd
Manchester University Press
Maverick House Publishers
Melisende UK Ltd
Mentor Books
Mercier Press Ltd
The Merlin Press Ltd
Merlin Publishing/Wolfhound
 Press
Microform Academic Publishers
The MIT Press Ltd
Myriad Editions
Nelson Thornes Ltd
New Internationalist Publications
 Ltd
New Island Books Ltd
Northumbria University Press
W. W. Norton & Company Ltd
The O'Brien Press Ltd
Open Gate Press
Open University Worldwide
The Orion Publishing Group Ltd
Orpen Press
Oxfam Publishing
Oxford University Press

Pagoda Tree Press
Palgrave Macmillan
The Penguin Group (UK) Ltd
Pluto Books Ltd
The Policy Press
Polity Press
Portobello Books Ltd
Princeton University Press
Profile Books
ProQuest
Quartet Books
The Radcliffe Press
Rand Publications
Random House UK Ltd
Roundhouse Publishing Ltd
Joseph Rowntree Foundation
Royal Irish Academy
Sage Publications Ltd
Sandstone Press Ltd
Saqi Books
Shepheard-Walwyn (Publishers)
 Ltd
Simon & Schuster (UK) Ltd
Social Affairs Unit
Spokesman
Stacey International
Rudolf Steiner Press Ltd
Sussex Academic Press
I. B. Tauris & Co Ltd
Taylor & Francis
Temple Lodge Publishing
Transworld Publishers Ltd
Trentham Books
Troubador Publishing Ltd
TSO (The Stationery Office Ltd)
University of Ottawa Press
University of Toronto Press
University of Wales Press
Vallentine Mitchell Publishers
Weidenfeld & Nicolson
John Wiley & Sons Ltd
The Women's Press
Y Lolfa Cyf
Yale University Press London
Zed Books Ltd

PSYCHOLOGY & PSYCHIATRY

American Psychiatric Publishing
 Inc
Ann Arbor Publishers Ltd
Anshan Ltd
Archive Publishing
Ashgrove Publishing
Atlantic Books
Austin & Macauley Publishers Ltd
Beautiful Books Ltd
Bedford Freeman Worth (BFW)
Nicholas Brealey Publishing
British Association for Adoption &
 Fostering
Cambridge University Press
Canongate Books
Capall Bann Publishing
Cengage Learning EMEA Ltd
Channel View Publications Ltd
Constable & Robinson Ltd
Cork University Press
Crown House Publishing Ltd
Darton, Longman & Todd Ltd
Delancey Press Ltd
Ashley Drake Publishing Ltd
Emerald Group Publishing Ltd
The Fostering Network
W. Foulsham & Co Ltd
Gibson Square
Gill & Macmillan
Gothic Image Publications
Granta Editions
HarperCollins Publishers Ltd
Harvard University Press
Hawthorn Press
Heart of Albion Press
Hinton House Publishers Ltd
Hodder Education
Human Kinetics Europe Ltd
John Hunt Publishing Ltd
Icon Books Ltd
Imprint Academic
Jones & Bartlett International
S. Karger AG
Karnac Books Ltd

Jessica Kingsley Publishers
Learning Matters Ltd
Little, Brown Book Group
Living Time® Media International
McGraw-Hill Education
Macmillan Publishers Ltd
Mainstream Publishing Co
 (Edinburgh) Ltd
Market House Books Ltd
The MIT Press Ltd
M&K Publishing
The National Academies Press
The National Autistic Society
 (NAS)
National Extension College Trust
 Ltd
Nelson Thornes Ltd
W. W. Norton & Company Ltd
Open Gate Press
Open University Worldwide
Orpen Press
Oxford University Press
Palgrave Macmillan
PCCS Books Ltd
The Penguin Group (UK) Ltd
Piatkus Books
Pipers' Ash Ltd
ProQuest
Roundhouse Publishing Ltd
The Royal College of Psychiatrists
Russell House Publishing Ltd
Sage Publications Ltd
Sheldon Press
Sherwood Publishing
Souvenir Press Ltd
Sussex Academic Press
Taylor & Francis
Troubador Publishing Ltd
United Writers Publications Ltd
University of Hertfordshire Press
Whiting & Birch Ltd
John Wiley & Sons Ltd
Wolters Kluwer Health (P & E) Ltd
The Women's Press

**REFERENCE BOOKS,
DIRECTORIES & DICTIONARIES**

Acumen Publishing Ltd
Adamson Publishing Ltd
Alban Books Ltd
Albyn Press
Ian Allan Publishing Ltd
Amber Books Ltd
American Psychiatric Publishing
 Inc
Anglo-Saxon Books
Anshan Ltd
Anthem Press
Antique Collectors' Club Ltd
Appletree Press Ltd
Ashgate Publishing Ltd
Atlantic Books
Atlantic Europe Publishing Co Ltd
Aurelian Information Ltd
Aurora Metro Publications Ltd
Austin & Macauley Publishers Ltd
AVA Publishing (UK) Ltd
Award Publications Ltd
Beautiful Books Ltd
Bender Richardson White
Bene Factum Publishing Ltd
Joseph Biddulph Publisher
BLA Publishing Ltd
A. & C. Black (Publishers) Ltd
Blackstaff Press
Bloomsbury Publishing Plc
BML
Bodleian Library Publishing
Boydell & Brewer Ltd
British Association for Adoption &
 Fostering
British Museum Press
Calypso Publications
*Cambridge Publishing
 Management Ltd*
Cambridge University Press
Camra Books
Capuchin Classics
Carel Press Ltd
The Catholic Truth Society
Caxton Publishing Group Ltd

CBD Research Ltd
Cengage Learning EMEA Ltd
Church House Publishing
James Clarke & Co
Collins & Brown
Commonwealth Secretariat
The Continuum International
 Publishing Group Ltd
Countryside Books
Crimson Publishing
D & N Publishing
Delta Alpha Publishing Ltd
J M Dent
Diagram Visual Information Ltd
Eric Dobby Publishing Ltd
Gerald Duckworth & Co Ltd
Earthscan
Edward Elgar Publishing Ltd
Encyclopaedia Britannica (UK) Ltd
Energy Institute
Equinox Publishing Ltd
Euromonitor International
Executive Grapevine International
 Ltd
Facet Publishing
Food Trade Press Ltd
W. Foulsham & Co Ltd
Four Courts Press
Friends of the Earth
Geography Publications
Stanley Gibbons
Gill & Macmillan
Gomer
*Graham-Cameron Publishing &
 Illustration*
Granta Editions
Green Books
Gwasg Gwenffrwd
Hachette Children's Books
Peter Haddock Publishing
Robert Hale Ltd
Harden's Ltd
HarperCollins Publishers Ltd
Harvard University Press
Haynes Publishing
Hemming Information Services
Hodder Education
How To Books Ltd
Hymns Ancient & Modern Ltd
Hypatia Publications
Icon Books Ltd
IHS Jane's
The Ilex Press Ltd
In Easy Steps Ltd
Indepenpress Publishing Ltd
International Network for the
 Availability of Scientific
 Publications (INASP)
IVP
IWA Publishing
Jarndyce Booksellers
Richard Joseph Publishers Ltd
Kew Publishing
Kogan Page Ltd
Kyle Books
Dewi Lewis Publishing
Lexus Ltd
The Lilliput Press Ltd
LISU
Logaston Press
Lomond Books Ltd
The Lutterworth Press
McGraw-Hill Education
Macmillan Education
Macmillan Publishers Ltd
Manchester University Press
Market House Books Ltd
Mentor Books
Mercury Books
Merlin Publishing/Wolfhound
 Press
The MIT Press Ltd
Mitchell Beazley
National Housing Federation
National Portrait Gallery
 Publications
The National Trust
Natural History Museum
 Publishing
New Internationalist Publications
 Ltd
Northumbria University Press

The Oleander Press
On Stream Publications Ltd
The Orion Publishing Group Ltd
Oxford University Press
Packard Publishing Ltd
Pagoda Tree Press
Palgrave Macmillan
The Penguin Group (UK) Ltd
Philip's
Polperro Heritage Press
Portland Press Ltd
Princeton University Press
ProQuest
Quiller Publishing Ltd
Radcliffe Publishing Ltd
Ripley Publishing Ltd
RotoVision SA
Round Hall
Roundhouse Publishing Ltd
Royal Irish Academy
RSC Publishing
Sage Publications Ltd
St Jerome Publishing Ltd
Scottish Cultural Press
Social Affairs Unit
Stacey International
Stainer & Bell Ltd
STRI (Sports Turf Research
 Institute)
I. B. Tauris & Co Ltd
Taylor & Francis
Thames & Hudson Ltd
Top That! Publishing Plc
Toucan Books Ltd
Trotman Publishing
Truran
TSO (The Stationery Office Ltd)
UCAS
Unicorn Press
University of Ottawa Press
University of Toronto Press
University of Wales Press
Merlin Unwin Books Ltd
Usborne Publishing Ltd
Veloce Publishing Ltd
Voltaire Foundation Ltd
Waterside Press
Waverley Books
Which? Ltd
Whittles Publishing
John Wiley & Sons Ltd
Witherby Publishing Group
Wolters Kluwer Health (P & E) Ltd
The Women's Press
Wordsworth Editions Ltd

RELIGION & THEOLOGY

Acumen Publishing Ltd
Alban Books Ltd
Anglo-Saxon Books
Anno Domini Publishing (ADPS)
Arena Books (Publishers)
Ashgate Publishing Ltd
Ashgrove Publishing
Atlantic Books
Atlantic Europe Publishing Co Ltd
Austin & Macauley Publishers Ltd
Authentic Media
Authorhouse UK Ltd
The Banner of Truth Trust
Bender Richardson White
Berghahn Books
Bible Reading Fellowship
Joseph Biddulph Publisher
BLA Publishing Ltd
Blackstaff Press
Blue Beyond Books
Blue Ocean Publishing
Borthwick Publications
Bryntirion Press
*Cambridge Publishing
 Management Ltd*
Cambridge University Press
Canongate Books
Capall Bann Publishing
Capuchin Classics
The Catholic Truth Society
Christian Education
Christian Focus Publications
Church House Publishing
Church of Ireland Publishing

Clairview Books Ltd
James Clarke & Co
Columba
The Continuum International
  Publishing Group Ltd
David C. Cook (UK)
Countyvise Ltd
Cyhoeddiadau'r Gair
Darton, Longman & Todd Ltd
The Davenant Press
Day One Publications
Gerald Duckworth & Co Ltd
Eagle Publishing Ltd
Equinox Publishing Ltd
Family Publications
Fastprint
Filament Publishing Ltd
Findhorn Press Ltd
Floris Books Trust Ltd
Four Courts Press
Garnet Publishing Ltd
GLMP Ltd
Godsfield Press Ltd
Gothic Image Publications
Gracewing Publishing
Graham-Cameron Publishing &
  Illustration
Gresham Books Ltd
Gwasg Gwenffrwd
Halban Publishers
HarperCollins Publishers Ltd
Harvard University Press
Hawthorn Press
Heart of Albion Press
Highland Books
Hodder Education
Hodder Faith
John Hunt Publishing Ltd
C. Hurst & Co (Publishers) Ltd
Hymns Ancient & Modern Ltd
Icon Books Ltd
Imprint Academic
Indepenpress Publishing Ltd
Irish Academic Press
The Islamic Texts Society
Ithaca Press
IVP
Janus Publishing Co Ltd
Jessica Kingsley Publishers
Kube Publishing Ltd
Liberties Press
Lion Hudson Plc
The Littman Library of Jewish
  Civilization
The Lutterworth Press
McCrimmon Publishing Co Ltd
Macmillan Publishers Ltd
Mandrake of Oxford
Maney Publishing
Melisende UK Ltd
Mercier Press Ltd
Microform Academic Publishers
Moorley's Print & Publishing Ltd
National Extension College Trust
  Ltd
Nelson Thornes Ltd
W. W. Norton & Company Ltd
The Open Bible Trust
Open Gate Press
Open University Worldwide
Oxford University Press
Palgrave Macmillan
Paragon Publishing
PCCS Books Ltd
The Penguin Group (UK) Ltd
Pickering & Chatto (Publishers) Ltd
Piquant Editions
ProQuest
Quantum Publishing
Redemptorist Publications
Roundhouse Publishing Ltd
Sage Publications Ltd
Saint Albert's Press
Saqi Books
Scottish Children's Press
Scottish Cultural Press
Scripture Union Publishing
Shepheard-Walwyn (Publishers)
  Ltd
Simon & Schuster (UK) Ltd
The Society for Promoting
  Christian Knowledge (SPCK)

Souvenir Press Ltd
Stacey International
Stainer & Bell Ltd
Rudolf Steiner Press Ltd
Sussex Academic Press
The Swedenborg Society
Ta Ha Publishers Ltd
Tabb House
I. B. Tauris & Co Ltd
Taylor & Francis
Temple Lodge Publishing
Thames & Hudson Ltd
Tharpa Publications
Thoth Publications
Trinitarian Bible Society
University of Wales Press
Vallentine Mitchell Publishers
Veritas Publications
Voltaire Foundation Ltd
Warburg Institute
Ward Lock Educational Co Ltd
Wild Goose Publications
John Wiley & Sons Ltd
Windhorse Publications
Worth Press Ltd
Yale University Press London

SCIENCE FICTION

Allison & Busby
Arena Books (Publishers)
Atlantic Books
Austin & Macauley Publishers Ltd
Authorhouse UK Ltd
Constable & Robinson Ltd
Gerald Duckworth & Co Ltd
Everyman's Library
Victor Gollancz Ltd
HarperCollins Publishers Ltd
Hodder & Stoughton General
Icon Books Ltd
Indepenpress Publishing Ltd
ISIS Publishing Ltd
Janus Publishing Co Ltd
Little, Brown Book Group
Liverpool University Press
Living Time® Media International
Macmillan Publishers Ltd
Orion Books Ltd
The Orion Publishing Group Ltd
Pan Macmillan
Paragon Publishing
Pipers' Ash Ltd
Random House UK Ltd
Sandstone Press Ltd
Sigel Press
Simon & Schuster (UK) Ltd
Transworld Publishers Ltd
Troubador Publishing Ltd
United Writers Publications Ltd

SCIENTIFIC & TECHNICAL

Anshan Ltd
Anthem Press
Archetype Publications Ltd
Atlantic Europe Publishing Co Ltd
Austin & Macauley Publishers Ltd
Bernard Babani (Publishing) Ltd
Biohealthcare Publishing (Oxford)
  Ltd
British Geological Survey
CABI
Calypso Publications
Cambridge University Press
Chalksoft Ltd
Commonwealth Secretariat
J M Dent
Donhead Publishing Ltd
Earthscan
Elsevier Ltd
Energy Institute
Food Trade Press Ltd
Forensic Science Society
The Geological Society
GLMP Ltd
Granta Editions
Greenleaf Publishing
HarperCollins Publishers Ltd
Haynes Publishing
Hodder Education
Human Kinetics Europe Ltd

IChemE
Icon Books Ltd
IHS BRE Press
Imperial College Press
Imprint Academic
In Easy Steps Ltd
Institute of Acoustics
Institute of Food Science &
  Technology
Institute of Physics & Engineering
  in Medicine
Institution of Engineering and
  Technology (IET)
Intellect Ltd
IOP Publishing
IWA Publishing
Jones & Bartlett International
Kew Publishing
Leatherhead Food Research
McGraw-Hill Education
Macmillan Publishers Ltd
Maney Publishing
Manson Publishing Ltd
Market House Books Ltd
Medikidz Ltd
Mentor Books
The MIT Press Ltd
The National Academies Press
Natural History Museum
  Publishing
Nelson Thornes Ltd
NMS Enterprises Limited -
  Publishing
Open University Worldwide
Packard Publishing Ltd
Palgrave Macmillan
Papadakis Publisher
Paragon Publishing
PC Publishing
Pickering & Chatto (Publishers) Ltd
Portland Press Ltd
Princeton University Press
ProQuest
Radcliffe Publishing Ltd
RSC Publishing
Sage Publications Ltd
Scion Publishing Ltd
The Society of Metaphysicians Ltd
Stacey International
Stobart Davies Ltd
STRI (Sports Turf Research
  Institute)
Tarquin Publications
Taylor & Francis
Trog Associates Ltd
TSO (The Stationery Office Ltd)
Usborne Publishing Ltd
David West Children's Books
Whittles Publishing
John Wiley & Sons Ltd
WIT Press
Wolters Kluwer Health (P & E) Ltd
Woodhead Publishing Ltd

SOCIOLOGY & ANTHROPOLOGY

Acumen Publishing Ltd
Anthem Press
Arena Books (Publishers)
Ashgate Publishing Ltd
Austin & Macauley Publishers Ltd
Beautiful Books Ltd
Berg Publishers
Berghahn Books
British Association for Adoption &
  Fostering
British Museum Press
Cambridge University Press
Jon Carpenter Publishing
Centre for Policy on Ageing
Channel View Publications Ltd
Countryside Books
Dunedin Academic Press
Earthscan
Emerald Group Publishing Ltd
Equinox Publishing Ltd
Garnet Publishing Ltd
Gibson Square
GLMP Ltd
Granta Editions
Gwasg Gwenffrwd

Harvard University Press
Hawthorn Press
Heart of Albion Press
Hodder Education
John Hunt Publishing Ltd
C. Hurst & Co (Publishers) Ltd
Icon Books Ltd
Imprint Academic
Institute of Education
  (Publications), University of
  London
Intellect Ltd
Irish Academic Press
Ithaca Press
Janus Publishing Co Ltd
Jarndyce Booksellers
Jessica Kingsley Publishers
Sean Kingston Publishing
Learning Matters Ltd
The Littman Library of Jewish
  Civilization
Liverpool University Press
McGraw-Hill Education
Macmillan Publishers Ltd
Manchester University Press
Mandrake of Oxford
The Merlin Press Ltd
Microform Academic Publishers
National Extension College Trust
  Ltd
Nelson Thornes Ltd
NMS Enterprises Limited -
  Publishing
W. W. Norton & Company Ltd
Open University Worldwide
Orpen Press
Palgrave Macmillan
Piatkus Books
Plowright Press
Pluto Books Ltd
The Policy Press
Polity Press
Princeton University Press
ProQuest
Joseph Rowntree Foundation
Russell House Publishing Ltd
Sage Publications Ltd
Saqi Books
Scottish Cultural Press
Shire Publications Ltd
Social Affairs Unit
Souvenir Press Ltd
Spokesman
Rudolf Steiner Press Ltd
Sussex Academic Press
I. B. Tauris & Co Ltd
Taylor & Francis
Thames & Hudson Ltd
Troubador Publishing Ltd
University of Hertfordshire Press
University of Ottawa Press
University of Toronto Press
University of Wales Press
Waterside Press
Whiting & Birch Ltd
John Wiley & Sons Ltd
Zed Books Ltd

SPORTS & GAMES

Ian Allan Publishing Ltd
J. A. Allen
Amber Books Ltd
Amolibros
Anova Books
Appletree Press Ltd
Atlantic Books
Aureus Publishing Ltd
Aurum Press
Austin & Macauley Publishers Ltd
A. & C. Black (Publishers) Ltd
Blackstaff Press
John Blake Publishing Ltd
Bodleian Library Publishing
Brown Dog Books
Butterfingers Books
Carel Press Ltd
Carlton Publishing Group
Christian Focus Publications
Cicerone Press Ltd
Coachwise Ltd
Collins & Brown

Copper Beech Publishing Ltd
Cork University Press
Countyvise Ltd
The Crowood Press Ltd
Cualann Press
D & N Publishing
The Derby Books Publishing Co
  Ltd
Diagram Visual Information Ltd
Ashley Drake Publishing Ltd
Gerald Duckworth & Co Ltd
Elliott & Thompson
Essential Works Ltd
FHG Guides Ltd
Filament Publishing Ltd
Footprint Travel Guides
W. Foulsham & Co Ltd
Gomer
Graffeg
Granta Editions
Hachette Scotland
Haldane Mason Ltd
Robert Hale Ltd
HarperCollins Publishers Ltd
Hart McLeod Ltd
Harvey Map Services Ltd
Haynes Publishing
Roger Heavens
Hodder Education
Hodder & Stoughton General
Alison Hodge Publishers
Human Kinetics Europe Ltd
Icon Books Ltd
Imray Laurie Norie & Wilson Ltd
Indepenpress Publishing Ltd
Janus Publishing Co Ltd
Jones & Bartlett International
Jessica Kingsley Publishers
Kyle Books
Dewi Lewis Publishing
Liberties Press
Little, Brown Book Group
Luath Press Ltd
The Lutterworth Press
Macmillan Publishers Ltd
Mainstream Publishing Co
  (Edinburgh) Ltd
Maverick House Publishers
Mentor Books
Mercier Press Ltd
Merlin Publishing/Wolfhound
  Press
Mitchell Beazley
Motor Racing Publications Ltd
Nelson Thornes Ltd
W. W. Norton & Company Ltd
The O'Brien Press Ltd
Octopus Publishing Group
The Oleander Press
The Orion Publishing Group Ltd
Pan Macmillan
Paragon Publishing
Pipers' Ash Ltd
Quantum Publishing
Quiller Publishing Ltd
Raceform Ltd / Racing Post Books
Random House UK Ltd
Reflections of a Bygone Age
Roundhouse Publishing Ltd
Russell House Publishing Ltd
Sandstone Press Ltd
Scala Publishers Ltd
Scottish Children's Press
Short Books Ltd
Sigma Press
Simon & Schuster (UK) Ltd
SLP Education
Smith Settle Printing &
  Bookbinding Ltd
Soccer Books Ltd
Souvenir Press Ltd
Sportsbooks Ltd
STRI (Sports Turf Research
  Institute)
Summersdale Publishers Ltd
Sussex Academic Press
Taylor & Francis
Top That! Publishing Plc
Transworld Publishers Ltd
Troubador Publishing Ltd
United Writers Publications Ltd
University of Wales Press

Merlin Unwin Books Ltd
Usborne Publishing Ltd
Veloce Publishing Ltd
Vertical Editions
Weidenfeld & Nicolson
David West Children's Books
John Wiley & Sons Ltd
Y Lolfa Cyf
Yore Publications

THEATRE, DRAMA & DANCE

Amolibros
Ashgate Publishing Ltd
Association for Scottish Literary
　Studies
Aurora Metro Publications Ltd
Austin & Macauley Publishers Ltd
Ruth Bean Publishers
Berghahn Books
A. & C. Black (Publishers) Ltd
Blackstaff Press
Bloomsbury Publishing Plc
Blue Ocean Publishing
Marion Boyars Publishers Ltd
Brown, Son & Ferguson, Ltd
Cambridge University Press
Capall Bann Publishing
Carel Press Ltd
Cló Iar-Chonnachta
Cois Life
Collins & Brown
The Continuum International
　Publishing Group Ltd
Cork University Press
Cressrelles Publishing Co Ltd
The Crowood Press Ltd
D & N Publishing
Dance Books Ltd
Ashley Drake Publishing Ltd
Dramatic Lines
Gerald Duckworth & Co Ltd
Faber & Faber Ltd
Filament Publishing Ltd
Samuel French Ltd
The Gallery Press
Gibson Square
GLMP Ltd
Granta Editions
Guildhall Press
Hanbury Plays
Ian Henry Publications Ltd
Nick Hern Books
Human Kinetics Europe Ltd
Indepenpress Publishing Ltd
Intellect Ltd
Irish Academic Press
Janus Publishing Co Ltd
Kenyon-Deane
The Littman Library of Jewish
　Civilization
Luath Press Ltd
Macmillan Publishers Ltd
Manchester University Press
Market House Books Ltd
Mercier Press Ltd
J. Garnet Miller
Moorley's Print & Publishing Ltd
Nelson Thornes Ltd
New Island Books Ltd
New Playwrights' Network
Northcote House Publishers Ltd
Northumbria University Press
W. W. Norton & Company Ltd
The Old Stile Press
Open University Worldwide
Peter Owen Publishers
Palgrave Macmillan

Paragon Publishing
Pipers' Ash Ltd
The Playwrights Publishing Co
ProQuest
Quartet Books
RotoVision SA
Russell House Publishing Ltd
SchoolPlay Productions Ltd
Scottish Cultural Press
Charles Skilton Ltd
SLP Education
Colin Smythe Ltd
Souvenir Press Ltd
Spokesman
Stainer & Bell Ltd
Rudolf Steiner Press Ltd
Sussex Academic Press
Taylor & Francis
Thames & Hudson Ltd
Trentham Books
Troubador Publishing Ltd
University of Exeter Press
University of Hertfordshire Press
University of Ottawa Press
University of Toronto Press
V&A Publishing
Joseph Weinberger Ltd
Yale University Press London

TRANSPORT

AA Publishing
Albyn Press
Ian Allan Publishing Ltd
Amber Books Ltd
Ashgate Publishing Ltd
Atlantic Books
Aurum Press
Barny Books
The Belmont Press
Brewin Books Ltd
Brooklands Books Ltd
Carlton Publishing Group
Caxton Publishing Group Ltd
Chatham Publishing
Colourpoint Books
Copper Beech Publishing Ltd
Countryside Books
Countyvise Ltd
Crécy Publishing Ltd
The Crowood Press Ltd
G. L. Crowther
D & N Publishing
The Derby Books Publishing Co
　Ltd
The Dovecote Press
Earthscan
Edward Elgar Publishing Ltd
Elm Publications
Emerald Group Publishing Ltd
Essential Works Ltd
Ex Libris Press
F+W Media International, LTD
　(formerly David & Charles)
Friends of the Earth
Gomer
Granta Editions
Robert Hale Ltd
Haynes Publishing
Ian Henry Publications Ltd
The Horizon Press
IHS Jane's
Imray Laurie Norie & Wilson Ltd
Irwell Press Ltd
Kogan Page Ltd
McGraw-Hill Education
Manchester University Press
Maney Publishing

Maritime Books
Merrell Publishers Ltd
Merton Priory Press Ltd
Middleton Press
Motor Racing Publications Ltd
NMS Enterprises Limited -
　Publishing
The Nostalgia Collection
Quantum Publishing
Quiller Publishing Ltd
Random House UK Ltd
Reflections of a Bygone Age
Roadmaster Publishing
Sheaf Publishing
Sheldrake Press
Shire Publications Ltd
Charles Skilton Ltd
Soccer Books Ltd
Special Interest Model Books Ltd
Stenlake Publishing Ltd
Troubador Publishing Ltd
TSO (The Stationery Office Ltd)
Twelveheads Press
Veloce Publishing Ltd
David West Children's Books
WIT Press
Witherby Publishing Group

TRAVEL & TOPOGRAPHY

AA Publishing
Amolibros
Chris Andrews Publications Ltd
Appletree Press Ltd
Arcadia Books Ltd
Arena Books (Publishers)
Aurora Metro Publications Ltd
Aurum Press
Austin & Macauley Publishers Ltd
BBH Publishing Ltd
Beautiful Books Ltd
The Belmont Press
Bene Factum Publishing Ltd
Berghahn Books
Black Dog Publishing Ltd
Blackstaff Press
Book Castle Publishing Ltd
Boydell & Brewer Ltd
Bradt Travel Guides Ltd
Nicholas Brealey Publishing
Bridge Books
Calypso Publications
*Cambridge Publishing
　Management Ltd*
Camra Books
Canongate Books
Capuchin Classics
Centre for Alternative Technology
　Publications
Channel View Publications Ltd
Cicerone Press Ltd
Cló Iar-Chonnachta
Coastal Publishing
Collins Geo
Compendium Publishing Ltd
Countryside Books
Crimson Publishing
Cualann Press
D & N Publishing
Day One Publications
Dedalus Ltd
Discovery Walking Guides Ltd
The Dovecote Press
Gerald Duckworth & Co Ltd
Eland Publishing Ltd
Elm Publications
English Heritage
The Erskine Press

Everyman's Library
Ex Libris Press
FHG Guides Ltd
Fiell Publishing Ltd
Footprint Travel Guides
W. Foulsham & Co Ltd
Garnet Publishing Ltd
The Geographical Association
Gibson Square
Gomer
Gothic Image Publications
Graffeg
Granta Books
Granta Editions
Green Books
Gwasg Gwenffrwd
Robert Hale Ltd
Halsgrove
HarperCollins Publishers Ltd
Haynes Publishing
Historical Publications Ltd
Hobnob Press
Alison Hodge Publishers
Holo Books
The Horizon Press
How To Books Ltd
Imray Laurie Norie & Wilson Ltd
Indepenpress Publishing Ltd
Instant-Books UK Ltd
The King's England Press
Little, Brown Book Group
Londubh Books
Luath Press Ltd
Macmillan Publishers Ltd
Mainstream Publishing Co
　(Edinburgh) Ltd
Maney Publishing
Melisende UK Ltd
Mentor Books
Merlin Publishing/Wolfhound
　Press
Merrell Publishers Ltd
Michelin Maps & Guides
Mitchell Beazley
Murdoch Books UK Ltd
John Murray Publishers
The National Trust
The O'Brien Press Ltd
The Oleander Press
The Orion Publishing Group Ltd
Pagoda Tree Press
Pan Macmillan
Paragon Publishing
The Penguin Group (UK) Ltd
Portobello Books Ltd
Prospera Publishing
Punk Publishing Ltd
Quadrille Publishing Ltd
Quiller Publishing Ltd
The Radcliffe Press
Reardon Publishing
Roadmaster Publishing
Alan Rogers Guides Ltd
Roundhouse Publishing Ltd
S. B. Publications
Scala Publishers Ltd
Sheldrake Press
Shire Publications Ltd
Sigma Press
Simon & Schuster (UK) Ltd
Charles Skilton Ltd
Slightly Foxed
Smith Settle Printing &
　Bookbinding Ltd
Souvenir Press Ltd
Stacey International
Stobart Davies Ltd
Strong Oak Press

Summersdale Publishers Ltd
teNeues Publishing UK Ltd
Thames & Hudson Ltd
Thorogood Publishing Ltd
F. A. Thorpe Publishing
Toucan Books Ltd
Transworld Publishers Ltd
Travel Publishing Ltd
Troubador Publishing Ltd
Unicorn Press
United Writers Publications Ltd
Weidenfeld & Nicolson
John Wiley & Sons Ltd
Willow Island Editions
Neil Wilson Publishing Ltd
Witherby Publishing Group

VETERINARY SCIENCE

J. A. Allen
CABI
Calypso Publications
Granta Editions
Luath Press Ltd
Manson Publishing Ltd
The National Academies Press
Quiller Publishing Ltd
Souvenir Press Ltd
TSO (The Stationery Office Ltd)
Whittet Books Ltd
John Wiley & Sons Ltd

VOCATIONAL TRAINING &
CAREERS

Amolibros
Austin & Macauley Publishers Ltd
Bene Factum Publishing Ltd
Nicholas Brealey Publishing
*Cambridge Publishing
　Management Ltd*
Cengage Learning EMEA Ltd
CILT, the National Centre for
　Languages
Crimson Publishing
Emerald Group Publishing Ltd
Ethics International Press Ltd
Filament Publishing Ltd
The Fostering Network
Gower Publishing Co Ltd
Hawker Publications
Hodder Education
How To Books Ltd
In Easy Steps Ltd
Institute of Education
　(Publications), University of
　London
Jones & Bartlett International
Jessica Kingsley Publishers
Kogan Page Ltd
McGraw-Hill Education
Macmillan Education
National Children's Bureau
National Extension College Trust
　Ltd
National Housing Federation
Need2Know
Nelson Thornes Ltd
Optimus Professional Publishing
Palgrave Macmillan
Practical Pre-School Books
Radcliffe Publishing Ltd
Russell House Publishing Ltd
Southgate Publishers
Trotman Publishing
UCAS
Which? Ltd

7.2 INDEX OF ISBN PREFIXES

978 0 906212 **2697**	978 0 948636 **2519**	978 0 9557559 **2291**	978 1 84148 **2067**	978 1 84583 **2704**	978 1 84995 **2761**
978 0 906290 **2734**	978 0 948667 **2349**	978 0 9559265 **2008**	978 1 84149 **2439**	978 1 84584 **2746**	978 1 85010 **2334**
978 0 906294 **2731**	978 0 948691 **2769**	978 0 9559541 **2574**	978 1 84150 **2389**	978 1 84589 **2070**	978 1 85015 **2252**
978 0 906301 **2122**	978 0 948817 **2310**	978 0 9561053 **2534**	978 1 84151 **2292**	978 1 84593 **2121**	978 1 85022 **2728**
978 0 906362 **2297**	978 0 948848 **2438**	978 0 9562821 **2154**	978 1 84158 **2082**	978 1 84596 **2456**	978 1 85035 **2774**
978 0 906391 **2456**	978 0 948877 **2043**	978 0 9564508 **2326**	978 1 84161 **2600**	978 1 84601 **2528**	978 1 85038 **2356**
978 0 906427 **2091**	978 0 9501861 **2313**	978 0 9564572 **2095**	978 1 84162 **2105**	978 1 84603 **2543**	978 1 85043 **2593, 2699**
978 0 906506 **2125**	978 0 9502121 **2309**	978 0 9565431 **2008**	978 1 84167 **2598**	978 1 84609 **2531**	978 1 85048 **2644**
978 0 906520 **2478**	978 0 9503647 **2685**	978 0 9565599 **2493**	978 1 84176 **2543**	978 1 84617 **2714**	978 1 85055 **2261**
978 0 906527 **2548**	978 0 9505458 **2644**	978 0 9566329 **2052**	978 1 84181 **2528**	978 1 84619 **2594**	978 1 85058 **2654, 2683**
978 0 906551 **2321**	978 0 9505570 **2107**	978 0 9567926 **2493**	978 1 84183 **2082**	978 1 84621 **2526**	978 1 85065 **2364**
978 0 906554 **2449**	978 0 9505828 **2236**	978 0 9568663 **2555**	978 1 84186 **2138**	978 1 84623 **2375**	978 1 85074 **2241**
978 0 906602 **2285**	978 0 9506431 **2728**	978 0 9668946 **2206**	978 1 84195 **2127**	978 1 84625 **2203**	978 1 85075 **2178**
978 0 906660 **2190, 2515**	978 0 9506563 **2250**	978 1 09 **2100**	978 1 84200 **2693**	978 1 84627 **2303, 2576**	978 1 85078 **2055**
978 0 906672 **2530**	978 0 9507735 **2723**	978 1 107 **2124**	978 1 84204 **2445**	978 1 84631 **2442**	978 1 85089 **2396**
978 0 906690 **2321**	978 0 9508285 **2108**	978 1 108 **2124**	978 1 84210 **2468**	978 1 84634 **2252**	978 1 85103 **2485**
978 0 906720 **2355**	978 0 9508674 **2601**	978 1 4039 **2551**	978 1 84212 **2541**	978 1 84643 **2151**	978 1 85116 **2144**
978 0 906731 **2153**	978 0 9509643 **2023**	978 1 4051 **2770**	978 1 84218 **2542**	978 1 84659 **2703**	978 1 85117 **2477**
978 0 906782 **2304**	978 0 9509773 **2099**	978 1 4052 **2230**	978 1 84222 **2132**	978 1 84661 **2407**	978 1 85124 **2097**
978 0 906798 **2039**	978 0 9510242 **2444**	978 1 4055 **2439**	978 1 84227 **2055**	978 1 84674 **2185**	978 1 85128 **2301**
978 0 906969 **2344**	978 0 9513240 **2120**	978 1 4073 **2033**	978 1 84229 **2718**	978 1 84680 **2606**	978 1 85137 **2331**
978 0 907018 **2694**	978 0 9515877 **2052**	978 1 4081 **2007**	978 1 84231 **2283**	978 1 84682 **2275**	978 1 85149 **2029**
978 0 907123 **2267**	978 0 9516129 **2186**	978 1 4085 **2510**	978 1 84234 **2248**	978 1 84686 **2067**	978 1 85158 **2456**
978 0 907345 **2430**	978 0 9516295 **2181**	978 1 4087 **2492**	978 1 84246 **2412**	978 1 84688 **2017**	978 1 85172 **2571**
978 0 907383 **2225**	978 0 9516960 **2570**	978 1 4129 **2623**	978 1 84255 **2540, 2541**	978 1 84689 **2591**	978 1 85175 **2365**
978 0 907461 **2693**	978 0 9517723 **2019**	978 1 4165 **2656**	978 1 84262 **2455**	978 1 84691 **2062**	978 1 85177 **2744**
978 0 907462 **2029**	978 0 9521964 **2648**	978 1 4169 **2656**	978 1 84264 **2247**	978 1 84697 **2082**	978 1 85182 **2275**
978 0 907476 **2642**	978 0 9522754 **2076**	978 1 4208 **2056**	978 1 84270 **2022**	978 1 84701 **2104**	978 1 85184 **2381**
978 0 907480 **2520**	978 0 9524749 **2692**	978 1 4259 **2056**	978 1 84277 **2780**	978 1 84709 **2668**	978 1 85196 **2566**
978 0 907526 **2681**	978 0 9526056 **2209**	978 1 4343 **2056**	978 1 84282 **2447**	978 1 84714 **2178**	978 1 85200 **2735**
978 0 907547 **2365**	978 0 9527302 **2305**	978 1 4347 **2179**	978 1 84285 **2290**	978 1 84715 **2440**	978 1 85205 **2323**
978 0 907554 **2292**	978 0 9528428 **2117**	978 1 4411 **2178**	978 1 84291 **2179**	978 1 84717 **2527**	978 1 85207 **2123**
978 0 907566 **2728**	978 0 9529782 **2549**	978 1 4426 **2739, 2740**	978 1 84298 **2363**	978 1 84720 **2234**	978 1 85223 **2194**
978 0 907579 **2189**	978 0 9530012 **2574**	978 1 4448 **2714**	978 1 84306 **2360**	978 1 84725 **2178**	978 1 85224 **2091**
978 0 907590 **2686**	978 0 9532440 **2396**	978 1 4450 **2396**	978 1 84310 **2416**	978 1 84730 **2747**	978 1 85228 **2670**
978 0 907595 **2651**	978 0 9532775 **2117**	978 1 4511 **2770**	978 1 84323 **2295**	978 1 84737 **2656**	978 1 85235 **2280**
978 0 907621 **2591**	978 0 9533478 **2779**	978 1 5121 **2770**	978 1 84326 **2239**	978 1 84738 **2656**	978 1 85249 **2126**
978 0 907631 **2667**	978 0 9535036 **2198**	978 1 55513 **2179**	978 1 84331 **2028**	978 1 84739 **2656**	978 1 85260 **2334**
978 0 907664 **2529**	978 0 9535353 **2046**	978 1 56292 **2179**	978 1 84334 **2772**	978 1 84744 **2439**	978 1 85265 **2479**
978 0 907768 **2186**	978 0 9535757 **2568**	978 1 56338 **2178**	978 1 84339 **2401**	978 1 84749 **2533**	978 1 85273 **2200**
978 0 907771 **2462**	978 0 9536757 **2052**	978 1 56750 **2389**	978 1 84340 **2026, 2169**	978 1 84762 **2180**	978 1 85278 **2234**
978 0 907845 **2374**	978 0 9536768 **2419**	978 1 56881 **2700**	978 1 84341 **2082**	978 1 84769 **2145**	978 1 85284 **2156, 2472**
978 0 907849 **2040**	978 0 9538460 **2037**	978 1 57113 **2104**	978 1 84351 **2436**	978 1 84772 **2531**	978 1 85297 **2244**
978 0 907861 **2724**	978 0 9539119 **2205**	978 1 57181 **2078**	978 1 84354 **2044**	978 1 84774 **2419**	978 1 85302 **2416**
978 0 907871 **2232**	978 0 9539852 **2648**	978 1 57439 **2770**	978 1 84358 **2090**	978 1 84782 **2714**	978 1 85304 **2600**
978 0 907926 **2323**	978 0 9540331 **2023**	978 1 58255 **2770**	978 1 84361 **2733**	978 1 84784 **2292**	978 1 85306 **2185**
978 0 907969 **2211**	978 0 9540499 **2513**	978 1 58562 **2020**	978 1 84371 **2178**	978 1 84788 **2077**	978 1 85310 **2591**
978 0 918438 **2362**	978 0 9540535 **2089**	978 1 58919 **2179**	978 1 84376 **2234**	978 1 84796 **2132**	978 1 85311 **2365**
978 0 930448 **2634**	978 0 9541544 **2677**	978 1 59339 **2239**	978 1 84377 **2284**	978 1 84797 **2194**	978 1 85312 **2768**
978 0 931250 **2362**	978 0 9542197 **2738**	978 1 59711 **2709**	978 1 84392 **2700**	978 1 84802 **2241**	978 1 85326 **2773**
978 0 931421 **2025**	978 0 9542330 **2052**	978 1 60160 **2707**	978 1 84395 **2714**	978 1 84806 **2370**	978 1 85328 **2424**
978 0 946015 **2273**	978 0 9542712 **2036**	978 1 60547 **2770**	978 1 84398 **2146**	978 1 84812 **2565**	978 1 85332 **2335**
978 0 946095 **2309**	978 0 9542813 **2709**	978 1 60831 **2770**	978 1 84400 **2589**	978 1 84819 **2416**	978 1 85340 **2565**
978 0 946139 **2236**	978 0 9542960 **2434**	978 1 60913 **2770**	978 1 84403 **2528**	978 1 84822 **2448**	978 1 85341 **2548**
978 0 946159 **2218**	978 0 9543127 **2570**	978 1 74045 **2490**	978 1 84407 **2225, 2700**	978 1 84829 **2027**	978 1 85356 **2501**
978 0 946211 **2046**	978 0 9543161 **2037**	978 1 74196 **2490**	978 1 84408 **2439**	978 1 84831 **2368**	978 1 85359 **2145**
978 0 946245 **2604**	978 0 9543811 **2326**	978 1 74245 **2528**	978 1 84409 **2265**	978 1 84834 **2380**	978 1 85361 **3027**
978 0 946284 **2194**	978 0 9543855 **2620**	978 1 74266 **2490**	978 1 84424 **2062**	978 1 84840 **2514**	978 1 85364 **2055**
978 0 946418 **2350**	978 0 9544075 **2082**	978 1 78032 **2780**	978 1 84425 **2334**	978 1 84842 **2345**	978 1 85375 **2132**
978 0 946439 **2410**	978 0 9544233 **2574**	978 1 78038 **2531**	978 1 84426 **2260**	978 1 84844 **2234**	978 1 85381 **2439**
978 0 946451 **2311**	978 0 9544334 **2300**	978 1 78040 **2401**	978 1 84445 **2425**	978 1 84851 **2295**	978 1 85383 **2225**
978 0 946487 **2447**	978 0 9544544 **2198**	978 1 78046 **2223**	978 1 84447 **2138**	978 1 84857 **2440**	978 1 85390 **2747**
978 0 946535 **2634**	978 0 9545335 **2433**	978 1 78049 **2410**	978 1 84449 **2531**	978 1 84859 **2174**	978 1 85398 **2039**
978 0 946590 **2698**	978 0 9545572 **2417**	978 1 78057 **2456**	978 1 84454 **2090**	978 1 84871 **2065**	978 1 85410 **2053**
978 0 946609 **2334**	978 0 9545870 **2042**	978 1 78076 **2593, 2699**	978 1 84455 **2191, 2726**	978 1 84873 **2537**	978 1 85411 **2642**
978 0 946616 **2346**	978 0 9546894 **2709**	978 1 78077 **2546**	978 1 84465 **2004**	978 1 84876 **2727**	978 1 85418 **2369, 2713**
978 0 946626 **2204**	978 0 9546912 **2052**	978 1 78100 **2234**	978 1 84474 **2400**	978 1 84880 **3026**	978 1 85424 **2437**
978 0 946640 **2436**	978 0 9547695 **2008**	978 1 81814 **2546**	978 1 84486 **2026**	978 1 84885 **2593, 2699**	978 1 85430 **2440**
978 0 946650 **2555**	978 0 9547757 **2692**	978 1 84011 **2705**	978 1 84489 **2014, 2351**	978 1 84893 **2566**	978 1 85437 **2698**
978 0 946947 **2021**	978 0 9547707 **2463**	978 1 84014 **2038**	978 1 84490 **2296, 2757**	978 1 84895 **2440**	978 1 85444 **2040**
978 0 946962 **2221**	978 0 9548708 **2463**	978 1 84017 **2637**	978 1 84494 **2108**	978 1 84901 **2177**	978 1 85450 **2236**
978 0 947548 **2468**	978 0 9548790 **2710**	978 1 84018 **2456**	978 1 84506 **2440**	978 1 84907 **2528, 2563**	978 1 85455 **2185**
978 0 947554 **2189**	978 0 9549137 **2574**	978 1 84022 **2773**	978 1 84508 **2147**	978 1 84908 **2543**	978 1 85458 **2191**
978 0 947645 **2503**	978 0 9549309 **2493**	978 1 84024 **2688**	978 1 84511 **2593, 2699**	978 1 84919 **2388**	978 1 85459 **2345**
978 0 947672 **3016**	978 0 9549727 **2134**	978 1 84033 **2681**	978 1 84513 **2053**	978 1 84926 **2062**	978 1 85486 **2675**
978 0 947731 **2107**	978 0 9550940 **2570**	978 1 84037 **2591**	978 1 84519 **2689**	978 1 84927 **2116**	978 1 85487 **2177**
978 0 947778 **2535**	978 0 9551032 **2429**	978 1 84046 **2368**	978 1 84520 **2077**	978 1 84929 **2174**	978 1 85506 **2178**
978 0 947971 **2524**	978 0 9551144 **2326**	978 1 84064 **2234**	978 1 84528 **2361**	978 1 84931 **2775**	978 1 85509 **2334**
978 0 947981 **2487**	978 0 9551566 **2052**	978 1 84067 **2138**	978 1 84529 **2177**	978 1 84934 **2754**	978 1 85514 **2505**
978 0 947988 **2762**	978 0 9552036 **2587**	978 1 84076 **2461**	978 1 84533 **2483, 2528**	978 1 84938 **2531**	978 1 85520 **2114**
978 0 948006 **2710**	978 0 9553648 **2574**	978 1 84078 **2376**	978 1 84539 **2464**	978 1 84939 **2022**	978 1 85521 **2038**
978 0 948080 **2723**	978 0 9553741 **2208**	978 1 84089 **2248**	978 1 84540 **2374**	978 1 84946 **2329**	978 1 85532 **2543**
978 0 948107 **2744**	978 0 9554273 **2198**	978 1 84091 **2176, 2528**	978 1 84541 **2145**	978 1 84949 **2589**	978 1 85534 **2754**
978 0 948183 **2173**	978 0 9554438 **2643**	978 1 84097 **2123**	978 1 84542 **2234**	978 1 84953 **2688**	978 1 85539 **2178**
978 0 948204 **2068**	978 0 9554514 **2139**	978 1 84101 **2079**	978 1 84545 **2078**	978 1 84956 **2718**	978 1 85549 **2049**
978 0 948238 **2086**	978 0 9555486 **2599**	978 1 84103 **2663**	978 1 84550 **2153**	978 1 84964 **2571**	978 1 85557 **2091**
978 0 948253 **2591**	978 0 9556055 **2037**	978 1 84113 **2329**	978 1 84553 **2243**	978 1 84965 **2156**	978 1 85566 **2104**
978 0 948285 **2244**	978 0 9556202 **2326**	978 1 84114 **2321**	978 1 84559 **2396**	978 1 84973 **2621**	978 1 85573 **2772**
978 0 948358 **2487**	978 0 9556400 **2417**	978 1 84119 **2177**	978 1 84560 **2470, 2471**	978 1 84980 **2234**	978 1 85575 **2410**
978 0 948543 **2006**	978 0 9556430 **2093**	978 1 84127 **2178**	978 1 84564 **2768**	978 1 84983 **2656**	978 1 85578 **2575**
978 0 948565 **2080**	978 0 9556476 **2717**	978 1 84135 **2058**	978 1 84569 **2772**		978 1 85584 **2680**
978 0 948578 **2250**	978 0 9557009 **2142**	978 1 84146 **2180**			978 1 85594 **2046**

7.4   INDEX OF COMPANIES & IMPRINTS

7.5 UK PUBLISHERS BY POSTCODE

LONDON & SOUTH-EAST ENGLAND

Brighton
BN1 1AD **3022**
BN1 1UJ **2381**
BN1 1WZ **3032**
BN2 1AH **2613**
BN2 1GJ **2379**
BN3 1DD **2611**
BN3 1FL **2493**
BN3 2FA **2586**
BN7 2NS **2372, 3018**
BN11 1BE **2057**
BN23 6NT **2179**
BN24 9BP **2689**
BN25 2UB **2629**
Bromley
BR3 5JS **2139**
Canterbury
CT11 9DA **2554**
Croydon
CR0 4PA **2264**
CR2 6NZ **2725**
CR5 2YH **2371**
CR9 5YP **2487**
Guildford
GU5 9SW **2207**
GU7 2EP **2346**
GU9 7HS **2539**
GU9 7PT **2038, 2298, 2448**
GU21 6LQ **2517**
GU29 9AZ **2478**
GU32 2EW **2328**
GU34 2PP **2200**
GU34 3HQ **2603**
Harrow
HA3 8RU **2075**
HA8 7UU **2745**
Hemel Hempstead
HP4 3BL **2585**
HP10 8EU **2413**
HP19 8TE **2393**
HP20 2NQ **3020**
HP23 5AH **3003**
Ilford
IG6 6DL **2405**
IG8 8HD **2356**
Kingston-upon-Thames
KT3 4LA **2465**
KT11 1LG **2114**
KT12 4RG **2013**
KT22 7RY **2427**
KT22 8BZ **2430**
London
E9 5LN **2472**
E14 5LB **2054**
EC1A 9DD **2158**
EC1A 9PN **2365**
EC1M 5QL **2402, 2711**
EC1M 5UX **2247**
EC1M 6BF **2222**
EC1M 6PE **3029**
EC1M 7BA **2669**
EC1N 8RT **2743**

EC1N 8SB **2137**
EC1N 8TS **2110**
EC1N 8XA **2225**
EC1R 0DU **3014**
EC1R 0HT **2015, 2320**
EC1R 0JH **2582, 2651**
EC1R 4QB **2106**
EC1R 4QL **2232**
EC1V 0AT **2249, 2630**
EC1V 0BB **2233, 2538**
EC1V 1LR **2414**
EC1V 1NG **2499**
EC1V 2NX **2495**
EC1V 3PZ **2142**
EC1V 3QP **2143**
EC1V 4JX **2658**
EC1V 4PY **2489**
EC1Y 7QE **2500**
EC1Y 1SP **2623**
EC2A 2BU **2435**
EC2A 3AR **2086**
EC2A 3DU **2713**
EC2M 5UU **2429**
EC3R 8DU **2390**
EC4A 2HS **2464**
EC4A 3AG **2096, 2102**
EC4M 9DQ **2617**
EC4Y 0DY **2439, 2564**
N1 2LZ **2206**
N1 7JQ **2277**
N1 9JB **2416**
N1 9JF **2780**
N1 9JN **2418**
N1 9PA **2562**
N1 9PF **2018**
N1 9RR **2452, 2552**
N1 9UN **2428**
N3 1DZ **2679**
N6 5AA **2571**
N7 8PL **2349**
N7 9BH **3025**
N7 9DP **2368**
N12 8EY **2209**
N13 9AJ **2227**
N19 4PT **2122**
N22 7BW **2326**
NW1 0ND **2053**
NW1 1DB **2632**
NW1 2DB **2112**
NW1 3BH **2315, 2337, 2351, 2352, 2354, 2491**
NW1 4DF **2296, 2757**
NW1 4ND **2588**
NW1 8PR **2565**
NW3 3PF **2712**
NW3 5HT **2410**
NW5 2DU **2242**
NW5 4QH **3011**
NW6 1DZ **2536**
NW6 1LU **2050**
NW6 3HR **2655**
NW6 6RD **2135**
NW8 6WD **2048, 2684, 2690, 2774**
NW10 3YB **2319**

NW11 7DL **2461**
NW11 8ED **2307**
SE1 0HX **2474**
SE1 2BH **2239**
SE1 7HR **2157**
SE1 7NX **2178**
SE1 7QY **2525**
SE1 8HA **2028, 2273**
SE1 8RD **2770**
SE1 8UG **2516**
SE1 8XX **2335**
SE10 8RF **2030**
SE10 9NA **2661**
SE11 5AY **2136**
SE11 5SD **2587**
SE19 1LP **2707**
SE19 3SR **3008**
SE23 3HZ **2759**
SE24 0PB **2359, 2579**
SE27 9NT **2693**
SW1A 1JR **2616**
SW1H 0QS **2401**
SW1H 9BN **2256**
SW1P 3AZ **2154**
SW1P 4RG **2698**
SW1P 4ST **2645, 2668**
SW1V 2SA **2022, 2597**
SW1V 2SS **2342**
SW1X 8PG **2618**
SW1Y 5HX **2174**
SW3 3ST **2466**
SW3 4AH **2012, 2657**
SW5 0RE **2545**
SW5 9JH **2064**
SW6 1RU **2409**
SW6 6AW **2440**
SW7 2AR **2619**
SW7 2RL **2744**
SW7 5BD **2507**
SW8 5WZ **2076**
SW11 5DH **2332**
SW11 6SS **2310**
SW12 0DA **2646**
SW14 8LS **2647**
SW15 1AZ **3031**
SW15 1NL **2103**
SW15 2PE **2197**
SW15 2TG **2490**
SW16 1WJ **2336**
SW19 1JQ **2146**
SW19 3NN **2724**
W1B 1AH **2369**
W1B 5DL **2073**
W1B 5SA **2667**
W1D 3QY **2087, 2092, 2344**
W1D 4SA **2175**
W1F 7BB **2634**
W1F 9JW **2318**
W1G 0DD **2278**
W1G 7AR **2240**
W1J 6HE **2205**
W1S 4EX **2606**
W1T 2LD **2590, 2771**
W1T 3JJ **2756**

W1T 3JW **2132**
W1T 3LJ **2531**
W1T 3QT **2523**
W1T 4AY **2420**
W1T 4EJ **2016**
W1T 5HJ **2034**
W1T 5JR **2276**
W1U 6BY **2403**
W1U 6NR **2248**
W1W 6AN **2482**
W1W 7AB **2032**
W2 4BU **2593, 2699, 2766**
W2 4QS **2164**
W2 5BP **2692**
W2 5RH **2628, 2703**
W4 5TF **2302**
W4 5YD **2696**
W5 4YX **2009**
W5 5SA **2596, 2721**
W6 7JP **2047**
W6 7NF **2061**
W6 7NJ **2385**
W6 7NL **2245**
W6 7PA **2406**
W6 7QH **2262**
W6 8JB **2327**
W8 4BH **2130, 2678**
W8 6SA **2230**
W8 9FA **2341**
W10 5ST **2534**
W11 2LW **2083**
W11 4QR **2303, 2576**
W12 8QP **2345**
W14 0RA **2026, 2069, 2169**
W14 9PB **2090**
WC1A 2QA **2580**
WC1A 2QS **2330**
WC1A 2TH **2566, 2691**
WC1B 3DA **2255**
WC1B 3DP **2007, 2077, 2777**
WC1B 3ES **2035**
WC1B 3JH **2138, 2470, 2471**
WC1B 3PA **2404**
WC1B 3PD **2673**
WC1B 3PL **2364**
WC1B 3QQ **2113**
WC1B 4HP **2177**
WC1E 7AE **2257**
WC1H 0AB **2750**
WC1H 0AL **2383**
WC1H 9HF **2641**
WC1H 9NE **2607**
WC1N 2BX **2039, 2235**
WC1N 3JZ **2044**
WC1V 6NY **2504**
WC1V 7QX **2709**
WC1X 8HB **2656**
WC1X 9DH **3013**
WC1X 9NG **2085**
WC2A 1PL **2424**
WC2A 1PP **2377**
WC2E 9DS **2544**

WC2H 0HE **2505**
WC2H 0LS **2589**
WC2H 7HH **2503**
WC2H 8JY **2176, 2293, 2481, 2483, 2528, 2563**
WC2H 9EA **2210, 2294, 2540, 2541, 2755**
WC2H 9HE **2373**
WC2N 6DF **2324**
WC2N 6RL **2147**
WC2R 0LX **2287**
WC2R 0RL **2559**
Luton
LU6 2ES **2109**
Medway
ME2 4HN **2019**
ME5 9AQ **2608**
Portsmouth
PO8 9JL **2479**
PO14 1BU **2094**
PO19 1RP **2688**
PO19 7DN **2548**
PO19 8SQ **2763**
Reading
RG1 4QS **2282, 2399**
RG8 8LU **2535**
RG9 4PG **2045**
RG14 5DS **2185**
RG19 6HW **2253**
RG20 6NL **2592**
RG20 8AN **2553**
RG21 4EA **2001**
RG21 6XS **2074, 2454, 2551**
RG22 4QB **2188**
RG27 0JG **2752**
Redhill
RH4 1DN **2705**
RH10 7WD **2686**
RH12 9GH **2600**
RH14 9QP **2599**
RH18 5ES **2160, 2680, 2706**
RH19 3BT **2751, 3006**
RH19 4FS **2181**
Romford
RM1 4LH **2343**
Slough
SL1 3UF **2274**
SL2 3PQ **2123**
SL6 2QL **2451**
SL9 8BA **2664**
SL9 9RZ **2105**
Southall
UB9 5NX **3005**
UB9 6AT **2778**
Southampton
SO24 9JH **2363, 2457**
SO40 7AA **2768**
Southend
SS1 1EF **2386**
SS3 0EQ **2450**
SS9 2LB **2492**
St Albans
AL1 1DT **2578, 2697**

AL1 3BN **2382**
AL1 4LW **2126**
AL6 9EQ **2508**
AL8 6HG **2251**
AL10 9AB **2738**
Tonbridge
TN1 1YS **2512**
TN4 9AT **2027**
TN11 8HL **2010**
TN16 1BZ **2270**
TN17 1HE **2610**
TN18 5AD **2216**
TN30 6BW **2281, 2309**
TN35 4PG **2670**
Twickenham
TW1 3QS **3030**
TW1 4HX **2052**
TW2 5RQ **2220**
TW9 1SR **2325**
TW9 2LL **2017, 2533**
TW9 2ND **2191, 2726**
TW9 3AE **2412**
TW9 3HA **2060**
Watford
WD6 3PW **2148**
WD17 1JA **2476**
WD19 4BG **2252**
WD25 9XX **2370**

SOUTH-WEST ENGLAND

Bath
BA1 2JQ **2550**
BA1 2NE **2701**
BA1 3JN **2286**
BA1 5BG **3026**
BA1 5DZ **3010**
BA1 6JX **2549**
BA2 3AF **2226**
BA2 3BH **2049**
BA2 3DZ **2271**
BA2 3LR **2115, 2518**
BA2 7JF **3028**
BA6 8AF **2120**
BA6 8XR **2297**
BA11 1DS **2150**
BA11 4EL **2348**
BA13 4JE **2224**
BA14 0AA **2577**
BA15 1ED **2250**
BA22 7JJ **2334**
Bournemouth
BH15 2RG **2675**
BH20 6AE **2167**
BH21 1HB **2036**
BH21 4JD **2218**
Bristol
BS1 2AW **2145**
BS1 6BE **2392**
BS1 6JS **2477**
BS8 1QU **2572**
BS8 3EA **2602, 2627**
BS16 3JG **2389**
Dorchester
DT1 3AR **2746**
DT7 3LS **2622**

Exeter
EX1 1HB **2425**
EX4 4QR **2737**
EX5 5HY **2374**
EX17 4LW **2672**
EX38 8ZJ **2408**

Plymouth
PL2 2EQ **2779**
PL6 7PP **2722**
PL14 4EL **2462**
PL15 8LD **2101**
PL19 9NQ **2521**
PL23 1EQ **2183**
PL28 8BG **2694**

Salisbury
SP3 5QP **2070**
SP3 6FA **2350**
SP7 9LY **2217**
SP10 5BE **2140**

Swindon
SN2 2EH **2241**
SN2 2NA **2506**
SN5 7YD **2151**
SN8 2AG **2005**
SN8 2HR **2194**
SN8 2LH **3012**
SN15 4BW **2567**

Taunton
TA4 1NE **2128**
TA4 1QF **3002**
TA6 4RR **2163**
TA19 0JT **2208**
TA21 9PZ **2321**

Torquay
TQ9 6EB **2305**
TQ9 7DL **2584**
TQ12 4PU **2254**

Truro
TR4 8ZJ **2731**
TR5 0RA **2728**
TR20 8BG **2735**
TR20 8XA **2355**
TR20 8XN **2366**

MIDLANDS

Birmingham
B1 2JB **2041**
B9 4AA **2717**
B29 6LB **2152**
B60 3HS **2561**
B61 0RU **2095**
B80 7LG **2107**
B91 1UE **2340**

Coventry
CV21 3HQ **2367**
CV31 1XN **2702**
CV32 4YS **2376**
CV34 4XE **2570**

Derby
DE6 1HD **2360**
DE7 5DA **2486**
DE21 4SZ **2211**

Dudley
DY8 3XY **2609**

Gloucester
GL5 1BJ **2333**
GL6 7RL **2671**
GL7 3QB **2196**
GL50 2JA **2234**
GL50 2JR **2677**
GL50 9AN **2601**
GL52 3LZ **2733**
GL53 7TH **2071, 2510**

Hereford
HR3 6QH **2444**
HR6 0QF **2299**
HR6 8NZ **2203**
HR9 5LA **2557**

Leicester
LE7 7FU **2714**
LE8 0RX **2727**
LE11 1UD **2640**
LE11 3TU **2438**
LE11 5DN **2715**
LE12 6UJ **2338**
LE67 9SY **2419**

Milton Keynes
MK2 2EB **2639**
MK7 6AA **2537**
MK8 0ES **2055**
MK9 2BE **2056**
MK11 1EB **2214**
MK18 1NT **2347**
MK43 7LP **2072**
MK45 4BE **2395**

Northampton
NN3 6RT **2301**
NN5 7HJ **2213, 2380**
NN7 3JB **3024**
NN12 6BT **2020, 2215, 2496, 2595, 2739, 2740**
NN14 4BW **2524**
NN17 4HH **2266**

Nottingham
NG1 9AW **2267**
NG2 3BP **2555**
NG6 0BT **2676**
NG7 2RD **2638**
NG7 3HR **2400**
NG12 5GG **2111**
NG12 5HT **2604**
NG14 5AL **2569**
NG17 9GU **2730**
NG32 2BB **2068**

Oxford
OX1 1AP **2459**
OX1 1BN **2423**
OX1 1ST **2391**
OX1 2JW **2329**
OX1 2PH **2040**
OX1 3HJ **2357**
OX1 5RP **2258**
OX2 0ES **2396**
OX2 0EW **2097**
OX2 0LX **2023**
OX2 0PH **2543, 2650**
OX2 0UJ **2441**
OX2 6DP **2547**
OX2 6JX **2749**
OX2 7DR **2437**
OX2 7ED **2033, 2067**
OX2 8EJ **2129**
OX3 0BP **2042**
OX3 0JP **2665**
OX4 1BW **2513**
OX4 1RE **2078**
OX4 2JY **2546**
OX4 3PP **2453**
OX5 1GB **2237**
OX5 1RX **2361**
OX7 3PH **2134**
OX7 6RU **3001**
OX10 8DE **2121**
OX12 8ED **2417**
OX12 8JY **2485**
OX14 1AA **2594**

OX14 3FE **2079**
OX14 4RN **2700**
OX15 0SE **2014**
OX15 5HX **2682**
OX16 9UX **2635**
OX18 4XN **2202**
OX20 1TW **2581**
OX28 4AW **3023**
OX28 4BN **2081**
OX29 8SZ **2421**

Shrewsbury
SY1 3TE **2059**
SY1 1JA **2591**
SY4 4UR **2687**
SY4 5JX **2443**
SY5 6LX **2708**
SY6 6WZ **2378**
SY8 1DB **2742**

Stoke-on-Trent
ST4 5NP **2723**
ST17 0TE **2192**

Wolverhampton
WV2 4NL **2263**

Worcester
WR6 6EN **2574**
WR9 7EE **2323**
WR13 6RN **2190, 2411, 2480, 2515**

EAST ANGLIA

Cambridge
CB1 1JT **2530**
CB1 2LG **2662**
CB1 2NT **2162, 2449**
CB1 3AN **2767**
CB2 1UR **2573**
CB2 8HN **2501**
CB2 8RU **2124**
CB4 0WF **2621**
CB4 0WS **2093**
CB4 1ND **2304**
CB4 3BW **2653**
CB5 8SW **2583**
CB6 2UA **2024**
CB7 4EH **2398**
CB21 6AH **2772**
CB22 5EN **2397**
CB23 7NU **3009**
CB25 9HP **3017**

Chelmsford
CM20 2JE **2558**
CM21 9JX **2467**
CM23 2EJ **2605**
CM24 8JU **2760**

Colchester
CO2 8HP **2575**
CO3 3HU **2633**
CO6 1JE **2159**

Ipswich
IP1 3RP **3007**
IP12 1AP **2718**
IP12 3DF **2104**
IP12 4SD **2029**
IP25 6QH **2556**
IP33 2BL **2037**
IP33 3PH **2246**

Lincoln
LN6 7FL **2720**
LN8 6NG **2187**
LN11 0BL **2339**

Norwich
NR2 3AD **2734**
NR3 1PD **2729**

NR3 3AX **2006**
NR14 7UR **3004**
NR16 2PB **2244**
NR26 8NB **3016**

Peterborough
PE2 6SG **3021**
PE2 6XD **2260**
PE2 9BF **2098**
PE2 9JX **2509**
PE11 1NZ **2144**
PE11 4TA **2753**
PE27 5BT **2375**
PE28 2NJ **2236**
PE28 5XE **2204**

Stevenage
SG1 2AY **2388**
SG1 2DX **2062**
SG8 5NJ **2775**
SG9 9AJ **3027**
SG12 9HJ **2773**
SG14 2JA **2648**
SG19 3JA **2008**

NORTH-EAST ENGLAND

Bradford
BD16 1AU **2685**
BD16 1WA **2238**
BD23 2QR **2748**
BD23 4ND **2455**

Doncaster
DN35 8HU **2666**

Durham
DH1 3NP **2004**
DH8 7PW **2292**

Harrogate
HG1 1BX **2272**
HG4 5DF **2099**

Huddersfield
HD8 0NQ **2631**

Leeds
LS3 1AB **2460**
LS6 4NB **2021**
LS8 2SP **2279**
LS12 4HP **2166**
LS19 7XY **2663**
LS28 6AT **2362**

Newcastle-upon-Tyne
NE1 2AJ **2268**
NE1 3DY **2494**
NE1 8ST **2522**
NE6 2HL **2781**
NE48 1RP **2091**
NE70 7JX **2025**
NE99 1DX **2732**

Sheffield
S1 4BF **2284**
S3 7WL **2644**
S3 8AF **2243**
S3 8GG **2308**
S8 0XJ **2498**
S10 5UD **2652**
SO23 9HX **2598**
S32 1DJ **2229**
S41 0FR **2475**
S63 9BL **2415**
S80 3LR **2058**

Wakefield
WF1 2LT **2231**
WF3 2AP **2477**
WF4 4PX **2764**
WF5 9AQ **2643**
WF8 4WW **2614**

York

YO10 5DD **2100**
YO10 5DX **2624**
YO16 6BT **2317**
YO18 8AL **2089**
YO24 1ES **2387**
YO30 6WP **2615**
YO30 7BZ **2184**
YO61 3ET **2171**
YO62 5BP **2520**

NORTH-WEST ENGLAND

Carlisle
CA2 5AU **2131**
CA3 9HZ **2568**
CA12 5AS **2484**

Chester
CH2 2PD **2716**
CH41 9HH **2186**

Isle of Man
IM2 4NR **2488**

Lancaster
LA1 4SL **2133**
LA7 7PY **2156**
LA12 9QQ **2710**
LA17 7WZ **2180**

Liverpool
L3 8EG **2384**
L69 7ZU **2442**

Manchester
M3 1LE **3015**
M13 9NR **2458**
M22 5LH **2189**
M23 9HH **2625**
M25 9JY **2063**

Preston
PR1 8JP **2195**
PR3 5LE **2719**

Stockport
SK4 4ND **2431**

Warrington
WA4 9DE **2283**

WALES

Cardiff
CF5 1GZ **2300**
CF10 4UP **2741**
CF14 2EA **2221**
CF14 7ZY **2219**
CF31 3AE **2642**
CF31 4DX **2118**
CF32 0TN **2051**
CF37 5PB **2080**
CF46 6RY **2003**

Llandudno
LL12 7AW **2108**
LL13 7NS **2560**
LL14 5HL **2659**
LL18 9AY **2290**
LL19 9SH **2704**
LL21 9WZ **2313**
LL53 5YE **2314**
LL53 6SH **2199**

Mid-Wales
LD7 1UP **3019**
SY20 9AZ **2141**
SY23 3GL **2358**
SY24 5HE **2776**

Newport (Gwent)
NP25 4TN **2529**

Swansea
SA6 6AE **2066**
SA18 3HP **2654, 2683**

SA33 5ND **2193**
SA44 4JL **2295**

SCOTLAND

Dumfries
DG10 9SU **2125**

Edinburgh
EH1 1JF **2519**
EH1 1TE **2127**
EH1 2ND **2447**
EH1 3QB **2223**
EH3 3UG **2456**
EH3 3YY **2497**
EH2 4PS **2306**
EH4 3BL **2011**
EH4 3DS **2502**
EH8 9LF **2228**
EH9 1QS **2082**
EH11 1SH **2269**
EH12 6EL **2065**
EH15 1JG **2212**
EH22 3LJ **2636, 2637**
EH52 5LY **2291**
EH52 5NF **2445**
EH54 8SB **2769**

Falkirk
FK16 6BJ **2331**

Glasgow
G2 3DH **2762**
G4 0HZ **2754**
G12 8QH **2043**
G13 1BQ **2765**
G40 2AB **2432**
G41 2SD **2116**
G64 2QT **2170**
G74 2JZ **2149**

Inverness
IV15 9WJ **2626**
IV20 1TW **2153**
IV36 2TF **2265**
IV36 2UA **2434**
IV42 8PY **2695**

Kilmarnock
KA5 6RD **2681**

Kirkcaldy
KY12 7XG **2198**

Orkney
KW6 6EG **2761**

Paisley & Isles
HS1 2QN **2002**
PA1 1NB **2316, 2353**
PA1 1TJ **2261**
PA75 6PR **2117**

Perth
PH2 1AU **2084**
PH20 1BU **2674**

Shetland
ZE1 0PX **2649**

NORTHERN IRELAND

Belfast
BT3 9LE **2088**
BT6 5NW **2426**
BT7 1AP **2031**
BT9 5BS **2660**
BT14 8HQ **2422**
BT16 2BB **2758**
BT23 4YH **2172**
BT48 0LZ **2311**